THE AA KEYGuide

On the Move

The Sights

What to Do

Walks and Tours

Eating and Staying

Planning

Country Atlas

KEYGuide

The AA KEYGuide Portugal

Contents

KEY TO SYMBOLS

- Map reference
- Address
- Telephone number
- Opening times
- Admission prices
- Bus number
- Train station
- Ferry/boat
- Driving directions
- Tourist office
- Tours
- Guidebook
- Restaurant
- Café
- Shop
- Toilets
- Number of rooms
- Parking
- No smoking
- Air conditioning
- Swimming pool
- Gym
- Other useful information
- Shopping
- Entertainment
- Nightlife
- Sports
- Activities
- Health and Beauty
- For Children
- ▷ Cross reference
- ★ Walk/drive start point

HOW TO USE THIS BOOK

Understanding Portugal is an introduction to the region, its geography, economy and people. **Living Portugal** gives an insight into the area today, while **The Story of Portugal** takes you through the country's past.

For detailed advice on getting to Portugal—and getting around once you are there—turn to **On the Move**. For useful practical information, from weather forecasts to emergency services, turn to **Planning**.

Out and About gives you the chance to explore Portugal through walks and drives.

The **Sights**, **What to Do** and **Eating and Staying** sections are divided geographically into eight regions, which are shown on the map on the inside front cover. These regions always appear in the same order. Towns and places of interest are listed alphabetically within each region.

Map references for the **Sights** refer to the atlas section at the end of this book or to individual town plans. For example, Sintra has the reference ✚ 344 A9, indicating the page on which the map is found (344) and the grid square in which Sintra sits (A9).

UNDERSTANDING PORTUGAL

Portugal has many faces—underdeveloped and unspoilt regions coexist with sophisticated coastal resorts that have been firmly on the tourist map for more than 40 years. Lisbon, the capital, happily combines modern development with old-fashioned, idiosyncratic charm, while regional capitals, such as Porto, Coimbra and Évora, each have their own distinctive personalities. But it's the coast and sea that define Portugal both physically and historically. In short, wherever you go, you will find variety and interest; there are truly many Portugals to discover.

Fishing boats moored in Setúbal, Portugal's third-largest port

An old cottage in the Algarve, with traditional painting scheme

Porto seen from the Douro, with its bridge in the background

LANDSCAPE

Portugal is a small country (89,106sq km/ 34,404sq miles), but it enjoys immense geographical diversity. North of the Rio Tejo, the hills and upland areas are a continuation of the *meseta*, the block of high plateau and mountains that occupies much of the Iberian peninsula. The climate here makes for a green, cultivated and heavily populated landscape, particularly in the Minho and Douro, though much of remote, mountainous Trás-os-Montes is good for little but sheep-grazing. Farther south in the Beiras, Estremadura and Ribatejo, the countryside is predominantly fertile and undulating, rich in woodlands, vines and olives.

South of the Tejo, the vast, sun-drenched and empty Alentejan plains are Portugal's granary, where huge wheat fields are interspersed with cork oak stands, olive groves and plantations. To the south, passes through the low hills lead to the fertile Algarve and the coast. This is a sinuous 1,793km-long (1,114-mile) ribbon that includes vast sandy beaches, dramatic cliffs, headlands and hidden coves, dunes, pinewoods and marshland.

ECONOMY

At the time of the 1974 Carnation Revolution, Portugal was economically at least 50 years behind the rest of Europe thanks to the policies of Salazar. Since then enormous strides have been taken, particularly since the country's entry to the European Union (EU) in 1986. For much of the 1990s, Portugal's economic growth was well above the EU average; now, its GDP stands at 70 per cent of those of the leading EU economies.

Portugal is the world's largest cork producer and among the largest producers of wine. Its leading industries include textile and footwear manufacture, papermaking and engineering. Tourism is increasingly important, while agriculture is notoriously inefficient. Many farms are little more than minute smallholdings.

POLITICS

Portugal is a republic. Administratively, the mainland is divided into 18 districts, responsible for their own health, education and financial affairs. Municipal power is in the hands of 305 *concelhos*, similar to district councils (boroughs), which are elected every four years. Madeira and the Azores are autonomous regions.

DEMOGRAPHY AND RELIGION

Portugal's population stands at around 10.5 million; the birth-rate, unlike that in many other southern European countries, is rising, albeit by a very low percentage (0.4 per cent). Most Portuguese still live on the land or in small towns, mainly close to the coast, with population levels highest in the Minho and lowest in the Alentejo.

The Portuguese are fervently Catholic; although it is falling, church attendance is much higher than in many other European Catholic countries. This is reflected in the large numbers of festivals, processions and religious pilgrimages that are still an integral part of daily life.

PORTUGAL'S REGIONS

THE MINHO AND TRÁS-OS-MONTES

The Minho is considered by many Portuguese to be the most beautiful and varied part of the country. Here you'll find the fertile river valleys of the Minho and Lima, huge stretches of sandy beaches along the Costa Verde, and the spectacular gorges and mountains of Peneda-Gerês, Portugal's only national park. The largest towns, historic Guimarães and Braga, Portugal's ecclesiastical heart, lie in the south of the region. The main coastal resort is Viana do Castelo, while Barcelos is famed for its exuberant weekly market, one of Europe's largest. Both river valleys are home to a string of lovely small towns, and the area is noted for its huge variety of traditional crafts.

The Trás-os-Montes, 'beyond the mountains', is a remote and sparsely populated region, unofficially divided into the southern and fertile Terra Quente (Hot Land), and the climactically extreme north, the Terra Fria (Cold Land), where life is still hard. The fortified frontier towns of Chaves and Bragança are the main northern bases, with Vila Real, the nearest town to the landmark Solar de Mateus manor house, dominating the southwest. Away from these, the main draws are the small towns and villages, such as Miranda do Douro on the Spanish border, and the magnificent countryside, where the way of life still seems relatively unchanged. The region has three natural parks: the Serra de Alvão in the west; the Parque Natural de Montesinho on the northern border with Spain; and the Parque Natural do Douro International, which straddles the Spanish border in the east.

Historic Elvas, the most beautiful of the Alentejo's frontier towns

This decorative tile is a tribute to fado, *Portugal's unique music*

You can buy a host of gourmet delights in Porto's old food stores

PORTO AND THE DOURO

Porto is Portugal's second-largest city, an unabashedly commercial hub near the mouth of the Rio Douro. Huge urban redevelopment has spruced up this once shabby city, and Porto today has plenty to offer in the shape of its historic riverside Ribeira area, Romanesque *Sé* (cathedral), clutch of fine buildings, good museums, and excellent shopping and entertainment. On the Douro's opposite bank is Vila Nova de Gaia, whose history is inextricably linked with the port trade and where you can learn about and sample the fortified wine that is undoubtedly Portugal's most famous export.

The Douro region lies on the north bank of the Rio Douro, a magnificent river that gives the area its name and cuts through some of Portugal's most impressive scenery. The landscape encompasses both rolling hills and steeply terraced vineyards dotted with port lodges, while the main towns include lovely Amarante and the buzzing coastal resorts of Póvoa de Varzim and Vila do Conde.

THE BEIRAS

The Beiras region is divided into three parts—the Beira Alta to the northeast, the Beira Baixa in the southeast, and the Beira Litoral along the coast. The Beira Alta and the Beira Baixa are the least visited of all Portuguese regions, with magnificent countryside that includes the Serra da Estrela, mainland Portugal's highest mountain range, and splendid and remote villages, such as Almeida, Belmonte, Trancoso and Monsanto. The main towns are Guarda, set at an altitude of more than 1,000m (3,280ft), and Viseu, birthplace of Grão Vasco, Portugal's greatest Renaissance painter. To the west, the Beira Litoral is dominated by the great university city of Coimbra, from where you can easily reach the Roman site of Conímbriga, Montemor-o-Velho and its castle, and the ancient forest of Buçaco. North from here is Aveiro, an estuary city surrounded by canals and lagoons; from Aveiro, a long sandy coast stretches north and south—head for the resort of Figueira da Foz to enjoy it at its best.

ESTREMADURA AND THE RIBATEJO

Estremadura and **the Ribatejo** are both packed with delights. Architecturally, Alcobaça and Batalha should be high on any visiting list, as should Tomar and the historic former headquarters of the Knights Templar (later the Order of Christ). East across the Serra de Aire lies Fátima, one of the Catholic church's most important shrines. North is the elegant inland town of Léiria. From here, it's a short hop to the coast, where a string of pretty resorts stretches south towards Lisbon. Pick of the bunch are Nazaré, Peniche—from where you can visit the offshore islands of Berlenga—and Ericeira. Inland gems include medieval Óbidos, the castle at Almourol, set on an islet in the Tejo, and pretty Abrantes.

LISBON

Lisbon is packed with history. Its main sights are its castle and Alfama area, the elegant Baixa, Chiado and Bairro Alto districts, Belém and the superb Mosteiro dos Jerónimos, the sleekly modern Parque das Nações complex, and some fine museums, like the Museu Calouste Gulbenkian and the Museu Nacional de Arte Antiga. Shopping and nightlife, which should include an evening of *fado*, Portugal's soul music, add another dimension to any visit.

Miradouro de Santa Luzia, Lisbon, has a great city view

Vineyards in the Serra da Arrabida. Portugal produces many fine wines

Praia de Dona Ana, Lagos, with its striking cliff formations

AROUND LISBON

Around Lisbon on either side of the Tejo estuary, there's the option of relaxing on the coast or visiting some of Portugal's finest royal palaces. The most important of these are at Sintra, a cool hillside oasis where you'll find the medieval Palácio Nacional and the 19th-century Palácio da Pena. There's another palace at Queluz, and one more at Mafra. From here, it's a short drive to the coast and Cabo da Roca, the westernmost point of mainland Europe. South are the fashionable resorts of Cascais and Estoril, while, across the Tejo, the dunes curve along the Costa da Caparica to remote, windswept Cabo Espichel.

THE ALENTEJO

The Alentejo region falls into two parts, Alto (Upper) and Baixo (Lower). It's a vast agricultural area, its rolling plains dotted with cork plantations and scattered towns and villages. Évora, one of Portugal's most attractive towns, is the main draw in the north, while Beja, once an important Moorish settlement, commands the south. The Alto Alentejo is home to some of the country's most picturesque hilltop towns, among them Elvas, with its superb fortifications, and Monsaraz, Marvão, Castelo do Vide and Évoramonte, all with fine medieval buildings and wonderful views. Lively Estremoz, famed for its market, and Vila Viçosa, seat of a royal palace, lie east of Évora, while the road west leads through picturesque Alcácer do Sal to the coast and the lovely Serra da Arrábida. South in the Baixo Alentejo, Serpa is another pleasant town, matched by nearby Mértola.

THE ALGARVE

The Algarve is Portugal's holiday playground. To the east of Faro the coast is fringed by long, sandy offshore islands, while to the west, bays, coves and cliffs predominate. The main towns are Faro, Portimão and Lagos, but in tourist terms, these are outshone by resorts such as Albufeira, Carvoeira, Praia da Rocha and Vilamoura, and the sporting enclaves of Vale do Lobo and Quinta do Lago. To escape the crowds, you'll need to head towards Sagres and the western coast around Cabo de São Vicente, or take in low-key Tavira in the east. The interior still has relatively untouched towns, such as Silves, and picturesque villages like Alte, Castro Marim and Estoi. For scenic beauty the Serra de Monchique hills take some beating, while, on the coast, the Parque Natural da Ria Formosa shouldn't be missed.

PORTUGAL'S REGIONS

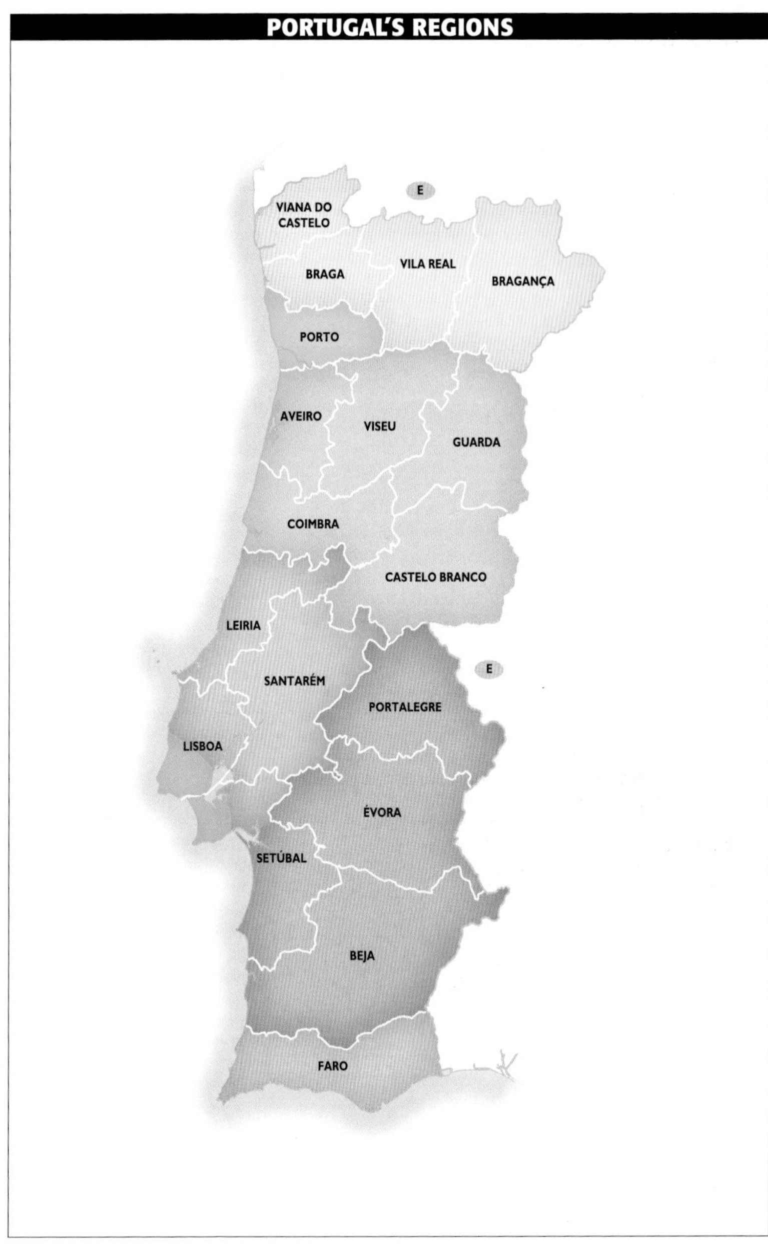

GETTING THE MOST FROM YOUR STAY

Many visitors to Portugal come for the sun, sea and beaches, but, given the country's relatively small size, it's quite possible to focus on more than one region or type of holiday. This is best done by car, as public transportation, though more than adequate for day-to-day use, can be patchy. Exploring some of the inland and more remote regions gives a whole new perspective and a far better insight into the country, with the chance to sample the delights of the more old-fashioned aspects of Portuguese life. From the Algarve resorts, a few hours' drive north opens up the sparsely populated Alentejo region, while Lisbon lies only a relatively short motorway drive away. From the capital, it's easy to head into the Beiras, Ribatejo and Estremadura, home of many of the country's great towns and monuments. Visitors to the north can combine the buzz of Porto with time spent in the beautiful Douro and Minho regions, while the remote wilderness of the Trás-os-Montes lies a relatively short drive to the east. Time anywhere away from Lisbon and the Algarve will give you a taste of the 'real' Portugal, and a chance to experience the sincere, welcoming kindness of the Portuguese themselves.

THE BEST OF PORTUGAL

THE MINHO AND TRÁS-OS-MONTES

Barcelos (▷ 67): Buy a ceramic cockerel at the Thursday market—the essential Portuguese souvenir.

Bom Jesus do Monte (▷ 69–70): Climb the steps of Portugal's great baroque architectural set-piece.

Camelo da Ampúlia, near Viana do Castelo (▷ 276): Eat the freshest of fish or try the best of Minho regional cookery while admiring the sea views.

Citânia de Briteiros (▷ 73): One of Portugal's most impressive archaeological sites, with extensive Celtic remains.

Guimarães (▷ 74–75): Head for a café table in the splendid Praça de Santiago and watch life go by.

Miranda do Douro (▷ 76): Stand above the Douro river and look across the dramatic gorge to Spain.

Parque Natural de Montesinho (▷ 76–77): Walk, drive or cycle through this unspoilt rural area.

Solar de Mateus (▷ 82): Stroll through the glorious formal gardens here, the finest in Portugal.

Above: Majestic Bom Jesus do Monte. Left: Barcelos's famous ceramic cockerels on display

PORTO AND THE DOURO

Café Majestic, Porto (▷ 276–277): Pause with coffee and a pastry served by uniformed waiters at this elegant café.

Cais da Ribeira (▷ 87): Explore the maze of narrow alleyways leading through old Porto down to the riverside.

Casa da Calçada, Amarante (▷ 299): Luxurious surroundings, superb service, great riverside views and beautiful gardens—the perfect overnight stop.

Fundação de Serralves (▷ 88): Exciting, cutting-edge modern art in Porto.

Ponte Dom Luís I (▷ 87): Walk across Porto's celebrated two-tiered bridge for great river and city views.

Torre dos Clérigos (▷ 87–88): Climb this tower in Porto for bird's-eye city views.

Vila Nova de Gaia (▷ 90): Find out about the story of port and enjoy a tasting at one of the port lodges.

Houses in the Ribeira, Porto's atmospheric old riverside quarter

THE BEIRAS

Almeida (▷ 96): Walk the 4km (2.5 miles) around the grassy walls for glimpses of town life from above and superb views across the plateau.

Coimbra (▷ 98–101): Visit the famous complex of the Velha Universidade.

Conímbriga (▷ 97): See the best of Portugal's Roman past at the archaeological site and museum.

Palace Hotel do Buçaco (▷ 301): Indulge yourself with a stay at this luxurious hotel, an ex-royal hunting lodge in the heart of the national forest near Luso.

Parque Arqueológico do Vale do Côa (▷ 106): 20,000-year-old art etched into the rock.

Serra da Estrela (▷ 105): Mainland Portugal's highest mountain range—dramatic scenery and crisp air.

A Taberna, Coimbra (▷ 279): Enjoy the best of traditionally cooked local dishes in the university city.

Viseu (▷ 107): Take in masterpieces by Grão Vasco, Portugal's greatest 16th-century painter.

Buçaco's Palace Hotel has old royal connections

THE BEST OF PORTUGAL

ESTREMADURA AND THE RIBATEJO

Alcobaça (▷ 110–111): Spend a few hours at this great monastery, one of Portugal's finest Gothic buildings.
Batalha (▷ 112–115): Marvel at the Manueline stonework in the Capelas Imperfeitas.
Castelo de Almourol (▷ 109): Take a tiny ferry across the Rio Tejo to visit the fairy-tale castle on its river island.
Ericeira (▷ 109): Sample some superb lobster and super-fresh fish in this fishing port north along the coast from Lisbon.
Estalagem de Santa Iria, Tomar (▷ 304): Escape the crowds and enjoy perfect peace at this hotel on a river island.
Fátima (▷ 116): Join the pilgrims at the country's greatest shrine.
Óbidos (▷ 117): Spend a night in this walled medieval town after the daytime crowds have gone home.
Peniche (▷ 122): Catch a boat to view the vast numbers of sea birds on the Ilha Berlenga.
Serra de Aire (▷ 122): Visit the dramatic limestone caves.
Tomar (▷ 118–121): Explore the Convento de Cristo, once the headquarters of the successors to the Knights Templar.

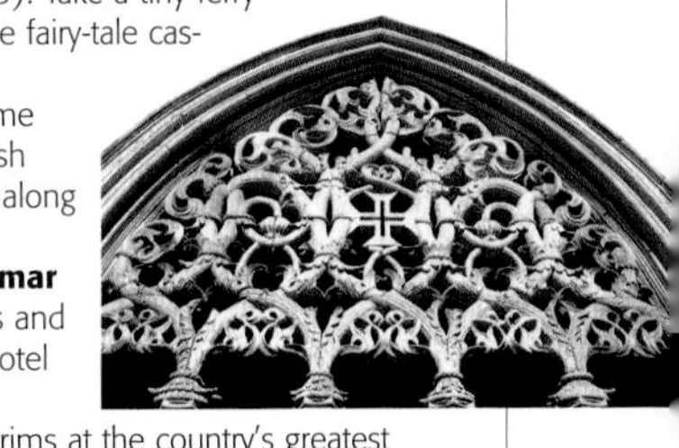

Left: A statue of Christ in Fátima. Right: Elaborate stonework, Batalha

Cyclists and pedestrians near a water feature in the Parque das Nações, Lisbon

A grim-faced gargoyle, from the Palácio Nacional da Pena, Sintra

LISBON

Alfama (▷ 128–129): Wander through the picturesque streets of Lisbon's medieval quarter.
Bairro Alto (▷ 131): Spend an evening eating, drinking and listening to *fado*, Portugal's unique soul music with a tradition all of its own.
Belém (▷ 132–135): Visit some of the capital's most significant monuments and important museums.
Castelo de São Jorge (▷ 136): Enjoy the space, the shady greenery and the great views of the city you get from its one-time citadel.
Chiado (▷ 208–210): Browse around some of Lisbon's most stylish shops.
Hotel As Janelas Verdes (▷ 307): Recover from a day's sightseeing as you relax in this elegant 18th-century mansion overlooking the Rio Tejo.
Museu Calouste Gulbenkian (▷ 138–141): A world-class collection of art spanning east and west.
Parque das Nações (▷ 142–145): Take in the Oceanário, stroll the riverside gardens and indulge yourself shopping.
Ribeira Market (▷ 146): Give your tastebuds a treat as you browse this great food market.

The Rossio, the main square of Lisbon's Baixa quarter

AROUND LISBON

Cascais (▷ 148): Indulge in some chic retail therapy.
Costa da Caparica (▷ 148): Catch the little train and hop off at one of the relaxing beaches.
Sintra (▷ 150–153): Visit two of Portugal's royal palaces—the Palácio Nacional de Sintra and the extraordinary neo-Gothic Palácio Nacional de Pena.

THE BEST OF PORTUGAL

THE ALENTEJO

One of Alcacér do Sal's celebrated stork nests, perched on top of a church tower. Below: The Kalifa carpet store in Arraiolos

Alcacér do Sal (▷ 155): Spot the storks' nests in this laid-back riverside town.
Arraiolos (▷ 155): Shop for local rugs and carpets.
Beja (▷ 155): See some of Portugal's finest *azulejos* (tiles) at the Convento de Nossa Senhora da Conceição.
Estremoz (▷ 157): Visit the Saturday market in the Rossio before exploring the Vila Velha (Old Town).
Évoramonte (▷ 157): Climb up to the castle for superb views across the Alentejo.
O Fialho, Évora (▷ 290): For the best in Alentejan cooking.
Vila Nova de Milfontes (▷ 164): Join Portuguese holidaymakers for a fabulous stay by the sea.

THE ALGARVE

Almancil (▷ 167): Visit the church of São Lourenço to see some of Portugal's best blue *azulejos* (tiles).
Carvoeiro (▷ 171): Take a boat trip to see the fabulous hidden coves and rock formations.
Faro (▷ 168–170): Explore the old town before indulging in some of the central Algarve's best shopping.
Parque Natural da Ria Formosa (▷ 172): Find out about the Algarve's environment.
Portimão (▷ 173): Where the locals shop.
Sagres (▷ 174): A great base from which to explore some unspoilt areas.
Silves (▷ 175): Spend time exploring this historic town, once the Algarve's Moorish capital.
Tavira (▷ 175): Enjoy the fine architecture and gentle pace of life.

Left: *Igreja de São Lourenço, Almancil, decorated with stunning blue* azulejos *(tiles). Below: The beach at Praia da Rocha, one of the Algarve's finest*

TOP 10 EXPERIENCES

Visit a port lodge and sample a few varieties of vintage port—try the delicate *porto branco* (white port) as a chilled aperitif.
Take a cruise up the Douro valley, the best way to appreciate this lovely area.
Eat a *pastel de nata,* a super-sweet, flaky-pastry custard tart, whose recipe is still a closely guarded secret, at the Antiga Confraria de Belém in Lisbon (▷ 282).
Visit the market at Barcelos for a real taste of rural Portugal.
Listen to *fado* at a *fado* house in the Bairro Alto in Lisbon, or in Coimbra, its other home.
Go to a soccer match at Lisbon's Estádio do Luz or Porto's Estádio das Antas.
Splash out on a night in a *pousada,* a state-run hotel in a historic castle or building.
See the world-class treasures at the Museu Calouste Gulbenkian in Lisbon.
Shop for local artisan work—there's a huge range of crafts in every region.
Visit Coimbra, a buzzing riverside university city that combines fine medieval buildings, churches and monuments with great shopping and eating opportunities.

Below: Tasting port on a terrace in Vila Nova de Gaia, high above the Douro. On the opposite bank of the river to Porto is the capital of Portugal's port trade

Living Portugal

A Minho cow with characteristic long horns

A traditional Alentejo shepherd leaning on his long crook

A barren landscape in the Algarve with only the occasional tree in view

Landscape and Nature

Portugal can be divided into a number of distinctive geographical zones, but overall the Atlantic is the predominant influence. This means much of Portugal enjoys a mild, rainy climate.

In the Minho region bordering northwest Spain, climate variations are similar to those of northern Europe. The Peneda-Gerês National Park—once the home of the brown bear—still shelters predators, such as the wolf and the royal eagle, as well as the rare Gerês fern. The highland plains and mountains extend into Spain, but gradually give way to lush pasture in central Portugal.

South of Lisbon, the endangered Iberian lynx roams the remoter parts of the arid Alentejo plains. This zone is at increasing risk of turning to desert in what is one of the world's most serious environmental problems. The Algarve, though, has a milder, more Mediterranean climate. More than 3,000 hours of sunshine a year help to warm the Atlantic waters as they round Cape St. Vincent and flow towards the Mediterranean. Farther north, the seas are cold and can be treacherous.

Rocks, trees and beach at Praia de São Rafael in the Algarve. This is prime tourist country, with more than 3,000 hours of sunshine every year, and so is a linchpin of Portugal's economy

World First

Environmental issues have not always been high on the Portuguese agenda, but the focus is shifting towards preserving the country's natural landscapes. Mata de Sesimbra, just south of Lisbon, has been selected as the site of a huge eco-friendly tourist resort. It will be the world's first-ever integrated sustainable building, tourism, nature conservation and reforestation project.

Planned facilities include four hotels, horseback-riding stables, cultural venues and a golf course. The development will use recycled materials from the area and is being built in consultation with advisers from Quercus—Portugal's largest environmental pressure group—and the World Wide Fund for Nature. It is hoped that the forest restoration project in particular will go some way to protecting areas for nesting birds, and recovering wetland and other important habitats.

A black stork, a welcome visitor

Celebrating the opening of the Ponte Vasco da Gama, Lisbon, the longest bridge in Europe

Looking over the Quinta do Castro vineyard to the river

Firefighters cope with a forest fire, Alcanede

Wine Country

Portugal has a wealth of indigenous grape varieties and pioneering wine-makers. Vineyards make their mark on the landscape in 47 different wine-growing regions, from the stepped terraces of the Douro valley to Dão high in the mountains of Beira Alta, the Alentejo plains and, overseas, the volcanic island of Madeira.

A number of mainland Portugal's finest grape varieties were wiped out by the devastating phylloxera outbreaks that spread across Europe in the 19th century. Now, however, scientists are busy recreating the old grape varieties from seeds recovered from the wreck of a ship that sank off the Portuguese coast more than 500 years ago. The scientists hope to grow a new vine using tissue culture created from the surviving seeds. Success would represent a scientific breakthrough, as well as enabling Portugal's vintners to revive a centuries-old wine.

Watery Grave

Europe's largest hydro-electric dam and reservoir, built to irrigate sun-baked southern Portugal, has paradoxically split the local community. The Alqueva floodgates were closed in 2002, damming the Guadiana river and creating an artificial lake covering 250sq km (96sq miles). Before the dam could be built, though, the village of Aldeia da Luz—and its graveyard—had to be relocated. A collection of Stone Age rock paintings and a Roman fort were also submerged.

Humans were not the only species to have relocation forced on them. Imperial eagles, Iberian lynx, black storks, wild boar and bats all lost their habitats in the area, along with some rare plant species. The government says the reservoir will boost agriculture, water sports and tourism, but it remains to be seen whether the benefits to farmers will outweigh the impact on the environment.

Space Age Solutions

Forests and woodland cover some nine per cent of the Portuguese countryside and the government is working hard to protect these natural habitats. But the forest fires that raged throughout much of southern Europe during the 2003 heat wave hit the country hard. Vast tracts of woodland were devastated and topsoil eroded.

However, the news is not all bad. In 2003, for the first time ever, European space agency satellites sent images to firefighters in Portugal, showing the spread of the blazes and helping the rescue services keep pace with the rapidly changing situation. As a result, the Portuguese are now better prepared for such an emergency; in 2004, prevention plans were in place including forestry patrols, while some 26,000 soldiers and engineers were drafted in to create firebreaks that would help to stop future blazes spreading.

Vasco da Gama Bridge

Opened in 1998, the Ponte Vasco da Gama is Lisbon's newest bridge and the longest in Europe. Nearly half of its 16km (10-mile) length-spans the Tejo estuary. The vast cable-stayed bridge enables north–south traffic to bypass Lisbon, alleviating the rush-hour congestion suffered by commuters on the older 25 de Abril Bridge and improving the air quality in the capital. It is now a landmark in its own right.

Despite its benefits, the project was not unopposed, particularly by ornithologists who were worried about the effect building work would have on the nearby bird sanctuary. In response, the Lusoponte consortium formed to build the bridge agreed to take special steps to avoid disturbing the flamingos, egrets and cormorants that feed in the area, and a great deal was done to minimize the impact on the local environment.

A beautiful decorated tile from Lamego

Nuns and a kneeling pilgrim approach Fátima's basilica

Statue of Our Lady of Fátima

Living Traditions

Handwoven woollens, a craft tradition that still flourishes

Traditional pottery from Monchique incorporates bright glazes and patterns

The towering statue of Cristo Rei (Christ the King) looking out over the Tejo estuary from Cacilhas serves as a constant reminder of Portugal's Catholic heritage. Although statistics suggest the Church's influence is in decline among the young, the crowds of pilgrims at the shrine of Fátima suggest little, if any, loss of faith.

Go into almost any Portuguese home and the chances are you will come across an ornamental cockerel, the national symbol. These cockerels come from Barcelos, where legend has it the miraculous crowing of a dead cockerel saved a pilgrim from the gallows five centuries ago. For all that time, the country was a monarchy, though it has now been a republic for nearly 100 years. Despite this, the claimant to the throne is a popular figure. Many other customs and traditions have similarly survived or adapted to meet the test of time.

The Altar of Portugal

The shrine of Fátima is the religious heart of Portugal and a place of devotion for Catholic pilgrims from all over the world. It receives some 2 million visitors every year. Controversy has been raging recently, though, after Fátima played host to an interfaith congress in 2003, attended by Buddhist, Hindu, Muslim, Orthodox and Anglican representatives. The shrine's rector, Monsignor Guerra, supports the idea of converting the sanctuary into a place where different religions can worship together. But many Catholics thought it was sacrilegious to see non-Catholics walking alongside priests in religious procession. Whatever the future may hold for Fátima, there is no doubt that this holy shrine still arouses fierce Catholic passions.

Dom Duarte, who will become king of Portugal in the event of the monarchy's restoration, and his wife

Port in bottle and cask, for centuries one of Portugal's most popular exports to a thirsty world

A decorated tile depicting a Portuguese ocean-going caravel

A university student from Porto in traditional celebratory dress

University Life

Held every May, the *Queima das Fitas* is the culmination of a set of university rituals that begin on enrollment day. They include the *latada* (baptism), when new students are given outrageous haircuts and embarrassing forfeits to carry out in public.

The best place to see the *queima* is in Coimbra, the home of Portugal's oldest university. The tradition gets its name from the symbolic burning of a *fita* (narrow ribbon) by students about to start their final-year examinations. Only after the ritual has been observed may finalists decorate their traditional folders with ribbons representing their particular faculties. The partying continues for a week, reaching its climax in a carnival-style procession through the city's streets—the last chance to let off steam.

Azulejos

The patterned glazed tiles that decorate the façades and interiors of many Portuguese buildings are the product of centuries of artistic tradition. At the Museu Nacional do Azulejo (National Tile Museum) in Lisbon, you can see murals that depict panoramic views of the capital before it was devastated by the great earthquake of 1755.

To see contemporary *azulejos* all you need to do is to take a trip on the Lisbon metro, which is decorated with tiles created by Lisbon-born artists Maria Keil and Rolando Sá-Nogueira. Keil's design at Intendente station is considered to be a masterpiece of tile art, marking the end of a long period of decline. For a different approach, head to Laranjeiras station, where Sá-Nogueira has used photo-realism to create mouthwatering depictions of lush ripe oranges—the fruit after which the district is named.

The House of Bragança

When you think of the royal houses of Europe, you may be forgiven for leaving Portugal off the list. But Dom Duarte Pio de Bragança is internationally recognized by monarchists as the rightful king, representing the nation at royal gatherings throughout Europe. Pretender to Portugal's abolished throne—a revolution in 1910 deposed the monarchy—Dom Duarte was born in exile in 1945. The family returned home five years later when the law banning the former royals was abolished. Married to Portuguese commoner Isabel de Heredia, the 24th Duke of Bragança now has three young children—eldest son and heir Afonso, Maria Francisca and Dinis. They are cherished by many Portuguese supporters, who regard them as living representatives of centuries of history, and who continue the campaign to see the monarchy restored.

Port

Port has been produced in the Douro valley since Roman times, although it did not really make an impact outside Portugal until the British began importing it in quantity from1703. Despite its popularity, the demands of today's highly competitive drinks market have forced the Portuguese to rethink port's image. Once deemed old-fashioned, this sophisticated fortified wine is now staging a comeback, particularly among younger people. Exports to North America are rising steadily, while the British are experimenting with alternatives to the classic vintages. Lower alcohol white port is perfect as a chilled aperitif, while cocktail lovers might like to try an Autumnal Equinox: Mix two measures of port to one of Grand Marnier and a half measure of an almond-based liqueur. Serve over ice and join the new wave of 21st-century port enthusiasts.

Fishermen mend their nets on the beach at Figueira da Foz as the sun sets

A gaily painted fishing boat hauled up on to the beach

Grilling fresh fish in the street

The Sea

Portugal's history has been inextricably linked to the sea since the Moors crossed the Strait of Gibraltar. They occupied the 'Al-Gharb'—the Moorish name for what is now the Algarve—for 500 years until the 12th century. Portuguese expansion began some 400 years later when the great explorers, such as Vasco da Gama, set sail, rounding the Cape of Good Hope and opening up new trade routes to the east.

Today, the sea continues to define the nation. The crowded, though beautiful, beaches of the Algarve stretching along the southern coast are a crucial source of tourist revenue. In contrast, the stormy seas of the Atlantic coast to the north are one of Europe's most important fishing areas, also making a vital contribution to the economy.

But disaster struck in November 2002. The sinking of a super-tanker off Spain's northwest coast was an environmental catastrophe as oil from the spill drifted southward. Local fishermen fear it will be many years before life in the sea recovers fully.

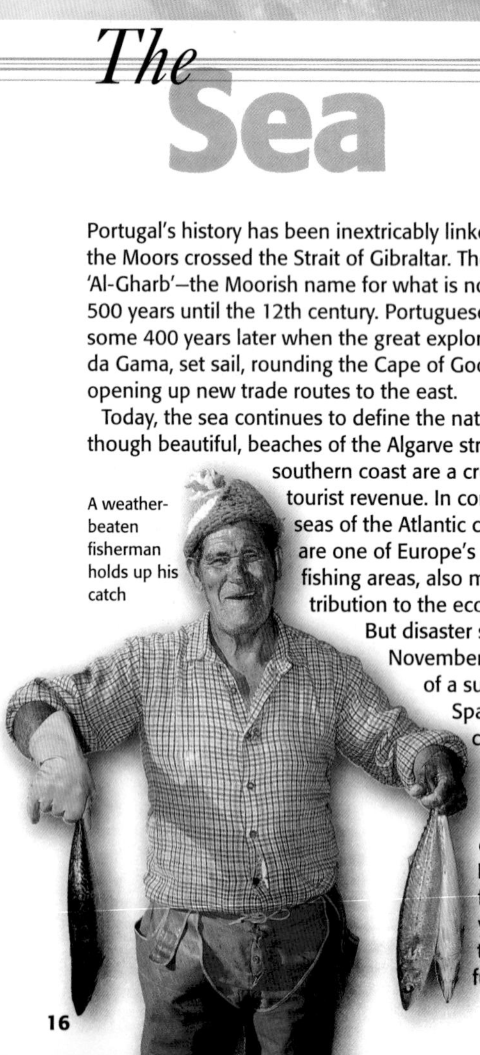

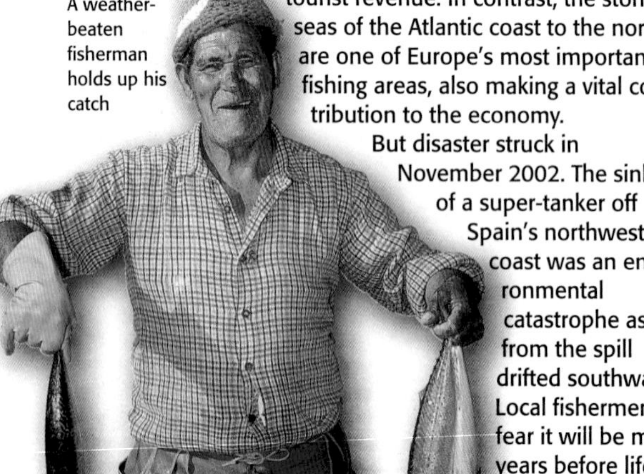

A weather-beaten fisherman holds up his catch

'365 Ways to Cook Salt-cod'

Dried salt-cod, or *bacalhau*, is arguably Portugal's most famous national dish. A popular saying states there is a different salt-cod recipe for every day of the year, and a glance at the average menu certainly seems to uphold this claim—the ubiquitous *bolinho de bacalhau* (codfish croquette) appears in restaurants throughout the country and is a tasty snack.

The story starts in the 1500s, when sailors learned to salt cod on their epic voyages, drying it out on deck until it was stiff as a board. On the beaches of Nazaré you can still see racks of fish drying in the sun the traditional way. What has changed, however, is that salt-cod now accounts for a quarter of Portugal's fish imports, as fishermen struggle to keep up with demand.

Natural erosion by wind and water has created the rock formations at Ponta da Piedade

A sperm whale on the move. Whale Watch Azores has spotted the largest number of whales in Europe over the years

Tiago Pires (right) and Justin Mujica (below right) cut a dash through the surf

Sea Arches

On the southern Atlantic coast at Ponta da Piedade, near the picturesque town of Lagos, there is a headland of sculptured cliffs comprising what may well be the largest collection of sea arches in the world. The rock is riddled with grottoes, deep holes and natural tunnels, all the hallmarks of centuries of natural erosion.

Now Lagos town council has decided to take action to protect this much-visited beauty spot. The lighthouse, cliff path and deep sandy creek—supporting countless forms of marine life—attract large numbers of tourists every year. The funds the council is raising will be used to prevent further erosion by regenerating the vegetation, for the building of designated paths and viewpoints for visitors, and for improved traffic controls and carparking facilities.

Plenty More Fish?

The Portuguese eat an annual average of 70kg (154 lb) of fish (the European average is 22.5kg/50 lb), making them the second-highest consumers of fish in the world. All along the coast there are numerous sea-dependent communities landing mackerel and sardines, but Portugal's fishermen are struggling to keep up with demand. They currently catch only 68 per cent of Portugal's fish supply—many sardines are now imported from Russia and cod comes from Norway.

Concerns about the rapid depletion of fish stocks in the North Atlantic have also led to cutbacks in quotas across the European Union, and Portugal's fishermen are suffering the consequences. The fishing fleet—local, coastal and offshore—is being downsized and the fisheries have agreed to maintain current landings in an attempt to aid stock renewal.

Whale-spotting

The Azores archipelago is one of the best places in the world to spot whales. Sperm whales thrive here, co-existing with the 24 other sea mammal species registered on and around the islands. When Europhlukes—a project funded by the European Commission—set to work compiling the largest whale and dolphin database in the world, Whale Watch Azores (WWA) jumped at the chance to become involved in this ambitious project.

WWA, which also runs whale-spotting tours around the islands, already has the largest sperm whale register in Europe. It has identified more than 1,500 examples, along with blue, sei, killer and pilot whales. Once the Europhlukes database is fully up and running, anyone will be able to submit photographs to the website and discover whether their particular whale, dolphin or porpoise has been spotted elsewhere in Europe.

World-class Waves

What do Sunset Beach, Hawaii, and Australia's Noosa have in common with the lively seaside resort of Figueira da Foz? The answer: all have hosted the World Surfing Championships. Hotshot Tiago Pires is Portuguese surfing's most famous export. This rising star has been winning competitions on the world circuit ever since he was crowned rookie of the year in 2000. But it is at home in Ericeira that you will find one of Tiago's best-loved surf spots. Known simply as The Reef, this finger of lava, sticking out at the southern tip of Ribeira Bay, is not for the inexperienced. Swells come in from the deep Atlantic, folding over the rocks into what Tiago warns is one of the fastest—and most dangerous—tubes in the world.

Ballet in action, Sintra (left) and (right) a decorated tile promoting *fado*

An imposing cinema frontage in the Baixa, Lisbon's oldest district

Models from Lisbon fashion week in Ana Salazar, José António Tenete and Fátima Lopes designs

The Modern Arts

Lisbon Fashion Week

ModaLisboa—first held in 1991—is Portugal's answer to the catwalk shows of London, Paris, New York and Milan. Lisbon is working hard to promote itself as a capital of fashion and its fashion week is rapidly achieving international status. More than 20,000 people now attend this event every year, and it has become a showcase for the talents of fashion designers and models alike.

At the cutting edge is Ana Salazar, widely considered to be the leading light of Portuguese fashion. Her contribution was recognized when she was awarded the Order of Infante D. Henrique by Portugal's president. Lisbon fashion week has also become a launching pad for new talent, propelling contemporary designers such as José António Tenente, Manuel Alves, Fátima Lopes and Maria Gambina onto the international fashion scene.

Portugal is not renowned for its contribution to the arts, but it can still claim its fair share of famous painters, poets, writers, musicians and dancers. Since the Middle Ages, a number of classic works have come to stand as cultural landmarks on the Portuguese arts scene.

Figurative art in Portugal can be traced back to Stone Age rock paintings and the *berrões*—roughly carved granite bulls and boars—probably used in fertility rituals as early as 4000BC. Literature, however, lagged behind. It was not until the 16th century that a poetic masterpiece was to appear. *The Lusiads*, an epic account of the voyages of discovery by Luis de Camões (*c*1524–1580), records the transition from medieval to Renaissance times. His portrait of Vasco da Gama rivals that of Virgil's Aeneas, while the theme he chose stands up to comparison with Homer's *Odyssey*.

In the 20th century, another Portuguese poet, Fernando Pessoa (1888–1935), made his mark. By creating a series of alter egos and publishing works under their names, he created a literary genre all of his own.

Mariza Nunes is the undisputed superstar of modern *fado*

A striking modern fountain in the square, Loulé, the Algarve

Nelly Furtado sings Euro 2004's anthem before the kick-off of the final between Portugal and Greece

Fado Diva

Hailed as the new Amália Rodrigues—Portugal's legendary *fadista*, or *fado* soloist—Mariza Nunes stands out from the crowd in more ways than one. *Fado* is Portugal's take on the blues, and Mozambique-born Mariza has both the voice and the looks to carry it off. Her peroxide-blonde braids may shock, but her vocal skills never fail to impress.

Fadistas are expected to stand stock still as they sing to hushed audiences in the bars and clubs of Lisbon and Coimbra. But Mariza defies convention. Always moving to the jazzed-up rhythms that set her style apart, she brings elements of gospel, soul and rock to this traditional song form that is unique to Portugal. In 2004, Mariza recorded a duet with Sting for the Olympic games in Athens, and is determined to continue promoting *fado* around the world, reaching ever wider, larger and more enthusiastic audiences.

Musical Oasis

On a farm in Castelo Branco, Maria João Pires has realized a life-long dream. The Portuguese piano virtuoso has opened a retreat where musicians can work in an environment perfectly in tune with their artistic needs. It took a great deal of work to get the project off the ground and turn Maria João Pires' dream into a reality. Lack of funding meant things got off to a shaky start, but the Portuguese government came to the rescue. Today, the Belgais Centre for the Study of the Arts has a concert hall with fantastic acoustics and a studio where Maria João Pires recorded *Moonlight*, her reinterpretation of the Beethoven sonatas that launched her career. Since then this musical oasis has gone from strength to strength, running courses for students from all over the world and providing encouragement to aspiring artists in these inspirational surroundings.

Nobel Laureate

When José Saramago won the 1998 Nobel Prize for Literature, he famously joked that 'this prize is for all speakers of Portuguese, but while we're on the subject, I shall keep the money'. Born in 1922 in Azinhaga, Portugal's greatest living author is still writing novels, plays, short stories, poetry and non-fiction. Many of his novels present alternative versions of historical events—what historians call counterfactuals—often with an intriguing supernatural twist.

A long-standing member of the Communist Party of Portugal, Saramago has also turned his attention to contemporary politics. *The Stone Raft*—a tale about Portuguese and Spanish society—follows four people whose lives are thrown into turmoil when the Iberian Peninsula breaks away from mainland Europe, spinning through the Atlantic towards the United States and triggering a geopolitical crisis.

Celestial Choreography

'If the gods wanted to see a dance performance, they would surely choose the Gulbenkian Ballet,' ran one recent review of this outstanding Portuguese dance company. The Gulbenkian Ballet has experienced rapid growth since 2003 under the artistic direction of prize-winning dancer-turned-choreographer Paulo Ribeiro. In 2004, it toured the European festival circuit performing *White*, choreographed by the director himself and with an original score performed by the Portuguese group Danças Ocultas.

Not one to rest on his laurels, Paulo Ribeiro now doubles as the general manager and programmer of the Centro Regional das Artes do Espectáculo das Beiras. Under his tutelage, the Centro Regional became a recipient of the prestigious Almada Prize awarded by the Instituto Português das Artes do Espectáculo.

José Manuel Barroso, a leading Portuguese politician and prime minister in 2004

Braga stadium packed with fans for the Euro 2004 championship match between Bulgaria and Denmark

Economy and Politics

Economic Goals

Braga municipal stadium is an architectural triumph. Built specially for the Euro 2004 football championships, it was carved out of the mountainside on the site of a former quarry. But this is not the only Euro 2004 success story. Although many critics said that in the midst of recession the government should be investing in hospitals rather than sport, Portugal now has seven new stadiums costing a total of 500 million euros to build. If this sounds like a lot of money, compare it to the 1.1 billion euros the new Wembley stadium in London is currently estimated to be costing. There is still more of which the Portuguese can be proud. Three of the sites have been awarded UEFA's highest, five-star, rating, rivalling the best stadiums in the rest of Western Europe.

Portugal has come a long way since 1986 when it joined the European Community. At the time it was seen as Spain's poor relation, but EU membership soon paid off for the country. Fast forward a few decades and you find a nation basking in the international spotlight as the host of the Euro 2004 football championships. A year earlier and the world's reporters were on Portuguese soil for a very different event. At Lajes air base in the Azores, US President George W. Bush was meeting Portuguese Prime Minister José Manuel Barroso and their British and Spanish allies. The islands were the stage for a crisis summit on the eve of the Iraq war in March 2003.

Not so long ago it would have been hard to imagine Portugal's economic and political standing being so high. In 2002 the country was reeling from the sudden resignation of Prime Minister António Guterres after his Socialist party had failed to find solutions for a stinging recession and high unemployment. In just a few years, the country has picked itself up and taken its first steps on the road to recovery.

Newspapers and magazines cater for all Portuguese tastes and interests

The two sides of life in the Algarve: A peasant farmer poses with his sheep (left) and a luxury hillside villa at Quinta do Lago (below)

Porto's new metro, a symbol of urban regeneration

Portugal's cork industry is under threat

Put a Cork in It

Generations of families in the Alentejo region of southern Portugal have earned their living as cork-makers. Portugal is the world's leading supplier, producing 50 per cent of all cork stoppers.

The industry currently keeps 15,000 people employed, but these jobs are coming under threat from a new trend in wine-bottling, with retailers opting for plastic- and screw-top alternatives to traditional corks. And there is another side to the story. According to the Worldwide Fund for Nature, it is not only Portugal's economy that could suffer. The harvesting of cork is environmentally friendly and, if the cork forests are not managed responsibly, they eventually could turn into desert. This would spell more trouble for many endangered species—such as the Iberian lynx—that are already battling for survival.

Farming Quotas

2003 was a bad year for Portuguese farmers, who lost out when Portugal was the only EU member state to vote against the reform of the Common Agricultural Policy. The agriculture minister said the resulting EU cuts in milk quotas for dairy farmers in the Azores—one of the poorest regions of Europe—would cripple the islands' economy. But quotas are not the only problem. High land prices mean most of Portugal's farms cover less than 5ha (12 acres), making it all but impossible for farmers to sell their livestock and produce at competitive prices, or to create opportunities for young people to join the industry. The reforms in Brussels have done little to address these concerns. Many farmers hope that the trend towards organic farming will save the day.

Job Creation

High unemployment has blighted Portugal's economy in recent years. But a new masters course in business start-up and management, run by the ISCTE Business School in Lisbon, has already had a positive impact on the job market.

One of the first students to graduate in 2003, Helena Serdoura, came from a business background as a partner in one of the few recruitment agencies for domestic workers in Portugal. The course helped her broaden and fine-tune her business skills through the study of marketing techniques and efficient and effective administration.

On graduating, Helen Serdoura set up Housekeeping, a school where domestic staff can improve their knowledge of cookery, flower arranging, etiquette, babysitting and first aid. Its doors opened in 2004 and, in just a few months, 70 people had completed training courses to boost their job prospects.

Regeneration

While holidaymakers may enjoy taking the old-fashioned trams down Avenida do Boavista to the seafront district of Foz do Douro, commuters in Porto had long been yearning for a quicker, smoother ride to work. Drivers crossing the river from Vila Nova de Gaia also longed for a day when traffic jams would be a thing of the past. Their wish came true with the opening of the Metro do Porto—the largest transport project under way in the EU—which carries 60 million passengers per year. Architect Eduardo Souto de Moura designed the 66 stations and engineer Adão de Fonseca built the Infante D. Henrique Bridge, which spans 371m (1,217ft) over the Douro. Once complete, the system will have four colour-coded lines intersecting at the central station of Trindade, dramatically cutting journey times for commuters and easing the city's traffic congestion.

A girl captured at a celebration to mark the anniversary of the 1974 Revolution, Porto

A Lisbon café scene. The Portuguese love to eat and drink, often late into the night

Traditional carpet-making in Arrailos, where this is a long-established craft activity

Faces of Portugal

A girl in elaborate folk costume

Moorish Legacy

In the small town of Arraiolos near Évora in central Portugal, local carpet-weavers make wall-hangings and floor-coverings using traditional Moorish techniques handed down from mother to daughter for more than 500 years. The authenticity of each *tapete de Arraiolos* (needlework rug) is guaranteed by the Arraiolos Producers' Association.

The roots of this flourishing art form can be traced back to the Inquisition, when the Moors, Jews and anyone else who was not a God-fearing Catholic were persecuted or forced to flee the cities. Some of the Moors sought refuge in the Alentejo plains, where they set about making rugs. Their legacy lives on to this day in Arraiolos, where it has spawned a prosperous cottage industry.

Perhaps as a result of Portugal's small land mass and population, its people have always been united by three factors: a common language, their Catholic faith and the sea. This cohesion helped Portugal become the first unified nation-state in Western Europe.

Despite this, the Portuguese can chart their ancestry back to a variety of ethnic groups. In the north, many families trace their roots back to the early Celtic tribes who settled in the area long before the Romans arrived. In contrast, the south bears witness to five centuries of Moorish occupation, particularly in the Algarve region. The language itself contains corruptions of Moorish expressions in words like *oxalá*, which means 'if only' in Portuguese and comes from the Arabic *Inshallah* (Allah willing).

In modern Portugal, regional differences owe more to tradition and climate than they do to wars and battles with prospective occupiers. The popular saying 'while Lisbon plays, Braga prays and Porto works' supports the theory that life up in the north has always been more conservative and devout than in the warmer, easygoing south.

Many older peasant women still stick to the traditional black

Tomar is the host to one of Portugal's liveliest traditional festivals

A bullfight in progress, the horseman showing off his riding skills

A traditional Algarve house, with its bright plasterwork

Historic Rivalry

Relations between Portugal and Spain, its only neighbour, have always been characterized by intense rivalry. A popular saying states that from Spain the Portuguese can expect 'neither a good wind nor a good marriage'.

The town of Olivença in the Alto Alentejo is a living reminder of this centuries-old aspect of Portuguese life. Both the town and 600sq km (231sq miles) of surrounding countryside were annexed by the Spanish in 1801 and, although Portugal has never got the land back, it has not stopped trying. The Grupo de Amigos de Olivença—Friends of Olivença—campaigns ceaselessly to end what it regards as the illegal Spanish occupation.

Other locals, however, take things more philosophically. They boast that the women of Olivença are unique in their combination of Portuguese beauty and Spanish grace.

Feast of São Gonçalo

The church of São Gonçalo in Amarante is the most famous building in this pretty town on the banks of the Tâmega river to the east of Porto. On the first weekend of June each year it becomes the focus for the Feast of São Gonçalo, the patron saint of the town and in charge of marrying off single women.

Just as in the rest of Portugal, folklore here goes hand in hand with the Catholic faith, in which it usually finds a basis and inspiration. As part of the festivities, the young couples of Amarante exchange lupin seeds—an ancient fertility symbol—or phallus-shaped cakes, incorporating a pagan custom into the saint's day celebrations. These little tokens represent their mutual love.

Rural v Urban

The village of Casais in the hill-country of Monchique in southern Portugal offers visitors a taste of the peace and tranquillity typical of rural life. But behind this seemingly idyllic façade, the reality is somewhat different. It seems that the lure of urban living may one day put an end to this pastoral existence and to the regional culture that accompanies it.

Abandoned farms and overgrown fields are both increasingly common sights throughout the *serra*, the mountainous border that separates the Algarve from the Alentejo. The lack of economic prospects is forcing many families to head for the towns and coastal areas in search of jobs that can guarantee them better living standards. Today, the rural population of Monchique stands at just 17 people per square kilometre (0.3sq miles).

Bullfighting Country

Vila Franca de Xira, north-east of Lisbon in the heart of Portugal's bull-fighting country, has an unrivalled reputation for bull rearing. Twice a year visitors gather here for the running of the bulls. For several days each July during the *Festa do Colete Encarnado* (Red Waistcoat Festival), there are bullfights and bull runs, when the young bulls are turned loose and the hot-headed, drunk, or just plain misguided attempt to dodge them as they thunder through the streets.

The festival gets its name from the traditional outfits worn by the *campinos* (cowboys), who watch over the bulls on the Ribatejo marshlands. The courageous Lusitano stallions traditionally ridden by Portugal's bullfighters are also bred in the area. Unlike his Spanish counterpart, the aim of the Portuguese *tourada* is not to kill the bull, but rather to show off his horse's schooling.

Soccer (left), windsurfing (below) and golf (bottom) are three sports particularly associated with Portugal

Two of Portugal's all-time footballing greats—Luis Figo (left) and, from a previous generation, Eusébio

Sporting Life

Portugal is a proud soccer nation with a world-class pedigree—the skills of 1960s player Eusébio, the 'black panther', rivalled those of Brazil's Pelé. It again confirmed its credentials when FC Porto romped to victory in the 2004 Champions League. And the eyes of the world remained fixed on the country as it hosted the third-largest sports event in the world. The national team made it through to the final of Euro 2004 and, although they were beaten by Greece, the smooth running of the tournament made the host nation a winner.

But there is much more to sport in Portugal than 'the beautiful game', even though football-crazy Portuguese might disagree. From stunning championship golf courses to world-class surfing beaches and great facilities for extreme sports, the possibilities are endless.

Above Par

Golf is big business in the Algarve, where, for many years, local courses have been designed on purely commercial grounds. However, growing concerns about the impact this has had on the local environment are now being taken seriously.

Vila Sol Golf Resort near Almansil, which has played host to two Portuguese Opens, has made high environmental quality a key selling point to the increasing numbers of golfers who are concerned about the long-term effects of their sport on the environment. At Vila Sol, treated waste water irrigates the course and much of the original forest has been retained in the roughs. There are sizeable populations of wild birds and reptiles, including ocellated lizards and chameleons, all of which make the resort an extra-special destination.

Sporting Chance

Named World Player of the Year by Fifa, soccer's governing body, in 2003, Portuguese midfielder Luis Figo is arguably one of the world's all-time great footballers. At the time of his signing to the Spain's Real Madrid in 2000, he was the world's most expensive player with a 55-million-euro transfer fee.

Figo has never forgotten his childhood in the working-class Lisbon suburb of Cova da Piedade. In 2003 he set up the Luis Figo Foundation, which aims to give needy children some of the opportunities that Figo had enjoyed. The foundation promotes sports initiatives to help keep youngsters off the streets. Although concentrating its initial efforts in the Lisbon area, there are plans to expand the project and help deprived children throughout the country.

The Story of Portugal

Celts, Romans and Visigoths

As part of the Iberian peninsula, Portugal shares much of its ancient history with Spain; indeed, it is hard to disentangle the two until the 12th-century creation of an independent Portuguese kingdom when the Christians drove out the Moors. Cut off from the rest of Europe by the northern mountains, this was a land apart.

Early settlers had occupied parts of the country as far back as 5500BC, but the historical dawn really broke with the establishment of a Celtic culture in the north around 700–600BC. Farther south, by 300BC, Phoenicians and Carthaginians, two great trading nations, had settled in turn around modern Lisbon. They were followed by the Romans, who arrived in 210BC.

In the fifth century AD, as the Roman empire fell apart, Vandals, Alans, Suevi and Visigoths crossed the Pyrenees from the north and settled in the area between the Douro and Minho rivers. By the sixth century, the Visigoths had gained the upper hand over their main rivals, the Suevi. They ruled from Toledo in modern Spain and had little interest, and less influence in what was to become Portugal. In the eighth century AD their lack of cohesion resulted in one faction asking the North African Moors for aid. By 711, however, the Muslim forces had turned on the Visigoths and were sweeping through Iberia.

The Living Legacy

There are no great Roman sites in Portugal, but, around the world, more than 200 million people daily commemorate the Roman occupation every time they speak. Portuguese is a Romance language, evolved from Latin, which developed over the seven centuries of Roman occupation. It is very similar to Galician, the language spoken in Spain's northwest corner. Over the years, words have crept in from the north, from Arabic, and from India and China, but Portuguese remains a Latin-based tongue, even though it sounds more like something from eastern Europe. It's the official language of Portugal's historic colonies, with Brazil leading the field, and ranks eighth among the most spoken languages world-wide.

This statue of a mounted knight is thought to date from Roman times

2000BC

Romans at war

Mosaic floors, a Roman legacy

Celtic ruins at Briteiros

Paved Streets and Plumbing

Scattered throughout the Minho are more than 40 *citânias*, fortified hill settlements constructed by the Iron Age Celts who arrived in Portugal from northern Europe around 700-600BC. By far the finest is at Briteiros, where the paved streets, drainage and circular huts are superbly preserved.

The Roman historian Strabo left a vivid account of the lifestyle of Portugal's Celtic inhabitants of around 20BC. They lived simply, drinking water and eating acorn bread. Beer and wine were saved for special occasions, when the whole community would assemble to dance to traditional music. On a more primitive note, the Celts also carried out mass human sacrifices, casting their auguries by inspecting the entrails of their still-living prisoners.

Viriatus—A Hero of His Time

In 193BC the Lusitani, a tribe based between the Tejo and Lima rivers, rose up against the Romans. This marked the start of a 50-year struggle against the might of the empire.

In 147BC Viriatus emerged as the rebel leader, raising an army, gaining territory and defeating the Romans time after time. The frustrated Roman Senate sent an army to put down the revolt once and for all, but Viriatus promptly succeeded in trapping its legions and forcing them to surrender. Cunningly, he used his prisoners as a bargaining tool, gaining Roman recognition for his rule. In 139BC, however, the Roman emissaries, ostensibly sent to negotiate with Viriatus, assassinated him. His followers were crushed by the legions and enslaved.

Bridging the Gap

In Chaves in the Trás-os-Montes you can walk across a bridge that's been standing since the end of the first century AD. Chaves was a military town, swarming with troops and an important metal-trading hub. Such was its importance that the Roman Emperor Trajan commissioned the construction of a 12-arched 140m-long (460ft) bridge that was strategically positioned on the road linking Braga and Astorga.

Two columns, inscribed with the names of governors and generals, still stand, along with milestones showing the distances to towns along the road. The bridge has carried heavy traffic ever since and has been strengthened many times. With the building of a new bridge upriver, it looks set to stand for a few more centuries.

Divine Swine

Prehistoric peoples focused their fertility rites on some pretty odd objects, and none more so than the pig. Held in reverence by the Celtic tribes, there are more than 200 sturdy granite pig statues in Trás-os-Montes, all of which are well over 2,000 years old. Crudely carved, but very definitely porcine, the *porcas* measure as much as 2m (6.5ft) in length and were probably worshiped as much for their strength and power as for their fertility and rich meat. They were originally placed in sacred enclosures, usually circular, but have migrated over the years, and are now proudly displayed in village squares, local museums and along roadsides. The biggest and best is at Murça, between Vila Real and Mirandela.

A Bragança *porca*

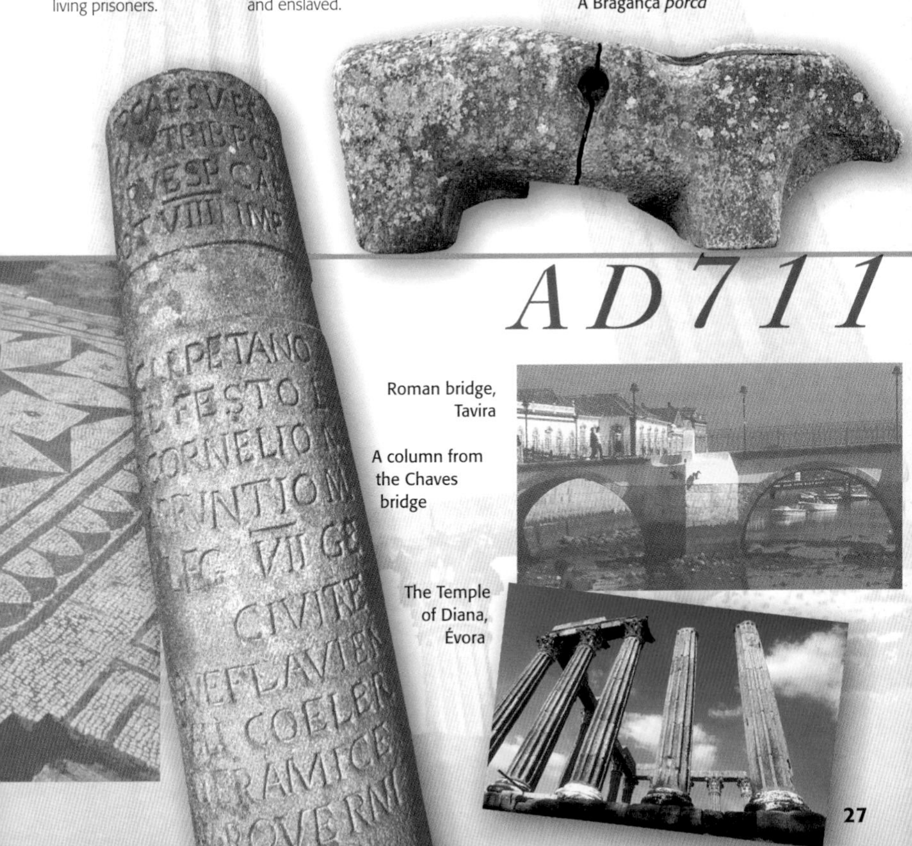

Roman bridge, Tavira

A column from the Chaves bridge

The Temple of Diana, Évora

The Moors

The damp green hills of northern Portugal held little attraction for the Moors, who were happy to concentrate their efforts on the well-watered Tejo valley, the rich lands of the Alentejo and, above all, the Algarve. This was the heart of their Portuguese territorial holdings. By the ninth century AD, the Algarve was a rich and important kingdom in its own right, entirely independent of neighbouring al-Andalus. Xelb, modern Silves, was its glittering capital, from where tolerant laws were issued to the *Moçárabes*, the Christians subject to Moorish rule. Agriculture and scholarship flourished, with towns growing up across the Moorish holdings.

Meanwhile, the Christians were regrouping up in the north in what they christened Portucale, the lands between the Minho and Douro. It was from here that Afonso Henriques launched his push southwards to drive out the infidels. Portuguese victory at Ourique in 1139 was a major blow for the Moors; by 1148 Lisbon was in Christian hands and Afonso Henriques' title as first king of Portugal had been confirmed by the treaty of Zamora. The following century saw steady Christian expansion; in 1249 Faro fell to them and Christian Portugal had established its mainland borders pretty much where they are today.

Guimarães castle

An Eastern Influence

The Moors inhabited Portugal for more than 500 years. They made their mark in scholarship and science, shipbuilding and construction, and, most lasting of all, in agriculture. They irrigated the land, damming and channelling water for use in irrigation and to power water mills. They practised crop rotation, introduced oranges and lemons, planted almond and fig groves, and raised cotton and rice. Their love of sweet things put sugar firmly on the Portuguese menu, while their spices pepped up the national diet. The Portuguese landscape, particularly in the Moors' stronghold of the Algarve, would look very different today without their legacy.

Oranges were one of the Moors' many gifts to the Algarve region

AD711

An imposing statue of Afonso Henriques, sword in hand

Queen of the South

Showpiece of the Moorish *al-Gharb* (Algarve), Xelb (modern Silves) was a thriving capital, with a population of more than 30,000, a huge castle and a stock of architectural treasures. In 1189 it was besieged by Sancho I, son of Afonso Henriques, looking for easy loot. The castle's water supply held out throughout the summer, but when the cisterns ran dry, the Moors were forced to surrender, encouraged by Sancho's promises of clemency.

What followed, though, was mayhem and massacre with more than 6,000 slain. In 1191 the Moors retook the city, but in 1249 Xelb became permanently Christian. A long period of decline followed—by the 1500s the population was just 140.

The First King of Portugal

Born in 1109, Afonso Henriques was the son of Henry of Burgundy and Tareja, the illegitimate daughter of Afonso VI, King of Léon and Castile of Spain. Henry died in 1114, leaving Tareja as regent of the embryonic kingdom.

By the time he was 30, Afonso Henriques had wrested power from his mother, established his capital at Guimarães, won a stunning victory over the Moors at Ourique, repudiated his vassalage to Léon and declared himself king of Portucale. In 1143, Léon, although reluctant to relinquish its influence over the kingdom, recognised Afonso's right to the throne. Papal approval quickly followed. Afonso went on to drive the Moors out of Santarém and Lisbon. By the time of his death in 1185, only the Alentejo and the Algarve remained in Moorish hands.

Sancho 1, Afonso Henriques' successor, continued his father's campaigns to drive out the Moors

The Battle of Ourique

According to legend, God was certainly on Afonso's side at the battle of Ourique in 1139. The legend has it that Christ appeared to Afonso in a vision immediately before the battle encounter and blessed his shield.

Guarded by this blessing, Afonso took on no fewer than five Moorish kings in single combat. He and his forces won a decisive victory. His deeds are commemorated on the Portuguese national flag, which has five shields on it. Some argue that the number represents the Moorish rulers Afonso defeated, some that it symbolizes the five wounds of Christ on the Cross.

A wall tile detail shows Moorish Lisbon under Christian attack

Ancient Honours

Warriors were needed to oust the Moors, and in 1166 Afonso Henriques raised an élite force of knights that was to become the great military *Ordem de Avis* (Order of Avis). Like the Knights Templar, it was a fighting monastic order, its members taking vows of poverty, chastity and obedience. Its prime obligation was to fight the Moors whenever the king should command it. The order was given the town of Avis as its headquarters, and later monarchs donated vast tracts of the reconquered lands to the knights.

In 1789 the order was secularized, though its members still came from the aristocracy. It still exists and is one of the oldest surviving orders of chivalry in Europe, with Portugal's president as its head. Membership is conferred on outstanding army officers.

1249

Almond trees, another Moorish import, in blossom

Moors confer

Portugal's flag features Afonso Henriques' shield

The Moorish-built castle, Sesimbra

The Great Age of Discoveries

With its borders settled and a stable monarchy on the throne, Portugal's main worry for the next 150 years or so was the Castile, its powerful and territorially ambitious neighbour to the east in Spain. The heroic Dom Dinis (reigned 1279-1325) got Castile to recognize Portugal's borders in 1297, but it was only Portuguese victory at the battle of Aljubarrota in 1385 that eventually led to a lasting peace.

With Castile put firmly in its place, it's hardly surprising that the thoughts of maritime Portugal turned seawards. The following century saw an unprecedented age of discovery and exploration. Prince Henry the Navigator, the son of João I and Philippa of Lancaster, had the ocean-going caravel designed and founded the School of Navigation at Sagres in the Algarve with the aim of making long-distance exploration feasible.

Between 1419 and 1497, Portuguese seamen discovered Madeira and the Azores, opened up the west coast of Africa, rounded the Cape of Good Hope, and found a sea route to India and beyond. As a result, Portugal became the world's premier trading nation. In 1494 Portugal and Spain signed the Treaty of Tordesillas. Negotiated by the Pope, this drew an imaginary line down the Atlantic, giving Portugal Brazil and the Orient. The Spanish took the rest of the Americas.

A Battle and a Promise

João I's proclamation as King of Portugal in 1385 led to an immediate confrontation with Castile, which backed the rival claimant to the throne. Juan I invaded the country at the head of a 30,000-strong, army.

On the eve of battle, João vowed to build a great abbey in honour of the Virgin Mary if he was victorious. The two armies clashed at Aljubarrota and, undoubtedly helped by England's timely loan of 500 archers, the Portuguese captured the Castilian standard within an hour. Juan was chased back into Castile, and Portuguese independence was secured for the next 200 years. Three years later, João kept his promise to the Virgin and the building of the great abbey at Batalha began.

João 1 (right) built Batalha Abbey (below) to fulfil a vow he made to the Virgin Mary

1249

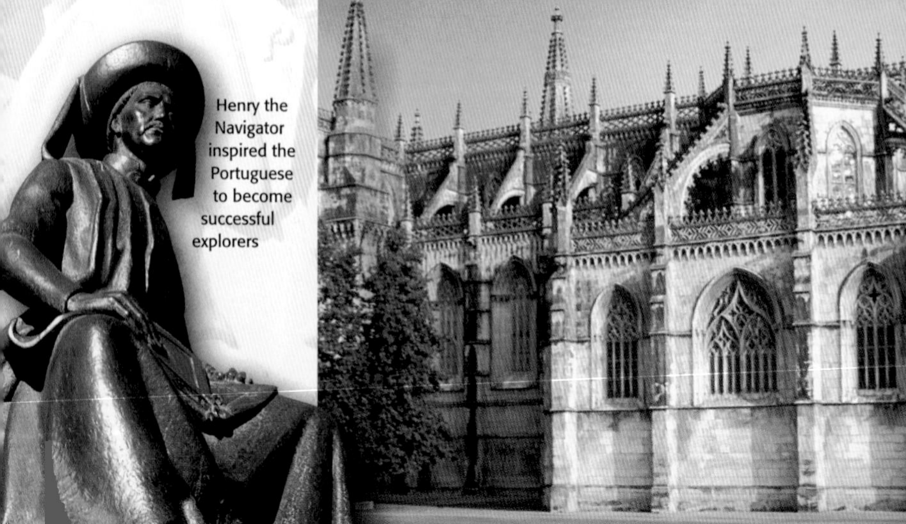

Henry the Navigator inspired the Portuguese to become successful explorers

Defending the Frontier

Dom Dinis inherited a country newly reconquered from the Moors; he also inherited one that needed stabilizing and strengthening. The biggest threat came from Castile in the east, and Dinis set about negotiating at once with his powerful neighbour. In the Treaty of Alcãnices in 1297, he got the Castilians to recognize Portugal's frontiers, but he took the precaution of backing this up with something more concrete. The result was a chain of more than 50 great castles along Portugal's eastern border. Many still stand, among them superbly sited Monsara; Belmonte, guarding the Serra da Estrela; Marvão and Castelo de Vide, within a stone's throw of Spain; and ancient Leiria in the east, though Dinis later rebuilt it as a royal residence.

Into the 'Sea of Darkness'

In the early 15th century, rounding Cape Bojador on the west African coast was the ultimate challenge. The southernmost point on sea-charts, it was the edge of the world, beyond which lay a 'sea of darkness'.

It was hardly surprising that sailors were scared of this stretch of water and its approaches. Between 1421 and 1433, no less than 14 expeditions failed to round the cape, and Henry the Navigator was losing patience with his lily-livered captains. In 1434 he dispatched the explorer Gil Eanes with instructions to round the cape without fail, promising him rich rewards if he succeeded. Eanes sailed south, doubled back from the Canaries and rounded the cape. The deadlock of superstition was broken and the way south was opened.

The English Connection

When the English nobleman John of Gaunt sent his archers to aid João I on the battlefield of Aljubarrota, it was a move that paved the way for one of Europe's oldest alliances. Suitably grateful for English help, João concentrated on cementing the ties between the two countries. In 1386, he signed the Treaty of Windsor and in 1387 he married Philippa of Lancaster, the daughter of John of Gaunt. They had five sons; their third son was the inspirational Henry the Navigator—a half-English prince.

Henry IV, Henry V and Henry VI of England successively ratified the Treaty of Windsor. Henry IV made João a Knight of the Garter, England's highest order of chivalry, to reward his loyalty.

Slave Trade

From the 1440s, Portuguese merchant ships were sailing west to the Atlantic islands and south down the west coast of Africa. Raid and trade was the name of the game, as the demand for labour to work the new sugar plantations in the Azores and Madeira grew.

Slavery had been a fact of life on the Iberian peninsula since Roman times, but figures rocketed in the 1450s, with slave numbers increasing by the year. North and west coast Africans were no longer domestic slaves, but worked as field hands, paid for in goods and shipped in often appaling conditions to the Azores, Madeira, Cape Verde and São Tomé. By the 1460s Madeira was the largest sugar producer in the western world.

Dom Dinis built a chain of castles along the eastern frontier

Afonso d'Alboquerque made Goa the Lisbon of the east

João and Henry IV of England at dinner

1520

Beatrix of Portugal married an English earl after Portugal and England became allies

The great compass rose, Sagres

The Torre de Belém, built to protect Lisbon's harbour

Spanish Domination

By 1520 Portuguese wealth and power may have been at its zenith, but with such a far-flung empire, there were hidden problems that were soon to bubble up to the surface. Very little of the money flowing into the country filtered down to the people at large, and there was no developing entrepreneurial class to handle the national finances. After the expulsion of the Jews and the establishment of the Inquisition, Portugal was left with a huge commercial empire, but not the financial expertise to run it.

By 1580 the money coming in from the empire was no longer enough to maintain it, and debts and costs were rising. Something had to give—and what gave was the monarchy. Three years after Dom Sebastião's death his uncle, Philip II of Spain, moved in, defeated the Portuguese at Alcântara and had himself crowned king in 1581. After a rosy start, Spanish domination brought few advantages. By 1640 the Portuguese had had enough. Conspirators threw out the Spanish governor and popular pressure persuaded the reluctant Duke of Bragança, head of Portugal's most powerful noble family, to take the throne as João IV.

Overstretched

Portugal ran its empire via the *feitorias* (factories), a series of fortified coastal trading posts that stretched round Africa to India and the Far East, Well fortified and easily resupplied by sea, the *feitorias* lulled the Portuguese into believing that they could maintain a grip on their vast possessions with minimal effort. For years, the system worked well enough, but by the mid-16th century it became clear that relying on 10,000 men to maintain this huge empire was simply not enough. The vital resupplying became more difficult and more expensive—the sea passage to Goa in India alone could take up to 18 months and it was as far again from Goa to Macau. The rewards, once so great, could no longer keep up with the expense.

Philip II of Spain forcibly united the two countries

A caravel, the ship that helped Portugal carve out an empire

1520

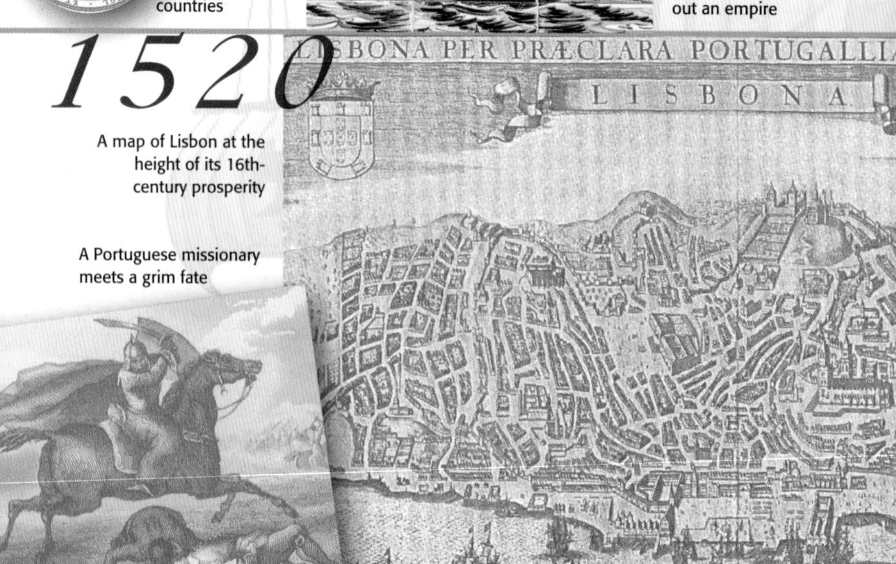

A map of Lisbon at the height of its 16th-century prosperity

A Portuguese missionary meets a grim fate

The Portuguese Inquisition

Auto da fé, trial by fire, is a not a Spanish phrase—it is Portuguese. The Inquisition in Portugal was just as feared and just as active as it was in Spain. It was set up in 1531 primarily to deal with those Jews who had supposedly embraced Christianity and so allowed to remain in the country after the mass expulsion of 1496, though its brief was broadened to investigate and punish all forms of heresy. Its investigations were basically unjust. Prosecutors, often acting on anonymous denunciations, were free to arrest anyone they chose, while the accused had no right to legal counsel or to question the accuser face to face. Known criminals often gave evidence unchallenged. Nor was there any right of appeal. Burning at the stake was the ultimate punishment.

A Portuguese Odyssey

Luís Vaz de Camões, Portugal's greatest literary figure, was born in 1525 and died in 1580. Outside Portugal, his fame rests on a single work, *Os Lusiadas (The Lusiads)*. This epic poem, glowing with patriotic fervour, celebrates Portuguese achievements in the great age of discoveries through the medium of Vasco da Gama's voyage to India. Da Gama is the poem's hero.

Camões was ideally placed to write about the east. His father had died in Goa and he himself spent 16 years travelling abroad. He lost an eye in Morocco, escaped shipwreck, was several times thrown in jail and enjoyed a passionate love affair with a local girl. He returned to Lisbon in 1570, publishing *Os Lusiadas* unsuccessfully in 1572 and died in poverty.

Disaster in Morocco

Things may have been going badly at home, but the deeply religious and equally bloodthirsty Dom Sebastião (reigned 1557–1578) was determined to resurrect the glory days of the Christian reconquest. Obsessed with war and bored with matters of state, Sebastião's ambition was to launch nothing less than an all-out crusade against the Muslims in North Africa.

In 1578, Sebastião managed to assemble a 14,000-strong army and set sail for Morocco. Near Alcázarquivir he met 40,000 Muslims who overwhelmed the Christian forces, killing Sebastião and 8,000 of his followers. Only three years later, the remnants of the Portuguese army were to stand little chance against Philip II of Spain when he marched into Portugal to claim the throne.

Diamond Trade

Until they were discovered in Brazil in 1725, diamonds came from India, with the Portuguese being the biggest shippers. Portuguese-Jewish diamond merchants settled in Antwerp in the early 16th century, where they mastered the technicalities of the trade, including the cutting and polishing of the stones. They were more than ready to handle the imports that poured out of India and through Lisbon to the north.

Most of the diamonds, along with sapphires and amethysts, originated in southern India, where the fabulous Koh-i-noor diamond was later found. Local Indian rulers acted as middlemen between the prospectors and the Portuguese, often keeping the biggest and best stones for themselves.

Camões, epic author

João de Barros became the first great historian of his country

1640

João de Castro saw Portuguese trade expand as viceroy in the east

Diamonds from India and then from Brazil added to Portugal's wealth

A Portuguese fortification in Morocco. Sebastião's crusade against the Moors there ended in disaster

The Road to Recovery

With the house of Bragança installed on the throne, relations with England back on course, and the discovery of gold and diamonds in Brazil, things were looking up. Money poured into the royal coffers, and just as quickly poured out again, as João V (reigned 1706–1750) embarked on an orgy of spending, squandering vast sums on lavish building schemes. His son, José I (reigned 1750–1777) was fortunate to have as his chief minister the Marquês de Pombal, a believer in enlightened despotism who dealt with the great Lisbon earthquake of 1755 and launched a massive modernization drive.

The rise of Napoleon led to a major new threat for the country. Lisbon was captured by the French in 1807, João VI fled to Brazil, and Portugal found itself embroiled in the Peninsular War. Two British generals, the Duke of Wellington and Lord Beresford, played the major role in expelling the French, but things remained unsettled until 1820, when Portuguese liberals drew up a new constitution. On his return from Brazil, the king accepted it, but his queen and younger son, Miguel, had other ideas. They led a reactionary movement that, after João's death in 1826, was to set the monarchy on an inexorable, though slow, slide to its eventual overthrow early the next century.

Sculptor Joaquim Machado de Castro designed the statue of José I, erected on the Praça do Comércio after the earthquake of 1755

Catherine of Bragança, wife of Charles II

A Nice Cup of Tea

Nearly 5,000 years ago, the Chinese were the first to enjoy a cup of tea, but it was only in 1560 that a European first sampled it—a Portuguese Jesuit called Jaspar da Cruz. Within a century, Portugal was importing tea from China to Lisbon They called it *chá*.

The Dutch caught the taste for tea as well and it was in Holland that a young exile, later Charles II of England, started to drink it. In 1662 Charles married the Portuguese Infanta Catherine of Bragança, also a confirmed *chá drinker*. Where king and queen led, the country followed. The royal stamp of approval was all it took to make tea as much enjoyed in England as it was in Portugal.

1640

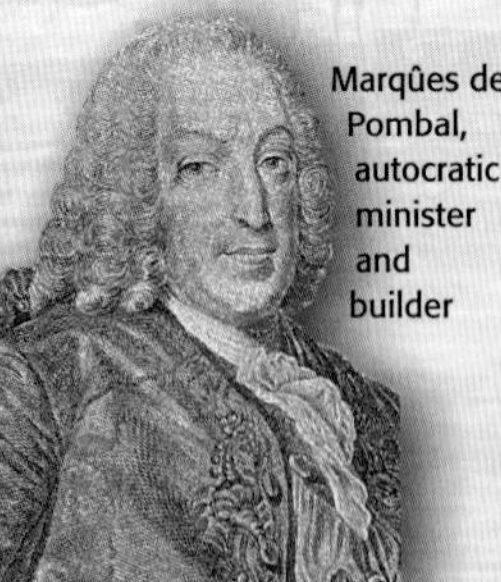

Marqûes de Pombal, autocratic minister and builder

Defending Torres Vedras, near Lisbon, against French attack

The Marquis de Campo Maior

With the royal family safely in Brazil, two British generals were the prime movers in the campaign to push Napoleon out of Portugal and Spain. They were Sir Arthur Wellesley, the future Duke of Wellington, and William Carr, Viscount Beresford.

Carr first encountered the Portuguese as governor of Madeira; it was love at first sight, and he immersed himself in learning the language and studying the country. It stood him in good stead in 1809, when he was given the task of reorganizing the Portuguese army, a task he achieved brilliantly, turning it into an effective fighting force fit to take part in the battle of Buçaco in 1811. He was made Marquis of Campo Maior and remained in Portugal as the country's administrator until 1821.

The Lisbon Earthquake

On 1 November 1755, as Lisbon churches were packed for the annual Mass for the dead, disaster struck in the form of a catastrophic earthquake, the aftershock of which was felt as far away as North Africa. For six minutes the ground heaved, while roofs and domes collapsed, killing hundreds, and a tidal wave swept in from the Tejo river, engulfing much of the lower part of the city. Candles, lit for the feast day, ignited fires that would burn for days. The chief minister, Sebastião José de Carvalho e Melo, later the Marquês de Pombal, stepped in, advising 'bury the dead, feed the living'. Thanks to him, nobody starved, there were no epidemics and, within 20 years, the Baixa, the historic heart of the city, had been triumphantly rebuilt.

Red, White and Ruby

Britain's on-and-off wars with France between 1679 and 1714 made port big business. French wine imports slumped, leaving a gap in the market that enterprising merchants quickly filled. Port flooded into Britain, encouraged by the Methuen Treaty of 1703, which lowered the import duty on it to a third of that on French wines. British entrepreneurs began establishing wine estates along the Douro, and names like Sandeman, Croft, Cockburn and Graham appeared. By 1756 the British had a stranglehold on the trade, and were passing off less-than-average port as the real thing. This led to the establishment of restrictions on what was port and what was not. The rules are still in force.

The Brazilian Question

With Napoleon's troops massing for invasion in 1807, the royal family, court and government hotfooted it across the Atlantic to Brazil and Rio de Janeiro. It was a bad move for the mother country; by 1815, Portugal, now administered by Beresford, was far weaker than its most important colony.

Trouble, in the shape of the liberals, loomed at home, and in 1821, João VI, weak, indecisive and suffering from piles, set sail for Lisbon with 4,000 officials and plenty of cash purloined from the Bank of Brazil. He left his son Pedro behind as regent. The next year, Pedro refused to return to Portugal. In 1822, he declared Brazilian independence. Portugal had lost its largest possession.

Napoleon's attempt to conquer Portugal was eventually thwarted

The Duke of Wellington, liberator of Portugal and Spain

Port ready for shipping

1826

Much of Lisbon was levelled by the great earthquake of 1755

Although much damaged, Lisbon's cathedral survived the 1755 earthquake

Extravagant João V squandered millions

Towards a Republic

When João VI died in 1826, his son and heir, Pedro, emperor of newly independent Brazil, installed his brother Miguel as regent in Portugal—but only on the condition he accepted a new, more liberal constitution. Miguel agreed, but once in power, promptly restored absolutist rule. Britain, Spain and France backed the liberals, who finally succeeded in installing Pedro (who had abdicated in Brazil) as king in 1834.

The rest of the century saw a constant tug of war between those who supported Pedro's 1826 constitution and the liberals, who clamoured for a return to the 1820 version they had devised, which was more democratic. By the 1850s, the two factions had settled into a fairly stable two-party system. The monarchy, meanwhile, now virtually bankrupt and humiliated as stronger European powers embarked on a scramble for territory in Africa, became increasingly unpopular and there was a growing surge of republicanism. Dom Carlos (reigned 1889–1908) clung to outdated ideas of kingship, attempting to rule dictatorially. In an attempted coup in 1908, he and his eldest son were assassinated. His successor, Manuel, hung on for another two years, until he was forced off the throne and into exile when the army and navy revolted.

The state opening of the Lisbon to Porto railway, 1856

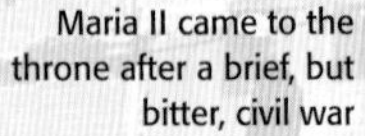

Maria II came to the throne after a brief, but bitter, civil war

Libertador and Usurpador

In February 1828, Pedro IV's brother Miguel, having promised to uphold the new constitution, arrived in Portugal. By July, he had overthrown it and had himself crowned king.

The move was not unpopular in Portugal itself, but Pedro, back in Brazil, saw it as a usurpation of his daughter Maria's rights—she had been married to Miguel at the age of seven. Pedro abdicated in Brazil and sailed for the Azores, where, in 1832, he set up a government-in-exile. From here, he captured Porto, but could get no farther until, with the help of the Duke of Terceiro's forces marching from the south, Lisbon fell to him in 1833. When Pedro died in 1834, Maria was put on the throne and Miguel went into exile.

1826

Pedro IV, a king with liberal principles for his times, died shortly after regaining the throne

The Saxe-Coburg-Gotha Connection

Pedro IV, king of Portugal and ex-emperor of Brazil, died in 1834, leaving his daughter Maria to inherit the throne. Her second husband died; in 1836 she married Ferdinand of Saxe-Coburg-Gotha, a cousin of Queen Victoria's adored consort, Prince Albert.

Ferdinand was to be an equally devoted husband. Like his cousin, he dabbled in the arts, helping to design the neo-Gothic Palácio da Pena at Sintra in the 1840s. He also had a hand in restoring the treasures of Mafra and Alcobaça, both of which had been damaged by anti-clericals, and still found the time to father 11 children. His eldest son, Pedro V, came to the throne when he was only 16, Ferdinand having been regent for the previous two years.

Retreat from Africa

From the 1860s Portuguese explorers were penetrating inland Africa from the coast, but so were the British, the French and, later, the Germans. Trouble loomed over rival territorial claims, and the 1884 Berlin Conference attempted to sort this out by partitioning the continent. Portugal was awarded Mozambique, Angola and Guinea, but only on condition it occupied the territories effectively.

Back in Africa, Portugal soon clashed with the British in the form of Cecil Rhodes in a disputed area of territory between Mozambique and Angola. Portugal protested at Rhodes' incursions; Britain claimed that the local chiefs had recognized its rights. Faced with the prospect of a disastrous war, Portugal climbed down in 1890.

The Iron Road

Portugal may have been a latecomer to the railway age, but the second half of the 19th century saw construction of lines all over the country. Tracklaying started in 1852 under British supervision with the construction of the Lisbon–Porto line, which was opened in 1856. This was soon followed by lines running to the east and south.

By the 1880s, Portugal was linked to the north and east with Spain by rail. In 1890 Lisbon's Rossio station opened, and both Lisbon and Porto acquired their own urban lines. By 1915, a network of tracks, some of them scenically stunning and still in use today, had opened up all but the most isolated parts of the country.

The Fall of the Monarchy

By 1910, following years of mounting republican agitation, revolution was in the air. It came at dawn on 4 October, when units of the army and navy rose, backed up by civilians. Lisbon's Rotunda was occupied and two warships bombarded the king's residence. By mid-morning, the republican flag flew above the city and Manuel left for Mafra. The following day, fishermen shipped the royal family out to their yacht, which sailed for Gibraltar. Before he left, Manuel wrote '…I am Portuguese and always will be…Viva Portugal'. He lived out his exile in England, dying at Twickenham in 1932, and was buried in the royal pantheon in the church of São Vicente de Fora, Lisbon.

Pedro IV, Emperor of Brazil, abdicated and returned to Portugal to win back the throne for his daughter

Manuel, Portugal's last king, was forced off the throne by a revolution in 1910

1910

A deserted stretch of the Mozambique coast. Portugal was to fight for years to hold onto its African colonies

The palace at Pena, Victorian Gothic at its best

Lisbon's Rossio station (left), a fitting tribute to the railway age

Dictatorship and Revolution

Between 1910 and 1926 the new Portuguese republic was in chaos; 45 governments came and went, and there were military risings, financial meltdown and rising hostility to the politicians throughout the country. Things came to a head in 1926 with the military-backed suspension of the republican constitution and the installation of General Carmona as president—he was to remain in office until his death in 1951.

The stage was set for the rise of António de Oliveira Salazar, a one-time economist from Coimbra University who was to control the country until 1968. In 1928 he was installed as finance minister, becoming prime minister—and dictator—in 1932. He balanced the books, but at a huge cost. Portugal's political, economic and cultural life was stifled for almost 40 years. Foreign investment was discouraged, censorship was absolute, agriculture stagnated and the poor were kept illiterate. The idea was to keep the masses in their place with a diet of '*fado*, Fátima and football'.

In a changing world, this could not go on for ever. There were demands for greater democracy at home, while resisting the clamour for independence in the colonies impoverished the country further. The result was revolution.

The Iron Hand

Salazar may have spurned the pomp and the rhetoric of fascism, but he admired Hitler and Mussolini—even keeping a photograph of the latter on his desk. Following the Nazi example, he set up the deeply-feared PIDE (*Polícia Internacional e de Defesa do Estado*), a special police force modelled on and initially trained by the Gestapo. Backed by a vast network of paid informers, the PIDE permeated every aspect of Portuguese society.

In 1936 Salazar set up a military-style youth movement, the *Mocidade Portuguesa*, and the paramilitary, extreme right-wing *Legião Portuguesa*; both adopted the Nazi salute and survived right up to the 1974 revolution.

António Salazar, longtime dictator

1910

A rebel barricade in the 1910 revolution

The children whose claim to have seen visions of the Virgin Mary made Fátima world-famous

World War II

It took a fine balancing act to keep Portugal out of World War II. Salazar, despite his admiration for Hitler and Mussolini, knew that neutrality was essential for his country. In 1939 he signed a mutual protection pact with the Franco regime in Spain to ensure this.

Portugal became a base for the rich, political refugees, spies and exiled royalty. The Germans were kept happy with supplies of tungsten, a vital mineral for war production, and the British by being allowed to set up military bases in the Azores. The Portuguese themselves were mainly pro-Ally, demonstrating their loyalties by drumming their feet or coughing loudly whenever Hitler or Mussolini appeared on cinema newsreels. The sight of George VI or Winston Churchill on screen was greeted with shouts of *'Viva... Benfica'*—there could have been no greater compliment than to compare the two men with Portugal's best-loved football team.

Salazar's Final Years

In August 1968, while enjoying the summer at Estoril, Salazar fell heavily from his canvas director's chair, striking his head on the tiled floor. The blow had no immediate effects, but by September crushing headaches proved to be the symptoms of a brain haematoma. The operation to drain it was successful, but it was followed by a massive haemorrhage on the other side of his brain. Marcelo Caetano took over as premier, but, such was the fear that Salazar inspired, nobody dared to tell him that his days of power were over. He lived for another two years, receiving ministers and even journalists, believing to the end he still had absolute control over Portugal. He died in July 1970.

The Carnation Revolution

Opposition to Marcelo Caetano, Salazar's successor, crystallized in the army with the formation of the *Movimento das Forças Armada* (MFA), a group of young officers disillusioned with the wasteful colonial struggle and conditions at home. After one abortive attempt, things came to a head in April 1974 under Major Otelo Saraiva de Carvalho. Just after midnight on 25 April, the start of the revolution was heralded by the radio broadcast of a banned protest song. Things went like clockwork, and by 3am Lisbon was secure. At 8am the MFA made its first broadcast, and within hours red carnations, the seasonal flowers, sprouted from rifle barrels all over the country—a symbol of revolution and regained freedom.

The End of Empire

By 1960 Portugal faced growing colonial problems. In 1961, India marched into Goa, dramatically ending more than 400 years of Portuguese rule. In Africa, Salazar attempted to defuse the freedom movements by combining a determined hearts-and-minds campaign with a ruthless military clamp-down on the guerrillas.

After the 1974 revolution, though, popular opinion at home was pressing for granting the colonies their independence. Exhausted by long years of war, the Portuguese withdrew from Angola in 1975, leaving the liberation movements to battle it out for power. Thousands of Angolans were killed in the ensuing war. In 1976 Portugal withdrew from East Timor, the result being more than two decades of bloody Indonesian rule.

Marcelo Caetano, Salazar's successor

Major Carvalho, leader of the coup that overthrew the dictatorship

1974

Graffiti daubed in a Lisbon square celebrate the anniversary of the 1974 revolution

Celebrating the overthrow of the Caetano regime

Tanks take to the streets in the 1974 revolution. Portuguese conscripts were tired of fighting unsuccessful colonial wars

Modern Portugal

1974–Today

The 1974 revolution heralded the start of Portugal's emergence as a fully fledged democracy onto the world stage. The teething troubles of the 1970s and early 1980s receded with Portugal's entry into the European Community in 1986, a move that brought unprecedented economic growth at every level. Portuguese self-confidence boomed with the huge success of Expo '98 in Lisbon, the problems of the last colonies were laid to rest, and inflation, infant mortality and illiteracy were tackled increasingly successfully.

The euro replaced the escudo as the national currency in 2002, and in 2004 the European Football Championships, held in the country, introduced yet more foreigners to the charms of Portugal as a tourist destination. Problems remain, but Portugal faces the future with growing optimism.

Macau peacefully reverted to Chinese rule in 1999

A Democratic State

Modern Portugal is a democracy, ruled by a government elected by citizens over the age of 18. It has a president, who is commander-in-chief of the armed forces, a prime minister, a council of ministers, an assembly (parliament) and an independent judiciary. The president is elected for five years and is advised by a 16-strong council of state. Guided by the assembly election results, he appoints the council of ministers, who present their programme to the assembly for debate.

Portugal has two autonomous overseas regions, Madeira and the Azores. Macau, Portugal's last dependency, reverted to Chinese rule in 1999.

Tourism

Tourists discovered the Algarve in the 1960s and, boosted by the opening of Faro airport, it did not take long for it to become a major holiday destination for foreign visitors. Today, tourism accounts for more than 25 per cent of Portugal's foreign investment and nearly 10 per cent of its GDP.

Visitors now regard Portugal as much more than a sun, sand and sea destination, with increasing numbers visiting Lisbon and exploring the country's interior. Badly planned coastal development was curbed when it became clear that it was destroying the very qualities that attracted visitors, and moves are being made to develop a greener and more sustainable tourist industry that helps to preserve the environment.

Poster, Euro 2004 football championships

Vasco da Gama mall, Lisbon (left), a tourist development in Alvo (above), and a villa at Quinto de Lago, show varied styles of modern Portuguese architecture

On the Move

ARRIVING

Arriving by Air

Most visitors to Portugal arrive by air, with numbers rising every year as the choice of budget airlines operating into the country expands and weekend breaks grow in popularity. Mainland Portugal has three international airports: Lisbon, Porto and Faro, serving respectively the central part, the north and the south of the country. If you're flying in from another continent, you'll arrive at Lisbon, the only airport with direct scheduled flights from the USA. Porto, in the north, is the gateway to Portugal's most heavily populated area, constantly busy with business travellers and a good jumping-off point for the Minho, Douro, Trás-os-Montes and the Beiras. Faro, serving the Algarve, is the busiest in terms of holidaymakers, and also makes a good entry point if you're planning to explore the southern third of the country. Some visitors to Portugal choose to fly to Spain and pick up an air, train or bus connection into Portugal from there.

LISBON

Lisboa Portelas lies 7km (4 miles) north of central Lisbon. It's a busy, crowded airport, with one terminal on three levels: arrivals on the ground floor and check-in and departures above.

International check-in desks are located behind and to the right of the shopping area on the second level, with a flight information board to the right of the main entrance. Allow plenty of time when departing, as the airport layout is confusing and check-in and security can be slow.

Portelas has an airport information desk (check-in level), visitor information office (arrivals hall), hotel reservation desk, car rental desks, shops, a bank, restaurants, snack bars and coffee shops, post office, lost luggage office and left luggage facilities. There is easy access to the surrounding motorway system from the airport.

PORTO

Aeroporto Francisco Sá Carneiro is 11km (7 miles) north of central Porto. The airport terminal is undergoing a major expansion, which will provide a greater range of facilities in more spacious surroundings;

GETTING INTO CITIES AND TRAVELLING ON FROM AIRPORTS

AIRPORT (CODE)	LISBON (LIS)	PORTO (OPO)
DISTANCE TO CITY	7km (4 miles)	11km (7 miles)
TAXI	Price: €15–€20 Time: 20–30 min	Price: €15–€18 Time: 30–45 min
TRAIN	Nearest metro station is the Gare do Oriente at the Parque das Nações (2.8km/1.7 miles); not recommended	N/A
BUS	Aerobus to Avenida da Liberdade, Rossio, Praça do Comércio and Cais do Sodré. Frequency: every 20 min 7.45am–8.45pm. Price: €2.35 (valid all day on all public transportation), €5.50 (valid for 3 days on all public transportation except the metro, where it is valid for one day) Additional Carris buses to the central area: 5, 22, 44, 45, 83. Frequency: every 20–30 min. Price: €1 Estoril–Cascais Shuttle. Frequency: every 45 min 7am–10.30pm. Price: €7	Aerobus to Avenida dos Aliados. Frequency: every 30 min 7.30am–7pm. Price: €2.60 Additional STCP buses to central areas: 56, 87. Frequency: every 30 min 7am–8pm. Price: €1.20
CAR	Central Lisbon: at airport roundabout take Avenida Almirante Gago Coutinho all the way to Rossio Other directions: Northwest: take A1 signed 'Lisboa/Porto' Northeast: take 2nd circular (ring road) then IC7 to A8 South: take 2nd circular to Ponte 25 de Abril or Ponte Vasco da Gama Cascais/Estoril: take 2nd circular to IC17 then M5	Central Porto: take IC1 and follow signs to city Other directions: North: take A3 (IP1) to Braga South: take A1 signed 'Porto/Lisboa' East: take A4 (IP4) to Vila Real/Bragança

Lisbon's airport, one of three that takes international flights

FARO (FAO)

4km (2.5 miles)

Faro €10–€12 (15 min), Albufeira €35–€40 (30 min), Carvoeiro €50–€60 (60 min), Portimão €50–€55 (70 min), Lagos €65–€75 (80 min), Vilamoura €25–€30 (30 min), Vila Real de Santo António €45–€55 (55 min)

N/A

EVA buses to central Faro: 1, 14, 16. Frequency: every 30 min 8am–7.45pm. Price: €1

Central Faro: take N125-10 link road, then N125
Other directions: take N125-10 link road, then either N125 east or west, or A22 (IP1) motorway east or west

AIRPORT LOCATOR

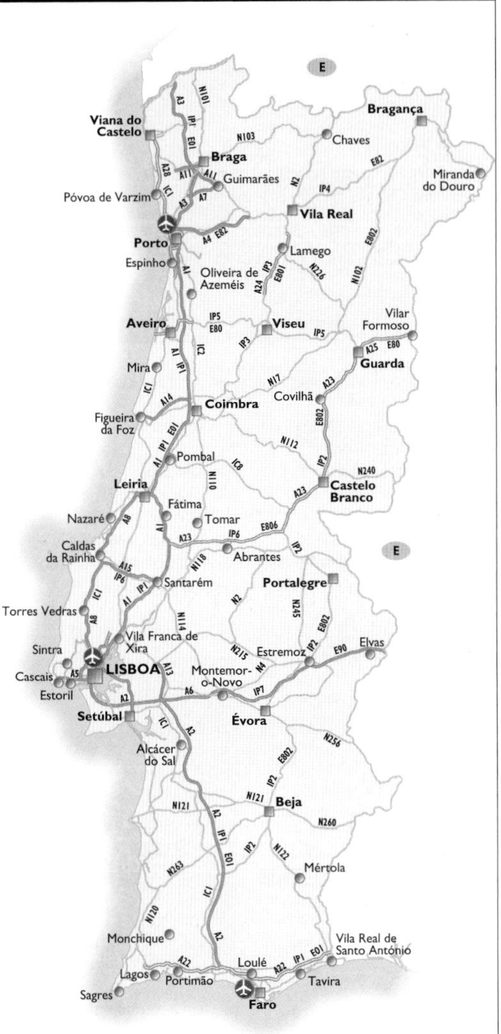

USEFUL AIRPORT CONTACTS

General		www.worldairportguide.com
Lisbon	tel 218 413 500 (general)	
	tel 218 413 700 (flights)	www.ana-aeroportos.pt
Porto	tel 229 432 400	www.ana-aeroportos.pt
Faro	tel 351 289 800800	www.ana-aeroportos.pt

Faro's baggage reclaim area can get very busy in high season

completion is due in 2005. Porto handles Portuguese domestic and European flights from its one terminal and classes itself as an international airport. Airport services include tourist information desks and car rental facilities.

FARO

Aeroporto de Faro is 4km (2.5 miles) west of central Faro. This modern airport handles international scheduled and charter flights and Portuguese internal flights. It can be extremely busy, particularly on weekends in the July and August high season; check-in and security can be very slow, especially for charter flights. Services include banking, a visitor information office, car rental desks (mainly located outside the terminal), self-service restaurant, snack bars, shops and a post office.

COPING WITH A DELAY

- In the high season, flight delays are inevitable, particularly at Faro, which has to cope with an exceptionally high volume of holiday flights.
- If your flight is delayed, the best plan is to stay landside for as long as possible.
- If the weather is fine, you could pass the time on the outdoor public terrace bar, which has an excellent view across the lagoon to the Praia de Faro beach.
- If the delay is longer than a couple of hours and you have checked in your bags, you could take a taxi to the beach itself for a last meal or swim.

FROM OUTSIDE EUROPE

If you're flying to Portugal from another continent, Lisbon is your arrival point. It is the only Portuguese airport, for instance, with scheduled flights direct to and from the USA—and these are limited in number. Continental has only one flight from Newark to Lisbon a day.

For US visitors, the alternative to flying direct is to fly to one of Europe's main hub airports, such as London Heathrow, Amsterdam Schiphol, Paris Charles de Gaulle or the Lufthansa hub, Frankfurt am Main, and then pick up a connecting flight with a European carrier from there. Obviously, this extra leg will add to the journey time—it's therefore sensible to plan flight connections so that you either have limited stop-over time, or instead you can plan things so as to spend some time in your stop-over point.

TAP, Portugal's national airline, flies direct to the UK and the USA

AIRLINES

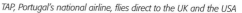

UK		
BMI Baby	tel 0870 264 2229	www.bmibaby.com
British Airways	tel 0870 850 9850	www.ba.com
British Midland	tel 0870 607 0555	www.flybmi.com
Easyjet	tel 0871 750 0100	www.easyjet.com
Flybe	tel 0870 567 6676	www.flybe.com
Monarch	tel 0870 040 5040	www.fly-crown.com
TAP Air Portugal	tel 0845 601 0932	www.tap.pt
USA		
Continental	tel 213/834-000	www.continental.com
TAP Air Portugal	tel 973/344-4490	www.tap.pt

Arriving By Road

Driving to Portugal takes time, so, if you are thinking of doing it, weigh up the pros and cons carefully. If you are coming from the UK, you can ferry your car to northern Spain. From elsewhere in Europe, though, you drive through several countries to reach your destination.

BY CAR

If you are driving to Portugal, you will need the following documents:

- Valid driver's licence.
- Original vehicle registration document.
- Motor insurance certificate (at least third-party insurance is compulsory).
- Passport.

USEFUL WEBSITES

Useful journey planning information can be found at:

- www.theAA.com
- www.autoroutes.fr
- www.autopistas.com
- www.brisa.pt

From the UK, you can cross the Channel either through the Channel Tunnel (Eurotunnel UK, tel 0870 535 3535; www.eurotunnel.com) or by ferry (see below). The major routes south to Portugal will take you through France and across Spain. There are two main options: south down the west coast of France on the E5, crossing the Spanish border at Irún; or through the Pyrenees on the E7, crossing into Spain at Candanchú. From Irún, head west across northern Spain on the A8 to Santander, then take the A67-N634 west to join the E1-A9 motorway south to Tui on the Portuguese border, where you'll pick up the A3 to Porto. The Pyrenees route takes you southwest via Zaragoza towards Madrid, then west to Salamanca, crossing the Portuguese border at Fuentes de Oñoro on the E80.

Traffic on the suspension bridge over the Rio de Arade, Portimão

BY BUS

International buses to Portugal from the UK are operated by Eurolines, the foreign arm of National Express (tel 0875 580 8080; www.eurolines.com). Destinations include Lisbon, Porto, Coimbra, Bragança, Guarda, Viseu, Beja, Faro and Portimão, with a return (round-trip) adult fare to Lisbon costing around €200; under-12s and senior citizens travel half-price. Passengers from the UK have to change buses in Paris, which sometimes involves a lengthy wait; it may be simpler to travel independently to Paris. Journey time is 40–45 hours, depending on your destination.

BY FERRY

If you're driving to Portugal from the UK, you can cut down on the driving time slightly by taking a ferry to northern Spain. The main international ferry access points are Santander and Bilbao, from where it is still a long day's drive through most of Spain to reach Portugal. There are no scheduled direct ferry services between Portugal and elsewhere in continental Europe, the UK or North America.

TRAVEL TIPS

- If you are travelling overland, pack a small bag with everything that you'll need for the journey easily to hand.
- Keep documents and money safely out of sight, especially if you're likely to fall asleep on a bus or train.
- If you're travelling with children, make sure you have plenty to keep them amused.
- Make sure you have change for the automatic motorway tolls, or buy a pass in advance.

FERRIES FROM THE UK

PLYMOUTH (UK) TO SANTANDER

Britanny Ferries (tel 44 (0) 870 366 5333; www.brittany-ferries.com) operates a twice-weekly service from Plymouth from March through November with a journey time of 24 hours. All passengers are obliged to book either a cabin or seat. Ferries dock in the heart of Santander. For the road route into Portugal from there, see above.

PORTSMOUTH (UK) TO BILBAO (SANTURTZI)

P&O Ferries (tel 44 (0) 870 520 2020; www.poferries.com) runs a year-round service to Bilbao with a journey time of 35 hours. Passengers must pre-book cabins. The service runs twice weekly, except in January, when there are two sailings only. Ferries dock at Santurtzi, 15km (9 miles) northwest of the city. From the port, follow the A8 west to Santander, then the route described above.

Arriving by Train

Though it takes time—and fares are quite high when compared to the cost of budget flights—travelling by train to Portugal can be quite an experience. The service itself is first rate.

From the UK you can travel by train to Portugal via Paris. The other rail option is to enter Portugal by train from Spain—a good choice if you want to see another European country during your visit. Bear in mind that journey times are long (25–28 hours from London to Lisbon) and fares are quite high compared with those of budget and charter flights.

The main route from Paris to Lisbon runs via Bordeaux, Biarritz, Irún, Donostia, Salamanca and Guarda; change at Irún for the Lisbon train and again at Guarda for connections to Porto and Coimbra. Travelling from Spain (Madrid), the rail route will take you through Cáceres to Marvão-Beirã, Abrantes, Entroncamento and so to Lisbon. From Lisbon you can connect with Porto, Coimbra and the south.

From the UK, it's best to use Eurostar via the Channel Tunnel as far as Paris, from where trains south are fast and frequent. Eurostar trains depart from Waterloo Station and link London with Paris in under 3 hours. You must check in 30 minutes before departure and are allowed two suitcases and one item of hand baggage, all of which should be clearly labelled with your name, address and seat number. You will need your passport to clear immigration and customs.

ARRIVING VIA SPAIN

If you want to combine visits to Portugal and Spain, there are easy connections from and to Madrid, Seville and Santiago. Direct train connections link Madrid and Lisbon (10 hours), Seville and Ayamonte on the Portuguese border (2 hours 30 min), and Vigo in Galicia and Valença on the border (45 min). Combining Portugal and Spain is also a good idea if you're renting a car, but check whether your rental agreement allows you to take the car from one country to the other.

TRAIN INFORMATION AND TICKETS

EUROSTAR

EPS House, Waterloo Station, London SE1 8SE, UK tel 08705 186186
www.eurostar.com

RAIL EUROPE

179 Piccadilly, London W1V 0BA, UK; International Rail Centre, Victoria Station, London W1V 1JY, UK
tel 08705 848848
www.raileurope.co.uk

RAIL PASSES

Portugal is a relatively small country with a somewhat fragmented rail system, and train travel is not expensive. In view of this, a rail pass makes sense only if you're visiting Portugal as part of a longer trip to Europe. If you're planning to make only one or two train journeys during your stay, it will probably work out cheaper to buy individual tickets as you need them.

Inter-Rail passes are valid for one month's unlimited train travel within a specified zone; you have to be a European citizen or have lived in Europe for six months to be eligible. The full fare is currently around €320, or €275 for those aged under 26; the ticket gives discounts on the cross-Channel services, including Eurostar. Portugal is in the same zone as Spain and Morocco.

Eurail passes are available for North American visitors, and must be purchased before arrival in Europe. They allow several days' consecutive travel, or journeys on a certain number of days within a fixed time period, in up to 17 countries. If you're planning to travel only within Portugal, a Eurail pass is unlikely to pay for itself. For more information see www.raileurope.com.

If you are a UK citizen holding a Senior Citizen Railcard, you are eligible, at a cost of €7, for a Rail Europe Senior Card, which gives a 30 per cent discount on rail fares through Europe, including Portugal.

EUROSTAR AND FAST EUROPEAN TRAINS

FACILITIES

- 1st- and 2nd-class seating.
- Bar/restaurant cars.
- Trolley service on day trains.
- Baby-changing facilities on day trains.
- Air conditioning.
- Telephone kiosks.
- Lavatories in each carriage (car).
- Lavatories for passengers with disabilities.

JOURNEY TIMES

- Total journey time from Waterloo to Lisbon is around 25–28 hours.
- Total journey time from Madrid to Lisbon is around 10 hours.
- Return (round-trip) ticket prices range from around €385–€410 (Waterloo–Lisbon) and €150–€200 (Madrid–Lisbon).

GETTING AROUND

Getting Around in Lisbon

Carris runs Lisbon's public transportation system, an integrated network that includes buses, trams and funiculars, or street elevators, all of which are frequent, inexpensive and reliable. You will be able to see everything you want by using just a few routes—but make sure they includes a tram ride, just for the experience.

BUSES

- *Autocarros* (single-decker buses) cover the whole city, and can be crowded. There are few seats, so be prepared to stand, and, although Lisbon has a low crime rate, watch your pockets and belongings.
- *Paragens* (bus stops) show the route number and list the stops along the line. The stop where you are is indicated inside the bus.
- Board at the front and validate your ticket. Exit towards the rear.

NIGHT BUSES

Carris operates a *madrugada* (night service) along the main routes; buses run between 11pm and 4am, depending on the route.

TRAMS

Lisbon's wonderful *eléctricos* (trams) are worth taking for the pleasure of the ride. They run along five routes and climb some of the steepest city gradients in the world.

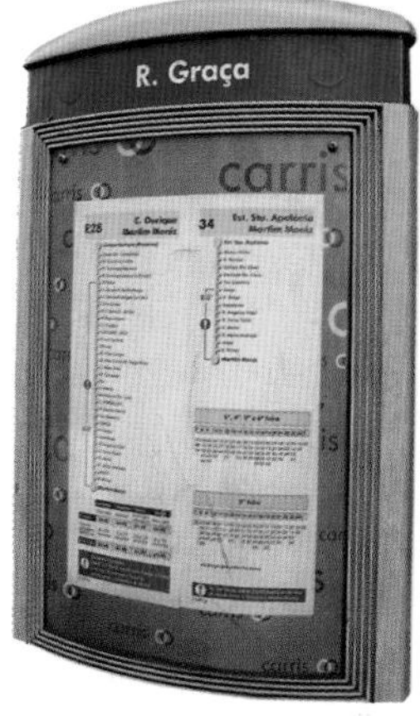

You must buy a ticket from a machine before you travel

One of Lisbon's famous trams at a stop in the Praça do Comércio

CARRIS INFORMATION

You can get information on Carris services at the Carristur office on the Praça do Comércio (tel 213 613 054, daily 8am–8pm, www.carris.pt), at the company's kiosks in Praça da Figueira, Restauradores and Cais de Sodre, or at any tourist office. Travel details, ticket information and free maps of the transport system are available.

TICKETS

Buy *bilhetes* (tickets) before boarding at the Carris kiosks and at shops and kiosks displaying the Carris logo. Single-journey tickets can also be bought on board for 90¢.

Bilhete turístico Carris
Travel pass valid for either 1 day (€2.50) or 3 days (€5.50) for buses, trams and *elevadores*.

Bilhete1dia Carris/Metro
1-day travel pass (€3) valid from purchase time until midnight on buses, trams, *elevadores* and the metro.

Bilhete de Bordo
Single-journey ticket (85¢) available on board and valid in only one zone.

BUCs
Single tickets in blocks of 10 (€8.50), available from kiosks.

Passe Turístico
4- or 7-day travel card valid on buses, trams and *elevadores* (€9.25 for 4 days, €13.50 for 7 days).

If you have any sort of combination ticket, it must be validated the first time you use it by stamping it in the machine next to the driver when you board.

TIP

If you're planning a lot of travel and sightseeing in Lisbon, consider investing in a *Cartão Lisboa* (Lisbon Card). This gives unlimited travel on buses, trams, *elevadores* and the metro, along with free—or substantially reduced—entry to many of the main sights (1-day €12, 2-day €18, 3-day €23).

Nos 28, 12 and 25 are old-fashioned, traditional trams that cover the heart of the old city. No. 18 runs west towards Belém, while No. 15 is a new 'supertram' that heads along the river from Cais de Sodre through Belém to Algés.

ELEVADORES

There are three useful funiculars, Bica, Glória and Lavra, which provide quick routes from the Baixa up to the Bairro Alto. Unfortunately, the walkway from the Santa Justa street elevator, which originally linked the Baixa with the Carmo church, has been shut for years as it is unsafe, but the ride is a pleasure in itself.

METRO (METROPOLITANO)

Lisbon's Metro, radically restructured for Expo '98, is a slick and efficient way of getting

A Lisbon metro sign. The subway is cheap and safe

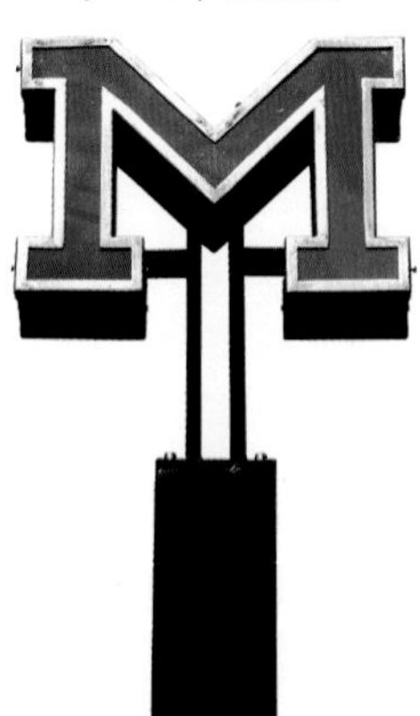

Local trains are the fastest way of getting to places like Sintra

around the city. There are four lines, with interchanges between them at Baixa-Chiado, Marquês de Pombal, Alameda and Campo Grande.

- Trains run 6.30am–1am.
- Entrances are marked with a white 'M' on a red background.
- Tickets cost 65¢ per journey or €6 for a *caderneta* (10-trip ticket).
- Validate your ticket in the box next to the entrance barrier.
- Clear information boards (green, blue, yellow or red according to the line you're on) indicate direction of travel by the name of the station at the end of the line.
- Metro maps are available at main stations.

LOCAL TRAINS

If you're visiting Cascais, Estoril, Queluz or Sintra, you can get there by local train. Trains run from Cais de Sodre to Estoril and Cascais, and also stop at Belém. For Queluz and Sintra, catch the train at Rossio station. The Lisbon Card also covers travel on these trains.

FERRIES

Ferries across the Rio Tejo leave from various points throughout the day. Fluvial river station, near the Praça do Comércio, links Lisbon with Cacilhas, Montijo and Barreiro; there's also a service from the Parque das Nações to Cacilhas, and from Belém to Trafaria. Buy your tickets at the ferry point; a return journey costs €1.10.

TAXIS

Lisbon taxis are cream or black and green. A green light indicates the taxi is occupied. All have meters—check to ensure yours is switched on; tips are discretionary. Taxi stands in the city include Rossio, Fluvial, Praça da Figueira, Chiado, Largo da Misericórdia and Avenida da Liberdade.

Taxis themselves are inexpensive, even though fares rise after 10pm and on weekends and public holidays. You can call a cab by telephoning:
Autocoope tel 217 932 7560
Rádio Taxis tel 218 119 000
Teletaxis tel 218 111 100.

SIGHTSEEING TOURS OF LISBON

Carris Tramcar Tour
Complete tour of Lisbon's central tram routes in a traditional tram with multilingual headphone commentary. Departures every 30 mins from Praça do Comércio, €12.

Cityline-Sightline Tour
City tour that includes Belém. Apr–end Oct every 30 min; Nov–end Mar every 60 min from BUS terminal (metro: Marquês de Pombal). Adults: €14; under-5s free.

Transtejo Rive
River cruises with English, French and Spanish commentary. Two departures from Fluvial daily Apr–end Oct, at 11am and 3pm. Adults €20; children (5–12) €8; under-5s free.

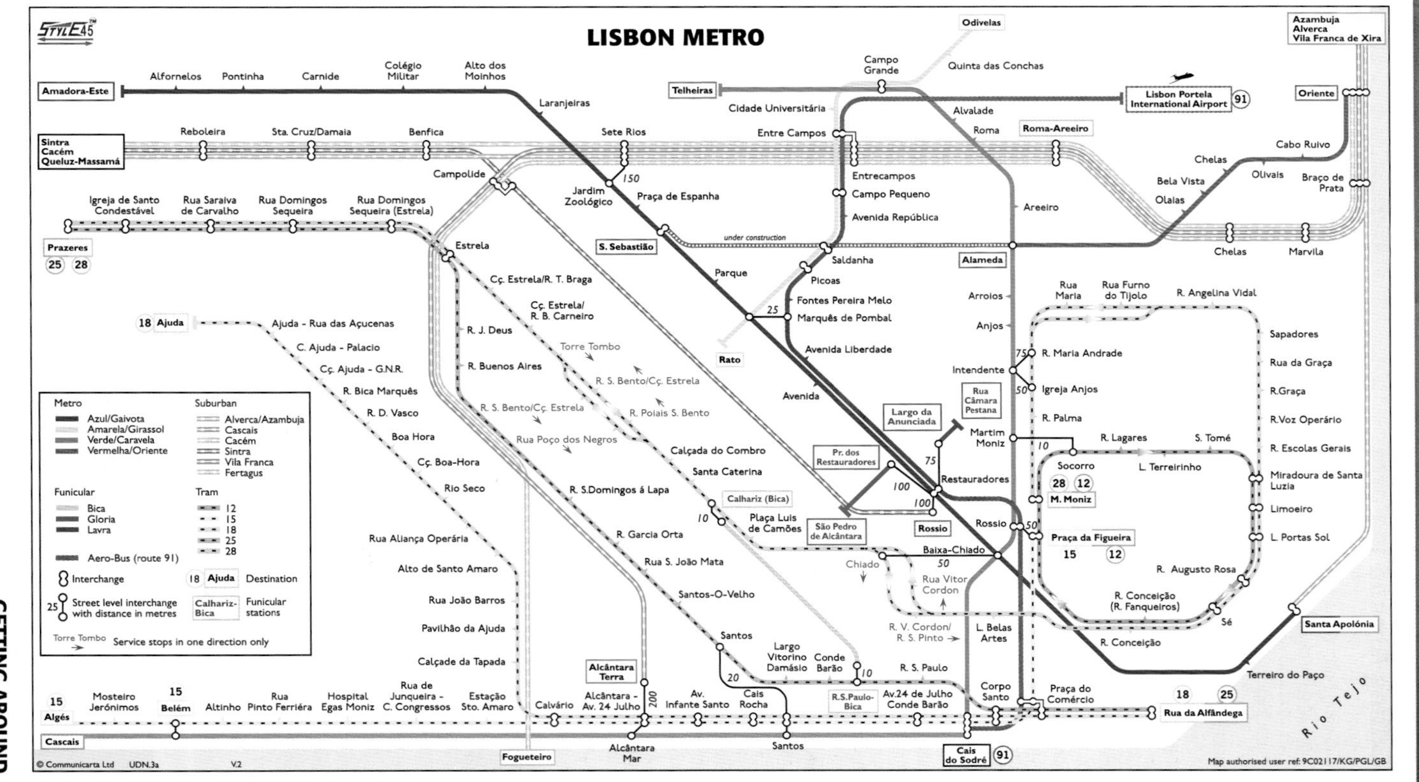
LISBON METRO
STYLE45
Amadora-Este
Alfornelos
Pontinha
Carnide
Colégio Militar
Alto dos Moinhos
Laranjeiras
Jardim Zoológico
Praça de Espanha
S. Sebastião
Parque
Rato
Marquês de Pombal
Avenida
Restauradores
Rossio
Baixa-Chiado
Terreiro do Paço
Santa Apolónia
Telheiras
Campo Grande
Cidade Universitária
Entre Campos
Campo Pequeno
Saldanha
Picoas
Fontes Pereira Melo
Avenida Liberdade
Odivelas
Quinta das Conchas
Alvalade
Roma
Areeiro
Alameda
Arroios
Anjos
Intendente
Martim Moniz
Roma-Areeiro
Chelas
Bela Vista
Olaias
Olivais
Cabo Ruivo
Oriente
Lisbon Portela International Airport
91
Azambuja
Alverca
Vila Franca de Xira
Braço de Prata
Marvila
Sintra
Cacém
Queluz-Massamá
Reboleira
Sta. Cruz/Damaia
Benfica
Sete Rios
Entrecampos
Avenida República
Campolide
under construction
Cais do Sodré
Corpo Santo
Praça do Comércio
Rua da Alfândega
Santos
Alcântara Mar
Alcântara Terra
Calvário
Fogueteiro
Belém
Algés
Cascais
Rio Tejo
Prazeres
Igreja de Santo Condestável
Rua Saraiva de Carvalho
Rua Domingos Sequeira
Rua Domingos Sequeira (Estrela)
Estrela
Ajuda
Ajuda - Rua das Açucenas
C. Ajuda - Palacio
Cç. Ajuda - G.N.R.
R. Bica Marquês
R. D. Vasco
Boa Hora
Cç. Boa-Hora
Rio Seco
Rua Aliança Operária
Alto de Santo Amaro
Rua João Barros
Pavilhão da Ajuda
Calçade da Tapada
Estação Sto. Amaro
Rua de Junqueira - C. Congressos
Hospital Egas Moniz
Rua Pinto Ferriéra
Altinho
Mosteiro Jerónimos
Alcântara - Av. 24 Julho
Av. Infante Santo
Cais Rocha
Largo Vitorino Damásio
Conde Barão
Av.24 de Julho Conde Barão
R.S.Paulo-Bica
R. S. Paulo
Santos-O-Velho
Rua S. João Mata
R. Garcia Orta
R. S.Domingos á Lapa
Rua Poço dos Negros
R. S. Bento/Cç. Estrela
R. Poiais S. Bento
Torre Tombo
Cç. Estrela/R. T. Braga
Cç. Estrela/ R. B. Carneiro
R. J. Deus
R. Buenos Aires
Calçada do Combro
Santa Caterina
Calhariz (Bica)
Plaça Luis de Camões
Chiado
Rua Vitor Cordon
R. V. Cordon/ R. S. Pinto
L. Belas Artes
São Pedro de Alcântara
Pr. dos Restauradores
Largo da Anunciada
Rua Câmara Pestana
Praça da Figueira
M. Moniz
Socorro
R. Lagares
L. Terreirinho
S. Tomé
R. Augusto Rosa
Sé
R. Conceição (R. Fanqueiros)
R. Conceição
R. Palma
Igreja Anjos
R. Maria Andrade
Rua Maria
Rua Furno do Tijolo
R. Angelina Vidal
Sapadores
Rua da Graça
R.Graça
R.Voz Operário
R. Escolas Gerais
Miradoura de Santa Luzia
Limoeiro
L. Portas Sol
150
25
200
20
10
50
75
100
12
15
18
28
Metro
Azul/Gaivota
Amarela/Girassol
Verde/Caravela
Vermelha/Oriente
Funicular
Bica
Gloria
Lavra
Aero-Bus (route 91)
Interchange
Street level interchange with distance in metres
Service stops in one direction only
Suburban
Alverca/Azambuja
Cascais
Cacém
Sintra
Vila Franca
Fertagus
Tram
Destination
Funicular stations
V2
UDN.3a
© Communicarta Ltd
Map authorised user ref: 9C02117/KG/PGL/GB

Getting Around in Porto

Sprawling Porto has a comprehensive public transportation network, which includes STCP buses and trams and an expanding, partly underground, state-of-the-art Metro system. Most main sights, however, are within the compact heart of the city, easily reached on foot, and so it's unlikely that you'll need to use many public transportation routes.

BUSES

An extensive bus service operates throughout Porto from 6am to 9pm; this reduces between 9pm and 1am, when the *madrugada* (night service) covers the principal routes until 5am. Buses can be crowded and there are few seats.

All tickets must be validated on boarding by stamping them in the machine at the entrance near the driver.

Bus stops show the bus number, destination, zone and whether it is a day, evening or night service.

Porto's buses are popular and there may be few free seats

METRO

Construction started on Porto's Metro system in 1999; it will eventually comprise four lines, covering 70km (43 miles) and with 66 stations. One line (Linha Azul) opened in 2002 and runs from Trindade in central Porto northwest to Senhor de Matosinhos, with a bus interchange at Viso. A second line came into operation in June 2004 (just in time for the Euro 2004 soccer championship), linking Trindade to the Antas stadium.

Trains run 6am–1am. Entrances are marked with a stylized wavy blue 'M' on a white background. There is a uniform fare, regardless of destination; single tickets cost 80¢. Visit www.metro-porto.pt.

TRAMS

There are two short tram routes, worth experiencing for their old-fashioned charm. No. 1E runs the 4km (2.5 miles) between

TIP

The *Passe Porto*, a 1- or 2-day combined travel and museum card, gives unlimited travel on both the bus and tram system, free entrance to eight museums and monuments, and discounts on other attractions, including river cruises and city tours. Buy it at the tourist information offices at Fenianos and Ribeira or the ICEP (Investimentos, Comércui e Turismo de Portugal) office on Praça Dom João I. It costs €5 (1-day) or €7 (2-day).

Metro at Câmara de Matosinhos surface station, Porto

Casa da Música Metro station

TRAVEL INFORMATION

The main place for transportation information is the Loja de Mobilidad (tel freephone 800 220 905; www.cm-porto.pt), the transportation shop in the visitor information office at Rua Clube dos Fenianos 25 (Apr–end Sep daily 9–7; Oct–end Mar Tue–Fri 9–5.30, Sat–Sun 9.30–4.30). It provides information on all forms of city transportation, including timetables and an excellent free booklet and map. There's another STCP office on Praça Almeida Garrett, opposite São Bento station.

TICKETS

You can buy *bilhetes* (single tickets) on the buses (€1) or booklets of 1, 2 or 10 tickets from STCP kiosks, newsagents and shops displaying the STCP logo. Pre-purchased tickets are considerably cheaper, costing 55¢ for 1 trip or €4.80 for 10 in the central zone. Metro tickets are available from automatic machines in the stations; they all combine with the STCP system and cost 80¢ for 1 journey and €7.20 for 10 in the central zone.

TRAVEL PASSES

- *Diário Porto* is valid for a day (€2.10) in the central zone.
- *Diário Rede Geral* is valid for a day in all zones including Vila Nova de Gaia (€2.60).
- *Andante Metro-STCP* is valid for 1 day on both the bus and metro system (€5).

Validate your ticket when you board the first time you use it.

Passeio Alegre and Infante, and No. 18 the 1km (half a mile) between Masserelos and Viriato. Single tickets (50¢) can be purchased on board; all travel cards include tram rides.

TAXIS

There are taxi stands in most of the main squares. Prices are low (€4–€5 for most central destinations). Ordinary taxis are metered; those distinguished by an 'A' *(carros de aluguer)* do not run on a meter and are best used for longer distances; negotiate a price before you take one.

You can call a cab by telephoning:
Raditáxis tel 225 073 900
Taxis Invicta tel 225 022 693
Taxis Unidos tel 225 029 898

FERRIES

A ferry service crosses the Douro between Cais do Ouro in Porto and Alfurada in Vila Nova da Gaia, departing every 15 mins between 6am–midnight. A single ticket, bought on board, costs 50¢.

CRUISES ON THE RIVER DOURO

Porto is the starting point for many of the river cruises up the Douro. They range from a 1-hour cruise around the city area to 3-day luxury cruises with visits to historic *quintas* (country estates) and fine dining included. Prices range from €7 for an hour's excursion to €345 for a 3-day luxury cruise. The main operators are:

- Douro Azul tel 351 223 402 500; www.douroazul.com.
- Rent Douro tel 224 769 063.

A sightseeing cruise on the Douro opens up a fresh city perspective

Car Rental in Portugal

If you decide to rent a car in Portugal, where rental rates are among the lowest in Europe, there's a wide choice. The major chains are all represented and have offices at airports, train stations and downtown in the major cities. You are likely to find the best value if you shop around beforehand, and book in advance before you leave home. The Algarve has numerous smaller, local and reasonably priced companies, but you may be unable to book them in advance from your home country. The solution is to travel from Faro airport to your destination by public transportation or taxi, completing your car rental deal on the spot on arrival. If your trip to Portugal is being organised by a specialist tour operator, it will be able to arrange car rental for you when you book your holiday or flight.

- Before you leave home, check your insurance to see if you will need any additional cover. You will generally be offered the option of a collision damage waiver, which is advisable in Portugal.
- You will need your credit card as a deposit when you pick up the car, and it's rare to pay additional charges for car rental with anything other than a credit card.
- Drivers of rented cars must be over 23 and carry a valid driver's licence.
- Photographic proof of identity is a legal requirement in Portugal; if you have an old-style driver's licence without a photo, make sure you carry a document that includes one (e.g. your passport) when you are driving.
- If there is to be more than one driver, you must specify this when you collect the car; the additional driver/s will also have to sign the rental agreement. If you intend to drive off public roads, check that the insurance covers this.
- Before you set off, thoroughly check both exterior and interior of the vehicle for any damage. If you find any, report it at once and get a company representative to look at it and make a note.
- You will be given the choice of returning the car with or without a full tank of fuel; it is cheaper to fill it up yourself just before you return it.

It's easy to rent cars or bicycles, but check the terms carefully

TIPS

If you're picking up a rental car in Lisbon with the intention of driving on, try to avoid an early morning or evening collection time. Traffic in and around the city is extremely heavy during the rush hour, when the main roads and the Tejo bridges can get clogged for hours.

Faro airport's car rental lot. Airports are convenient for car rental

CAR RENTAL COMPANIES

Book your rental car before you leave home, either by phone or on-line. Major international rental groups are listed below.

	TELEPHONE UK	TELEPHONE US	WEBSITE
Alamo	0870 400 4562	800/462-5266	www.alamo.com
Avis	0870 606 0100	800/230-4898	www.avis.com
Budget	01442 276266	800/527-0700	www.budget.com
Hertz	0800 317540	800/654-3131	www.hertz.com
National	0870 536 5365	800/227-7368	www.nationalcar.com
Thrifty	01494 751600	800/367-2277	www.thrifty.co.uk www.thrifty.com

Driving

Up until the 1990s, Portugal had one of Europe's least developed road networks, with just one (incomplete) motorway open between Lisbon and Porto. Since then, a massive injection of European Union funding into road construction has given the country a network of motorways and main highways that has provided faster and easier access to main towns and cities as well as to previously remote areas. Portugal is now served by an adequate road system, with dual carriageways (divided highways) and motorways linking the main cities and towns, and minor roads connecting smaller towns and villages.

Driving makes sense if you are concentrating on smaller cities and towns and rural areas. But be aware that Portuguese roads are of variable quality and are often in bad condition. You may encounter winding roads with poor surfaces and maintenance, bad illumination and signing, and heavy and slow-moving traffic.

The sharp rise in car ownership has also brought congestion problems, particularly in and around cities and on smaller roads. In addition, Portuguese driving has a justified reputation as being among the worst in Europe; statistically, Portugal is consistently number one in terms of traffic accidents and deaths per capita, and also leads the field in the number of pedestrians being run over. Much is being done to tackle the problem, with better policing and prosecution and a concerted effort to educate drivers. Portugal is one of the few European countries where driving tips are a daily feature of the morning TV news programme.

Roads are still of mixed quality despite extensive motoway building

The best bet is to stick to motorways for long journeys and to steer clear of the cities, particularly Lisbon and Porto. One-way systems, narrow streets, heavy traffic and lack of parking make city driving stressful, and even smaller towns are best avoided during the busy morning and early evening periods. Be prepared for exceptionally heavy traffic on summer weekends, when roads and motorways around big cities are heaving, and the roads in the Algarve, Portugal's major holiday playground, have to contend with a massive influx of both Portuguese and foreign drivers.

BRINGING YOUR OWN CAR

BEFORE YOU LEAVE:

- Have headlights adjusted for driving on the right.
- Contact your motor insurer or broker at least 1 month before taking your car to Portugal.
- Have your car serviced.
- Check the tyres and tyre pressures.
- If you don't have a rear-view mirror on the left side, have one fitted.
- Ensure you have adequate breakdown cover (AA Five Star 0800 444500; www.theAA.com).

YOU WILL NEED:

- A valid driver's licence; Portuguese law requires everyone to carry photographic proof of identity at all times. If you have an old-style licence without a photo, make sure you have your passport with you when you're driving.
- Vehicle registration document.
- Motor insurance certificate; third-party insurance at least is compulsory.
- A first-aid kit, fire extinguisher and spare bulbs.
- It is compulsory to carry a warning triangle and to display a nationality sticker (unless you have Euro-plates).

DOCUMENTS

Carry documents with you whenever you are driving; if you are stopped, the Guarda Nacional Republicana (GNR) will want to see them. Both UK and US driver's licences are valid in Portugal, but it is recommended that you also carry a translation. For UK drivers, the new licences with photographs and the pink, EU-style ones include a translation; if you hold an older, green licence, it is a good idea either to update your licence or apply for an International Driving Permit. Holders of US driver's licences should also apply for an International Driving Permit. Though these permits are not compulsory, they can smooth out problems and also act as another form of identification. Permits can be obtained from many national motoring organizations including the AA and AAA.

RULES OF THE ROAD

Some of the following rules of the road are flagrantly ignored by most Portuguese motorists. They are the law, and foreign drivers should observe them.

- Drivers must be at least 18 years of age and hold a full driver's licence.
- Drivers who have held a licence for less than a year must not exceed 90kph (55mph) or any lower speed limit.
- Drive on the right.
- Unless otherwise indicated, give priority to all vehicles approaching from the right at intersections.
- Vehicles already using a roundabout take priority over those entering it.
- Seatbelts are compulsory.
- Children aged under 3 are prohibited from sitting in the front seat unless in an approved child seat.
- All children between 3 and 12 must use an approved restraint system wherever they are sitting.
- Speed limits: built-up areas 50kph (31mph); outside built-up areas 90kph (55mph) or 100kph (62mph); motorways *(autoestradas)* 120kph (74mph). Minimum speed on motorways is 40kph (24mph).
- You must use dipped headlights in poor daytime visibility, in tunnels and on zero-tolerance IP roads at all times.
- Drinking and driving: For levels of alcohol in the blood from 0.05 to 0.08 per cent, penalties include a fine and withdrawal of driver's licence for one month to one year; for more than 0.08 per cent, a fine and withdrawal of licence from two months to two years.
- All road fines have to be paid on the spot to the police officers concerned. If you refuse to pay, or cannot pay, you will be asked for a deposit based on the maximum fine for the offence committed. If you refuse to pay that, your vehicle will be impounded by the police and not released until you can make the full payment.

TIPS FOR TOWNS

- Study a city map before you reach your destination, so that you can recognize major landmarks that will help you orientate yourself (e.g. a castle, cathedral, river, major boulevard).
- Work out by which road you are entering the town to help you decide on left and right turns.
- Remember to watch for badly placed signs.
- Be aware that traffic lights are often small and poorly sited.
- Slow down, take your time and watch for other drivers.
- If you make a mistake, remember that most drivers are used to dealing with the unexpected and will eventually make room or give way to you.

City parking is difficult and traffic jams all too frequent

IN THE SERVICE STATION

How far is it to the next service station, please?
Quantos quilómetros faitam para a próxima bomba de gasolina?
Fill the car up, please.
Encha se faz favor.
Could you check the oil?
Não se importava de ver o nivel do óleo?
Could you check the tyre pressures?
Não se importava de ver a pressão dos pneus?
I'm having car trouble. Could you give me a hand?
Tenho uma avaria. Poderia ajudar-me?

Could you contact the rescue service for me, please?
Poderia avisra o pronto socorro da ACP?
Which garage can help me?
Que oficina poderá me ajudar?
Can you fix it?
Poderia consertar isso?
When will my car be ready?
Quando o meu carro fiça pronto?
How much will it cost?
Quanto é que vai custar?
Can I have a receipt for the insurance?
Pode dar-me un recibo para a companhia de seguros?

DRIVING DISTANCES AND TIMES

Use the chart below to work out the distance in km (green) and estimated duration in hours and minutes (blue) of a car journey.

	Aveiro	Beja	Braga	Bragança	Chaves	Coimbra	Évora	Faro	Guarda	Guimarães	Leiria	Lisboa	Miranda do Douro	Portimão	Porto	Sagres	Valença do Minho	Viana do Castelo	Vila Real de Santo Antonio	Vilar Formoso	Viseu
Aveiro		601	202	531	441	104	521	826	308	211	204	436	558	821	123	914	331	235	835	359	137
Beja	337		909	1023	1037	518	123	233	639	1056	356	312	1001	524	810	309	1017	922	213	730	732
Braga	114	513		410	223	307	745	1038	441	024	429	635	540	1032	059	1126	123	121	1038	533	347
Bragança	309	582	234		147	538	859	1256	344	341	659	837	130	1250	407	1344	534	532	1235	435	407
Chaves	263	595	134	100		438	913	1209	435	247	559	737	317	1203	304	1257	345	347	1247	503	304
Coimbra	60	297	175	316	260		438	722	246	255	121	259	542	717	208	810	416	320	731	337	134
Évora	300	78	435	504	517	260		356	516	932	317	226	838	632	647	725	854	758	336	607	609
Faro	473	143	596	725	681	413	221		912	1329	601	416	1234	118	939	212	1146	1051	057	1059	905
Guarda	176	373	263	209	257	155	295	516		418	407	545	322	907	351	1000	605	603	852	051	131
Guimarães	122	613	22	207	156	164	535	756	241		417	623	604	1324	047	1417	145	144	1306	509	323
Leiria	116	221	251	392	336	76	184	337	231	240		232	704	605	330	658	537	441	609	458	255
Lisboa	258	179	369	483	427	167	136	239	322	358	142		907	410	536	504	758	756	524	636	432
Miranda do Douro	335	562	318	84	184	320	484	705	189	340	396	511		1229	537	1323	704	702	1214	306	421
Portimão	468	303	591	720	676	408	366	73	511	751	341	234	700		934	054	1141	1045	215	1053	859
Porto	78	458	55	231	172	120	380	541	216	44	196	314	315	536		1027	207	112	939	442	220
Sagres	518	177	641	770	726	458	416	123	561	801	391	284	750	50	586		1234	1139	308	1147	952
Valença do Minho	197	577	78	312	210	239	499	660	341	98	315	447	396	655	119	705		056	1146	656	510
Viana do Castelo	145	525	76	310	212	187	447	608	339	97	263	445	394	603	67	653	52		1051	654	332
Vila Real de Santo Antonio	481	124	596	706	717	421	202	53	497	735	345	303	686	126	541	176	660	608		943	943
Vilar Formoso	224	421	311	257	283	203	343	616	48	289	279	370	174	611	264	661	389	387	545		222
Viseu	91	423	212	231	172	88	345	509	85	190	164	255	244	504	131	554	290	198	545	133	

WARNINGS AND SAFETY

- Be aware constantly of overtaking vehicles, especially on corners and double white lines.
- Some roads (usually IP numbers) are classified as zero tolerance. If they display blue signs showing dipped headlights, this is a mandatory instruction no matter what the weather. If you drive without lights on these roads, you are liable to be stopped by the traffic police and will receive an on-the-spot fine of €25 (Portuguese citizens lose their licence for one month).
- Speed limits and other road rules are enforced by radar traps and unmarked police cars.
- Beware of radar-controlled traffic lights in smaller towns and villages, where green lights will change to red if you're over the speed limit (50kph/31mph). The threat of this often leads to erratic driving by local motorists. Such traffic lights are usually signified by a warning sign: *velocidade controllada* + the speed limit.
- Roads and non-motorized vehicles (e.g. bicycles, donkey carts) are not well lit at night, so drive with caution, keeping a special eye-out for pedestrians, who often wear dark clothes.
- Be patient on rural roads, where there are likely to be horse-drawn vehicles, donkeys and farm animals.
- Watch out for drivers of both cars and agricultural vehicles in remote areas; they rarely signal their intentions.
- Drivers will often get far too close to the car in front, even on motorways.
- Traffic signs and signposts can often be difficult to spot.
- Never leave any property visible in the car when you're not using it and always lock the car when you leave it, if only for a few moments.
- Lower the aerial (antenna) and tuck in the side mirrors when you park.

EXAMPLES OF TYPICAL ROAD SIGNS

Motorway traffic restrictions

No agricultural traffic

Motorway speed limit

Toll road

Zero tolerance

Meter parking

Pedestrian crossing

Street signs to places of interest

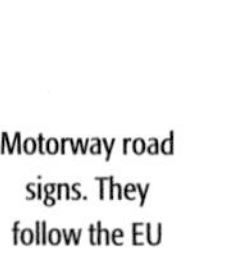

Motorway road signs. They follow the EU common model

Motorway toll boths. The system is effective, but expensive

MOTORWAYS (AUTOESTRADAS)

Portugal's motorway system is built and run by a private company, Brisa (freephone 808 508 508; www.brisa.pt). Motorways run from north to south of the country, from Valença on the Spanish border to Lagos in the Algarve. They link the cities of Braga, Aveiro, Coimbra, Leiria and Lisbon with the Algarve, and there is a further network around Lisbon. In addition, the A23 runs northeast from Entroncamento to Vilar Formoso on the Spanish border; the A6 links Lisbon with Badajoz in Spain; and the A22 runs from the western Algarve to the Spanish frontier at Vila Real de Santo António.

All motorways are clearly signposted and approached via slip roads leading to the toll booths. Take the ticket from the automatic booth on the left of the car and the barrier will lift. Keep your ticket safe while you're on the motorway, as you will need it to pay when you come off it. Cash payment is made to the official in the booth at the exit; the amount due is displayed on a screen outside the payment window.

All toll booths have a *Via Verde* (Green Channel), controlled by CCTV, that enables tolls to be automatically deducted from your bank account. This channel is available only if you have previously registered with *Via Verde* and obtained a green channel identification disk. You can find out more about the scheme on www.viaverde.pt (Portuguese only).

Slip roads onto and off Portuguese motorways are short and you may have to stop and wait before you can join the main carriageway. Watch for drivers coming up fast and driving close behind you; Portuguese drivers will often pull out suddenly with no warning.

Autoestrade have service areas approximately every 50km (30 miles) with fuel stations, bar/restaurants, rest areas, shops and lavatories. Some of them also have hotels.

Toll charges on motorways are relatively high; the cost of travel from Lisbon to Porto, for example, will be around €18.

ROAD CLASSIFICATION

EM – Estradas Municipales
These vary in width and condition, but are usually fairly narrow, with few markings or guardrails.

EN or N – Estradas Nacionales
2-lane roads where the width may vary. They normally have horizontal and vertical markings and signs, although these can be in poor condition. Some of these roads, such as the N125 in the Algarve, have a notorious reputation for accidents.

IC – Itinerários Complementares
Can have either 2 or 4 lanes, and often pass through populated areas.

IP – Itinerários Principais
Controlled-access 3- or 4-lane roads linking major towns and cities, characterized by heavy traffic and impatient drivers. The IP5, linking Aveiro with the Spanish frontier, has a particularly bad reputation, as does the Amarante–Bragança IP4.

A – Autoestradas
Toll motorways, all built within the last 20 years.

PROBLEMS

If your car breaks down, turn on your hazard warning lights and place the warning triangle 50m (55 yards) behind the vehicle. If you're driving your own car, you can get help from ACP (Automóvel Clube de Portugal; www.acp.pt), which has reciprocal breakdown assistance arrangements with overseas motoring organizations. It provides 24-hour help: tel 228 340 001 (north of Coimbra) or 219 429 103 (south of Coimbra). Many car insurance policies will cover your car in Portugal, but it's worth taking out extra insurance in case of breakdown.

If you have an accident, call the police (tel 112) but do not admit liability. Witnesses should remain

to make statements, exchange details (name, address, car details, insurance company's name and address).

If the Guarda Nacional Republicana (GNR) stop you, they will want to see your personal and car documentation. They may give no reason for this, but you are most likely to have been pulled over for speeding or some other infringement of the law, such as driving without lights on a zero-tolerance road. The officers will calculate an on-the-spot fine from the official police highway code book, and will issue a receipt for the money. Most police patrolling major roads speak English, so do not attempt to plead ignorance. Remember that the Portuguese have a high respect for all officials; the more polite and helpful you are if stopped, the quicker you will be on your way.

PARKING

Parking in Portugal's bigger towns and cities is difficult. Traffic is heavy, streets are congested and often medieval, and picturesque towns were not built to accommodate modern vehicles. Only top-rank hotels have private parking, and you can spend hours trying to find central parking anywhere. The smaller much-visited historic towns and villages, such as Évora, Beja and Marvão, have good-sized parking areas on the outskirts, and are small enough for the old hearts of the towns to be easily accessible on foot from these. In larger places, you may have a long walk in from the parking area. Coimbra is one of the few places to have instituted a 'park and ride' system; this may be copied by other towns.

You often need to be up early to find a free meter bay in the busy cities

If you rent a scooter, make sure they give you crash helmets

- Unemployed men sometimes earn a little money by pointing out empty parking spaces to drivers. In return for a tip of around €1, they will keep an eye on your vehicle for you.
- The best time to arrive in a town is during the lunch hour, when streets are quiet and there may be more spaces.
- Downtown parking areas, where they exist, are usually expensive, but it is often worth paying the price for peace of mind. The nearer they are to historic sights, the more expensive they will be.
- If you can find metered parking, it's good value.
- If you arrive at night, check your chosen parking street has no restrictions that will come into force before you return the next morning. Cars may be towed away to make space for weekly markets.

BUYING FUEL

- Fuel stations are generally open from 7am until midnight; some remain open 24 hours.
- The types of *gasolino* (fuel) normally available are *super* (four star), *sem chumbo* (unleaded) and *gasóleo* (diesel).
- Fuel is normally priced around 95¢ per litre for unleaded and 70¢ for diesel.
- Many fuel stations still have an attended service. For a full tank, ask for *cheio, se faz favor*.
- 24-hour pumps are sometimes automatic. These take €5, €10 and €20 notes (bills) and will dispense fuel until the money runs out. They can be temperamental, however, and will often reject all but the most pristine notes.

MOTORCYCLES AND SCOOTERS

If you're staying on the coast, particularly in one of the Algarve resorts, you may be tempted to rent a scooter or 80cc motorcycle to get around. These are readily available, but take things easy if you have little or no experience, or have not ridden one in Portugal before: Be extremely wary of other road-users. That said, a motorcycle or scooter is economical, fun and easier to park than a car.

You'll need to be at least 18 (over 23 for motorcycles exceeding 125cc) and to have held a full motorcycle licence for at least a year. Rental starts at around €20 a day and usually includes third-party insurance, helmet rental and locks.

BICYCLING

Bicycling is a great way to see some areas of Portugal, but it is not recommended away from quiet country roads, or in the busy and hilly northwest. Remember, too, Portugal can get very hot in high summer. Tourist offices can help with tracking down rental outlets—rental rates start at around €10 a day—and may also have information on routes, although designated bicycle routes are virtually non-existent. Bicycles may be taken on local trains for a small fee.

Trains

Trains in Portugal are operated by CP—Caminhos de Ferro Portugueses (tel 808 208 208; www.cp.pt). Its network, augmented in some areas with connecting buses, covers much of the country, and includes some wonderfully scenic lines. There are different types of trains and services. Local trains can be snail-like, and so you may find some destinations easier and faster to reach by bus, although trains are often cheaper. Full timetable information may be hard to track down if you want to get from one part of the country to another, although complete train timetables (€5) and those for individual lines are sometimes available at main stations. The best policy is to plan your journey in advance, using the excellent English-language website.

DIFFERENT TYPES OF TRAIN

- Both Porto and Lisbon have a local network of commuter trains; the Cascais and Sintra lines out of Lisbon are particularly useful for visitors.
- Some minor lines have been replaced by buses operated by CP; train tickets and passes are valid on these.
- Narrow-gauge lines still exist in the north and are part of the network. The Tâmega, Corgo, Tua valley and Douro, all superbly scenic lines, fall into this category.
- Stations can be some distance from the town or village they serve; connecting transportation is not guaranteed.

The vast tile-decorated booking hall at Porto's São Bento station

STATIONS

Lisbon and Porto have more than one *estação de comboios* (station), each with amenities such as bars, cafés, newsstands and left-luggage facilities. In the rest of the country, major cities have one station. Smaller stations generally have little more than a ticket office and waiting room; some may even be unmanned. Some Portuguese stations are decorated with *azulejos* (tiles) showing local scenes.

TICKETS

- Portuguese trains have first- and second-class *bilhetes* (tickets), which can be purchased on-line (www.cp.pt) and at railway stations. Different price structures exist for different train categories, with regional trains being the cheapest. Overall, rail travel is relatively inexpensive.
- Rail-pass holders must pay supplements on the faster services, such as the *inter-regionales*, *intercidades* and the *Alfa* between Lisbon and Porto.
- Groups of 10 or more are eligible for a *bilhetes de grupo* (combined ticket), providing the distance travelled is a minimum of 75km (47 miles) for a single

TYPES OF TRAIN

REGIONAL AND INTER-REGIONAL	INTERCIDADES	ALFA
Most Portuguese trains fall into these categories. They run throughout the country, using both first- and second-class carriages (cars) with an acceptable level of comfort. Regional trains stop at most stations; inter-regional ones are faster, stopping only at major stations. On-board facilities are basic, but do include lavatories.	These are fast, comfortable intercity trains, on which advance reservation is mandatory; this adds around 60 per cent to the price of a normal ticket. On-board facilities include bar/café, telephones and lavatories. Both first- and second-class seats are available. Such trains link: Lisbon–Porto–Braga; Lisbon–Guarda; Lisbon–Covilhã; Lisbon–Alentejo; Lisbon–Algarve. A second-class return (round-trip) ticket between Lisbon and Porto costs €32.	This fast, luxurious service operates between Lisbon and Porto, with stops at Coimbra and Aveiro. Advance booking is essential, and some Alfa trains are made up of first-class carriages (cars) only, with all the facilities to be expected on a premier service. A second-class return (round-trip) ticket between Lisbon and Porto on the Alfa costs €45.

(one-way) journey or 150km (94 miles) for a round trip. This gives reductions of between 20 and 30 per cent and must be applied for 4 days in advance.

- The *Cheque Trem* (Rail Cheque), obtainable in four different values, can be in an individual's name or a company's name and has no time limit; it gives a reduction of 10 per cent and can be used for purchasing tickets and for many other railway services. Check the CP website for more information.
- CP issues *bilhetes turisticos* (tourist tickets) valid for 7, 14 and 21 days of unlimited travel; prices range between €110 and €275.
- Travel is cheapest on 'Blue Days', usually Monday afternoon through Thursday. Fares go up over the weekend, and on national holidays and the days preceding them.
- There is no reduction for *ida e volta* (return, or round-trip journeys).
- Children between 4 and 11 pay 50 per cent of the full price; under-4s travel free.
- Senior citizens (over 65) are entitled to a 50 per cent discount on production of proof of age.
- Passengers travelling without a ticket will incur an on-the-spot fine payable to the conductor.
- Some country stations are unmanned; in this case, you can buy your ticket on the train without a penalty.

AT THE STATION

- Every station has a *bilheteira* (ticket office) or *máquina das*

RAIL NETWORK

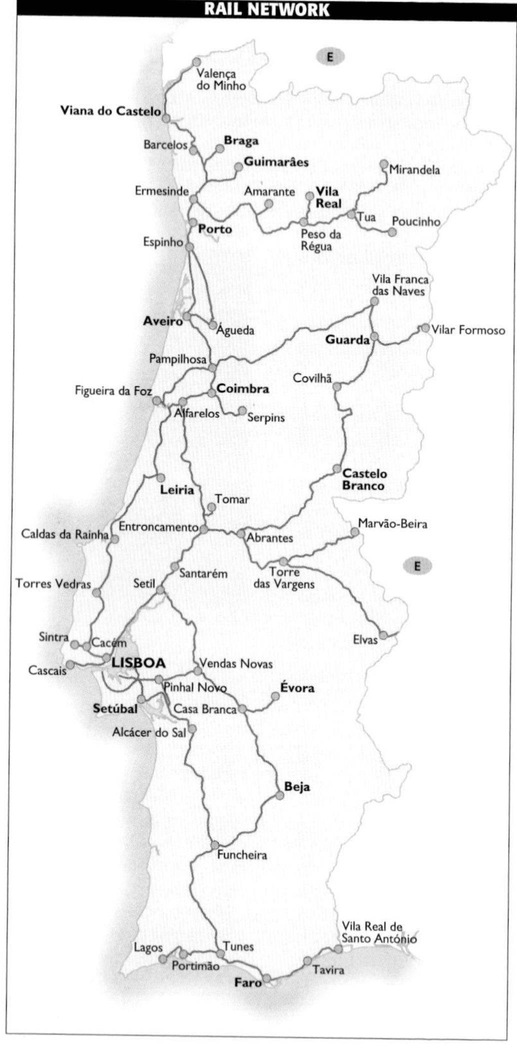

RAIL PASSES

INTER-RAIL PASS	EURAIL PASS	EURAIL FLEXIPASS
(for European residents) Valid for one month's unlimited train travel within a specified zone. Unless you are going to be making a lot of train journeys, you will almost certainly be better off buying individual tickets. For information: www.inter-rail.co.uk	(for non-European foreigners) Valid for train and ferry travel on Eurail group transportation for periods of 15 or 21 days, or 1, 2 or 3 months. Useful if you're visiting Europe for a long trip and planning to travel around a lot. For information in the US: tel 800/438-7245; www.raileurope.com/us	(for non-European foreigners) As Eurail Pass, but valid for 15 or 21 days within a 2-month period

bilhetes (ticket machine), which will accept notes (bills) as well as coins in payment. At the ticket window, prices are displayed on a readout at the cash register—useful for establishing the cost if you don't speak Portuguese. Check your tickets if you want a return (round-trip) ticket to make sure that you were understood properly and have been issued with the correct type. In Portuguese a one-way ticket is *ida*, and a return *volta*.

- Major stations have information screens giving travel details of arrivals and departures; if you can't see your train on the board, point at the ticket and ask the way to the appropriate *plataforma* (platform).
- Timetables are normally posted on the walls inside the station; if you have to make a connection, use these to find the time and platform of your next train.
- For lost property, call the station at either your arrival or departure point.

Regional trains can be slow, while the country's inter-city services are faster

RAIL JOURNEY TIMES

This chart shows the duration in hours and minutes of a train journey between various destinations in Portugal.

	Abrantes	Aveiro	Barcelos	Beja	Coimbra	Entroncamento	Figueira da Foz	Guarda	Guimarães	Leiria	Lisboa	Marvão-Beira	Mirandela	Pampilhosa	Portimão	Porto-Campanha	Setúbal	Tomar	Valença do Minho	Viana do Castelo
Aveiro	232																			
Barcelos	504	204																		
Beja	C545	C559	805																	
Coimbra	216	038	232	517																
Entroncamento	022	130	323	400	059															
Figueira da Foz	242	142	340	611	039	147														
Guarda	419	228	504	830	158	302	314													
Guimarães	515	203	128	820	238	349	401	543												
Leiria	406	307	505	C658	141	310	050	459	640											
Lisboa	A147	A230	A430	B230	A159	A102	A252	A410	A509	236										
Marvão-Beira	116	409	633	1036	334	139	447	559	654	744	A255									
Mirandela	1000	553	539	C1152	633	738	852	915	531	1037	A842	1327								
Pampilhosa	236	023	216	C549	009	114	058	149	249	219	224	417	628							
Portimão	C833	C823	1115	310	652	631	C833	C1005	C1108	C908	448	C1200	1333	716						
Porto-Campanha	319	042	053	C630	108	216	215	336	103	351	310	503	434	113	C855					
Setúbal	C353	C427	630	152	356	C253	405	C607	C736	C440	B114	C532	1037	C413	422	507				
Tomar	059	233	427	C424	149	022	228	352	515	413	134	219	804	201	C701	316	C332			
Valença do Minho	641	320	108	C947	410	522	529	710	320	802	627	854	705	357	1250	206	C850	616		
Viana do Castelo	532	232	027	C906	257	439	404	525	148	620	526	652	624	316	1126	122	C736	534	039	
Vilar Formoso	531	335	559	941	238	357	344	028	617	456	509	709	1118	226	1012	405	C707	504	712	554

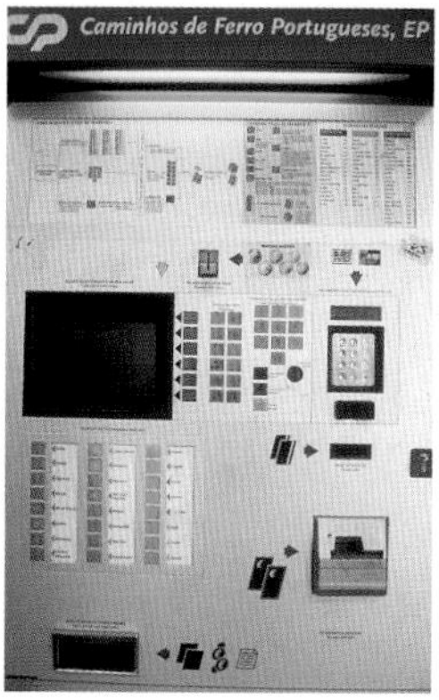

Always buy a ticket—travelling without one means a heavy on-the-spot fine

Buses

Portugal has a good bus network at local, regional and national level. You should be able to travel almost anywhere using buses, which are often faster than the equivalent trains.

Porto is experimenting with environment-friendly buses

- Buses in Portugal are operated by various different companies, all private, mainly running services within their own region. Privatization has led to hot competition between operators, with a proliferation of more frequent services on the more popular routes, and the inevitable cut-backs or even cessation of many local services.
- There is no national long-distance bus company. Portugal's network of long-distance express buses is run by many different companies, although these do combine their timetables and fare structures. Journeys should be booked, and seats reserved, in advance. For information and reservations, tel 969 502 050 (some operators may speak English). You can also check times, and book and pay for tickets, on line at www.rede-expressos.pt (Portuguese only, but simple to operate). Express buses are comfortable, with air conditioning; smoking is not permitted.
- From larger towns and cities, services may be run on identical routes by several different companies; these will all leave from different bus stations, depending on the operator—Porto alone has nearly 20 companies, each with its own terminal.
- In smaller towns, *estação de camionetas* (local bus stations) are the places to get information and book tickets.
- Be aware that companies, routes, addresses and timetables may change every year; check with local tourist offices for the latest information.
- Local services are geared to the population's needs, so many buses operate to suit working, market and school hours.
- Bus services are far less frequent, and sometimes non-existent, on Saturdays and Sundays.

Airport shuttles are efficient

In the country, bus services may be infrequent at weekends

Taxis

Taxis are available in cities and towns, including some surprisingly small places. Fares in Portugal are relatively low by European standards. If you don't have a car, this makes taxis a good option for getting around in rural areas, especially as, away from the major towns and cities, it is acceptable to negotiate for a few hours' hire.

- Portuguese taxis are generally metered, with a minimum fare of around €1.50.
- Any luggage carried in the boot (trunk) is charged for as an extra.
- Additional charges are made between 10pm and 6am.
- Taxi hire in the Algarve is the most expensive in the country.
- Tipping is not obligatory, but 10 per cent of what is on the meter is appreciated—Portuguese taxi drivers are often very helpful.

Bear in mind the basic rules of taxi travel:

- Check that the meter is working, switched on and set to minimum fare before you set off.
- If there's no meter, agree the price with the driver before you drive off, writing it down if there's any language problem.
- In big cities, get your bearings on a map so as to check landmarks en route to ensure you're not being driven an unnecessarily long way round.
- After paying, check your change.
- At airports and railway stations, wait at the official stand, sometimes controlled by an official.
- It's sometimes easier to telephone for a taxi or go to a stand than to rely on flagging one down on the street; bus and train stations are also good places to find taxis.

Taxi fares are usually metered

Internal Flights

As a small country (Lisbon and Porto are only 300km/185 miles apart), Portugal has little in the way of internal flights, although there are regular services to both Madeira and the Azores (see box below).

Lisbon is connected to Porto and Faro by air, but there are no direct flights from Porto to anywhere other than Lisbon.

Air Luxor
Reservations: 0870 750 5747
www.airluxor.com
Services:
Lisbon to Porto
Lisbon to Funchal
Lisbon to Porto Santo

PGA Portugalia Airlines
Reservations: tel 0870 755 0025
www.pga.pt
Services:
Lisbon to Porto
Lisbon to Faro
Lisbon to Funchal
(Operates flights jointly with TAP Air Portugal on some internal routes.)

TAP flies direct to Madeira and the Azores from Lisbon and Porto

GETTING TO MADEIRA AND THE AZORES FROM PORTUGAL

The easiest way to get to Madeira and the Azores is by plane. TAP Air Portugal operates flights from Lisbon and Porto to Madeira, and from Lisbon to Ponta Delgado on São Miguel in the Azores. Air Luxor also has regular flights between Lisbon and Madeira. SATA Air Açores connects both Lisbon and Porto to Ponta Delgado, from where it runs inter-island flights to the other islands in the group.

- Air Luxor www.airluxor.com
- SATA Air Açores www.sata.pt
- TAP Air Portugal www.tap.pt

VISITORS WITH A DISABILITY

In Portugal, the major problems for people with a disability often lie not so much in the transportation, accommodation and public buildings as in the actual nature of the old cities and towns. Things are progressing, but disability facilities in Portugal overall still lag behind those in northern European countries and North America. This is partly offset by the helpfulness of the Portuguese themselves, who will make great efforts to render your visit as stress-free and uncomplicated as possible.

- If you have a disability, plan your trip carefully in advance. Aim to travel with able-bodied friends, or consider booking via a specialist tour operator. Contact both your departure and arrival airports and the airline you are flying with in advance of your date of travel to let them know what assistance you will need. It can be a problem getting this organized without advance notice.
- Taxis can take wheelchairs folded and stored in the boot (trunk), but Portuguese taxis are normal saloon (sedan) type cars, and so getting in and out of them may be difficult. Lisbon, Braga and Coimbra have taxi services for passengers with disabilities: tel 218 155 061(Lisbon), 253 684 081 (Braga), 239 484 522 (Coimbra).
- Dial-a-ride bus services exist in Lisbon: tel 213 613 161, or log on to www.carris.pt. The service operates Mon–Fri 6.30am–10pm, Sat–Sun 8am–10pm and each trip costs €1.50. Rides require 2 days' notice and you may be asked for a medical certificate.
- Buses do not have wheelchair access.
- Dogs for the blind travel free.
- Drivers from the UK can use a disabled person's parking badge in Portugal.
- You should be aware that many streets in old quarters of towns and cities are cobbled. They are often very steep.
- Official buildings tend to have good access.
- Major museums are making headway in providing wheelchair access, but coverage is patchy.
- Access steps are the major problem in cathedrals and churches.
- Book well ahead and be specific about your requirements.
- For a relaxed holiday, steer clear of big cities and use a car to explore rural areas, the coast and the smaller towns and villages.

Firms like Wheeling Around the Algarve organize personal help

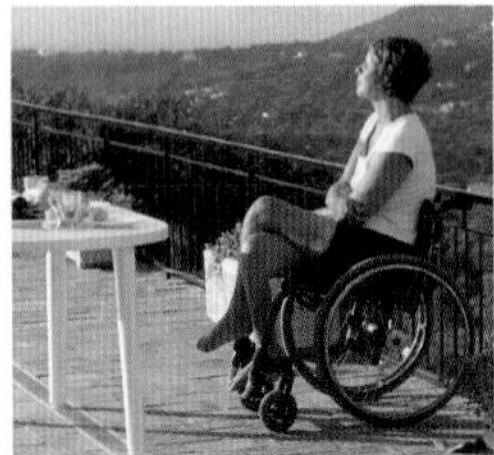

Avoid problem places and you'll have a relaxed holiday

USEFUL CONTACTS

Holiday Care
7th Floor, Sunley House,
4 Bedford Park, Croydon,
Surrey CR0 2AP, UK
Tel 0845 124 9971;
fax 0845 124 9972
www.holidaycare.org.uk
Publications and information on accessibility.

Society for Accessible Travel and Hospitality (SATH)
Lots of tips for travellers with mobility or visual impairment.

Secretariado Nacional de Reabilitação
Conde de Valbom 63,
1000 Lisboa
Tel 217 929 500
www.snripd.msst.gov.pt
Government-run site that provides information on transportation facilities (Portuguese only). Also publishes the *Accessible Tourism Guide*, with comprehensive listings of hotels, travel agents, restaurants, clubs etc.

Wheeling Around the Algarve (Rodando Pelo Algarve)
Rua Casa do Povo 1, Apartado 3421, 8135-905 Almancil
Tel 289 393 636; fax 289 397 448
www.player.pt
This highly personal company helps people with disabilities holidaying in the Algarve. It will arrange everything from airport transfers and villa rentals to wheelchair hire and sporting and leisure activities, and is contactable 24 hours a day, 7 days a week.

This chapter is divided into the eight regions of Portugal (▷ 5–7). Places of interest in each region are listed in alphabetical order. At the start of each regional section, the major sites in the region are listed.

The Sights

THE MINHO AND TRÁS-OS-MONTES

There's a huge contrast in these adjacent northern regions, which cover some of Portugal's most heavily populated areas and some of its remotest. Historic cities like Bragança are the perfect foil to the grandeur of the mountains, while riverside towns such as Barcelos are counterbalanced by remote Miranda do Douro and the beautiful coastal town of Viana do Castelo.

MAJOR SIGHTS

Fruit and vegetables on sale in the Thursday market, Barcelos

The picturesque old quarter of Chaves is just above the river and its Roman bridge, which was built by order of Emperor Trajan

BARCELOS

340 B3 Torre de Menagem, Largo da Porta Nova, 4750 Barcelos, tel 053 811 882 Barcelos
www.rtam.pt

Try to visit Barcelos on a Thursday, when this attractive town bursts with vibrant life during its vast weekly market, or *feira*, which is one of the largest in Europe. Here you can buy anything from fruit and vegetables, grown by farmers on the surrounding smallholdings, to live rabbits, sportswear, clothes and CDs, as well as the wonderful handicrafts for which the Minho is famous. It's also the place to pick up a red-and-black ceramic cockerel, the town's emblem. Legend has it that a Santiago pilgrim, wrongly accused of theft, declared that the judge's roast chicken dinner would stand up and crow if he was sentenced to hang. The cock crowed, the pilgrim was set free and a monument was erected in memory of the miracle, which you can still see in the archaeological museum in the ruins of the old ducal palace. The palace stands high above the River Cávado and is backed by the beautiful 13th-century Igreja Matriz, whose interior, rich with blue *azulejos* (tiles), glitters with gold. There are more tiles and ceramics in the Museu de Olaria, which has a huge range of Minho examples. Another of the town's highlights, the 1704 Templo de Bom Jesus da Cruz, overlooks the Campo, site of the *feira*. Its white and granite exterior sets the standard for church design all over the Minho. Take time to stroll through the tempting shopping streets and walk along the riverbank.

A brightly decorated ceramic cockerel, the famous town emblem of Barcelos

BRAGA AND BOM JESUS

See pages 68–71.

BRAGANÇA

See page 72.

CAMINHA

340 B2 Rua Ricardo Joaquim Sousa, 4910 Caminha, tel 258 921 952 Caminha
www.rtam.pt

Caminha, a relaxed river port and historically important frontier town, stands at the confluence of the River Coura with the mouth of the Minho. The town still guards the border between Portugal and Spain, and you can take a ferry across the river to the Spanish town of La Guardia. It's a peaceful place to stop if you're heading south, with a clutch of monuments around its spacious main square, the Praça Conselheiro Silva Torres. Here you will find a fine 16th-century granite fountain, a stately town hall and a clock tower that once formed part of the 14th-century fortifications. The road through the arch leads to the town's main attraction, the magnificent Igreja Matriz. Built between the 15th and 16th centuries, at the height of the town's prosperity, the Renaissance building's carved south door is framed by pilasters supporting a gallery with statues of St. Peter and St. Paul. Inside, there is a superb maplewood ceiling, a fine carved pulpit and intricate decorative *azulejos* (tiles).

CHAVES

341 D2 Terreiro de Cavalaria, 5400-531 Chaves, tel 276 340 661
www.rt-atb.pt

For centuries the town, only 12km (7.5 miles) from the Spanish border, was fought over by the Spanish and Portuguese. Today, things are more peaceful, and modern Chaves is proud of its links with Spanish Galicia, celebrated during the *Festas da Cidade* in July. A market town and capital of the northern Trás-os-Montes, Chaves is also well known for being a spa resort—the hot springs bubble up from the ground at 73°C (163°F) and have valuable therapeutic properties. The area also produces gastronomic delights, including some of Portugal's finest hams, sausages and red wines.

The old quarter stands just above the River Tâmega, with the spa to the west below the old walls. The area is dominated by two 17th-century fortresses, the Forte de São Francisco, now a luxury hotel, and the Forte de São Neutel, where concerts are sometimes held. There's an interesting museum, the Museu da Região Flaviense in the Praça de Luis Camões (Tue–Fri 9–12.30, 2–5.30, Sat–Sun 2–5.30, €1), which traces the history of the town from its foundation as a Roman spa—a good place to visit once you have seen the Ponte Trajana, named after Emperor Trajan. The main churches, the Igreja da Misericórdia with its huge tile panels, and the severe Igreja Matriz, its apse still proudly retaining its Romanesque elements, are both worth a visit.

Braga and Bom Jesus

Portugal's religious capital, with a superb cathedral and more than 35 churches, is the largest city in the Minho, with one of Portugal's best-known religious monuments nearby. It's a historic town that is embracing the 21st century.

The baroque façade of the Hospital de São Marco, Braga

A medieval tomb in the Capela dos Reis, Braga Cathedral

The Gothic-style Capela dos Reis was built in the 16th century

RATINGS	
Cultural interest	●●●●●
Historic interest	●●●●●
Specialist shopping	●●●●
Walkability	●●●●

TIPS

- Driving into and out of Braga is confusing—arrive either early or during the middle of the day when there's less traffic.
- There's a large underground parking area below the Praça de República on the Avenida Central, a few minutes' walk from the highlights.
- Braga's most important festivals celebrate *Semana Santa* (Holy Week, the week before Easter), the *Festas de São João* (the Festival of St. John, 23–24 Jun) and *Bom Jesus* (Sacred Jesus, six weeks after Easter at Whitsun). It's a wise precaution to reserve accommodation well in advance if you are planning to stay in the city during these times.
- Bom Jesus is very crowded at weekends.

SEEING BRAGA AND BOM JESUS

Braga makes a good base if you are touring the southern Minho, particularly if you are relying on public transport. If you are simply making a brief visit for a few hours, start exploring from the Praça de República, an arcaded square at the top of the old town. From here, follow Rua do Souto downhill; Braga's highlights are on or around this lively shopping street, which runs down to the Porta Nova and traverses the whole of the old city. The baroque staircase and pilgrim church of Bom Jesus do Monte are on a hillside 5km (3 miles) east of the city; you can drive right up to the church near the top of the hill or alternatively there are regular buses from Braga to the foot of the staircase at the bottom of the hill, where a funicular runs up to the church.

HIGHLIGHTS

SÉ

✉ Rua Dom Paio Mendes, 4700-422 Braga ☎ 253 263 317 🕒 May–end Sep daily 8.30–6.30; Oct–end Apr daily 8.30–5.30 🎟 Museum and chapels €2

Braga's cathedral was founded immediately after the Christian reconquest in 1070 on the site of a Moorish mosque. Little remains of the original French-influenced Romanesque building, but the south doorway on the side wall to the right of the main façade is decorated with quirky scenes from the legend of Renard the Fox. The main east front has a portico with Gothic arches, built in the 16th century for Archbishop Diogo de Sousa by Basque workmen. As you approach, it's more likely your eye will be drawn to the cathedral's roofline, topped with pinnacles and balusters. This, too, was commissioned by the Archbishop and is the work of João de Castilho, who was to go on to work on Lisbon's Mosteiro dos Jerónimos (▷ 134), one of the greatest of all Manueline buildings.

The interior is surprisingly small, a plain nave contrasting with the rich baroque woodwork and a Manueline font, with its elaborate, twisted carving. Walk down the nave to the crossing, with its 1970s stained glass, for a close-up of the high altar, where the plain granite walls provide the perfect backdrop for a lovely 14th-century statue of

the Virgin and an altar carved with scenes from the Ascension. The *azulejos* (tiles) in the chapel to the left date from the 18th century. Turn your back on the altar for a view of the ornate double baroque organs in the Coro Alto, a masterpiece dripping with gold and covered with trumpets and angels.

A door below the Coro leads into the cloisters, giving access to a courtyard surrounded by three chapels. The Capela dos Reis, where you will find the 16th-century tombs of the cathedral's founders, Henry of Burgundy and his wife Tareja, the parents of Afonso Henriques, the first king of Portugal, is the most important. From the cloisters, stairs lead up to the Treasury, one of the richest in Portugal, where the compulsory guided tour whisks you past treasures spanning 800 years of masterful craftsmanship. There's a plethora of vestments, plates and reliquaries; highlights include a 10th-century Mozarabic ivory chest, a stupendous 18th-century silver-gilt monstrance studded with diamonds, and a rock crystal cross from the 14th century.

BOM JESUS DO MONTE

340 C3 • Bom Jesus do Monte Church: Oct–end Apr daily 8.30–5.30, May–end Sep daily 8.30–6.30 Funicular €1

The church and ornamental approachway of Bom Jesus, one of Portugal's most famous buildings and a triumph of baroque architecture, were commissioned by Archbishop Maura-Teles in 1723 and completed in 1783. A harmonious mix of whitewashed plaster and

The interior of Braga's great cathedral is richly decorated

BASICS

340 C3

Praça da República, 4710-251 Braga, tel 053 262 550; Mon–Fri 9–7, Sat 9–12.30, 2–5.30

Braga

www.cm-braga.pt

Run by the city council, this fast site, also in English, covers everything that visitors need to know about the city—its history, culture, infrastructure, accommodation, restaurants, entertainment and shopping

MORE TO SEE

ANTICO PAÇO EPISCOPAL

Largo do Paço, 4700-415 Braga
253 601 187 Mon–Fri 9–12, 2–8
Free

This huge fortress-like building consists of three blocks, dating from the 14th, 17th and 18th centuries. They now contain the municipal library and some of the university faculties. The medieval north wing has a fine reading room with a gilt coffered ceiling. The palace overlooks the pleasant Jardim de Santa Bárbara.

MUSEU DOS BISCAÍNHOS

Rua dos Biscaínhos, 4700-415 Braga
053 204 650 Tue–Sun 10–12.15, 2–5.30 €2
www.ipmuseus.pt

An absorbing museum of the decorative arts housed in the 17th- and 18th-century bishops' palace. Rooms are filled with contemporary furniture, paintings, carpets and sculpture, all in keeping with the date and style of the building. The ground floor retains its original flagstones, laid to allow carriage access to the stables. Behind the palace are tranquil green gardens.

PRAÇA DE REPÚBLICA

The main square connects the old and new city, overlooked by two linked arcades sheltering several wood-panelled historic cafés, once the meeting points for Braga's intellectuals. Behind stands the Torre de Menagem, once part of the defensive wall system. The square also has a superb trio of modern fountains.

granite, the double staircase leads up to a grandiose church, commemorating through simple allegory at each landing the life and sacrifice of Christ. You can approach the church up the stairs, or by the Via Sacra, a sacred path lined with chapels whose wooden tableaux show scenes from the Passion of Christ. Each landing of the staircase has a fountain, which is intended to recall the five wounds of Christ, the five Senses and the three Virtues. Pilgrims crawl up the steps on their knees, but most visitors come simply to enjoy the surrounding woods and gardens and the superb views. There are even finer vistas at the Santúario do Sameiro, about 2km (1 mile) farther on, a shrine built in the 1830s. Its vast 1950s concrete esplanade and heavy statuary bear witness to the importance given to the shrine by the Salazar regime.

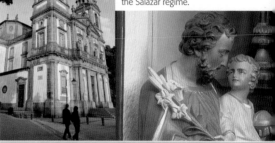

Exterior of the Bom Jesus do Monte church, Braga

Religion is everywhere; these statues are part of a shop front

BACKGROUND

Braga, Roman Bracara Augusta, has a long history, much of which is entwined with that of the Catholic church in Portugal, starting from the time of the Christian reconquest of the 11th century. The city was probably a Celtic foundation. After a long period of Roman occupation, it fell to the Suevi and then to the Visigoths before being captured by the Moors. Recaptured by the Christians in 1070, its archbishops pressed hard for recognition as the Primates of the Spains, Iberia's most important religious position, against the rival claims of Toledo and Tarragona.

Eventually, Braga's name became synonymous with Catholicism in Portugal. The Portuguese saying 'while Coimbra studies and Lisbon plays, Porto works and Braga prays' neatly sums up its traditional position in Portuguese life, as demonstrated by the city's many fine examples of Renaissance and baroque buildings, erected at the most potent time in Portugal's ecclesiastical history. The superb ornamental stairway of Bom Jesus do Monte, just outside the city, is a splendid example of the architectural achievements of the period.

Braga is still the seat of the Portuguese archbishops, and the religious processions and celebrations here are among the most fervent in the country. Over the past decades, however, the city has been keen to shake off its traditional conservative and religious image and has been working hard to promote more commercial assets, particularly the thriving industries on the outskirts. The prominent role Braga played in the 2004 European Football Championships certainly brought the city's secular side well to the fore. Its continued diversification demonstrates that Braga is much more than simply a deeply religious and politically reactionary town.

Statues of two of the apostles at the Igreja de São Marco, Braga (right); the double stairway by which you access Bom Jesus do Monte (far right) has more than 1,000 steps

Inside and outside the medieval walls of Bragança's citadel

RATINGS	
Cultural interest	●●●●
Historic interest	●●●●●
Walkability	●●●●

TIPS

- Winters in the Terra Fria area of Trás-os-Montes are bitter and summers are scorching; aim to visit Bragança in spring or autumn.
- If time is short, concentrate on the Cidadela, and, to get a real sense of the place, perhaps return in the evening when the crowds have left.
- The heart of old Bragança is remarkably compact, so park your car and explore the city on foot.

BASICS

341 F2 Avenida Cidade de Zamora, 5301 Bragança, tel 273 381 273 Oct–end Apr Mon–Fri 9–12.30, 2–5; May–end Sep Mon–Fri 9–7, Sat 9–6

www.bragancanet.pt/braganca
Packed with information on the town and surrounding area, in Portuguese only

BRAGANÇA

A fortified frontier town in an unspoilt area has become the remote and evocative capital of the Trás-os-Montes. It's an excellent base from where to explore the Terra Fria.

The medieval city of Bragança is named after the Bragança dynasty, which acquired the dukedom in 1442. During the 17th-century Spanish occupation, it was the Braganças who became dominant; João IV gained the throne in 1640, and the family remained the Portuguese ruling house until the fall of the monarchy in 1910. In recent years Bragança has benefited immensely from EU funding, while, thankfully, retaining its old spirit.

THE CIDADELA

On a hillock to the east of the town is one of Portugal's most evocative sites, a circle of medieval walls that encloses a clutch of whitewashed houses over which loom a massive castle and keep. The huge Torre de Menagem, built in 1187, dominates the open space at the top of the hill—33m (108ft) high with 15 turrets around its walls. Inside, the two halls are lit by Gothic windows and there are superb views from the top of a small military museum. Opposite this is the Igreja de Santa Maria, a Romanesque church remodelled in the 18th century, when the doorway niches and vaulted painted ceiling were installed. Squashed up beside the church is the Domus Municipalis, built in the 13th century as a council chamber and one of few surviving Romanesque civic buildings in Europe. Pentagonal in shape, it has an arcaded first floor and an underground reservoir beneath. It was here that the *homens bons* (good men) met to dispense justice. Wrongdoers could have found themselves in the *pelhourinho* (pillory) near the castle—it's supported by a prehistoric granite pig, thought to be a fertility symbol and one of more than 200 found in the region.

MUSEU DO ABADE DE BAÇAL

The quality of the exhibits in Bragança's Abade de Baçal museum in Rua Conselheiro Abilio Beca (Tue–Fri 10–5, Sat–Sun 10–6, €2) reveals the role the town played as an administrative, fiscal and judicial capital. In a sensitively converted 18th-century palace, once the bishop's home and backed by splendid gardens, the museum focuses predominantly on Celtic art from the surrounding area, but some rooms contain sculpture, religious art and fine textiles as well. There's also an appealing collection of local costumes and topographical paintings of the Trás-os-Montes.

Citânia de Briteiros, the largest Celtic site in Portugal

Many of the Costa Verde's fine beaches remain uncrowded, although Mar, in the background, is still a prosperous fishing port

CITÂNIA DE BRITEIROS

340 C3 Alameda de São Damaso 83, 4810-286 Guimarães or Praça de Santiago, 4810-300 Guimarães, tel 253 412 450 or 253 518 790
www.cm-guimaraes.pt

The Minho is scattered with the remains of *citânias*, Celtic hilltop settlements, and none is better than Citânia de Briteiros, which occupies a superb position in the oak-forested hills between Braga and Guimarães. These Iron Age villages were mainly established between 600 and 500 BC and remained occupied through to the third century AD.

Briteiros, one of Portugal's most impressive archaeological sites, is thought to have been the last stronghold to fall to the Romans, and its walls, streets and huts provide an insight into a forgotten way of life. Excavations here began in the 1870s and still continue today. Paved streets run through the settlement, with hut outlines on either side. A couple have been reconstructed so you can see the stone benches that hugged the circular walls and the central pillar that supported the thatched roofs. At the communal bathhouse, below the main settlement, you can see water tanks and an ancient oven that was once used for heating water to produce steam.

COSTA VERDE

340 B3 Rua do Hospita Velho (off Praça da Erva), 4930 Viana do Castelo, tel 258 822 620 Viana do Castelo
www.rtam.pt

The Costa Verde, the Green Coast, runs north through the Minho from Porto to the Minho river and the Spanish border, a stretch that includes beautiful beaches and a clutch of lively resorts. The main holiday towns are Viana do Castelo (▷ 83) and Póvoa de Varzim (▷ 92), both packed and bustling in summer, but there is an endless choice of quieter places, where you can have a stretch of sand virtually to yourself. You need to leave the main N13 and take minor roads down to the sea to see the best of the area. A string of popular resorts, north of Porto, lead up to Póvoa, but north of here things are less developed, particularly the protected area south of the River Neiva, where you can still see traditional farms scraped out of the dunes.

Other villages worth seeing are Esposende, a low-key resort, and Mar, still a thriving fishing community with a sideline in seaweed gathering—the seaweed is used as fertilizer. North of Viana, dunes and pines run down to the sea; Afife and Carreço have great beaches, though you will find more facilities in Praia de Âncora. Bear in mind that it rains along this green stretch of coastline even in summer, so expect a few cloudy days, rain or wind.

FREIXO DE ESPADA-À-CINTA

341 F4 Avenida do Emigrante, tel 279 653 480
www.bragancanet.pt/freixo

In a fertile bowl surrounded by grim yet beautiful mountains, Freixo was founded by Dom Dinis in the late 13th century. The king is said to have cut an ash down on this spot, giving the town its name, Freixo de Espada-à-Cinta, meaning 'tree of the sword'. The town's church is a late Gothic structure whose doorway is decorated with late 15th-century motifs in the shape of twisted columns and pinnacles. Inside, there's fine network vaulting and the chancel has a superb *retábulo* (altarpiece) by the great 16th-century artist Grão Vasco.

GUIMARÃES

See pages 74–75.

LINDOSO

340 C2 Park office: ADERE Peneda-Gêres, Largo da Misericórdia, 4980 Ponte de Barca, tel 258 452 250
www.adere-pg.pt

A true mountain village, Lindoso perches on granite slopes deep in the heart of the Parque Nacional da Peneda-Gerês (▷ 78–81). Despite the presence of a dam and some modern buildings, it is a traditional settlement. Like so many villages in the area it is dominated by a clutch of *espigueiros*, grain storehouses built on stilts in the 18th and 19th centuries. They all have roof crosses to bring blessings on the crops and are clustered together to make communal farming easier.

Lindoso's Castelo (May–end Sep Tue–Fri 10–12.30, 2–6.30, Sat–Sun 10–12.30, 2–6; Oct–end Apr Tue–Fri 9.30–12.30, 2–5, Sat–Sun 10–12.30, 2–4.30) is a crenellated medieval keep. It houses a little museum that provides park information.

A traditional stone grain store on stilts, Lindoso

Guimarães

The birthplace of the Portuguese nation is a historic town, dominated by a ducal palace and an ancient castle. A fine collection of squares, churches and an impressive museum await.

The Paço dos Duques and the Largo da Oliveira, Guimarães

SEEING GUIMARÃES

The historic heart of Guimarães consists of tranquil squares linked by arcades and cobbled streets and lined with buildings painted in honey shades. The southern end is bordered by wide avenues surrounding the town gardens, while the imposing castle and the Paço dos Duques de Bragança stand to the north.

Enter the old city at the southern end from the Largo República do Brasil. The Museu Alberto Sampaio is almost immediately on your right, while farther up, the street widens into the Largo da Oliveira, a square linked by arcades to the adjoining Praça de Santiago. From here, you can walk up Rua de Santa Maria to the castle and the palace. There are some stylish shops here, though there are more interesting ones along and around Rua Paio Galvã, outside the historic town to the west.

RATINGS

Cultural interest	●●●●
Historic interest	●●●●●
Photo stops	●●●●
Walkability	●●●●

TIPS

- It is possible to see Guimarães in a day, but you will absorb more of the city's atmosphere if you stay overnight.
- Parking is difficult anywhere near the old part of town—use one of the underground parking areas outside the old city walls and walk from there.
- If you are planning to stay, book well in advance, particularly during the July and August festival period.

BASICS

340 C3 Alameda de São Damaso 83, 4810-286 Guimarães; Praça de Santiago 37, 4810-300 Guimarães, tel 253 412 450 or 253 518 790; Mon–Fri 9.30–12.30, 2–6.30, Sat 10–6, Sun 10–1 Guimarães

www.cm-guimaraes.pt
A good, fast site, with a wide range of information for visitors, but only in Portuguese

Afonso Henriques (right) is commemorated at the castle

HIGHLIGHTS

PAÇO DOS DUQUES DE BRAGANÇA

4810 Guimarães 253 412 273 Sep–end Jun daily 9.30–12.30, 2–5.30; Jul–end Aug daily 9.30–12.30, 2–7 €3, free Sun am

This fortified palace, with its steep roof, crenellations and numerous chimneys, wouldn't look out of place in northern Europe. It was built in the early 15th century by Dom Afonso, Duke of Burgundy and the illegitimate son of João I, whose familiarity with French architecture is evident from the palace's exterior. Used as a royal residence for a century, the palace fell out of favour when the court moved to Vila Viçosa (▷ 165), and was restored only in the 1930s under the Salazar regime. It is still an official presidential residence. The interior is a procession of vast rooms, with fireplaces big enough to roast an ox, and hung with tapestries woven to cartoons by Rubens. The furniture, paintings, weapons and porcelain date mainly from the 17th and 18th centuries.

LARGO DA OLIVEIRA AND PRAÇA DE SANTIAGO

The Largo da Oliveira is dominated by two superbly contrasting buildings, the Igreja de Nossa Senhora da Oliveira (Our Lady of the Olive Tree) and the old council chambers, in an arcaded building remodelled in the 17th century. The church gets its name from a legendary olive tree, planted to provide oil for the church lamps. The tree died, but in 1342 it burst miraculously back into life after a cross was hung from one of its branches. The adjoining square, Praça de Santiago,

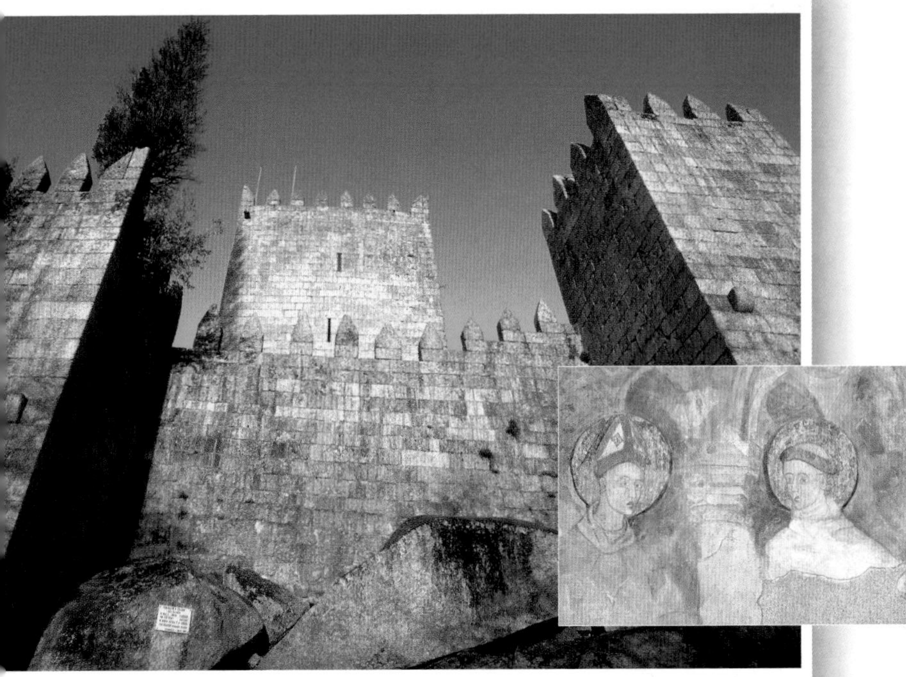

The castle keep and a wallpainting (inset) from Igreja São Francisco

with its old stone houses and wooden balconies, dates back to the 13th century. It was named after St. James who, according to legend, brought a statue of the Virgin to the spot to replace a pagan shrine.

MOSTEIRO DE SANTA MARINHA DE COSTA

✉ 4810 Guimarães 🕑 Chapel: Mon–Fri 11–7, Sat–Sun 10–8

On the slopes of the 617m (2,020ft) Penha, 2km (1 mile) to the southeast of Guimarães, stands the monastery of Santa Marinha de Costa, founded in 1154 by Queen Mafalda, Afonso Henriques' wife, in honour of Santa Marinha, the patron saint of pregnant women. The church's elaborate façade is rococo, but the interior is a beguiling mix of different architectural styles. The monastery was extensively damaged by fire in 1951, but was sensitively restored. It is now a hotel.

MUSEO ALBERTO SAMPAIO

✉ Rua Alfredo Guimarães, 4810 Guimarães ☎ 253 423 910 🕑 Tue–Sun 10–12.30, 2–5.30 ✋ €2, free Sun am

The collection of the Alberto Sampaio museum is beautifully presented in the cloisters and chapterhouse of the Oliveira. The highlight of the silver collection, one of Portugal's finest, is a silver-gilt *Triptych of the Nativity*. This miracle of metalwork is said to have been looted by João I's troops after the Portuguese victory over the Castilians at Aljubarrota in 1385. Look out, too, for the tunic worn by João I at the same battle, a silver-gilt and enamel Gothic chalice and an ornate Manueline cross engraved with scenes from the Passion of Christ.

BACKGROUND

Guimarães was the birthplace of Afonso Henriques, who became the first king of Portugal in 1143. Although the capital was soon transferred to Coimbra (▷ 98–101), Guimarães has always retained its sense of historic pride, as evidenced by the city motto *Portugal nasceu aqui* ('Portugal was born here'). Today, this beautifully preserved city is surrounded by modern development. Home to the University of the Minho, it also has a thriving cultural scene and better-than-average nightlife.

MORE TO SEE

CAPELA DO SÃO MIGUEL

✉ 4810 Guimarães ☎ 253 412 273 🕑 Daily 9.30–12.30, 2–5 ✋ Free

A tiny 12th-century Romanesque chapel between the castle and the *paço*. Afonso Henriques is said to have been baptized here.

CASTELO

✉ 4810 Guimarães ☎ 253 412 273 🕑 Daily 9.30–12.30, 2–5.30 ✋ Free

The 10th-century castle was extended by Afonso Henriques and restored in the 1940s. It's an impressive 28m (92ft) high, with seven towers and superb views.

IGREJA DE SÃO FRANCISCO

✉ 4810 Guimarães 🕑 Tue–Sat 9.30–12, 3–5, Sun 9.30–1 ✋ Free

The chancel is worth a special look for its beautiful 18th-century tile decoration. Look out, too, for the elaborately painted panelled ceiling in the sacristy and the stately cloisters.

MUSEU ARQUEOLÓGICO MARTINS SARMENTO

✉ Rua Paio Galvão, 4810 Guimarães ☎ 253 415 969 🕑 Tue–Sun 9.30–12, 2–5 ✋ €1.50

The museum houses finds from archaeological digs around the cloisters of São Domingo. The fascinating range of exhibits dates from pre-Roman times.

A craftsman from Miranda do Douro shows off his metalwork

The stone houses of Rio de Onor in Parque Natural de Montesinho, a hamlet that straddles the Portuguese border with Spain

MIRANDA DO DOURO

341 G3 Largo do Menino Jesus da Cartolinha, 5210 Miranda do Douro, tel 273 431 132

The frontier town of Miranda do Douro faces the barren stony hills of Spain across a rocky gorge, a position that has made it strategically important for more than 600 years. In 1762 this role ended when an explosion during a Franco-Spanish attack destroyed 200 houses and much of the castle, and the town became a half-forgotten backwater. However, since 1955, when the Douro dam was built, the town has thrived and there is a steady stream of cross-border traffic attracted by the promise of low Portuguese prices. You will see hard evidence of this in the new town, which is packed with cut-price stores.

To sample the charm of Miranda, head for the old town, with its stately buildings and narrow cobbled streets lined with whitewashed, granite-trimmed houses. High on the list of things not to miss is the Sé (cathedral), for several centuries the main cathedral of the Trás-os-Montes. It was built as the result of Pope Paul III's response to a local request to make Miranda the seat of a bishopric. Work started in 1552. It's an austere and beautiful building, the Gothic interior is full of light and the severity of its granite floor and walls contrast with sumptuous gilding of the high altar, dedicated to the Assumption of the Virgin. Behind the Sé, you will see the ruins of the old episcopal palace. The *praça* (square) in front has superb views across to Spain.

Near here, in the Praça Dom João III, is the Museu da Terra de Miranda (Mon–Tue 10–6, Wed–Sun 9.30–12.30, 2–6, €1.50), a splendid collection of local bits and pieces that sheds light on the town and region. Look out for the costumes worn by the *pauliterios*, stick-dancers unique to the town, and for the thick woollen capes for which the region is traditionally famous.

Don't miss The little statue of the infant Jesus to the right of the high altar in the *Sé*, locally much venerated, comes with a full wardrobe of tiny suits, hats and shoes.

PARQUE NACIONAL DA PENEDA-GERÊS

See pages 78–81

PARQUE NATURAL DO DOURO INTERNACIONAL

341 E4 Park office: Rua de Santa Marinha, Mogadouro, tel 279 340 030 www.rt-nordeste.pt/douro.php

A fine example of international cooperation, the Parque Natural do Douro Internacional spans both the Spanish and Portuguese sides of the upper valley of the Douro. Established in 1998, the park covers a huge area running from Barca de Alva in the south up to Mirando do Douro in the north. Hidden for centuries beyond the Trás-os-Montes mountains, the entire region has remained relatively untouched by 20th-century industry and agriculture, helping to preserve a huge variety of flora and fauna. With unemployment here among the highest in Portugal, the park authorities are particularly anxious to develop ecotourism in the area as well as encouraging sustainable low-key agriculture.

Meteorologically, the area has a Mediterranean microclimate, ensuring the survival of species that have vanished farther south. If you enjoy spending time in the great outdoors, the park has plenty to keep you occupied. It's particularly good for birdwatching, with over 170 species, both resident and summer visitors, including Europe's largest group of Egyptian vultures. Botany enthusiasts should aim to visit in spring, when the hillsides are covered in almond blossom and there is an abundance of orchids, cistus and aromatic field plants. The main park office is in Mogadouro; the staff provide maps and advice on where to go and what to see, and will help you find guided tours or walks.

PARQUE NATURAL DE MONTESINHO

341 E2 Park office: Parque Natural de Montesinho, Apartamento 90, Lote 5, Bairro Salvador Nunes Teixera, 5301 Bragança, tel 273 381 234 Closed Nov–end Mar www.bragancanet.pt/vinhais/vslomba/pnm.html

Covering more than 750sq km (290sq miles) between Bragança and the Spanish border, the Parque Natural de Montesinho is the only place in the Trás-os-Montes that remains untouched by rapid development. The population of around 8,000 is scattered among the park's 92 villages, where the way of life is traditional, hard and extremely basic.

The village of Rio de Onor, straddling the border, provides a fascinating insight into the local way of life, the subject of many anthropological studies. Spanish and Portuguese people have intermarried for generations, virtually creating their own autonomous state, with its own system of justice and mutual cooperation. Here, and in other villages, such as Guadramil, donkeys are a frequent means of transport and it is common to see women washing clothes in the river. The beautiful landscape, with rich woodlands and heather-clad moors, supports birds of prey and animals such as wild

The intricate carved doorway of Igreja de São Salvador, Bravães, is, like the church, from the 12th and 13th centuries

The medieval stone bridge gave Ponte de Lima its name

boar and wolves. Serious and well-equipped walkers can enjoy long-distance hikes between the villages, and there are plenty of shorter walks, bicycling trails and horse-riding establishments to choose from. You can rent traditional houses by the week, and some villages have rooms for rent and simple cafés. Bragança itself (▷ 72) and the village of Vinhais to the west make the best bases for exploring the area.

PONTE DA BARCA

340 C2 Largo da Misericórdia, 4980 Ponte da Barca, tel 258 452 899
www.rtam.pt

The town gets its name from the boats that used to ferry passengers across the River Lima before the bridge here was built in the 15th century—this was a major crossing point for pilgrims on their way to Santiago de Compostela in Spain. Above the bridge, mansion-lined old streets lead past the town pillory and the 18th-century arcaded market, to a pleasant *praça* (square) and a couple of churches.

Walk or drive the 4km (2.5 miles) downriver to the hamlet of Bravães, where you will find one of Portugal's greatest architectural achievements, the Romanesque Igreja de São Salvador. This was built between the 12th and 13th centuries according to a French design, a style that had travelled down the Camino de Santiago—the pilgrim way of St. James that runs through here. Plain and stark, its granite solidity is offset by the carving around the remarkable doorway. It is sculpted with monkeys, doves and geometric motifs, while the tympanum (cross-stone) rests on the heads of two wide-horned cattle, still found in the Minho. Above this, two angels adore a Christ Pantocrator, a sculpted figure of the Glorious Christ, enclosed in a stone oval, with his hand raised in blessing. Inside the dark interior, lit by seven slit windows, are fine frescoes of St. Sebastian and the Madonna.

PONTE DE LIMA

340 C2 Praça da República, 4990 Ponte de Lima, tel 258 942 335
www.rtam.pt

Some 30km (20 miles) east from the coastal town of Viana do Castelo (▷ 83), this beautiful and peaceful little town is a beguiling mix of quiet old mansions, green shady gardens and riverside walks. It gets its name from the medieval stone bridge across the river, built to replace a Roman bridge that formed part of the military route from Astorga to Braga. Traces of the Roman occupation can still be seen in the form of five arches and a few milestones built into the bridge.

On the riverside, and just below the bridge, is the Largo Principal, a laid-back square surrounded by outdoor cafés, behind which lie the streets of the old town. Here you'll find superb buildings representing every definable era of vernacular architecture—Romanesque, Gothic, Manueline and baroque—along with churches, fountains and pockets of greenery. The Alameda, a tree-lined promenade, runs beside the river, which you cross to visit the Museu Rural (Tue–Sun 2–6, free), housing a collection of rural implements. Lima's other main site is the Igreja-Museu dos Terceiros (Tue–Fri 2–5.30, free), a church and conventual complex with fine woodwork and 16th-century *azulejos* (tiles).

The countryside around is dotted with *solares* and *quintas*, both types of manor house. Many provide accommodation as well as producing the famous *vinho verde*, a slightly sparkling, low-alcohol, dry white wine characteristic of the region.

SOLAR DE MATEUS

See page 82.

TORRE DE MONCORVO

341 E4 Rua Manuel Seixas, Torre de Moncorvo, tel 279 252 289
www.bragancanet.pt/moncorvo

The road from the south climbs steeply through the mountains to Moncorvo, a fortress-like town near the edge of a high plateau in the northeast of the Trás-os-Montes. Below are the fertile valleys of the Douro and Sabor rivers, while above the town arid and stony mountains stretch towards Spain. To the east lie the hills of the Serra de Reboredo and around the town the slopes burst into white blossom in spring when the almond trees come into flower.

Legend has it that the trees were first planted to assuage the nostalgia of a northern princess. She had married a Moorish prince, and, though happy during summer, pined in winter for the snows of her native land. The prince hurried south to the Algarve and brought back hundreds of almond trees, whose blossom reminded her of the snow-covered hills of home. The town is still famous for both the trees and their fruit, attracting spring visitors to admire the spectacle and buy the locally produced sugared almonds.

Moncorvo's main monument is the Igreja Matriz. The largest church in the region, it was built between 1544 and 1650. The façade is dominated by a central tower and a Renaissance doorway, while inside you will find a fine 17th-century altar. Behind the church, a maze of medieval streets surround the central *praça* (square).

Parque Nacional da Peneda-Gerês

Portugal's only national park preserves a traditional way of life. A wilderness area, it's a paradise for walkers and outdoor enthusiasts.

Distinctive Minho cattle graze in the park (left)
The River Cávado (above) flows through the park's heartland

SEEING THE PARQUE NACIONAL DA PENEDA-GERÊS

The Parque Nacional da Peneda-Gerês covers a crescent-shaped tract of land in the northern Minho, with its two arms encircling the southwest tip of the Spanish province of Orense. A staggering landscape of rock and scree, valleys and reservoirs, its separate mountain areas, the *serras* of Peneda, Soajo, Amarela and Gerês, are divided by three river valleys—the Lima, Homem and Cávado. Road access is restricted in certain areas of the park and there are few north–south through routes; as a result, the quickest way for drivers to get from the northern Peneda section to the Gerês is through Spain. The western section of the Gerês *serra* is the wildest area, where roads skirt the southern edge of the massif.

To explore the southern section of the park, head for the spa town of Caldas do Gerês, where there is plenty of accommodation and some stunning local drives and walks. To head north, you need to backtrack to join the N101 to Ponte da Barca (⊳ 77), from where a fairly good road leads up the Lima valley to the village of Lindoso (⊳ 73) near the Spanish border. From here you could head through Spain and re-enter the park at Ameijoeira to explore the wild Serra da Peneda.

To make the most of the glorious scenery, though, it is best to do as much walking as you can—there is a huge range of hiking trails to choose from, of all lengths and standards. It's well worth consulting the park offices, as the staff there are very good at helping you to plan suitable routes. They also give out details of guided walks and can help you find a private guide, whose walking expertise and local knowledge will help you search out the hidden highlights of the area.

RATINGS	
Good for kids	●●●●
Outdoor pursuits	●●●●●
Photo stops	●●●●●
Walkability	●●●●

Attractive Caldas do Gerês (right) with its spa hotel (below) lies at the foot of a wooded gorge; a traditional granite grain store (bottom)

BASICS

PARK OFFICES

BRAGA
340 C3 Avenida António Macedo, Quinta das Parretas, 4710 Braga, tel 253 203 480
www.adere-pg.pt

PONTE DA BARCA
340 C2 ADERE Peneda-Gerês, Largo da Misericórdia, 4980 Ponte da Barca, tel 258 452 250
www.adere-pg.pt

INFORMATION POINTS

CALDAS DO GERÊS
340 C2 Avenida Manuel Francisco da Costa, Caldas do Gerês, tel 253 390 110
May–end Sep Mon–Tue, Thu–Fri 10–12.30, 2–6, Sat 10–12, 2.30–6, Sun 10–12, 2.30–5; Oct–end Apr Mon–Tue, Thu–Fri 9.30–12.30, 2–5.30, Sat 10–12.30, 2–5, Sun 10–12.30, 2–4.30

MEZIO
Rua Arcos de Valdevez, Mezio, tel 258 526 751
May–end Sep Mon–Tue, Thu–Fri 10–12.30, 2–6, Sat 10–12, 2.30–6, Sun 10–12, 2.30–5; Oct–end Apr Mon–Tue, Thu–Fri 9.30–12.30, 2–5.30, Sat 10–12.30, 2–5, Sun 10–12.30, 2–4.30

HIGHLIGHTS

SERRA DO GERÊS

You must be prepared to do some hiking and climbing if you want to penetrate deeper into this dramatic mountain area, though it is possible to appreciate its scale from the Vale do Rio Cávado (▷ 83). Alternatively, start exploring from the Confluente de Canicada, where there are two lakes formed by a dam some 10km (6 miles) to the west. From here, head for Caldas do Gerês, a relaxed and faded little spa town at the bottom of a wooded gorge, whose waters are thought to aid in the treatment of liver and digestive disorders.

A hydrangea-lined road climbs steadily through the town, crossing the River Homem as it races through its rocky gorge, and continuing to the Spanish border. Just before, a track heading to Campo do Gerês crosses the Roman road that linked Braga and Astorga—you can still see the distance markers with their commemorative inscriptions. Below is the intense blue of the Represa de Vilarinha das Fumas, a superb reservoir in a rocky, wild landscape.

If you go south from Gerês and turn right towards Campo do Gerês, there are stunning mountain views to be had, though the road is twisty. From its highest point you can walk to the Miradouro de Junceda, one of the area's most dramatic viewpoints. If you have time, drive on to the other end of the Vilarinha reservoir, perhaps taking the track to walk up and join the Roman road.

Roadside orange-sellers (below left); delicious honey for sale (below right); a stallholder in Caldas do Gerês shows off the local produce (bottom)

SERRA DA PENEDA

For a taste of the wild Peneda section of the park, you could enter at Lamas de Mouro and make an immediate detour to Castro Laboeiro, an ancient village that was once famous for its dogs, bred to protect sheep from wolves. The ruined castle has great views and there are some excellent walks around the village. Head south down a wooded valley and you will reach the Santuário de Nossa Senhora da Peneda, in Peneda. Set at the foot of a cliff, the pilgrimage site is modelled on Bom Jesus near Braga (▷ 69–70); in September, hundreds come to pay their respects here.

From here, the scenery gets wilder and wilder, with tiny fields hewn out of the landscape between great granite boulders. Keep an eye out for traditional *espigueiros*, granite grain stores, in the villages. There are some scattered in the terraced fields around Roucas, while farther on, Soajo has a superb group. From Soajo you can join the road running up the Lima valley to Lindoso (▷ 73).

BACKGROUND

Peneda-Gerês lies in the northern district of Braga, Viana do Castelo and Vila Real. Historically, this border country was one of the great through routes between Portugal and Spain, and the valleys and passes here are crisscrossed by footpaths that formed part of the Camino de Santiago, the great pilgrim route to the shrine of St. James at Santiago de Compostela in Galicia. The park itself was established in 1971 and covers 72,000ha (178,000 acres) of the countryside. In common with national parks in other countries, it aims not only to protect an area of outstanding natural beauty from the threat of development, but also to conserve the archaeological sites, plus the flora, fauna and bird life. A considerable number of people live in the villages within the park, but such communities are dwindling and ageing, and traditional customs are consequently in danger of dying out. The park authorities are trying to strike a balance—protecting the environment and traditional way of life, while catering for the ever-increasing number of visitors that come to spend time in the park each year.

TIPS

- Pick up walking leaflets in English at the information points and park offices—they have details of footpaths of all lengths from short strolls to three- to four-day hikes.
- Take warm and waterproof clothes, a compass, water and food if you are going on a long walk. Let someone know where you are going and what time you expect to be back.
- The weather can change suddenly in mountainous areas, while large areas of the park are buried in snow in winter.
- When driving, bear in mind that map distances are deceptive—the roads here are slow, steep and tortuous, so allow extra time.

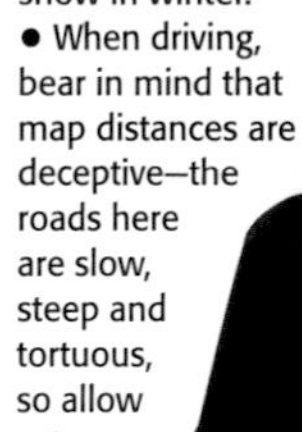

With its beautiful formal gardens and elaborate façade, Solar de Mateus is a triumph of Portuguese baroque architecture

RATINGS

Cultural interest	●●●●●
Historic interest	●●●●
Photo stops	●●●●●

TIPS

- The solar is signposted 'Palácio de Mateus' from the outskirts of Vila Real—take the Bragança road out of town and look for signs to Mateus.
- Arrive early in summer to avoid the crowds and find a parking space.
- Both the Vila Real tourist office and the solar have details of cultural events.

BASICS

340 D3 • Fundacão da Casa de Mateus, 5000 Vila Real

259 323 121

Jun–end Sep daily 9–7.30; Oct, Mar–end May daily 9–1, 2–6; Nov–end Feb daily 10–1, 2–5; guided tours only of up to 10 visitors and 3 tours in house simultaneously only, so book ahead in summer

House and garden: €6.25. Garden only: €3.50

All visits are by guided tour (approx. 30 minutes) and most guides speak some English

No guidebooks; coffee-table book available at €40

Small café selling coffee, soft drinks and cakes

Shop selling books, wine and jam

Very limited at the top of the entrance drive

SOLAR DE MATEUS

This perfect example of an 18th-century Portuguese manor house set in beautiful formal gardens is renowned worldwide as the symbol of Mateus Rosé.

The Casa de Mateus was built in the 1740s by the third Margado de Mateus; his descendants still live in one wing. The architect is unknown, but is thought to have been Nicolau Nasoni, an Italian who had immense influence on the development of Portuguese baroque.

THE FAÇADE

This is one of the finest examples of Portuguese baroque architecture. Its central section is set back, with the main door at first-floor level. This is flanked by two windows, approached by a double balustraded stairway and surmounted by a tall emblazoned pediment with allegorical statues on either side. Severe classical wings, topped by pinnacles, enclose a courtyard leading to an archway beneath the main stairs. This leads to the inner courtyard, with a further double staircase. To the left of the palace is a baroque chapel, built in 1750.

THE INTERIOR

The hall, like many of the other rooms, has a fine chestnut carved ceiling. It leads into the richly draped Four Seasons Room. From here, the Blue Room, with its Chinese ceramics, leads to the Dining Room, with a rich collection of silver and china. In the Four Corners Room, look out for the Indo-Portuguese wood and ivory portable desk. Two rooms in the south wing have been converted into a museum, where the highlight is the original printing plates made by Jean Fragonard to illustrate an 1817 edition of *Os Lusíadas* by the poet Luís de Camoês.

THE GARDENS

These were altered considerably in the 1930s, when the reflecting pool was added. The parterres, planted with shrubs and flowers and surrounded by topiary or box hedges, perfectly mirror the house's architecture. The planting is dominated by camellias, hydrangeas and roses. Make sure to take the time to explore the wisteria-hung pergola, the dense cedar tunnel, the three-tiered pools and the adjoining old threshing floor, with its views to the Serra do Marão and the famous vineyards stretching out in front.

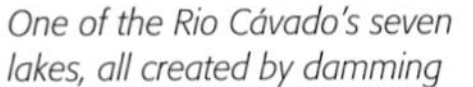

One of the Rio Cávado's seven lakes, all created by damming

There are magnificent views of Viana do Castelo from the basilica of the church of Santa Luzia, though it is a stiff climb to the hilltop

VALE DO RIO CÁVADO

340 D2 Praça da República 1, 4710-251 Braga, tel 053 262 550
www.cm-braga.pt

For a superb mix of high mountains, wooded slopes, attractive villages and lake scenery, head for the upper valley of the River Cávado, which runs along the southern edge of the Serra do Gerês to Braga. Above Braga, the river cuts through and is enclosed by a rocky valley that was first dammed in 1946, creating a series of beautiful lakes, set in an upland landscape. There are seven dams in all, helping to generate enough waterpower to produce around 18 per cent of Portugal's hydroelectricity. The main road (N103) climbs east through a series of villages. Reservoir views open up below until you reach the plateau, where the vast expanse of the largest lake in the valley, the Barragem do Alto Rabagão, comes into view. There is little in the way of tourist development here, and the locals have managed to preserve their traditional way of life—you can still see primitive earth dams in the fields, designed to trap the water for summer grazing. It's worth making a detour off the main road north to Montalegre, an ancient village with a ruined 14th-century castle that has breathtaking mountain views. Boticas and Vilarinho, unspoilt villages both on a minor road south of the reservoir, are also worth visiting.

VALENÇA DO MINHO

340 B2 Avenida de Espanha, 4930 Valença do Minho, tel 251 823 329 Valença do Minho
www.rtam.pt

The old town of Valença is a picturesque jumble of narrow cobbled streets, lined with splendid buildings and enclosed in a massive double fortress, itself enclosed in two massive linked fortresses overlooking the River Minho towards Spain. The fortress is largely 17th century, its star-shaped design and series of ramparts heavily influenced by the French military architect Vauban. A town grew up within the citadel, its two sections linked by a causeway across a dry moat. Enter through gates in either the south or east walls to wander around the streets and admire the views from the ramparts.

VIANA DO CASTELO

340 B2 Rua do Hospita Velho (off Praça da Erva), 4930 Viana do Castelo, tel 258 822 620 Viana do Castelo
www.rtam.pt

Within easy reach of one of northern Portugal's finest beaches, Viana do Castelo has a reputation for being one of the Minho's best resorts. Backed by the wooded Monte de Santa Luzia, crowned with an impressive basilica, there is plenty to explore and its elegant and historic heart is packed with good shops and restaurants. It comes alive during the August *romaria*, a three-day carnival with daily street parades, *gigantones* (giant figures), bands, fireworks and dancing in the streets.

Viana's history is entwined with the sea. Money from its maritime activities funded the town's fine buildings, seen at their best in and around the central square, the Praça da República. Here you will find the 1589 Misericórdia, a Flemish-Venetian-influenced almshouse whose façade is decorated with a massive colonnade and loggias. Near this is the 16th-century town hall, embellished with ground-level arches and the town's caravel coat of arms.

Just off the square is the Igreja Matriz, a truly lovely church whose architectural shapes and detail are a happy mix of rounded, solid Romanesque forms and delicate Gothic touches. The Museu Municipal (Tue–Sun 9–12, 2–5, €2) was formerly an 18th-century palace. It is perfectly preserved, its interior walls covered with *azulejos* (tiles) depicting hunting and fishing scenes. It showcases a celebrated collection of superb glazed earthenware.

Southeast on the waterfront, ferries run across the Lima and the smart marina is backed by pleasant gardens. Take the ferry to reach the Praia do Cabedelo, a curving expanse of smooth sand with good surf and summer watersports and bars. There's good walking on the slopes of Monte de Santa Luzia, where paths wind through eucalyptus woods with superb views—these are even better if you climb the steps to the dome of the basilica at the summit.

VILA REAL

340 D3 Avenida Carvalho Araújo 94, 5000 Vila Real, tel 259 322 819 Vila Real
www.cm-vilareal.pt

Vila Real lies above the River Corgo, with the ranges of the Marão and Alvão mountains behind. Seat of the region's university, the town is a pleasant base for a couple of nights, especially if you are car-less as it is the hub of the regional transport system. At its heart you will find some gracious buildings, including the town hall and the 15th-century *Sé* (cathedral), but its selling point is the lively atmosphere, best appreciated at the morning market and along the streets in the late afternoon. The town's main claim to fame is that it is the birthplace of explorer Diogo Cão, who discovered the Congo River in 1482.

PORTO AND THE DOURO

Portugal's second-largest city is superbly set on the River Douro, the houses of its historic Ribeira clinging to slopes tumbling down to the water. Its treasures include a fine cathedral and excellent museums. The city's name remains inextricably associated with port, although the trade is focused on Vila Nova de Gaia, across the river.

MAJOR SIGHTS

Amarante's bridge leads to the Rua de Janeiro and the church

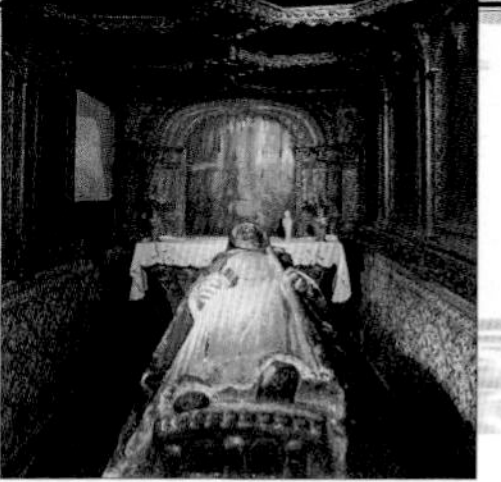

The tomb of São Gonçalo, Amarante's patron saint

The abbey at Paço de Sousa, once Benedictine headquarters

AMARANTE

340 C3 Câmara Municipal, Praça da República, 4600 Amarante, tel 255 420 246 Amarante
www.cm-amarante.pt

The beautiful old town of Amarante stands on the banks of the River Tâmega, a tributary of the Douro, in a scenic valley of wooded slopes and vines. This is wine country, birthplace of the light and sparkling *vinho verde*, and the surrounding countryside is dotted with fine old *solares* (manor houses), many of which are happy to provide accommodation for overnight visitors.

Historically, Amarante's big moment came during the Peninsular War, when, in 1809, a heroic show of defence by the townspeople succeeded in halting Marshal Soult and his French forces as they retreated in the face of Beresford's advancing British columns. Amarante held out for two weeks, its inhabitants escaping to safety before the French planted explosives, blew up the defences and took the town. You can still see French bayonet marks in the paintings inside the church of São Gonçalo, the town's patron saint, made as the French feverishly searched for hidden treasure.

The church and former monastery dedicated to Gonçalo are Amarante's main sights, an interesting complex standing beside the graceful old bridge, which is now the Museu Municipal (Tue–Sun 10–12.30, 2–5.30, €1.50). The museum is mainly devoted to the Cubist painter Amadeo de Souza Cardosos (1887–1918), who was born in the town and is one of the few Portuguese artists to have become famous worldwide.

Cross the bridge to reach Rua de Janeiro, lined with old buildings whose balconies hang over the Tâmega. The river is lined with waterside cafés and beaches, and you can rent boats and pedalos here. It is not always tranquil—look out for the plaques on buildings throughout town marking the high flood levels in record years—1909, 1939, 1962 and 2001. Downstream from the bridge, the Parque Florestal is green and cool in summer, while the swimming pool complex is great for kids. You'll find good local craft shops in town and the surrounding villages, while Amarante itself has a twice-weekly market (Wednesday and Saturday).

PAÇO DE SOUSA

340 C4 Avenida Sacadura Cabral 90, Penafiel, tel 255 712 561
www.penafieldigital.com.pt

On the banks of the River Sousa, the village of Paço de Sousa is dominated by the monastic church of São Salvador, formerly the headquarters of the Benedictine order in Portugal. It was the Benedictine monks who initially terraced the valley slopes for vines, their other legacy being the fine Romanesque churches they left behind throughout the area. Their great medieval church at Paço has a simple façade with a rose window, while inside, the tomb of Egas Moniz, a Portuguese hero whose name is synonymous with loyalty, can be found in the right of the three shadowy aisles. In 1127 Egas negotiated peace with the King of Léon on behalf of his master, King Afonso Henriques, thus allowing the monarch to concentrate his military efforts on defeating the Moors in the south. Three years later, Afonso conveniently forgot the settlement and war again threatened. Egas journeyed to Toledo and offered up himself and his family for the punishment due to Afonso. His loyalty was rewarded when the Spanish monarch sent him home unharmed.

PENAFIEL

340 C4 Avenida Sacadura Cabral 90, Penafiel, tel 255 712 561 Penafiel
www.penafieldigital.com.pt

Wine-lovers should head straight for Penafiel, the heart of the *vinho verde* wine country. A laid-back, relaxed little town, it has just one cultural sight, the Museu Municipal (Mon–Fri 9.30–12, 2–5.30, €1.50), with a well-presented, though small, collection of archaeological finds from the nearby Celtic settlement of Mozinho. Look out for some exquisite gold jewellery.

There are plenty of opportunities to sample wine—the Quinta da Aveleda, just outside the town, is a good option, and the tourist office will advise where else you can try. Penafiel also makes a good base from which to track down some superb Romanesque churches —the ones in Abragão, Gandra and tiny Boelhe are within easy reach.

The tomb of Egas Moniz, one of Portugal's medieval heroes, in the church at Paço de Sousa

Porto

A dynamic and earthy metropolis with a superb historic heart and a vibrant cultural and entertainment scene, Portugal's second-largest city stands at the mouth of the River Douro.

RATINGS	
Cultural interest	●●●
Historic interest	●●●●
Photo stops	●●●●●
Specialist shopping	●●●●

BASICS

340 B4

Rua Clube dos Fenianos 25, 4000-172 Porto or Rua Infante d Henrique 63 4050-297 Porto, tel 223 393 470 or 222 009 770; Oct–end Jun Mon–Fri 9–5.30, Sat– Sun 9–4.30; Jul–end Sep daily 9–7

Estação de Campanhã, Estação de São Bento

www.portoturismo.pt
This is a fast, easy-to-use site available in three languages—Portuguese, English and Spanish. Updated daily, it covers every aspect of visiting the city, with good practical and cultural information and links to other sites

SEEING PORTO

Porto is a big, sprawling city, but it is easy for visitors to get around as most of the main sights are clustered together. If you are touring, it makes sense to tackle the place before you pick up your car: There is a shortage of parking in the city, while the entire central area is a confusing grid of one-way streets.

Porto revolves round the Avenida dos Aliados, which ends at the Praça da Liberdade, a square that is the hub of the city's public transport system and only a couple of minutes from the Estação de São Bento, one of Porto's two mainline stations. South from here, the city's historic core tumbles down the hill-side towards the Cais de Ribeira, the old waterfront, with the *Sé* (cathedral) complex looming above to the east.

This is the most interesting quarter, so take time to explore it thoroughly before heading uphill via the Bolsa to the streets east of the Liberdade. Here you can climb the Clérigos tower for a bird's-eye view of the city. To get to other sights, use the bus or the metro system, which is currently being expanded.

HIGHLIGHTS

SÉ

89 B3 • Terreiro da Sé, 4050-572 Porto 222 059 028 Cathedral: Nov–end Mar Mon–Sat 8.45–12.30, 2.30–6, Sun 8.30–12.30, 2.30–6; Apr–end Oct Mon–Sat 8.45–12.30, 2.30–6, Sun 8.30–12.30, 2.30–7. Cloisters: Nov–end Mar Mon–Sat 9–12.15, 2.30–5.15, Sat 2.30–5.15; Apr–end Oct Mon–Sat 9–12.30, 2.30–6, Sun 2.30–6 €2

There are expansive river views from the flagstoned Terreiro da Sé, the sweeping open space, complete with pillory, in front of Porto's cathedral. The *Sé*, like so many of Portugal's ancient cathedrals, is half-church, half-fortress, an austere but pleasing granite Romanesque

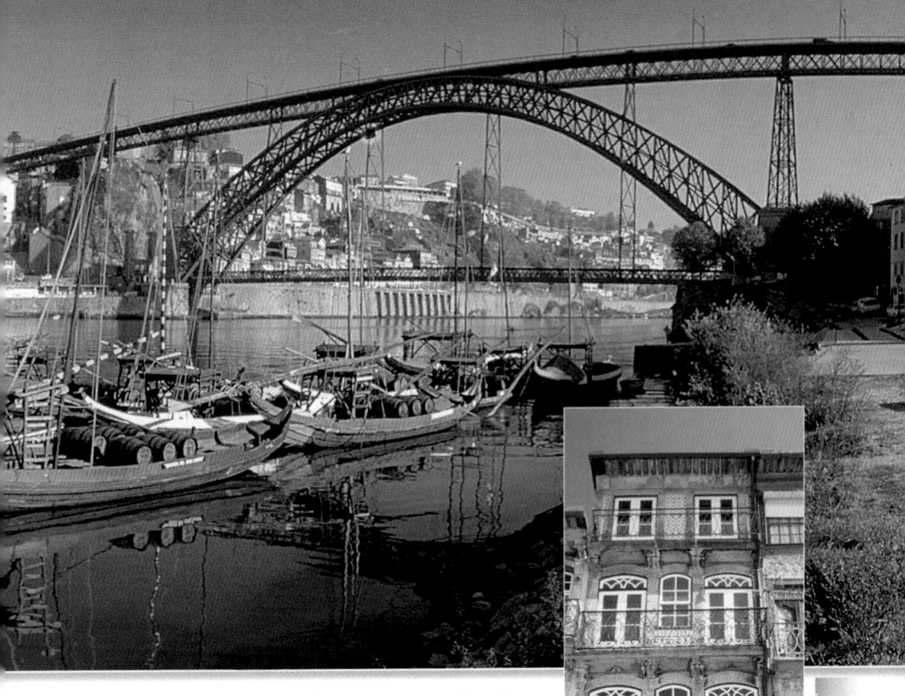

building, founded in the 12th century by Dona Teresa, mother of Afonso Henriques. The interior was remodelled in the 18th century. Gleaming in the north transept to the left of the high altar is a superb silver altarpiece, dating from the mid-17th century.

More instantly appealing than the church are the cloisters, begun in 1385 and adorned with glowing panels of 18th-century *azulejos* (tiles). From here, a fine staircase designed by the Italian architect Nicolau Nasoni, who was responsible for introducing baroque architecture into the country between 1735 and 1748, leads to the chapter- house and terrace—there are more great river and city views from here. Outside, pause to admire the classical façade of what was once the archbishop's palace, designed by Nasoni in 1772. Round the back, surrounded by a tranquil garden, is the Museu Guerra Junqueiro, Rua Dom Hugo 32 (Tue–Sat 10–12.30, 2–5, Sun 2–5, 75c). It houses a fine collection of Islamic Iberian art.

RIBEIRA

89 B4 • Cais de Ribeira 4050-029 Porto A good variety of shops, including craft shops

From the Terreiro da Sé you plunge down into the heart of Porto's oldest district, a confusing maze of narrow streets, winding steps and alleyways. Despite a recent clean-up, it is still a resolutely raucous and vibrant area, revolving around the waterfront Cais da Ribeira, where you will find a lively weekday market. West of here, the Praça da Ribeira, lined with tall, rickety old houses, is the main square, from which precipitous streets run uphill towards the more modern parts of the city. There's a great view of the two-tiered Ponte Dom Luís I bridge—walk across the bottom level to reach the port warehouses of Vila Nova de Gaia (▷ 90–91). Head west from the Praça da Ribeira and up Rua da Alfândega to take in the Casa do Infante, said to be the birthplace of Prince Henry the Navigator in 1394.

TORRE DOS CLÉRIGOS AND IGREJA DOS CLÉRIGOS

89 B2 • Rua São Felipe de Nery, 4050 Porto 222 001 729 Church: Nov–end Mar Mon–Sat 9–12, 3.30–7.30, Sun 10–1, 8.30–10.30; Apr–end Oct Mon–Sat 9–12, 3.30–7.30, Sun 10–1, 8.30–10.30. Tower: Nov–end Mar daily 10–12, 2–5; Apr–end Jul, Sep–end Oct daily 9.30–1, 2–7; Aug daily 10–7 Tower: €1 3, 6, 20, 52, 78

A few minutes' walk west of the Praça da Liberdade, the baroque Torre dos Clérigos soars 75.6m (248ft) into the air. It was once the

Fishing boats moored on the Douro, with the graceful Ponte Dom Luís I in the background (top) and houses in the Ribeira, Porto's oldest district (above)

tallest structure in Portugal, and the bird's-eye view of the city and beyond from the top is excellent for getting your bearings. It, too, was designed by Nasoni. The Igreja dos Clérigos, right beside the tower, was the first oval-plan church to be built in Portugal, and is lavishly adorned with a riot of festoons and garlands.

THE BOLSA

89 A4 • Rua Ferreira Borges, 4050-253 Porto 226 399 000 Nov–end Mar daily 9–1, 2–6; Apr–end Oct daily 9–7 €5 1, 57, 91

Up the hill and west of Ribeira is Porto's temple of commerce, the Stock Exchange, a building that typifies Porto's 19th-century commercial acumen and industry. Built to impress, its neoclassical façade is the perfect expression of financial solidity and probity. Designed and erected in 1834, it is elaborately decorated inside with a profusion of precious stone, marble and wood, seen at its most lavish in the wonderfully kitsch Arabian Hall, a wonderful pastiche of Granada's Alhambra in Spain, complete with Moorish-style stuccowork, lavish stained glass and elaborately carved woodwork.

The baroque Torre dos Clérigos (above left), for long the tallest building in Portugal, and the Praça da Liberdade (above centre), old Porto's main square. The cloisters (above right), liberally decorated with 18th-century blue tiles, are a major feature of the cathedral, whose exterior (opposite) is pleasingly austere and Romanesque

There is more jaw-dropping ostentation next door in the Igreja de São Francisco (Nov–end Mar daily 9–1, 2–6; Apr–end Oct daily 9–7, €3), which was built for the Franciscans and began life as a plain Gothic structure with a fine rose window. The interior underwent a formidable reconstruction in the 18th century, and is now filled with golden rococo carving, the altars, walls and vaulting dripping with *putti* (cherubs), vines, garlands and depictions of wildlife. It is said that the clergy were so shocked by its extravagance when it was unveiled that the church was promptly deconsecrated—it remains so. Don't miss the museum, beneath whose floor lies a vast *ossário*, an ossuary or bone deposit, where thousands of bones were buried before public cemeteries were instituted in Portugal in 1845.

TIPS

- It is worth investing in the *Passe Porto*, a 1- or 2-day discount card. This lets you travel free on public transport and gives you free or discounted admission to monuments and museums and discounts in shops, restaurants and on river cruises. It is available at tourist information offices (1-day €5, 2-day €7).
- River cruises are the best way to see Porto's bridges and the Douro valley. Timings and services vary throughout the year, with few running during the winter months. Contact Barcadouro (tel 222 008 882) for further details or ask at the tourist office.
- Wear comfortable, flat shoes—Porto is very hilly, with steep cobbled streets in the historic areas.

FUNDAÇÃO DE SERRALVES

89 A4 • Rua Dom João de Castro 210, 4150-417 Porto 226 156 571 Oct–end Mar Tue–Wed, Fri–Sun 10–7, Thu 10–10; Apr–end Sep Tue–Fri 10–7, Sat–Sun 10–6 €5 3, 19, 21, 30, 35 Good art books and museum souvenirs

www.serralves.pt

Porto's modern art museum, the Fundação de Serralves, stands in a sculpture-dotted park a short distance west of the heart of the city. The permanent collection is focused on the relationship between Portuguese artists and their international counterparts from the late 1960s to the present day, and is displayed in a clean-cut ultra-modern building designed by renowned Portuguese architect Alvaro Siza. The museum also hosts temporary exhibitions in the 1930s art deco Casa de Serralves, which forms part of the museum complex.

BACKGROUND

Porto grew in importance during the Roman occupation, when two settlements grew on opposite banks of the River Douro. In 1095 the area passed to Henry of Burgundy by marriage. Under Afonso Henriques, it became the base for the Christian reconquest, and Porto eventually gave its name to the entire country.

In 1387 Porto was the setting for the marriage of João I and Philippa of Lancaster, and their son, Henry the Navigator, was

born in the city. Its harbour and shipbuilding industry rapidly developed and trading links were forged with many European nations–in particular England, through treaties signed in 1654 and 1703. During the Peninsular War, British troops under Wellington recaptured the city from its French occupiers in 1809; in 1820, Porto's citizens played a major part in forcing the adoption of a more liberal constitution for the whole country.

Today, Porto is Portugal's second city, a bustling, earthy mix of merging urban areas that for many years was so busy making money that its historic treasures were neglected and began to decay. Its naming as European City of Culture in 2001 was the spark for a massive urban renewal. The Ribeira quarter, a World Heritage Site, got a major face-lift, many buildings were restored, and streets and squares pedestrianized, creating a maritime promenade linking the heart of the city with the sea.

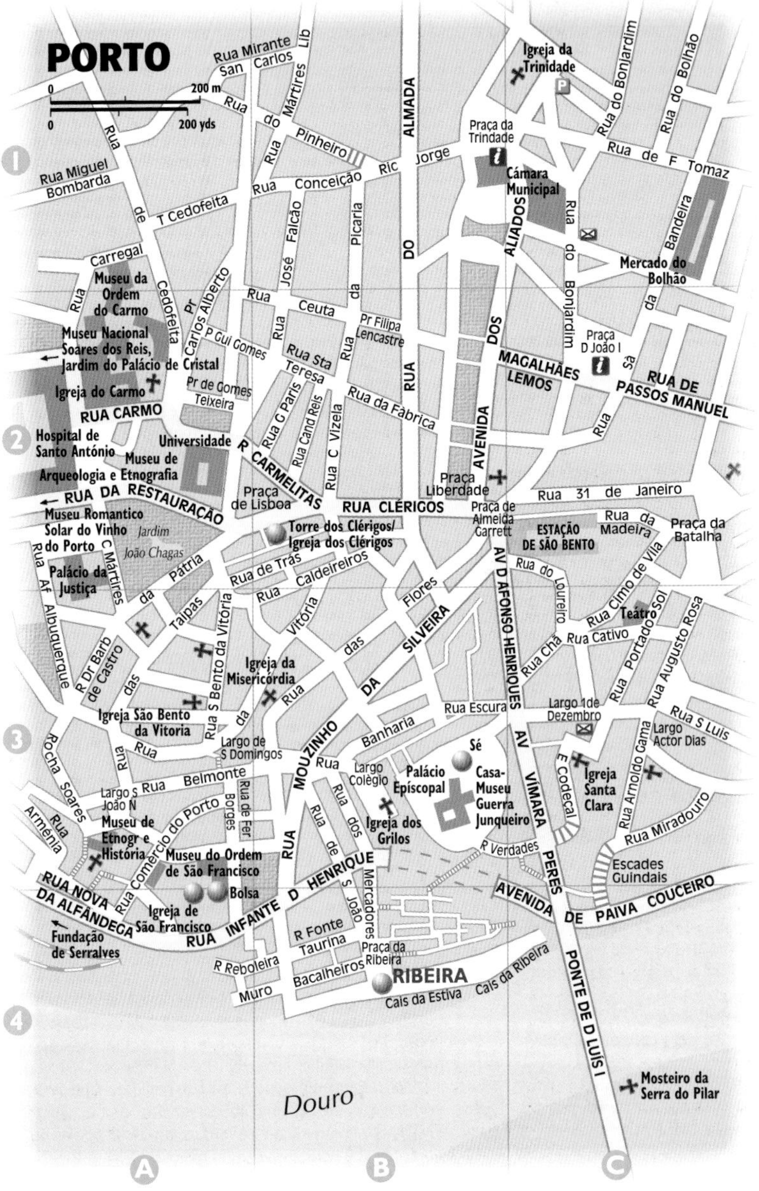

PORTO

0 200 m
0 200 yds

Rua Mirante
San Carlos
Rua do Mártires Lib
Rua do Pinheiro
ALMADA
Igreja da Trinidade
Praça da Trinidade
Rua do Bonjardim
Rua do Bolhão
Rua de F Tomaz
Rua Miguel Bombarda
Rua de Cedofeita
T Cedofeita
Rua Conceição
Ric Jorge
Câmara Municipal
Rua José Falcão
Rua da Picaria
Rua do Bonjardim
ALIADOS
Rua da Bandeira
Mercado do Bolhão
Carregal
Museu da Ordem do Carmo
Pr Carlos Alberto
Rua Ceuta
Pr Filipa Lencastre
Museu Nacional Soares dos Reis, Jardim do Palácio de Cristal
P Gui Gomes
Rua Sta Teresa
Praça D João I
MAGALHÃES LEMOS
RUA DE PASSOS MANUEL
Igreja do Carmo
Pr de Gomes Teixeira
Rua da Fábrica
RUA CARMO
Rua G Paris
Rua Cand Reis
Rua C Vizela
AVENIDA DOS
RUA DO
Hospital de Santo António
Universidade
R CARMELITAS
Museu de Arqueologia e Etnografia
Praça Liberdade
RUA DA RESTAURAÇÃO
Praça de Lisboa
RUA CLÉRIGOS
Praça de Almeida Garrett
Rua 31 de Janeiro
Museu Romantico
Solar do Vinho do Porto
Jardim João Chagas
Torre dos Clérigos/ Igreja dos Clérigos
ESTAÇÃO DE SÃO BENTO
Rua da Madeira
Praça da Batalha
Rua C Mártires
Rua Af Albuquerque
Palácio da Justiça
Rua da Pátria
Rua de Trás
Rua Caldeireiros
Rua do Loureiro
Rua Cimo de Vila
Rua Taipas
Rua Vitória
Flores
Teatro
Rua Portado Sol
Rua Cativo
Rua Augusto Rosa
R Dr Barb de Castro
Rua S Bento da Vitória
Igreja da Misericórdia
Rua das Flores
DA SILVEIRA
AV D AFONSO HENRIQUES
Rua Chã
Largo 1de Dezembro
Igreja São Bento da Vitoria
Rua Escura
Rua S Luis
Largo Actor Dias
Rocha Soares
Largo de S Domingos
MOUZINHO
Banharia
Sé
AV VÍMARA PERES
E Codecal
Rua Arnoldo Gama
Igreja Santa Clara
Largo S João N
Rua Belmonte
Rua de Fer
Borges
Largo Colégio
Palácio Episcopal
Casa-Museu Guerra Junqueiro
Rua Arménia
Museu de Etnogr e História
Rua do Comércio do Porto
Rua dos Grilos
Igreja dos Grilos
Rua Miradouro
Museu do Ordem de São Francisco
RUA INFANTE D HENRIQUE
R Verdades
Escades Guindais
RUA NOVA DA ALFÂNDEGA
Bolsa
Rua S João
Mercadores
AVENIDA DE PAIVA COUCEIRO
Igreja de São Francisco
Fundação de Serralves
R Fonte Taurina
Praça da Ribeira
R Reboleira
Bacalheiros
RIBEIRA
Cais da Ribeira
Muro
Cais da Estiva
PONTE DE D LUÍS I
Mosteiro da Serra do Pilar
Douro
1 2 3 4
A B C

Vila Nova de Gaia

The heart of the centuries-old port trade, Vila Nova is famous for its wine lodges—the best place to learn about the history of this great fortified wine and sample a wide variety of vintages.

Tasting port in Gaia (above left); port barrels (above right)

RATINGS	
Historic interest	●●●●
Specialist shopping	●●●●●
Value for money	●●●●●
Walkability	●●●●

TIPS

- If time is short, join a tour from Porto: one takes in Porto and Gaia; the other is a mini-train trip from the Sé (cathedral) to Gaia—ask at Porto's tourist office.
- If you have a head for heights, approach Gaia by walking across the upper level of the Ponte Luís I, which has great views across to Gaia and back to the Ribeira waterfront.
- You can get top-quality port at good prices in Gaia.

BASICS

340 B4

Avenida Diogo Leite 242, 4400 Vila Nova de Gaia, tel 223 703 735

Oct–end Jun Mon–Fri 9–5.30, Sat–Sun 9–4.30; Jul–end Sep daily 9–7

There are 16 lodges open for tours

www.portoturismo.pt
This comprehensive, regularly updated site is in Portuguese, Spanish and English. It gives details of opening hours and information on the port lodges that provide guided tours and tastings

SEEING VILA NOVA DA GAIA

It is easy to make your way across the river from Porto to visit Vila Nova de Gaia. Despite its close proximity to Porto, it's a city in its own right, usually known simply as Gaia. The wine lodges are in rows stretching back from the water's edge, so it's a case of choosing two or three to visit—though check with the tourist office for opening times first. Try to visit one of the large producers, such as Sandeman or Graham, and a smaller one like Barros or Ramos Pinto. For historical interest, Cockburn's, still British-owned and run, is well worth checking out, while Ferreira has one of the best tasting rooms, beautifully decorated with lovely *azulejos* (tiles). Take a stroll around the streets to soak up the historic atmosphere—if you are feeling energetic, you could climb up to the Mosteiro da Serra do Pilar for superb views of Gaia, Porto and the river. However, note that the monastery church is open only on Saturday and Sunday mornings.

HIGHLIGHTS

THE PORT WINE LODGES

There are 16 wine lodges in Gaia that run tours and offer port tastings. Port's production area was the world's first demarcated wine zone; until 1987, the wine could be called port only if it had been matured in Vila Nova de Gaia. Traditionally, port was produced up-river and shipped down to Gaia; production still takes place on the *quintas* of the Douro valley, which are now also allowed to mature their port on site. The port producers are proud of their long history and welcome visitors into their lodges and warehouses.

HOW PORT IS MADE

Port is a fortified wine, which means that brandy is added to the grapes during production. This both strengthens the product and halts the fermentation, leaving half the natural grape sugar in the wine. The climate and geography of the valley play a key role: Temperatures are extreme, with broiling summers and bitter winters, and the soil is thin and poor, forcing the vines to root as deep as 6m (20ft) into the rock to find the moisture they need in order to grow and flourish.

The harvest takes place from mid-September to mid-October, when the grapes are picked, crushed and fermented at a controlled temperature, then stored up-river to settle and clear until the following spring. Once in Gaia, port is left to mature for as long as it takes to produce wines of the required quality and then is shipped all over the world.

There are several varieties of port: white, a subtly mellow yet dry wine mainly drunk chilled as an aperitif; ruby, a clear intense red; tawny, an older, more complex port; and late-bottled vintage and vintage port. Vintages are declared only in years when the quality is particularly high; the wine must then remain in cask for two more years before it can be bottled and left to mature.

BACKGROUND

Port's story as a recognized variety of wine dates back to the early 18th century, when English merchants based in Porto spread the word of its quality. It was an opportune moment—imports of French claret into England were impossible as the two countries were at war. In consequence, port drinking soon became all the rage, helped by the 1703 Methuen Treaty, which reduced the import duty on the wine.

The port trade boomed. Profits were so high that many rogue producers attempted to pass off inferior wines from other parts of the country as the genuine article. The port producers' response was to set up the Companhia General de Agricultura dos Vinhos do Alto Douro in 1756, which demarcated the port area and regulated how the wine was to be produced and then matured. Gaia had plenty of land available to build warehouses to mature huge quantities of port and was perfectly positioned on the River Douro to take a leading role in the export trade. It maintains that role today.

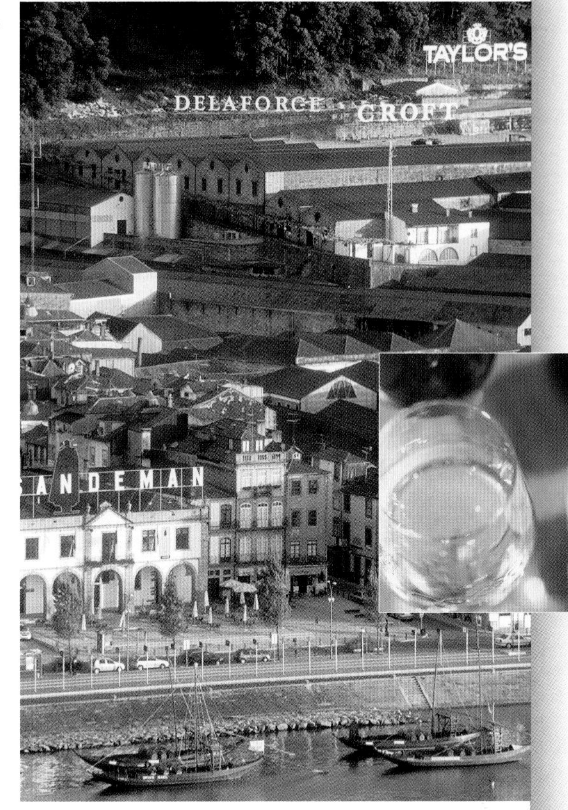

Wine lodges line the Douro; white port (inset) is a good aperitif

THE WINE LODGES

BARROS
✉ Rua Dona Leonor de Freitas 182, 4400 Vila Nova de Gaia ☎ 223 752 320 ⏲ June–end Sep daily 9.30–7; Oct–end May daily 10–6
www.porto-barros.pt
This lodge is one of the few remaining family-owned companies in Gaia, running low-key tours and tasting sessions—old tawnies are their forte.

COCKBURN'S
✉ Rua Dona Leonor de Freitas 4400, Vila Nova de Gaia ☎ 223 776 545 ⏲ Mon–Fri 10–12, 2.30–4
www.martinez.pt
Cockburn's was founded in 1815. Despite now being part of the huge Allied Domecq group, it still retains its individuality. The guided tours are very informative, and there are lots of chances to sample the port.

GRAHAM'S
✉ Rua Rei Ramiro 514, 4400 Vila Nova de Gaia ☎ 223 776 330 ⏲ Oct–end Apr Mon–Fri 9.30–1, 2–5.30; May–end Sep daily 9.30–6
www.grahams-port.com
Founded in 1820, Graham's is a traditional working lodge with an attractive tasting terrace overlooking the river across to Porto. Free guided tours are preceded by a video explaining port production, and there is a small museum as well as thousands of barrels of port, which you have the chance to taste.

RAMOS PINTO
✉ Avenida Ramos Pinto 480, 4400 Vila Nova de Gaia ☎ 223 707 000 ⏲ Mon–Fri 9–1, 2–5
www.ramospinto.pt
Ramos Pinto was founded in 1880 specifically to supply the Brazilian and other South American markets with port, and during a tour of the lodge you will see old posters, photographs and other memorabilia, before sampling some of the port. The lodge has a superb library and extensive vaulted cellars.

SANDEMAN
✉ Largo Miguel Bombarda 3, 4400 Vila Nova de Gaia ☎ 223 740 533 ⏲ Nov–end Mar Mon–Fri 9.30–12.30, 2–5; Apr–end Oct daily 10–12.30, 2–6 €3 (redeemable against the price of a bottle of port)
www.sandeman.com
The pick of the bunch if you want to visit a lodge, Sandeman's runs guided tours of the cellars and regular tastings. There is also a fascinating museum, which tells the story of the wine-producing area up-river from Porto.

Póvoa de Varzim, a good base for a traditional beach holiday

Once a convent and now a reformatory, the massive building of the Convento de Santa Clara is a landmark in Vila do Conde

PÓVOA DE VARZIM

340 B3 Praça Marquês de Pombal, 4490 Póvoa de Varzim, tel 252 298 120
www.cm-pvarzim.pt/turismo

If what you want is a straightforward holiday resort with a real Portuguese twist, Póvoa de Varzim is a good option. With more than 7km (4.5 miles) of clean, pebble-and-sand beach, a wide selection of hotels and restaurants to suit every budget, and a clutch of traditional buildings, it is a good beach base for a few days. The long esplanade, dotted with fountains, is backed by high-rise hotels and apartments, but the town has enough atmosphere to outweigh what it lacks in style. At the southern end you'll find the fishing harbour, a fine 18th-century fortress and the casino, a big draw for Portuguese holidaymakers. Behind this strip are the vestiges of the original town, with some nice hidden streets and squares, good churches and the interesting small Museu Municipal (Tue–Sun 10–12.30, 2.30–6, €1.50), which has archaeological displays and a variety of exhibits connected with local seafaring.

Póvoa has a procession of summer festivals, including a classical music event in July. To catch the best, try and be there on 15 August, the Feast of the Assumption of the Virgin, when there are processions to the fishing boats in honour of the Virgin, and spectacular fireworks.

VILA DO CONDE

340 B3 Rua 25 de April 103, 4480 Vila do Conde, tel 252 248 473

Around 30km (20 miles) north of Porto, the ancient port of Vila do Conde, a down-to-earth boatbuilding and fishing town that has retained its compact old quarter and some attractive buildings, makes a great contrast to neighbouring Póvoa. It's on the mouth of the Rio Ave, and you can still see fishing boats tied up alongside the riverbank with their fresh catches for sale, as well as the busy boatyard. It was here that a replica of the first caravel to round the Cape of Good Hope was built in 1987—it is now moored in South Africa where it finished its journey.

The area is dominated by the dome of the 17th-century Capela do Socorro, while the narrow cobbled streets are lined with a pleasing mix of simple whitewashed houses and fine mansions. You can't miss the huge bulk of the Convento de Santa Clara, now a reformatory, with its Gothic church and cloister. Behind it, you will find the remnants of the old aqueduct that supplied the convent with water. Walk downhill from here to reach the Igreja Matriz, a mixture of ornate Portuguese and more restrained Spanish styles—perhaps the latter are the result of Basque workmen being involved in the construction.

Vila has a couple of museums worth visiting: the Museu Rendas (Mon–Fri 9–12, 2–6, Sat–Sun 3–6, free), where you can see the town's famous lace; and the Museu Ciênca (Tue–Sun 10–6, €2.50), a life science workshop with plenty of hands-on exhibits.

VILA NOVA DE GAIA

See pages 90–91.

A stained-glass window in the Igreja Matriz, Vila do Conde

THE BEIRAS

This region is packed with variety. Its scenic draws include the mountains of the Serra da Estrela, Portugal's highest inland range, a coastline that encompasses lagoon-set Aveiro, and the Buçaço national forest. Portugal's oldest university is in Coimbra, an elegant contrast to Viseu and Guarda. These larger places are balanced by delightful smaller towns, such as Lamego, Almeida, Monsanto and the resort of Figueira da Foz.

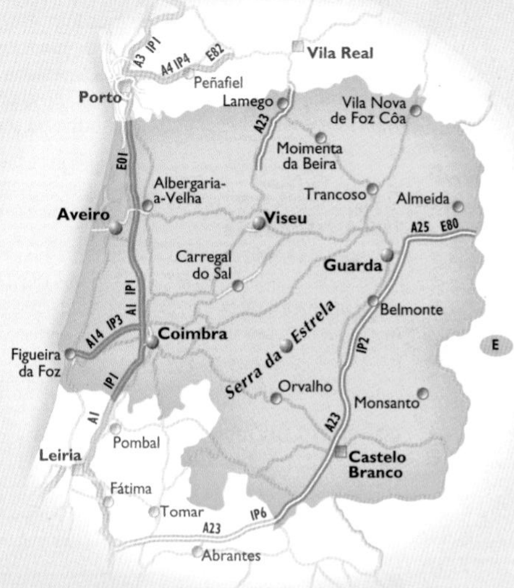

MAJOR SIGHTS

Aveiro

A thriving city in a unique canal and lagoon setting, Aveiro offers excellent shopping and dining with easy access to some superb beaches.

The decorated prow of a traditional Aveiro fishing boat

RATINGS	
Chainstore shopping	●●●●
Cultural interest	●●●●
Photo stops	●●●●●
Specialist shopping	●●●
Walkability	●●●●●

BASICS

342 B5
Rua João Mendonça 8, 3800 Aveiro
234 420 760
Oct–end May Mon–Sat 9–7; Jun–end Sep daily 9–8
Aveiro

www.rotadaluz.aveiro.co.pt
A fast site with an English-language option, packed with information on Aveiro and its surroundings, including its history, gastronomy, museums and surrounding countryside

TIPS

- If you are driving, the IP5 takes you straight into the city.
- City parking is difficult. There is limited parking by the Canal das Pirâmides just off the IP5, otherwise head through the town towards the N109 or N1.
- Outside the peak season between July and September, it is still possible to rent a boat to tour the Ria Aveiro—ask at the tourist office.

SEEING AVEIRO

Begin by strolling round the narrow traditional streets that back the Rossio, central Aveiro's attractive palm-fringed square. The streets all eventually lead to the fish market, close to a canal inlet. Walk back to the Praça Humberto Delgado and the main bridge, and cross the central canal to visit the Misericórdia before heading northeast along Rua Homem Cristo, one of Aveiro's main shopping streets.

At the next bridge you could cross and turn left to take in the city's main market, or head right along Avenida 5 de Outubro to the Convento do Jesus and the museum. After visiting the collections, stroll around the fine buildings, spacious streets and pleasant green spaces in the area. Leave time to take a trip on the lagoon, the best way to catch a glimpse of life in Aveiro. There are superb beaches to the north and south of the town.

HIGHLIGHTS

THE OLD QUARTER

The huddle of streets on the north side of the main canal make up Aveiro's old quarter. Admire the *moliceiros* (flat-bottomed boats) along the waterside before exploring the backstreets, where rows of neatly tiled houses face each other. This area is seen at its best in the evening, when it throngs with people drinking in the lively bars before they head off to eat in the many excellent fish restaurants.

CONVENTO DO JESUS

Rua Santa Joana, 3800 Aveiro 234 652 850 Tue–Sun 10–5.30 €2
The Convento do Jesus, built between the 15th and 17th centuries, and with a baroque façade added in the 18th, is now Portugal's second largest museum after the Museu Nacional de Arte Antiga in

Lisbon (▷ 137). The richness of the collections owes much to the Infanta Joana, daughter of Afonso V, who lived in the convent from 1471 until her death 18 years later. Some time after she died, the convent's church was sumptuously decorated as a fitting place for her tomb, and now forms part of the museum. The exuberant chancel is covered in intricately carved gilt wood, while the *azulejos* (tiles) decorating the walls depict scenes from Joana's life. The chancel contains her tomb, carved by João Antunes in the early 18th century.

From the church you can visit the Renaissance-style cloisters, whose highlight is the distinctive side chapel containing fine Renaissance tombs—off here, the refectory is entirely covered with flower-strewn 17th-century *azulejos*. The museum proper has other remembrances of Joana, notably her portrait, attributed to Nuno Gonçalves, and an oratory in the room where she died. Other highlights on show include primitive Portuguese paintings, wooden baroque statues, rich church vestments and delicate porcelain and ceramics.

THE RIA AVEIRO AND THE BEACHES

The tidal lagoon known as the Ria Aveiro is best explored on a boat trip from Aveiro. It is bordered by salt marshes, woods and small villages, while to the west, a narrow strip of land separates it from the sea. This is some of Europe's most spectacular dune land, and you can explore the habitat and learn about the area's flora and fauna at the Reserva Natural das Dunas de São Jacinto.

On the landward side, the settlements vary in size from small fishing ports like Bico and São Jacinto to bigger towns such as Ilhavo, where you will find a good fishing museum, and Vista Alegre, with its famous china factory and museum, the perfect place to watch craftsmen at work and buy the finished product direct. If you are looking for a beach, try Praia da Barra, Costa Nova or Torreira.

BACKGROUND

Aveiro was an important fishing port throughout the Middle Ages until disaster struck. In 1575, a storm altered the course of the River Vouga and the harbour silted up as a result. It was not until 1808, when a breakwater was built to open up a new passage from the lagoon to the sea, that Aveiro's fishing industry was reborn. A ceramic industry was also established and the new money that flooded into Aveiro paid for the construction of many of the city's finest buildings.

Today, Aveiro is still primarily a fishing port, its catches coming from both its lagoon and the sea. It is also Portugal's third-largest industrial town, dedicated to shipping, fish processing, engineering, and iron and steel production. Traditional industries also survive, including salt farming from the lagoon, the production of fertilizer utilizing the local seaweed, and rice-growing.

BOATS

The shallow Ria Aveiro—its average depth is just 2m (6.5ft)—led to the development of the flat-bottomed *moliceiros*. Beautifully painted with traditional designs, these boats are used to collect seaweed from the lagoon bottom for use as fertilizer. Their numbers are declining, but you are sure to see some moored on the canal—the best place to find them is below the main bridge and Praça Humberto Delgado.

Joana's tomb (above); the canal at night (bottom left); and stopping for a chat in the city (bottom right)

MORE TO SEE

IGREJA DA MISERICÓRDIA

✉ Rua Coimbra, 3800 Aveiro 🕘 Daily 10–12.30, 2.30–5.30 ✋ Free

A church with a lovely tiled façade and 17th-century doorway. There are more decorative tiles inside and an interesting church wardens' pew.

SÉ

✉ Rua Batalhão Cacadores, 3800 Aveiro 🕘 Mon–Sat 9–12.30, 2.30–6, Sun 10–12.30, 3–6 ✋ Free

Once part of a convent, Aveiro's cathedral has a baroque façade but a stylistically mixed interior.

Almeida's elaborate defensive walls were built in the 1700s and the six mighty bastions date from the same period

The hotel at Buçaco, once a popular royal hunting lodge

ALMEIDA

343 E5 Portas de São Francesco, 6350 Almeida, tel 271 570 020

Tucked away in barren upland country in the east of the mountain Beiras and only 15km (9.5 miles) from the Spanish border, Almeida is a compact border town entirely enclosed within the star-shaped walls of a military fortification built in the 18th century. The Dutch design was heavily influenced by the work of the French military architect Vauban, and consists of a twelve-pointed star with six bastions and six curtain walls pierced by two superb double gates whose tunnels run under the grass-topped outer walls. Almeida played a key part in the Peninsular Wars, falling twice to the French, who were eventually thrown out by Wellington in 1811; plaques in the town commemorate Lord Beresford, one of Wellington's chief subordinates and organizer of the Portuguese forces.

Park outside the walls and walk through the approach tunnels into the town. Built in the 18th century, the harmonious streets and squares have a logical layout, filled with homogeneous buildings. These open up as you head towards the ruins of the castle, destroyed by the French.

Don't miss The Casamatas were once home to 5,000 troops; for a great overview, take the 4km (2.5-mile) trail along the grass-covered walls.

AROUCA

342 C4 Praça Barndão de Casconcelas, 4544 Arouca, tel 256 943 575

The monastic settlement of Arouca sits in a small green valley surrounded by agricultural terraces and wooded hills. The huge Convento da Arouca was founded in the eighth century AD and what you see today is baroque laid over late-medieval foundations. The single-naved abbey church is rich with silver and precious wood. This is the burial place of Queen Mafalda, daughter of Sancho I, who retired here after the death of her husband, Dom Henriques I de Castilha. Some of Mafalda's possessions are in the Museu de Arte Sacra here, notably a 13th-century silver diptych, as well as Portuguese primitive paintings from the 15th and 16th centuries.

AVEIRO

See pages 94–95.

BELMONTE

343 E6 Castelo de Belmonte, 6250 Belmonte, tel 275 911 488

The little agricultural town of Belmonte was established between the 11th and 12th centuries as a stronghold against the Moors. It is dominated by its castle, gifted by Afonso V in the 15th century to the Cabral family, who transformed it into a fortified manor house. Pedro Alvares Cabral, the discoverer of Brazil, is said to have been born in the castle—a statue of the Virgin that accompanied him on his voyages is in the Igreja Matriz, down the hill. South from here is the Jewish quarter, a warren of ancient alleys with more than 120 resident Jewish families. There has been a Jewish community in Belmonte since at least the 13th century. For more history, take in the ancient Romanesque church of Santiago, transformed in the 15th century as a burial place for the Cabrals—Pedro Alvares is buried here.

BUÇACO

342 C6 Avenida Emídio Navarro, 3050 Luso, tel 231 939 133 Luso (3km/2 miles from Buçaco)

The northernmost peak of the Serra do Buçaco is crowned by the *Mata Nacional* (National Forest), a 105ha (250-acre) wood, best appreciated on foot (▷ 243). This beautiful forest is encircled by stone walls and carefully planted with native and exotic trees and shrubs, the background for artificial lakes, rushing water and splashing fountains.

Benedictine monks established the first hermitage here in the sixth century AD. The wall was built around the forest in 1622 when women were forbidden entry on pain of excommunication according to the rule of the Barefoot Carmelite order. Nearby, you can still see the remains of the 17th-century Carmelite convent. The Carmelites also planted a huge variety of trees, a tradition that was continued after the religious orders were abolished in 1834. The woods now contain around 400 native tree species, 300 or more non-natives, banks of camellias, rhododendrons, magnolias and superb tree ferns.

Between 1888 and1907 King Carlos built a palatial hunting lodge here. A pastiche of Manueline style, it is now a luxury hotel. You can park here if you want to walk in the forest.

This elegant statue doubles as a lamp in what is now a luxury hotel in Buçaco

Vintage car fans will have a field day at the Museu do Automóvel

Fine topiary in Castelo's Jardim do Antigo Paço Episcopal

The Casa dos Repuxos, one of the Roman villas at Conímbriga

CARAMULO

342 C5
www.serra-caramulo.com

Walkers will love this magnificent upland country, a verdant mountain area scattered with tiny villages and rich in thickets of rhododendrons, azaleas and hydrangeas. The town of Caramulo, at 800m (2,620ft), is a good base from which to explore the Serra do Caramulo and its main peak, Caramulino (1,075m/3,520ft). It is also a spa town, laid out amid parks and gardens, with a couple of good museums. The Museu do Caramulo (daily 9–12.30, 2–6, €5) has a rich art collection—Tournai 16th-century tapestries depicting the Portuguese arrival in India, furniture and porcelain, and some remarkable pieces of 20th-century art, including works by Picasso and Dalí and a portrait of Queen Elizabeth II by Graham Sutherland, donated in recognition of the centuries-old alliance between England and Portugal. More specialized is the nearby Museu do Automóvel (daily 9–12.30, 2–5.30, €2), a collection of vintage cars and motorcycles, all beautifully maintained in full working order. The oldest exhibit is an 1899 Peugeot, and there is a large group of shiny 1950s Harley Davidsons.

CASTELO BRANCO

343 D7 Alameda da Liberdade, 6000 Castelo Branco, tel 272 330 339
Castelo Branco
www.cm-castelobranco.pt

The capital of the Beira Baixa, Castelo Branco, a frontier town guarded over by an ancient Templar castle high above the town, is only 18km (11 miles) from the Spanish border. Centuries of invasion, particularly by Napoleon's troops in 1807, have ensured that little remains of the castle and old town, but it is worth heading up the hill to take in the sweeping views from the Miradouro de São Gens, a flower-decked esplanade to the left of the castle ruins.

Below the medieval city are the broad streets and shady squares of modern Castelo, a buzzing and wealthy agricultural hub—local cheese and honey bring in the money, and the olive oil is considered to be some of the best in Portugal. Civic pride is also in evidence in the 17th-century Palácio Episcopal and its surrounding buildings, now the Museu Tavares Proença Júnior (Tue–Sun 10–12.30, 2–5.30, €2), with a local collection of intricate *colchas* (bedspreads) for which the town is famous. These striking embroideries are still traditionally made by young girls for their trousseau—the clothes and linens collected together by a bride before her wedding day. Next to the palace, and once solely reserved for the bishop, is the Jardim do Antigo Paço Episcopal, a 17th-century formal parterre garden—a pleasant surprise in this remote eastern corner of the country. The flower beds are approached from an elegant double stairway, decorated with *azulejos* (tiles), a splendid mix of statuary, brilliant flowers, water and fountains.

COIMBRA

See pages 98–101.

CONÍMBRIGA

342 C6 Museu Monográfico de Condeixa, 3150 Condeixa-a-Nova
Ruins: Oct–end Apr daily 9–1, 2–6; May–end Sep daily 10–8. Museu Monográfico: Oct–end Apr Tue–Sun 10–1, 2–6; May–end Sep Tue–Sun 10–8
€3.50
www.conimbriga.pt

Conímbriga, an ancient settlement 16km (10 miles) from the modern city of Coimbra, was founded by the Celts and later flourished as a Roman city between the second and fourth centuries AD. The archaeological site here is by far the most important example of a Roman settlement in Portugal, largely because Conímbriga, a major staging post on the route between Lisbon and Braga, was abandoned in the 460s and thus stayed untouched rather than being fought over.

Before they fled the threat of the barbarian Suevi, the Roman inhabitants constructed a massive wall right through the heart of the city in an attempt to keep out the invaders. To build this, houses were pulled down for use as construction materials, and you can see pillars, stone blocks and bricks taken from the dwellings still embedded in the wall as it survives today.

Most of the excavations lie around the wall, and it will take you an hour or so to explore them. One of the highlights is the ruins of the Casa de Cantaber, with its central atrium (an inner open courtyard), arcaded porticoes, pools and impressive private baths. Opposite is the Casa dos Repuxos, a second century AD house with an atrium and a *triclinium* (dining room). Its superb mosaic floors, decorated with hunting and marine scenes, have been wonderfully preserved along with the original fountains that have now been restored to working order.

Elsewhere there are remnants of the aqueduct that supplied the town with water, the forum and the baths. A museum of finds from the site is laid out thematically and according to location. Highlights here are jade jewellery, surgeons' instruments and delicate glass. It is worth buying the guidebook, as the exhibits are labelled only in Portuguese.

Coimbra

A vibrant and historic city and Portugal's oldest university town, come to Coimbra for plenty of good shopping, splendid monuments and museums, and a buzzing, student-orientated nightlife.

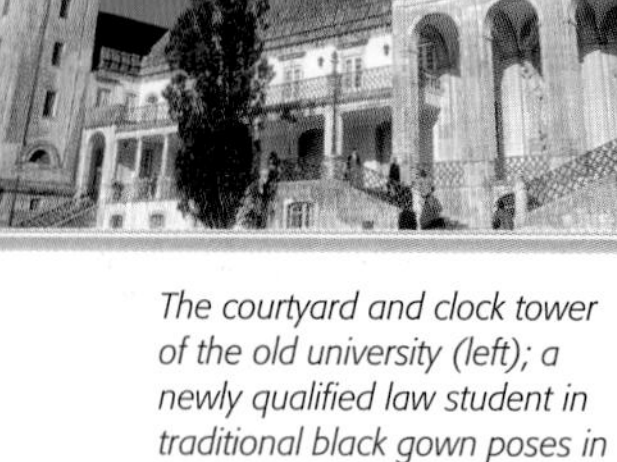

The courtyard and clock tower of the old university (left); a newly qualified law student in traditional black gown poses in front of the university buildings (middle); and the ornate ceiling of the Biblioteca Joanina (right)

RATINGS	
Cultural interest	●●●●
Historic interest	●●●●●
Specialist shopping	●●●●
Walkability	●●●●

TIPS

- Most of the streets in the heart of the city are pedestrianized, so driving in Coimbra can be a nightmare. Use one of the signposted parking areas—you will need to arrive early in the day to get a space. Alternatively, park across the river and walk into town.
- May, the end of the academic year, is a great time to visit. There are concerts, parades and student ceremonies all over the old city, and the streets are wonderfully vibrant and busy.
- Old Coimbra is very steep—wear flat, comfortable shoes to cope with the cobbles, or take a No. 1 tram from the Largo da Portagem to avoid the climb.
- Take a river trip on the Mondego—a great way to relax after a morning spent walking.

SEEING COIMBRA

The nucleus of old Coimbra spreads down a steep hill towards the River Mondego, the university buildings crowning the summit. Most of the highlights are in this relatively small area, which has always been traditionally divided into A Cidade Alta, the upper town that is home to the university and religious buildings, and A Cidade Baixa, the lower area, with excellent shops along pleasant pedestrianized streets.

The best place to start exploring Coimbra is at the university—it is the easiest place to find and the splendid views will give you a chance to get your bearings. After visiting the university buildings and the nearby Sé Velha (Old Cathedral), make your way through the maze of ancient cobbled streets downhill towards the lower town. Here, the Praça do Comercio is the hub—the main shopping streets, Rua Visconde da Luz and Rua Ferreira Borges, run just east of the square into the Largo da Portagem. From here, you can cross the river over the Ponte Santa Clara, which has great views back over the old city. On the other side of the river, you will find the two Conventos de Santa Clara, as well as the Portugal dos Pequenitos (Portugal for the Little Ones) theme park, which will keep kids happily entertained for hours.

HIGHLIGHTS

VELHA UNIVERSIDADE

101 C2 • Largo da Porta Ferréa, 3000 Coimbra 239 859 900 Oct–end Mar daily 9.30–12, 2–5.30; Apr–end Sep daily 9–7.30 Library, chapel and Sala dos Capelos: adult €4, under 14s and over 65s €2.50. Library only: adult €2.50, concessions €1.35. Chapel only: adult €2.50

The old university buildings, once part of the royal palace, lie around the Patio das Escolas, or Paço dos Estudos. Little has changed here since 1540, when João III donated the buildings. Step through the Porta Férrea on the east side, though, and you are definitely back in the mid-20th century, surrounded by unstylish concrete buildings, the unfortunate outcome of a Salazar-inspired modernization in the monumental style typical of his era. Rather, concentrate on the harmonious architectural ensemble around the patio, beginning by admiring the views over the city and river from the front of the terrace, approached on the right by a wonderfully complicated flight of zigzag, terraced steps, before turning round to face the square. Towering above the other buildings looms a 1733 clock tower, once used to summon the students to lectures and affectionately nicknamed *A Cabra* (The Goat).

On the left is the Capela de São Miguel, a Manueline chapel, while on the right is the elegant façade of the university lecture rooms and offices, pierced by the 17th-century *porta férrea* (iron gate), the main entrance to the university courtyard. Linking these two wings is the Paços da Universidade, the original palace building, which was given a colonnade, known as the Via Latina, in the late 18th century.

SALA DOS CAPELOS

To the right of the central range of the main university complex is the Sala dos Capelos, which gets its name from the *capelos* (caps) given to students on graduation. The huge hall, hung with portraits of Portuguese monarchs, is still the venue for graduation ceremonies. It has a fine painted Manueline ceiling, as does the adjoining examination room. The building also contains lecture halls and tutorial rooms—you can usually peek in or get behind the scenes down in the basement at the students' bar.

BIBLIOTECA JOANINA

The undisputed highlight of the university is its old library, the Biblioteca Joanina, behind the right-hand wing. It was gifted to Coimbra in 1724 by João V, and consists of three rooms richly decorated in the baroque style. Look out for the *trompe l'oeil* design, which draws the eye towards the donor's portrait in the final room. The opulent gilding and lacquerwork is heavily influenced by Chinese

THE REPUBLICS AND STUDENT LIFE

There are around 20,000 students at Coimbra University, some of whom live in unique establishments known as republics. These were devised at the end of the 18th century to emulate some of the ideals of the French Revolution, notably *liberté*, *égalité*, *fraternité* (freedom, equality, brotherhood). Over the years they evolved into communes and today the republics generally consist of between 15 to 20 students, who rent huge apartments and pool their living expenses. A maid who prepares the communal meals is usually included in the budget.

You can identify the republics in the old town by the flags hanging from their façades. It is quite common, too, to see the students clad in their voluminous black capes, which are fringed with ribbons to identify the faculty to which they belong: blue for arts, yellow for medicine and red for law. Some of the capes are distinctly ragged, the cuts round the hems denoting the number of times the owner has been rejected by a loved one.

BASICS

342 C6

Largo da Portagem, 3000 Coimbra; Largo Dom Dinis, 3000 Coimbra; or Praça da República, 3000 Coimbra; tel 239 855 930, 239 832 591 or 239 833 202

Oct–end Mar Mon–Fri 9–1, 2.30–6, Sat–Sun 10–1, 2.30–5.30; Apr–end Sep Mon–Fri 9–6, Sat–Sun 10–1, 2.30–5.30

Basófias River Tours: Parque Dr. Manuel Barga, tel 966 040 695, Oct–end Mar 2–3 departures daily; Apr–end Sep 3–5 departures daily

Coimbra A, Coimbra B, Coimbra Parque

www.cm-coimbra.pt
A busy site, with an English-language option, that covers Coimbra and the surrounding area. It's a bit tricky to navigate, but has plenty of information to browse through once you come to terms with how it works

An elegant loggia outside the Museu Nacional Machado de Castro (below), where the little statue of a knight (bottom) is a Roman exhibit; the battlemented west façade of the Sé Velha (right), with a window almost as big as the door beneath it

MORE TO SEE

CONVENTO DE SANTA CLARA-A-NOVA

101 B3 • Santa Clara, 3000 Coimbra 239 441 674 Church: daily 8.30–6. Cloisters: daily 9.30–12, 2–5 €1

The convent was built in 1560. The church, a good example of Portuguese baroque, contains the original 14th-century tomb of Queen Isabel as well as her 17th-century silver replica tomb in the chancel.

JARDIM BOTÂNICO

101 C3 • Calçada Martim de Freitas, 3000 Coimbra 239 822 897 Mid-Sep–end Feb daily 10–5; Mar–end Jun daily 10–7; Jul–mid Sep daily 9–8 €2

These terraced botanical gardens were once among the most important in Europe; this is where new plant discoveries were acclimatized. There are also many rare tropical trees.

MUSEU ACADÉMICO

101 C1 • Largo Dom Dinis, 3000 Coimbra 239 827 396 Mon–Fri 10–12.30, 2–5.30 €1

A museum that concentrates on university life and traditions.

MUSEU NACIONAL MACHADO DE CASTRO

101 C2 • Largo Dr. José Rodrigues, 3000 Coimbra 239 823 727

decorative techniques and style. The library contains more than 30,000 books arranged on two levels with ladders for reaching the higher shelves. Back on the main Patio das Escolas is the entrance to the Capela de São Miguel, an elaborately decorated church with painted ceiling, *azulejos* (tiles) and intricately twisted columns—the gilding and decoration of the organ is particularly extravagant.

SÉ VELHA

101 B2 • Largo da Sé Velha, 3000 Coimbra 239 825 273 Mon–Thu 10–6, Fri 10–2, Sat 10–5 Free

Forbidding yet serene, the superb Romanesque Sé Velha (Old Cathedral) squats halfway up the hill on a sloping square. Commissioned by Afonso Henriques and built between 1140 and 1175, this is Portugal's oldest cathedral and one of the country's most important Romanesque buildings. Once standing at the frontier of the Christian and Moorish worlds, it has a fortress-like appearance little altered over the centuries. It is modelled on Cluny and other churches in the Auvergne, the probable birthplace of Bernard and Robert, the cathedral's two French architects, and has remained untouched, the simplicity of the overall design accentuated by a few flourishes.

One of these flourishes is the north doorway, added in 1530. Despite being a relatively recent part of the building, it is in worse condition than other older areas. Also admire the tower on the east side, with its beautifully integrated arcaded gallery. Inside, the sense of solidity continues, the simplicity of the plain design of the nave highlighted by a wide gallery above the aisles. The rich, gilt Gothic altarpiece, carved by the Flemish masters Olivier de Ghent and Jean d'Ypres, stands out.

To the right of the chancel, the Capela do Sacramento (Chapel of the Sacrament) contains another alterpiece by Tomé Velho, a pupil of Coimbra's famous sculptor, João de Ruão, who was responsible for the Renaissance-Manueline font to the front of the cathedral. You can enter the late 13th-century Gothic cloisters from the south aisle—the chapterhouse, off to one side, is the burial place of Dom Sesnando, the first Christian governor of Coimbra. He was reputedly a Moor who converted to Christianity.

MOSTEIRO DE SANTA CRUZ

101 A2 • Praça 8 de Maio, 3000 Coimbra 239 822 941 Mon–Sat 9–12, 2–5.45, Sun 4–6 Cloister: €1

Santa Cruz is an excellent place to admire the work of three of Coimbra's major 16th-century sculptors: Nicolas Chanterene, João de Ruão and João de Castilho. Though their work on the porch has sadly deteriorated, the detailed carving of the pulpit inside the church is a superb example of the Coimbra school. The sculptors also worked on the tombs of Afonso Henriques and Sancho I on either side of the high altar, rich with early Renaissance decoration.

Just off the church is the Claustro do Silêncio (Cloister of Silence). Designed by Marcos Pires in 1524, its airy arches and elaborate stonework are acknowledged to be some of the purest examples of the Manueline style. The low-relief sculptures illustrate scenes from the Passion of Christ, while the *azulejos* (tiles) date from the 16th and 17th centuries.

BACKGROUND

Coimbra is an ancient city, once inhabited by the Romans and occupied by the Moors. The historic university traces its origins back to 1290. João III donated a palace to it in 1537 and it was the country's only university until 1911. Perhaps because of lack of competition, the university had a chequered history of corruption until 1772, when the Marquês de Pombal introduced reforms as well as commissioning some of its most beautiful buildings.

The university has always been associated with political activism, its students opposing the Salazar regime from the 1950s. After the 1974 revolution, it expanded. Today it remains the country's most prestigious seat of learning.

Closed until 2006 €3

A superb museum in the old episcopal palace.

PORTUGAL DOS PEQUENITOS

101 B3 • Rossio de Santa Clara, 3000 Coimbra 239 801 170 Mid-Sep–end Feb daily 10–5; Mar–end Jun daily 10–7; Jul–mid-Sep daily 9–8 €4

A theme park containing scale models of great Portuguese buildings plus examples of vernacular and colonial architecture.

SÉ NOVA

101 C1 • Largo da Sé Nova, 3000 Coimbra 239 823 138 Tue–Sat 9.30–12, 2–5.30 75c

The cathedral was built by the Jesuits in 1598; the niches in the façade contain statues of Jesuit saints. There is one vast nave with a barrel vault topped by a high lantern. The main altar and side chapels are baroque; look out for the gilt wooden altarpiece and silver throne.

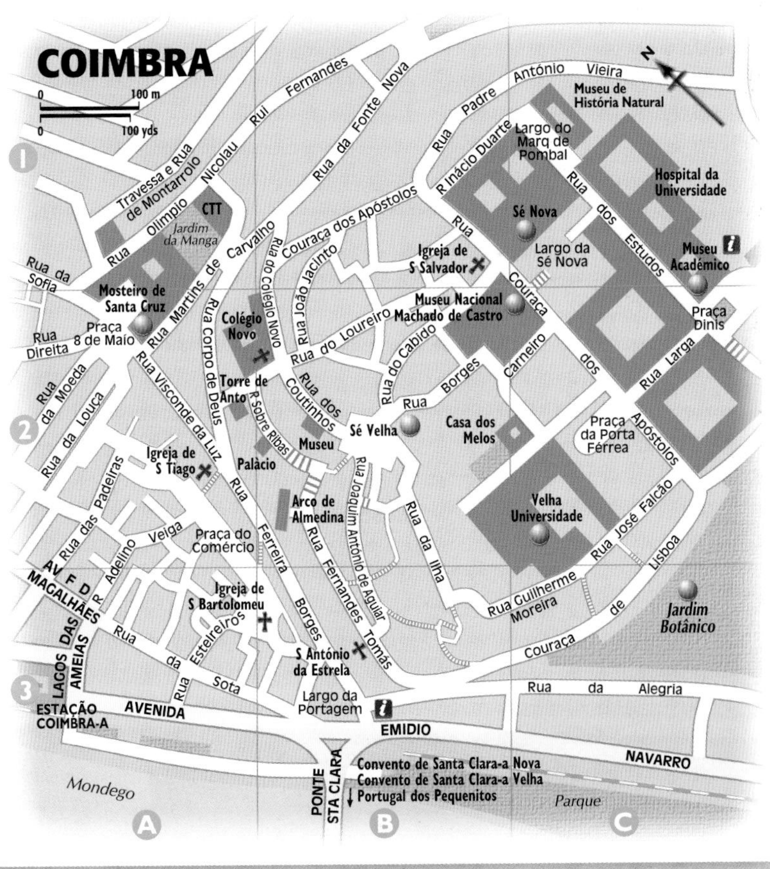

Holidaymakers sunbathe and swim at Figueira da Foz

Fine tiles decorate the stairs to Nossa Senhora dos Remédios

Elegant townhouses like this are typical of the spa resort of Luso

FIGUEIRA DA FOZ

342 B6 Avenida 25 de Abril, 3080 Figueira da Foz, tel 402 827 610 Jun–end Sep Mon–Fri 9–12.30, 2–5.30, Sat–Sun 2.30–6.30; Oct–end May Mon–Fri 10–12.30, 2.30–6.30, Sat–Sun 2.30–6.30 Figueira da Foz www.figueiraturismo.com

Figueira da Foz—'Fig Tree at the Mouth of the River'—stands at the mouth of the Mondego. It is an important deep-sea fishing port and a major resort. Don't expect anything picturesque; this is a modern and unpretentious town, with more than a touch of industry on the outskirts and a long promenade backed by modern apartment blocks. What Figueira does have though is two superb beaches, great restaurants, bars, a casino and clubs. It also has a couple of small museums: the Casa do Paço in Largo Prof. Vitor Guerra (Mon–Fri 9.30–12.30, 2–5.30, free), whose walls are completely covered with Delft wall tiles, part of a ship's cargo that arrived in Figueira in the 17th century; and the Museu Municipal in the Rua Calouste Gulbenkian (Tue–Fri 9.30–5.15, Sat–Sun 2.15–5.15, €1.50), which focuses on local archaeology.

LAMEGO

340 D4 Avenida Visconde Guedes Teixera, 5100 Lamego, tel 54 612 005 www.cm-lamego.pt

Wealthy Lamego is isolated in the Beira hills, its riches based on wine and its position on major trade routes. The elegant and prosperous old part of town is scattered with beautiful patrician buildings and dominated by the splendid *Sé* (cathedral), predominantly Renaissance in style, but still retaining its 13th-century Romanesque bell-tower and tranquil cloister. Facing this across the spacious Largo do Camões is the town's museum (Tue–Sun 10–12.30, 2–5, €2)—the star attraction is five panels from an altarpiece by Grão Vasco. Northwest from here, down a tiny street lined with shops, loom the walls of the ancient citadel—walk through to reach the castle, which dates from the 12th and 13th centuries.

Back in the heart of town, allow time to wander round the hidden corners and stately mansions. The tree-lined Avenida Dr. A. de Sousa draws the eye west to Lamego's great shrine of Nossa Senhora dos Remédios, approached by a magnificent 18th-century baroque stairway, embellished with statues, fountains and chapels, and modelled on Bom Jesus (▷ 69–70). This is one of Portugal's most important pilgrimage sites and thousands of sick people visit it every year. The main pilgrimage takes place in early September.

LUSO

342 C6 Avenida Emídio Navarro, 3050 Luso, tel 231 939 133 Luso www.turismo-centro.pt

Luso, just 3km (2 miles) down the hill from the National Forest at Buçaco (▷ 96), is a spa town, its health-giving waters bottled and sold all over Portugal. It's a lovely place to cool off and escape from the summer heat, with a gentle pace of life and easy access to the attractive countryside.

The town is dotted with turn-of-the-20th-century spa buildings and elegant villas, and there are some evocative 19th-century-style tea-rooms and a rather restrained casino. Most people come to take the waters—it's easy to book, and you can have hydrotherapy, massage and other treatments, or swim in a pool fed by the mineral springs.

MONSANTO

343 E6 Rua Marques da Gracioça, tel 277 314 642 Sat–Sun 10–1, 2–6 Monsanto

Ancient Monsanto clings to the foot of a granite outcrop in the middle of a plain. Founded in prehistory, it was occupied by the Romans and in 1165 handed over to the Knights' Templar, who built the impregnable citadel, its ruins now half-lost amid the surrounding boulders.

Up here, in the Beira Baixa hills near the Spanish border, the views are immense, on clear days stretching even as far as the Serra da Estrela (▷ 105). Beneath the fort and the ruined chapel of São Miguel, the granite houses huddle between massive boulders along streets seemingly hewn from the living rock, and you may meet the occasional pig or chicken as you pick your way through the narrow alleys. The town is inevitably something of a tourist honeypot, so come early or late to see it at its best.

The ruins of the chapel of São Miguel in the remnants of the castle in Monsanto

GUARDA

The highest town in Portugal has remained unspoilt through history. It is a good base from where to explore the Serra da Estrela and has a lively student population.

Cold, windswept and forbidding, Guarda is the highest town in Portugal (1,056m/3,465ft), a dour mountain place where bitter winters are the norm. During the second half of the 20th century the town expanded down the hill and the student population swelled as well, bringing a touch of liveliness to this old settlement. There is plenty to keep you occupied, with a maze of old streets to explore and a good choice of restaurants for lunch.

SÉ

The weighty stone cathedral in the Praça Luís de Camões (Tue–Sun 9–11.30, 2.30–5, free) dominates Guarda's central square, its castellated façade flanked by heavy octagonal towers. It took so long to complete that it is virtually an architectural textbook, with Gothic, Renaissance and Manueline elements all in evidence. Construction started in the 14th century and was finally completed in 1540. The main façade is pure Gothic, with a Manueline window inserted later, but the side elevations are altogether lighter, with soaring pinnacles, flying buttresses and grotesque gargoyles. Step inside, and you will find yourself in a lofty space, the twisted pillars and arched vaulting heavily influenced by the Manueline style. Gleaming out of the gloom at the far end of the cathedral is the superb *retábulo* (altarpiece), a Renaissance masterpiece of white, marble-like Ançã stone from Coimbra province, gilded in the 18th century. The high-relief figures, 100 in all, are the work of João de Ruão, a leading light in the Coimbra sculpture school. For a bird's-eye view of the town and its surroundings, climb the staircase in the south transept to reach the cathedral's roof.

MUSEU DA GUARDA

This museum in the Rua Alves Roçadas (Tue–Sun 10–12.30, 2–5.30, €2) is housed in the old bishop's palace outside the original fortifications. It has the usual mixture of local archaeological finds, art and sculpture, as well as some everyday objects spanning the centuries—an interesting retreat from the wind on chilly days.

Guarda's cathedral towers into the sky, its cross (inset) sitting on top of an obelisk

RATINGS	
Historic interest	●●●●
Outdoor pursuits	●●●●●
Value for money	●●●●
Walkability	●●●●

TIPS

- **Guarda is a confusing city to drive through—come early or during the siesta hours, when there is less traffic.**
- **The Serra da Estrela has its own information office, about 100m (110 yards) from the tourist office, at Rua Dom Sancho I (tel 271 225 454).**

BASICS

343 E5 | Praça Luís de Camões, 6300 Guarda, tel 271 205 530 | Mon–Sat 9–12.30, 2–5.30 | Guarda | www.mun-guarda.pt/turismo

A statue of Dom Sancho I outside the cathedral commemorates the town's founder

A narrow tunnel links the two parts of Feira's medieval castle

The exterior of Feira's Europarque Visionarium, home to a fascinating collection of interactive exhibits that bring science to life

THE SIGHTS

MONTEMOR-O-VELHO

342 B6 Castelo de Montemor, Paço das Infantas, 3140 Montemor-o-Velho, tel 239 680 380 Montemor www.turismo-centro.pt

It is impossible to miss the dramatic, crenellated silhouette of Montemor-o-Velho as you approach Coimbra from the west along the flatlands of the Mondego valley. Montemor has a chequered past—founded by the Romans, the town passed several times from the Moors to the Christians and back again until finally it was secured by the Christians in 1064. The castle became a strategic outpost in the push south against the Moors, and by the 13th century it was the royal residence of choice.

Today, you can wander round the medieval nucleus, take in the great views over the river valley and pop into the ancient church of Santa Maria da Alcáçova, founded in 1095. Inside, twisted columns support an intricate wooden ceiling, and there are beautiful Moorish-style *azulejos* (tiles) and good stone architectural Manueline touches.

Montemor maintains firm links with the surrounding countryside. There is a great twice-monthly Wednesday market, when the town is packed with farmers—local delicacies on sale include duck, lamprey and eels. A walk in the surrounding fields should yield some good sightings of storks; bird enthusiasts can book a birdwatching afternoon (tel 239 499 020).

PINHEL

343 E5 Câmara Municipal, Rua Silva Gouveia 1, 6400 Pinhel, tel 271 410 000

Remote Pinhel, once a fortified outpost on the way to Spain, is a quintessential Beira Alta town, where sightings of foreign visitors are rare and the pace of life is snail-like compared to that of the cities. This is all part of the region's contrasting charm.

In the old part of town, superb mansions, decorated with coats of arms and fronted by delicate wrought-iron balconies, are evidence of Pinhel's wealth in days gone by. Walk through the main street to find the best examples, set around the beautifully planted central square and lining the adjoining streets. Farther on, the narrow alleys of the oldest part of town run down the hill from the ruins of the old castle, a forbidding tower enlivened by a Manueline window.

Pinhel lies at the heart of a successful olive oil and wine area—you will see vineyards on the approach to the town, and you can sample the excellent red made by the local co-operative.

SANTA MARIA DA FEIRA

340 C4 Praça da República, 4524 Santa Maria da Feira, tel 256 372 032 www.cm-feira.pt

Feira, as it's mostly known, has two contrasting attractions—an old castle and Portugal's biggest and newest science museum, packed with interactive, state-of-the-art displays.

Head first for the Castelo da Feira (daily 9–12, 2–6, €1.25), standing on a wooded height facing the main town. It was built back in the 15th century; the keep has pepperpot turrets and there are hefty perimeter walls. A sunken gateway leads into the castle proper, whose highlight is a vast Gothic hall. Climb up from here for great views from the upper platform—you can see the Ria Aveiro (▷ 95) in the distance. From the keep a heavily fortified tunnel links the two parts of the castle—look out for the narrow arrow slits and hidden entrances. Then move on to the science park.

Grandly named Europarque Visionarium (Mon–Fri 9–6, Sat–Sun 2–8, adult €6.50, under-14s €5), is a complete contrast with its distinctly 21st-century feel. It is an architecturally stunning museum with an interactive twist that brings science to life. The visit starts with an audio-visual introduction, which fills you in on all the exhibits and displays. The emphasis is on Portugal, with excellent material on the great voyages of discovery, but everything is accessible in English as well as Portuguese.

SERNANCELHE

343 D4

High in the Serra de Lapa, in the dour upland country typical of the Beira Alta, stands the plain old granite town of Sernancelhe, an agricultural hub that brings together people, mules and donkeys from far and wide for its weekly Thursday market. Head for the old part of town and you will find yourself in the main *praça* (square), ringed with fine stone mansions, many dating from the 16th and 17th centuries and embellished with coats of arms. This pleasing ensemble is dominated by the Igreja Matriz, a beautiful Romanesque church whose façade is decorated by three free-standing statues set in niches on either side of the door—art historians maintain they are the only examples of such statues in Portugal.

Sernancelhe had many Jewish residents in the Middle Ages. You can still wander round the old Jewish quarter of the town—look out here for houses with a pair of unequal-sized doors, a wide one for use by tradespeople and a narrower one reserved for the immediate family.

The views from and around Torre are fabulous, while the tasty sheep's cheese the area produces (inset) is nationally famous

SERRA DA ESTRELA

Majestic scenery and untouched villages characterize this high granite massif, home to mainland Portugal's highest peak. Enjoy outdoor activities all year round.

The Serra da Estrela is the westernmost of the high *serras* that spread across the Iberian peninsula. It's a granite massif containing some of Portugal's most imposing peaks, including Torre (1,993m/6,538ft), the highest on the mainland. Much of it is a high plateau cut by valleys, in two of which rise two major rivers, the Mondego and the Zêzere. The high tops are a forbidding jumble of rocks and scree; the lower slopes are forested. The crops in the valleys vie for space with the local sheep, whose wool has long been the backbone of the area's economy.

THE SOUTHERN SERRA

You can cross the entire mountain range from Covilhã to Seia during the summer, a beautiful drive that takes in the full range of mountain scenery in the park as well as Torre and some attractive villages. Follow the N339 uphill through Penhas de Saúde, then branch left to follow the road to Torre—you can drive right to the top for superb views over the mountains. En route in a desolate area of worn granite, you will pass the huge statue of Our Lady of the Holy Star, the scene in August of a lavish religious procession. Northeast of Torre, look out for the narrow rock cone known as the Cântaro Magro (Slender Pitcher), which conceals the source of the Zêzere. The scenery here is extraordinary, a wilderness of granite and lakes—the largest is Lagoa Comprida. From here, the road drops rapidly into the Mondego valley and the village of Sabugeira, where you can taste and buy the local rye bread, spicy sausage and *Queijo da serra*, the strong local sheep's cheese that is a national favourite.

THE NORTHERN SERRA

You will see the best of the *serra* by driving from Covilhã to Caldas de Manteigas (▷ 236–237), but, if you head northwest from Manteigas on the N232 to Gouveia, you will get a taster. The town has lost its isolated atmosphere, but there are some fine buildings to explore. Linhares to the north is a traditional village overlooking the Mondego with a castle and some superb paintings in the church. Animals live in the heart of the settlement, and donkeys are still the main transport.

RATINGS	
Good for kids	●●●
Outdoor pursuits	●●●●●
Photo stops	●●●●●
Value for money	●●●●●
Walkability	●●●●●

TIPS

- The weather can deteriorate rapidly, so wear sensible footwear and clothing. Take a good map, a compass, and food and water with you. Let someone know where you are going and when you expect to be back.

BASICS

COVILHÃ
343 D6 Avenida Frei Heitro Pinto, 6200 Covilhã, tel 275 319 560
www.rt-serradaestrela.pt

GOUVEIA
343 D5 Jardim Lopes da Costa, 6290 Gouveia, tel 238 492 185
www.rt-serradaestrela.pt

PARQUE NATURAL DA SERRA DA ESTRELA
343 D5 Rua 1° de Maio, 6260 Caldas de Manteigas, tel 275 980 060
www.rt-serradaestrela.pt

SEIA
343 D6 Praça da República, 6270 Seia, tel 238 317 762
www.rt-serradaestrela.pt

Explaining the stone engravings at the Vale do Côa

The squat, serviceable walls of the old fortress at Trancoso

Vila Nova's square, dominated by the church and town pillory

TRANCOSO

343 E5 Largo das Portas d'El-Rei, 6420 Trancoso, tel 271 811 147 www.cm-transcoso.pt

Trancoso feels a long way from anywhere, an atmospheric fortress town on the boulder-strewn *planalto* (high plateau) of the Beiras. It was captured by the Moors in the 10th century, whose legacy is evident in the squat design of the castle, its sturdy battlements echoing those on top of the town gates. By the 12th century Trancoso was in Christian hands, and it was here, in 1282, that the marriage of Dom Dinis to St. Isabel took place. Wander round the town's walls, perhaps bypassing the main gates and ducking through one of the narrow entrance passages to enter its heart, where you will find a collection of churches, chapels and fine mansions. There are echoes of the Peninsular War in the shape of a central house known as the Quartel do General Beresford—named after one of Wellington's leading generals and organizer of the Portuguese forces in the struggle against Napoleon—and a clutch of beguiling squares.

Trancoso has a good Friday market and some interesting shops selling local produce such as cheese, ham and sausage.

VALE DO CÔA, PARQUE ARQUEOLÓGICO DO

341 E4 Avenida Gago Coutinho e Sacadura Cabral 19, 5150 Vila Nova de Foz Côa, tel 279 768 260 www.ipa.min-cultura.pt/pavc

In 1992, during the construction of a dam on the River Côa, archaeologists working with an environmental impact study group discovered a huge cache of Palaeolithic outdoor art in what is now known as the Parque Arqueológico do Vale do Côa. The biggest such find ever made in Europe, it contains 28 different areas that extend for 17km (10 miles) along the steep and rocky river valley. New discoveries are being made all the time—depictions of horses, deer, the extinct ox-like auroch and goats all etched and scratched into the rock. These 20,000-year-old carvings are unique. Similar ones exist at other European archaeological sites, but Vale do Côa's are the only examples outside rather than inside caves.

Vale do Côa also contains later rock art spanning the Neolithic era, Bronze Age and Iron Age. There are even some 17th- and 18th-century rock engravings. When the carvings were discovered, the site was under threat from the EDP, Portugal's national electricity company, which wanted to build a dam there to generate hydroelectric power. Archaeologists, environmentalists, art historians and locals joined forces to fight against the dam's construction. Their campaign was successful and in 1995 the plan was abandoned. The area became a World Heritage Site in 1998.

Three sites are accessible by guided tour, led by multilingual archaeology students. Canada do Inferno, Penascoso and Ribeiro de Piscos all have interpretation offices, clarifying the site area and its art, from where you can take a tour of the site in an eight-seater 4WD vehicle. Advance booking is compulsory—book well ahead in summer—and the tours involve walking in what can be difficult terrain. Wear boots and waterproofs in winter, and take a sun hat and plenty of water in summer; temperatures in the valley can exceed 40°C (104°F) in the hottest months.

If you have time to take only one tour, Penascoso is probably the best bet—the engravings here are by far the most legible. Try to go in the afternoon when the angle of the light is best, and look out in particular for the vivid depiction of horses.

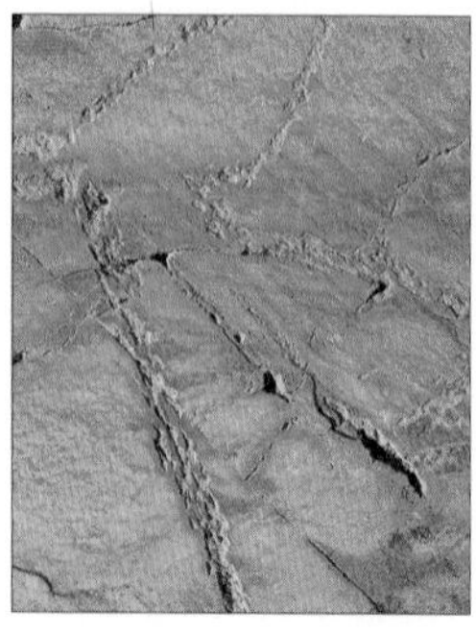

Penascoso's horse engravings are extremely well preserved

VILA NOVA DE FOZ CÔA

341 E4 Rua Castelo Melhor, 5150 Vila Nova de Foz Côa, tel 279 765 243

If you are planning on making several visits to the Parque Arqueológico do Vale do Côa, Vila Nova de Foz Côa is a good base. It is a pleasant little town, remarkably unaffected by its close proximity to a World Heritage Site.

The town's main attraction is the 16th-century Igreja Matriz, fronted by the town pillory from the same period. The church's granite façade is a remarkable example of Manueline decoration, with pilasters around the door, itself topped by an archivolt below a beautiful limestone Pietà. Inside, the three naves are covered by a painted wooden ceiling, the leaning columns giving the impression the building is open to the sky. The pillory, with its ropework decoration, statues and columns, is also a classic example of the Manueline style.

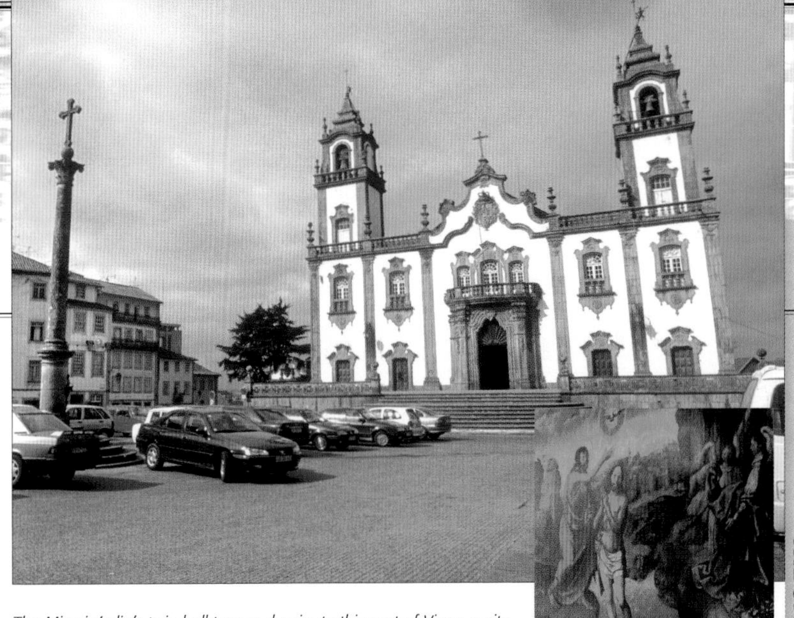

The Misericórdia's twin bell-towers dominate this part of Viseu, a city that also gave its name to the Viseu school of painting (inset)

VISEU

Visit Viseu, the heart of the Dão wine region and prosperous capital of the Beira Alta, to see superb paintings by one of Portugal's greatest old masters.

Modern Viseu stands on the site of a Roman settlement, built close to the camp of Viriatus, leader of the Lusitanian rebels against Rome. The ruins of this camp lie to the north—it was there that Viriatus fought his last battle. The town prospered on agriculture in the Middle Ages, the wealth funding the building of the cathedral, churches and fine mansions, all of which were enclosed within the city's stout defensive walls. Today, Viseu is the regional capital. It is also the heart of the Dão wine area, producer of excellent reds exported worldwide.

MUSEU DE GRÃO VASCO

As its name implies, Viseu's star turn alongside the cathedral in the Praça da Sé (Tue 2–6, Wed–Sun 10–6, €1.50) is mainly devoted to the art of the great Portuguese painter Grão Vasco. It is the only place in Portugal where you can see a large and representative collection of his work.

The museum's collection was originally distributed around the cathedral, the episcopal palace and other churches in the region. Gathering the works together has given art historians the chance to trace the evolution of Vasco's style and learn more in general about Portuguese art of the period. The pictures you will see here were originally panels that made up a series of large altarpieces designed for the cathedral in Viseu and other churches in the region. Concentrate on the pictures that once hung in the chancel of Viseu's *Sé* (cathedral), which depict detailed scenes from the life of Christ.

SÉ

The *Sé*, remodelled between the 16th and 18th centuries, is Romanesque, and has retained its weighty twin towers, though the façade was altered in the 17th century. The vast hall-church has a wonderful Manueline roof of intricate ropework supported on Gothic pillars. Shining through the dimness is a glittering 18th-century baroque altarpiece, with a serene 14th-century Madonna as its focus. There is also a fine gallery and a restrained Renaissance cloister, decorated with 18th-century *azulejos* (tiles). The first floor is home to the cathedral's small museum.

RATINGS

Cultural interest	●●●●●
Good for food	●●●●●
Historic interest	●●●●●

TIP

• Driving into Viseu is quite confusing; head for the heart of the city and park before trying to get your bearings.

BASICS

343 D5

Avenida Calouste Gulbenkian, 3500 Viseu, tel 232 420 950 Apr–end Dec Mon–Fri 9–12.30, 2.30–6, Sat 10–12.30, 2.30–5.30, Sun 10–12.30; Jan–end Mar Mon–Fri 9–12.30, 2.30–6

www.rt-dao-lafoes.com

THE VISEU SCHOOL

Like Lisbon, Viseu had a flourishing school of painting during the 16th century, led by Gaspar Vaz, who died around 1568 and Vasco Fernandes, who lived from 1480 to around 1543. Vaz studied in Lisbon, where he was much influenced by Flemish artists, particularly Van Eyck, though his work is distinctly Portuguese in style. Fernandes, who earned the nickname Grão Vasco (the Great Vasco), is one of Portugal's finest painters. He combines a great sense of composition and drama with rich shades, fine detail and a gift for realism inspired by local people and landscapes.

ESTREMADURA AND THE RIBATEJO

This region is home to some of Portugal's most famous sights—the churches at Batalha and Alcobaça, the shrine of Fátima, and Tomar's impressive Convento do Cristo. The rolling hills of the Serra de Aire are riddled with stunning caves and grottoes, while the coast and its hinterland boast some beguiling towns and resorts.

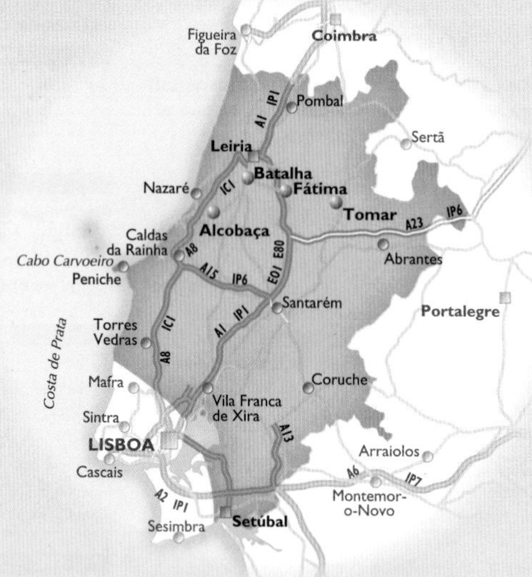

MAJOR SIGHTS

THE SIGHTS

Abrantes, high above the Tejo, was a defensive stronghold

The Castelo de Almourol, with its nine towers, was built in 1171

Waves pound the rocks below the fishing port of Ericeira

ABRANTES

345 C8 Largo de Paio, 2200 Abrantes, tel 241 362 555 Abrantes www.cm-abrantes.pt

Abrantes, set high on a hill above the Tejo, is historically renowned for its role as a defensive outpost. Romans and Moors established strongholds here, though today's castle dates from the early 14th century. It later fell into disrepair and was partly ruined by the time it was taken by the French in 1807 during the Peninsular War. General Wellesley, later to be the Duke of Wellington, then recaptured it and made it his headquarters for a brief period in 1809.

Climb up through the narrow, flower-hung streets to the castle, where there are great views along the river and south over a landscape planted with olives and dotted with white villages. Inside the fortress you can visit the Igreja de Santa Maria, now the town's archaeological museum. Highlights of the small collection are some rare 16th-century Hispano-Moorish *azulejos* (tiles) and a beautiful 15th-century statue of the Virgin and Child. The two large white churches visible from the battlements are the Igreja da Misericórdia and the Igreja de São João Baptista, both remodelled in the 16th century.

Glazing a parrot in Caldas da Rainha, known for quirky ceramics

ALCOBAÇA

See pages 110–111.

BATALHA

See pages 112–115.

CALDAS DA RAINHA

344 A8 Praça 25 de Abril, 2621 Caldas da Rainha, tel 262 839 700 Caldas da Rainha

Caldas da Rainha is a bustling spa and market town, a good stopping-off point en route to Alcobaça (▷ 110–111). It got its name, meaning 'Queen's Hot Springs', in 1484, when Queen Leonor, the wife of João II, was intrigued by the sight of peasants bathing in sulphurous-smelling waters by the side of the road. The locals explained to the queen that the waters were good for the treatment of rheumatism and Leonor decided to try them for herself. She funded a hospital in the town, and for the next four centuries Caldas was popular as a bathing retreat with royalty and the nobility. Its zenith came in the 19th century, but the spa still continues to attract visitors.

Caldas is also noted for its ceramics, some of the quirkiest in the country, in the shape of mythical beasts and peculiar vegetation. You can see examples of these in the Museu da Cerâmica (Tue–Sun 10–12.30, 2–6, €2). Take time, too, to enjoy the lovely town park and the market, held daily in the Praça da República.

CASTELO DE ALMOUROL

344 C8 Castelo de Almourol, tel 249 720 358 Oct–end Apr daily 9–5; May–end Sep daily 9–7 Entrance: free. Ferry: 50c www.ippar.pt

The fairy-tale castle of Almourol crowns the slopes of a green island in the middle of the Tejo. This commanding site was probably fortified in pre-Roman times and may have been used by the Moors—documents show that a castle stood here as early as 1129. In 1171 Gualdin Pais, Master of the Templars from Tomar (▷ 118), built the existing castle, a copy-book design that was new to Portugal, with double perimeter walls, a tall square keep—85 steps take you to the top—and nine small towers around the walls. The castle was never tested during conflict, but it was the setting for many romantic tales, such as Francesco de Morais' *Palmeirim de Inglaterra* (*Palmeirim of England*), a story crammed with fights and duels around the castle. The castle is reached by ferry, a romantic approach to what is indisputably an enchanting building.

ERICEIRA

344 A9 Rua Dr. Eduardo Burnay 46, 2655 Ericeira, tel 261 863 122 www.ericeira.net

North along the coast from Lisbon, perched on a cliff facing the Atlantic, is the resort town and fishing port of Ericeira. To see the fishing boats setting off or returning to be hauled up the beach, head for the Largo das Ribas, a lively square that overlooks the fishermen's beach, sheltered by a long jetty and the surrounding cliffs. From here, thread your way through the narrow cobbled alleys, lined with white houses, to the central Praça da República, the main town square, from where it's a short stroll to the Igreja Matriz, filled with blue-tiled decoration.

Ericeira has great fish restaurants, noted for their crayfish and lobster, and two bathing beaches to the north and south of the fishing beach. To escape the weekend crowds, walk north along the coast to Praia do São Sebastião, a stretch of unspoilt sand with crashing surf.

Alcobaça

Portugal's largest church and finest example of Gothic architecture is a memorial in stone to a tragic medieval love story.

The monastery's Claustro do Silencio (Cloister of Silence)

RATINGS	
Cultural interest	●●●●●
Historic interest	●●●●●
Photo stops	●●●●
Walkability	●●●●

TIPS

- It is difficult to park near the monastery; instead, park on the town's outskirts and stroll through the streets to reach the church.
- Alcobaça makes a good overnight stop with the bonus of seeing the church ahead of the day trippers.
- Climb the hill overlooking the town for fine views of the monastery complex.
- For a superb contrast, combine Alcobaça with a visit to Batalha, 20km (12.5 miles) to the north (▷ 112–115).

SEEING ALCOBAÇA

Walking to the monastery will give you an idea of the sheer scale of the building; pause in the square outside to marvel at the 18th-century façade, flanked by its two wings. Entry to the cloisters and monastic buildings is through a door just inside the church and to the left. Take in the church, then explore the rest of the monastery. Allow between one and two hours for a visit.

HIGHLIGHTS

THE CHURCH

Filled with light, the lofty interior of the church is a supreme example of the uncluttered style of pure Gothic architecture, a contrast to the fussiness of the façade, which was reworked in the baroque style. The church is divided into a central nave with two side aisles, which are separated by solid pillars supporting magnificent vaulting. The aisles are nearly as long as they are high, giving the church a unique perspective. The crossing transept is backed by the high altar with a superb ambulatory behind. It contains the 14th-century tombs of Dom Pedro and Dona Inês de Castro, the ill-fated protagonists of one of the most tragic of all medieval love stories.

Inês was the daughter of a Galician noblemen and thus considered politically unsuitable to be the wife of Dom Pedro, the eldest son of Afonso IV and so heir to the Portuguese throne. When Pedro's first wife died, he married Inês in secret at remote Bragança, and installed her at Coimbra, provoking his father to such a rage that he had her murdered in 1355. When Afonso died two years later, Pedro immediately had the assassins killed and in 1361 ordered Inês' exhumation. Her corpse was crowned before being buried at Alcobaça. Pedro is buried opposite her, the tombs, on his orders, lying foot to foot, so that the two can rise and face each other on Judgement Day.

Inês, supported by six angels, reclines upon her tomb, which is carved with a plethora of biblical scenes, animals, heraldic symbols and ornate decoration. At the foot, a dragon, representing Hell, consumes the damned, her murderers among them. Pedro's equally fine sepulchre has a wheel of fortune at the head and scenes from his life and death. Touchingly, the tombs are inscribed with the epitaph *'Até ao Fim do Mundo'* ('To the End of the World').

THE ABBEY BUILDINGS

You enter the monastic buildings through the Sala dos Reis (Royal Hall), built in the 18th century, and decorated with statues of Portuguese kings carved by the monks and blue *azulejos* (tiles) telling the story of the monastery's foundation. This opens into the Claustro do Silencio (Cloister of Silence), commissioned by Dom Dinis in the 14th century. The traceried windows contrast with the plain arches of the upper storey, added 299 years later. The small hexagonal building jutting out on the east side of the cloister was the *lavatorium* for pre-meal handwashing, positioned, as was customary, opposite the entrance to the refectory, a vaulted hall with a simple reader's lectern, from where the monks were entertained with readings during mealtimes. Off here is the large kitchen, whose size gives a clue as to why the monastery had a reputation for good living. The huge room has a vast chimney and a stream running through. This not only provided water for the cooks, but also delivered fish straight to the kitchen from the ponds outside. Back in the cloister, take the narrow stairs up to the left to a monks' dormitory. The one you see, another grandiose space 60m (195ft) long, is one of the many original sleeping areas. The tour finishes in the chapterhouse.

GINGINHA

Apart from the monastery, Alcobaça is best known for *ginginha*, a cherry liqueur, made from locally grown fruit—you can sample and buy it at many places in town. The Museu da Junta Nacional do Vinho, outside town on the Leiria road, tells you more about how it is made. Look out, too, for the attractive blue pottery that is made in and around Alcobaça.

The interior of the monks' washroom (above left) and fine Gothic stonework (above right). Alcobaça is Gothic at its finest. The tombs of Dom Pedro and Dona Inês de Castro, Alcobaça's star-crossed lovers (bottom)

BACKGROUND

The monastery owes its existence to Afonso Henriques, first king of Portugal, who is said to have vowed that he would found a monastery here if he captured Santarém from the Moors. Building started in 1178, the church was completed in 1253 and, by the end of the century, Alcobaça was the richest and most powerful monastery in Portugal. It continued to thrive, and soon more than 900 monks were in residence, celebrating Mass and chanting their prayers around the clock.

By the 18th century, however, Alcobaça was more famed for the profligacy of its monks' lifestyle than for its spirituality, though the monastery's hospitality and charity remained bywords, with visitors being plied with the best of food and wine. The place was also famous for its superb library and for the Royal Pantheon, the burial place of Portugal's kings and queens.

In 1834, Portugal abolished the religious orders, the monks left and Alcobaça's collections were broken up to go into museums in Portugal or sold. Alcobaça was designated a World Heritage Site in 1985.

BASICS

344 B8

Praça 25 de Abril, 2461 Alcobaça, tel 262 582 377

Mosteiro de Alcobaça, 2461-901 Alcobaça

262 583 469 or 262 505 120

Oct–end Mar daily 9–5; Apr–end Sep daily 9–7

Entrance to church: free. Monastery complex: adult €3, under-14s free; Sun 9–2 free

Good English-language pamphlet €1; also available in Portuguese, French, Spanish and German

Small shop selling postcards, books and expensive museum souvenirs but very little relevant to Alcobaça itself

On the square facing the church

www.ippar.pt
Excellent website with an English-language option and information about the church and monastery

Batalha

Batalha's abbey is an expression in stone of national pride and a celebration of Portuguese independence from Spain. It is the country's finest example of Gothic-Manueline architecture.

The entrance to the Capela do Fundador, one of the glories of the great abbey at Batalha

RATINGS	
Cultural interest	●●●●●
Historic interest	●●●●●
Photo stops	●●●●
Walkability	●●●●●

SEEING BATALHA

Apart from the abbey itself, there is little to see at Batalha, so concentrate on this magnificent building. If driving, you should be able to park without difficulty within easy walking distance. Start your visit by tackling the church and the Capela do Fundador (Founder's Chapel), before moving into the cloisters, chapterhouse and monastic buildings. To visit the Capelas Imperfeitas (Unfinished Chapels), you have to exit the main complex and walk round to the east end of the church.

HIGHLIGHTS

THE CHURCH

The exterior of this soft yellow abbey church is a profusion of pinnacles, flying buttresses, spires, parapets and towers, the ultimate expression of a peculiarly ornate form of French Gothic. Most of it was built between 1388 and 1434, with later 15th- and early 16th-century additions in the Portuguese Manueline style. The interior is plain, its strong vertical lines soaring up from solid pilasters to accentuate the vaulting in a manner reminiscent of British cathedrals of the time, such as York and Winchester. The chancel is lit by stained-glass windows, used here for the first time in Portugal and designed and installed by craftsmen from Flanders and Germany.

THE CAPELA DO FUNDADOR

From the right-hand aisle you enter the Capela do Fundador, a square chamber surmounted by an octagonal lantern topped by a cupola. Beneath the lantern are the tombs of Dom João I and Philippa of Lancaster; their four younger sons (the eldest, Duarte, is interred in the sanctuary) are buried in recessed and ornamented bays along the south and west walls. Second from the right is the canopied tomb of Prince Henry the Navigator, the driving force behind the development of Portuguese navigational techniques and a key player during the great age of discoveries. The beginning of this momentous era coincided with the building of Batalha, and consequently the abbey reflects Portugal's growing national self-confidence and wealth.

Light filters through the stained-glass windows into the Capela do Fundador (above left), where João I and Henry the Navigator are both buried. Elaborate exterior detail adds to the grandeur (above right)

THE CLAUSTRO REAL AND THE SALA DO CAPÍTULO

The Claustro Real (Royal Cloister) was originally a simple Gothic construction, but, during the reigns of Afonso V and Manuel, it was completely revamped with a triumphantly successful series of Manueline flourishes, notably the stone tracery added to the original plain windows. These grilles are considered a high point of Manueline

BASICS

342 B7 • Mosteiro de Santa Maria da Vitória, 2440-109 Batalha

244 765 497

Oct–end Mar daily 9–5; Apr–end Sep daily 9–6

Church: free. Monastery complex: adult €3, under-14s free; Sun 9–2 free

Good English-language pamphlet €1; also available in Portuguese, French, Spanish and German

Small shop selling postcards, books and expensive museum souvenirs but very little relevant to Batalha itself

P

www.ippar.pt

Excellent website run by the Ministry of Culture, with an English-language option and full information about the church and monastery

The Capela do Fundador (right) was largely built between 1388 and 1434. It was the first time stained glass was used in Portugal. The sarcophagus of Dom João (below) lies within and his wife, Philippa of Lancaster, is buried close by

TIPS

- Avoid visiting during the weekends of 13 May and 13 October, the most important pilgrimage weekends in nearby Fátima, when thousands of pilgrims also make the day trip to Batalha.
- Accommodation is limited, so it is best to visit Batalha as a day trip—Leiria, Fátima and Nazaré are within easy distance, or it's feasible to travel from Lisbon.
- Combine a visit to Batalha with a trip to contrasting Alcobaça, 20km (12.5 miles) to the south (▷ 110–111).

MORE TO SEE

CLAUSTRO DE DOM AFONSO V

These fine and restrained Gothic cloisters, built during the reign of Afonso V, contrast with the flamboyance of the Claustro Real.

LAVABO

This is a beautiful structure in the northwest corner of the Claustro Real, opposite the refectory, which was used by the monks for ablutions before their meals. The focal point of the washroom is a superbly ornate three-tiered fountain and the exterior arches are decorated with exquisite Manueline ropework.

decoration. They are adorned with distinctive crosses, symbols of the Order of Christ, and armillary spheres, similar to those at Tomar (▷ 118–121), while the columns are decorated with elaborate ropework, pearls and shells.

THE CHAPTERHOUSE

Opening off the east side of the cloister is the chapterhouse, an early 15th-century innovative vaulted structure, whose unsupported ceiling spans 20m (65ft) or more. It was a radical design when it was built, and there were great fears that the roof would collapse. Construction was considered so dangerous that only criminals condemned to death worked on it, and the architect slept there for a night to allay fears after the scaffolding came down. Today, it's a national shrine containing Portugal's Tomb of the Unknown Soldiers (there are two of them), guarded day and night by the Portuguese army. There is a museum in memory of Portuguese soldiers who have died in war, in the refectory on the other side of the cloister.

THE CAPELAS IMPERFEITAS

At the east end of the church are the Capelas Imperfeitas. (Unfinished Chapels). Commissioned in 1437 by Dom Duarte, eldest son of João and Philippa, as a royal mausoleum, they were totally remodelled by Dom Manuel's architects. This is Manueline at its most flamboyant, a riot of stone decoration. The doorway, around 15m (50ft) high, which gave access to the east end of the church, is a superb example of the style, its arches and pillars heavily carved with strange vegetation and animals. The tombs of Dom Duarte and his queen, Leonor of Aragon, lie side by side in one of the seven hexagonal chapels that surround the central octagonal space.

BACKGROUND

In 1383, the death of Dom Fernando, the last ruler of the House of Burgundy, marked the start of a period of feverish political intrigue as rivals tried to secure the throne. Fernando's widow, strongly pro-Spanish, betrothed her daughter to Juan I of Castile, the dead king's nephew, but João, Grand Master of the Order of Avis, also laid claim to the throne.

On 13 August 1385, the armies of the two pretenders clashed at Aljubarrota, south of Batalha. The odds were firmly stacked against João, who, knowing that defeat would mean Spanish domination of Portugal, vowed to the Virgin Mary that he would build her a great church if she brought him victory . She seemingly heard his prayers, because the Spanish were defeated and Portuguese independence was consequently secured for almost 200 years.

In 1386 work started on the building of Batalha under the Portuguese architect Afonso Domingues; it continued from 1402 to 1438 under a Catalonian, Huguet. It was he who designed the Capela do Fundador and started work on the Capelas Imperfeitas. Afonso V had the cloisters built and there was further work done on the capelas. They were never completed, however, as Batalha was abandoned by João III for his new Mosteiro dos Jerónimos in Lisbon (▷ 134).

Batalha's monastery, named for Our Lady of Victories, quickly fell into disrepair following its dissolution in 1834. In 1840 restoration began, but modern pollution has taken its toll on the soft limestone used to build the monastery, which is also threatened by the vibration caused by the constant heavy traffic on the nearby NI. Batalha was named a World Heritage Site in 1983.

AN OLD ALLIANCE

A contingent of English longbowmen fought at the battle of Aljubarrota in 1385, and English architects and builders were involved in the construction of Batalha. The latter had accompanied Philippa of Lancaster to Portugal for her marriage to João in 1386, a union that was part of the terms of the Treaty of Windsor, 'an inviolable, solid, perpetual and true league of friendship' between the two countries. It's a friendship that's continued ever since, strengthened by Charles II's marriage to Catherine of Bragança in 1661 and then by the Methuen Treaty of 1703.

At 600 years plus, the alliance is the longest-standing in Europe. It enabled the British to establish military bases in the Azores during World War II, though Portugal was officially neutral. The Portuguese offered the British facilities there again during the 1982 Falklands War.

Religious souvenirs dominate the shops (above)
A pilgrim approaches the Basilíca on her knees (left)

FÁTIMA

Portugal's most celebrated shrine is visited by Roman Catholics from all over the world. The Virgin Mary is said to have appeared to three peasant children here in 1917.

On 13 May 1917, three peasant children, Francisco, Jacinta and Lúcia, were watching over their parents' sheep near Fátima when they saw a flash of lightning and 'a lady brighter than the sun' standing in the branches of an oak tree. She asked them to return on the same day monthly for six months, at the end of which she would tell them who she was and what she wanted. Although only the children could see the Virgin, and Lúcia was the only one who could hear her speak, the crowds swelled. In October more than 70,000 were present.

The Virgin, so it is said, revealed three secrets to Lúcia. The first was a prophesy of peace, the second predicted the coming of Communism in Russia and the third foretold the 1981assassination attempt on Pope John Paul II. Over the following years the cult grew, and the Basilica was completed in 1953. Francisco and Jacinta died shortly after the last apparition; Lúcia, a nun, is still alive. Today, the shrine attracts thousands of pilgrims, the crowds thickest and the atmosphere most charged on the 12th and 13th of every month.

THE ESPLANADE AND BASÍLICA

The Esplanade can hold up to a million people. It measures 540m by 160m (1,772ft by 525ft), sweeping down a slope and up to the Basilíca at the far end. Twice the size of St. Peter's Square in Rome, the proportions are such that you only grasp its size once you realize how long it takes to walk from one end to the other. The neoclassical Basilíca, with its open altar in front and a vast tower, has a semi-circular peristyle curving round from each side. It can accommodate more than 300,000. Francisco and Jacinta are buried inside.

CAPELA DAS APARIÇÕES

The Capela das Aparições (Chapel of the Apparitions) is far more compact in comparison to the surrounding expanses. It is built on the spot where the Virgin appeared, a simple, clean-cut modern structure, with plain benches occupied by devoted pilgrims. A constant stream of them wait to light candles before the statue of Our Lady of Fátima. Nearby stands an oak; it replaces the original, which was destroyed by early pilgrims in search of souvenirs.

RATINGS

Cultural interest	●●●●
Specialist shopping	●●●●●
Value for money	●●●●●

TIPS

- To appreciate Fátima fully, visit it when the shrine is packed with thousands of fervent devotees. There are celebrations on the 13th of every month, but the biggest are on 13 May and 13 October.
- From May to October there's a candlelit procession every evening at dusk.

BASICS

342 B7 Avenida Dom José Correia da Silva, 2495 Fátima, tel 249 531 139

www.santuario-fatima.pt
The official Shrine of Our Lady of Fátima site; English-language option

www.rt-leiriafatima.pt
A regional tourism site; English-language option

The Praça Rodrigues Lobo, the heart of Leiria's old town

Looking down from the heights to the town beach, Nazaré

Medieval walls straddling the hillside surround pretty Óbidos

LEIRIA

342 B7 Jardim Luís de Camões, 2401 Leiria, tel 244 848 770 Leiria www.rt-leiriafatima.pt

Leiria, at the confluence of the rivers Liz and Lena, is an inland town with easy access to the beautiful Pinhal de Leiria, an extensive pine forest that stands high on the cliffs above some of Estremadura's most beautiful and unspoilt beaches. Penetrate the unprepossessing outskirts to the graceful old town, where you will find fine squares and cobbled streets dotted with gardens. Leiria's main attraction is its Castelo (Oct–end Mar Mon–Fri 9–5.30, Sat–Sun 10–5.30; Apr–end Sep Mon–Fri 9–6.30, Sat–Sun10–6.30, €1.50), which occupies a commanding site that made the castle strategically important during the reconquest. It was captured from the Moors by Afonso Henriques in 1135, and rebuilt during the 14th and 15th centuries.

Within the walls you will find the keep and a royal palace built by Dom Dinis for Queen Isabel, his beloved queen for whom he also built the castle of Óbidos. It is fronted by a superb loggia overlooking the town. Lower down from here, head for the spacious Praça Rodrigues Lobo, the heart of the old town, lined with homogenous arcaded buildings, from which a tangle of pretty streets radiate.

Leiria is particularly noted for its lively festivals and wide range of folk arts. Local wares include bright pottery and glass, woven textiles and willow baskets.

NAZARÉ

342 B7 Avenida da República, 2450 Nazaré, tel 262 561 194 www.rt-leiriafatima.pt

Despite the huge influx of summer visitors, Nazaré just about manages to hang on to its original role as a picturesque fishing village—there's still a harbour, and you will see boats drawn up on the beach and women stalking regally along with trays of fish on their heads. But summer brings big crowds, here for the superb beaches and buzzing fish restaurants.

The main town beach—the safest place to swim on this dangerous coast—is backed by a wide esplanade. This opens up into a couple of laid-back squares, lined with tempting bars and scattered with outdoor cafés. For a change of scene take the funicular (May–end Sep, 7am–midnight, 50c) up to the Sítio headland, 110m (360ft) above the town. This was the site of the original settlement, out of the reach of marauding pirates, and it's home to the church of Nossa Senhora da Nazaré, a 17th-century building decorated with *azulejos* (tiles). They commemoratate the legend of Dom Fuas Roupinho, a long-ago knight who was saved from tumbling over the cliff in pursuit of a deer in the mist by a warning vision of the Virgin Mary.

ÓBIDOS

344 A8 Rua Direita 51, 2510 Óbidos, tel 262 955 060 Óbidos www.cm-obidos.pt

Postcard-pretty Óbidos attracts coachloads of visitors every day, so you may want to arrive early, visit out of season or spend the night to best appreciate it. The town, surrounded by its medieval walls, stood on the edge of the sea until the 15th century, while Peniche (▷ 122), 23km (14 miles) to the west and now on the coast, was an island. From 1282 the town was the traditional wedding gift of the kings of Portugal to their wives; the first donor, Dom Dinis, built the massive castle here, which is now one of Portugal's most celebrated *pousadas*.

A long central street cuts through the town, from where steep alleyways, flights of steps and tiny cobbled squares open up, all dripping with flowers and lined with brilliantly whitewashed buildings. It is a pleasure to explore the network of streets and squares, and you can also walk right around the town's perimeter walls, admiring the surrounding countryside and catching glimpses of life behind the tourist façade as you go—aim to stay until dusk, when sensitive floodlighting adds another dimension to the town.

The Igreja de Santa Maria, on a small *praça* (square) shaded by trees, was where the 10-year-old Afonso V married his 8-year-old cousin, Isabel, in 1444. Inside, the Renaissance church is lined with 17th-century blue *azulejos* (tiles).

A gaily dressed local dried-fruit seller plies her trade by the roadside, Nazaré

Tomar

The main attraction of this pretty riverside town is the Convento de Cristo, an architectural tour de force that embodies in its grandeur the religious, political and miltary power of a medieval knightly order.

The Convento de Cristo (left) and folk dancers, Praça da República (above)

The Charola (above) and typic Manueline decoration (right)

SEEING TOMAR

Most of what's worth seeing lies on the west bank of the river, an attractive grid of streets, some running parallel with the river and others running down to it. Above looms the spectacular Convento de Cristo on a hill that provides excellent views of the town and its surroundings. If time is short, concentrate your energies here—you should allow at least an hour, and more likely two, to explore the church and the castle. You could then make your way downhill past the church of Nossa Senhora da Conceição to the Praça da República, a good point to start a tour round the town. Don't miss taking a stroll along the river, taking in the Parque do Mouchão, Tomar's town park on a river island.

RATINGS

Cultural interest	●●●●●
Historic interest	●●●●●
Photo stops	●●●●
Walkability	●●●●

TIPS

- When visiting the Convento de Cristo you have the choice of two routes, marked by red or blue arrows at infrequent intervals throughout the building. The red route will take you to the highlights; the blue covers everything there is to see.
- Tomar has a fine large market every Friday, spread out on either side of the river.
- During summer, a tourist train trundles round Tomar, dropping off visitors at all the main sites. Departures from Praça da República are at hourly intervals (10am–noon, 4–7).

HIGHLIGHTS

CONVENTO DE CRISTO

✉ Castelo dos Templários, 2300 Tomar ☎ 249 313 481 🕐 Oct–end Mar daily 9–5.30; Apr–end Sep daily 9–6.30 (last admission 30 min before closing) 🎟 Adult €3, under-14s free; Sun 9–2 free

THE CHAROLA

The term *charola* is used to describe the round structures that were at the heart of Templar worship. Like all circular churches, the one at Tomar is modelled on the Church of the Holy Sepulchre in Jerusalem, for whose protection the Knights Templar were founded. From here, the knights drew their spiritual strength, attending Mass on horseback, and passing solitary nights of vigil before their initiation. Tomar's Charola is a Romanesque 12th-century construction, an eight-sided building that contains the high altar of the church, which stretches to the west. It was ornately decorated during the 16th century with paintings and polychrome wooden statues. The central temple stands in a virtually circular 16-sided chapel, which acts as a cloister.

THE CHURCH AND CHAPTERHOUSE

In 1492 Dom Manuel, later Manuel I, became Grand Master of the Order and instigated a series of alterations that radically changed the building. He extended the convent by building a nave westwards from

BASICS

344 C7

Avenida Dr. Cândido Madureira, 2300 Tomar; Rua Serpa Pinto 1, 2300 Tomar

249 329 000 or 249 329 823

Tomar

www.rttemplarios.pt
A good, fast site, crammed with information, which covers Tomar and the surrounding area. Portuguese only

The Igreja de São João Baptista is on the east side of the main square

FESTA DOS TABULEIROS

Every four years or so Tomar celebrates the *Festa dos Tabuleiros*—literally, the Festival of the Platters. It keeps alive a tradition started by the saintly Queen Isabel in the 14th century as a way of distributing bread, wine and meat to the poor. Today's celebration takes place over five days, when more than 400 young women and their partners process through the streets. Each girl, dressed in white, carries an immense edifice on her head as tall as herself. This *tabuleiro* is constructed of 30 small loaves, entwined with flowers and leaves and threaded on vertical canes. It is surmounted by a white dove, the symbol of the Holy Spirit, and weighs up to 15kg (33lb)—hence the need for the accompanying young man to steady the load. The festival also includes dancing in the streets, feasting, drinking and fireworks.

the Charola, enlarging the church and creating two different levels. The upper one was to serve as the church's choir, the lower as the chapterhouse.

Internally, these plain vaulted extensions contrast admirably with the excesses of the Charola, but it's the exterior decoration that's impressive. The doorway, and particularly the window, is considered to be a crowning example of Portuguese Manueline ornamentation, liberally embellished with maritime motifs. The ropework, so typical of the style, is prominent, but look out, too, for the seaweed, coral, cables and anchor chains as well as Manuel's armillary spheres—navigational instruments that were the monarch's personal emblem.

THE MAIN CLOISTER

João III was responsible for the next big building project between 1557 and1566. He transformed the place from the purely political headquarters of the order into a monastic complex, adding dormitories, kitchens and no less than four new cloisters, making a total of seven. The grandest by far is the two-floor Main Cloister to the southwest of the church and Charola. João turned his back on the home-grown Manueline style, and looked to Italy for inspiration. The Main Cloister is thus an example of pure Renaissance classicism, with Ionic and Tuscan columns influenced by the ideas and principles of the Italian architect Andrea Palladio. The rounded arches, balustrades and alternating square and round apertures are perfectly balanced, while the spiral stairways in the corners add a quirky twist. These lead to the second floor and up to roof level, giving views of the whole Convento de Cristo. It is a good vantage point from which to admire the cloister's fountain.

The matchbox museum, home to Europe's largest collection

ADDITIONAL CLOISTERS, CELLS AND CONVENT BUILDINGS

Take your time exploring the rest of the complex, a compelling and confusing labyrinth of cloisters, corridors, kitchens and monks' cells, surrounded by terraced gardens, with orange trees, box hedges, pergolas and decorative *azulejos* (tiles). Each of the cloisters is different—particularly beautiful are Santa Barbara, with its squat arches; the verdant Cemetery Cloister, with its Gothic pointed arches; and the Washing Cloister, lined with *azulejos*, where the domestic chores of washing and drying the laundry were carried out. Both of the latter cloisters were commissioned by Henry the Navigator, who was Grand Master, and thus head, of the Order of Christ between 1417 and 1460. On the third floor, an immense corridor cuts through the building from north to south, with another branching off at right angles. Both are lined with surprisingly well-appointed and spacious monks' cells; there's a small chapel at the crossing, designed for the use of monks who were unable to get to the main church to pray.

BACKGROUND

The Order of the Knights Templars, forerunners of the Order of Christ, was founded in Jerusalem shortly after the creation of the Crusader Latin Kingdom of Jerusalem in 1118. The knights' remit was to guard the holy places, and their beliefs were shrouded in mystery and secrecy—some said they had searched for and found the Ark of the Covenant and the Holy Grail, others that they had discovered how to turn base metals into gold through the use of the legendary philosopher's stone. Whatever the truth, the order was formally established in 1128, creating an independent organization of knight-monks, answerable only to the popes.

The Templars prospered rapidly, accruing property, riches and power to such an extent that they were seen as a threat by

The two-floor Main Cloister is overshadowed by the bell-tower

Europe's temporal rulers. In contrast, the Portuguese kings saw them as an essential tool in consolidating the Christian reconquest, and hence their role became entwined with the drive to expel the Moors. They established their headquarters at Tomar in 1158, and the building of their castle and church there started two years later.

In 1312, Philip IV of France, determined to put an end to the Templars' power, disbanded the order. In 1319, Dom Dinis, following the French example, created his own new order, the Order of Christ, to which he transferred all the possessions and privileges the Templars had once enjoyed. Tomar was kept as the Order of Christ's headquarters, and ultimately the order became heavily involved in the country's overseas expansion, answerable only to Portugal's monarchs. It continued to build at Tomar, adding to the Templar structures to create the existing castle and monastic buildings.

In 1834, the Portuguese religious orders were abolished and the Convento de Cristo afterwards was variously used as a residence of the counts of Tomar and a religious seminary. It became a national monument in 1910 and a UNESCO World Heritage Site in 1983.

MORE TO SEE

CAPELA DE NOSSA SENHORA DA CONCEIÇÃO

Rua Convento de Cristo, 2300 Tomar · Oct–end Mar daily 9–12.30, 2–5; Apr–end Sep daily 10–12.30, 2–6 · Free

Standing on its own down the hill to the north of the Convento de Cristo, this serene little 16th-century Renaissance church was begun by João de Castilho and finished by Diogo de Torralva. It has three vaulted aisles.

IGREJA SANTA MARIA DO OLIVAIS

Rua Aquiles da Mota, 2300 Tomar · Mon–Fri 10–5, Sat–Sun 10–6 · Free

This 13th-century church stands on the site of the original church built for the Templars as part of their foundation. Gothic in style, it has a fine rose window and an interior that was remodelled in the 16th century. It is the burial place of Gualdim Pais, the founder of the Templar castle, and during the age of discoveries was the mother church for all the churches the Portuguese founded overseas.

IGREJA DE SÃO JOÃO BAPTISTA

Praça da República, 2300 Tomar · Daily 9.30–6 · Free

Standing on the east of Tomar's main *praça* (square), the Gothic church of São João Baptista has some nice Manueline elements, most notably the belfry with its beautiful and flamboyant door. The interior features fine pictures and good-quality *azulejos* (tiles).

MUSEU DOS FÓSFOROS

Várzea Grande, 2300 Tomar · 249 322 427 · Daily 10–5 · Free

An unusual museum that claims to have the largest match-box collection in Europe.

SINAGOGA (MUSEU LUSO-HEBRAICO ABRAHAM ZACUTO)

Rua Joaquim Jacinto 23, 2300 Tomar · Daily 10–1, 2–6 · Free

Tomar's early 15th-century synagogue is the oldest in Portugal, its domed ceiling suppported by free-standing columns. It was closed following the expulsion of the Jews in 1496, but somehow survived. It contains a collection of 13th- to 14th-century Hebrew inscriptions.

Ourém's castle, destroyed by Napoleon but now restored

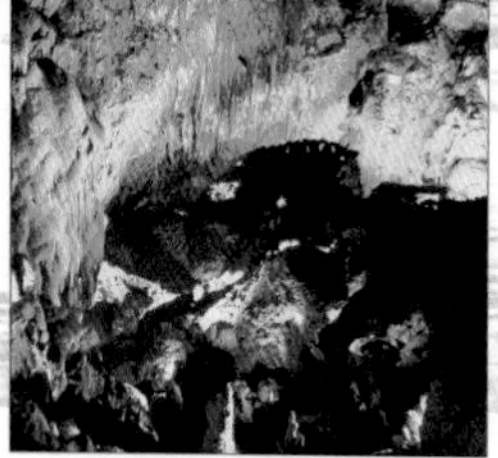
Spectacular stalactites in the Grutas de Mira de Aire

The Igreja da Marvila, Santarém, covered with elaborate wall tiles

OURÉM

342 B7 2490 Ourém, tel 249 544 654

If you are on the way from Tomar (▷ 118–121) to Fátima (▷ 116), Ourém makes a pleasant place to pause and stretch your legs. Ignore the workaday and modern section of the town, the Vila Nova, and head up the hill to the fortified medieval area, home to a ruined castle, collegiate church and an attractive village. The castle courtyard still retains the old Moorish cisterns dating from the ninth century AD, but Ourém's heyday was in the 15th century, when Dom Afonso, son of the Duke of Bragança, converted the existing castle into a palace and built several grand monuments—Afonso is buried in the crypt of the church. Destroyed by Napoleon's troops during the Peninsular War, the castle has now been restored, and there are fine views west to Fátima and north to Pinhel (▷ 104) from its parapet.

PARQUE NATURAL DAS SERRAS DE AIRE E CANDEEIROS

344 B8

The undulating upland limestone country between Fátima and Batalha has been designated a natural park to preserve both the landscape and way of life. It's a good mix of rugged hills and high farmland, with some well-marked hiking trails and interesting and beautiful flora in spring and early summer. Most visitors head here to visit the network of spectacular underground caves in the chalk of these limestone hills, most of which were discovered in the second half of the 20th century.

The caves have now been opened up to the public and the stalactites and stalagmites are beautifully floodlit. The best known and most easily accessed cave is the Grutas de Mira de Aire (Oct–end May daily 9.30–5.30; Jun, Sep daily 9.30–7; Jul, Aug daily 9.30–8.30, €3.50), a labyrinthine system crammed with dramatically lit rock formations and an underground lake. There are more caves at Santo Antonio, São Mamede, Alvados and Moeda.

PENICHE (CABO CARVOEIRO AND ILHA BERLENGA)

344 A8 Rua Alexandre Herculano, 2520 Peniche, tel 262 789 571

Until the 15th century, Peniche was an island, but the sands slowly seeped in and it's now joined to the mainland by a narrow isthmus fringed by shelving beaches. It's an active fishing port where traditional boat building still goes on, and you can stroll along the waterfront to get a glimpse of the boatyards at work. The old town, huddled inside its walls, is dominated by the vast 16th-century *fortaleza*, one of Portugal's most notorious political jails under the Salazar regime. It is now a small museum. Drive north along the coast and you will reach Cabo Carvoeiro, a peninsula with some extraordinary flat laminated rock formations. From here, there are views across the sea to the Ilha Berlenga, the main island of a tiny archipelago that's now a nature reserve. Its coastline, indented with inlets and grottoes, is one of the best places for scuba diving in Portugal. If you are interested in birds, this is a great place to see cormorants, puffins and gulls, or you can take a boat trip to explore the best of the island's coastline (boats run 15 May–15 Sep; crossing time is about an hour. Contact Viamar, tel 262 785 646, for reservations). Visitors are limited to 300 daily.

SANTARÉM

344 B8 Rua Capela e Ivens 63, 2000 Santarém, tel 243 391 512
Santarém
www.cm-santarem.pt

Santarém, capital of the Ribatejo, sits high on a hill on the north bank of the Tejo at the heart of the region's flat plains and bull-rearing country, which stretches out to the south and east. The quiet streets of the old town wind up to the Portas do Sol, a splendid *miradouro* (viewpoint) with sweeping views over the town and surrounding landscape. From here, head downhill to the two main churches: the Igreja da Marvila, with its Manueline doorway and stunningly tiled interior; and the 14th-century Igreja de Graça, with a rose window and unfussy nave. Santarém is famous for festivals. The best are *Feira Nacional da Agricultura* in June, and November gastronomy festival in , which celebrates the best of traditional Portuguese cooking.

TOMAR

See pages 118–121.

A sculpted face mask from Peniche's local museum

LISBON

Set on hills overlooking the beautiful River Tejo, Lisbon is one of Europe's most beguiling capitals, packed with contrasting delights and retaining its own individual character. The narrow streets of the historic Alfama district, the elegance of the Baixa, the castle, the churches and the superb waterfront all bear witness to the city's history, to which fine museums and the style and buzz of the Parque das Nações provide the perfect foil.

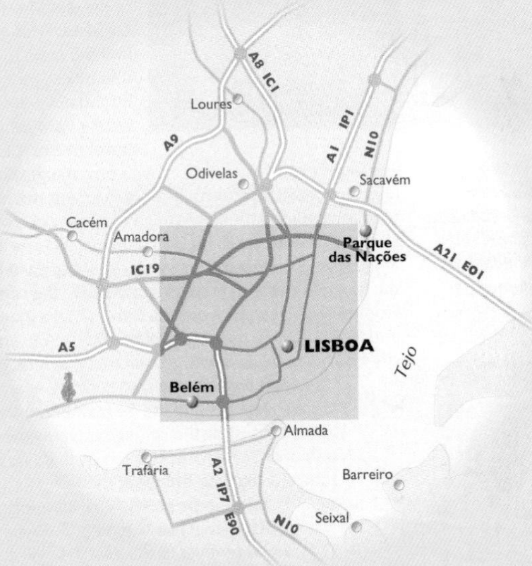

MAJOR SIGHTS

THE SIGHTS

Lisbon

🞣 127 D4 ℹ Praça do Comércio, tel 210 312 810/15 Ⓜ Cais do Sodré
🞣 127 D3 ℹ Palácio Foz, Praça dos Restauradores, tel 213 463 314 Ⓜ Restauradores
🞣 127 F3 ℹ Estação de Santa Apolónia, Terminal Internacional, tel 213 658 435
www.atl-lisbon.pt, www.visitlisboa.com

The Baixa district (above), a marvel of 18th-century town planning, with Lisbon's cathedral and one of the city's celebrated trams (below) and the futuristic architecture of the Parque das Nações (bottom)

SEEING LISBON

The city is a superb mix of the old and the new, spreading across hills running down to the shining waters of the Tejo estuary. Its districts are linked by steep cobbled streets, traversed by clanking trams and funicular railways, and lined with traditional shops and cafés.

Head first for the Baixa, a grid of elegant 18th-century streets built after the great earthquake of 1755, whose architectural flourish is the huge expanse of the waterfront Praça do Comércio. This is where you will find the main tourist information office—pick up maps and information, and invest in a Lisboa Card, which lets you travel free on public transport and gives excellent reductions on entry charges to many museums and other attractions. In Comércio, too, you can hop on a tram for a guided multi-language tour that covers much of downtown Lisbon—an excellent way of getting your bearings. For an alternative overview, try the parapets of the Castelo de São Jorge, the Moorish castle to the east, high above the central Baixa area. From here you can pick out the Baixa's main square, the Rossio, and look across to the slopes of the Bairro Alto, the hub of the city's nightlife, packed with restaurants and *fado* houses.

Below the castle, the slopes of the Alfama, a warren of narrow alleys around the *Sé* (cathedral) that make up Lisbon's oldest district, plunge towards the riverfront. North of this central core is the Avenida da Liberdade, linking the old city with the more modern areas that contain some of Lisbon's most prestigious museums. West along the river is Belém, with its stunning Mosteiro dos Jerónimos (▷ 134), while up-river to the east you will come to the Parque das Nações (▷ 142–145), built for Expo '98 and now a vibrant riverside entertainment and shopping area.

If it's your first visit you shouldn't miss the main attractions, but make time for simply wandering, making sure not to bypass Lisbon's many *miradouros* (lookouts), with their superb views across the city. Like many historic cities, Lisbon is best explored by walking its streets, but you can save your feet by hopping on a tram or using the funiculars. The Glória runs from Praça dos Restauradores, the third largest of the city's

INFORMATION AND LISTINGS

Follow Me Lisboa is a monthly free listings guide available from tourist offices. *Agenda Cultural Lisboa* is also a monthly dedicated to cultural listings.

central squares, to Rua São Pedro de Alcântara in the Bairro Alto, while the Bica links Rua de Boavista to Rua do Loreto. Before you leave, take the ferry or a river trip to see Lisbon from the water, the best way to appreciate its setting.

BACKGROUND

Legend has it that Lisbon (Lisboa in Portuguese) was founded by Ulysses, one of the Greek heroes of the Trojan Wars, but it was the Phoenicians who probably were the first to settle there around 1200BC. Greeks and Carthaginians followed, before the arrival of the Romans in 205BC. Their prosperous city of Olisipo was founded around 60BC by Julius Caesar.

The Romans were forced out by the Visigoths, and barbarian rule lasted until the area was captured by the Moors early in the eighth century AD. They rechristened the city Lishbuna. It and its rich hinterland prospered thanks to the trade links that were established with the Arab world. The Moors held the city for some four centuries until their expulsion and the establishment of the Portuguese monarchy in 1147. It became the capital in 1255, when Afonso III moved here from Coimbra.

Two centuries later, the city boomed as the departure point for the voyages of the great age of discoveries, when mariners such as Vasco da Gama opened up new trade routes to the east and the Americas. The city's population grew as well, from an estimated 65,000 in 1527 to around 165,000 in 1620. Wealth from overseas paid for the construction of some of the city's grandest and most historic monuments, notably at Belém, where Portugal's finest examples of the home-grown Manueline architectural style are found.

Building continued in the early 18th century, funded by the gold and diamonds pouring in from Brazil, but, in 1755, disaster struck. On 1 November Lisbon was hit by a massive earthquake, which destroyed an estimated two-thirds of the city and killed nearly 40,000 *Lisboetas*. Most of the city's population was attending Mass at the time—1 November is All Souls' Day—and the damage caused by the earthquake was exacerbated by the fires sparked off by thousands of candles. Within only a decade the city had been triumphantly rebuilt with the construction of a new and architecturally fabulous downtown area—the Baixa district (⊳ 130).

This 18th-century core still defines the city, though it continues to expand. Since the 1980s, Lisbon has undergone a massive regeneration, the most obvious beneficiaries being the Parque das Nações, created to house Expo '98, and the *Estádio da Luz* (Stadium of Light), which was revamped for the 2004 European Football Championship. This raised Lisbon's profile still further and helped to attract increasing numbers of international visitors.

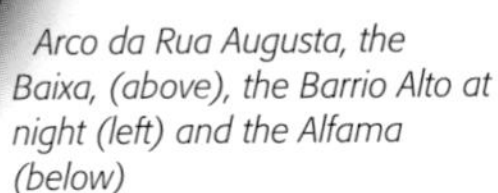

Arco da Rua Augusta, the Baixa, (above), the Barrio Alto at night (left) and the Alfama (below)

LISBOA CARD

This discount card is available from the tourist information offices and gives free travel on buses, trams, funiculars, the metro and trains to Sintra and Cascais, and free entry, or reductions on the admission charge, to 25-plus museums and other attractions. Available for 1, 2 or 3 days (€13, €21.50 or €26.55).

SIGHTSEEING TOURS

- CARRISTUR operates multilingual bus and tram tours 10–4 year-round from the Praça do Comércio; tickets available from the driver (tel 213 582 324, www.carris.pt, adult €12.47–€14.96; child €6.23–€7.48).
- Cityline runs hop-on-hop-off tours from the Praça Marquês de Pombal year-round, with Portuguese and English commentary (tel 213 191 090, www.cityline-sightline.pt €14).
- Cityrama runs half-day tours with hotel pickups as well as day trips to Fátima, Mafra, Sintra, Nazaré and Óbidos, and Lisbon by Night (tel 213 864 322, www.cityrama.pt €30–€80).
- The Art Shuttle May–Sep hop-on-hop-off minibus service covers the main museums and attractions (tel 800 250 251, www.artshuttle.net, €2–€4).
- Transtejo has daily river cruises May–Oct (tel 218 820 348).

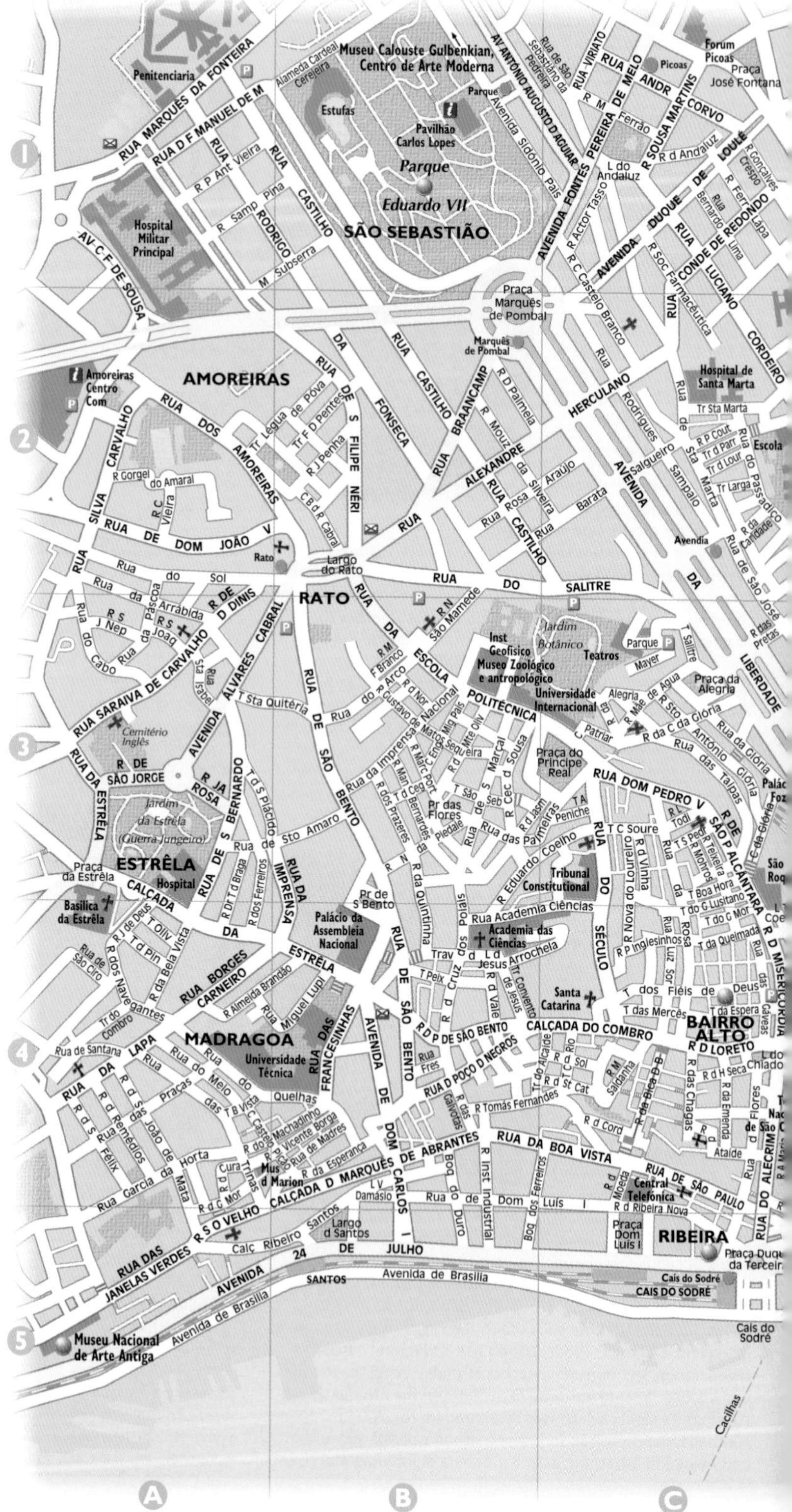

Penitenciaria
Museu Calouste Gulbenkian,
Centro de Arte Moderna
Estufas
Pavilhão
Carlos Lopes
Parque
Eduardo VII
SÃO SEBASTIÃO
Parque
Picoas
Forum
Picoas
Praça
José Fontana
RUA MARQUÊS DA FONTEIRA
RUA D F MANUEL DE M
Hospital
Militar
Principal
AV C F DE SOUSA
RUA RODRIGO
RUA CASTILHO
AVENIDA FONTES PEREIRA DE MELO
AV ANTÓNIO AUGUSTO D AGUIAR
Avenida Sidónio Pais
RUA VIRIATO
RUA ANDR
CORVO
RUA SOUSA MARTINS
AVENIDA DUQUE DE LOULÉ
RUA CONDE DE REDONDO
RUA LUCIANO CORDEIRO
L do
Andaluz
Praça
Marquês
de Pombal
Marquês
de Pombal
Amoreiras
Centro
Com
AMOREIRAS
RUA DOS AMOREIRAS
RUA SILVA CARVALHO
RUA DE S FILIPE NÉRI
RUA DA FONSECA
RUA BRAANCAMP
RUA ALEXANDRE HERCULANO
AVENIDA
Hospital de
Santa Marta
Escola
RUA DE DOM JOÃO V
Rato
Largo
do Rato
RATO
RUA DO SALITRE
RUA DA ESCOLA POLITÉCNICA
RUA DAS AMOREIRAS
AVENIDA DA LIBERDADE
Inst
Geofísico
Museo Zoológico
e antropológico
Jardim
Botânico
Teatros
Parque
Mayer
Praça da
Alegria
Universidade
Internacional
RUA SARAIVA DE CARVALHO
AVENIDA ÁLVARES CABRAL
Cemitério
Inglês
R DE
SÃO JORGE
R JA
ROSA
Jardim
da Estrêla
(Guerra Junqueiro)
RUA DA ESTRÊLA
RUA DE S BERNARDO
RUA DE SÃO BENTO
RUA DA IMPRENSA
Praça do
Príncipe
Real
RUA DOM PEDRO V
R DE SÃO P ALCÂNTARA
ESTRÊLA
Praça
da Estrêla
Hospital
Basílica
da Estrêla
CALÇADA DA ESTRÊLA
Palácio da
Assembleia
Nacional
Rua Academia Ciências
Academia das
Ciências
Tribunal
Constitucional
RUA DO SÉCULO
Santa
Catarina
BAIRRO
ALTO
R D LORETO
CALÇADA DO COMBRO
RUA BORGES CARNEIRO
MADRAGOA
Universidade
Técnica
RUA DAS FRANCESINHAS
AVENIDA DE DOM CARLOS I
RUA DA LAPA
RUA D POÇO D NEGROS
RUA DA BOA VISTA
CALÇADA D MARQUÊS DE ABRANTES
Museu
d Marion
Central
Telefónica
RUA DE SÃO PAULO
RUA DO ALECRIM
Largo
d Santos
Praça
Dom
Luís I
RIBEIRA
Praça Duque
da Terceira
R S O VELHO
RUA DAS JANELAS VERDES
AVENIDA 24 DE JULHO
SANTOS
Avenida de Brasília
Cais do Sodré
CAIS DO SODRÉ
Cais do
Sodré
Museu Nacional
de Arte Antiga
Cacilhas
1
2
3
4
5
A
B
C

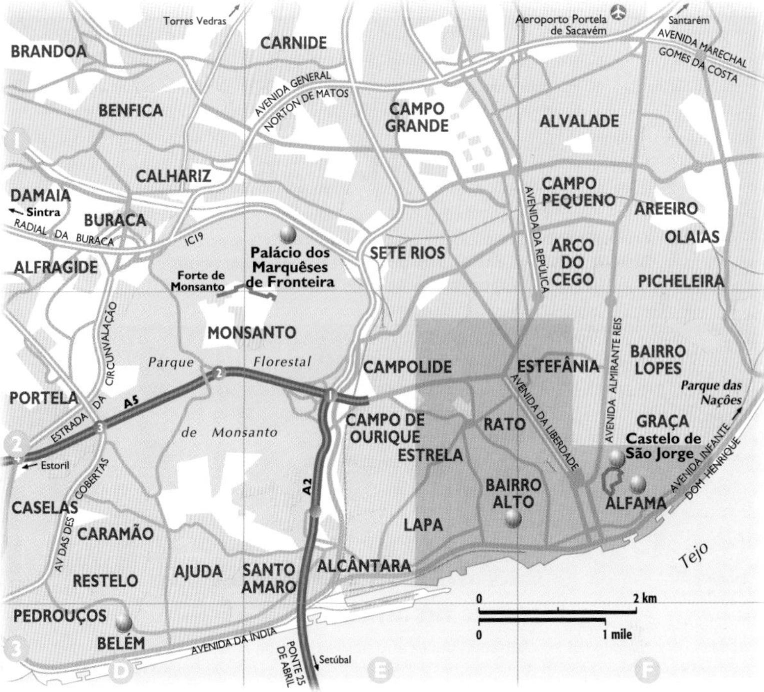

Torres Vedras
BRANDOA
CARNIDE
Aeroporto Portela de Sacavém
Santarém
AVENIDA MARECHAL GOMES DA COSTA
AVENIDA GENERAL NORTON DE MATOS
BENFICA
CAMPO GRANDE
ALVALADE
CALHARIZ
DAMAIA
Sintra
BURACA
RADIAL DA BURACA
IC19
CAMPO PEQUENO
AREEIRO
OLAIAS
AVENIDA DA REPÚBLICA
ALFRAGIDE
Forte de Monsanto
Palácio dos Marquêses de Fronteira
SETE RIOS
ARCO DO CEGO
PICHELEIRA
CIRCUNVALAÇÃO
MONSANTO
AVENIDA ALMIRANTE REIS
Parque Florestal de Monsanto
CAMPOLIDE
ESTEFÂNIA
BAIRRO LOPES
Parque das Nações
PORTELA
A5
ESTRADA DA CIRCUNVALAÇÃO
CAMPO DE OURIQUE
RATO
AVENIDA DA LIBERDADE
GRAÇA
Castelo de São Jorge
ESTRELA
AVENIDA INFANTE DOM HENRIQUE
Estoril
A2
BAIRRO ALTO
ALFAMA
CASELAS
AV DAS DESCOBERTAS
CARAMÃO
LAPA
Tejo
RESTELO
AJUDA
SANTO AMARO
ALCÂNTARA
0 2 km
0 1 mile
PEDROUÇOS
BELÉM
AVENIDA DA ÍNDIA
PONTE 25 DE ABRIL
Setúbal

Coliseu
Martim Moniz
Convento Nossa Senhora da Graça
RUA DA VOZ DO OPERÁRIO
Rua da Verónica
T do Rosário
T das Freiras
R dos Cavaleiros
C de Santo André
C da Graça
R M P de Lima
P do Colégio
Castelo
T de S Vicente
Campo de Santa Clara
Panteão Nacional
SANTA APOLÓNIA
Rossio (Praça Dom Pedro IV)
Pr da Figueira
MOURARIA
Castelo de São Jorge
L R Freitas
L Sta Marinha
Igreja de São Vicente de Fora
Igreja da Madre de Deus
Museu Nacional do Azulejo
RUA DA BETESGA
L S C do Castelo
Museu-Escola de Artes Decoratives
L dos C de Ferro
Museu Militar
Museu Arqueológico de Carmo
RUA DA PRATA
ALFAMA
R S Estêvão
Rua dos Remédios
R J DO TABACO
Baixa-Chiado
BAIXA
CHIADO
L Loios
R S Tiago
L d C d Dentro
Alfândega Geral
R de São Pedro
DOM HENRIQUE
Casa do Fado
Doco do Terreiro do Trigo
Sé
R do Barão
Santo António
R de S João da Praça
R C D SANTAREM
AVENIDA INFANTE
C das Cebolas
Biblioteca Pública
Museu Nacional
RUA DO COMÉRCIO
RUA DA ALFANDEGA
Município
Pr do Município
Ministérios
Praça do Comércio
Doca da Marinha
Terreiro do Paço
DO ARSENAL
DA RIBEIRA DAS NAUS
Cais das Colunas
Estação Fluvial Terreiro do Paço
0 500 m
0 500 yds
Tejo
Seixal
Barreiro
Montijo

LISBON

Alfama

Lisbon's evocative and atmospheric medieval quarter is a magical blend of historic buildings and picturesque streets, with great photo opportunities at every turn.

The Miradouro de Santa Luzia (left), traditional housing in the Alfama (middle), and the Casa dos Bicos (right), a16th-century architectural curiosity

RATINGS	
Cultural interest	●●●●
Historic interest	●●●●●
Photo stops	●●●●●
Walkability	●●●●●

TIPS

- **If you get lost in the Alfama don't worry. Simply head downhill to get your bearings; you'll eventually emerge near the waterfront.**
- **Pickpockets can be a problem, so keep a close eye on your bag, wallet and camera. Narrow, ill-lit and deserted streets and alleys are best avoided after dark.**
- **Catch the tram up to the Graça and walk downhill to avoid having to walk uphill.**

BASICS

127 E4

www.visitlisboa.com
Lisbon's official tourist site, crammed with useful information on every aspect of the city. Portuguese-, English-, French-, Spanish- and German-language options

SEEING THE ALFAMA

Although buses and trams serve the area, walking is by far the best option—the labyrinth of narrow alleys cannot be accessed by vehicle in many parts. Begin at the *Sé* (cathedral), then walk up the hill towards the Graça, before cutting down past Igreja de São Vicente de Fora to explore Lisbon's oldest district. There is plenty to see along the way, including some great photo stops at the *miradouros* (viewpoints). These are also good for a refreshment pause, though you might want to wait and find somewhere for lunch in the Alfama itself. Give yourself the time to explore the district to the full and to take in its buzzing street life.

HIGHLIGHTS

THE SÉ

127 E4 • Largo da Sé, 1100 Lisboa 218 866 752 Museum and cloisters: Mon–Sat 10–5. Cathedral: Mon 9–5, Tue–Sat 9–7 Museum and cloisters: €1 37; Tram: 28, 12

Lisbon's cathedral—the *Sé*—stands on the site of the city's main mosque. It was founded by Afonso Henriques in 1150. Like the other great Portuguese Romanesque cathedrals in Évora (▷ 158–161) and Coimbra (▷ 98–101), it's a fortress-like building, redolent of the troubled times when it was constructed. It has been damaged over the centuries by earthquakes, the worst occurring in 1755 when the south tower collapsed and the chancel, chapels and high altar suffered structural and fire damage. Restoration continued on and off into the 19th century, resulting in a building whose Romanesque appearance was virtually lost under baroque and neoclassical additions. This was put right in the 1930s, when the baroque trappings were removed and the rose window and squat towers were restored.

Off to the right, you'll find the treasury and cloisters. The latter were built in the 13th century. Traces of Roman Olisipo, Visigothic remains and sections of the mosque's walls have been found here.

MUSEU-ESCOLA DE ARTES DECORATIVAS

127 E4 • Largo das Portas do Sol, 1100-411 Lisboa 218 814 600 Tue–Sun 10–5 €3; 20 per cent reduction with a Lisboa Card 37; Tram: 28, www.fress.pt

Founded in 1947 by the banker Ricardo do Espírito Santo Silva, the Museum of Applied Arts is home to both a great furniture collection

Founded in 1150, Lisbon's fortress-like cathedral (left) now looks more like it did in medieval times as much intrusive restoration has been removed

A detail from the cathedral's celebrated rose window (below)

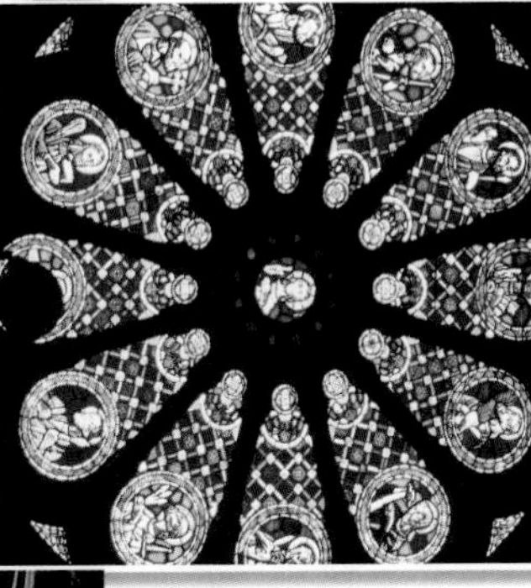

and working craft studios—you can buy their products in the museum shop. The collection is beautifully displayed in a series of reconstructed rooms, lavishly decorated with contemporary tiles and objets d'art. Other highlights include early Chinese export ware, and some exquisite silverware—don't miss the travelling toilet case, inspired by those in the French court at Versailles, but made in Lisbon.

IGREJA DE SÃO VICENTE DE FORA

127 F3 • Largo de São Vicente, 1100 Lisboa 218 824 400 Tue–Sun 9–12, 3–6 Church: free. Monastery and cloisters: €1 12; Tram: 28

A church dedicated to St. Vincent, patron saint of Lisbon, was first built on this site in 1147; in1580, Philip II brought in his architect Juan Herrera to build something more in the Italian Mannerist style. Severely damaged in the 1755 earthquake, the church was restored and is now one of Lisbon's finest examples of baroque architecture. The soaring nave, with a fine coffered vault, leads the eye up to the gilded high altar with its *baldachino* (canopy), while the walls are decorated with superb tiled panels. In the cloisters, you will find still more tiles decorated with court and hunting scenes from La Fontaine's fables. The refectory is the pantheon of the Bragança dynasty.

BACKGROUND

Under the Moors, this was the grandest area of the city, and this continued during the early years of Christian rule, but a succession of earth tremors caused the nobility to move away, leaving the Moorish character of the district untouched. This can be seen today in its labyrinthine streets, their twists and turns designed to confuse enemies, and the distinctly Arabic latticed window shutters on many houses. Because it is built on rock right against the castle hill, the area suffered relatively little damage in the 1755 earthquake and remained a vibrant, heavily populated blue-collar district. This still applies, though an element of commercialization is creeping in as Lisbon's young professionals snap up top-floor apartments and the number of visitors continues to rise.

MORE TO SEE

CASA DOS BICOS

127 E4 • Rua dos Bacalhoieros, Campo das Cebolas, 1100 Lisboa 218 810 900 Mon–Fri 9.30–5.30 Free 37; Tram: 28

A 1523 merchant's house built by Brás de Albuquerque. The name comes from the *bicos* (pyramidal spikes) that decorate the façade. When it was restored in 1983, Roman and Moorish remains were found underneath.

IGREJA DE SANTO ANTÓNIO

127 E4 • Largo de Santo António da Sé, 1100 Lisboa 218 869 145 Daily 8–12.30, 3–7 Free 37; Tram: 28

This small baroque church replaced one destroyed in 1755 and reputedly stands on the site of the birthplace of St. Anthony of Padua in 1195. There is an adjoining museum packed with mementoes of the saint.

PANTEÃO NACIONAL DE SANTA ENGRÁCIA

127 F3 • Campo de Santa Clara, 1170 Lisboa 218 881 529 Tue–Sun 10–5 €1 12; Tram: 28

This church was designated the national pantheon in 1916. There are great views over the Alfama and the Tejo from the dome. The *Feira da Ladra*, Lisbon's flea market, is held outside on Tuesdays and Saturdays.

Dom José's statue (inset) stands in front of a triumphal arch in the Praça do Comércio (above)

RATINGS	
Historic interest	●●●●●
Specialist shopping	●●●
Walkability	●●●●●

TIPS

- Street vendors sell roast chestnuts here in winter.
- Late afternoon is a good time to explore the area and see the streets at their liveliest.

BASICS

127 D4

Rossio, Baixa-Chiado

Dom Pedro IV still surveys the Rossio regally

THE BAIXA

Rebuilt after the great earthquake, the streets, squares and houses of this district at the heart of Lisbon are a superb example of 18th-century town planning.

In 1755 Lisbon suffered one of Europe's most catastrophic recorded earthquakes, which killed thousands and destroyed much of the historic heart of the city, including the entire area behind the waterfront. The Marquês de Pombal, Portugal's first minister, decided to rebuild in the style of the time. The result is the Baixa, a carefully planned network of 18th-century streets lined with elegant, classical buildings. The main axis is the Rua Augusta, an arrow-straight thoroughfare of tiled façades, mosaic pavements and idiosyncratic shopfronts.

PRAÇA DO COMÉRCIO

Rua Augusta leads south through an over-the-top monumental arch, the Arco Triunfal, finally completed in 1873, to the Praça do Comércio, a vast waterfront square that stands on the site of the Terreiro do Paço. Pombal wanted a square that would rival any in Europe, and this huge space was the result. Lined on three sides with arcades, its fourth side is open to the Tejo, Lisbon's sea gateway.

PRAÇA DOM PEDRO IV

The district's other great open space, the Praça Dom Pedro IV, known simply as the Rossio, owes much to Pombal's 18th-century remodelling. The grand building on the north side is the Teatro Nacional de Dona Maria, built in the 1840s on the site of the old Inquisitor's palace. The statue in the middle is of Dom Pedro IV.

The Rossio opens out to the northwest into the Praça dos Restauradores and the neo-Manueline façade of Rossio station. At the top you will find the Elevador do Glória, a ramshackle funicular that links Restauradores with the Bairro Alto.

ELEVADOR DE SANTA JUSTA

Just off the Rua do Our, you will find the Elevador de Santa Justa, one of Lisbon's best-loved landmarks. Opened in 1901, the 45m-tall (147ft) elevator was constructed to link downtown Baixa with the Largo do Carmo above. It was designed by Raul Mesnier de Ponsard, a disciple of Gustave Eiffel, who designed the Eiffel Tower in Paris. The viaduct linking the tower with the Carmo is closed, but a ride up the elevator still gives you great views of the Baixa.

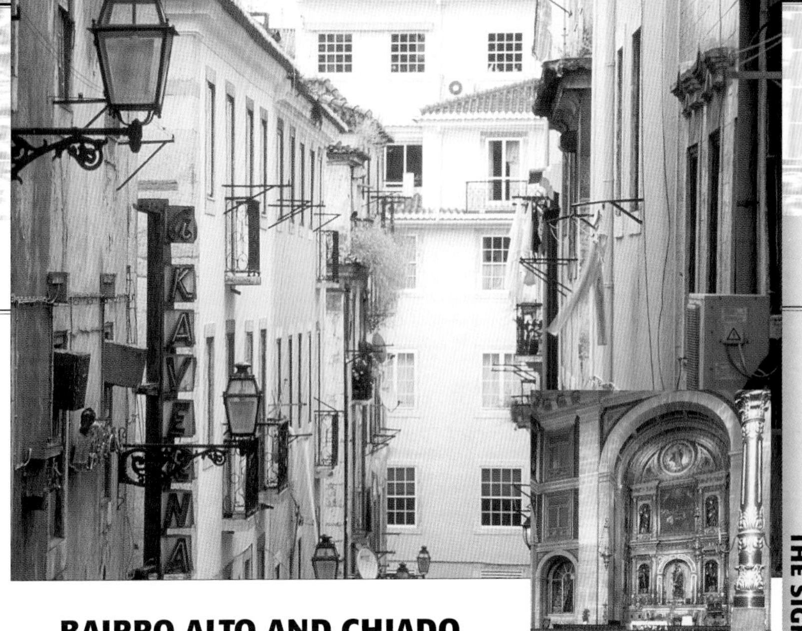

BAIRRO ALTO AND CHIADO

A typically narrow Bairro Alto street (above)
The Igreja de São Roque (inset)

The narrow streets of the Bairro Alto are where you'll find some of Lisbon's best nightlife, while Chiado has traditional shops, stylish cafés and elegantly restored buildings.

BAIRRO ALTO

First laid out in the 1500s, Bairro Alto by day is a quiet residential area that's home to a broad cross-section of *Lisboetas*. It has three pleasant squares: the Largo de Trindade Coelho, bordering the upper Chiado; the Praça Luís de Camões, a square at the southern end of the *bairro* (district); and the Jardim de São Pedro de Alcântara, a garden *miradouro* (viewpoint) with great vistas over the Avenida da Liberdade district. These squares are linked by a maze of alleys and streets, where it's as easy to get lost as in the Alfama (▷ 128–129). Here you will find some of the city's quirkier shops—alternative fashion outlets, specialist record shops and second-hand booksellers near the Trindade. By night it's very different, as thousands of people throng the streets, bars and restaurants. The Bairro Alto is also one of the traditional strongholds of *fado*, Portugal's unique contribution to popular song, and the area still has more than 20 *fado* clubs, some aimed at tourists, others packed with intently listening Portuguese.

CHIADO

This district's focal point is the Largo do Carmo and the main streets of Rua Garrett and Rua do Carmo, which are both lined with some sumptuous stores. Big international names stand alongside traditional Portuguese shops selling luxury goods of all kinds, as well as the pick of the pan-European chain stores and an elegant mall at the bottom of Rua Garrett.

MUSEU ARQUEOLÓGICO DO CARMO

127 E4 • Largo do Carmo ☎ 213 460 473 Oct–end Mar 10–5; Apr–end Sep 10–6 €2.50

The museum is in the ruins of the Gothic Convento do Carmo, which was destroyed in the 1755 earthquake. The entire nave is open to the sky, with tombs on either side of the main altar. One is the resting place of Ferdinand I; nearby lies Gonçalo de Sousa, chancellor to Henry the Navigator, who is commemorated by a statue on top of his tomb. Among the rest of the somewhat eclectic collection here, look out for the pre-Columbian mummies, an Egyptian sarcophagus, Iron Age flints and arrowheads, Roman coins and ancient ceramics.

RATINGS

Chainstore shopping	●●●●●
Cultural interest	●●●●●
Specialist interest	●●●●●
Walkability	●●●●●

TIPS

- Use the *elevadores* to get up the hills.

BASICS

126 C4, 127 D4
Baixa-Chiado

The Elevador de Santa Justa

Belém

The departure point for the voyages of discovery, Belém's buildings span more than 600 years, including the best of Manueline architecture and a clutch of superb monuments and museums on the waterfront.

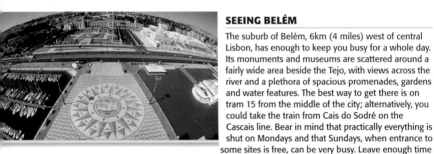

A compass (above) and world map (inset, right); part of the memorial to Portugal's greatest explorers (right)

SEEING BELÉM

The suburb of Belém, 6km (4 miles) west of central Lisbon, has enough to keep you busy for a whole day. Its monuments and museums are scattered around a fairly wide area beside the Tejo, with views across the river and a plethora of spacious promenades, gardens and water features. The best way to get there is on tram 15 from the middle of the city; alternatively, you could take the train from Cais do Sodré on the Cascais line. Bear in mind that practically everything is shut on Mondays and that Sundays, when entrance to some sites is free, can be very busy. Leave enough time to stroll along the waterfront and enjoy the plants and flowers in Belém's two parks, the tropical Jardim do Ultramarino and the Jardim Botânico da Ajuda.

RATINGS	
Cultural interest	●●●●●
Good for kids	●●●●
Historic interest	●●●●●
Walkability	●●●●●

HIGHLIGHTS

PADRÃO DOS DESCOBRIMENTOS

Avenida de Brasilia, 1400-038 Lisboa 213 031 950 Sep–end Jun Tue–Sun 9–5; Jul–end Aug Tue–Sun 9–6.30 €2; free with Lisboa Card 27, 28, 43, 49, 51; Tram: 15 Linha de Cascais Belém Surrounding streets

The idea for a monument commemorating the great age of Portuguese discoveries was first mooted in 1940 during the Exhibition of the Portuguese World, for which the Belém area was radically reconstructed. The first Padrão was temporary and the swooping white edifice you see today was erected in 1960. The jutting pediment resembles the prow of a Portuguese caravel, with a trio of curving forms behind the wind-filled sails. Its hard lines are softened by the figures crowded on the sloping prow. Dominating them is Henry the Navigator (1399–1460), holding a ship in his hand. Behind him, the 32 other figures include Manuel I, whose reign (1495–1521) coincided with some of the greatest voyages, and Luís de Camões, Portugal's most famous poet. You can take a lift to the top for great estuary views; the exhibition space inside stages temporary shows on aspects of Lisbon's history. The pavement in front combines a design of a compass and a world map showing the great Portuguese voyages and their dates, making it possible to trace their steady progress south, east and west. It was a gift from South Africa to commemorate the 500th anniversary of the death of Henry the Navigator.

The Torre de Belém

TORRE DE BELÉM

Avenida de Brasilia, 1400-038 Lisboa 213 620 034 Nov–end Apr Tue–Sun 10–5; May–end Oct Tue–Sun 10–6 €3; free with Lisboa Card 27, 28, 29, 43, 49, 51; Tram: 15 Linha de Cascais to Belém Poor selection of expensive souvenirs Surrounding streets
www.mosteirojeronimos.pt

Built between 1515 and 1519, the Torre de Belém, one of Portugal's most potent national symbols, originally stood well out into the river, a fortress designed to safeguard the western

approaches to Lisbon's harbour. The great earthquake of 1755 substantially altered the course of the River Tejo, and the Torre today stands on the water's edge, though still surrounded on three sides by the sea. It was designed for Dom Manuel I by Francisco de Arruda, who had previously worked on Portuguese buildings in Morocco, and the Moorish influence is evident in much of the architectural detail, seen at its best in the turrets with their rounded domes. The combination of these elements with Gothic, Venetian and Byzantine touches makes it unique. It is also the only complete example of the Manueline style to survive in Portugal, the others being remodelled earlier buildings or completed at a later date.

Look out for the armillary spheres in the decoration, which represent navigational instruments and were Dom Manuel's personal badge, and the cross of the military Order of Christ of which he was the Grand Master. Don't miss the intricate stone ropework, so typical of Manueline decoration, or the first European sculpture of a rhinoceros under the northwest corner watchtower. There's a serene Gothic statue of the Virgin of Calm Voyages set in a niche on the second-floor terrace—from here, steps lead up to the top of the tower with wide views across the Tejo. You can reach the terraces via the surprisingly plain and unadorned interior, whose chief point of interest is the 'whispering gallery', the acoustics of which amplify the tiniest whisper.

Exquisite stained glass in the Mosteiro dos Jerónimos

MOSTEIRO DOS JERÓNIMOS

Praça do Império, 1400–206 Lisboa 213 620 034 Nov–end Apr Tue–Sun 10–5; May–end Sep Tue–Sun 10–6 Church: free.Cloisters: €3; €2 with Lisboa Card, free on Sun 27, 28, 29, 43, 49, 51; Tram: 15 Linha de Cascais to Belém Sells expensive museum reproductions, china and T-shirts from all over Portugal, plus some books (but no guides) Surrounding streets www.mosteirojeronimos.pt

The Mosteiro dos Jerónimos is both the triumphant symbol of Portugal's great seafaring age and Lisbon's finest monument. It was built on the site of an earlier church founded by Henry the Navigator, where Vasco da Gama spent his last night on shore before setting out on his voyage east. Dom Manuel I vowed to erect a larger church if the voyage was successful, though it took until 1551 before the entire complex was more or less complete. The main architects were Diogo da Boitaca, pioneer of the Manueline style, and João de Castilho, a Spaniard. The west door, by Nicolau Chanterène, shows Manuel and his second wife, their patron saints, the four evangelists and the apostles. Look for the Manueline details here and throughout the church and its cloisters. You will also see these on the south entrance, the work of da Boitaca and de Castilho. The central statue is of Prince Henry the Navigator, the bearded figure between the two doors.

Inside, heavily decorated columns soar towards the superb rib-vaulted ceiling. Under the gallery to the left, you will find the tomb of Vasco da Gama, while that of the poet Luís de Camões lies across the aisle. Da Gama's sarcophagus is supported by lions and decorated with his coat of arms, ropework and six-sailed caravels. Touchingly, he wears a beret with a pompon on top, while his pointed shoes—also with pompons on the toes—point heavenwards.

The double-floored cloister is reached by exiting the church. The combination of different architectural influences, the Gothic and Renaissance contrasting with innovative touches such as the recurring anchors, ropes and maritime motifs, makes it a perfect example of Manueline style. The upper floor, besides being the best place to get an overview of the cloister, gives access to the church's organ gallery, well worth taking in for its superb view over the interior of the church and for a close-up of the carving on the columns.

MUSEU DA MARINHA

Praça do Império, 1400–206 Lisboa 213 620 019 Oct–end Apr Tue–Sun 10–5; May–end Sep Tue–Sun 10–6 €2.50; 10 per cent reduction with Lisboa Card 27, 28, 29, 43, 49, 51; Tram: 15 Linha de Cascais to Belém Moderate–expensive Expensive museum reproductions, china and T-shirts from all over Portugal, some books (but no guides) Surrounding streets

Lisbon's Naval Museum is in the west wing of the Mosteiro dos Jerónimos, to where it moved in 1962 following a fire in its original

MORE TO SEE

CALOUSTE GULBENKIAN PLANETARIUM

Praça do Império, 1400-206 Lisboa 213 620 002 Oct–end Jun Sat–Sun 3.30–5; Jul–end Sep Wed–Thu 2.30–4, Sat–Sun 3.30–5; English shows on Sat and Sun, phone for details €3; 50 per cent reduction with Lisboa Card 27, 28, 29, 43, 49, 51; Tram: 15 Linha de Cascais to Belém

Informative shows about the stars and heavens, some of which are slanted towards the use of celestial navigation during the age of discoveries.

CENTRO CULTURAL DE BELÉM

Praça do Império, 1400-206 Lisboa 213 612 490 Daily 11–8 Varies according to exhibitions and performances 27, 28, 29, 43, 49, 51; Tram: 15 Linha de Cascais to Belém

A modern cultural venue that stages exhibitions, concerts and live weekend entertainment.

MUSEU DE ARTE POPULAR

Avenida de Brasilia, 1400-038 Lisboa 213 012 821/675 Tue–Sun 10–12.30, 2–5 €3; 20 per cent reduction with Lisboa Card 27, 28, 29, 43, 49; Tram: 15 Linha de Cascais to Belém

An eclectic collection of folk art, which includes clothing, toys, tools, fabrics and furniture. Good for an insight into the diversity of this small country.

home in the Arsenal. It's among Europe's finest maritime museums, with a huge collection. In the sections relating to the age of discoveries, you will find fascinating models, globes and maps, as well as the museum's oldest treasure, a polychrome wooden carving of the Archangel Gabriel said to have accompanied Vasco da Gama on his great voyages. The Oriental room also contains astrolabes and instruments for navigating by the stars. Heavily gilded royal barges contrast with deep-sea fishing equipment, and the flying boat flown by two Portuguese pilots across the Atlantic to Brazil in 1922 is lovingly preserved. In the adjoining children's museum, the Museu das Crianças, there are plenty of interactive displays to keep kids entertained.

A model caravel in the Museu da Marinha (left), the coach museum (below left) and the monastery cloister (below right)

MUSEU NACIONAL DOS COCHES

Praça Afonso de Albuquerque 213 610 850/2/4 Tue–Sun 10–5.30 €3; €2 with Lisboa Card 27, 28, 29, 43, 49, 51; Tram: 15 Linha de Cascais to Belém Sells expensive museum reproductions, china and T-shirts from all over Portugal, plus some books (but no local guides) Surrounding streets
www.museudoscoches-ipmuseus.pt

Once the Royal Riding School, this richly decorated 18th-century building is now the National Coach Museum. It forms part of the complex of the Palácio do Belém, the official residence of the Portuguese president. Carved gilded wood, painted panels and opulent hangings adorn a huge collection of vehicles. There are also equally impressive displays of sedan chairs, cabs and prams. Examples to look out for include the 18th-century coaches built for the Marquês de Frontes, Portugal's ambassador to the Holy See, a carriage sent by Philip III of Spain in 1619, and a 19th-century English coach, built in London and last used for Queen Elizabeth II's state visit to Portugal in 1957.

BACKGROUND

The area of Belém was once a maritime settlement right on the water known as Restelo and was quite separate from the city of Lisbon. Manuel I changed its name to Belém in the early 1500s, by which time the district was synonymous with maritime exploration. In 1493 Columbus paused here on his way back to Spain from the Americas, and in 1497 it was the starting point for Vasco da Gama's journey to discover a sea passage to India. The Mosteiro dos Jerónimos was built to give thanks for da Gama's successful voyage.

The Salazar regime revamped the waterfront and laid out the pools and gardens fronting Jerónimos. The Padrão went up in 1960, and in 1992 the Centro Cultural de Belém (▷ margin text opposite) was built to mark Portugal's presidency of the European Union. Little remains of old Belém except for the houses on the Rua de Belém, but the area attracts thousands of visitors who come to enjoy the monuments and museums.

MUSEU DO DESIGN

Praça do Império, 1400-206 Lisboa 213 612 934 Daily 11–7.15 €3; 20 per cent reduction with Lisboa Card 27, 28, 29, 43, 49, 51; Tram: 15 Linha de Cascais to Belém

An important collection from 1937 to the present. Each section includes furniture, lighting, homewares, glass and jewellery.

MUSEU NACIONAL DE ARQUEOLOGIA

Praça do Império, 1400-206 Lisboa 213 620 000 Tue 2–6, Wed–Sun 10–6 €3; 20 per cent reduction with Lisboa Card 27, 28, 29, 43, 49, 51; Tram: 15 Linha de Cascais to Belém
www.mnarqueologia-ipmuseus.pt

For those interested in Portugal's Roman heritage, there are Roman mosaics, sarcophagi and sculpture from all over the country.

A 15th-century statue by Raphael (left) in the Museu da Marinha

São Jorge (above) and looking down from the castle (inset)

CASTELO DE SÃO JORGE

The birthplace of the city is an oasis of peace and cool greenery with superb views over the busy streets and the River Tejo below.

RATINGS	
Cultural interest	●●●
Good for kids	●●●●
Historic interest	●●●●
Photo stops	●●●●●

TIPS

- **The castle and its gardens are a great place to spend a couple of hours during the hottest part of the day.**
- **The paving is uneven, so watch your step and wear comfortable, flat shoes.**

BASICS

127 E4 • Castelo de São Jorge, 1100–129 Lisboa

218 800 620

Olisipónia: Mar–end Oct Thu–Tue 10–6.30; Nov–end Feb Thu–Tue 10–5.30. Câmara Escura: Jun–end Oct daily 10–1.30, 2.30–6.30; Nov–end May daily 10–1.30, 2.30–5.30

Olisipónia: €3; 30 per cent reduction with Lisboa Card. Câmara Escura: €2

37; Tram: 28, 12

Casa do Leão: an elegant and expensive restaurant in one of the surviving rooms of the Alcáçova

Small self-service café with hot and cold drinks, snacks and ice-cream

Small shop with a limited selection of souvenirs

The Castelo de São Jorge has long been a defensive stronghold—a fort stood here even before the coming of the Romans in 138BC. They built a citadel on the site of the present castle, from which the Roman city spread down the hill. The Moors built a castle over the earlier Roman fortification with the Alcáçova in the middle—the palace that still stands today. Portugal's kings lived here from 1279 to 1511, moving out only after the construction of the Palácio de Ribeira.

THE RAMPARTS, WALLS AND GARDENS

Topped with battlements and crowned with 10 towers, the inner walls surround two courtyards, from where stairs provide access to the wall-top walkways. From these you can climb the towers, one of which contains an old-fashioned camera obscura. This gives bird's-eye views of the streets and people far below. More stairs lead down the hill to the outlying Torre de São Lourenço. The entire complex had a thorough facelift before Expo '98, as did the surrounding gardens, and it is now one of the best-kept parts of central Lisbon.

THE ALCÁÇOVA AND OLISIPÓNIA

The Alcáçova was the original Moorish palace, which served as the royal residence from the 14th to the 16th centuries. Little of it remains today and what there is has been heavily restored, but you will get a good idea of its original size and state in the series of chambers now housing the Olisipónia, a multimedia exhibition focusing on the history of the capital.

A series of screens and sound effects leads you through a 25-minute run-down of the city's past, with some good information on Portugal's golden age in the 15th and 16th centuries and some fascinating insights into the great earthquake of 1755. Unusually for Portugal, there is an English audio commentary.

Don't miss Take in the show at the Olisipónia for an informative overview of Lisbon's history.
Walk along the castle's ramparts for some of the best views over Lisbon and its river.
Explore the medieval quarter of Santa Cruz within the outer walls.

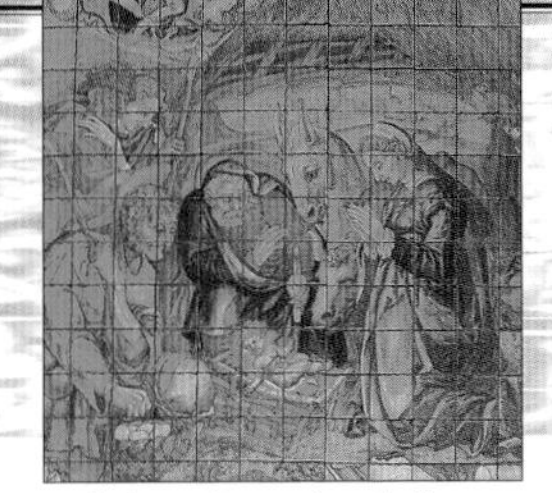

A tile from the National Tile Museum

MUSEU CALOUSTE GULBENKIAN

See pages 138–141.

MUSEU DO CENTRO DE ARTE MODERNA

See page 146.

MUSEU DO CHIADO

127 D4 • Rua Serpa Pinta 6, 1200-444 213 432 148/9 Tue 2–6, Wed–Sun 10–6 €3; 20 per cent reduction with Lisboa Card Baixa-Chiado Tram: 28, 38, 100

Founded in 1914 as Portugal's national museum of contemporary painting and sculpture, the Museu do Chiado was totally revamped after the Chiado fire of 1988. Reopened in 1994, with a contemporary facelift by the French architect Jean Michel Wilmotte, it now concentrates on Portuguese art between 1850 and 1950. The collection covers every movement, from romanticism, naturalism, modernism and surrealism to abstractionism. Artistically, works such as *A Sesta* by Almada Negreiros and *O Desterrado* by Soares dos Reis are the best, but most visitors will find scenes of Lisbon, such as Carlos Botelho's *Lisboa e o Tejo*, more interesting.

MUSEU NACIONAL DO AZULEJO AND IGREJA DA MADRE DE DEUS

127 F3 • Rua da Madre de Deus, 1900-312 Lisboa 218 100 340 Tue 2–6, Wed–Sun 10–6 €3; 20 per cent reduction with Lisboa Card Arroios then 18, 42, 104, 105

The museum traces the history of the *azulejo* from the 15th century to the present day. Highlights include the blue-and-white Lisbon cityscape, showing the city prior to the 1755 earthquake. There are additional stunning *azulejos* in the adjoining church.

Intricate designs in silver, the work of Renaissance craftsmen

MUSEU NACIONAL DE ARTE ANTIGA

Portugal's national art museum is located in a beautifully converted 17th-century palace with a tranquil garden.

126 A5 • Rua das Janelas Verdes, 1249-017 Lisboa 213 912 800 Tue 2–6, Wed–Sun 10–6 €3; 20 per cent reduction with Lisboa Card 27, 40, 43, 49, 60; Tram: 28

The Museu Nacional de Arte Antiga is the place to come to see the best of Portuguese painting, enjoy an overview of other European painting schools, and take in a comprehensive collection of furniture, textiles and objects from all branches of the decorative arts. The museum's strengths are its Portuguese paintings and the Far Eastern collections, particularly the examples of late 16th-century Japanese Namban art, dating from the time the Portuguese were in Japan. They arrived there in the early 1500s and stayed until the Japanese closed the country to Europeans.

PORTUGUESE PAINTING—FLOOR 3

This covers the 15th- and 16th-century schools, when Portuguese painting was heavily influenced by Flemish artists such as Jan van Eyck and Rogier van der Weyden. The big names are Nuno Gonçalves, Grégorio Lopes and Frei Carlos. Gonçalves' star piece is the *São Vicente Polyptych*, a six-panel altarpiece showing a crowd paying homage to St. Vincent, Lisbon's patron saint.

EUROPEAN PAINTING—FLOOR 1 (GROUND)

The Flemish and German schools are strong here, the *Temptation of St. Anthony* by Hieronymous Bosch being an outstanding example of that artist's surrealistic style. Look out, too, for works by Cranach, Dürer, Raphael and Zurbarán.

FAR EASTERN ART—FLOOR 2

This is an outstanding collection of decorative art, including porcelain and metalwork, dating from the colonial period in Africa and the Far East. The ceramics and silverware rival the exhibits in the Gulbenkian (▷ 138–141), particularly the Chinese porcelain and the huge steely and lustrous 1756 silver dinner and decorative table service by F. T. Germain of Paris.

Don't miss The 16th-century Japanese screens on floor 2 depict the arrival of the Portuguese in Nagasaki; they are full of quirky European figures with long pointed noses and stork-like legs.

Museu Calouste Gulbenkian

Lisbon's only world-class museum, housed in a sleek building in lovely gardens, is home to a comprehensive but compact collection of great art, with examples from every century and from all over the world.

RATINGS

Cultural interest	● ● ● ● ●
Historic interest	● ● ● ●
Value for money	● ● ● ● ●

BASICS

126 B1 • Avenida de Berna 45, 1067-001 Lisboa

217 823 000

Tue 2–6, Wed–Sun 10–6

Adult €3.50, under-12s €2; 20 per cent reduction with Lisboa Card

Praça de Espanha, São Sebastião

16, 26, 31, 46, 56

Self-service restaurant serving mediocre food and snacks throughout the day

Café serving coffee, drinks and snacks; part of the restaurant

Shop selling a wide selection of art books, almost exclusively in Portuguese, and some good-quality and expensive museum reproduction souvenirs. Some smaller, less expensive objects aimed at children. No museum guidebooks or postcards

TIPS

- There is no floorplan or guidebook available, so it pays to study the wall plan in the entrance hall before you start your visit.
- Allow around 2–3 hours for a leisurely visit.
- Leave time to enjoy the fine gardens that surround the Fundação Calouste Gulbenkian's buildings.
- Combine visiting the Gulbenkian with the Museu do Centro de Arte Moderna (▷ 146), which is also part of the foundation and situated close by to it.

The entrance to the museum (above)

SEEING THE MUSEU CALOUSTE GULBENKIAN

The Museu Calouste Gulbenkian is part of the Fundação Calouste Gulbenkian, a few minutes' walk north of Parque Eduardo VII. The collection is relatively small, but every exhibit is a superlative example of its type. Though there is no audio-guide, floor plan or guidebook available on site, the exhibits are clearly laid out in geographical and chronological groups: there are two main sections, one of which is devoted to European art and the other to the art of the ancient and oriental worlds. All the exhibits are labelled in Portuguese and English.

HIGHLIGHTS

EASTERN ISLAMIC AND ARMENIAN ART—ROOMS IV AND V

Two interconnecting galleries hold the Eastern Islamic and Armenian collections, providing an overview of all that's best from these regions, with particular emphasis on works from the 15th to 17th centuries. The silk and wool carpets, some laid flat, others used as wallhangings, are a high point, as are the numerous examples of wall tiles from the Ottoman Empire—one particularly beautiful 15th-century panel of faience tiles with a turquoise, blue and white underglaze stands out.

Don't miss the Persian and Turkish ceramics, especially the mainly blue-and-white Turkish Izmet bowls. These have a definite Ming influence, probably owing to traders' contact with China as Chinese pottery started to travel west along the so-called Silk Road. An entire case is filled with exquisite Egyptian glass mosque lamps made in the 14th century—gilded, translucent and iridescent, they represent staggering technical expertise for the period in which they were created.

FAR EASTERN ART—ROOM VI

The exhibits include deep Ming bowls with a translucent celadon green glaze, though more eye-catching by far are the Chinese porcelain vases and covered pots, mainly dating from the 17th and 18th centuries. Two outstanding sets are made of enamelled porcelain, one decorated with chrysanthemums in clear pink, turquoise and green on a white ground, the other with pink and green flowers and natural motifs on a black glaze. On the right as you leave the gallery, don't miss the intricate 14th-century Chinese coromandel screen, inlaid with lacquer and paper designs.

Renoir's Madame Monet *(above)*
A modern sculpture (below)

EUROPEAN ART—ROOMS VII–XVII PAINTING
Highlights from the painting collection include Ghirlandaio's *Portrait of a Young Woman*; she is wearing a pink dress with green sleeves, while her coral necklace draws attention to the delicate wisps of hair around her face. More pretty girls feature in a trio of portraits by the English artists Gainsborough, Romney and Lawrence, while Rembrandt's *Pallas Athene*, a dark depiction of the goddess with a superb shield and plumed helmet, is more sombre. Rubens is represented by a sympathetic portrait of his second wife Helena Fourment, and there is an atmospheric Turner, *The Mouth of the Seine*, all swirling water and pearly tints. Venice fans shouldn't miss the side room devoted to Guardi—19 real or imagined Venetian scenes, including one showing Palladio's design for the Rialto bridge. Corot, Monet, Renoir and Dégas represent the French Impressionists; outstanding here are two winter scenes, a Millet pastel of *Snow-Covered Haystacks* contrasting finely with Monet's *Ice Floating*.

SCULPTURE, FURNITURE AND PORCELAIN
Sculptures include a 15th-century Luca della Robbia medallion from Florence, a Rossellino bas-relief of the Madonna and Child, and Houdon's marble *Diana* (1780). The French Louis XV and Louis XVI furniture is superb and includes chairs,

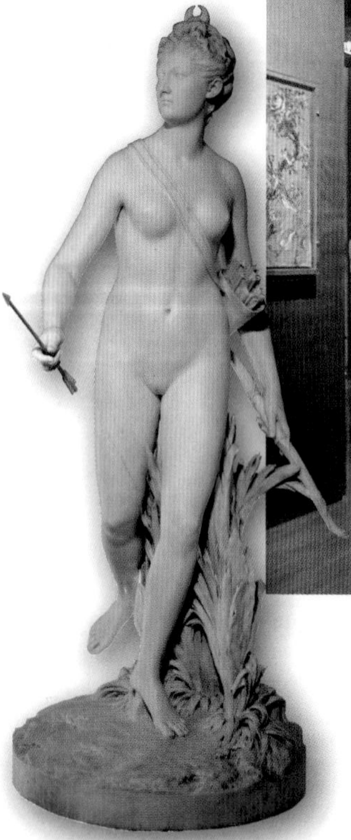

The gallery of 18th-century French decorative arts is full of treasures

cupboards, sideboards and inlaid tables, set off by wall hangings and tapestries. There's more French pre-Revolutionary opulence in the shape of silver and gold tableware, together with a large display of Sèvres porcelain, some with a blue and some with a green background glaze.

Nicholas Houdon's impressive marble statue of Diana *(above)*

RENÉ LALIQUE

The final room is devoted to work by the art nouveau jeweller and designer René Lalique, and includes 169 pieces of his jewellery, intricate and sinuous designs embellished with enamel, gold, diamonds, pearls and other gems.

Perfection in jewellery by René Lalique (above)

Fragments of a Mughal carpet with a classic geometric pattern (below), which was woven in either Kashmir or Lahore in India during the early part of the 17th century

BACKGROUND

The museum is part of the Fundação Calouste Gulbenkian, a cultural foundation that funds the art collections, the Centro de Arte Moderna, an orchestra, a choir and a ballet company, and runs three concert halls and two exhibition galleries in Lisbon. The foundation is active throughout Portugal, funding museums and libraries and giving charitable grants to a huge range of projects. This is all possible thanks to Calouste Gulbenkian (1869–1955), an Armenian-born oil magnate, who made millions in the Middle East. Art collecting was his passion, and the Museu Calouste Gulbenkian is the result of years of astute buying and a deep pocket. During World War II the British seized control of his assets, and it was neutral Portugal that provided one of the most important 20th-century cultural patrons with a home.

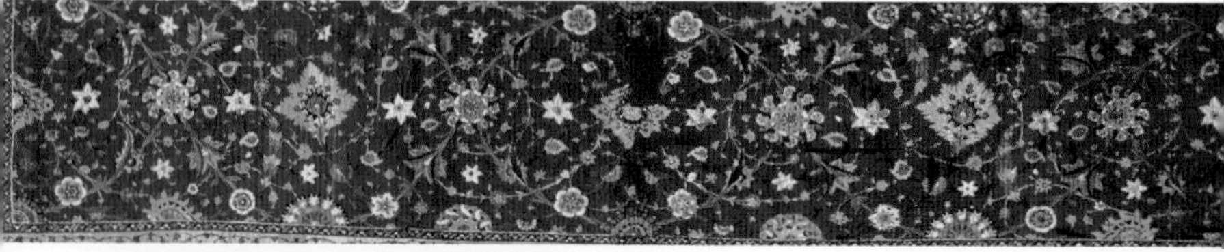

Rembrandt's celebrated Portrait of an Old Man *(above) and a lamp from a mosque dating from around 1400 (below)*

GALLERY GUIDE

1. Egyptian art
2. Graeco-Roman art
3. Mesopotamian art
4. Oriental-Islamic art
5. Armenian art
6. Art from the Far East
7. Work in ivory; Illuminated manuscripts
8. 15th-, 16th- and 17th-century painting and sculpture
9. Renaissance art
10. 18th-century decorative art: France
11. 18th-century painting and sculpture: France
12. 18th- and 19th-century silverwork: France
13. 18th- and 19th-century painting: England
14. 18th-century painting: Italy
15. 19th-century painting and sculpture: France

Finding the way around the Gulbenkian Museum can be confusing. Use this floor plan as your guide to locating specific galleries

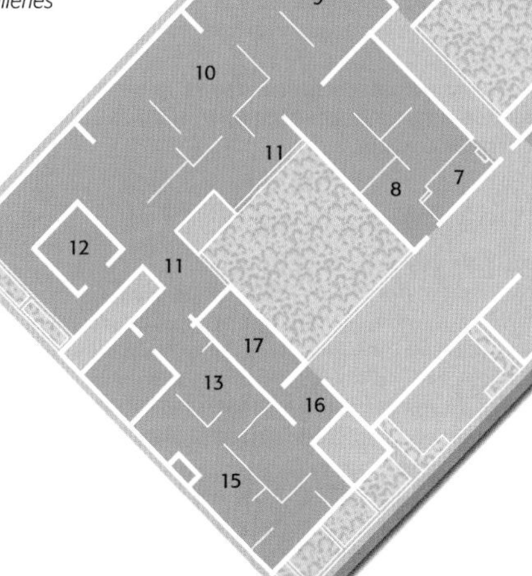

EGYPTIAN ART–ROOM 1

A small collection of superlative quality—look for a 16th-century BC carved ivory spoon; a relief stela, showing an offering being made to the Pharaoh (1580BC); and bronze cats (664–525BC).

GRAECO-ROMAN ART–ROOM II

Highlights here are an Attic Greek vase (450BC) decorated with scenes of chariots and games, the Roman iridescent glassware, a Greek silver pitcher (third century BC) and intricate Roman jewellery (second century BC–fourth century AD)

MESOPOTAMIAN ART–ROOM III

Look out for an Assyrian bas-relief from the palace of Assurbanipal in Nimrud showing a bearded warrior wearing a feather-trimmed cape (ninth century BC).

IVORIES AND ILLUMINATED MANUSCRIPTS–ROOM III

Medieval Books of Hours, missals and gospels, all lavishly embellished and decorated.

Parque das Nações

A stunning waterside site, whose attractions include Europe's finest oceanarium, lots of fun for the kids, and no-hassle shopping. This is a perfect family day out.

RATINGS	
Chainstore shopping	●●●●●
Good for kids	●●●●●
Specialist shopping	●●●●●
Value for money	●●●
Walkability	●●●●

BASICS

127 F2 • Alameda dos Oceanos, 1990-223 Lisboa
218 919 333
Oriente line to Oriente
www.parquedasnacoes.pt

SEEING THE PARQUE DAS NAÇÕES

It's an easy journey by metro to the state-of-the-art Oriente station in the Parque das Nações, from where you have only to walk through the huge and tempting Vasco da Gama shopping mall to reach the park itself. The site is rambling, and distances can be deceptive, but judicious use of the miniature train and the cable car will help you to get around. Aim to visit the Oceanário before the queues build up, then spend the rest of the day exploring everything else. Although the crowds are thinner during the week, the atmosphere is best at the weekends when thousands flock here to enjoy the attractions and wander along the waterside promenades. You can also visit the park without going into Lisbon, as it's easily accessible from the motorway system.

Oriente station, with Parque das Nações in the background, built for Expo '98

THE SIGHTS

HIGHLIGHTS

OCEANÁRIO

✉ Parque das Nações, 1800 Lisboa ☎ 218 917 002/6 🕐 Oct–end Apr daily 10–7 (ticket office closes at 6pm); May–end Sep daily 10–8 (ticket office closes at 7pm) 🎫 Adult €9, child (4–12) €4.50, under-3s free, family (2 adults and 1 child) €20; tickets can be booked online at www.oceanario.pt Ⓜ Oriente 🚌 28 📖 Illustrated floor plan in English €1.50 🎁 Excellent shop selling a wide range of ocean-related books, souvenirs, stationery and stuffed toys 🚻 🅿 www.oceanario.pt

Designed by the American architect Peter Chermayeff, the Oceanário opened in 1998 as part of Expo '98. Its role was to provide Lisbon with a permanent reminder of the Expo by neatly linking the country's maritime past with the future role of the oceans. The building crouches on the water's edge like some futuristic underwater machine, but it's the marine life inside that attracts the crowds.

The huge central tank, visible from two levels, contains more than 7 million litres (1.8 million US gallons) of salt water and is inhabited by a range of fish and sea creatures from the world's oceans—sharks, rays and great schools of smaller fish living at different depths. This is surrounded by four areas representing various oceanic ecosystems: the Atlantic, the Antarctic, the Pacific and the Indian. These exhibits have both above- and below-water habitats, allowing visitors to see birds, animals and vegetation typical of these zones above ground as

TIPS

- The *posto de informacão* (information desk) is outside the Vasco da Gama shopping mall, and has plans of the park and details of events.
- If you want to see everything, consider purchasing the Cartão do Parque (adult €15.50, child €8.50). It gives access to the main sites and discounts elsewhere.
- If you don't feel like walking, a hop-on-hop-off miniature train makes the round trip through the park between 10am and 5pm. It leaves hourly on the hour from outside the Atlantic Pavilion (adult €2.50, under-14s €1.50). You can also rent bicycles (€5 per hour); ask at the information desk.
- It may take more than an hour to get into the Oceanário at peak times, so it can pay to get to the park early and head there first.

The oceanarium, built for Expo '98 and one of the world's finest

well as the marine life under the water. The puffins and guillemots in the Atlantic zone are very popular, as are the Magellan penguins hopping around the snow in the Antarctic zone and the fish-eating sea otters of the Pacific. All these creatures can be viewed underwater once you descend to the lower level, where sunlight filters through the water onto the weeds and coral, and shoals of fish glide by.

Additional tanks cover sea habitats as diverse as living coral reefs to mangrove forests. Highlights here are the Australian dragon fish, their camouflage so perfect that they're almost impossible to detect against the seaweeds they live in; the luminous tropical jellyfish; vivid anemones and an astounding range of crabs. There are more than 15,000 animals and plants here, with 450 different species represented. Educational interactive exhibits include information on fishing, ocean products, currents, winds, tides and conservation. Everything is clearly labelled in Portuguese and English.

The striking Sun Man *sculpture by Jorge Viera*

MORE TO SEE

CABLE CAR

✉ Parque das Nações, 1800 Lisboa 🕐 Mon–Fri 11–7, Sat–Sun 10–8 💲 One way: adult €3, child (4–13) €1.50, under-4s free. Round trip: Adult €5, child (4–13) €2.50, under-4s free

A cable car runs the length of the waterfront between the Oceanário and the Torre Vasco da Gama, with a bird's-eye view of the park.

PAVILHÂO ATLÂNTICO

✉ Parque das Nações, 1800 Lisboa ☎ 218 918 409

This is Portugal's largest indoor arena, used for sporting events, conferences and concerts.

TORRE VASCO DA GAMA

✉ Parque das Nações, 1800 Lisboa ☎ 218 918 000 🕐 Daily 10–8 💲 Adult €2.49; child (5–14) €1.25

Once part of the oil refinery that originally occupied the site, the Vasco da Gama Tower provides spectacular views over Lisbon, the Tejo and south into the Alentejo.

CENTRO DA CIÊNCIA VIVA

Alameda dos Oceanos, Parque das Nações, 1990-223 Lisboa 218 917 100 Mon–Fri 10–6, Sat–Sun 11–7 Adult €5, child (7–17) €2.50, under-6s free, family ticket (2 adults and 2 children) €11 Oriente 28 Explanatory English leaflet €1.50 Good book and gift shop with plenty of reasonably priced souvenirs P
www.pavconhecimento.pt

This is another great attraction for families. It's a science park that aims—and succeeds—in getting the message across to ordinary people that science and technology are fun. There are plenty of permanent interactive exhibits, ranging from how holograms work to technology in everyday life, while kids can spend hours in the cybercafé with its free Internet access. Run by the Portuguese Ministry of Science and Technology, the site also has thematic exhibitions, drawing on the resources of the world's major scientific institutes. Highlights among these are the Unfinished House, designed by the Cité des Sciences in Paris, San Francisco's Exploratorium, and the See, Do, Learn display jointly conceived by the universities of Cardiff and Helsinki. All of these are interactive exhibits and learning zones where visitors can enjoy a real hands-on experience of science at its liveliest. Everything's clearly labelled in both English and Portuguese.

The exploding fountain in the park (above left) keeps kids amused for hours as it changes colour, while the giant Vasco da Gama shopping mall (above right) caters to adult tastes

THE WATERFRONT AND GARDENS

The Tejo is up to 10km (6 miles) wide here and walkways, planted with shrubs and trees from Portugal's former colonies, run all along the water's edge from west of the Oceanário to beyond Ponte Vasco da Gama. At weekends, thousands of locals flock here to relax and enjoy the fine views; during the week, though, it's one of the city's most peaceful areas. Don't miss the Jardim da Agua, where ponds are linked by stepping stones and and jets fountains spray cooling water.

BACKGROUND

Until the early 1990s the area now containing the Parque das Nações was an industrial wasteland, scarred by derelict warehouses, an oil refinery and the municipal abattoir. The site was chosen as the hub of Expo '98, Lisbon's international World's Fair, which launched the country firmly into the European mainstream. The fair ran from May to September 1998 and was a huge success, attracting many thousands of visitors.

Once Expo closed, the site was reopened as an urban district and given its present name. Construction around the park is ongoing, with the ultimate aim of creating a large-scale and well-planned residential and business zone, focused around the existing park and its huge riverside gardens. The area contains two of Lisbon's largest concert venues and a multitude of shops, cafés and restaurants. It is served by excellent public transport links via Santiago Calatrava's stunning Estação do Oriente rail, metro and bus station.

MORE TO SEE

BIL

Parque das Nações, 1800 Lisboa 218 922 521/2 Mon–Thu noon–2am, Fri noon–4am, Sat 11am–4am, Sun 11am–2am Varies

A vast bowling alley with 30 AMF lanes and other state-of-the-art facilities, such as arcade games and amusements.

MICOLÂNDIA

Parque das Nações, 1800 Lisboa 218 940 277 Oct–end Apr Tue–Fri 2.30–7.30, Sat–Sun 10–8 €2 for 30min, each additional 15 min €1

A children's play area with inflatable bouncy castles, slides, mazes, tunnels and plastic ball pools.

One of the light, airy galleries of the modern art museum

Features in the gardens of the Palácio dos Marquêses de Fronteira are adorned with ornately decorated tiles

MUSEU DO CENTRO DE ARTE MODERNA

126 B1 • Rua Dr. Nicolau de Bettencourt 217 823 474 Mon–Fri 10–6, Sat–Sun 11–7 Adult €5, child (7–17) €2.50, under-6s free, family ticket (2 adults and 2 children) €11 Praça de Espanha 16, 26
www.pavconhecimento.pt

Lisbon's modern art complex is part of the Fundação Calouste Gulbenkian (▷ 138–141). You can walk through the grounds from the Gulbenkian Museum to reach it, taking in the outdoor sculpture collection, including works by Henry Moore, along the way. The light and airy modernist building is the perfect setting for the 20th-century art by Portuguese artists, including works by José de Almada Negreiros (1873–1970); look out for his *Self-Portrait* (1925), showing him and friends in the Café A Brasileira in Lisbon. Other artists to look out for are the Futurists Amadeu de Sousa Cardosa and Guilherne Santa-Rita, and Paula Regeo, a contemporary painter now living in England.

PALÁCIO DOS MARQUÊSES DE FRONTEIRA

127 E1 • Largo de São Domingo de Benfica 217 782 023 Palace: guided tours only. Oct–end May 11, noon; Jun–end Sep 10.30, 11, 11.30, noon. Gardens: Tue 2–6, Wed–Sun 10–6 Palace and gardens: €5. Gardens: €2.50 Sete Rios 46, 72

This small, pink country house was originally built in the 1670s, more than130 years after St. Francis Xavier supposedly said Mass in the chapel before his voyage to India. The palace was damaged in the 1755 earthquake, so what you see today dates from the late 18th century. It's particularly noted for its *azulejos* (tiles), which decorate both the interior of the house and the gardens. The big attraction inside is the Sala das Batalhas, where tiled panels illustrate battles against the Spanish during the 1640–1668 Wars of Restoration. Other blue-and-white tiles were imported in the early 17th century from Delft in the Netherlands. Outside, the gardens are laid out in the Italian Renaissance style, with parterres, topiary and fountains, while Portuguese *azulejo* panels adorn the walls, terraces, fountains and benches.

PARQUE EDUARDO VII AND THE ESTUFAS

126 B1 • Praça Marquês de Pombal 1070-099 Lisboa 213 882 278 Estufas: Oct–end Apr daily 9–5; May–end Sep daily 9–6 €2 Marquês de Pombal 1, 11, 12, 20, 36, 44, 49, 53

There's no better place to spend a couple of tranquil hours than in Lisbon's main park, the Parque Eduardo VII, which lies at the northern end of the monumental Avenida da Liberdade. It opened in 1903, the year Edward VII of England visited Portugal to reconfirm the Anglo-Portuguese alliance (in existence since 1382), and was named in his memory. The layout is formal in the extreme, revolving around two broad mosaic-paved walkways, intersected by minor paths and lined with neatly trimmed hedges. The big neo-baroque building by the eastern entrance is the Pavilhão Carlos Lopes, a sports pavilion re-named in memory of Portugal's marathon champion. Walk north from here for some great city views and to explore the *estufas* (greenhouses). Three interconnect, the *estufa fria* (coldhouse), the *estufa quente* (hothouse) and the *estufa doce* (containing plants that thrive in arid conditions). Opened in 1930, they are crammed with flowers, shrubs and trees, planted around running water, ponds and fountains.

PARQUE DAS NAÇÕES

See pages 142–145.

RIBEIRA MARKET

126 C5 • Avenida 24 de Julho, Cais de Sodré, 1200-479 Lisboa Mon–Sat 5am–2pm Cais de Sodré

You will get a real taste of Lisbon life around the Ribeira market and Cais de Sodré—everyone from commuting professionals to schoolkids and sailors shops here. Cais de Sodré is one of the main transport hubs, jam-packed in the rush hour with commuters. From here you can take a train to Estoril and Cascais, get the metro or take a ferry across the Tejo.

The station is across the road from the Ribeira market, Lisbon's main food market, a two-floor building filled with stands selling gleaming fresh fish, exotic fruits and vegetables. The best range of goods is on show in the late morning when the food market is still in full swing and the flower sellers are setting up. There is a cultural venue on the upper floor, with an exhibition and performance area and a good range of cheeses, wines and local dishes to sample.

West of the market, much of the waterfront has been redeveloped, and the trendy bars and restaurants are popular with joggers and skateboarders. A couple of blocks away, you will find the Bica, with its smart eateries and-food stores. Take the Elevador da Bica from the Rua de São Paolo in Santos to Calçada do Combro in the Bairro Alto before strolling to Miradouro da Santa Catarina, a popular meeting place, with wonderful views across the river.

AROUND LISBON

Superb coastal scenery lies on either side of the Tejo estuary, with headlands poised above wild seas, and summer beach pleasures at the resorts of trendy Cascais and elegant Estoril. Inland rise the Sintra hills, home to cool shade, gardens and royal palaces. There are more regal delights at Mafra and Queluz, while south of the river, Sesimbra and the Costa da Caparica draw the weekend crowds.

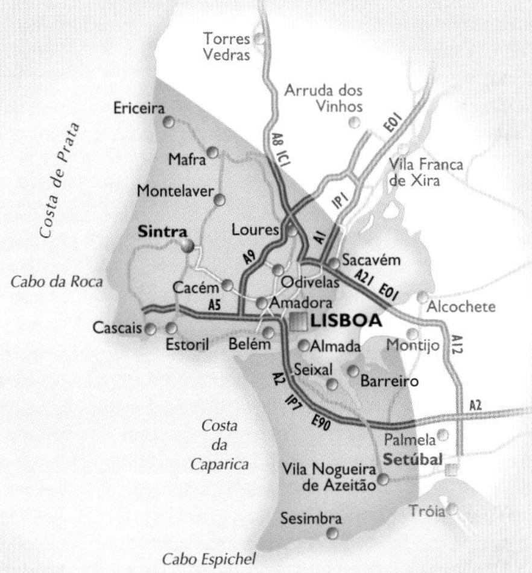

MAJOR SIGHT

THE SIGHTS

The lighthouse at Cabo Espichel, on its windy headland

Charming Cascais is a busy fishing port and tourist resort

The Costa da Caparica has many uncrowded beaches

CABO ESPICHEL

344 A10 Avenida dos Náufragos, Sesimbra, tel 212 288 540
www.costa-azul.rts.pt

A lonely road runs through tiny villages and increasingly windswept and barren country to Cabo Espichel, where a lighthouse looms high above the pounding sea. To the right stands a grand baroque church fronted by a large square, down either side of which run lines of shabby 18th-century pilgrim lodgings.

The church is dedicated to Nossa Senhora do Cabo (Our Lady of the Cape), the patron saint of local fishermen. In its gloomy interior, candlelight flickers off the gilded surround of the image of Ave Maris Stella (Our Lady Star of the Sea). Large crowds gather here for the feast of Nossa Senhora do Cabo on the third Sunday in September, when fishermen pray for safety and good catches in the year ahead. This remote cape was also one of the locations in Wim Wenders' film *A Lisbon Story*.

CABO DA ROCA

344 A9 Cabo da Roca, Azoia, Colares 2705-001, tel 219 280 081
Sintra or Cascais, then bus 403
www.estorilcoast-tourism.com

The headland of Cabo da Roca lies at the end of the Serra de Sintra, where the hills flatten out to meet the sea. Wild and rugged, with spectacular views up and down the coast, it's the westernmost point of continental Europe. There's little to see apart from the lighthouse and a monument inscribed with words by Luís de Camões, Portugal's national poet. The tourist office will sell you a certificate to prove you have stood this far west, but time is better spent admiring the views up and down the coast. Unspoilt beaches lie north and south: Praia Grande to the north and Guincho, popular with surfers, to the south. Further north is the picturesque village of Azenhas do Mar, its rows of cottages seemingly tumbling down the cliffs to the seawater swimming pool below the cliffs.

CASCAIS

344 A9 Avenida Combatentes da Grande Guerra, 2750 Cascais, tel 214 868 204 Cascais
www.estorilcoast-tourism.com

Cascais, popular with Portuguese, expatriates, and foreign visitors, is both a holiday resort and a busy fishing village. Fishermen's boats are still drawn up on the sand of one of the beaches and early risers will see the boats chug out at dawn. The massive bulk of the Cidadela fortress, built in the 16th century to protect the bay and the Lisbon approaches, dominates the waterfront, behind which lie the narrow streets of the old town. The streets form an attractive flower-hung maze, lined with chic shops, bars and restaurants. The main area to head for in the evenings lies in the newer quarter on and around the pedestrianized Rua Federico Arouca to the east.

Cascais is well endowed with parks and gardens—the attractive Parque Municipal de Gandarinha contains the mansion of the counts of Guimarães, now a museum with an eclectic, mainly 19th-century collection (Tue–Sun 10–5, €1.50). Across the park is the Museu do Mar (Tue–Sun 10–5, €1.50), which is crammed with sea-related exhibits, such as model boats, old fishing lines and nets, mariners' clothes and equipment. The town has three beaches and a swanky yacht marina, but bathing is not recommended, so, if you want to swim, take the miniature train (daily every 45 minutes 11.15–1.30, 3–4.30, free) that chugs west to the Boca do Inferno. Be prepared for big summer crowds in Cascais, particularly at the weekends, when it's packed with visitors from Lisbon.

COSTA DA CAPARICA

344 A10 Avenida da Liberdade 18, Caparica, tel 212 900 071
www.costa-azul.rts.pt

If you're looking for a typical Portuguese beach area, head for the Costa da Caparica, the largely unspoilt stretch of coastline running south from the estuary of the Tejo. It's easily reached from Lisbon by car, by bus from Praça de Espenha in central Lisbon, or by taking the ferry from Lisbon to Cacilhas, from where there are regular bus connections to Caparica itself.

Vast beaches stretch down the coastline from this lively resort. They are linked by a miniature railway running through the dunes, which stops 18 times between Caparica and Fonte da Telha to the south. The railway provides easy access to the beach, which grows increasingly wilder and more deserted the farther south you head, but you will find wooden beach bars and restaurants at every stop.

Each section has its own character, with families tending to stick to the northernmost areas, the well-heeled young heading for the stretch between Praia da Riviera and Praia do Rei, and the southernmost beaches being reserved for nudists. The sea is clean, but remember that undertows can be dangerous, particularly for small children, so take extra care if you plan to swim. To catch a glimpse of the unspoilt beauty of this coastline, take the train at least as far as Praia da Mata (stop 8), the first point with little building except for the occasional beach bar.

The casino at Estoril, once the haunt of spies and exiled royalty

A shady passage leading from Mafra's palace to the monastery

Sesimbra's well-preserved castle dates from Moorish times

ESTORIL

344 A9 Arcadas do Parque, 2769 Estoril, tel 214 663 813 Estoril
www.estorilcoast-tourism.com

Classy Estoril gained its reputation in the post-World War II years, when it was a bolt-hole for rich expatriates and exiled royalty. It's still a smart resort, with plenty of grand hotels and exclusive villas within a stone's throw of its long sandy beach. This is backed by a promenade running west; you can stroll all the way to Cascais in an hour or so, pausing at one of the pleasant waterfront bars along the way. The town's main attractions are its golf course and the casino in the Parque do Estoril, beautifully planted with tropical trees and scattered with fountains.

MAFRA

344 A9 Avenida 25 de Abril, 2640 Mafra, tel 261 812 023
www.mafra.net

Gold from Brazil paid for João V's astonishing architectural legacy. Built between 1717 and 1755, the Palácio e Convento de Mafra (Wed–Mon 10–5.30, €3, Sun free) is modelled on Madrid's El Escorial. Its focus is the magnificent basilica, flanked on either side with wings containing the royal apartments and backed by monastic quarters. More than 50,000 builders were employed on site, constructing a building 220m (720ft) long and 68m (220ft) high, with 880 rooms, 4,700 doors and windows and 29 courtyards. The basilica's dome is one of the world's largest, and its posession of six organs unique, while its bell-towers contain 114 bells—free bell-ringing concerts are held every Sunday at 4. Palace tours take in the royal apartments, including the Hunting Trophy Room, where all the furniture is made of deer antlers and upholstered in deerskin; and the library, a rococo showpiece with elaborate stuccowork and a chequered marble floor. Mafra is also the venue for an autumn International Festival of Music, when baroque and contemporary concerts take place in the basilica and library.

PALÁCIO NACIONAL DE QUELUZ

344 A9 Largo do Palácio, 2745-191 Queluz 214 343 860 Palace: Wed–Mon 10–5 (last admission 4.30). Gardens: Jan–end Apr, Oct–end Dec Wed–Mon 10–5; May–end Sep Wed–Mon 10–6 Palace: €3, free Sun. Gardens: 50c Queluz-Belas Cozinha Velha, in palace's original kitchens; open for lunch and dinner
www.ippar.pt

This elegant, pink-washed palace started life as a hunting lodge until Dom Pedro III embarked on its rebuilding in 1747. This transformed the lodge into a palace, now considered the country's finest example of rococo architecture, with rambling 18th-century formal gardens to match. In 1760 Dom Pedro married his niece, the future Queen Maria I, and it was here she spent 27 declining years, driven increasingly mad by grief following the death of her son. More renovations followed her death and Queluz eventually became state property in 1908. Today, it's preserved as a museum portraying 18th-century aristocratic life, decorated with fine pieces from the former royal collections. The mirror-lined Throne Room, the elegant public rooms and the Ambassador's Chamber, where visiting diplomats and foreign dignitaries were received, trace the development of Portuguese taste from the rococo to the neoclassical. Don't miss the gardens, where the pools, fountains, terraces and parterres form the perfect background to the palace itself.

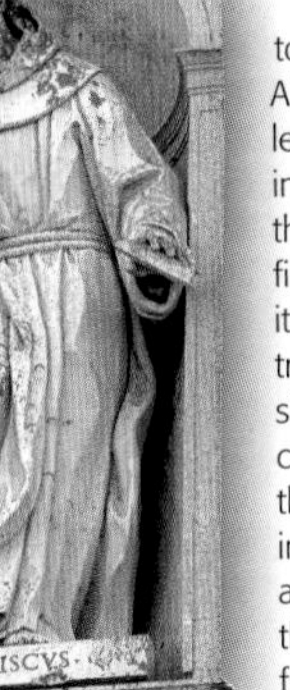

A statue of St. Francis in Mafra's magnificent Palácio e Convento

SESIMBRA

344 A10 Avenida dos Náufragos, Sesimbra, tel 212 288 540
www.costa-azul.rts.pt

Encircled by sheltering cliffs, Sesimbra is a beguiling resort. Historically, it was the site of a Moorish settlement, and you can still visit the Moorish castle (Sun–Thu 7–7, Fri–Sat 7–8, free) high on a hill behind the town. Around the narrow streets and *praça* (square) of the old town, apartment blocks and hotels spread across the hillside, while the palm-lined promenade is thronged with visitors enjoying fresh fish at the café-restaurants.

Follow the signs to the Porto do Abrigo and you leave the holiday industry behind—this is a serious fishing port with its ocean-going trawlers. Both sides of town come together in the early morning, when beach and streets are thronged with fishermen maintaining their nets.

Sintra

The summer residence of the kings of Portugal and of the Moors before them, Sintra, set in the wooded mountains with wonderful views out to sea, is a World Heritage Site with outstanding palaces, gardens and museums.

The imposing exterior of the Palácio Nacional de Sintra

The architecture shows a mastery of elaborate details

Balustrades and domed turrets (right) add to the Moorish feel

RATINGS	
Good for kids	●●●●●
Historic interest	●●●●●
Outdoor pursuits	●●●●●
Photo stops	●●●●●

BASICS

344 A9

Praça da Republica 23, 2710-616 Sintra, tel 219 233 919

Oct–end May daily 9–7; Jun–end Sep daily 9–8

Sintra

Illustrated leaflets available for both palaces in Portuguese, English, French, German, Spanish, Italian and Japanese, €1. General guidebooks available at souvenir shops in Portuguese, English, French, Spanish and German, prices vary

www.cm-sintra.pt
An excellent section for visitors in Portuguese, English or German. It covers every aspect of tourism in and around Sintra, including suggested itineraries, practical information and hotel and restaurant listings

SEEING SINTRA

Sintra is made up of three separate villages, spread out over lush, wooded hills and along valleys. This makes driving the best way to explore all the sights quickly, though a half-hourly tourist bus links all the main attractions. Trains from Lisbon arrive in Estefânia. Sintra-Vila, where you will find the Palácio Nacional de Sintra and the Quinta da Regaleira, is a short walk uphill, while the third village, São Pedro de Sintra, is 20 minutes on from there. The Palácio Nacional de Pena is on top of a hill some distance away from Sintra-Vila. Visiting the gardens of Monserrate and the Convento dos Capuchos means taking a taxi, unless you prefer a 9km (5.5-mile) hike through the hills.

Sintra also has excellent sports facilities, with golf, tennis, horse-riding and swimming in the area (the sea is within easy reach). Its arts scene is lively—the International Music Festival (June–July) is one of Portugal's most prestigious, and a two-month-long ballet festival is held here in August and September. São Pedro de Sintra is a good place for antiques and boutique shopping and holds an excellent market every second Sunday.

HIGHLIGHTS

PALÁCIO NACIONAL DE PENA

2710-609 Sintra 219 105 340 Tue–Sun 10–5.30 €6; 40 per cent reduction with Lisboa Card Sintra then Scotturb bus 434

www.ippar.pt

There's been a building on the site of the Palácio Nacional de Pena, high above Sintra-Vila, since the 14th century. It was originally a chapel with an adjoining late-Gothic cloister, which fell into disrepair after it was damaged in the 1755 earthquake. In 1836, Queen Maria II married Prince Ferdinand of Saxe-Coburg-Gotha, an enthusiastic Romantic. He commissioned the German architect von Eschwege to design today's extraordinary palace, which fortunately has been preserved despite the overthrow of the monarchy in 1910.

What you'll see is a fantasy of neo-Gothic, an over-the-top combination of Manueline decoration, Germanic embellishments and Moorish features. There are turrets, cupolas, domes and battlements every-

TIPS

- Use the 434 bus to get around; a hop-on-hop-off Sintra ticket costs €3, while a day rover includes all Scotturb bus routes and costs €6.50. Use it to go on to Cascais via Cabo da Roca, returning to Lisbon on the Cascais line.
- If you take a taxi to Monserrate or Capuchos check the price first with the driver as meters aren't always used; the price should be approximately €10. Taxis wait outside the station and in the Praça de República in Sintra-Vila.
- Book ahead if you want to stay in Sintra.

where, and the interior is no less bizarre, a celebration of late-Victorian taste where every surface is lavishly decorated. It's been described as 'a textbook of 19th-century decorative arts and the Belle Époque in transition to the 20th century', and bears more than a passing resemblance to the fantasies of Ludwig II, the 'mad king' of Bavaria, who was responsible for the castle at Neuschwanstein. Highlights include some remarkable stuccowork, splendid bathrooms and kitchens, and some mildly erotic unfinished paintings by Carlos I, the last king of Portugal. Don't miss the wooded garden below the palace, an oasis of verdant shade and soothing water.

PALÁCIO NACIONAL DE SINTRA

Largo Rainha Dona Amália, 2710-616 Sintra 219 106 840 Mon–Tue, Thu–Sat 10–5.30, Sun 10–2 €3; free with Lisboa Card Sintra
www.ippar.pt

A pair of extraordinary conical chimneys surrounded by a riot of decorative architecture dominates the heart of Sintra-Vila. This is the Palácio Nacional de Sintra, a summer pleasure palace built largely during the late 14th and 15th centuries by Dom João and his successor, Dom Manuel. Stylistically, it's a happy blend of Gothic and Manueline styles with plenty of Moorish touches, and wouldn't seem out of place in a theme park.

There's a set route through the palace, taking in all the main rooms, with tantalizing glimpses of hidden courtyards and superb views over the surrounding landscape. Pause first in the Hall of Swans, the magnificently tiled hall whose ceiling is decorated with painted swans, adorned with golden necklaces. During João I's reign it was the main reception chamber and is the largest room in the palace. It overlooks a central patio, with a stucco-embellished grotto, which once acted as a cooling fountain.

A view of Sintra-Vila, the great palace prominent, taken from higher up the hill. Building started here in the 14th century

Steps lead up from here to the Hall of Magpies, a private antechamber. Here both frieze and ceiling are painted with a flock of jaunty magpies, each holding in its beak the legend *'Por bem'* ('For the best'). It was reputedly painted on the orders of Dom João to put a

GUIDE TO PÁLACIO NACIONAL DE SINTRA

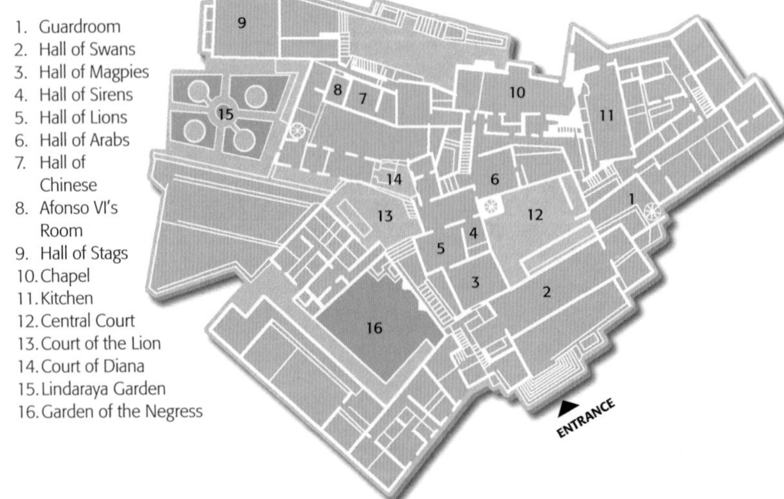

stop to the gossiping of the court ladies—Philippa of Lancaster, João's wife, had found out from this about the king's affair with one of her ladies-in-waiting.

From here a succession of smaller rooms and corridors leads to the stupendous Hall of Stags, lined with blue *azulejos* (tiles), its coffered ceiling displaying the armorial bearings of 72 noble families. The views towards the sea are fabulous—it is said that the kings could watch their fleets setting out to Africa, Brazil and India from here.

The so-called Initiation Well in the fascinating gardens of Quinta da Regaleira

QUINTA DA REGALEIRA

✉ Rua Barcosa du Bocage, 2710-567 Sintra ☎ 219 106 650 ⌚ Daily 10–5.30; guided visits (book in advance) 11, 12.30, 2.30, 4 ✋ Unaccompanied €5; guided visits (must be pre-arranged) €10 🚉 Sintra

The Quinta da Regaleira, a short walk from Sintra-Vila's main square, is an elaborate private estate that achieved World Heritage status in 1995. It's a fine example of turn-of-the-20th-century revivalist neo-Manueline architecture, built by the wealthy landowner António Carvalho Monteiro (1850–1920) and designed by the Italian architect Luigi Mannini (1848–1936), who was also responsible for Buçaco (▷ 96). The extraordinary main house, all towers and ornate stonework, has some elaborate rooms—look out for the rococo wooden ceilings and incredibly detailed mosaic floors, showing hunting scenes and still lives of dead game.

It's the gardens that steal the show, a maze of paths on a steep hillside planted with camellias, hydrangeas and tree ferns, and dotted with lakes, fountains, terraces and statuary. They are full of Masonic themes and imagery, the highlight being the Initiation Well, inspired by the Freemasons and Knights Templar, which is approached through a revolving stone door. Well-trodden, moss-covered steps lead to the foot of the well and through an eerie tunnel.

BACKGROUND

The Romans used Sintra as a defensive post, but it was the Moors that fell in love with this green, well-watered spot, building a palace here before the 10th century. It fell to the Christians in 1147, and Sintra palace became the property of the kings of Portugal, a situation that remained unchanged until the monarchy was overthrown and the last king forced into exile in 1910. The kings used the palace both as a hunting base and as a refuge from Lisbon's summer heat, enlarging it and laying out attractive, cool gardens. Wealthy aristocrats followed in the royal footsteps, and by the 19th century the Sintra hills were dotted with vast mansions and huge villas, some of which are still privately owned.

MORE TO SEE

CASTELO DOS MOUROS

✉ Parque de Sintra, 2710 Sintra ☎ 219 237 300 ⌚ Oct–end May daily 10–7; Jun–end Sep daily 10–8 ✋ €3 🚉 Sintra

The ruins of the Moorish castle, which was captured by Afonso Henriques, lie between the two palaces. They consist of two defensive positions, each set on rocky crags, with a mosque between them. It is worth the steepish climb for the extraordinary views west to Cascais and Cabo da Roca, south across the Tejo and north as far as Peniche and the Berlenga Islands.

CONVENTO DOS CAPUCHOS

✉ Serra de Sintra, 2710 Sintra ☎ 219 237 300 ⌚ Daily 9.30–6; guided tours at 10, 11, 1.30, 2.30, 3.30, 4.30. Book ahead by phone ✋ €3.50 🚉 Sintra

An evocative hermitage around 9km (5.5 miles) from Sintra. The cells are cut from the rock and lined with cork from the surrounding woods. It is thought to have been the poorest convent in Portugal and was occupied from the mid-16th century to 1836.

MONSERRATE

✉ Est. de Monserrate, 2710-405 Sintra ☎ 219 232 863 ⌚ Oct–end May daily 9–7; Jun–end Sep daily 9–8 ✋ €3 🚉 Sintra

A vast garden just outside town planted with subtropical trees, shrubs and plants. It was home from 1793 to1799 to William Beckford, a rich homosexual who fled England to escape hanging. More planting was done under Sir Francis Cook, who built the folly-like mansion.

MUSEU DE ARTE MODERNA

✉ Avenida Heliodoro Salgado, 2710-575 Sintra ☎ 219 248 170 ⌚ Tue–Sun 10–6 ✋ €3, free on Thu 🚉 Sintra

A huge collection of modern art. Exhibits change every two months, but paintings by David Hockney, Roy Lichtenstein, Andy Warhol and Jackson Pollock are usually on show.

A statue in the Quinta da Regaleira gardens, which, like the house, were created at the start of the 20th century

THE ALENTEJO

The Alentejo sprawls across sparsely populated rural southern Portugal, where large areas of wheatlands and pasture are punctuated by cork oaks and olives. Impressive Évora is the main hub, a civilized town set off by the wild country to the east, also home to some superb settlements. Other historic towns include Beja, Mértola and Vila Viçosa, site of a royal palace, while, to the west, a string of resorts runs down the coast.

THE SIGHTS

MAJOR SIGHTS

Alcácer do Sal founded its fortunes on salt

Carpets have been woven at Arraiolos since the 17th century

Inside the chapterhouse of Beja's convent, now a museum

ALCÁCER DO SAL

344 B10 Rua da República, 7580 Alcácer do Sal, tel 265 622 565 www.costa-azul.rts.pt

Laid-back and slightly scruffy, Alcácer do Sal is at the head of the estuary of the River Sado, a vast wetland nature reserve. The town runs along the banks of the river and up the hill behind, looking towards the paddy fields and salt flats that have ensured local prosperity. The Moors built a castle here, high on a bluff above the river, which was temporarily taken in 1158 during Afonso Henrique's first big push south, finally becoming Christian in 1217. Since then, the town has quietly prospered, with salt, bulls and horses traditionally bringing in the money.

Stroll along the riverfront promenade, where you'll find local ladies ladling out freshly boiled shrimps—the town's delicacy—before heading into the medieval warren of narrow streets. Climb up to the castle, now a *pousada*, for a good view over the rooftops, their chimneys crowned with the nests of Alcácer's resident stork population. If you're interested in nature, it's worth heading into the Sado estuary to see more storks, herons, marsh harriers and flamingos—you can even view the lagoons from a hot-air balloon (details from the tourist office).

ARRAIOLOS

345 C9 Praça Lima Brito, 7040 Arraiolos, tel 266 499 105 www.cm-arraiolos.pt

If you want to visit a typical Alentejo town head for Arraiolos, perched on a hill above the rolling plain. Sparkling white houses, picked out with blue or yellow trim, line the cobbled streets leading up to the old walls that enclose the castle and its surrounding dwellings and church. You'll notice the large number of shops selling carpets—these have been manufactured here since the 17th century, when an industry was set up to make hemp-and-linen embroidered rugs, which were used as wall hangings and table and chest covers. The patterns originally followed Persian and Indian designs, using animal and plant motifs, but this intricacy gradually gave way to something simpler and more geometric, with yellow and blue the dominant shades. If they appeal, buy them here—prices are high, but you won't find them less expensive anywhere else.

The surrounding countryside has a desolate beauty, the huge wheat fields scattered with holm oak and cork, while other areas are dedicated to wine production. From Arraiolos, you can follow the circular wine route from village to village; pick up a leaflet at the tourist office.

AVIS

345 D9 Câmara Municipal, 7480 Avis, tel 242 412 024 www.rtsm.pt

After the long slog across the Alentejan plateau, with only cork and olive trees for interest, Avis comes as a welcome sight and a good place for a break. It's an old settlement, retaining traces of its ramparts and medieval towers—you'll get a good view of these as you approach on the N244. This road crosses the vast lake at the confluence of the Seda and Avis rivers, formed when a hydro-electric dam was built 15km (9 miles) downstream.

Backwater it may seem now, but Avis played a significant role in shaping Portuguese history. It was here, in the early 13th century, that the Order of Avis, the oldest order of chivalry in Europe, was founded by Afonso Henriques to fight the Moors. In 1385, the Grand Master of the Order, João, was proclaimed king, the first monarch of the House of Avis, which was to rule Portugal until 1580. João I was one of Portugal's great rulers; in 1387 he married Philippa of Lancaster, so strengthening the Anglo-Portuguese alliance further.

BEJA

346 D11 Rua Capitão João Francisco de Sousa 25, 7800 Beja, tel 284 311 837 Beja www.rt-planiciedourada.pt

Beja, the capital of the Baixa Alentejo, lies in the heart of this southern region and makes a good stopping-off point. First Roman, then Visigothic, Moorish and finally Christian, it's a prosperous agricultural town, neatly laid out on a rise in the plains. Its main sights all lie within the appealing old part of town.

Head first for the Convento de Nossa Senhora da Conceição in the Rua Conde de Boavista, now home to the Museu Regional (Tue–Sun 9.45–1, 2–5.30, €1, free on Sun). The convent's Manueline architectural flourishes attest to its 15th-century foundation, while the interior highlights include a cloister and chapterhouse totally covered with bright *azulejos* (tiles) and an over-the-top rococo chapel, complete with flying gilded cherubs. The exhibits are pushed to compete with this, but provide an insight into much of Beja's past.

From the convent, take a pleasant stroll through the heart of the town to the Castelo, whose tower has good views. The nearby Ingreja Santo Amaro, now an archaeological museum, is a rare reminder of Visigothic Portugal; parts of this basilica date back as far as the sixth century AD.

The Judiaria was the Jewish quarter of Castelo de Vide

Distinctive terracotta pottery from Flôr de Rosa

The Aqueduto da Amoreira, Elvas, was built in 1622

THE SIGHTS

CASTELO DE VIDE

345 E8 Posto de Turismo de Castelo de Vide, 7320 Castelo de Vide, tel 245 901 361
www.rtsm.pt

The hills of the Serra de São Mamede are where you will find a pair of picturesque hilltop villages, Marvão and Castelo de Vide. Castelo's streets huddle along the hillside from the spacious main square, an elegant expanse with a church and some fine 17th-century buildings. Walk behind the church and dive into the maze of narrow streets of the Judiaria, the old Jewish quarter. Winding, flower-hung alleys are lined with blindingly white houses, many retaining their Gothic doorways and windows. Streets are steep, climbing towards the castle—one leads past a fine granite Renaissance fountain to the 13th-century synagogue, the oldest surviving in Portugal. At the top, the castle squats firmly within the fortified walls of the original medieval settlement—head for the room with the Gothic cupola and cistern, from where there's a wonderful view of the village below.

CRATO

345 D8 Flôr da Rosa, 7430 Crato, tel 245 997 341
www.rtsm.pt

Crato is an ancient agricultural town on the plateau to the west of Portalegre (▷ 162–163). It was a textile boom town in the 16th century and its surviving monuments date mainly from that time. There are three fine churches and a clutch of mansions, though the most interesting structure is the Varanda do Grão Prior in the main square, a type of loggia built for the outdoor celebration of Mass. Far older than all this was the castle, now an overgrown ruin but once the seat of a priory of the Knights Hospitallers of St. John of Jerusalem, a military religious order that was to evolve into the Knights of Malta.

The village of Flôr de Rosa is only 2km (1 mile) away. The highlight here is the beautifully restored *mosteiro* once owned by the Knights—it's now a *pousada*. The village manufactures its own distinctive pottery—if you're tempted to buy a *caçoila*, a round cooking pot, bear in mind that they are fragile and will need to be packed carefully.

CROMELEQUE DO ALMENDRES

345 C10 Details on the sites from the Évora Tourist Information Office, Praça do Giraldo 73, 7004 Évora, tel 266 702 671

West of Évora (▷ 158–161) is an area rich in megalithic monuments—cromlechs, dolmens and caves, all dating from between 4000 and 2000BC. Almendres is easy to visit—take the N114 towards Montemor-o-Novo and after 10km (6 miles) bear left to the village of Guadalupe and follow the signs. You will find a 2.5-m-high (8ft) menhir near the village, while the impressive stone circle, composed of 95 granite monoliths, is farther along the rough road. It stands in a clearing among the cork oaks, a 60m by 30m (197ft by 98ft) oval that's best explored on foot

Nobody really knows the significance of these stone circles, though it is thought that they probably had a religious or astronomical purpose. All were erected between 4000 and 2000BC but the remains are hard to date with any more accuracy. It's a lovely area, rich in bird life—look out for hoopoes in spring and early summer. If the weather's wet, leave the car as the road can be very muddy.

ELVAS

345 E9 Praça da República, 7350 Elvas, tel 268 622 236 Elvas
www.rtsm.pt

If you visit only one of the Alentejan fortified towns, it should be Elvas, one of Portugal's mightiest frontier posts, whose star-shaped walls and forts make it one of Europe's most complex military fortifications. It has been a stronghold since time immemorial, though little remains of its earliest walls. Wrested from the Moors in 1230, its later history was shaped by incessant friction with Spain that culminated in a massive 17th-century defensive building scheme under the French military architect Vauban. This incorporated the existing defences into the complex system of forts, walls and bastions that still surrounds the town.

Begin exploring in the Praça da República, dominated by the stylistically eclectic church of Nossa Senhora da Assunção (Wed–Mon 9.30–12.30, 2.30–7), the town's cathedral until 1882 when the bishopric moved. It was designed by Arruda, who was also responsible for the town's Aqueduto da Amoreira. Up the hill is the Nossa Senhora da Consolação (Wed–Mon 9.30–12.30, 2.30–7), an octagonal church of immense interior beauty, modelled on a Knights Templar design. Inside, its walls and eight-sided ceiling are covered with yellow-and-blue 17th-century *azulejos* (tiles), and there's a superb pulpit, fronted by a graceful iron balustrade. Outside in the Largo de Santa Clara stands the town's pillory, still topped by metal shackles. Walk farther up the hill to explore the Castelo (daily 9–5), built by the Moors on a Roman site—there are superb views towards Spain from the terrace.

Market Saturday is always busy at historic Estremoz

Marvão's 13th-century castle was built to guard the frontier. Its waterless remoteness meant it was hard to keep garrisoned

ESTREMOZ

345 D9 Praça da República 26, 7100 Estremoz, tel 268 333 541
www.cm-estremoz.pt

Estremoz stands at the heart of a marble-quarrying area, a pleasing city whose Saturday market is one of Portugal's biggest and liveliest. If you catch it, it's a great place to buy the bright local pottery, made here since the 16th century and sometimes decorated with marble chips.

The town is neatly divided into two, the lower quarter focused around the huge marketplace, the Rossio, lined with cafés and the marble-faced former Câmara Municipal. It's also where you will find the Museu Rural (Mon–Sat 10–12.30, 2–5.30, €1), a good place to see the full range of local pottery, as well as displays of Alentejan tools, textiles and objects. There are more local exhibits at the Museu de Alfaia Agrícola in the Rua Serpa Pinto (Mon–Fri 8.30–12.30, 2–4, Sat–Sun 2–5, €1).

You can walk from the Rossio up the hill to the Vila Velha (Old Town), once one of Portugal's major fortified citadels and a splendid contrast to the 'new' town below. Bulky walls surround the nucleus of this historic heart, whose focus is a harmonious open square around which stand Gothic and Manueline buildings. Immediately eye-catching is the 13th-century Torre de Menagem, a beautiful building that's now one of Portugal's most famous *pousadas*. Go inside and climb the main tower for views of the town below and surrounding countryside beyond. Don't miss the Capela da Rainha Santa Isabel to the right behind the *pousada*, a beautiful chapel with *azulejos* (tiles) depicting stories from the life of the saintly queen. One tells the story of the Miracle of the Roses, when a skirtful of bread she was taking to the poor against her husband's wishes miraculously turned to roses when he demanded to see what she was carrying. Near here, the fine old almshouses are now the Museu Municipal (Oct–end Apr Tue–Sun 9–12.30, 2–5.30; May–end Sep Tue–Sun 9–12.30, 3–6.30, €1), with displays of historic pottery figures.

ÉVORA

See pages 158–161.

ÉVORAMONTE

345 D9 Rua de Santa Maria, Évoramonte, tel 268 959 227

If you are driving north from Évora on the E802, you will pass through rolling country, dotted with whitewashed villages and softened by stands of cork oaks and olive groves. Some 15km (9 miles) southwest of Estremoz is a castle surrounded by walls and battlemented towers. This is Évoramonte, a historic, fortified medieval town and castle on a steep 474m-high (1,558ft) hill. The Romans were the first to fortify the site and, as elsewhere, they were followed by the Moors, who were evicted by Afonso III. Dom Dinis ringed the hilltop with walls in the 1200s, but the castle gained its present appearance when João III reconstructed it after an earthquake in the 16th century. He built the solid rounded towers at the corners, and added the huge ropework course to the outer walls. The knots are Bragança dynasty symbols derived from a play on words on their motto *'Despois vós, nós'* ('After you, us'); *'nós'* can mean both 'us' and 'knots'. There's not much to see inside but, if the weather's clear, it's worth climbing the battlements, from where you are supposed to be able to see from one side of Portugal to the other.

Stone knots, a Bragança dynastic symbol

MARVÃO

345 E8 Posto de Turismo, 7300 Marvão, tel 245 993 886
www.cm-marvao.pt
www.rtsm.pt

Perched high on the eastern frontier, little Marvão is a compact fortified town with a superb castle and some of the finest panoramas over mountainous border country in the Alentejo. For the best views, stay the night and get up early to see dawn breaking over Spain.

Encircled Marvão was settled by the Romans, Visigoths and Moors, fell to the Christians in 1166 and got its castle under Dom Dinis in 1229. From then on it was a key border fort, but, isolated, windy and waterless, it was always difficult to keep manned. The garrison was often made up of exiled soldiers and malcontents, who chose service here rather than face prison. In the town, pop into the old church of Santa Maria, now the tourist office and a small museum, and look out for the Manueline doors and wrought-iron balconies that adorn many buildings. The castle has fortified gates, parapet walkways, crenellated watchtowers and an underground cistern, which provided catchment water for the medieval garrison. It's a really great place for children to explore.

Évora

With its fascinating medieval core surrounded by walls, fine monuments and museums, the Alentejo's capital is a relaxed shopping town that rivals Portugal's biggest cities.

The Templo Romano at night (above left); a traditional store (middle); statues of the apostles decorating the cathedral doorway (right); houses built into Évora's aqueduct (facing)

RATINGS	
Cultural interest	●●●●
Historic interest	●●●●
Specialist shopping	●●●●●
Walkability	●●●●●

TIPS

- Do not drive into the middle of Évora outside the winter; instead, use one of the numerous well-signposted parking areas outside the walls of the old city.
- Évora has a particularly lively *passeio* (early evening promenade), when it seems as if the whole city is out on the streets. See this at its best in and around the Praça do Giraldo.

BASICS

345 D10 Praça do Giraldo 73, 7004 Évora, tel 266 702 671
Oct–end Apr daily 9–12.30, 2–5.30; May–end Sep Mon–Fri 9–7, Sat–Sun 9–12.30, 2–5.30
Évora

www.cm-évora.pt
Portuguese-only site run by the city council

SEEING ÉVORA

Aim to spend a night in Évora to give yourself enough time to explore the city properly and for the pleasure of enjoying it after dark, when many of the buildings are floodlit. If time is short, arrive early in the day and allow the whole morning to see the main sights, leaving after a late lunch.

Whatever your schedule, you'll probably have to leave your car outside the city walls, so start by walking up the hill to the Praça do Giraldo, the main square, where you can drop into the tourist office for local information. From here, head up one of the steepish streets to the top of the hill, where you'll find most of Évora's main sights—the *Sé* (cathedral), the Templo Romano and the museum. Spend time visiting these, then head back down the hill, perhaps stopping along the way for a drink in one of the outdoor cafés in the Giraldo.

South of here, and down the hill from the left-hand corner of the Praça do Giraldo, is the church of São Francisco and the extraordinary Capela dos Ossos. If you are shopping, the best streets are Rua da República, Rua dos Mercadores and Rua João de Deus. All three streets run off the Praça do Giraldo.

HIGHLIGHTS

TEMPLO ROMANO

161 B2

For a chronological tour, start at the Templo Romano, just west of the Sé on top of the hill. This architectural fragment is the best-preserved Roman ruin in Portugal. The temple was probably built in the second or third centuries AD for worshipping Jupiter—though locals believe it was a temple to goddess Diana. What's left comprises 14 elegant columns raised on a high plinth, the carving of the marble Corinthian capitals being wonderfully preserved. Somewhat dwarfed by the surrounding monuments during the day, the Templo Romano comes into its own at night when floodlights bring a touch of drama to the ruins.

SÉ

161 B2 • Largo da Sé, 7004 Évora 266 759 330 Daily 9–12, 2–5 Free

The Sé is a fortress-like construction that, with its rounded arches, is typical of the Portuguese Romanesque style. Building started around

1185 on the site of the former mosque and continued into the 13th century. The result was a church that combines Romanesque and Gothic elements, as on the main façade where the plain and solid towers flank an intricate doorway, carved with figures of the Apostles by late 13th-century French and Portuguese sculptors.

Inside, Gothic features dominate in the high nave, with its barrel vaulting and beautiful transept dome, while there are Romanesque echoes in the clerestory arcade running high above the nave and behind the apse. Don't miss the rose windows—the north one shows the Morning Star and the south the Mystic Rose. Elsewhere in the cathedral, be sure to take in the Gothic cloister, built between 1322 and 1340, where the elegant tracery contrasts with the solid granite stonework. You will get a good view of the bell-tower, pure Romanesque, from the southwest corner and it's also worth visiting the terrace for views of the town.

An even better townscape opens up from the terrace over the main door, which you'll cross on your way to the Museu de Arte Sacra and the choir in the gallery. Pause to examine the choir stalls with their lively carvings of agricultural scenes before tackling the museum. This is crammed with rich textiles, vestments and a mass of ecclesiastical silver, jewellery and statues—look out for the mind-boggling solid gold rosary and the chalice studded with emeralds and diamonds.

The cathedral's façade, a mix of Romanesque and Gothic styles

CONVENTO DOS LOIOS

161 B2 • Largo do Conde de Vila Flor, 7004 Évora 266 704 714 Tue–Sun 10–12.30, 2–6 (sometimes closed without notice) €3

The Convento dos Loios, a church and monastery dedicated to St. John the Baptist, dates from 1585. It was owned by the dukes of Cadaval, and is now one of Portugal's most appealing *pousadas*, so, unless you're staying, it's off-limits. You can, however, visit the convent's church, rebuilt after the 1755 earthquake, whose nave is totally covered from floor to ceiling with *azulejos* (tiles) telling the story of St. Laurence Justinian, Patriarch of Venice. The nave contains some fine Renaissance tombs and you can peer through a floor grille to the ossuary containing the bones of the monks who lived and died here.

IGREJA DE SÃO FRANCISCO

161 B3 • Praça 1° de Maio, 7004 Évora 266 704 521 Daily 9–1, 2.30–6 Free

South of the Praça do Giraldo you will find Évora's other main attraction, the church of São Francisco and its gruesome adjunct, the Capela dos Ossos (Chapel of Bones). The Franciscan church was built in the early 16th century and is fronted by an unusual portico, whose diversely shaped arches—pointed, rounded and horseshoe—are crowned with battlements and pinnacles. The lofty building is typical of the Franciscan style; the order's churches were used for preaching, so there had to be room for the crowds who came to hear Mass from miles around.

CAPELA DOS OSSOS

161 B3 • Praça 1° de Maio, 7004 Évora 266 744 307 Daily 9–12.50, 2.30–5.50 €2

The chapterhouse of the Igreja de São Francisco gives access to the Capela dos Ossos, built between 1460 and 1510 for the bones of more than 5,000 monks, collected from various resting places across Évora, where they were taking up valuable space. Walls and columns are entirely covered with neatly arranged tibias, femurs, vertebrae and skulls, a macabre design highlighted by the welcoming inscription over the door, which reads *'Nós ossos, que aqui estamos, Pelos vossos esperamos'* ('We bones here are waiting for your bones'). There's a certain grimness,

Two evocative Évora figurines perched on a high pinnacle

MORE TO SEE

ANTIGA UNIVERSIDADE

161 C2 • Rua Duques de Cadaval, 7004 Évora 266 740 800 Mon–Fri 8–9, Sat 10–2, 3–6, Sun 10–2, 3–6 €1.50, free Sat am

University buildings with a lovely inner courtyard and a fine 16th-century cloister with an attractively arched gallery.

AQUEDUTO DO AGUA PRATA

161 A1 • 7004 Évora

A magnificent medieval aqueduct running into the city from the northwest—walk west from the Giraldo along Rua do Cano to traverse it and admire the houses that have been built in its arches.

LARGO DA PORTA DE MOURA

161 C2 • 7004 Évora

This is Évora's most picturesque square and is divided into two unequal-sized sections, the larger one containing a Renaissance fountain. The whole square is bordered by fine 16th-century houses with Manueline-Moorish arcades.

MOURARIA

161 B1 7004 Évora

The name was coined to define the old Moorish quarter to the north of the cathedral complex. It consists of picturesque cobbled alleys and tiny squares.

too, in the braids of hair hung about the entrance, left here by young women as good-luck offerings before they marry.

BACKGROUND

Évora was an important city in Roman times, when it was the political heart of Iberia. When Rome fell, the city declined, its fortunes reviving only during four centuries of Moorish occupation. It became an important agricultural and trading hub, a tangle of typically Moorish streets growing up around the old Roman core. By the mid-12th century, internal squabbles were weakening the Muslims, prompting Afonso Henriques to attack. In 1165 the town became the seat of the royal House of Avis and remained the capital of choice through to the 16th century. Scholars, writers, architects and artists flocked to the court, enriching Évora with churches, monuments and stately mansions. In 1559 Dom Henriques founded a prestigious Jesuit university, but this proved to be the final flowering of Évora's golden age as in 1580 Portugal was annexed by Spain.

Although the country regained its independence in 1640, later monarchs moved the court closer to Lisbon, the university closed, and Évora became a backwater. It was this obscurity that preserved Évora until the 20th century, when intensive restoration began, culminating in the city becoming a World Heritage Site in 1986. The university reopened in the 1970s, and Évora is once again a successful regional capital, a university city and an agricultural hub.

PRAÇA DO GIRALDO

161 B2 • Praça do Giraldo, 7004 Évora

This beautiful central square, with its arcaded shops, lies at the heart of the city. The fountain standing on the site of the Roman triumphal arch dates from the 18th century.

The interior of the macabre Capela dos Ossos

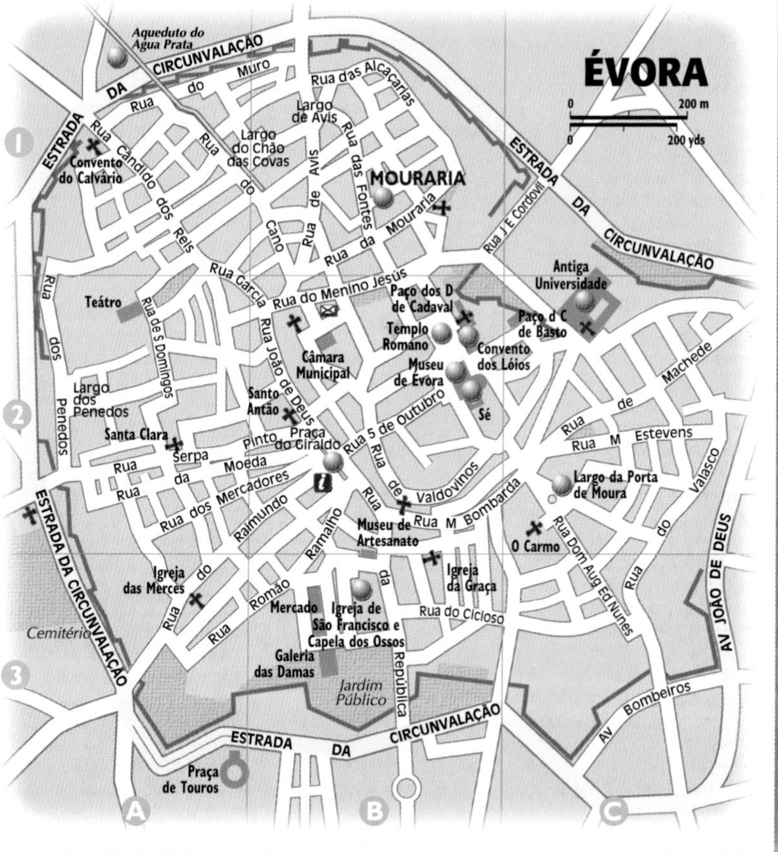

ÉVORA
0 200 m
0 200 yds
Aqueduto do Agua Prata
Estrada da Circunvalação
Rua do Muro
Rua das Alcaçarias
Largo de Avis
Largo do Chão das Covas
Convento do Calvário
Rua Cândido dos Reis
Rua do Cano
Rua de Avis
Rua das Fontes
MOURARIA
Rua da Mouraria
Rua J E Cordovil
Antiga Universidade
Rua dos Penedos
Teátro
Rua de S Domingos
Rua Garcia
Rua do Menino Jesús
Paço dos D de Cadaval
Templo Romano
Convento dos Lóios
Paço d C de Basto
Câmara Municipal
Rua João de Deus
Museu de Évora
Sé
Rua de Machede
Largo dos Penedos
Santo Antão
Santa Clara
Serpa Pinto
Praça do Giraldo
Rua 5 de Outubro
Rua M Estevens
Rua da Moeda
Rua dos Mercadores
Rua de Valdovinos
Largo da Porta de Moura
Rua do Valasco
Rua do Raimundo
Rua do Ramalho
Museu de Artesanato
Rua M Bombarda
O Carmo
Rua Dom Aug Ed Nunes
Igreja das Merces
Rua do Romão
Igreja da Graça
Rua do Cicloso
Av João de Deus
Mercado
Igreja de São Francisco e Capela dos Ossos
Cemitério
Galeria das Damas
Jardim Público
Rua da República
Av Bombeiros
Praça de Touros

Inside the Igreja Matriz, Mértola, which was once a mosque

A winding cobbled street in the tiny hilltop village of Monsaraz

The castle at Palmela now houses an elegant *pousada*

MÉRTOLA

347 D12 Largo Vasco da Gama, 7750 Mértola, tel 286 612 573
www.rt-planiciedourada.pt

Mértola stands at the confluence of the Guadiana and Oeiras rivers. Here, the river valley breaks the monotony of the plains, with the little white town rising on the slopes above. At the highest point stands the 12th-century castle—it's partly ruined but excavations around it are slowly revealing traces of a Roman and Moorish past. For more insight, visit the small Museu Arqueológico (Mon–Sat 9–12.30, 2–5.30, €2.50), which has a nicely presented collection of local finds. Also don't miss the Igreja Matriz, the parish church, which started life as a mosque. It's a wonderful building, virtually square, with a typically Moorish forest of columns supporting the central space. Behind the high altar you'll see the *mihrab*, the niche from where prayers to Allah were chanted.

MONSARAZ

345 E10 Largo Dom Nuno Álvares, Monsaraz, tel 266 557 136

The Alentejo is scattered with villages and it's hard to choose which to visit. Don't miss Marvão (▷ 157) or Monsaraz though. Monsaraz has a superb hilltop settlement with a castle encircled by walls. With just four streets, all cobbled, there's not much to see, but it's a great place to wander. Walk up the Rua Direita to see the best of the village houses, many dating from the 16th and 17th centuries and adorned with the exterior staircases and wrought-iron balconies typical of the area. On the way you will pass the Igreja Matriz, with a 14th-century carved tomb, and the Antigo Tribunal, once the town's courthouse—on the left, with pointed arches over the doors and windows. At the end, the street widens into a square, with an 18th-century pillory.

The castle was built by Dom Dinis in the 14th century, some 200 years after Monsaraz was captured from the Moors and became a Knights Templar fortress. Part of the Templar fort has been turned into a bullring, but time is better spent admiring the incredible views of the surrounding landscape dotted with cork stands and olive groves.

MOURA

347 D11 Largo Santa Clara, 7860 Moura, tel 285 251 375
www.rt-planiciedourada.pt

Moura, surrounded by silvery-grey olive groves, is a pretty, low-key spa town, its clutch of mansions and monuments testifying to a wealthy past. It's named after a Moorish girl, who threw herself in despair from the castle after her lover was slain by Christian knights who went on to occupy the town. The Moors were here from the eighth century AD up to 1233, and the Mouraria quarter, all narrow streets and low houses decorated with tiles, is the oldest part of town.

More elegant is the spacious pedestrian main square, home to a fine Câmara Municipal, which stands facing the Gothic church of São João Baptista. As you enter the church through the lovely Manueline doorway you are met by twisted white marble columns and soaring vaulting, the simplicity lifted by the vivid tiles in the chapels to either side of the high altar.

Outside, to the right, is the entrance to the thermal baths, nestling in a pretty garden. You can still enjoy the waters, which are recommended for the treatment of rheumatism.

PALMELA

344 B10 Castelo de Palmela, 2950 Palmela, tel 212 332 122
www.costa-azul.rts.pt

In Portuguese minds the pretty town of Palmela is associated with one thing—wine. By the middle of the 18th century wine was being produced here on a large scale, and the town's September grape festival is the big date in the local calendar. The red and white wines from the area are noted for their distinctive taste and full body, the Periquita grape variety producing a deep red and the Fernão Pires a smooth white. *Adegas* (wine cellars) around the town run tours and tastings.

The town stands on a spur of the Arrábida hills, its huge castle dominating the horizon. After several attempts, it was finally taken from the Moors in 1196 and became a stronghold of the Knights of St. James, a military order involved in the reconquest. The castle is a mixture of styles and eras, dating from the 14th to 18th centuries, its main attraction being the *pousada* in the conventual buildings and the superb panoramic view from the top of the keep—worth every one of the 64 steps. Near the castle, too, is the church of São Tiago (St. James), its clean Romanesque and Gothic lines accentuated by the *azulejos* (tiles) on the walls. There are more tiles in the church of São Pedro below.

PORTALEGRE

345 E8 Palácio Póvoas, Rossio, 7300 Portalegre, tel 245 331 359
Portalegre
www.cm-portalegre.pt
www.rtsm.pt

Capital of the Alto Alentejo, Portalegre crouches in the shadow of the Serra de São Mamede. It's an attractive town,

Elegant Portalegre is still attractive despite modern traffic

Quinta da Bacalhoa's gardens owe much to Italy and India

Serpa's little church shows unmistakable Moorish influence

whose mansions, the legacy of its 17th- and 18th-century industrial heyday, give the historic heart of the place an air of faded elegance that has survived even the incursions of modern traffic.

Portalegre built its wealth on textiles, concentrating on intricate tapestry and fine silk, and the surviving Fábrica Real de Tapeçarias still takes tapestry commissions from all over Europe, knotting more than 5,000 shades of wool 250,000 times for each square metre. You can see some of the historic products in the Museu do Guy Fino in the Rua da

A fine modern tapestry from Portalegre

Figueira (daily 9.30–12.30, 2.30–6, €2). To see what the fruits of 17th-century industry built, walk up the Rua 19 de Junho, a narrow and now sadly traffic-clogged street that's lined with splendid mansions. This leads to the Largo da Sé and the 16th- to 18th-century cathedral.

The square is overlooked by the former seminary. This now houses the Museu Municipal (Wed–Mon 10–12.30, 2–6, €1.50), an eclectic collection of religious art, ivories, ceramics and some examples of early carpets from Arraiolos (▷ 155).

QUINTA DA BACALHOA

344 B10 Quinta da Bacalhoa, Vila Nogueira, tel 212 180 011
Tue–Sat 9–5
www..azeitao.net

For a contrast to the wild beauty of the Serra de Arrábida, make a point of stopping at the Quinta da Bacalhoa, a villa with a classic Renaissance garden and wine estate on the Setúbal road. It was built in the 1550s by the son of Afonso de Albuquerque, a viceroy of India and great seaman. Afonso the younger visited Italy, where he saw the great gardens laid out by the ducal families and absorbed stylistic ideas that he was to blend with Indian and Moorish inspiration at Bacalhoa. From the villa's loggias and balconies a series of geometric parterres opens up, delineated and planted with box hedging and dotted with fountains and topiary. One of the most important design elements is the reflecting pool, an idea borrowed from India. There is no floral planting, but additional shades are supplied by the *azulejos* (tiles) in the loggias, patios and buildings.

SANTIAGO DO CACÉM

346 B11 Praça do Mercado, 7560 Santiago do Cacém, tel 269 826 696
www.costa-azul.rts.pt

Heading south through the Alentejo from Lisbon, Santiago do Cacém makes a good stop. It's a pleasant town with a highly impressive Moorish castle, a laid-back atmosphere and easy access to one of Portugal's most compelling Roman sites. Begin by heading up to the castle, rebuilt by the Knights Templar and encircled with battlements—there are superb views of the sea from here. Wander round the old lower town and visit the Museu Municipal in the Praça de Municipio (Tue–Fri 10–12, 2–5, Sat–Sun 2.30–5, free), an excellent regional museum housed in what was once one of the Salazar regime's most notorious prisons. One of the cells has been chillingly preserved, but more appealing are the mock-ups of Alentejan interiors—there's a great country kitchen complete with copper pans.

From here head out to Miróbriga, the ruins of a Roman town that thrived between the first and fourth centuries AD. It's a romantic grassy site, where you can follow what was a Roman road from the Temple of Jupiter and the Forum, at the highest point, to the baths, where the heating systems and the water channels are still visible.

SERPA

347 D11 Largo Dom Jorge de Melo, 7830 Serpa, tel 284 544 727
www.rt-planiciedourada.pt

Serpa, overlooking a classic Alentejan landscape of vast rolling wheatfields dotted with cork oaks and planted with olives and vines, has all the classic ingredients of a plains' market town—a walled heart around a castle and narrow streets. It's a good stop if you are heading south to the Algarve.

To see the best of Serpa, walk through the fortified gate in the ramparts into the middle of town, where you will find the main square and parish church. Turn down to the right to reach the mainly Moorish castle—climb up to the sentry path for splendid views. You can learn more about Serpa's past in the Museu Etnográfico in the Largo do Corro (Tue–Sun 9–12.30, 2–5.30, free), where agricultural and domestic implements, costumes and craft exhibits illustrate aspects of the local story.

Looking down on Portinho da Arrábida from the serra above

Vila Nova de Milfontes clusters round the Mira's sandy estuary. The town is the Alentejo's liveliest tourist resort

THE SIGHTS

SERRA DA ARRÁBIDA

344 B10 Praça da República, 2901 Setúbal, tel 265 534 402
www.costa-azul.rts.pt

The Serra de Arrábida is a range of mountainous hills, stretching some 35km (21 miles) along the coast from Sesimbra (▷ 149) to Setúbal. It's a beautiful area, its landscape and vegetation more Mediterranean than Atlantic, with scented undergrowth, cypresses, pines and dramatic cliffs running down to sheltered coves. Away from the sea on the northern side of the hills, the land is fertile and dotted with vineyards, olive trees and orchards, the villages prosperous and the country scattered with long-established *quintas* (estates). Since 1976 much of the area has been a natural park, formed to protect the landscape, flora and fauna, buildings and traditional way of life.

The N379/N10 across the hills and along the coast runs through Portinho da Arrábida, a coastal village on a white-sand bay guarded by a 17th-century fort, and along a corniche road on the crest of the *serra*, with great views north and south over the landscape to the coast. The Convento da Arrábida (by appointment only, tel 212 180 520, Wed–Sun 3–4, €3), a Franciscan foundation, is also along the same road.

SERRA DE SÃO MAMEDE

345 E8 Rua General Conde Jorge de Avilez 22, 7301 Portalegre, tel 045 236 31
www.rtsm.pt

Tucked up against the Spanish border, the Serra de São Mamede, a green and hilly oasis, comes as a welcome relief after the flatlands to the south. This rocky lump is a geological aberration, the altitude, granite and impermeable soil creating sufficient humidity for a lush range of green vegetation to thrive. You can explore the entire range in two to three hours by car, stopping to enjoy the fresh mountain air and take in the picturesque villages of Marvão (▷ 157) and Castelo de Vide (▷ 156) along the way. The road climbs steeply from Portalegre (▷ 162–163), through chestnut and cork oak to reach an undulating plateau where you will see irrigated fields, olives, vines and timeless hamlets, along with pigs, chickens and mules. The highest point is São Mamede (1,025m/ 3,336ft), signposted off the main road, from where there are incredible views over the Alentejo and east towards the Spanish sierras. The whole area is tiny, a miniature mountain wilderness with good walking on well-marked trails. Most of the walks are circular and vary from around 8 to18km (5 to 11 miles)—pick up a leaflet at any of the local tourist offices.

SETÚBAL

344 B10 Casa do Corpo Santo, Praça do Quebedo, 2901 Setúbal, tel 265 534 402 Setúbal
www.mun-setubal.pt

Setúbal, Portugal's third-largest port and a major industrial town, doesn't pretend to be a prime tourist destination, but if you are heading south from Lisbon it makes a good stop. This honest maritime city has a beguiling old town, good shopping and some interesting monuments and museums. It's also an excellent place if you are interested in outdoor activities—from the port, you can explore the Sado estuary and go dolphin-watching or snorkelling, while the tourist office will fill you in on walking, jeep safaris and hot-air ballooning in the area. Setúbal's greatest building is the extraordinary Igreja de Jesus in the Rua Acácio Barradas (Tue–Sun 9–12, 2–5, free), designed in 1491 by the architect Boytac—Portugal's first building with Manueline decoration. The essentially late-Gothic interior, approached through a flamboyant doorway, is embellished by extraordinary columns of twisted granite that support the spiral vaulting ribs. The town's less-than-riveting museum (Tue–Sat 9–12, 1.30–5, free) is next to the church; other low-key museums include the Museu Arqueológico in the Avenida Luísa Todi (Tue–Sat 9–12.30, 2–5.30, free), where you will find displays on the fishing trade, and the Museu Michel Giacometti in the Largo Defensores da República (Tue–Fri, Sun 9–12, 2–6, free), a big ethnographical collection.

VILA NOVA DE MILFONTES

346 B12 Rua António Mantas, 7645 Vila Nova de Milfontes, tel 283 996 599
www.vnmilfontes.net
www.cm-odemira.pt

The southern Alentejo coast is popular with Portuguese holidaymakers, many of whom spend their summer vacations at Vila Nova, a good-value, no-frills seaside town on the sandy estuary of the River Mira. It's the Alentejo's liveliest and most crowded resort, with a wide range of modern hotels, good restaurants and some far funkier clubs than you might expect in this largely rural region. It's still essentially Portuguese, with an old heart and a castle, giving it a more genuine atmosphere than resorts in the Algarve. Escape the crowded beaches in high summer by heading southward down the coast, where the sea and scenery are wilder.

The impressive frontage of the Paço Ducale (above) and the less inspiring Praça da República, with the castle behind (inset)

VILA VIÇOSA

The seat of the Bragança dynasty and site of their last palace, this is a prosperous and attractive town with an ancient hilltop castle and walled village.

The dukes of Bragança established their seat at Vila Viçosa in the 15th century. It was the fourth duke who began work on the ducal palace, and with building under way, the town became the base for a burgeoning court. The Braganças eventually moved on to grander palaces in Lisbon (▷ 123–145), Mafra (▷ 149)), Queluz (▷ 149) and Sintra (▷ 150–153), stripping their original seat of many of its treasures. But they retained a fondness for the place, often returning to hunt from their simple country home. Portugal's last two kings, Dom Carlos 1 and Manuel II, were particularly fond of Vila Viçosa. Manuel's will established the Fundação da Casa de Bragança, and the doors of the palace opened to the public in the 1940s.

THE PAÇO DUCALE

✉ Terreiro do Paço 🕐 Oct–end Mar Tue–Sun 9.30–1, 2–5; Apr–end Sep Tue–Fri 9.30–1, 2.30–5.30; Sat–Sun 9.30–1, 2.30–6. Guided tours only; last tours leave 60 min before closing. 🖐 Palace: €5. Armoury: €2.50. Coach Museum: €1.50. Chinese Porcelain Collection: €2.50. Treasury: €2.50. Child (under10) free

Situated in the aptly-named Terreiro do Paço, the Paço Ducale sprawls over two wings and three floors of an elegant, flat-fronted building set back from a spacious square that's dominated by a fine equestrian statue of João IV.

Before you go in, admire the Porta dos Nós, a splendid gateway that's one of the last remnants of the original 16th-century wall—its Manueline knots are a play on the Bragança motto *'Despois vós, nós'* ('After you, us'). Knots were chosen as the family's emblem because *'nós'* can mean both 'us', 'we' and 'knots'. Inside, the tour takes you through a series of lavishly decorated rooms. Of these, the Sala dos Duques stands out, both for its gilded and painted ceiling showing the Bragança dukes and the splendid 17th-century tapestries, designed by Rubens. Far more evocative, though, are the private apartments of Dom Carlos I and his wife Maria-Amélia, left virtually untouched since the couple left for Lisbon on 1 February 1908. The king was assassinated that afternoon.

Porcelain fans will enjoy the huge collection, mostly dating from the 17th to 19th centuries. It's particularly strong on Chinese ware, but there are fine examples from all the major European manufacturers—look out for Meissen, Limoges, Worcester, Dresden and Delft. From here, move to the Coach Museum in what were the royal stables—more than 70 beautifully maintained and venerable carriages, coaches and landaus are housed here.

RATINGS

Cultural interest	●●●●
Historic interest	●●●●
Photo stops	●●●●
Walkability	●●●●

TIPS

- Allow an hour for the main palace, 45 minutes to an hour for the armoury, 30 minutes for the coach collection, and the same for the Chinese porcelain and treasury respectively.
- Apart from a couple of expensive options, there's little accommodation in the town, so it's best to visit for the day from Évora or Estremoz.

BASICS

✚ 345 E9 ℹ Praça da República, 7160 Vila Viçosa, tel 268 881 101 🕐 Daily 9–12.30, 2–4

www.cm-vilavicosa.pt Town council, Portuguese-only site

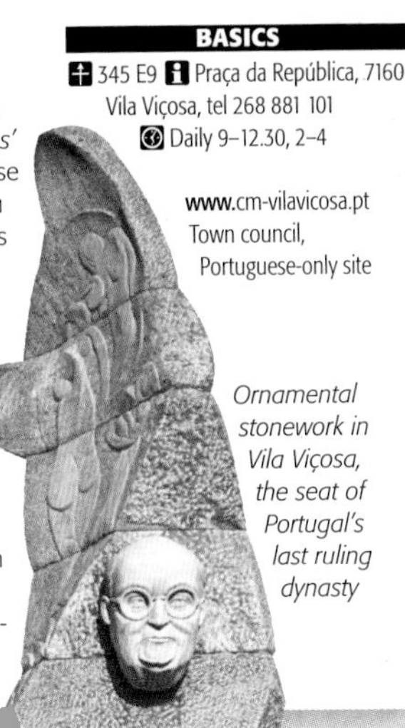

Ornamental stonework in Vila Viçosa, the seat of Portugal's last ruling dynasty

THE ALGARVE

Long sandy beaches, headlands, sheltered bays and coves are the hallmarks of the Algarve's coast, which draws hundreds of thousands of visitors. Glitzy developments, manicured golf courses and bustling towns like Faro, Lagos, Albufeira and Portimão contrast with the untouched seaboard north of Sagres. Inland, the hills of the Serra de Monchique dominate an unspoilt rural hinterland where the traditional pace of life is unchanged.

MAJOR SIGHTS

THE SIGHTS

Local fishing boats drawn up on the fishermen's beach, Albufeira. The town is one of the Algarve's most popular tourist resorts

São Lourenço's stunning *azulejos* were painted in 1730

ALBUFEIRA

346 C13 Rua 5 de Outubro, 8200 Albufeira, tel 289 585 279, free information number 800 296 296
www.rtalgarve.pt

Since the 1960s, when it was still essentially a fishing village, Albufeira has changed beyond recognition, evolving into one of the most popular package-tour destinations in the Algarve. There's little left today of the traditional way of life, and the old village, nestling between two headlands, is virtually swamped by high-rise apartments and hotels, while development creeps farther inland every year.

Despite this, you can still see the fishermen on their beach in the early morning, and Albufeira manages to hang on to some of its charm. This is best seen in the steep cobbled streets and distinctive architecture of the old town, revolving around the main square, Largo Duarte Pacheco. This is the hub of the town, lined with outdoor cafés and bars, where you can eat an English breakfast or drink a pint of Guinness. From here the main street leads towards the sea, plunging through a tunnel to reach a terrace above the town beach, with its high cliffs and smooth sand. Wander along a corniche-type street above the main beach to reach the Gruta do Xorino, a sea-cave with crystal waters. For a change of pace, the town has a couple of good churches and a small archaeological museum in the Travessa da Bateria (mid-Sep–end May Tue–Sun 10–5; Jun–mid-Sep Tue–Sun 2.30–8.30, free) devoted to local finds; more interesting are the early photographs, which show the town untouched by tourism. A good time to hit the old town, particularly Rua Candido dos Reis, is the early evening when the shops are open, the bars are buzzing, and the whole town is gearing up for eating, drinking and dancing. Most bars stay open well after midnight, while summer clubs along Montchoro are open until around 6am.

ALMANCIL

346 C13 Free information number 800 296 296
www.rtalgarve.pt

On the eastern outskirts of Almancil (Almansil), a service town on the N125, is the church of São Lourenço (Tue–Sat 10–1, 2.30–5, Mon 2.30–5, €1.50), whose interior is one of Portugal's most outstanding examples of 18th-century tilework. Every inch of the walls and ceiling is covered with glowing blue-and-white *azulejos* (tiles) depicting stories from the life of the martyr, St. Laurence. The tiles were painted in 1730 by Policarpo de Oliveira Bernardes, acknowledged to be one of the country's finest artists. Look out for the background details of local life in the big panels and the wonderful *trompe l'oeil* colonnades on the ceiling.

ALTE

346 C13 Estrada da Ponte 17, 8100 Alte, tel 289 478 666, free information number 800 296 296
www.rtalgarve.pt

Head inland from Albufeira and you will soon be in unspoilt countryside, where almonds, citrus trees and olive groves cover the hillsides and village life remains largely untouched by tourism. One of the prettiest of these villages is Alte, a bus-tour stop and a popular weekend destination for locals—to see it at its best, avoid these busy times. The well-tended village nestles in the limestone hills of the area known as the Barrocal and sprawls along a hillside, its narrow cobbled streets crammed with hidden corners and photo opportunities. The exhibition in the tourist office will fill you in on local history—from here head uphill to explore the town and take in the Igreja Matriz, built in the 16th century with a fine Manueline doorway and a wealth of 18th-century woodwork and *azulejos* (tiles).

From the heart of the village it's a five-minute walk out to a couple of natural springs, the Fonte Pequena and Fonte Grande, a local beauty spot where picnic tables are set under the trees beside a series of shallow canals. For the more energetic there's a good waymarked walk through the hills west to São Bartolomeu de Messines. This path is part of what will ultimately be a trans-Algarve hiking trail.

CACELA VELHA

347 D13 Free information number 800 296 296
www.rtalgarve.pt

To get a taste of what the eastern Algarve once looked like, head for Cacela Velha, a tiny whitewashed village on a dead-end road 10km (6 miles) east of Tavira (▷ 175). Perched on a bluff above the eastern end of the Parque Natural da Ria Formosa (▷ 172), it's little more than a handful of cottages, a church and an 18th-century fort. Below the village lies the lagoon and beach—you can walk down through the dunes and olive trees to wade out to the barrier island at low tide, or catch the ferry at the hamlet of Fabrica. At sea level, beaches stretch east along the coast for miles; even in high summer a short walk should get you away from the crowds thronging the better-known resorts and their beaches.

Faro

The Algarve's capital has a picturesque old quarter, an atmospheric harbour filled with yachts and fishing boats, fabulous shopping and a buzzing nightlife.

The Largo da Sé in the heart of the old town (above left); noted artist Arco de Repousa created this fine decorative tile showing a scene from local history (middle); one of Faro's three fine beaches (right)

RATINGS	
Historic interest	●●●●●
Outdoor pursuits	●●●●●
Specialist shopping	●●●●●
Walkability	●●●●●

BASICS

346 D13
Rua da Misericórdia 8, 8000 Faro
289 803 604, free information number 800 296 296
Oct–end Apr Mon–Fri 9.30–5.30, Sat–Sun 9.30–12.30, 2–5.30; May–end Sep daily 9.30–7
Faro

www.rtalgarve.pt
The main website for the entire Algarve, full of useful practical information

SEEING FARO

Most visitors flying into Faro bypass the town, but it makes an ideal stopover for a night or so if you're arriving late or leaving on an early morning flight. Head first for the harbour, from where you can explore the historic old town before strolling through the pedestrianized shopping streets to the Museu Regional. From here it's a 10- to 15- minute walk northwest to the churches.

HIGHLIGHTS

CIDADE VELHA

169 A3

Faro's old town is still completely enclosed within walls, a dense complex of narrow streets and ancient houses with the majestic Largo da Sé and cathedral (Mon–Sat 10–12.30, 1.30–5, €2) at its heart. Walk up through the Arco da Vila, the 19th-century town gate designed by the Italian Francisco Fabri, to the harmonious cathedral square, planted with orange trees and lined with 18th-century buildings, one of which was the episcopal palace. The cathedral is a hybrid of Gothic, Renaissance and baroque architecture, the result of rebuilding after the 1755 earthquake. The interior is richly gilded and there's a fine old organ and some 18th-century *azulejos* (tiles). Climb the tower for superb views.

Behind the Largo da Sé is the Largo Dom Afonso III, dominated by a statue of Afonso III, where you will find the Museu Arqueológico (Oct–end Apr Mon, Sat 2–5.30, Tue–Fri 9.30–5.30; May–end Sep Mon, Sat 2.30–6, Tue–Fri 10–6, €2). The museum, the Algarve's oldest, is in the 16th-century Convento de Nossa Senhora da Assunção, an elegant building with an airy internal courtyard. The museum concentrates on Roman and medieval finds, many from the excavations at Estói (▷ 171). Look out for the statues from the site. Take care not to miss the star turn, a superb third-century AD mosaic showing Neptune and the four winds, found near Faro station. Take a different route back to the Arco da Vila for fascinating glimpses of everyday life in this picturesque district.

THE HARBOUR AREA

Sleek yachts are moored in Faro's harbour, the focus of a bustling area that buzzes throughout the day and into the evening. The harbour is backed by attractive gardens and cafés. Two child-friendly

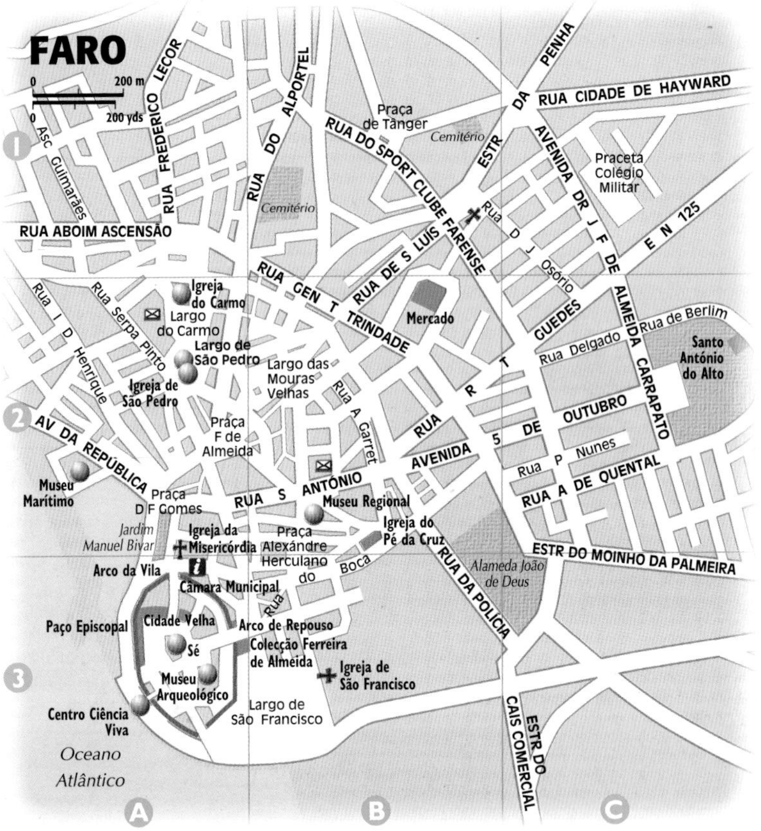

FARO

0 200 m
0 200 yds

Asc Guimarães
Rua Frederico Lecor
Rua do Alportel
Praça de Tânger
Cemitério
Rua do Sport Clube Farense
Estr da Penha
Rua Cidade de Hayward
Avenida Dr J F de Almeida Carrapato
Praceta Colégio Militar
Cemitério
Rua Aboim Ascensão
Rua D J Osório
E N 125
Rua Gen T Trindade
Rua de S Luís
Rua I D Henrique
Rua Serpa Pinto
Igreja do Carmo
Largo do Carmo
Largo de São Pedro
Igreja de São Pedro
Largo das Mouras Velhas
Mercado
Guedes
Rua Delgado
Rua de Berlim
Santo António do Alto
Rua A Garrett
Rua R T
Rua 5 de Outubro
Praça F de Almeida
Av da República
Museu Marítimo
Praça D F Gomes
Rua S António
Avenida
Rua P Nunes
Rua A de Quental
Museu Regional
Jardim Manuel Bivar
Igreja da Misericórdia
Praça Alexándre Herculano
Igreja do Pé da Cruz
Rua da Polícia
Estr do Moinho da Palmeira
Arco da Vila
Câmara Municipal
Rua do Boca
Alameda João de Deus
Paço Episcopal
Cidade Velha
Arco de Repouso
Colecção Ferreira de Almeida
Sé
Igreja de São Francisco
Museu Arqueológico
Centro Ciência Viva
Largo de São Francisco
Estr do Cais Comercial
Oceano Atlântico

attractions are located here—the Museu Marítimo (Capitania do Porto do Faro, Rua da Comunidade Lusiada, tel 289 894 990, call ahead for appointment, free), and the Centro Ciência Viva in the Rua Comandante Francisco Manuel (mid-Sep–end Jun Tue–Fri 10–5, Sat–Sun 3–7; Jul to mid-Sep Tue–Sun 4–11, adult €2.50, child (under 12) €1. The former concentrates on model boats and fishing, while the science exhibit, along the waterfront, is more ambitious, with plenty of interactive action. Don't miss the flight simulator.

Take a stroll beside the sea and railway before cutting up into the old town, or perhaps catching a ferry to one of the offshore beaches. Alternatively, head inland from the Jardim Manuel Bivar into Faro's shopping area, an attractive spread of pedestrianized streets where you'll find the best of the international chain stores alongside some highly individual and typically Portuguese shops.

THE BEACHES

The beaches mostly fall inside the eastern end of the Parque Natural da Ria Formosa and are long and low sandbars, reached through marshy channels. Ferries run from the jetty in Faro harbour to both Farol, on the Ilha da Culatra, and the Ilha Deserta (or Ilha da Barreta), the most southerly point in mainland Portugal, with water sports, restaurants and bars. Farol tends to be quieter, but the best time to visit both is during the week rather than at weekends. Outside high season, there are not many people around during mid-week, so, if you are planning a beach day, this is a good time to go.

If you have a couple of hours to spare before a flight, the Praia de Faro, close to the airport, is worth investigating. It's another typical lagoon stretch, with a sweep of beautiful sand and a sheltered inland side. Out of season it's quiet, but far more developed than the offshore beaches, with bars, restaurants and holiday houses.

A pair of storks nest on the 19th-century gateway to the old town

TIPS

- It is hard to find parking in central Faro—arrive early and you may be able to park along the harbour's edge near the bus and train stations.
- Ferry services to the island beaches run from mid-Jun to end Sep, with four departures daily.

Jardim Manuel Bivar (below left), a street in the old town (below right) and the Igreja do Nossa Senhora do Carmo (bottom)

BACKGROUND

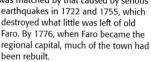

The Faro area was colonized by the Romans, based at Milreu. Ultimately control passed to the Moors, for whom it was a major port. It was reconquered by Afonso III for the Christians in 1249 and thrived, emerging by the 15th century as one of the most important towns in southern Portugal.

In 1580 Philip II of Spain usurped the Portuguese throne, giving the English the perfect excuse to attack the Algarve, which was now nominally part of Spain. The Earl of Essex landed in Faro in 1596, sacking the city and looting the bishop's palace, which he then made his headquarters. The contents of the library were sent back to England as a gift for Essex's friend Thomas Bodley, founder of the Bodleian Library in Oxford. Essex eventually withdrew, setting fire to the city as a parting gesture. The devastation that resulted was matched by that caused by serious earthquakes in 1722 and 1755, which destroyed what little was left of old Faro. By 1776, when Faro became the regional capital, much of the town had been rebuilt.

The town got an extra boost with the opening of the Lisbon–Faro railway in 1889, with holiday visitors starting to arrive as a result. But, though there was some low-key tourism in the first half of the 20th century, it was only with the construction of the airport in 1965 that Faro and the Algarve really took off as a holiday destination. Today, nearly 5 million tourists pass through the airport annually and mass tourism has brought increasing prosperity to the city and the surrounding area.

MORE TO SEE

IGREJA DE NOSSA SENHORA DO CARMO

169 A2 • Largo do Carmo, 8000 Faro Oct–end Apr Mon–Fri 10–1, 3–5; May–end Sep Mon–Fri 10–1, 3–6 Church: free. Capela dos Ossos: €1

An early 18th-century baroque church with a carved, gilt high altar. The main attraction is the Capela dos Ossos (Chapel of the Bones), a side chapel lined with decorative displays of monks' bones—these were disinterred from a cemetery in the 19th century and put on display to act as a reminder of mortality.

IGREJA DE SÃO PEDRO

169 A2 • Largo de São Pedro, 8000 Faro Daily 9–12, 2–5 Free

A beautiful 16th-century church decorated with a frieze of polychrome *azulejos*. The side chapels have more superb blue-and-white tiles and gilt altarpieces.

MUSEU REGIONAL

169 B2 • Praça da Liberdade 2, 8000 Faro 289 827 610 Mon–Fri 9–12, 2–5 €1.50

This is a good place to catch a glimpse of the Algarve as it was, before the days of tourism, with ethnographical displays of local objects and tools, mock-ups of traditional rooms and houses, and photos of old Faro.

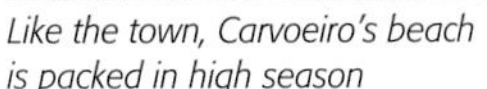

Like the town, Carvoeiro's beach is packed in high season

The Reserva Natural do Sapal wetlands near ancient Castro Marim are home to more than 150 bird species

CARVOEIRO

346 C13 Praia do Carvoeiro, 8400 Lagoa, tel 282 357 728, free information number 800 296 296 www.rtalgarve.pt

A narrow fertile valley leads down to the sea from the inland wine town of Lagoa to Carvoeiro, once an unspoilt fishing village, now a resort on the package tour circuit. To see it at its best means coming out of season, when the tiny triangular beach is empty and the old streets on either side of the cove, lined with painted houses, are crowd-free.

In summer, Carvoeiro is heaving with visitors, many based in the sprawl of apartment blocks and villa complexes either side of the old town, and you will be pushed to park or find a peaceful spot on the beach. The best bet is to hop on one of the fishing-boat ferries that ply the coast, dropping visitors off at a series of sandy coves, many with spectacular cliffs and rock formations. The pick of these is Algar Seco, where winds and tides have chiselled away at the cliffs, forming grottoes and pinnacles. The clear water makes it ideal for snorkelling. Other nearby beaches include the Praia da Paraiso, just west of the village; Centianes; Benagil, still largely unspoilt; and Marinha, a beautiful and relatively undeveloped spot. Be warned that signposting to the beaches is generally inadequate, and parking difficult everywhere in high summer.

CASTRO MARIM

347 D13 Rua José Alves Moreira 2–4, 8950 Castro Marim, tel 281 531 232, free information number 800 296 296 www.rtalgarve.pt

Two castles bear witness to the past strategic importance of Castro Marim, a little village on a hill overlooking the marshlands of the River Guadiana, which here acts as the border between Portugal and Spain. The main castle, to the north of the town, was built in 1319 as the headquarters of the Order of Christ, the successors to the Knights Templar, and remained their base until the order moved north to Tomar (▷ 118–121) in 1334.

The castle was built on an earlier 12th-century Moorish fortification, which you can still see within the main walls; it's now a small archaeological museum. The walls themselves were erected in the 17th century and are topped with ramparts, from where you'll get great views of the river, the shimmering salt-flats, the roofs of the town below and the sea to the south. Here, too, you can pick up information on the surrounding Reserva Natural do Sapal, a nature reserve that protects the wetlands around the town and along the river. It's a varied habitat, with more than150 species of birds, including flamingos, storks, avocets, ducks and waders.

Across the town are the remnants of the 17th-century fort of São Sebastião, another great lookout point.

ESTÓI

346 D13 Free information number 800 296 296 www.rtalgarve.pt

The sugar-pink Palacio d'Estói is a real sleeping beauty's palace. This neglected building and its overgrown garden date from the 1740s, when the Conde de Cavalhal constructed a miniature version of the royal rococo palace of Queluz (▷ 149) here. Today, both palace and gardens are crumbling, though it may be that the building will be turned into a *pousada* or a conference venue, a plan outlined on a board by the entrance.

The house is shut, but there is free entrance to the overgrown gardens (Mon–Sat 9–12.30, 2–5.30). Palm and orange trees line the approach avenue, at the end of which a double stairway, decorated with tiles and statuary, leads up to the reflecting pool and terrace in front of the palace. There are statues, busts, huge vases and pots dotted around, and the air is perfumed with the scents of oranges and aromatic plants. The village is also worth a quick inspection, particularly the Igreja Matriz on the main square—it was built after the 1755 earthquake and designed by Fabri, who worked in Faro.

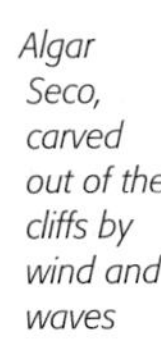

Algar Seco, carved out of the cliffs by wind and waves

The Ponta da Piedade rocks, a half-hour boat trip from Lagos

The fishermen's quarter, Olhão, seen from the church tower

The striking logo of the Parque Natural da Ria Formosa

FARO

See pages 168–170.

LAGOS

346 B13 Largo Marquês de Pombal, 8600 Lagos, tel 282 764 111, free information number 800 296 296 Lagos
www.rtalgarve.pt

The biggest town in the western Algarve, Lagos is a vibrant place packed with history, making it a good base for a couple of nights if you want a buzz of life that the smaller western villages don't provide. The area has been settled since Phoenician times, but it won European fame in the 15th century when the port was the departure point for Henry the Navigator's explorers as they set off on the great voyages of discovery. Lagos is on the River Bensafrim, with most sights of interest found inside the medieval walls that still encircle the old town.

Start your visit at the waterfront, backed by gardens and guarded at the sea end by the trim little 17th-century Forte da Ponte da Bandeira. Walk up-river from here beside the solid town walls to reach a square, the Praça Infante Dom Henrique, with its fine bronze statue of Henry the Navigator. The old custom house is also here. Its small arcade was once the site of Europe's first slave market, operating from 1444 to 1756.

From here, walk through to the Museu Regional in the Rua General Alberto da Silveira (Tue–Sun 9.30–12.30, 2–5, €1.50). Exhibits include much of local interest, including a model Algarve village, but also such curiosities as an eight-legged goat. The superb church of Santo António, a riot of baroque gilding built between 1710 and 1720, is part of the museum.

East from here are shopping streets, pretty squares and a huge range of bars, cafés and restaurants. The best of these are around two pleasant mosaic-paved squares, the Praça Luis de Camões and the Praça Gil Eanes. For a change of pace, you could take the half-hour boat trip to the Ponta da Piedade (Bridge of Piety), a spectacular rock formation with stacks, arches and grottoes. Near here, a string of delightful cove beaches is enclosed by headlands with coastal views. East of Lagos, across the river, the Meia Praia is a 4km (2.5-mile) stretch of soft sand. Kids will enjoy a trip to Lagos Zoo (Oct–end Apr daily 10–5; May–end Sep daily 10–7; adult €6, child under 12 €4, family €15), an environmentally conscious zoo for small mammals, birds and farm animals.

A gilded cherub in Igreja Santo António, Lagos

OLHÃO

346 D13 Largo Sebastião M. Mestre 6A, 8700 Olhão, tel 289 713 936, free information number 800 296 296 Olhão
www.rtalgarve.pt

Down-to-earth Olhão is the biggest fishing port in the Algarve, and a good base from which to explore the Parque Natural da Ria Formosa. Its highlights are the waterfront and harbour area, with superb fish and produce markets and tranquil gardens, and the Praça da Restauração, reached through the warren of twisting streets that make up the fishermen's quarter. Climb up the tower of the early 18th-century Igreja Matriz for terrific views over the roof terraces of the whitewashed cube houses, reminiscent of North African buildings and reflecting Olhão's old trading links.

PARQUE NATURAL DA RIA FORMOSA

346 C14 Quinta do Marim, Quelfes, 8700 Olhão, tel 089 704 134
Daily 9.30–12.30, 2–5

Just west of Faro towards Manta Rota is the Parque Natural da Ria Formosa, established in 1987 to protect the barrier islands and lagoons that run along the east end of the Algarve. The lagoons, riddled with tidal flats, islets, channels and salt marshes, form what is a unique ecological environment and an important bird nesting area. Residents, over-wintering and migratory birds all feed here, while the dunes and marshlands themselves support rich vegetation.

Around 7,500 people live within the park, most working in lagoon-related activities—nearly 80 per cent of Portuguese clams and other shellfish come from here. During the summer the population triples, and the park authorities have the task of balancing environmental needs with the demands of tourism.

To promote this work, the Environmental Education Centre was set up near Olhão. Other attractions include a traditional water mill powered by the tides and a lagoon on which an old tuna fishing boat sails filled with visitors who want to explore this fascinating place further. Don't miss the Portuguese water dogs, a unique web-toed species bred for work with fishing boats.

Looking across the Arade from Portimão to the old fort. Founded in 1461, the town is the second biggest in the area

The long, gently shelving beach at Praia da Rocha, ideal for kids

PORTIMÃO

346 B13 Avenida Zeca Afonso, 8500 Portimão, tel 282 470 732, free information number 800 296 296
Portimão
www.cm-portimao.pt
www.rtalgarvept

Romans and Moors inhabited the Portimão area, but the present city on the banks of the River Arade was established by charter in 1463, flourishing during the era of the great voyages of discovery. The 1755 earthquake destroyed much of the town and the subsequent economic decline was halted only towards the end of the 19th century, when fishing and fish-canning took off here.

Today, Portimão is thriving, a mainly modern town that's the second largest in the Algarve. Its economy is now driven by tourism, canning and construction, with the traditional fishing industry playing an increasingly minor role. The famous open-air sardine restaurants along the riverfront, grilling fish fresh off the boats, have been moved, with a smart marina taking their place. The area behind Rua Serpa Pinto is still probably the pleasantest part of town, with its shady gardens, bars and restaurants. The marina and quayside area are also the departure point for boat excursions, which cruise both east and west along the coast or up the river valley to historic Silves (▷ 175).

West from here is the heart of town, its largely pedestrianized streets and good shops pulling in the crowds–Portimão also has several out-of-town malls. The main church of Nossa Senhora de Conceição is a few blocks back from the water; its Manueline doorway dates from the 15th century, but much of the rest of the building postdates the 1755 earthquake.

PRAIA DA ROCHA

346 B13 Avenida Tomás Cabreira, 8500 Portimão, tel 282 419 132, free information number 800 296 296
www.rtalgarve.pt

Praia da Rocha is the oldest-established Algarve resort, popular from the start of the 20th century. It was home to a largely British colony of writers and artists from the 1930s to the 1950s and boomed in the following two decades, when it became known as the 'Queen of the Algarve'. Now this famous holiday resort is largely given over to high-rise hotels, faceless apartment blocks, home-from-home bars and noisy discos.

Nothing, however, can detract from the dramatic rock formations and the glorious beach, the widest cliff-backed stretch of sand in Europe. It was created artificially in 1969 when a million tonnes of sand were moved here, pushing the sea back some 150m (490ft) and leaving the rock stacks, formerly lapped by water, high and dry.

Access to the beach is from various points along the Avenida Tomas Cabreira, which runs along the clifftop from the Fortaleza de Santa Caterina. Built in 1691 to protect the river mouth, the fort is a great place from which to watch the fishing boats come into port, or to take in the sunset. Walk down the avenue to admire the remaining turn-of-the-20th-century villas, relics of when Praia da Rocha was a hotbed of international partying.

QUARTEIRA

346 C13 Praça do Mar, 8125 Quarteira, tel 289 389 209, free information number 800 296 296
www.rtalgarve.pt

Nowadays, Quarteira, the first of the Algarve resorts to be developed in the 1970s, comes in for a lot of criticism. It's big, its high-rise buildings are ugly and the town is often noisy during the summer high season, but it's blessed with a long, gently shelving beach, perfect for little ones to play, paddle and swim safely. The resort's other main selling points are its relaxed family atmosphere and realistic prices.

The glorious beach is fronted by a palm-lined promenade, with a small fishing harbour at the west end. The streets are buzzing with life, there's a good daily market, and on Wednesdays the town plays host to one of the biggest and liveliest Gypsy markets in the Algarve.

QUINTA DO LAGO

346 C13 Quinta do Lago, 8135 Almansil, tel 289 396 097, free information number 800 296 296
www.rtalgarve.pt

The quiet roads of Quinta do Lago are lined with villas hidden by trees, expensive luxury hotels and country clubs. This purpose-built resort caters for the rich, who pay for privacy, exclusivity and access to the best golf courses in the Algarve. If you are staying at one of the hotels, the resort office will fill you in on what's happening; if you are visiting for the day, head down to the beach at the western end of the Parque Natural da Ria Formosa.

Take the walkway across the lagoon and mud flats to reach the superb beach or head out along one of the nature trails to explore the marshlands, lakes and woods. Here you can see the salting tanks dating from Roman times, or do some birdwatching–it's a good place to spot flamingos. Golf, tennis or riding are all on offer, but if you prefer to shop, the complex also has some of the region's classiest designer stores.

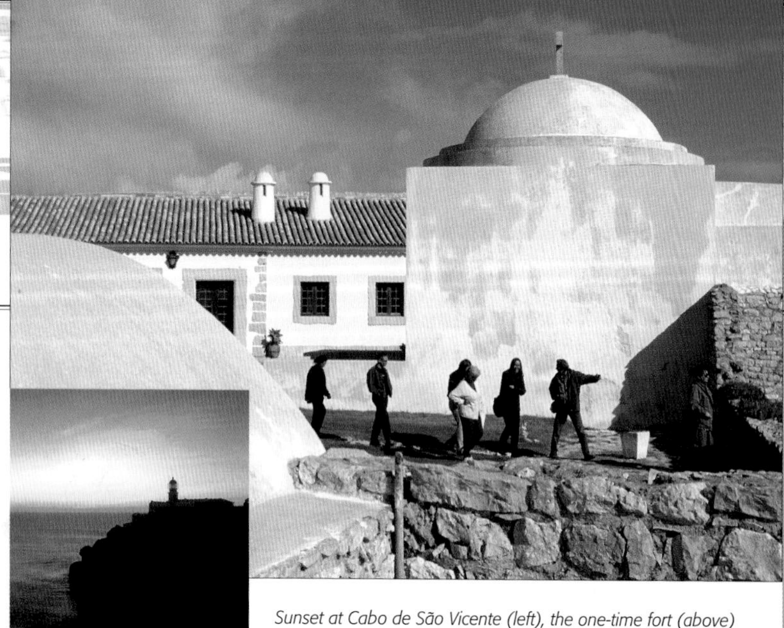

Sunset at Cabo de São Vicente (left), the one-time fort (above)

SAGRES & CABO DE SÃO VICENTE

This old fort dating from the time of Henry the Navigator and the great age of discoveries is a must-see along a stretch of magnificent coastal scenery.

RATINGS	
Good for kids	●●●●
Historic interest	●●●●●
Outdoor pursuits	●●●●●
Photo stops	●●●●●

MORE TO SEE

SAGRES
A sprawling, friendly little town with good restaurants, beaches and plenty of places to stay.

THE BEACHES
There are superb beaches in and around Sagres. Try Mareta and Baleeira within the town, or head out to Tonel or Belixe. Both stay relatively uncrowded.

TIPS

- Cabo de São Vicente can get very crowded with day trippers in the summer.
- If you take a tour of the lighthouse, tip the keeper when he's finished.

BASICS

346 B13 Rua Comandante Matoso, 8650 Sagres, tel 282 624 873, free information number 800 296 296
Mon–Sat 9.30–1, 2–5.30

www.rtalgarve.pt
A highly detailed and efficient site with English-language option
www.sagres.net
English-language site packed with lots of useful local information

Known to the Romans as the Promontorium Sacrum (Sacred Promontory) and to ancient Portuguese mariners as O Fim do Mundo (End of the World), Cabo de São Vicente is the southwesternmost point of mainland Europe. Its fame dates from the time when Prince Henry the Navigator set up his celebrated School of Navigation at Sagres in1415. Henry gathered the best astronomers, cartographers and navigational instrument-makers of the day around him to launch the great age of discoveries; the revolutionary ocean-going caravel was also designed and subsequently developed here.

FORTALEZA DE SAGRES

8650 Sagres 282 620 140 Oct–end Apr daily 10–6.30; May–end Sep daily 10–8.30 €2.60
www.ippar.pt.

It's generally agreed that Henry's School of Navigation occupied the headland at Sagres, though his fort was sacked by Sir Francis Drake in 1587. The present one dates from 1793. The entire area is surrounded by massive walls and bastions. Walk through and you will find yourself in a vast and windswept space, with a range of modern buildings ahead and the tiny church of Nossa Senhora da Graça, where Henry certainly worshipped, to the right. Before visiting the church, climb the ramp to the right of the entrance for an overview of the area—below is the outline of the 39m-diameter (127ft) *Rosa dos Ventos*, a wind, or compass, rose thought to have been used to help teach navigation. Unearthed by accident in 1921, it certainly dates from Henry's time, but how it worked is still a mystery.

CABO DE SÃO VICENTE

Whatever the weather, mainland Europe's remotest point has great views, fresh air and wild sea. You can walk into the lighthouse complex—once a fortress—and peer down to the rocks and pounding surf, or photograph the superb views up and down the coast. The lighthouse's lamp is the most powerful in Europe. The place is not officially open to the public, but the keeper sometimes gives tours.

The Serra de Monchique, good walking country

Historic Silves is dominated by its cathedral and Moorish castle

Tavira is a peaceful riverside town that's fun to explore

SERRA DE MONCHIQUE

346 B13 Largo dos Chorões, 8550 Monchique, tel 282 911 189, free information number 800 296 296
www.rtalgarve.pt

Just 25km (15 miles) from the teeming coast, the hills of the Serra de Monchique are a different world—this is rural Portugal, with unspoiled countryside and small traditional villages that are untouched by the commercialization found along much of the coast. The hills are mainly wooded, with almonds, olives and mimosa giving way to eucalyptus and pine trees on the higher slopes. Above the tree line are the peaks of Foia, at 902m (2,960ft) the highest point in the Algarve, and Picota, 774m (2,540ft). You can drive to the top of each to enjoy the magnificent views over the western Algarve, but this is excellent walking country and it's quite feasible to hike up them.

The main settlement and start point for walks in the *serra* is Monchique, a small hill town that's renowned for its handicrafts and its fine 16th-century church. A few miles below is the tiny spa settlement of Caldas de Monchique, where the mineral-rich waters gush out at 32°C (90°F). Popular in the 19th century, the spa retains a faded fin de siècle elegance; the waters are used to treat rheumatism and respiratory illnesses. From the hills, you can head west towards Aljezur, a magnificent drive on a twisting road that takes you down to the wild west coast.

SILVES

346 C13 Rua 25 de Abril, 8300 Silves, tel 282 442 255, free information number 800 296 296
www.rtalgrave.pt

Silves, known to the Moors as Xelb, is historically the Algarve's most important city. It was the Islamic capital of Al-Gharb, a major fortress, river port on the Arade and a trading hub, whose wealth and influence were renowned all over Europe. After the 13th-century expulsion of the Moors, the town declined, the river silted up and by the 16th century Silves was a forgotten backwater, its population, once 30,000, shrinking to 150.

Cork processing revived the town in the 19th century, and today Silves thrives on tourism, citrus growing and farming, with thousands of visitors heading here to see the city walls and castle, one of Portugal's best preserved Moorish monuments. You will have to climb steeply uphill to reach the castle (Sep–end Jun daily 9–5.30; Jul–end Aug 9–8, €1.50), now little more than a shell, with magnificent views from the walls. Just outside is the *Sé* (Mon–Fri 8.30–6.30, free), a fine twin-towered Gothic cathedral built on the site of the Moorish mosque. It was the Algarve's most important church until the bishopric moved to Faro in 1577.

Downhill from here is the Museu Arqueológico (Mon–Sat 9–6, €2), whose displays trace local history through Phoenician, Roman and Moorish times. There is more history in the town's one-time cork factory, the Fabrica Inglês (daily 9am–midnight), which has been revamped as a cultural and leisure venue. It is near the river, where there's a morning market.

Though Silves castle is a shell, its walls are well preserved

TAVIRA

347 D13 Rua da Galeria 9, 8800 Tavira, tel 281 322 511, free information number 800 296 296 Tavira
www.com-tquira.pt

Tavira, on the banks of the River Gilão, is a prosperous town that made its money from tuna fishing 300 years ago and has managed to withstand the impact of 20th-century mass tourism. It can no longer be described as undiscovered, but it has kept its soul and retained its fine buildings, narrow streets, old-fashioned shops, cafés and traditional way of life. From the river, spanned by a 'Roman' bridge that's actually 17th century, you can explore the heart of town, a tangle of narrow streets and old houses that contrast with broad riverside avenues. Tavira is rich in churches, with more than 25 to view; pick of the bunch are the beautiful Igreja da Misericórdia, built between 1541 and 1551 by Pilarté, a mason who worked at Belém, and Santa Maria do Castelo, famous for the tombs of seven Christian knights slain by the Moors. The killings were the catalyst for the Christian revolt that expelled the Muslims

The Moorish castle ruins, set in immaculate gardens, lie just up the hill, a good place for a pause, as are the riverside gardens that run down from the main Praça da República. From here, a miniature train runs seawards to the ferry departure point for the Ilha de Tavira, where there's a superb sandy beach with good walking through the dunes.

A lone golfer on the 16th hole of Vale do Lobo's Royal Course

Vila Real's fine buildings, a tribute to 18th-century elegance

The huge marina at Vilamoura, one of the largest in Europe

VALE DO LOBO

346 C13 Free information number 800 296 296
www.vdl.com

Like Quinta do Lago (▷ 173), Vale de Lobo caters for the rich, who come here to play golf and relax in secluded and well-heeled surroundings. Similar in style to Quinta, Vale de Lobo has a wonderful beach, which may be worth investigating in high season—the resort villas all have their own pools, which usually means that the beach is uncrowded. Golfers should enquire at the resort office about playing, but note that green fees are high, the courses exclusive and advance booking a must. The resort has several classy hotels and country clubs, and is well served by international-style restaurants, bars and shops—if you're staying here, there's no need to venture out at all.

VILA REAL DE SANTO ANTÓNIO

347 D13 Centro Cultural António Aleixo, Rua Teófilo Braga, 8900 Vila Real de Santo António, tel 281 542 100, free information number 800 296 296
Vila Real de Santo António
www.rtalgarve.pt

For a taste of 18th-century rationalism, head for Vila Real de Santo António on the banks of the River Guadiana, opposite Spanish Ayamonte. Founded in 1773 to replace an earlier settlement swallowed up by waves and shifting sand, it was the brainchild of Portugal's chief minister, the Marquês de Pombal, who was also responsible for rebuilding Lisbon's Baixa district (▷ 130). A grid design was drawn up, precut stone was shipped in and the entire town was virtually completed in six months. Arrow-straight streets of wonderfully homogenous buildings converge on the central square, the Praça Marquês de Pombal, with its church, town hall and former barracks. Stroll around the town and along the riverbank, or hop on the ferry and enjoy a few hours in Spain. Boats run up-river, too, an idyllic cruise through undulating countryside. Vila Real's stores are popular with Spanish shoppers looking for bargains.

VILA ROMANA DE MILREU

346 D13 Ruínas de Milreu, Estói, 8000 Faro, tel 289 803 604
Oct–end Apr Tue–Sun 9.30–12.30, 2–5; May–end Sep Tue–Sun 9.30–12.30, 2–6
www.ippar.pt

Mosaic flooring in the baths

Just down the hill from the palace at Estói (▷ 171) are the ruins of Milreu, a first- to third-century AD villa and bath complex that's the Algarve's most important Roman excavation. You will need a little imagination to work out the site, most of which is occupied by what was a huge third-century AD country house, complete with a central pool and garden backed by a colonnaded peristyle. Surrounding this are the fragments of a large bath complex, still retaining its tubs and heating furnaces.

The sheer numbers of changing rooms and pools have given rise to the theory that Milreu was once a spa and temple complex—it has been proved that a large sanctuary was built here in the fourth century AD. It is all somewhat confusing, so concentrate on the lively mosaics scattered throughout the villa, all that's left of its archaeological treasures, most of which are now in museums in Faro and Lagos. The mosaics accurately and creatively depict dolphins, many varieties of fish, shells and seaweed. Some scholars think this concentration may provide a clue to the villa's owner, who could have been a fish-processor with a factory on the coast. Be sure to peek inside the 16th-century house built on top of part of the ruins, a fine example of vernacular architecture incorporating Roman masonry.

VILAMOURA

346 C13 Free information number 800 296 296
www.rtalgarve.pt

Hotels, shops, a casino, restaurants and bars surround the huge marina here. The resort's story dates back to the 1970s, when visitors began to flock to the Algarve. It continues to expand, with villa and hotel developments radiating ever farther inland. The main attraction is golf; there are five courses, all challenging and all beautifully maintained. The marina is the watersports' hub, with everything from jet skiing to big-game fishing, while inland there's horseback-riding and tennis. Northwest of the marina is the Museu Cerra da Vila (Oct–end Apr 10–1, 3–5; May–end Sep 10–1, 3–8, €4), a Roman archaeological site with an adjoining small museum with local finds.

Vilamoura has two great beaches, the 3km-long (2-mile) Praia de Marinha and Falésia. The latter is reached via a walkway over an inlet and consequently is usually less crowded.

This chapter gives information on things to do in Portugal other than sightseeing. Portugal's best shops, arts venues, nightlife, activities and events are listed region by region.

What to Do

SHOPPING

Until Portugal joined the European Union in 1986, shopping was confined largely to small specialist stores, with only Lisbon and Porto offering much besides. That's all changed now, and most larger towns have malls on their outskirts with a vast range of goods on offer. Lisbon and Porto still rule the luxury market, but other towns are catching up, particularly in the heavily populated north and the prosperous Algarve. A plethora of tiny, specialist stores still exists, alongside the larger outlets, in towns and cities, while remote villages have some wonderful general stores catering to the needs of the locals.

DEPARTMENT STORES AND SHOPPING MALLS

Department stores are virtually non-existent in Portugal, where the emphasis has always been on individual, specialist retail. If you're visiting Lisbon, El Corte Inglés, the giant Spanish chain store, has a big and popular branch there.

Since 1987, when the Amoreiras shopping mall, Portugal's first, opened in Lisbon, the Portuguese have fallen in love with huge shopping complexes that are as much day-out destinations as retail outlets. These all have branches of Portuguese and international chain stores—which you often won't find in traditional downtown locations. They frequently have longer opening hours than the shops in the heart of the city, and there's normally a huge supermarket or hypermarket attached. In addition to food, they sell clothes, white goods and electronic equipment. The two main chains are Continente and Pingo Doce.

OPENING HOURS

Small shops open around 9, close between 12 and 2, and re-open until around 6 or 7. Outside large cities, shops tend to close for the weekend at Saturday lunchtime.

Traditional shops may have random closing times; a *volto jà* (back soon) sign on the door should be taken with a pinch of salt. Small shops often close for a month in summer.

PAYMENT

Credit cards are increasingly accepted, though not for small transactions or on the same scale as in other European countries. Market traders are paid in cash. Personal cheques are not generally accepted.

TAX REFUNDS AND SALES

Residents of non-EU states can claim back IVA (VAT) for goods purchased at shops that are part of the tax-free scheme. Such stores will have a sticker

NAME	Menswear	Womenswear	For children	Shoes	Cosmetics and toiletries	Accessories	Household items	Stationery	Books, music and DVDs	CONTACT NUMBER
Alain Manoukian		✔		✔		✔				217 110 953
Atlantis							✔			214 608 506
Bata			✔	✔						217 168 161
Bertrand									✔	214 607 092
O Boticário					✔					214 607 020
Casa Alegre							✔			218 955 604
Cortefiel	✔	✔				✔				214 679 188
Façonnable	✔									214 601 129
FNAC									✔	213 221 800
Hera				✔						214 601 676
Jakadi			✔	✔		✔				218 955 681
Lanidor		✔								214 600 131
Papelaria Fernandes								✔		214 608 515
Parfois						✔				214 607 084
Pull & Bear	✔	✔		✔		✔				214 601 060
Spal						✔				214 601 269
Vista Alegre							✔			213 831 910

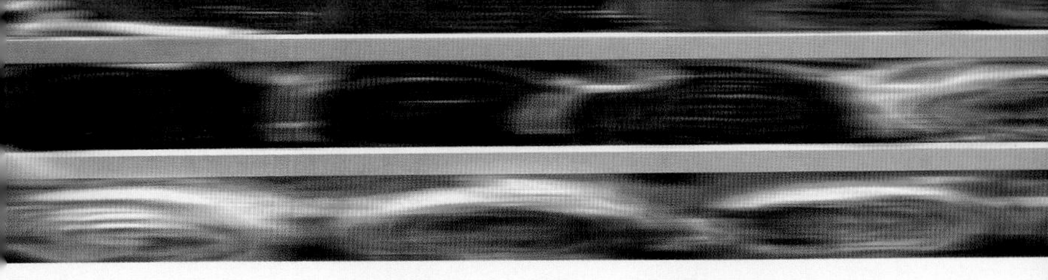

displayed in the window. Claims are made by filling in a form available at the tax-free counter at the airport when you are departing.

HANDICRAFTS
Portugal has a very strong and flourishing tradition of handicrafts and artisan work, best seen at the weekly markets all over the country and in particular the big fairs. You'll also find specialist outlets for different handicrafts in their location of manufacture.

CERAMICS AND POTTERY
Ceramics generally are excellent value. *Azulejos* (decorated tiles) are a major Portuguese product, and retailers will be able to arrange shipping if you're buying in bulk.

Portugal's main porcelain manufacturer is Vista Alegre, whose high-quality products are exported worldwide. Selection and prices are better in Portugal than overseas, and a visit to their factory near Aveiro is well worthwhile.

TEXTILES
Portugal produces superb textiles, many of whose designs are traditionally associated with a particular place. Lace and embroidery are often used as decoration on textile products, with the finest lace coming from the coastal areas. The silk-embroidered linen *colchas* (bedspreads) from Castelo Branco are among the best-known and loveliest textiles in Portugal, while Arraiolos is famous for its linen-based wool-embroidered carpets.

LEATHER
Shoe and leather goods are major industries. Prices are extremely competitive, but check for quality if they seem too good to be true.

JEWELLERY
Portugal has a tradition of filigree work, and you'll find intricate pieces made from fine gold wire in different shapes. Brooches and earrings are both good buys.

WOODWORK AND BASKETWARE
Wooden cupboards, chairs and trays are made in different regions, often beautifully decorated in bright designs. Easier to transport is basketwork, and you'll find finely made baskets in a variety of shapes and sizes on sale in markets and shops all over the country.

FOOD AND WINE
Every region in Portugal has its own special foods and wines, which you'll find in markets, at food shops and at local delicatessens. You can also buy wine and olive oil direct from many producers—look for signs or ask at the local tourist information office.

You will encounter branches of chain stores listed in this chart in shopping districts and malls throughout the country

Take home an unusual ceramic

DESCRIPTION	
Stylish clothes and accessories for women	www.alain-manoukian.com
Fine crystal and porcelain	www.atlantis-cristais-de-alcobaca.pt
Reasonably priced footware for men, women and children	www.bata.com
Bookshop including a limited selection of English-language books	www.bertrand.pt
Perfume and cosmetics	www.boticario.br
Inexpensive modern tableware and household accessories	www.vistaalegre.pt
Department store selling classic clothes for men and women	www.cortefiel.es
Classic wear for men	www.faconnable.com
Books, music, DVDs, camera and computer equipment, and performance tickets	www.fnac.pt
Footwear for men and women	www.hera.online.pt
Stylish clothes for children	www.jakadi.fr
Women's clothes, especially woollen items	www.lanidor.pt
Stationery, pens, paper, paints and art equipment	www.papelariafernandes.pt
Costume jewellery and handbags	www.parfois.com
Streetwear for young adults	www.pullbear.com
Porcelain and crystal	www.spal.pt
Quality dinner services and porcelain in classic designs	www.vistaalegre.pt

ENTERTAINMENT

If you're looking for a break from sightseeing or lazy beach days, you'll find a good range of entertainment on offer in Portugal. Lisbon is the main live performance arena, but Porto and other large provincial cities have a variety of theatre and concerts. Don't miss the chance to hear some *fado*, Portugal's soul music, or to take in some regional music, often performed on traditional instruments unique to the country.

CINEMA

Multiplexes have proliferated all over the country in recent years, many of them located in major shopping malls. If you don't speak Portuguese the big bonus is that all films are shown in their original language, so you'll be able to catch the latest international

Fado clubs in Lisbon are concentrated around the Bairro Alto district

blockbusters almost everywhere, as well as art-house films from all over the world in the bigger cities.

Prices are low (around €5), with further reductions on Mondays, though you need to arrive at the cinema early to be sure of getting a seat.

Online film listings and ticket sales are available at www.publico.pt, www.iol.pt and www.lusomundo.net, though you'll need some knowledge of Portuguese to negotiate the sites.

Details of films are shown in weekend or Friday newspapers, and in weekly and monthly listings magazines.

CLASSICAL MUSIC, BALLET AND DANCE

There is usually a good selection of classical music concerts during the main season, which runs from October to May. Lisbon has three orchestras, which perform in the city and at venues across the country. Concerts are often staged in historic settings, such as monasteries, cathedrals, palaces and castles, so it's worth finding out what's on simply to enjoy fine music in beautiful surroundings.

Portugal's national ballet company, the Companhia Nacional de Bailado, performs classical ballet during the winter months, while the internationally acclaimed Ballet Gulbenkian showcases contemporary works.

Modern dance fans should try to catch a performance by companies like the Companhia Portuguesa de Bailado Contemporâneo, which stages highly theatrical works that include a strong dash of African influence.

FADO

This is Portugal's soul music, an urban invention involving singer and guitar, and expressing the uniquely Portuguese concept of *saudade*, a sadness or yearning that has a beauty all of its own. There are two *fado* traditions, from Lisbon and Coimbra respectively, so you'll hear the best in either of these cities.

Lisbon's version is purely vocal and can be sung by men and women, while Coimbra's includes guitar pieces as well as song, and is performed exclusively by men.

You'll hear *fado* at specialist clubs, where eating and drinking are very much part of the proceedings. Some clubs are expensive, some real tourist traps, and there's no real way of knowing whom or what you'll hear on a given night. That said, in Lisbon, some well-known *fadistas* run their own clubs. The music is performed by a solo singer, usually accompanied by the *guitarra* (despite its name not a guitar but a type of six-stringed 18th-century cittern)

The Seteais Palace in Sintra, near Lisbon, hosts ballet performances

and the *viola de fado* (similar to the Spanish guitar). For the Portuguese, the words are an essential part of *fado*, but even if you don't speak the language, the combination of voice and instruments can be truly spine-tingling. In Lisbon, head for the Bairro Alto for a good range of *fado* clubs; in Coimbra, it's associated with the university.

CONTEMPORARY LIVE MUSIC

International bands and stars tend to concentrate on Lisbon and Porto, where they often perform in stadiums and large concert halls. Artists include

big names from Brazil, giving a chance to hear something not normally on offer in other European cities. Portugal's main cities, too, are places to hear a wide range of musical styles, often fuelled by a steady supply of African, Cape Verde and Brazilian musicians. Concerts are advertised in listings magazines, by posters and by flyers in bars—or ask at tourist offices. Local rock is performed all over the country, often in bars where you can relax with a drink, and jazz takes the stage at some of the summer music festivals.

FOLK AND REGIONAL MUSIC

Characteristic songs, ensembles and instruments survive in

Traditions are kept alive with popular regional folk dancing

each region of the country, and tend to be at their best in rural inland areas such as the Trás-os-Montes, the Beiras and the Alentejo.

Many towns and villages have their own *ranchos folclóricos*, troupes who perform at festivals and keep the old traditions going. They often play uniquely Portuguese instruments, such as the *gaita-de-foles* (bagpipes) in the Trás-os-Montes and Minho, the *flauta pastoril* (whistle), and drums, such as the *adufe* (square drum), *bombo* (bass drum) and *caixa* (snare drum). Ask at local tourist information offices about performances or check out www.attambur.com for festival listings and music samples you can download.

THEATRE

Unless you are a Portuguese speaker, you are unlikely to want to go to the theatre in Portugal. Many places, however, double up as venues for music or dance, so in the bigger cities it's worth checking listings or asking at the tourist office to see if anything appeals.

LISTINGS IN LISBON

The best listings magazine is the *Agenda Cultural*, a free monthly that's published in Portuguese only, though much of the information also appears in the *Follow me Lisboa* booklet (in English) produced by the tourist board; you can pick up both at city tourist offices. Both the Gulbenkian and the Belém Cultural Centre publish a schedule of their concerts, exhibitions and events, which you can collect from their reception desks. Two newspapers, the *Díario de Notícias* and *O Independente*, publish Friday supplements with full entertainment listings.

LISTINGS IN PORTO

Listings can be found in the free monthly arts listings booklet *cultura.norte*, and in the quarterly *Agenda do Porto* (www.agendadoporto.pt). Both are available from tourist information offices. The newspaper *Público* publishes a listings supplement on Fridays and you can also find information in the *Jornal de Notícias*, Porto's leading paper.

LISTINGS IN THE ALGARVE

There are entertainment listings in the free monthly papers *Welcome to the Algarve* and the *Algarve Guide*.

LISTINGS ELSEWHERE

In other towns and cities throughout the country it's worth checking the listings in the local newspapers to find out what's on, particularly for late-night music events and details of what's happening on the club scene. In smaller places, local tourist information offices will be able to help, while bars are always good places to pick up flyers.

TICKETING IN LISBON

You can book ahead for different events at the following ticket outlets:

ABEP (Agência de Bilhetes para Espectáculos Públicos)
Praça dos Restauradores
213 240 130
Mon–Sat 9am–9.30pm
Restauradores

Dance and theatre are just some of the entertainments on offer

Agência de Bilhetes Alvalade
Praça de Alvalade 6, Edificio Centro Comercial Alvalade, Loja 43, Alvalade
217 955 859
Daily 11–9.30
Alvalade

FNAC Centro Comercial Colombo
Avenida do Colégio Militar, Loja (shop) A-103
217 114 240, 217 114 241
Daily 10am–midnight
Colegio Militar

FNAC Chiado Armazéns do Chiado
Rua do Crucifixo 2
213 221 811, 213 221 812
Daily 10–10

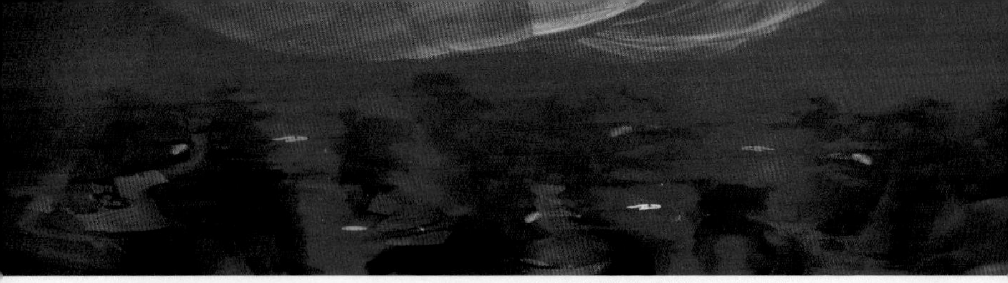

NIGHTLIFE

Nightlife in Lisbon and Porto is up there with the best in Europe, with a plethora of late bars and clubs offering something for every taste. Outside these two main cities (with the exception of the university city of Coimbra during term time) you'll find things quieter during the week, when choice will be limited to a couple of music bars, but there'll be something on offer at the weekends. The Algarve is packed with night-time options, and you'll find plenty to choose from at other popular summertime coastal resorts. Don't miss the chance to participate in local celebrations, when small communities let their hair down in uniquely Portuguese style.

BARS AND NIGHTCLUBS

There's a fair amount of cross-over between bars and clubs, with many bars hosting live music some nights of the week.

Cocktail hour in Albufeira after a hard day's sunbathing

Most clubs open around 8pm, with things getting going near midnight and continuing until 3am or later. Lisbon and Porto can be packed throughout the night at weekends with club-bers moving on from one venue to another.

In Lisbon, the traditional place for night-time action has always been the Bairro Alto, though this area now concen-trates more on late bars than dance venues. You'll find the best, brashest and most excit-ing of these down by the waterside, notably around Santa Apolónia and the Doca de Santo Amaro beneath the Ponte 25 de Abril. Lisbon's other hot spots are around the Avenida 24 de Julho and in Alcântara.

In Porto, many of the main dance venues are outside the heart of the city, though you'll find late music bars and some clubs clustered around the Ribeiro waterfront. Across the river, there's clubbing to be done in Vila Nova de Gaia, while summer sees the scene shifting towards the beach-side clubs at Foz do Douro.

If you're in the Algarve, you'll find clubs and bars of every type, ranging from the packed discos of Albufeira to pricey and romantic music bars in the more sophisticated resorts.

Check with local tourist information offices or listings magazines (▷ 181) for the latest news and opening times, and keep an eye out for posters and flyers in bars.

Many clubs operate what's known as the *consumo mínimo* system, specifying a minimum amount that you have to spend while in the club. In other words, it's a disguised admission charge, though it may include the price of one or more drinks. On entering you are handed a card, which is stamped every time you order a drink. On the way out you pay the minimum *consumo* stamped on the card–even if you've had nothing to drink. In a few of the most exclusive clubs, the *consumo mínimo* can vary hugely from person to person (from €10 to €250) as it is used to deter less 'desir-able' or less 'well-dressed' customers.

In the listings in this guide, the *consumo mínimo* is treated as an admission charge.

GAY AND LESBIAN NIGHTLIFE

Over the last decade or so attitudes to gay and lesbian people have lightened up considerably in what is still a conservative society.

Lisbon has long been a gay-friendly city, and the Algarve, too, offers a relaxed welcome at clubs and bars, though it's best to keep a low profile in conservative, church-going country places.

You can dance the night away until the small hours

To check out what's on, pick up a copy of the quarterly gay men's magazine *Korpus* or, for women, *Zona Livre*, available in newsagents.

In Lisbon, most gay bars and clubs are found in the Bairro Alto and Príncipe Real. The Centro Comunitário Gay e Lesbico de Lisboa (tel 218 873 918) is a good starting point for contacts and information.

It's also worth checking out the English-language website www.portugalgay.pt for information on what's on.

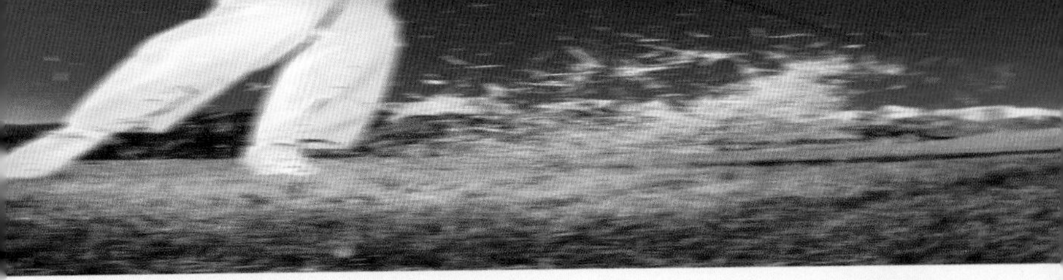

SPORTS AND ACTIVITIES

Portugal has some of Europe's finest year-round facilities, seen at their best in the superb golf courses and tennis complexes in the Algarve. There's a great number of activites visitors can take part in: hiking, horseback riding, off-road driving, bicycling, swimming and watersports. In the cities, too, leisure and sports facilities are burgeoning and fitness fans should be able to find something to suit. Soccer is by far Portugal's most popular spectator sport, with millions keenly following their heroes. Roller-hockey is another popular spectator sport, with the Portuguese women's team winning the world championships in 2003.

BULLFIGHTING

The heart of bullfighting in Portugal is the Ribatejo, where the animals are bred. Portuguese bullfighting differs from the Spanish version in that the bull is not killed in the ring, but wrestled to the ground. The bull, its horns padded or sheared, first faces a mounted *toureiro* in 18th-century costume, who plants *farpas* (darts) in its back in a superb display of horsemanship. An eight-strong team of *moços-de-forcado* then moves in and overwhelms the bull by brute force, pinning it to the ground between them.

Serious golfers will be in heaven in this major golfing country

If you want to see a bullfight, head for the Ribatejo, avoiding the tourist displays occasionally put on in the Algarve. The season runs from April to October, with *festas* at Vila Franca de Xira and Santarém.

Other Ribatejo towns and villages also stage bull-running through their streets, similar to that at Pamplona in Spain.

FISHING

Portugal's northern rivers are rich in trout, with those of the Minho offering the best fishing. If you're interested, you'll need a permit, available from local town halls.

GOLF

Portugal has some of Europe's finest golf courses, beautifully laid out and designed by the top names in the sport. The pick of the bunch are found all along the Algarve coast, with a high concentration in the central area, particularly at Vilamoura, Quinta do Lago and Vale de Lobo. Farther north, you'll find lovely courses in the Lisbon area; these have the benefit of being quieter than those in the Algarve and offering excellent value for money.

If you just want a game of golf, rather than booking a golfing holiday, ask at the local tourist office for details of the nearest course. Portuguese clubs are private, and can be expensive, but it's often possible to play a round and rent clubs and a golf cart.

The Portuguese Open Championships are held in the Algarve during April at different courses, among them Penina, Vila Sol and Quinta do Lago South. For tickets and further information, contact your own club, a specialist travel operator, or www.theworldofgolf.com or www.portugalvirtual.pt/golf.

GYMS AND FITNESS

The keep-fit culture was late in reaching Portugal, and it's still rare to see people jogging, even in the larger cities. But gyms do exist, and the number is growing. Local tourist offices should be able to point you in the right direction.

Gyms in Lisbon and Porto have all the usual indoor fitness facilities, plus some extras. They are normally open from around 7am to 10pm Monday to Friday, with shorter hours at the weekend.

Taking a trip on horseback makes a change from the beach

HORSEBACK RIDING

Increasing numbers of riding companies are opening all over the country, organizing riding excursions or holidays through some of the most beautiful areas. You may even get the chance to ride the Lusitanos, Portugal's famous breed of horse, ambling through the rolling Alentejo or galloping flat out along a stretch of unspoilt beach.

Whether you're interested in a gentle hack or a comprehensive riding holiday, ask at local tourist information offices.

ROLLER-HOCKEY

Portugal excels at this fast-moving sport, with local teams forming a national league whose matches are played on Saturday or Sunday afternoons and evenings. Roller-hockey is particularly popular in the north, where you'll find the strongest teams; ask at local tourist offices in bigger towns if you want to catch a match. The season runs from September until June and there are two European cups.

SOCCER

The successful staging of the European Football Championship in 2004 put Portuguese soccer firmly on the map, and provided the impetus for the upgrading or construction of stadiums. Importantly, many of these were designed to be used for other sporting events as well as *futebol* (soccer).

Soccer is dominated by two Lisbon teams, Benfica and Sporting Lisbon, and FC Porto from Porto. Virtually everyone supports one of these three clubs, so even reputable local teams, such as Sporting Braga and Guimarães, barely get a look in. The league season runs from September until May, and matches are played on Sunday afternoons or evenings.

Except for big matches, tickets are generally inexpensive (€3–€30) and easy to obtain either direct from kiosks at the grounds or from ticket agencies. Matches are prominently advertised in the sporting press, particularly *Bola,* or you can catch the latest news at www.portuguesesoccer.com or www.infordesporto.pt/futebal.

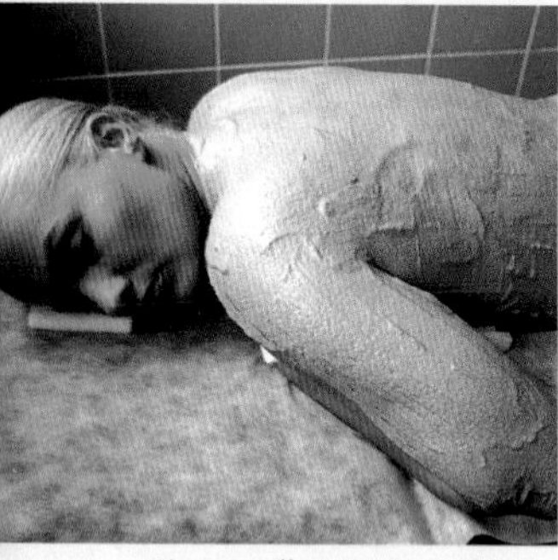

Give yourself a treat at one of the many thermal spas

SPAS

Taking the waters is an integral part of Portuguese culture, and you'll find spas all over the country. Few are of the five-star health-farm type—though these are starting to appear—but as a real Portuguese experience and a chance to enjoy some inexpensive pampering they're hard to beat. Note, though, that some are well off the beaten track.

The Portuguese believe firmly in the benefits of mineral-rich water, whether it's to improve their health by drinking it, or using its beneficial qualities to treat specific medical conditions such as allergies, arthritis and rheumatism, or digestive and breathing problems.

If you want to alleviate a medical condition, you'll need to see a doctor on arrival, who will work out the regime best suited to your needs. If you just want to wallow in a steaming hot tub, make a reservation and lie back and enjoy.

Portuguese spas are overseen by an umbrella organization, the Termas de Portugal (Avenida Miguel Bombard 110, 2º Dtº, 1050-167 Lisbon, tel 217 940 574, 217 940 505, fax: 217 938 233), which can help with information and bookings.

SURFING AND WINDSURFING

With its west-facing Atlantic position, it's not surprising Portugal has superb surfing—it's a year-round sport up and down the coast. If you're an experienced surfer, simply ask at local tourist offices for advice on good locations; if not, don't try to go it alone as currents and tides can be very dangerous, and you'll need professional help to get going.

Windsurfing is also an option; you can rent boards at many places in the Algarve, at the bigger resorts in the north of the country and around Lisbon. Popular locations are Guincho, north of Lisbon, and Ericeira, farther north up the coast. Several companies offer surfing camp holidays with tuition. For general information, go to www.surf-experience.com or www.purevacations.com/surf/portugal.

SWIMMING AND WATER SPORTS

Swimming and the water are the obvious major draws for many visitors to Portugal, and you'll find superb beaches along the entire coastline.

Swimming in the pool or the sea is usually the major part of a holiday

With its year-round balmy climate, the Algarve is the top draw for most visitors, and swimmers can take to the water here all year. Most Algarve hotels have swimming pools, and if you're renting a villa at the top end of the range, you're likely to have one of your own.

Farther north, sea swimming is more of a summertime activity, and you could find the water off the northern coast cold, so if you're holidaying with small children it would be better to head south of Lisbon.

Portuguese beaches are not well endowed with lifeguards and currents can be strong, particularly along the west coast, so swim from beaches only where there are plenty of other people about, rather than take risks at a secluded spot. With tides scouring in from the Atlantic, water quality is good on the whole, though it's best to avoid swimming near major cities, ports or industrial coastal areas. Inland, some hotels have swimming pools and you'll find municipal pools in the larger towns; enquire at local tourist offices about facilities.

Larger coast resorts also offer jet-ski and motor-boat rental, and in some areas you may be able to rent a small sailing boat; tourist offices will be able to help and it's worth scanning the local press for details.

Scuba-diving can be an unforgettable experience, and divers are well catered for in the clear waters of the Algarve, with equipment hire and PADI diving courses on offer.

TENNIS

Many hotels and villa complexes have their own tennis courts, and you'll find tennis clubs in larger towns and cities. Book in advance during the summer, remembering that evenings, when courts are floodlit and temperatures drop, are a good (although popular) time for a game. In the south, tennis coaching and holidays can be organized by the clubs attached to the resorts in the central Algarve, notably at Quinta do Lago and Vale de Lobo.

WALKING AND HIKING

Walking as a recreational pursuit is still a relatively new concept in Portugal, and the networks of good trails and paths found in other European countries do not exist as yet. But there's still plenty of choice if you're looking for gentle strolls near the coast, or want to experience the grandeur of the upland interior in the northern and central parts of the country.

The best way to undertake some serious walking is by booking a holiday with a specialist company, which will have researched good continuous routes and will often provide guided tours. If you're in the Algarve you'll find superb walking in the hills behind the coast; there are several good English-language publications detailing routes, or local tourist offices will be able to supply leaflets for some areas. Elsewhere there will be local companies offering day walks, while some tourist offices can provide leaflets detailing safe walking routes.

There are fine hard and grass courts at clubs throughout the country

Discover Portugal's rural pleasures on your own, or join a tour

PARKS–THE TOP FIVE

Parque Nacional da Peneda-Gerês (▷ 78–81)
Portugal's only national park, set in the north, with superb mountain scenery on an impressively grand scale.

Parque Natural do Douro Internacional (▷ 76)
A scenic and remote area spanning the Portuguese–Spanish border in the northeast.

Parque Natural de Montesinho (▷ 76–77)
A remote upland park in the far northeast that retains an unspoilt and traditional way of life.

Parque Natural da Ria Formosa (▷ 172)
The Algarve's own park, with coast, dunes, grass and woodlands.

Parque Natural da Serra da Estrela (▷ 105)
A central mountain park that includes mainland Portugal's highest point, Torre, at 1,993m (6,538ft).

FOR CHILDREN

Children are very much part of the mainstream of life in Portugal, fussed over by people of all ages, and happily participating in most everyday activities. This means that adult tolerance levels are high, but the downside is that there are relatively few child-specific facilities and amusements. Nor should you expect too much in the way of child concessions, baby-changing facilities or children's menus. There's plenty for kids to do, though, particularly on the coast and in the larger cities, where there are museums and other attractions. Older children might appreciate Portugal's great outdoors, with its opportunities for walking, horseback riding, quad-biking and water sports.

FAMILY-FRIENDLY AREAS

If you're visiting with younger children, a beach holiday makes sense, with the Algarve and its hundreds of attractions heading the list. Resorts here are well geared to children, there's a wide range of types of beach to choose from, and there are waterparks and other attractions for a change of pace. The balmy climate allows for year-round holidaying; visiting outside the high summer months means that you will pay less and also benefit by escaping the high temperatures that small children will find hard to tolerate.

Waterslides are a good idea when you've had enough of the beach

Also bordered by wonderful sandy beaches, the west coast has lively resorts where there are more opportunities for children to experience real Portuguese life. Bear in mind, though, that sea temperatures are lower here than in the south, and some rain is almost inevitable, even in summer.

For older children, a judicious mix of sightseeing and country and seaside activities can work wonders—the Beira Alta, the Trás-os-Montes and the Minho might well appeal to those in their early teens.

BEACHES

Seaside resorts everywhere are busy throughout the peak holiday period of July and August, with the Algarve's season lasting a bit longer, from May until October.

Small children will be happy in the eastern Algarve, where there are miles and miles of gently shelving sandy beaches, beach games and playgrounds. Older children may well prefer more scenic areas, such as the coves and cliffs of the western Algarve and southern Alentejo.

If you're planning a beach holiday farther north, bear in mind that the water can be cold and that there are dangerous currents and undertows in many places. Because of this it's best to stick to busier beaches, even if your children are strong swimmers. Boat trips are often popular with children of all ages—ask at local tourist offices.

Birds create a show: whether toucans…

THEME PARKS

Portugal's biggest and best waterparks are in the Algarve, but you'll also find adventure and theme parks in other regions, though not on the same scale as in many other European countries. Ask at tourist information offices for details of children's attractions.

CITIES

Portuguese cities don't usually have the wealth of children's indoor attractions that other European cities offer, but Lisbon has plenty to keep them entertained. Getting around, by tram, funicular, open-top bus or ferry, is fun, while the Parque das Nações has plenty to keep kids busy.

…or parrots, and are part of a theme patk experience

Elsewhere, holidaying in cities with children can be hard work, but shopping malls often have amusements, and films and cartoons are shown in English throughout the country. Tourist offices will advise on child-orientated attractions.

FESTIVALS AND EVENTS

Like many European countries, Portugal stages arts festivals throughout the year. There is also a huge number of local, traditionally Portuguese festivals, which can range from tiny but exuberant village celebrations to huge week-long fairs and pilgrimages that draw thousands. Most reflect important themes in Portuguese life, and there's no better way of experiencing what makes the country tick than mingling with the crowds. Ask at tourist offices for up-to-the-minute information, keep an eye out for posters, or go to www.rede-almanaque.pt/feiras, a comprehensive site listing festivals all over the country.

RELIGIOUS

Religious festivals are linked both to the great feasts of the church calendar and to religious shrines, many devoted to the Virgin Mary. Of these,

A typical parade at the Festa das Cruzes, Barcelos

Fátima (▷ 116) tops the list, with those in Viana do Castelo in the Minho and Lamego in the Beiras mixing let-your-hair-down celebration with religious fervour. The festivals of Santo António and São João are similar, and the minor festivals in smaller towns and villages are a highly enjoyable blend of religion and party time.

TRADITIONAL

Some of Portugal's most lively celebrations are the *feiras* (festivals), which combine the best of traditional country fairs with serious festivities. At one of these you can experience an exciting blend of agricultural show, folk festival and amusement park, with eating and drinking high on the agenda.

ARTS FESTIVALS

Many of Portugal's major arts festivals take place in and around Lisbon and Porto, and feature classical music, jazz and film. Ask at any local tourist information office for details of what's on where and when.

THE BIGGEST AND BEST

Carnaval
Celebrates the start of Lent with street processions in towns all over Portugal; see the best in Lisbon and the major resorts along the Algarve (Feb–early Mar).

Queima das Fitas (Coimbra)
Marks the end of the academic year in Coimbra with traditional customs, partying and plenty of Coimbra-style *fado* (mid-May).

Fátima
Portugal's most famous pilgrimage in honour of the Virgin Mary (13 May). A second major pilgrimage takes place in October.

Feira Nacional da Agricultura (Santarém)
A huge country show with the accent on traditional farming, bullfighting and dancing (10 days from 1st Fri in Jun).

Santos Popularos
Celebrations all over Portugal in honour of St. Anthony (12–23 Jun), St. John (23–24 Jun), and St. Peter (28–29 Jun). Lisbon focuses on St. Anthony, Porto on St. John.

Romaria da Nossa Senhora da Agonía (Viana do Castelo)
Weekend-long pilgrimage and festivities with dancing, music parades and fireworks (nearest weekend to 20 Aug).

Romaria da Nossa Senhora dos Rememédios (Lamego)
Pilgrimage and *festa* with religious processions, parades, car-racing, rock music and non-stop partying (pilgrimage 6–8 Sep, but other events take place over a fortnight).

Traditional costumes from the Trajes de Festas Populares in Bragança

Feiras Novas (Ponte de Lima)
Huge market and fair—music, *gigantones* (carnival figures), fairground and bands (2nd and 3rd weekend in Sep).

Feira Nacional do Cavalo (Golegã)
Portugal's biggest horse fair, with mounted parades of magnificent beasts, bull-running and lively street partying (first 2 weeks in Nov).

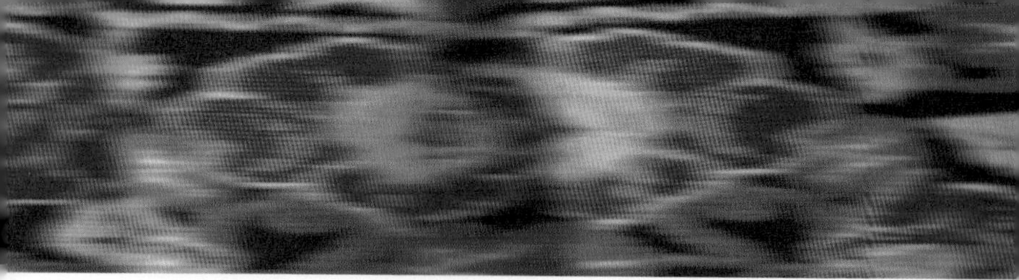

THE MINHO AND TRÁS-OS-MONTES

WHAT TO DO

The Minho and the Trás-os-Montes have plenty on offer: good regional shopping, great festivals, outdoor activities in beautiful surroundings, spas and more than a touch of culture and nightlife. The region is noted for its textile production, and you'll see traditionally produced linen goods in markets all over the area. These weekly markets are one of the glories of Portugal that you really shouldn't miss; if you can't make it to the one held in Barcelos, the biggest and most famous of them all, you'll find one in every town of any size, and its smaller cousin in remote villages. They showcase all the best in local produce, whether that's food, artisan work or textiles. The Minho produces excellent leather goods, sometimes available at factory outlets, and you'll find distinctive local pottery everywhere.

KEY TO SYMBOLS

- **Shopping**
- **Entertainment**
- **Nightlife**
- **Sports**
- **Activities**
- **Health and Beauty**
- **For Children**

BARCELOS

BARCELOS MARKET

Campo da República, Barcelos

This is one of the best ceramics markets in Portugal. Traditional (and inexpensive) earthenware with cream patterns and the ubiquitous red-, black- and white-painted cockerels are well-known tourist purchases, sold alongside basket ware, hand-painted tin objects, household goods and plenty of fresh produce.

Thu

CENTRO DE ARTESANATO DE BARCELOS

Largo da Porta Nova, Barcelos

Tel 253 811 882

Within the 16th-century Torre da Menagem, this great craft shop offers both quality and good value. Two floors are crammed with a range of goods; perhaps most interesting of all are the comic green- and brown-glazed figurines from the heirs of the famous Rosa Carvalho—the mother of Portuguese ceramicists.

Fri–Wed 9–12.30, 2.30–6, Thu 9–6

From Praça da República, take Rua Dom António Barroso towards the river; it is in the same tower as the tourist office, opposite Santa Cruz church

VATICANO

Rua Candido da Cunha 118, Barcelos

Tel 253 812 962

The young partying set comes from across the region to this landmark bar and club. Begin in the outer area with a drink, before moving into the dance area to be blasted with house and trance or maybe a live band.

Fri–Sat midnight–7am €5 (includes drinks)

AMIGOS DA MONTANHA

Rua Custódio José Gomes Vilas Boas 47, Barcelos

Tel 253 831 647, or mobiles 962 767 420 and 917 793 805

www.amigosdamontanha.bcl.pt

For hiking, bicycle riding or canoeing, the best company in town is surely Amigos de Montanha. It has a fixed calendar of events; for details or to arrange an activity, telephone or visit the office or go to the website.

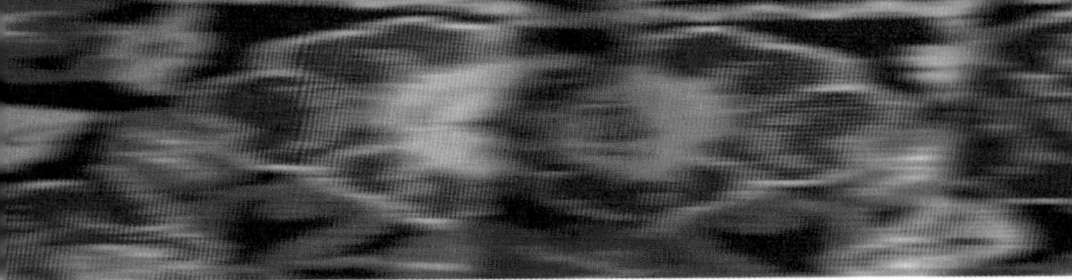

Central office: Wed 6.30–7.30pm, 9.30–10.30pm. Mobile phone lines: 9–7 Mountain-biking, canoeing €20; white-water rafting €45; hiking information free On the street leading to the medieval bridge

BRAGA

BRAGA MARKET

Parque de Exposições, near the São João bridge

The Braga weekly market sells the usual fare, but, thanks to its proximity to the northern shoe and textile factories, has a good selection of these. You can often find international brands at knock-down prices.

Tue

JOSÉ GONÇALVES

Rua da Boavista 69–71, Braga
Tel 253 612 428

Among Braga's most important craft products are its fine folk guitars. This workshop near the Campo da Vinha specializes in classical guitars, the smaller *cavaquinhos*, *bandolinas* and *guitarras*.

Mon–Fri 10.30–1, 2–7, Sat 2–7

BAR DO LIP

Rua Dom Pedro V 154 A, Loja (shop) 3, Braga
Tel 253 260 969

This American-inspired bar, decorated with pictures of John Wayne, Marilyn Monroe, Elvis Presley and other stars of the silver screen, keeps to its 'gringo' theme by playing a selection of 1950s and 1960s rock and blues, with live bands or karaoke on alternate Friday and Saturday nights.

Mon–Sat 10pm–2am Mon–Thu admission free, Fri–Sat €5

BARBIÉRI CAFFÉ

Avenida Central 42–44, Braga
Tel 253 614 381

A few doors down from Insolito (another nightspot), this club begins the evening with dance classes. After midnight the Latin rhythms continue on the ground floor, while upstairs often hosts themed parties.

Tue, Fri–Sat midnight–5am Tue €3 (includes drinks), Fri–Sat €1.50

CAFÉ ASTÓRIA

Avenida Central 5, Praça da República, Braga
Tel 965 065 601

One of Braga's landmark cafés, the Astória recently branched out by opening a nightclub on its first floor. Hosting regular themed parties and playing a vibrant mix of house and techno sounds, it has become a popular city hot spot.

Jun, Jul Fri–Sat midnight–5am; Sep–end May Sat midnight–5am €5 (includes drinks)

Traditional ceramic cockerels for sale at Barcelos market

BRACALANDIA

Avenida João Paulo II, Braga
Tel 253 603 260
www.bracalandia.com

This mini-theme park is a great day out for children of all ages. Flying elephant rides, roller-coasters, carousels, log flumes, Apache camps and Blackbeard pirate hideouts are just a few of the attractions on offer. You need not worry about food and drink for the children, as a variety of on-site bars and restaurants serve refreshments throughout the day.

2nd weekend Jun–2nd weekend Sep and Easter holiday daily 10–8; 3rd weekend Mar–1st weekend Jun and 3rd weekend Sep–last weekend Oct Sat–Sun and national holidays 10–8 Adult €14, child (5–12) €12

INDIANA BILL

Rua Nova de Santa Cruz 128–132, Braga
Tel 253 679 918

Have some fun with the kids at this pirate-themed adventure playground, with its climbing frames, swings and slides. When appetites build up, there is a snack bar on site.

Mon–Fri 2.30–7.30, Sat–Sun and national holidays 10.30–7.30 €3 per hour

BRAGANÇA

BRAGANÇA MARKET

Around Municipal Stadium, Avenida Abade de Baçal, Bragança
Tel 273 381 273 (tourist office)

In the west of town, this market sells all the usual products, including ceramics, household goods and fresh produce.

3rd, 12th and 23rd of month, or nearest Mon when these dates fall over weekends

MUNICIPAL MARKET

Forte São João Deus, Bragança
Tel 273 325 474

Worth a quick stop, the stalls here sell a selection of regional crafts, cured meats and cheeses, plus some less visitor-orientated foods, such as a selection of dried tripe for making your own sausages at home.

Mon–Fri 8–7, Sat–Sun 8–1

ROSÁRIO AND JULIETA

Shopping Loreto, Shop 26, Avenida Sá Carneiro, Bragança
Tel 919 130 366 or 919 130 346

To see two local ceramicists in action visit Rosário and Julieta, who produce, among other things, hand-painted plates and models of the local *pombais* (dovecotes). Don't be put off by the grim mall in which the workshop is housed.

Mon–Fri 9–7 The mall is on the ground floor of the tallest building on Avenida Sá Carneiro. Go up the main steps and, once inside, the shop is round to the left

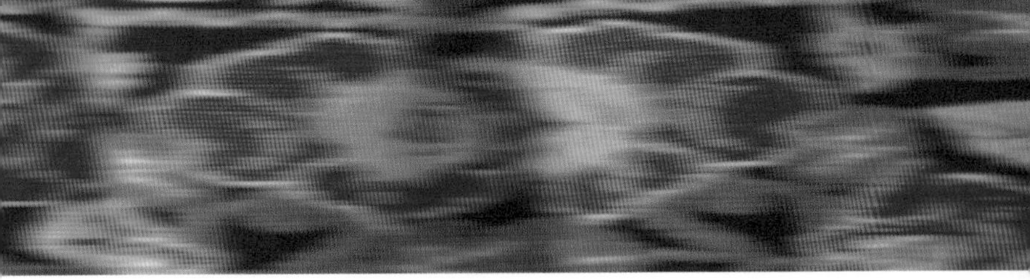

CENTRO HÍPICO DE FRANÇA

França

Tel 273 919 141

For great horse-riding in the Montesinho Natural Park, with its forested hillsides and undulating grassland, contact the Centro Hípico, some 15km (9 miles) outside Bragança in the direction of Portelo. Both guided and independent rides can be arranged.

Apr–end Oct 10–12, 2–7.30; Nov–end Mar 10–12, 2–5.30 €8 per hour França village is north of Bragança on the EN103-7

PARQUE NATURAL DE MONTESINHO

Park office: Bairro Salvador Nunes Teixeira, Lote 5, Apartado 90, Bragança

Tel 273 381 234 or 273 381 214

www.icn.pt

The wild reserve that stretches north of Bragança to the Spanish border is filled with heather- and broom-covered mountains and alder- and willow-filled valleys, creating a pleasurable terrain for hiking and walking. The park office has detailed information.

Mon–Fri 9–12.30, 2–5.30

CHAVES

CHAVES MARKET

Next to stadium, Chaves

Tel 276 340 661 (tourist office)

This is a good place to buy local crafts, such as baskets made in the surrounding villages, or the distinctive black Chaves pottery, which is fired in an ash- and earth-covered pit to achieve its dark lustre.

Wed

NORTE AVENTURA

Turismo e Animação Lda, Largo de São Roque, Loja R/C D to, Chaves

Tel 966 047 700

Norte Aventura provides qualified guides and instructors for all kinds of outdoor pursuits, such as hiking, mountain-biking and four-wheel driving, or more strenuous outdoor activities like rock-climbing, canoeing, abseiling or white-water rafting.

Office: Jun–end Oct Mon–Sat 10–1, 3–7.30; Nov–end May Sat 10–1, 3–7.30 Prices depend on activity

VIDAGO PALACE GOLF CLUB

Parque de Vidago, Vidago

Tel 276 909 662 or 276 999 404

www.portugalgolf.pt

For a game of golf, head 20km (12.5 miles) south of Chaves to the spa village of Vidago. The Palace Hotel has a hilly nine-hole course, played over two rounds, with a par of 33. The September competitions are well known to visitors from Lisbon and Porto. The club house serves light meals.

Jun–end Sep 9–8; Nov–end May 9–7 18 holes €25; club and trolley rental €17.50 Southwest from Chaves on IP3 to Vidago, then signed

Rolling hills are the mark of the Parque Natural de Montesinho

TERMAS DE CHAVES

Largo das Caldas, Chaves

Tel 276 332 445

The natural spring here is one of the hottest in Europe, bubbling out of the ground here at 73°C (163°F). The spa, which is on the south bank of the river, is generally full of elderly patients on extended courses of treatments, but casual visitors can take a swig from the waters.

1 Mar–30 Nov daily 8–8 €4–€16 according to treatment

GUIMARÃES

GUIMARÃES MARKET

Praça de São Tiago and Largo da Oliveira

This market sells clothes, shoes and regional products, such as carved wooden animal yokes, woven textiles, leatherwear, pottery and, sometimes, linen, special to Guimarães. Hand-spun, hand-woven and then embroidered, the quality is excellent.

1st Sat of month

A OFICINA

Rua Paio Galvão, 11, Guimarães

Tel 253 515 250

For a good selection of Guimarães' famous linens, including tablecloths, napkins and hand towels, try this municipal outlet, which was established to promote the town's artisans. Other regional crafts include fine gold- and silversmithing, embroidery and pottery.

Mon–Fri 9–8, Sat 9–7

ULTIMATUM JAZZ CAFÉ

Rua Rei do Pegú, Guimarães

Tel 253 415 294

Playing a mix of classical, jazz and piano-bar tunes, the Ultimatum hosts live bands on Thursdays and Fridays and puts on a disco on Fridays and Saturdays, starting at 1am and playing a blend of pop-rock and Latino sounds.

Tue–Sun 8pm–4am Tue–Thu entry free, Fri–Sat €5 for women, €8 for men (includes drinks)

CENTRO DE ACTIVIDADES LÚDICAS E DESPORTIVAS

Laje do Mocho, São Torcato

Tel 253 553 139

This 8ha (20-acre) adventure park provides professionally organized activities as diverse as paintballing, orienteering, mountain-bicycling, archery, rock-climbing, abseiling and 4x4 adventure treks.

May–end Oct 9–7; Nov–end Apr 9–5 €10–€12.50 according to activity São Torcato is north of Guimarães on the EN207

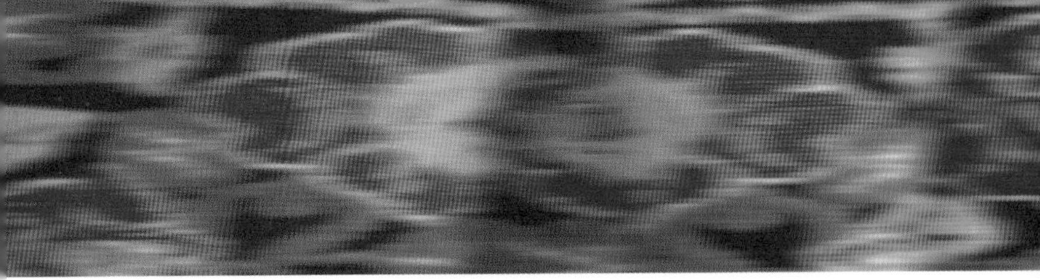

TERMAS DAS TAIPAS

Taipas
Tel 253 577 898
www.termasdeportugal.pt
For a day of relaxed pampering, take the waters at one of Portugal's finest spas. Within a leafy park on the right bank of the River Ave, the Termas das Taipas claims to help rheumatism, skin allergies and respiratory problems.
Mar–end Dec Mon–Fri 9–11, 5–7 €4.50–€10 according to which treatment you have

MIRANDA DO DOURO

ASSOCIAÇÃO PARA O ESTUDO E PROTECÇÃO DO GADO ASININO

Avenida do Ciclo Preparatório, Sede da Junta de Freguesia, Sendim
Tel 273 739 307 or 914 093 724
www.aepga.pt
Created for the study and protection of donkeys and to promote their importance in traditional rural society, this sanctuary offers donkey rides through the Miranda plain, as well as educational farm tours.
Daily 9.30–12.30, 2.30–6 €30 for approximately 4-hour excursion 26km (16 miles) south of Miranda do Douro on IC5

EUROPARQUES PORTUGAL

Centro Ambiental Luso-Espanhol, Parque Náutico, Miranda do Douro
Tel 273 432 396
Miranda do Douro's most impressive sight is undoubtedly its dramatic river gorge and the dam standing 80m (264ft) high, which lies just east of town. You can take a one-hour cruise in the international waters of the river from the Parque Náutico, beside the dam on the Portuguese side.
Boats leave Mon–Fri 4pm, Sat–Sun 11am and 4pm €12

PARQUE NATURAL DO DOURO INTERNACIONAL

ICN (Instituto da Conservação da Natureza): Rua do Convento, Palácio da Justiça, Miranda do Douro
Tel 273 431 457
www.icn.pt
The park encompasses the stretch of the River Douro that marks the frontier with Spain. It is outstandingly attractive, especially in late February and March when the steep river valley is covered in blossoming almond trees. Several hikes have been waymarked through the park, following ancient pathways but they are not always easy to navigate. If you are visiting independently rather than taking a guided tour, contact the ICN office, which will provide directions, maps and details of the hike.
Mon–Fri 9–12.30, 2–5.30

Donkeys have always been important to rural dwellers

SILBOTE

Hotel Residencial Planalto, Rua 1º de Maio 25, Miranda do Douro
Tel 273 431 362
www.hrplanalto.pt
This company organizes hiking trips, donkey rides and mountain-bicycling in the Miranda.
Daily

PONTE DE BARCA

MINHO ALEGRE

Lugar do Romão, Touzedo, São Lourenço, Ponte da Barca
Tel 258 455 500
If you would like to hike in the area, but are worried about getting lost if you set out alone, why not take a trip with one of Minho Alegre's multilingual guides. As well as walks through the Gerês National Park, the company organizes canoeing, bicycling and horse-riding, all of which should be booked at least three days in advance.
Phone lines: 9am–10pm. There is no central office €20–€60, according to activity

PONTE DE LIMA

JOAQUIM CERQUEIRA DA SILVA

Lugar do Boudilhão, Moureira do Lima
Tel 966 721 154
For an insight into the craft of artisan shoemaking, visit the workshop of Sr. Cerqueira da Silva, which specializes in *chinelas de lavradeiras*, wooden-soled clogs with finely embroidered uppers traditionally worn by women working in the fields.
Daily 10–6 Head out of town on the EN202 towards Viana. Turn right at sign for Moureira do Lima, and on reaching the village follow sign to Boudilhão. After the sign take the first left, first right and right again

PONTE DE LIMA MARKET

Tel 258 942 335 (tourist office)
Given its charter in 1125, this is the country's oldest market. Every other Monday it spreads itself over the dry sandy river bed of the River Lima, selling everything from farm equipment and wine barrels to clothes and fresh bread.
Alternate Mon

CENTRO EQUESTRE VALE DO LIMA

Quinta da Sobreira, Feoinelos, Ponte de Lima
Tel 258 743 620
The countryside here is ideal for riding and this is one of the best riding stables around. The horses are well behaved and the people welcoming.
Daily 9–6 €10 per hour Southwest of Ponte de Lima on the EN203 towards Feitosa. Watch for the sign off to the Centro Equestre, which is just before the Galp service station

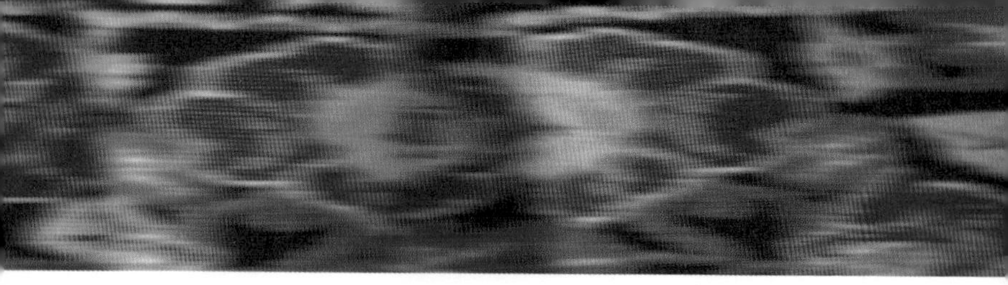

CLUB NÁUTICO

Arcozelo, Ponte de Lima
Tel 258 944 899
Walk across the river to Arcozelo and turn left downstream. Near the N201 bridge is the Club Náutico, which rents kayaks and canoes.
Jul–end Sep daily 10–1, 4–7; Oct–end Jun Sat–Sun 10–1, 4–7
€3 for 1.5 hours

GOLF DE PONTE DE LIMA

Quinta de Pias, Fornelos, Ponte de Lima
Tel 258 900 250
www.golfe-pontedelima.com
A short distance south of town, this nine-hole, par-71 course (18 holes if played over two rounds) has great views. The modern club house includes a restaurant, sauna and golf equipment shop.
Daily 8.30–6.30 18 holes €48; club rental €25; trolley €5 South of Ponte de Lima on EN307. Golf club is signposted

WHAT TO DO

VIANA DO CASTELO

ISILDA PARENTE

Lugar da Portela, Perre
Tel 258 841 047
For fine embroidery typical of the Minho, it is worth heading out to the village of Perre, some 5km (3 miles) east of Viana, and in particular to the shop of artisan Isilda Parente. Among other things, she specializes in the elaborately decorated local costumes of the north.
Mon–Fri 8.30–12, 1–5 East of Viana on the N202 to Santa Maria de Portuzelo. Turn left to Perre

VIANA DO CASTELO MARKET

Campo da Agonia, Viano do Castelo
Tel 258 822 620 (tourist office)
Held in the west of town, Viano do Castelo's market sells all the usual things, but specializes in an immense range of shoes and textiles from Portugal's northern factories, all sold at low prices.
Fri

TEATRO MUNICIPAL SÁ DE MIRANDA

Rua Sá de Miranda, Viana do Castelo
Tel 258 822 644 (general) or 258 809 382 (ticket office)
www.cm-viana-castelo.pt/teatro
Along from the railway station, this splendid, ornate, three-tiered Italianate theatre opened in 1885. It was restored to its former glory in the 1990s and now hosts concerts, opera, dance, drama and a range of other events, including occasional cinema showings.
Ticket office: Mon–Fri 9–8, Sat–Sun and national holidays 2pm–show time on performance day only €6–€40 according to performance In the auditorium

Canoeing on one of Portugal's many rivers can be fun for all

GLAMOUR

Rua da Bandeira 179–185, Viana do Castelo
Tel 258 822 963 or 914 058 272
Many of the hottest bars and clubs lie outside the city limits, but for somewhere near the middle try Glamour, just up from the Praça da República. It plays a mix of music, with occasional themed parties and live bands.
Mon–Sat 10pm–4am €4–€6 (includes drinks)

QUINTA DO SANTOINHO

Estrada Nacional 13, Darque
Tel 258 800 363 or 258 322 159
www.avic.pt/santoinho
For a Minho extravaganza come to Santoinho, a huge rustic barn of a place dedicated to all things *minhoto*. The entry price covers a meal of limitless fresh sardines and *vinho verde* straight from the barrel, plus a show of traditional dancing to well-loved local tunes.
Aug Tue, Thu, Sat 8pm–1am; May–end Jul and Sep–end Nov Sat 8pm–1am Adult €14, child (4–10) €6.50 5km (3 miles) from Viana, south on the EN13

CAVALEIROS DO MAR

Edifício do Parque, Estrada da Papanata 204–Loja B, Viana do Castelo
Tel 258 824 445
www.cavaleirosdomar.com
For outdoor activities in the coastal region of the Minho, this company offers plenty of choice. On-land options include hiking, archery, rock-climbing and four-wheel-drive excursions, or head out to sea for fishing or coastal sightseeing trips.
Office: Mon–Fri 9–1. Phone lines: daily 9–8 €15–€40 according to activity: hiking, 2–5-hour routes, minimum 6 people, €15 pp; canoeing, half-day, minimum 6 people, €25 pp inc. lunch; boat excursion, departs 9am and 4pm, minimum 4 people, €35 pp; sea-fishing, 4-hour trip, departs 9am, minimum 2 people, €40 pp

KARTÓDROMO

Praia da Amorosa (Chafé)
Tel 258 824 455
www.kartodromodeviana.com
Next to the Praia da Amorosa, just to the south of Viana do Castelo, this is the largest go-kart track in Portugal and Spain. Opened in 2000, it consists of two tracks, one measuring 468m (510 yards) and the other 1,117m (1,217 yards). The venue has hosted many national and international competitions.
Wed–Sun 9.30–12.30, 2.30–6.30 €10 for 10 minutes Leave IC1 at Castelo de Neiva exit. At Castelo de Neiva head towards Praia da Amorosa. Kartódromo is signed

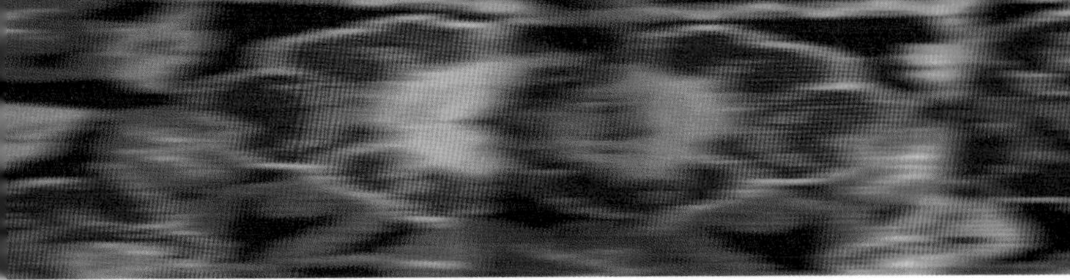

FESTIVALS AND EVENTS

MARCH

BRAGA JAZZ
Dates vary, Auditório Grande, Pavilhão Municipal de Exposições de Braga, Avenida Dr. Francisco Pires Gonçalves, Braga
Tel 255 262 550
www.cm-braga.pt
A popular annual jazz festival set up in 2000 to promote contemporary Portuguese musicians and to bring international jazz names to the north of the country. It runs for three days in the main auditorium of the Braga exhibition centre.
€7–€10

MAY

FEIRA DAS CANTARINHAS
2–4 May, Bragança
Tel 273 381 273 (tourist office)
Bragança's largest yearly market attracts vendors and shoppers from all over the region. The huge street fair sells all kinds of crafts and hand-made goods, including ceramics, metalwork, baskets and textiles.

FESTA DAS CRUZES
3 May, Barcelos
Tel 253 811 882 (tourist office)
The first of the big *romarias* that mark the summer months in the Alto Minho, this festival commemorates the 'miracle of the cross', when a 16th-century cobbler had a vision of a cross engraved in the ground. There are fireworks, dances, regional costumes and flowers strewn on the streets.

JUNE

VACA DAS CORDAS/CORPUS CHRISTI
Ninth Thursday after Easter, usually early June, Ponte de Lima
Tel 258 942 335 (tourist office)
This age-old tradition, similar to Spanish bull-running, involves crowds of young men taunting a bull—restrained by ropes—as it runs through the town and down to the river. The next day is the festival of Corpus Christi, when the streets are carpeted with flowers.

SÃO JOÃO PADROEIRO DE BRAGA
23–24 June, Braga
Tel 253 262 550 (tourist office)
This festival is dedicated to the patron saint of Braga, but has its roots in the pre-Christian summer solstice celebration. Illuminated with lights and fireworks, the city is in full party mode with folk-dancing, parades and funfairs.

FESTA DE SÃO PEDRO
28–29 June, Vila Real
Tel 259 322 819
The town's biggest and liveliest yearly festival. As well as bands, amusements and *farturas* (deep-fried, stick-shaped doughnuts), there is a large market—a good place to buy the distinctive local black pottery and fine embroidery from surrounding villages.

JULY

MIMARTE—FESTIVAL DE TEATRO DE BRAGA
First two weeks in July, Braga
Tel 253 262 550 (tourist office)
www.cm-braga.pt
Braga's festival of performing arts takes place on the streets and aims to bring theatre to the people. Acts include jugglers, mime artists, circus and dance performances.

AUGUST

FESTIVAL OF THE GUALTERIANAS
First weekend in August, Guimarães
Tel 253 412 450 (tourist office)
Celebrated since 1452, this is the most important festival in Guimarães, held in honour of São Gualter, the patron saint. For three days the town is filled with folk-dancing, rock concerts, fireworks and, on the Monday, a grand parade.

FESTA DE SANTA BARBARA
Third Sunday in August, Miranda do Douro
Tel 273 431 132 (tourist office)
Watch the *pauliteiros* (stick dancers) perform a rhythmic dance while clacking their wooden sticks to the accompaniment of drums, bagpipes and tambourines.

SEPTEMBER

FEIRA MEDIEVAL
Early September, Guimarães
Tel 253 412 450 (tourist office)
The medieval fair involves costumed participants who set up stands selling traditional products, while jesters, jugglers and acrobats entertain.

DECEMBER

FIESTA DOS RAPAZES
27–30 December, Miranda do Douro
Tel 273 431 132 (tourist office)
This festival has its roots in ancient rites of passage, as energetic, unmarried men leap bonfires and don masks and robes of rags. With cow bells jangling from their belts they 'accost' young women—accompanied by the *pauliteiros* (stick-dancers).

The Festival of Nossa Senhora da Agonia in Viana do Castelo

WHAT TO DO

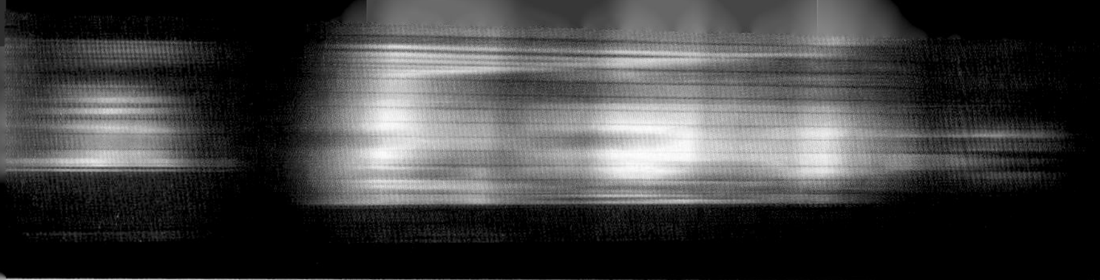

PORTO AND THE DOURO

WHAT TO DO

Shopping is good everywhere here, with quirky individual shops in Amarante, and everything in Porto from elegant specialist stores to huge state-of-the-art shopping malls. Look for regional pottery, textiles and food, or prowl the malls for excellent-value clothes and leather goods. The region's fame is inextricably linked with the port and wine trade and you can buy both, as well as learning about production methods and areas—tourist offices have an excellent range of information. If you want to be active, there's golf or more extreme sports, such as rock-climbing, abseiling and white-water rafting. Porto is the place for culture, with music and theatre, cinemas showing the latest releases, and great festivals, ranging from film, rock and Celtic music to traditional events like São João in June, where you could find yourself being hit on the head with a plastic hammer for good luck.

KEY TO SYMBOLS

 **Shopping**
 **Entertainment**
 **Nightlife**
 **Sports**
 **Activities**
 **Health and Beauty**
For Children

AMARANTE

GOLF CLUB OF AMARANTE

Quinta da Defeza, Fregim
www.portugalgolf.pt
Outside Amarante towards Fregim, this hilly course has 18 holes (par 68) and great views. Book a game on the website.
Tue–Fri 9–7, Sat–Sun 8–7 18 holes Mon–Fri €37, Sat–Sun €47; club rental €20; hand trolleys €3

DOURO

QUINTA DO PANASCAL

Valença do Douro
Tel 254 732 321 or 223 742 800
www.fonseca.pt
There is no need to book ahead at this *quinta*, which has free guided tours of the extensive vineyards and traditional winery. Wine can be purchased in the shop (cash only).
May–end Sep daily 10–6; Oct–end Apr Mon–Fri 10–6 From Régua take the N222 towards Pinhão. The estate is in the village of Valença do Douro

QUINTA DE SÃO DOMINGOS

Juncal de Cima, Peso da Régua
Tel 254 320 260/264
www.castelinho-vinhos.pt
This renovated *quinta* has one of the largest visitor facilities in the region. No booking is required for their free tours and tastings of port and Douro wines, which can be bought in the shop (cash only).
Daily 9–6 On the left on the road heading out towards Vila Real

PORTO

ARMAZÉM DOS LINHOS

Rua de Passos Manuel 19, Porto
Tel 222 004 750
Perpendicular to the main Santa Catarina shopping street is Passos Manuel, home to this great linen shop, in business since the late 19th century. As well as embroidered and regional pieces, it also stocks the famous decorative printed cotton from Alcobaça.
Mon–Fri 9.30–12.30, 2.30–7, Sat 10–1

ARTE FACTO

Rua da Reboleira 37, Ribeira, Porto
Tel 223 320 201
In an elegant 18th-century building a block back from the river, this shop stocks a great selection of good-quality local crafts. It hosts frequent craft exhibitions and workshops.
Tue–Fri 10–12, 1–6, Sat–Sun 1–7

CASA MARGARIDENSE

Travessa de Cedofeita 20-A, Porto
Tel 222 001 178
In business since the 1800s, this shop is a museum piece. Its wooden cabinets are lined with bowls of quince jam, covered, as is the custom, with

a circle of greaseproof paper; it also specializes in light, airy *pão de ló*, a sponge cake made to a secret recipe.
Tue–Fri 10–1, 2–7.30, Sat 10–1

FERNANDO S. DIAS DOS SANTOS
Rua dos Clérigos 45–47, Porto
Tel 222 006 053
Amid several craft shops near the Torre dos Clérigos, this shop is one of the oldest, dating back to the 18th century. As well as the usual selection of pottery and textile goods, it also sells a great collection of national costumes as worn in different parts of the country.
Mon–Fri 9–12.30, 2–7, Sat 9–12.30

GALERIA DE ARTESANATO 'O GALO'
Rua Mouzinho de Silveira, Porto
Tel 223 325 294
In one of the roads leading down from São Bento station, this place attracts ceramics lovers with its shelves full of regional pottery, decorative plates and abstract artistic pieces. The permanent exhibitions display comical figurines by the descendents of the famous Rosa Ramalho, along with pieces by Mistério and José Franco.
Mon–Fri 10–12.30, 1.30–7, Sat 10–1

GARRAFEIRA DO CARMO
Rua do Carmo 17, Porto
Tel 222 003 285
Garrafeira do Carmo sells a variety of LBVs, tawnies and vintage ports—some dating back to 1900—as well as high-quality table wines at reasonable prices.
Mon–Fri 9–1, 2–7, Sat 9–1

GARRAFEIRA TIO PEPE
Rua de Santos Pousada 290, Ramalde, Porto
Tel 226 184 656
www.garrafeiratiopepe.pt
This giant wine emporium, to the north of the city, is an excellent place to stock up if you have a car with you (there's parking). Trained staff guide you through the huge range of ports and wines.
Mon–Fri 9.30–12.30, 2.30–7.30, Sat 10–1 Bus 35 from Avenida dos Aliados Francos Two streets over from the Avenida do Aeroporto, near the Nó de Francos roundabout

LIVRARIA LELLO & IRMÃO
Rua das Carmelitas 144, Porto
Tel 222 002 037
This neo-Gothic literary cathedral, with stained-glass ceiling and sweeping carved staircases, opened in 1906 and justifiably claims to be the world's most palatial bookshop. Booklovers can browse through any of the 60,000 titles that fill the ornate shelves. It also sells books in English, French and German.
Mon–Fri 10–7.30, Sat 10–7

Attractive shopfronts line the Rua Formosa in Porto

MERCADO DO BOLHÃO
Rua Formosa, Porto
Tel 222 097 200
Stalls in the market's open central courtyard and tiered verandas, busiest in the morning, sell everything from bread, cheeses and cured meats to household goods, pets and flowers. A selection of crafts, including ceramics and basketry, is also on sale.
Mon–Fri 8–5, Sat 8–1

A PÉROLA DO BOLHÃO
Rua Formosa 279, Porto
Tel 222 004 009
For quality groceries, including superb cured sausages, try this place across from the market. The art nouveau building has a decorative façade with two blue-shawled oriental figures, intended to symbolize the places where its teas, coffees and spices originated.
Mon–Fri 9–1, 2–7.30, Sat 9–1

COLISEU DO PORTO
Rua de Passos Manuel 137, Porto
Tel 223 394 940 or 223 394 949
www.coliseudoporto.pt
This large theatre has attracted a variety of international stars over the years. and stages international rock gigs, dance shows and classical concerts.
Ticket office: Mon–Sat 2–8, 9–10; closed Aug €10–€40 In auditorium

TEATRO NACIONAL DE SÃO JOÃO
Praça da Batalha, Porto
Tel 223 401 910
www.tnsj.pt
Opened in 1798, this theatre has had a turbulent history. Gutted by fire and then turned into a sleazy cinema, it was bought by the government and restored. Reopened as the National Theatre of São João in 1995, it now hosts prestigious theatrical events.
Ticket office: Tue–Sat 1–10, Sun 1–7 €10–€50 In auditorium

ANIKI BÓBÓ
Rua da Fonte Taurina 36–38, Ribeira, Porto
Tel 223 324 619
This split-level club is a long-standing Ribeira landmark and attracts an arty, student crowd. In the lower part there is a dance floor while upstairs the calmer bar area sometimes hosts live drama performances or art exhibitions on Thursdays.
Tue–Sat 10pm–4am €5

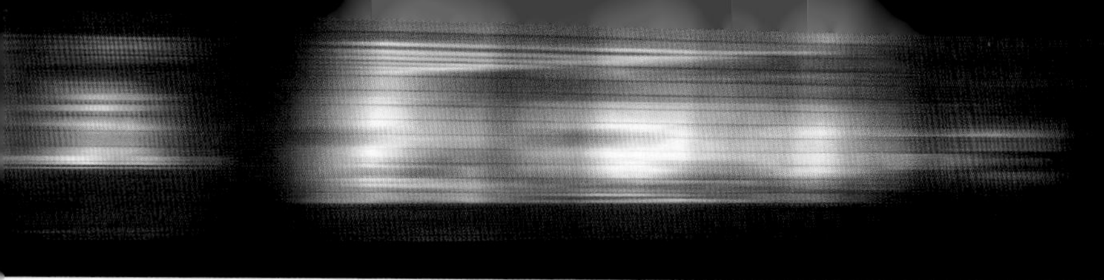

SWING

Rua de Julio Dinis 766, Boavista, Porto
Tel 226 090 019

Off the Rotunda da Boavista is Porto's oldest club, which has remained fashionable since day one. Music styles vary during the week from 1980s student nights to dance and commercial club, and attract a mixed crowd, old and young, gay and straight.

Daily midnight–7am €7.50, or €12.50 on special events nights (includes drinks)

VIA RÁPIDA

Rua Manuel Pinto de Azevedo 567, Unit 5, Ramalde, Porto
Tel 226 109 427

Models and model agencies run several of the bars in this landmark warehouse-style club. There are frequent fashion shows and label-sponsored parties. Music is revivalist and house.

Fri, Sat midnight–7am 10
Bus 41 from the Science Faculty

ESTÁDIO DO DRAGÃO

F. C. Porto (club), Avenida Fernão de Magalhães, Antas, Porto
Tel 225 070 500 or 707 200 384 (club hotline)
www.fcporto.pt

Home to frequent national football champions F. C. Porto, this impressive stadium (picture ▷ 194) was completed in 2003 to host the opening match of the 2004 European Football Championship. Seating 52,000, it is part of the 'sport city' complex of multi-purpose pavilions, shops and housing. For match details see *Público* or *Jornal de Notícias*.

Ticket office for matches: daily 10–1, 3–7 Tickets €15–€50 Antas
Bus 21, 78

OPORTO GOLF CLUBE

Paramos, Espinho
Tel 227 342 008
www.portugalgolf.pt

This is the oldest golf club in the country. The first of its 18 holes, a par 4, is cunningly set against the strong *nortada* (prevailing north winds), providing a challenge for any player. The club house has good facilities, although the restaurant is open only to members.

Tue–Sun 8am–sundown 18 holes Tue–Fri €50, Sat–Sun €60; club rental €20; hand trolley €5 Take IC1 north for almost 20km (12.5 miles), leaving at Espinho exit. The course is just south of the town

FERREIRA

Avenida Ramos Pinto 70, Vila Nova de Gaia, Porto
Tel 223 746 107 or 223 746 106
www.2000yearsvintage.com

Ferreira is Portugal's best-selling port and remarkably the only major company to be founded by a native Douro family. Its founder, Dona Adalaide, began with a modest handful of vineyards, but became so successful that it is said she ended up owning vineyards stretching from Porto to Spain. Come and taste the results.

Daily 10–12.30, 2–6 €2.50 including visit and tasting Bus 57 or 91 from Rua Mouzinho da Silveira, just down from São Bento train station

Fortifying the port at Taylor's, an institution in Porto for 300 years

ROTA DO VINHO DO PORTO

Rua da Ferreirnha, Edificio do Solar do Vinho do Porto, Porto
Tel 222 071 600
www.ivp.pt

This information office provides details about driving tours, wineries, festivals and other wine-related events in the port region.

Mon–Fri 9–12.30, 2–5.30

ROTA DOS VINHOS VERDES

Comissão de Vinicultura da Região dos Vinhos Verdes, Rua da Restauração 318, Porto
Tel 226 077 300
www.vinhoverde.com

This organization provides suggested driving routes through the *vinho verde* region, taking in some of the most interesting *quintas*. Some tours providing English commentaries, offering the best wine-tastings with great places to eat, are singled out for you.

Mon–Fri 9–12.30, 2–5.30

TAYLOR'S

Rua do Choupelo 250, Vila Nova de Gaia, Porto
Tel 223 742 800
www.taylor.pt

Of all of the old English-run lodges this 300-year-old company probably provides the best tour and tasting of quality late-bottled vintage ports. Its website gives plenty of information on the port-producing process and the various types of port.

Jul, Aug Mon–Fri 10–6; Sep–end Jun Mon–Sat 10–6 Visit and tasting free
Bus 57 or 91 from Rua Mouzinho da Silveira, just down from São Bento train station

INDIANA BILL

Avenida Fontes Pereira de Melo 459, Porto
Tel 226 162 878

This themed adventure playground is an ideal place for young children to let off steam. It has a jungle theme, with climbing frames, swings, slides and an on-site snack bar.

Mon–Fri 3.30–7.30, Sat–Sun and national holidays 10.30–7.30 €3.50 per hour

FESTIVALS AND EVENTS

FEBRUARY–MARCH

FANTASPORTO
Porto
www.fantasporto.com
Porto's international arts film festival has been running since 1981 and is considered by many to be the world's top sci-fi and fantasy film forum. The festival also includes related events such as lectures, exhibitions and film workshops.

APRIL

FESTIVAL INTERCÉLTICO DO PORTO
Early April, Porto
Rua Duque de Saldanha 97, Porto (information)
Tel 225 193 100
The country's largest gathering of all things Celtic attracts groups from home and abroad, including Scottish and Irish bands.

MAY

QUEIMA DAS FITAS
Early May, Porto
The end of the academic year and start of the examination period is marked by the Burning of the Ribbons, a week of rock concerts, beer-drinking and parties, culminating in a massive parade where final-year students dress up in their robes and top hats.

JUNE

ROMARIA DE SÃO GONÇALO
First weekend in June, Amarante
São Gonçalo, associated with matchmaking and fertility, is remembered in Amarante's most important yearly festival, with bands, folk-dancing, processions and market stands. Saturday night is marked by a massive firework display on the river and Sunday by a solemn procession in honour of the saint.

Porto's streets get packed during the São João festivities in June

FESTAS DA CIDADE–SÃO JOÃO
23–24 June, Porto
On the night of São João, crowds take to the streets, often in carnival costume, to enjoy *sardinhadas* (sardine barbecues), parades and dances. Watch out for the plastic hammers that are used to hit passers-by on the head, supposedly a way of wishing them good fortune.

AUGUST

NOITES RITUAL ROCK
Porto
Rua Dom Manuell II
Held in the Crystal Palace Gardens, this is the place for Portuguese rock bands to get some exposure. Almost anyone who has made it on the national music scene has played here.

FESTAS DE SÃO BARTOLOMEU
Sunday following 24 August, Foz de Douro
A unique festival that takes place in the old fishing village of Foz do Douro. People dress up in imaginative, multi-hued paper costumes to parade through the streets before taking a symbolic and cleansing plunge into the ocean.

SEPTEMBER

FESTIVAL DE JAZZ DO PORTO
End September, Porto
Concerts usually held in the Rivoli Teatro Municipal, Praça Dom João I
Tel 223 392 200 (information)
Started in 1993 and organized by Culturporto, this festival attracts top names from the national and international jazz world and showcases new and established talents.

OCTOBER–DECEMBER

CARTOON WORLD FESTIVAL
Museu Nacional de Imprensa, EN108, 206, Freixo, Porto
Tel 225 300 648
This unusual festival was launched in 1999 by the National Printing Museum with the aim of putting Porto firmly on the world cartoon map and has proved to be extremely successful. It hosts exhibitions of cartoons from around the world as well as offering live sessions with famous international cartoonists.
Admission free

WHAT TO DO

THE BEIRAS

Coimbra, Aveiro, Guarda and Viseu are the main towns in the Beiras, and the places to head for in search of tempting retail therapy. As far as outdoor activities are concerned, there is a great variety, with everything from river and water sports to horseback riding through the woods beside the River Lamego. Or you could spend time on the golf courses, or just messing about in boats—take a cruise on the river at Coimbra, go canoeing, or try a trip in one of Aveiro's traditional brightly painted *moliceiros*. You'll be spoilt for choice in the evenings—you could try a classical music concert or traditional Coimbra *fado*, visit some funky clubs, have a casino flutter, or have a bop at Portugal's biggest disco. Festivals include the fabulous *Carnaval* at Figueira and Portugal's best academic shindig at Coimbra.

KEY TO SYMBOLS
- Shopping
- Entertainment
- Nightlife
- Sports
- Activities
- Health and Beauty
- For Children

AVEIRO

FÁBRICA VISTA ALEGRE
Vista Alegre
Tel 234 320 600
Some 6km (4 miles) south of Aveiro, the village of Vista Alegre is home to this prestigious porcelain works. There is a small museum recording the factory's history.
Museum: Tue–Fri 9–12, 2–4.30, Sat–Sun 9–12.30, 2–5.30. Shop: Mon–Sat 9.30–6.30 Take the N109 south out of Aveiro, past Ilhavo

MARIA DA APRESENTAÇÃO DA CRUZ
Rua D. Jorge de Lencastre 37, Aveiro
Tel 234 422 323
Aveiro's most famous food is its *ovos moles*, literally 'soft eggs', sweet cakes that this family store has been producing according to a closely guarded recipe since 1882. They are sold in traditional wooden painted barrels.
Mon–Sat 9–8, Sun 9.30–3

FISH BAR
Praça do Peixe, Aveiro
Tel 234 383 392
Of the many bars in the lively Praça do Peixe, this one has good buzzing vibes. There's always the option of leaving the energetic to dance below, while you retire upstairs for a hearty *caldo verde* (soup) or beef sandwich before moving on to the celebrated shots bar.
Mon–Sat 8.30pm–2am €5 (includes drinks)

OITO GRAUS OESTE
Cais do Paraíso, Aveiro
Tel 234 423 217
Aveiro's biggest disco, south of the central canal, down from the Rossio. The terrace overlooks the river and two floors play 1980s and 1990s hits. There's live music Thursdays and house music Fridays.
Wed–Sat midnight–6am
Wed–Thu free, Fri–Sat €5 (includes drinks)

SALPOENTE
Canal de S. Roque 83, Aveiro
Tel 234 382 674
Above its restaurant (▷ 279), Salpoente has a popular bar

with views over the salt pans, and live music on Friday and Saturday nights. Originally a salt warehouse, it has displays of regional costumes and salt-workers' tools.
Fri–Sat 11.30pm–2am €3 (includes drinks)

AVEIROSUB
Aveineda José Estevao 724, Gafanha da Nazaré, Aveiro
Tel 234 367 555
Outside Aveiro towards Praia da Barra, this place offers scuba-diving lessons and organizes diving trips either in the lagoon or open sea, depending on weather conditions. Introductory lessons, including trial dives, are available for beginners.
Phone lines: Mon–Sat 9–12.30, 2–7 Day's diving (2 dives) €50; dive course (20 theory lessons, 6 pool lessons, 5 open sea lessons) €350; introductory dive €35

BUGA
Centro Comercial Forum, Aveiro
Tel 967 050 441
BUGA (Bicicleta de Utilização Gratuíta de Aveiro) is Aveiro's free bicycle scheme, which has been running since 2000. Head for the blue-and-white BUGA stands, insert 50¢ into the slot, then take the bicycle and use it within the city limits, returning it to any of the stands when finished.
BUGA shop: Mon–Fri 10–12.30, 1.30–6, Sat–Sun 9–7 50¢ coin needed; if no bicycles are available at the stands please contact the shop

ECO RIA
Rua Cândido dos Reis 59B, Aveiro
Tel 967 088 183
Or at Torreira Campsite (24 hours)
Tel 234 838 397
As well as regular boat trips in launches and *moliceiros* from May to the end of September, Eco Ria offers sea- and lagoon-fishing trips in July and August. Sea bass and eels are the fish most commonly caught, along with a variety of other seafood.
Office: Mon–Fri 9–12.30, 2–5.30. *Moliceiro* trips: Jun–end Sep daily 10–6, every hour. Motor launch trips: Jun–end Aug daily, depart 12.30 return 2.30 *Moliceiro* trips €7 per person, minimum 8 people; motor launch trips €20 per person including lunch (book 5 days in advance); fishing trips all year, 5 hours including lunch €25 per person (book a week in advance)

COIMBRA

A CAMPONESA
Rua da Louça 80, Coimbra
Tel 239 827 947
This long-established wine store, with an ancient (and still functioning) cash register and a large gilt clock fitted among the original wooden shelves and counters, stocks a great selection of port and wines from several of Portugal's wine-producing regions. You can come and take a look even if you don't want to buy.
Mon–Fri 9.30–1, 3–7, Sat 9.30–1

Coimbra's fado has its own distinctive style. It is performed by men only

O CANTINHO DA ANITA
Rua Sargento Mor 2, Coimbra
Tel 239 827 415
Behind the medieval-looking exterior is a fine craft shop selling traditional Coimbra ceramics, splendid imitation 17th-century Viuva Lamêgo tiles, and quality cotton embroidery and weavings.
Jul, Aug Mon–Fri 9–7, Sat 9–1; Sep–end Jun Mon–Fri 9–1, 3–7, Sat 9–1

TEATRO ACADÉMICO GIL VICENTE
Praça da República, Coimbra
Tel 239 855 630
www.uc.pt/tagu
The theatre hosts a varied selection of shows and events, including classical music, dance, cinema and plays.
Ticket office: Mon–Sat 5–10, Sun (on show days) 5–10 €10–€30
In auditorium

A CAPELLA
Capela Nossa Senhora da Vitória, Rua Corpo de Deus, Largo da Vitória, Coimbra
Tel 239 833 985
Housed in a 14th-century chapel, this unusual bar has dark wooden floors and projected images of Coimbra on the walls. There are live *fado* shows in summer and jazz and ethnic music nights in winter.
1 May–30 Oct daily *fado* shows from 10pm; Nov–end Apr Thu–Sat *fado* shows from 10pm, Tue Lisbon *fado*, Wed jazz, Sun ethnic sounds
Admission on *fado* nights €5 (includes drinks)

VIA LATINA
Rua Almeida Garrett 1, Coimbra
Tel 239 833 034
Just off the Praça da República, this is one of the city's most popular clubs, especially among the student crowd. During the week there are often university parties and at the weekend national and international DJs play mainly house and dance sounds.
Mon–Sat midnight–6am €5 (includes drinks)

BASÓFIAS
Estrada Nacional da Luz, Urbanização Madacelo, 1-Armazém, Coimbra
Tel 239 912 444
Basófias runs boat trips on the River Mondego, departing from beside the Parque Dr. Manuel Braga. Along the way you'll get great views of the historic buildings on the far bank.
Tue–Fri 3, 4.30 and 6, Sat–Sun 11, 3, 4.30, 6 and 7.30 €8.20

GOLF QUINTA DAS LÁGRIMAS
Santa Clara, Coimbra
Tel 239 808 388
www.quintadaslagrimas.pt
The golf academy at Quinta das Lágrimis on the banks of the River Mondego has superb views over to Coimbra's historic heart. As well as a nine-hole pitch-and-putt course, it has a driving range, putting and chipping greens.
Tue 12–6, Wed–Sun 10–6 Daily green fee €10; club rental €5 per club Cross the Santa Clara bridge, turn left then right at the sign

O PIONEIRO DO MONDEGO
Rua da Calçada, Penacova
Tel 239 478 385
Rent a kayak for a trip on the River Mondego between Penacova and Coimbra. You can paddle up to 25km (16 miles), which takes around four hours, but there are shorter options. A minibus collects you at the eastern corner of Parque D. Manuel Braga at 10am.
Phone lines: Jun–end Sep daily 8–10, 1–3, 8–10 €15 including transportation

TERMAS DA CURIA
Curia
Tel 231 512 185
www.termasdacuria.com
The thermal spa at Curia has been going since the 19th century, when the curative properties of its waters were internationally recognized. You can have massages, saunas and beauty treatments. There's also a hotel, bicycles, mini-golf and swimming pools.
Mon–Sat 9–12.30, 4.30–7.30, Sun 9–12.30 €7–€17.50 according to which treatments you take Take the IC2 north out of Coimbra. Turn left at the sign to Curia and follow signs for '*Termas*', 25km (16 miles) north of Coimbra

PORTUGAL DOS PEQUENITOS
Rua de Santa Clara, Coimbra
Tel 239 801 170
This theme park has become Coimbra's most-visited attraction (though perhaps it is somewhat overrated). It provides lots of fun for all the family, with child-size models of Portugal's most famous monuments and several areas dedicated to the country's former colonies.
Jul to mid-Sep daily 9–8; Mar–end Jun daily 10–7; mid-Sep to end Feb daily 10–5 Adult €6, child (6–13) €3, under 5s free

FIGUEIRA DA FOZ

CASINO DA FIGUEIRA DA FOZ
Rua Dr. Calado 1, Figueira da Foz
Tel 233 408 400
www.casinofigueira.pt
From the beginning of the 20th century, this casino attracted Portugal's aristocracy to its salons. These elegant gaming rooms now sit inside an ultra-modern glass and foil façade alongside modern slot machines, an excellent restaurant, a nightclub and dancing show girls.
Daily 3pm–2am. Shows: Tue–Sun 11pm €5 for show (includes drinks)

A miniature house at the Portugal dos Pequenitos theme park

CENTRO DE ARTES E ESPECTÁCULOS DA FIGUEIRA DA FOZ
Rua Abade Pedro, Figueira da Foz
Tel 233 407 200
www.figueira.net/cae
Figueira's main venue for drama, classical and contemporary music and dance performances was built in a modern style in white concrete and glass in 2000. Inside is an 800-seat auditorium, a small cinema and a light and airy exhibition hall, and there's an outdoor amphitheatre.
Ticket office: Tue–Fri 10–6, Sat–Sun and national holidays 2–6 (until midnight on show days). Tickets also available on-line €10–€40 In auditorium

LITTLE HAVANA
Rua Cândido dos Reis 86A, Figueira da Foz
Tel 233 422 610 (tourist office)
With its Latin theme, Little Havana brings a taste of Cuba to the Atlantic coast. Palm trees, vibrant tones and free-flowing margaritas and *mojitos* are enhanced by live bands playing salsa and popular Latin American tunes.
Tue–Sun 8pm–4am Free

PERFUMARIA PUB
Rua Dr. Calado 37, Figueira da Foz
Tel 233 426 442
With two floors, gentle lighting and unobtrusive music, this pub-like bar is one of Figueira's oldest and is an ideal place for a quiet drink. Beware of the tight spiral staircase.
Daily 9.30pm–6am Free

CAPITÃO DUREZA
Rua Dr. José Francisco Nico 4–3, Figueira da Foz
Tel 919 079 852 or 914 929 407
www.capitaodureza.com
Operating throughout central Portugal, this activities company provides events year round. With qualified instructors and the latest equipment, it organizes white-water rafting, paintballing, canoeing, kayaking, canyoning, abseiling and other sports and events.
Phone lines: 9–9 €24–€60 according to which activity you choose

JOGOS DE PRAIA
Figueira da Foz
Tel 233 422 610 (tourist office)
During July and August the beaches of Figueira come alive with the *Jogos da Praia*, liter-

ally 'beach games'. As well as the *Mundialito* (▷ 203) there is beach volleyball, aerobics classes and fashion shows.

ROTASDOMUNDO
Rua Miguel Bombarda 25, Figueira da Foz
Tel 233 411 635
If you fancy taking a ride along the sea front, you can rent bicycles by the day or the hour from this travel agent. Safety helmets are not provided.
Mon–Fri 9.30–1, 2.30–6.30 Day €15, hour €2.50

TOURADA
Praça de Touros, Figueira da Foz
Tel 233 422 610 (tourist office)
During the season (July and August), the municipal bullring, just off Rua do Viso, hosts an impressive line-up of top *talento taurino*. For more detailed information, contact the tourist information office.
€15–€60 according to the status of the bullfighters

GUARDA

CASA ESPIGADO
Rua da Torre 21, Guarda
Tel 271 212 269
Founded in 1916, this shop is packed with all things metal. Copper, stainless steel, wrought iron and tin have been made into all manner of practical and curious items, which the friendly owner is pleased to explain, though he speaks only Portuguese.
Mon–Fri 9.30–1, 3–7, Sat 9.30–1

A CATEDRAL
Rua dos Cavaleiros 18, Guarda
Tel 271 22 33 86
The best bars in Guarda are dotted around the old town in former townhouses, and so all of them are quite small inside. This bar, decorated with large, religious themed paintings from which it gets its name, is one of the most popular. Because of this beware that it can get quite cramped.
Tue–Sat 10pm–3am €1 (includes drinks)

O TROVADOR
Rua D. Dinis 9, Guarda
Tel 271 215 170
This homelike bar, just off the Rua D. Francisco de Passos, mainly attracts a student crowd. It has five rooms whose stone walls are decorated with a collection of stringed instruments. Although it's fairly quiet during the week, it really comes to life at weekends, with karaoke and live bands.
Wed–Sat 10pm–3am

CENÁRIOS DOURO
Praceta Aureliano Barrigas 6, 1st floor, Vila Real
Tel 259 33 81 35
www.cenarios.com

You can try your hand at kayaking on the open sea

This company specializes in all kinds of activities along the River Douro, as well as hot-air balloon trips over the upper Douro valley and the beautiful Parque Natural do Duoro.
€82–€270 depending on the balloon size

UNIVERSO TT
Rua Almirante Gago Coutinho 10, 2nd floor, right-hand door, Guarda
Tel 969 774 445 or 969 105 015
www.universott.com
For exciting Landrover excursions through the Mondego valley or Malcate Serra, or along themed frontier castle, wool or cheese routes, try this company. It also organizes outdoor activities, such as hiking and hot-air balloon flights.
Daily 10–7. Phone lines: daily 9–9
Half-, 1- and 2-day trips available from €25

LAMEGO

BARBA E CABELO
Rua da Olaria 7–9, Lamego
One of the best shops on the Rua da Olaria, this tiny place at the bottom of the hill was once home to the town barbers. With only the old chair remaining, the rest has been replaced with regional artisan products and gift items, including baskets and linens.
Mon–Fri 10–12.30, 2.30–7, Sat 10–1

CAVES DA MURGANHEIRA
Abadia Velha, Ucanha
Tel 254 670 185 or 254 670 186
Murganheira is Portugal's largest producer of sparkling wine. There is no need to book a tour, and there is a shop too.
Mon–Fri 9–10, 11–2, 3–4 Tasting and tour free; groups of up to 4 people
Southeast of Lamego off the N226

LUSO

GRANDE HOTEL DE LUSO
Rua Dr. Cid de Oliveira 86, Luso
Tel 231 937 937
If a bicycle ride in the Buçaco National Forest sounds like your thing, this hotel rents out bicycles by the hour. The park is criss-crossed with tracks and dotted with chapels, ponds and fountains. Of the many trails one of the best is the Vale dos Fetos (Valley of Ferns). Ask at the hotel for more details.
€3 per hour

TERMAS DO LUSO
Tel 231 937 910
www.termasdoluso.com
The medicinal properties of the waters at Luso were discovered in the late 1700s, with the first spa building opening in the 1850s. Facilities include a swimming pool, a cleansing high-powered Vichy shower, and massage.
2 May–31 Oct Mon–Sat 8–12, 4–7
Massage €15; Vichy shower €7.80

VISEU

CASA DA RIBEIRA

Largo da Nossa Senhora de Conceição, Viseu
Tel 232 427 400
Viseu is well known for its lace and basketware, both of which can be found at Casa da Ribeira, the town outlet for regional crafts. You can see craftsmen working, while items on sale include quality glassware, pottery and textiles.
Tue–Sat 9–12.30, 2–5.30

THE DAY AFTER

Complexo Turistico de Viseu, IP3 towards Lamego
Tel 232 450 645
www.thedayafter.pt
This nightclub is probably Portugal's biggest and attracts all ages and tastes. It has different areas playing all kinds of music. The Tequila Club plays commercial pop, the American bar concentrates on hip-hop and rock, and at the Torre Millenium, salsa, danceteria, techno and house blast out. Once you've done with dancing, there's a bowling alley, go-karts and all-night restaurants.
Wed–Sat 9pm–6am Wed–Fri free; Sat €8 for men, €5 for women Take IP3 north out of Viseu towards Lamego. The Day After is on the left-hand side

OBVIAMENTO OK

Largo do Pintor Gata 26, Viseu
Tel 232 426 635
This bar plays pumping house music to a young crowd. As well as drinks, it serves snacks late, which can be a lifesaver for hungry dancers near dawn.
Mon–Sat 8.30pm–4.30am Free

CENTRO HÍPICO MONTEBELO

Farminhão, Viseu
Tel 232 856 474
www.centrohipicomontebelo.pt
This equestrian centre is 10 minutes' drive from Viseu, and has fine views of the surrounding countryside. It has covered and outdoor arenas, paddocks and a club house. Horses can be hired by the hour.
Tue–Sun 9–8 €20 per hour Take the IP3 south out of Viseu. Turn off at São Miguel de Outeiro/Sabugosa. The centre is signed

GOLFE MONTEBELO

Farminhão, Viseu
Tel 232 856 464
www.golfemontebelo.pt
www.portugalgolf.pt
This hilly course has the magnificent Serra da Estrela and Serra do Caramulo as a backdrop. The 18 holes are set around pines, oaks and clumps of gorse with frequent dog-legs, streams and lakes.
May–end Sep 8–8; Oct–end Apr 8–7 18 holes Mon–Fri €30, Sat–Sun €45; club rental €15; buggy €30

Thousands of people tee off in Portugal every summer

Take the IP3 south out of Viseu. Turn off at São Miguel de Outeiro/Sabugosa. The golf course is signed from there

PALÁCIO DOS DESPORTOS

Quinta de Santa Luzia, Estrada de Nelas, Viseu
Tel 232 461 111
www.visabeiraturismo.pt
This multipurpose sports venue has large pavilions, gyms, three heated indoor swimming pools, and squash courts. There are aerobic and step classes, while a bar provides a good place in which to relax after a punishing work-out.
Mon–Sat 8am–11pm, Sun 8am–10pm €5–€42.50 according to activity 3 indoor On the EN231 just to the south of the town

PALÁCIO DO GELO

Quinta de Santa Luzia, Estrada de Nelas, Viseu
Tel 232 461 111
www.visabeiraturismo.pt
This is Portugal's largest ice-rink where you can spend an afternoon if it rains during your holiday. You can rent skates. In the same building, there is a small shopping mall, a restaurant, a multiscreen cinema, a bowling alley and several amusement arcades.
Mon 10–5, 6.15–11, Tue 10–5, 8.10–11, Wed 10–5, 8–11, Thu 10–5, 6.15–7.30, 8.10–11, Fri 10–4, 9.30–11, Sat 2–4.30, 8–11, Sun 12.15–5.30, 7–11 €2 for half an hour, including skate rental On the EN231 just to the south of the town

PALÁCIO DA SAÚDE

Quinta de Santa Luzia, Estrada de Nelas, Viseu
Tel 232 461 111
Whether you prefer a sauna, Jacuzzi, Scottish bath, Turkish bath, hydro-massage, solarium, or relaxation rooms, you name it, the 'Palace of Health' has everything you could need to relax. The facilities are modern and spotlessly clean.
Mon–Sat 8am–11pm, Sun 8am–10pm €7–€60 according to treatment On the EN231 just to the south of the town

TERMAS ALCAFACHE

Rua do Balneáreo, Alcafache
Tel 232 479 797
www.termasdealcafache.pt
Southeast of Viseu, this tranquil spa in the pine forests of the Dão valley opened in 1962 and has undergone various improvements since. It offers the usual medicinal treatments for joint and respiratory complaints, as well as relaxing mud baths and hydro-massage.
1 May–30 Nov €3–€10.60 according to treatment and time of year From Viseu take the EN231 south. Turn left to Nelas, then left to Alcafache, 8km (5 miles) from Viseu

FESTIVALS AND EVENTS

JANUARY

FESTA DAS CAVACAS
Second week in January, Aveiro
Tel 234 423 680 (tourist office)
The old town is lavishly decorated in honour of São Gonçalo. In a curious custom, special loaves of bread known as *cavacas* are thrown to the crowds from the top of a chapel in thanks for the safe return of the town's fishermen.

FEBRUARY

CARNAVAL
Figueira da Foz
Tel 233 422 610 (tourist office)
Carnaval is a big event in Figueira and its exotic Rio-style parades on carnival Saturday and Shrove Tuesday attract visitors from all around the country. Decorated floats, glitzy costumes, scantily clad samba dancers, and parading soap stars are the main attractions.

MARCH/APRIL

FEIRA DE MARÇO
Late March–late April, Aveiro
Tel 234 423 680 (tourist office)
Held in Aveiro since the mid-15th century, the fair has all the usual festival attractions, such as folk-dancing, street parties and, at weekends, lavish parades and processions.

MAY

FEIRA DE SANTA CRUZ
3 May, Lamego
Tel 254 612 005 (tourist office)
One of Lamego's liveliest events, the fair serves primarily to show off regional livestock breeds, but also includes horse parades and races in which the locals fight it out amid much friendly banter.

FESTA DE SANTA JOANA
First weekend in May for two weeks, Aveiro
Tel 234 423 680 (tourist office)
Held in honour of Santa Joana, the beatified daughter of Afonso V who lived in an Aveiro convent for 20 years. The most important day is 12 May, with its procession in honour of the saint.

JUNE

FESTAS DA VILA
13–24 June, Figueira da Foz
Tel 233 422 610 (tourist office)
Held in honour of São João, the patron saint of Figueira, this two-week festival, with its regional crafts, gastronomic delicacies and concerts, culminates on 24 June with an impressive parade of folk-dancing and costumes.

FESTA MEDIEVAL
Coimbra
Tel 239 832 591 (tourist office)
This one-day *festa* is Coimbra's opportunity to step back into the past as theatre groups put on street performances and medieval-looking stands sell traditional foods. Telephone the tourist information office to check the date as it changes from year to year.

JULY–AUGUST

EXPODOURO
Early July for 1 week, Largo da Feira, Lamego
Tel 254 612 005 (tourist office)
One of the north's largest exhibitions of regional products. The wine section is excellent and there are also displays featuring local crafts and traditional gastronomy.
Mon–Fri 6pm–midnight, Sat–Sun 3pm–midnight

MUNDIALITO DE FUTEBOL DE PRAIA
Figueira da Foz
Tel 233 422 610 (tourist office)
Held every year on the sands of the main beach in Figueira da Foz, the World Beach-Soccer Championships attract teams from around the world and hoards of enthusiastic fans. Accommodation can be at a premium, so book ahead.

FESTA DA RIA
Mid-July to end August, Aveiro
Tel 234 423 680 (tourist office)
Aveiro's most important festival celebrates its canals and the decorative *moliceiros* boats, originally used for the collection of seaweed. The boats compete to be the best decorated and regattas are held.

AUGUST–SEPTEMBER

NOSSA SENHORA DOS REMÉDIOS
Last Thursday in August–8 September
Lamego
Tel 254 612 005 (tourist office)
This is Lamego's biggest yearly *festa*. The mix of religious and secular celebrations, including car-racing, rock concerts and parades, is rounded off on 8 September by a procession of religiously themed, ox-drawn carts and penitents climbing the church steps on their knees.

FEIRA DE SÃO MATEUS
24 August–21 September, Viseu
Tel 232 420 950 (tourist office)
Held yearly at the Campo de Feira de São Mateus, this festival honours St. Matthew with folk music, dancing, amusements and plenty of fireworks. It also includes a massive agricultural and crafts market.

DECEMBER

MAGUSTO DA VELHA
26 December, Guarda
Tel 271 205 530 (tourist office)
The *Magusto da Velha* (literally 'Old Lady's Roasted Chestnuts') celebrations began after an old lady left instructions in her will that each year 50kg (110lb) of chestnuts should be roasted and tossed from the church tower. This still happens every Boxing Day.
Take the EN16 west, then north, out of Guarda. Take the road to Aldeia Viçosa signed to the left after about 15km (9 miles)

WHAT TO DO

ESTREMADURA AND THE RIBATEJO

There's a full range of consumer choice plus some good markets in Estremadura and the Ribatejo, but for something specific to the region, look for glass and crystal—you'll find the finest at Alcobaça. As elsewhere, there's plenty of attractive local pottery on sale too. Popular towns like Óbidos and Nazaré sell giftware from all over the country, though you'll need to trawl through a lot of tawdry stuff to hit the jackpot. Fátima is packed with religious souvenir shops, with some good pieces among the mostly kitsch objects. Daytime activities largely focus on water-based pursuits, with canoeing on the River Nabão at Tomar, and some good options on the coast, including water parks to keep the kids happy and great surfing at Peniche. Also at Peniche, you can go scuba-diving, deep-sea fishing, or enjoy a boat trip out to the Berlenga Islands. Back on dry land, there's golf and bicycling, but for a really unforgettable experience don't miss exploring the fabulous and imaginatively lit limestone caves of the Serra de Aire. Evenings might include a concert in Óbidos, or simply enjoying an atmospheric and welcoming bar anywhere in the region.

KEY TO SYMBOLS

- Shopping
- Entertainment
- Nightlife
- Sports
- Activities
- Health and Beauty
- For Children

ALCOBAÇA

ATLANTIS CRISTAIS DE ALCOBAÇA, S. A.

Casal da Areia, Cós, Alcobaça
Tel 262 540 200
www.atlantis-cristais-de-alcobaca.pt

Founded in 1945, Atlantis is Portugal's best-known manufacturer of fine lead crystal. Made with the purest sand, potash and litharge (lead monoxide), its crystal pieces vary from tableware to figurines and vases. You can visit the working factory, explore the small historical museum and buy some crystal to take home from the shop.

Factory visits: Mon–Sat 10.30, 11.15, 12, 2.30, 3.30, 5. Closed Aug. Shop and museum: Mon–Sat 10–7 Adult €1.25, child (under 12) free Take the N8-4 north out of Alcobaça. Turn right to Maiorga and Cós

LOUÇA E AZULEJOS DE ALCOBAÇA

Rua Frei Fortunato 39–41, Alcobaça
Tel 914 577 789

This shop, near the Igreja da Conceição in the old part of town, is a good place to buy Alcobaça's traditional blue-and-white pottery. It also sells a selection of painted faïence ceramics and attractive 17th-century and art nouveau tiles.

Mon–Sat 10.30–1.30, 2.30–8, Sun 2.30–7

FÁTIMA

FUNPARQUE

Boleiros
Tel 249 521 030
www.funpark.pt

This outdoor adventure park offers a range of activities for all ages. There is a go-kart track of 1,130m (1,230 yards), rough-terrain kartbugs, paintballing, abseiling, mountain-bicycling and lots more. When you want to take a break, there is a restaurant and a park with designated barbecue areas.

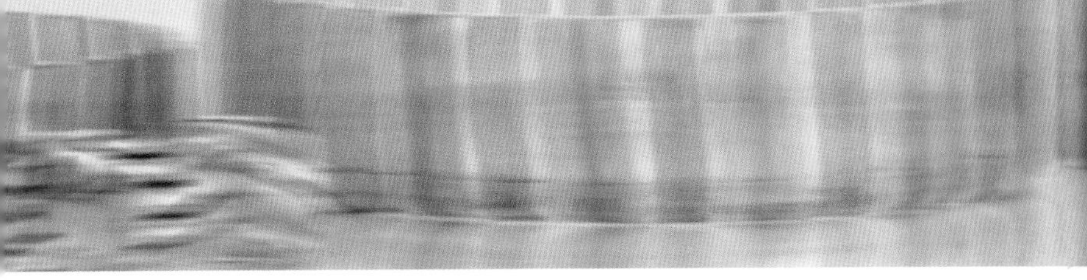

Apr–end Oct Wed–Mon 10–10; Nov–end Mar Wed–Sun 10–8 Go-karts €15 for 15 min, €27.50 for 30 min At the Pastorinhos roundabout, head south on the EN360, following signs to FunParque and the Kartódromo

GRUTAS DE MIRA DE AIRE
Avenida Dr. Luciano Justo Ramos
Tel 244 440 322
Portugal's largest cave system stretches for 4km (2.5 miles), though tours cover only about 700m (760 yards). The caverns are lit to a depth of 110m (360ft) and the final cave, with artificial fountains and waterfalls, has an elevator back to the surface.
Jul, Aug daily 9.30–8.30; Apr, May daily 9.30–6; Jun, Sep daily 9.30–7; Oct–end Mar daily 9.30–5.30 €4.50 Take the N360 south out of Fátima, then turn left onto the N243 towards Porto de Mós. The caves are on the left

GRUTAS DA MOEDA
São Mamede
Tel 244 704 302
www.grutasmoeda.com
These caves, about 3km (2 miles) from Fátima, were discovered unexpectedly in 1971 by two hunters. The huge galleries stretch for 350m (380 yards) and are endowed with emerald-green lakes and spectacular stone formations, including a limestone column believed to be around 30,000 years old.
Jul–end Sep 9–7; Apr–end Jun 9–6; Oct–end Mar 9–5 €4 From Fátima's northern roundabout follow signs to the A1. Just before joining the A1 turn right. The caves are signed

LEIRIA

PARQUE AQUÁTICO-MARIPARQUE
Avenida Marginal, Praia da Vieira Aptdo 62, Vieira de Leiria
Tel 244 440 700
Great for a day out with the kids, this water park is about 25km (18 miles) north of Leiria. Situated on the beachfront at Praia da Vieira, the complex includes chutes, rapids, twisting toboggans and junior pools. Bars and a restaurant provide refreshments.
Jun–end Sep daily 10–6 Adult €5–€7.50, child €2.50–€6 (half- and full day) Take the IC1 north out of Leiria. Turn left to Monte Real/ Vieira de Leiria and then follow signs to Praia da Vieira

MARINHA GRANDE

JASMIM-VICRIMAG
Estrada de Leiria 227, Apt. 87, Marinha Grande
Tel 244 575 590
www.jasmimglass.com
One of many glass producers in the area, Jasmim opened in 1996 with the aims of reviving ancient hand-blown glass-making methods and using environmentally friendly materials. Visitors can see artists at work and there are English-speaking experts available to answer any questions.
Daily 10–7

Go to Marinha Grande if you are looking for exquisite glassware.

MUSEU DO VIDRO
Palácio Stephens, Marinha Grande
Tel 244 560 209
This museum was opened in 1998 to commemorate 250 years of glass production in Marinha Grande. Its stunning glass collections are housed in the 18th-century Palácio Stephens, named after the Englishman who was to re-establish glass-making in the town in 1769.
Jun–end Sep daily 10–7; Oct–end May Tue–Sun 10–6 €1.50

ÓBIDOS

RUA DEREITA
Óbidos
This street is full of small shops selling an assortment of curios and souvenirs. It is worth looking around for a bit as it is possible to find some examples of tasteful regional crafts among the trinkets. The town's weekly market is on Saturday.

ABRIGO DA BIQUINHA
Rua da Biquinha, Óbidos
Tel 262 959 449
One of the town's oldest and best-loved bars is set on a series of levels, the small rooms giving the place a homelike feel. Be sure to try the local *ginjinha de Óbidos* (cherry brandy), along with their excellent *linguiça* (spicy sausage).
Jul–end Sep daily noon–3am; Oct–end Jun Mon–Sat 8pm–3am

ADEGA COOPERATIVA DE CADAVAL, CRL
Largo da Adega Cooperativa, Cadaval
Tel 262 696 137 or 262 959 231 (tourist information on tastings at other vineyards in the area)
Grapes are brought from the gentle slopes of the Serra do Montejunto to this cooperative by some 650 growers. The resulting wines have won numerous prizes at the yearly *Festival do Vinho Português*. Book a couple of days in advance for tastings.
Visits and tastings: Mon–Fri 9–noon, 2–5 €2 Take the A8/IC1 south from Óbidos to Bombarral, then the N115 to Cadaval

GOLFE DA PRAIA D'EL REY
Vale de Janelas, Óbidos
Tel 262 905 005
www.praia-del-rey.com
www.portugalgolf.pt
Opened in 2003, this golf course is part of the 5-star Praia d'El Rey Golf and Country Club. Its 18 championship holes (par 72) look across the

dunes to the ocean, and the club house has a restaurant, indoor pool and health club.
Apr–end Oct daily 8–8; Nov–end Mar 8–6.30 18 holes Mon–Fri €75, Sat–Sun and national holidays €95; club rental €30; trolley €5; cart €35 Indoor Take the EN114 west out of Óbidos. Turn right at Serra d'El Rei and follow signs to the resort

ÓBIDOS TUR
Animação Turística Ltd, Casal de Soitão, Óbidos
Tel 969 052 148
This company organizes horse-drawn buggy and carriage rides to local places of interest. Trips last between 10 and 60 minutes, depending on the route you take. A couple of the drivers speak English and there is also a route information board at the departure point.
May–end Sep daily 10–6 Routes and prices include: aqueduct €15, village of Pinhal €25, Igreja da Pedra €35, village of Aldeia da Pedra €60
Departures from the Óbidos car park at the entrance to the town

PENICHE

ESCOLA DE RENDAS DA CAMARA MUNICIPAL DE PENICHE
Rua Alexandre Herculano, Peniche
Tel 262 785 934
As with many other Portuguese fishing villages, such as Vila do Conde in the north, Peniche is famous for its bobbin lace. The tourist office is also home to the town's lace school, which demonstrates how lace has been made here since 1919.
Mon–Fri 9–12.30, 2–5.30

DANAU BAR
Praia do Baleal, Baleal
Tel 262 709 818
This surfer-style hangout, just north of Peniche at the Baleal beach, is one of the most happening bars in town. Built totally of wood, and with great decks overlooking the beach, it often has live bands and karaoke at weekends.
Jun–end Sep daily 9am–4am; Oct–end May Wed–Mon 10am–4am
Praia do Baleal is to the north of Peniche. The all-wooden Danau is at the right-hand end of the beach

BALEAL SURF CAMP
Rua dos Amigos do Baleal 2, Praia do Baleal
Tel 969 050 546
www.balealsurfcamp.com
Peniche is one of the hottest spots in Portugal to catch the waves, and this company organizes individual lessons and week-long surf camps from its beachfront base at the Praia do Baleal. It also rents equipment and can arrange basic accommodation.
Apr–end Oct daily 10–8; Nov–end May daily, call to arrange times 2-hour lesson €30; 1-week course Mon–Fri with 2 hours of lessons a day €120; 1-week surf camp including lessons as above plus equipment, insurance and accommodation in dormitory room €395, private room €445

Ride the waves at Peniche, famous for its high rollers

BERLENGA ISLANDS TOURS
Largo da Ribeira, Peniche
Tel 918 619 311 or 917 601 114
These clear-watered islands are designated bird sanctuaries. You can visit the largest island, but are restricted to waymarked paths. Five-hour trips are available from several companies at the harbour.
Mon–Fri 9–8 Berlenga trips €17 pp, minimum 10 people, or €170 for boat. Departures weather dependent

BERLENGA SUB
Largo da Ribeira Velha 24, Marina de Peniche
Tel 965 107 728
This company organizes great scuba-diving trips around the Berlenga Islands just off the coast. You must be a qualified diver and be able to produce a valid diver's certificate.
Apr–end Jul daily 9–8; Aug book 1 month in advance; Sep book 1 week in advance €30 along the coast, €40 to the Berlenga Islands

NAUTIPESCA
Largo da Ribeira Velha, office A1, Peniche
Tel 917 588 358
Based in the old harbour, this outfit organizes coastal and open-sea fishing, providing all the necessary equipment.
Office: Jun–end Sep. Phone lines: daily 9–9. Trips run daily at any arranged time, depending on the weather Coastal trip Mon–Fri €60, Sat–Sun €80; open-sea trip €150

TOMAR

TEMPLAR
Alameda 1 de Março, Centro Comercial dos Templários, loja 309, Tomar
Tel 249 323 414
www.templar.online.pt
Canoeing, mountain-bicycling, archery, hiking and abseiling are just a few of the outdoor activities organized by Templar. They also offer a range of water sports, such as diving, water skiing and boardsailing.
Mon–Fri 10–1, 2–6 Prices vary according to the activity chosen; €150 for package of mixed activities

VIA VENTURA
Rua Marquês de Pombal 2–1º B, Tomar
Tel 249 324 464 or 939 641 425
In the summer, rent a canoe from Via Ventura for a trip out to sea, or a bicycle if you'd rather stay on land. The company also organizes 4x4 excursions through the year.
Daily 9–6.30 Bicycle rental including helmets €15; canoeing, including all equipment €20; 4x4 trips €60, including lunch and a guide

FESTIVALS AND EVENTS

Decorative headdresses are part of the Festa dos Tabuleiros in Tomar

EASTER

SEMANA SANTA
Óbidos
Tel 262 955 060 (tourist office)
The most important religious and cultural event in Óbidos is its Easter celebration, attracting thousands of visitors and pilgrims from all over the country. Saints and images are taken out of their churches and paraded through the streets. The most moving is the Via Sacra procession, re-enacting Christ's last hours before the Crucifixion.

MAY

PILGRIMAGES
12–13 May (see also October), Fátima
The pilgrimages mark the alleged first and last appearances of the Virgin Mary to three shepherd children (▷ 116). Though it is always busy, Fátima is transformed during these days as literally thousands of road-weary pilgrims from across the country and around the world crawl the last kilometre up to the basilica on their knees.

JULY

FESTA DOS TABULEIROS
2nd Sunday in July (every 4 years, next in 2007), Tomar
Tel 249 322 427
The unique Festival of the Trays honours both the Holy Spirit and the saintly Dona Isabel (married to Dom Dinis, a medieval king of Portugal). It is particularly famous for the massive headdresses of bread and paper flowers topped with a white dove—the *tabuleiros*—which the women of the town wear as they take part in processions through the streets.

AUGUST

SEMANA INTERNACIONAL DE PIANO
Around 1st week August, Óbidos
Tel 262 959 231
www.sipo2003.com
Held in several locations in Óbidos, including the Auditório da Casa da Música, this piano festival brings international names to the concert stage. In addition to concerts, the maestros give master classes and lectures, which culminate with the students' concert on the festival's last day.

FESTA DE NOSSA SENHORA DA BOA VIAGEM
First Friday in August for 4 days, Peniche
Tel 262 789 571 (tourist office)
Amid the many festivities, the highlight of the Festival of Our Lady of the Good Voyage—patron saint of Peniche's fisherman—is on the Saturday night when a statue of the Virgin Mary is carried down to the ocean and taken by a procession of illuminated trawlers out to Cabo Carvoeiro.

OCTOBER

FESTIVAL DE MÚSICA ANTIGA
1st week in October, Óbidos
Tel 262 955 060 (tourist office)
Started in 1982, this Festival of Ancient Music, supported by the Gulbenkian Foundation, provides a week of free evening performances. Concerts are held in various churches and auditoriums, and involve singers, chamber orchestras, string quartets and guitarists.

PILGRIMAGES
12–13 October (see also May), Fátima

NOVEMBER

FESTIVAL INTERNACIONAL DO CHOCOLATE
Early November, Óbidos
Tel 262 955 060 (tourist office)
www.festivalchocolate.com
A must for chocoholics everywhere, this festival brings national and international chocolate chefs to Óbidos. Prizes are awarded for Best International Chocolate Recipe, Chocolatier of the Year and Artistic Pieces in Chocolate. There are also exhibitions, demonstrations, and free samples to take away or devour on the spot.

Too good to eat? Not for visitors to the Festival do Chocolate in Óbidos

LISBON

Shopping in Lisbon is wonderfully varied. Here you'll find Portugal's biggest and best malls, while there's a great range of idiosyncratic specialist shops throughout the city where you can track down things that are quintessentially Portuguese. In this attractive capital city you can also find goods from all over the country, so if you're looking for a specific craft from somewhere you're not visiting, there's a good chance you'll be able to find it here. The same goes for food and drink, with a vast selection of port, wines and delicacies for sale. Don't miss the chance to browse the markets, where you'll find everything from fresh food to clothes, antiques and trinkets. Once you've finished shopping, there's a full range of sightseeing trips, including tram tours and river cruises. If you're a sports fan catch a soccer match at the Estádio da Luz, or, if you want to be sporty, you could play golf at Belavista, rent a sailing boat, go for a swim, bicycle at the Parque das Nações, or go roller-blading or skating. Save some energy for the evening, which could include enjoying a *fado* performance, or dancing the night away at one of the city's cutting-edge clubs.

KEY TO SYMBOLS
- Shopping
- Entertainment
- Nightlife
- Sports
- Activities
- Health and Beauty
- For Children

SHOPPING

ACCESSORIES

AZEVEDO RUA
Praça Dom Pedro IV 69–73, Baixa
Tel 213 470 817
The place for hats of every kind. A family business since 1886, this Baixa institution has original wood cabinets, stuccoed ceilings and a vast inventory, including Panamas, straw hats, berets, bonnets, tams and bowlers. It is one of the few remaining hatters to make tri-horned bullfighter hats.
Mon–Fri 9.30–7, Sat 9.30–1
Rossio

CASA BATALHA
Centro Comercial do Chiado, Loja 10-A, Rua do Carmo, Chiado
Tel 213 427 313
Established in 1635 and owned by its founding family, Casa Batalha is known throughout the country for quality costume jewellery and accessories. Its premises were destroyed in the 1988 Chiado fire; the shop is now in the Armazéns do Chiado mall.
Daily 10–10 Baixa-Chiado

LUVARIA ULISSES
Rua do Carmo 87a, Chiado
Tel 213 420 295
During the 19th century this area boasted several prominent glove stores; today, only Ulisses remains. Opened in 1925, this tiny walk-in cubby of a shop retains its period interior and the personal service of days gone by. It has a wonderful selection of gloves in leather, silk, satin and cashmere.
Mon–Sat 9.30–7 Rossio

RETROSARIA BIJOU
Rua da Conceição 91, Baixa
Tel 213 425 049
Haberdashery may not be high on the souvenir list, but this lovely art deco shop offers a

glimpse of how shopping once was, with its old wooden counters and personal service. Founded in 1922, it stocks all kinds of buttons, ribbons, cords, cottons and threads.
Mon–Fri 9–7, Sat 9–1 Baixa Chiado

BOOKS

LIVARIA BERTRAND
Rua Garrett 73–75, Chiado
Tel 213 468 646
www.bertrand.pt
This bookstore, Portugal's oldest, was founded in 1773 and still retains much of its 19th-century interior, with fine wooden shelving and counters. While most books are in Portuguese, it is still a good place to find coffee-table picture books on a variety of Portuguese themes that make excellent gifts or souvenirs.
Mon–Thu 9–8, Fri–Sat 9am–10pm, Sun 2–7 Baixa-Chiado

DEPARTMENT STORES

EL CORTE INGLÊS
Avenida António Augusto de Aguiar
Tel 213 711 700
www.elcorteingles.pt
This gigantic department store, part of the Spanish chain, offers a full range of quality and designer items: clothing, accessories, perfumes and cosmetics, electrical appliances and household goods. In the basement there is a wonderful gourmet delicatessen section, restaurants and a multiscreen cinema showing films in their original language (usually English).
Daily 10am–midnight São Sebastião Bus 46, 205

FASHION

ALFAIATARIA NUNES CORRÊA
Rua Augusta 250, Baixa
Tel 213 240 930
Named after its founder, who was known as the 'prince of tailors', and opened in 1856, this classic men's outfitter clothed the men of Portugal's royal family for over half a century and dictated fashion among high society. Come here for quality off-the-rack and bespoke suits and shirts.
Mon–Fri 9–7, Sat 9–1 Rossio

ANA SALAZAR
Rua do Carmo 87
Tel 213 472 289
www.anasalazar.pt
Probably Portugal's best-known fashion designer, Ana Salazar is considered to be the pioneer of Portuguese fashion by both the national and international press. She set up her own label in the 1980s and opened a Paris showroom in 1985. Her designs often make intriguing use of stretch fabrics in neutral tones of grey, earthy browns and maroons.
Mon–Fri 10–7, Sat 10–7 Baixa-Chiado

Get your hands on one of Ana Salazar's stunning designs

JOSÉ ANTÓNIO TENENTE
Travessa do Carmo 8, Chiado
Tel 213 422 560
After working under Ana Salazar, Tenente opened his own store in 1990. Since then he has become one of the country's leading international designers. His cotton shirts and suits are popular, thanks to their sleek, innovative design, as is his fabulous selection of accessories.
Mon–Sat 10.30–7.30 Baixa-Chiado

ROSA AND TEIXEIRA
Avenida da Liberdade 204
Tel 213 110 350
Amid the stylish designer shops of the Avenida da Liberdade, this popular boutique is one of the most highly regarded classical menswear stores in the city. In addition to their own-label off-the-rack clothing, they offer bespoke tailoring and a long line-up of designer names.
Mon–Sat 10–7.30 Avenida

FOOD AND DRINK

A CARIOCA
Rua da Misericórdia 9, Bairro Alto
Tel 213 420 377
This superb coffee house opened its doors in 1936 and is, to this day, one of the city's best. Behind its original façade and fittings, it sells all manner of coffee, freshly ground or as whole beans, plus some fine teas and a great selection of quality chocolate.
Mon–Fri 9–7, Sat 9–1 Baixa-Chiado

CONFEITARIA NACIONAL
Praça da Figueira 18-B
Tel 213 424 470
Founded in 1829 and selling all kinds of delicious confectionery, this store is worth a visit just for its interior. The wood-and-glass cabinets and antique mirrors make the perfect setting for the rows upon rows of tempting sweets made to traditional recipes. The almond cookies are particularly good.
Mon–Sat 8–8 Rossio

MANUEL TAVARES
Rua da Betesga 1A, Baixa
Tel 213 424 209
www.manueltavares.com
On the southeast corner of Praça da Figueira, this traditional grocery store and deli has been in business since 1860. The original decorative wooden shelves are crammed with products from around the country: cheese, wine, dried fruits, Madeira honey cake and

a tempting counter full of elaborate confectionery.
Mon–Fri 9.30–7.30, Sat 9.30–1
Rossio

HOME FURNISHINGS

CASA DAS VELLAS LORETO
Rua do Loureto 53, Bairro Alto
Tel 213 425 387
This shop has been selling candles since 1789. The small but perfectly formed teak-and-mahogany interior, with antique clock and pointed flame-like arches, is lined with glass cabinets full of every size and shade of candle imaginable: religious, moulded, scented, large and small. All are produced on the premises.
Mon–Fri 9–7, Sat 9–1 Baixa-Chiado Tram 28

PARIS EM LISBOA
Rua Garrett 77, Chiado
Tel 213 424 329
Walking up the exclusive Rua Garrett in the Chiado, it is difficult not to notice the sinuous art nouveau exterior of this textile shop, which is just as grand inside as it is out. In business since 1888, it now specializes in quality towelling products made in factories in the north of the country.
Mon–Sat 10–7 Baixa-Chiado

SANTOS OFÍCIOS
Rua da Madalen 87, Baixa
Tel 218 872 031
This shop, opened in 1995 to promote quality, hand-selected crafts, is housed in an 18th-century stable, opposite the church of Madalena in the Baixa. Representing all regions of Portugal, it stocks an eclectic mix of pottery, rugs, embroidered linens, figurines, tiles and sculptures. A full shipping service is available.
Mon–Sat 10–8 Baixa-Chiado

SOLAR
Rua Dom Pedro V 68–70, Bairro Alto
Tel 213 465 522
Rua Dom Pedro, leading into Rua do Alecrim, is home to many antiques shops; one of the best known is Solar, with a fine collection of salvaged, hand-painted tiles, some of which date back to the 15th century. It also has a good selection of furniture and pewter ware.
Mon–Fri 10–7, Sat 10–1
Restauradores then Gloria elevator
Bus 58

VISTA ALEGRE
Largo do Chiado 18, Chiado
Tel 213 461 401
www.vistaalegre.pt
Producing exquisite porcelain since 1824, Vista Alegre is renowned for its high-quality, classic designs, which the company supplied to many European royal families. Its luxury headquarters, here in the Chiado, displays its wares just like fine jewels, spotlighting them in a lavish setting of polished marble and glass. There are also smaller branches in all the major city malls.
Mon–Sat 9.30–7 Baixa-Chiado

The Centro Comercial Amoreiras is the most elegant of Lisbon's malls

VIÚVA LAMEGO
Calçada do Sacramento 29, Chiado
Tel 213 469 692
www.viuvalamego.com
If you have admired the fine faïence tiles that grace many of the city's façades and would like to buy some, the central outlet of the Sintra-based Viúva Lamego tile factory is the place to go. Producing hand-painted tiles since 1849, they specialize in the reproduction of 16th- to 18th-century motifs.
Mon–Fri 10–7, Sat 10–7 Baixa-Chiado

JEWELLERY

OURIVESARIA W. A. SARAMENTO
Rua da Áurea 251 (also known as Rua do Ouro)
Tel 213 426 774
Often known by its old name of Rua do Ouro (Gold Street), this street was traditionally home to jewellers and goldsmiths. W. A. Saramento, founded in 1870, is still producing fine filigree and stonework, and has some exquisite pieces on display.
Mon–Fri 10–1.30, 3–7, Sat 10–1.30
Baixa-Chiado

MARKETS

FEIRA DA LADRA
Campo de Santa Clara, Graça
This is the city's main flea market, selling the usual junk: old record-players, car stereos and old trinkets passed off as genuine antiques. It also has records, CDs and lots of South Americans selling their crafts.
Tue 8am–1pm, Sat all day
Tram 28

MERCADO ABASTECEDOR DA RIBEIRA
Avenida 24 de Julho
Tel 213 462 966
Lisbon's largest covered market is just down from the Cais do Sodré station and is one of the city's most important fresh fish outlets. It is also good for other fresh produce, including fruit, vegetables and regional cured meats and cheeses.
Mon–Sat 6am–2pm Cais do Sodré

SHOPPING MALLS

CENTRO COMERCIAL AMOREIRAS
Avenida Duarte Pacheco
Tel 213 810 200
www.amoreiras.com
The oldest of the city's now numerous malls is housed in

the distinctive, post-modern Torres das Amoreiras. Despite the fact that there are now many more malls, it remains popular with many *Lisboetas*, who think it is more refined than some of the newer mega-malls. It has a multiscreen cinema.
Daily 9am–11pm Marquês de Pombal, Rato Bus 11, 23, 48, 53, 58, 74, 75, 83

CENTRO COMERCIAL COLOMBO
Avenida do Colégio Militar, Benfica
Tel 217 113 600
www.colombo.pt
To the north of the city, this terracotta temple to modern consumerism stands opposite the Benfica stadium. When completed in the late 1990s, it was the biggest mall in Portugal and Spain housing three floors of shops, galleries, food halls and entertainments, including a roller-coaster.
Daily 10am–midnight Colégio Militar-Luz

CENTRO COMERCIAL VASCO DA GAMA
Parque das Nações, Avenida Dom João II
Tel 218 930 600
www.centrovascodagama.pt
At the Expo '98 site east of the heart of the city, the Vasco da Gama mall has all the main chain stores, plus a few smaller names. Avoid weekends when it gets really crowded.
Sun–Fri 10am–11pm, Sat 10am–midnight Oriente

ENTERTAINMENT

CINEMAS

EL CORTE INGLÊS
Avenida António Augusto de Aguiar
Tel 707 232 221
www.warnerlusomundo.pt
A new cinema complex in the basement of the huge department store shows all the latest blockbusters in their original language. A small supplement buys a VIP ticket, which entitles you to a pre-film drink and priority seating.
Ticket office: Mon–Fri 1.30pm–12.30am, Sat–Sun 11am–midnight
€5, VIP €8 In auditorium
São Sebastião Bus 46, 205

INSTITUTO DA CINEMATECA PORTUGUESA
Rua Barata Salgueiro 39
Tel 213 596 262
Housed in a late 19th-century house just off the Avenida da Liberdade, Portugal's national film theatre screens contemporary Portuguese films and international classics.
Mon–Sat 6.30pm and 9.30pm
€5 In auditorium
Avenida

The Coliseu dos Recreios is an architectural gem with drama thrown in

QUARTETO
Rua Flores Lima 16
Tel 217 971 244
Here is a cinema with all the charm of yesteryear: four small screens, a bar selling drinks and newspapers, and an interval in which to enjoy them. Though it screens some big films, it generally concentrates on less commercial offerings.
Ticket office: daily 1.30pm–midnight
€5 In auditorium Roma
Bus 17, 27

LIVE PERFORMANCE VENUES

COLISEU DOS RECREIOS
Rua Portas de St. Antão
Tel 213 240 585
www.coliseulisboa.com
Opened in 1890, this was one of the first public buildings in Portugal to use wrought iron, both in its structure and as an architectural feature. A little faded yet still grand, it frequently hosts ballet performances and contemporary music concerts.
Box office: Mon–Sat 1–7.30 or until half an hour before start of performance €20–€50 In auditorium
Restauradores Bus 36, 59; tram E15

FUNDAÇÃO CALOUSTE GULBENKIAN
Avenida da Berna 45
Tel 217 823 030
www.gulbenkian.pt
The most important cultural venue in the country, the Gulbenkian Foundation has its own orchestra, choir and dance company, which stages regular performances throughout the year. It also hosts national and international art exhibitions.
Box office: Mon–Fri and weekends of performances 1–7 and one hour prior to start of performance
€15–€40 In auditorium
São Sebastião Bus 56

PAVILHÃO ATLÂNTICO
Parque das Nações
Tel 218 918 409
www.pavilhaoatlantico.pt
Built for Expo '98 within the Parque das Nações complex, this blue, mushroom-like pavilion plays host to big international stars, rock concerts, Broadway shows and international sporting events.
Box office: daily 1–7 or until half an hour after start of performance. Tickets also available at FNAC stores around the city that accept credit cards
€20–€50 Estação do Oriente
Bus 26

TEATRO NACIONAL DE SÃO CARLOS
Rua Serpa Pinto 9, Baixa
Tel 213 253 000
www.saocarlos.pt
Opened in 1793, the splendid gold-leaf and red-velvet audi-

torium of the Teatro Nacional de São Carlos has been the stage for the country's most prestigious opera productions and major symphony concerts ever since.
Box office: Mon–Fri 1–7 or until half an hour before start of performance. Opera season: Oct–end Jun €20–€60 In auditorium Baixa-Chiado Bus 58; Tram 28

NIGHTLIFE

BARS

DOCA DE ALCÂNTARA
Alcântara
Particularly popular in summer, this converted dockside warehouse under the 25 de Abril bridge houses a selection of restaurants and bars, with outside terraces looking over the marina and river beyond. Try Doca de Santo, with live music from Sunday to Thursday nights.
Restaurants: 12–2.30, 7.30–10.30. Bars: 9pm–2am or later at weekends Alcântara Bus 28; tram E15

SÉTIMO CÉU
Travessa da Espera 54, Bairro Alto
Tel 213 466 471
Always keeping up with the latest trends in both interior decoration and music, Sétimo Céu is one of the most popular gay bars in the city. It specializes in excellent Brazilian *caipirinha* cocktails—*cachaça* (sugar-cane liquor), sugar and limes on ice.
Daily 10pm–2am Restauradores then Glória elevator Bus 58; tram E28

SOLAR DO VINHO DO PORTO
Rua de São Pedro de Alcântara 45, Bairro Alto
Tel 213 475 707
www.ivp.pt
This 18th-century mansion is home to the Port Wine Institute, established in 1933 to control port quality and promote the drink around the world. Its club-like atmosphere makes it an ideal place to try the many ports on offer. You can take a tutored tasting of port wine, or choose your own to sample.
Mon–Sat 11am–midnight Prices per glass start at €1 Baixa-Chiado, Restauradores then Glória elevator

JAZZ

CHAPITÔ
Rua Costa do Castelo 1–7
Tel 218 867 334
This relaxed outdoor bar just below the castle has exceptional views over the city. Next door is a circus school, so there are often juggling, tap-dancing and clowning shows as well as live bands from 11pm Thursday to Saturday.
Mon–Fri 7pm–midnight, Sat noon–2am Bus 37; tram E28

Why not end the evening with a visit to a chilled-out jazz bar?

HOT CLUB
Praça da Alegria 39
Tel 213 467 369
Opened more than 60 years ago, the Hot Club is Lisbon's best choice for dedicated jazz enthusiasts. With live shows every week, many great names have played gigs here.
Jam sessions: Tue–Wed 10pm–2am. Concerts: Thu–Sat 10pm–2am €7–€10 (concert days) Avenida

CLUBS

KAPITAL
Avenida 24 de Julho 68, Santos
Tel 213 957 101
Kapital is an elite and trendy hangout for Lisbon's rich and beautiful; admittance to this three-floored club is a lottery and ultimately down to the whims of the doormen. Casual yet smartly dressed couples and attractive single women seem to stand the best chance.
Daily 11pm–6am Charge at discretion of doorman Santos Bus 28; tram E15

PLATEAU
Avenida 24 de Julho, Escadinhas da Praia 7, Santos
Tel 213 965 116
Plateau was Lisbon's first true nightclub and as such enjoys legendary status. Decorated with oriental objects, it plays mainly 1980s revivalist, pop and rock to the mixed beautiful crowd lucky enough to make it past the doormen.
Wed–Sat midnight–6am Charge at discretion of doorman Santos Bus 28; tram E15

TRUMPS
Rua da Imprensa Nacional 104 B, Bairro Alto
Tel 213 971 059
www.trumps.pt
At the top end of the Bairro Alto, Trumps is Lisbon's best known gay club. It has a huge dance floor downstairs, where commercial mainstream sounds play, and a gentler chill-out area upstairs with mellow music and snooker.
Tue–Sun 10pm–6am Admission €10 (includes drinks) Bus 58

SPORTS AND ACTIVITIES

BICYCLING

TEJO BIKE
Parque das Nações
Tel 218 919 333
www.parquedasnacoes.pt
A great way to get around the Parque das Nações is by bicycle. Rent one from the Rossio dos Olivais (between the river and back entrance of the shopping mall), or at Praça Sony towards the bridge. Children's equipment is available.
15 Apr–15 Sep 10–8, 16 Sep–14 Apr 10–6 Adult €2.50 for 30 min, €5

for 1 hour, additional 30 min €1.50; child €1.50 for 30 min, €3 for 1 hour, additional 30 min €1; tandems €4 for 30 min, €7 for 1 hour, additional 30 min €3

BULLFIGHTING

PRAÇA DE TOUROS

Campo Pequeno, Avenida João XXI–Avenida da Républica
Tel 217 932 143 or 217 932 093

For a chance to appreciate the renowned horsemanship of Portuguese bullfighters, the restored 19th-century neo-Moorish bullring at Campo Pequeno is worth a visit in season. Note that in Portugal, unlike in Spain, the bulls are not killed in the ring, but skilfully wrestled to the ground.

Season: Apr–end Sep. Bullfights: Thu 8pm €20–€50 according to the line-up Campo Pequeno Bus 27, 36, 45

GOLF

CLUBE DA BELAVISTA

Avenida Avelino Teixeira da Mota, Chelas
Tel 218 310 860 or 916 660 900
www.portugalgolf.pt

Close to the airport, Belavista is the only golf club within the city. It's a short and fairly difficult course, owing to its undulating terrain and artificial lakes. Be sure not to miss the excellent clubhouse restaurant.

Jun–end Sep 7am–7.30pm; Oct–end May 8–5 18 holes €28; club rental €20; buggy €33.50 Aveiro Bus 10, 68

SOCCER

ESTÁDIO DE ALVALADE

Sporting Clube de Portugal, Edifício Visconde de Alvalade, Rua Professor Fernando da Fonseca, Campo Grande
Tel 217 516 000
www.sporting.pt

Home ground to Sporting Lisbon (Benfica's city rival), this green-and-white-tiled stadium seats 54,000. The complex includes restaurants, bars, a bowling alley and cinemas. For match information see local press or the club's official website.

Ticket office: daily 11.30–7.30, match days 11.30–9pm kick-off €10.50–€50 Campo Grande Bus 1, 36

ESTÁDIO DA LUZ

S. L. Benfica (club), Avenida General Norton de Matos, Benfica
Tel 218 627 000 (general) or 217 210 522 (ticket office)

The Estádio da Luz (Stadium of Light) is the world-famous home of Benfica soccer club. For match information see the local press.

Ticket office: daily 11.30–7.30, match days 11.30–9pm kick-off €10.50–€50 Colégio Militar-Luz Bus 4, 64, 65, 109

Benfica football club's emblem and motto grace the grounds' entrance

TOURS

CITYLINE

Avenida Praia da Vitória 12B
Tel: 213 191 090
www.cityline-sightline.pt

The most frequent and comprehensive city tours are offered by multinational giant Cityline, starting at its Marquês de Pombal terminus by the park. Some of the most popular routes are the Avenida, Baixa, Belém and Estrêla, before returning to the Marquês de Pombal.

Apr–end Oct, every 30 min between 9 and 6; Nov–end Mar departures every 60 min between 10 and 6 Adult €14, child (under 5) free Marquês de Pombal

PRAÇA DO COMÉRCIO

Tel 966 298 558

Take a panoramic, open-top bus ride around the city's main sights, starting on the east side of the Praça do Comércio. Or, for a tour with a nostalgic difference, try one of their lovingly restored, early 20th-century wooden trams, complete with their original brass fittings, which will take you along the city tram routes.

Departure times are regular but they do vary. For tickets and information see the above address or go to the tourist information office Baixa–Chiado

TRANSTEJO

Estação Fluvial do Terreiro do Paço, Praça do Comércio
Tel 218 820 348
www.transtejo.pt

These river cruises take two-and-a-half hours and are a superb way of seeing the city from a different perspective. The fabulous view of Lisbon's hills, dotted with churches and the castle, is especially good in late afternoon, when the light is fantastic. Commentary is in English, French and Spanish.

Apr–end Oct daily 11am and 3pm Adult €20, child (5–12) €8, under 5s free Baixa-Chiado Bus 45, 46, 58, 59

HEALTH AND BEAUTY

HEALTH CLUB MESTRE SILVA

Hotel Sheraton, Rua Latino Coelho 1 (first floor)
Tel 213 147 353

Just off Avenida Fontes Pereira de Melo, the Sheraton has one of the few health clubs open to non-members in the city. The club has a full range of facilities, including a gym, massage, sauna, Turkish baths and a heated outdoor pool set attractively into a plant-filled rooftop deck.

Mon–Fri 7am–9pm, Sat–Sun and national holidays 10–8 €5–€45 according to which activity you choose Outdoor Picoas

FOR CHILDREN

JARDIM ZOOLÓGICO
Estrada de Benfica 158–160, Parque das Laranjeiras
Tel 217 232 900
www.zoolisboa.pt
Home to some 400 species, Lisbon zoo is set in lovely gardens and has a variety of attractions to entertain children. There are dolphin and sea-lion shows, a birds of prey and macaw presentation, hands-on farm animals and a cable car.
Apr–end Sep 10–8; Oct–end Mar 10–6 Apr–end Sep adult €11.50, child €8.50; Oct–end Mar Mon–Fri adult €10.50, child €7.70, Sat–Sun adult €11.50, child €8.50 Jardim Zoológico Bus 16, 26, 31, 41, 54, 55, 58, 63, 68, 70, 72 Sete Rios

MICOLANDIA-PARQUE DO GIL
Parque das Nações
Tel 218 940 277
This excellent children's playground at the far end of the Parque das Nações towards the bridge is named after Gil, the Expo '98 mascot. It has bright inflatables, ball pools, slides, tunnels and mazes, and a bouncy castle.
May–end Sep Mon and Wed–Fri 3–8, Sat–Sun and national holidays 10–8; Oct–end Apr Mon and Wed–Fri 2.30–7.30, Sat–Sun and national holidays 10–8 Child (4–12) €2 first 30 min, then €1 every additional 15 min Oriente Bus 28

OCEANÁRIO
Parque das Nações
Tel 218 917 002 or 218 917 006
www.oceanario.pt
This cleverly designed oceanarium, the largest in Europe, is not to be missed. It has a huge central tank that can be viewed from two different floors, and is home to countless sea creatures, such as manta rays, sharks and eels. Four smaller tanks house more species from four different oceans.
Late Mar–end Sep 10–7; Oct–late Mar 10–6 Adult €9, child (4–12) €4.50, under 3s free; 1 free visit with Cartão do Parque Oriente Bus 28

TELEFÉRICO
Parque das Nações
Tel 218 965 413
www.parquedasnacoes.pt
Running about 20m (65ft) above the ground from the Torre de Vasco da Gama towards the Oceanário, Lisbon's cable car gives amazing views of the river, the Ponte Vasco da Gama and the whole of the Parque das Nações. Stretching up 140m (458ft) into the sky, the tower is Lisbon's tallest building and well worth a visit. Its circular viewing platform has a revolving restaurant.
Jun–end Sep Mon–Fri 11–8, Sat–Sun 10–9; Oct–end May Mon–Fri 11–7, Sat–Sun 10–8 Adult one way €3.50, return €5.50, child (5–15) one way €1.80, return €3, 1 return trip free with Cartão do Parque

FESTIVALS AND EVENTS

EASTER

CARNAVAL
Date varies
Tel 210 312 810 (tourist office)
Celebrated throughout Portugal with fireworks and parades, Carnaval in Lisbon is based around the Avenida da Liberdade, where a long-planned parade of bright costumes, samba dancers and decorated floats makes its way along the avenue to loud applause.

MARCH

LISBON HALF-MARATHON
Date varies, usually end of March (check with tourist office)
Tel 210 312 810 (tourist office)
Lisbon's most important participatory sporting event takes up to 35,000 runners from the far side of the Ponte 25 de Abril across to Alcântara, up to the Praça do Comércio and back down the river to finish in Belém. You must register in advance to participate.

MODA LISBOA
Dates vary, usually end of March (check website)
Tel 213 213 000
www.assoc-modalisboa.pt
Held in various venues around the city, this is Lisbon's most important fashion event. Shows and other fashion-related activities are spread over several days, attracting all the top national designers and international names from New York, Paris, Milan and London.

APRIL

ESTORIL OPEN TENNIS CHAMPIONSHIPS
Early April, Club de Tenis do Complexo, Desportivo do Jamor, Cruz Quebrada
Tel 214 146 041
Held at the Jamor sports venue, to the west of the city, the Estoril Open is Portugal's top tennis competition, attracting international players.

JUNE

FESTAS DOS SANTOS POPULARES
June
Tel 210 312 810 (tourist office)
These are some of the city's traditional festivals. Alfama, Mouraria and Madragoa are decorated with bunting and host all sorts of events.

Santo António
12–13 June
Held in honour of Lisbon's patron saint and marking the beginning of the *Festas dos Santos Populares*; Alfama's streets are decorated and host sardine barbecues.

São João
23–24 June
Similar to Santo António, with street parties and parades.

São Pedro
25 June–1 July
Marks the end of the festivities, as fishing boats sail over to Montijo on the far bank of the River Tejo to be blessed.

AROUND LISBON

There's enough shopping, activities and entertainment around Lisbon to keep you happy for weeks. Shopping is excellent, with elegant malls packed with designer names, individual boutiques selling quirkier products and some great market opportunities. There's a huge range of sports, too: golf, bicycle riding, hiking, tennis and water sports, including spectacular windsurfing and surfing at Guincho. Evenings bring plenty to entertain, with summer arts and music festivals at Sintra that are among the best in Portugal.

KEY TO SYMBOLS

-  **Shopping**
- **Entertainment**
- **Nightlife**
- **Sports**
- **Activities**
- **Health and Beauty**
- **For Children**

CARCAVELOS

CARCAVELOS SURF SCHOOL

Windsurf Café, Praia de Carcavelos, Avenida Marginal, Carcavelos
Tel 214 578 965 or 966 131 203
www.windsurfcafe.com

Surfing is big in Portugal, and Carcavelos beach is popular with both pros and beginners. If you're a beginner, you could arrange lessons with a professional teacher. These are available at the Windsurf Café, the hippest of the Carcavelos beachfront bars, just below the skate ramps.

Wed–Fri 5pm–7pm, Sat–Sun 11–1, 4–6. Closed Aug Registration €5; 1 lesson €25; set of 4 lessons €75

CASCAIS

BOCA DO INFERNO

Estrada da Boca do Inferno, Cascais
Tel 214 868 204 (tourist office)

The 'Mouth of Hell', where surf rushes into a crevasse in the rocky coastline, is Cascais' most popular attraction. Around it a small craft market has grown up, which offers a good selection of pottery, woollens and textiles.

Daily 10–7

CASCAIS MUNICIPAL MARKET

Avenida 25 de Abril, Cascais
Tel 214 868 204 (tourist office)

The municipal market lies behind the Cascais Villa Shopping Mall. Although the inside stands are open all week, the best days to come are Wednesday and Saturday, when the central courtyard is filled with stalls selling fresh local produce and flowers.

Wed and Sat morning

CASCAIS OPEN-AIR MARKET

Praça de Touros, Cascais
Tel 214 868 204 (tourist office)

Held in the area surrounding the bullring west of town, this market sells clothes, shoes and other textile products, as well as ceramics, wooden home utensils and trinkets.

1st and 3rd Sun of month Take the special Buscas from the station to the bullring €1.10

CASCAIS VILLA SHOPPING MALL

Avenida Dom Pedro I, Lote 1 and 2, Cascais
Tel 214 838 610
www.cascaisvilla.com

This fairly small shopping mall, at the end of the Marginal guarding the entrance to Cascais, has all the usual national and international chains, a supermarket and multiscreen cinemas showing mainly English-language Hollywood blockbusters.

Daily 10am–11pm

CASCAISHOPPING
Estrada Nacional 9, Alcabideche
www.cascaishopping.pt
Since it was extended in 2003, this mall now has around 160 shops housing branches of major international stores, such as FNAC, Mango, Habitat, Benetton, Zara and many more. It also has two large food halls and multiscreen cinemas.
Daily 10am–11pm Bus 417 from Cascais

CENTRO CULTURAL DE CASCAIS
Avenida Rei Humberto II de Itália 27–50, Cascais
Tel: 214 849 900
www.cm-cascais.pt
At the heart of cultural activities in Cascais is the CCC, housed in funky renovated buildings near the castle. A full line-up of events includes classical music, dance, theatre, exhibitions and, in summer, live performances in the Largo de Camões.
Tue–Sun 10–6 €5–€10, although many events are free In auditorium

BAR DO GUINCHO
Estrada do Abano, Praia do Guincho Norte, Cascais
Tel 214 871 683
www.bardoguincho.pt
Overlooking the pounding Guincho surf, this is a good place for a snack lunch or full meal. It is also a hot nightspot, snug with a log fire in winter and cool and breezy in the summer. During weekends, it hosts live bands and karaoke.
Sun–Thu noon–2am, Fri–Sat noon–4am Bus 415, 405 from Cascais

COCONUTS
Avenida Rei Humberto II de Itália, Cascais
Tel 214 823 490 (Estalagem Farol Hotel) or 214 844 109
Cascais' best-known club is perched on the rocks above the ocean, just past the marina. With several bars and lounge areas it plays club sounds from top DJs. Thursday is ladies' night, when female guests are served free drinks.
Tue–Sat 11pm–6am Usually €10 (includes drinks) but can be as high as €250 to discourage undesirable patrons

CENTRO HÍPICO DA QUINTA DA MARINHA
Quinta da Marinha
Tel 214 869 084
www.quintadamarinha-centrohipico.pt
Horse-racing began here in 1924 and today this venue is one of the largest and best equipped in the country, with paddocks, show grounds, outdoor arenas, a racing track and horses to rent by the hour.
Tue–Sun 9–1, 3–7 €30 per hour

You can cycle along the coast on a designated track from Cascais

PRAIA DO GUINCHO
Tel 214 868 204 (tourist office)
The wild and stunning Guincho beach, with its backdrop of golden cliffs, is a windsurfer's paradise. Be warned, though: The beach is often blasted by strong winds and crashing rollers, and there is an undertow that can be dangerous. This makes bathing a risk for any but the strongest swimmers, but sand and dunes still make it a great spot for kids.
Bus 415, 405 from Cascais

OITAVOS GOLFE
Quinta da Marinha, Casa da Quinta 25
Tel 214 860 600
www.portugalgolf.pt
Designed by Robert Trent Jones and considered one of the best courses in Europe, Oitavos has 18 holes and a par of 71. The chic club house, with outdoor terraces and panoramic plate-glass windows, looks straight out over the ocean.
May–end Oct daily 8–8; Nov–end Dec, Mar, Apr daily 8–7; Jan, Feb daily 8–6 18 holes Mon–Fri €90, Sat–Sun €150; club rental €20; electric trolley €10; buggy €32

SPORTACCESS
Casa da Guia, shop 11, Estrada do Guincho
Tel 214 847 909
There is a great bicycle track running for about 8km (5 miles) from Cascais along the coast and past the dunes to Guincho beach. To rent bicycles, contact Sportaccess, which lets them out for the hour, half- or full day. They also have child seats and bicycles for children aged 10 years and older.
Tue–Fri 10–6, Sat–Sun 10–7
1 day €15–20 depending on type of bicycle, half-day €10; 1 hour €3; helmets €1 Bus 405, 415 from Cascais

VISCONDE
Rua Visconde da Gandarinha 166, Cascais
Tel 214 849 470
www.mestresilva-healthclubs.com
This is one of the few health clubs in the area open to non-members. As well as a great outdoor pool surrounded by grassy lawns, there is a heated indoor pool, gym, squash court, sauna and Turkish bath.
Mon–Fri 7am–10pm, Sat–Sun 9–8
€11–€35 according to activity
Outdoor and indoor

JARDIM DA GANDARINHA
Parque Municipal da Gandarinha, Cascais
Tel 214 868 204 (tourist office)
This large park is great for kids when it's time to relax and

take a break from shopping or the beach. In addition to spacious grassy lawns, there are adventure playgrounds with slides, swings and climbing frames, a lake with ducks and swans, dirt tracks for bicycle riding, and an aviary. Spectacular peacocks wander freely through the park.

ESTORIL

CASINO ESTORIL

Praça José Teodoro do Santos, Estoril
Tel 214 667 700
www.casinoestoril.pt

The casino at Estoril has more than 1,000 gaming machines, as well as traditional gaming tables. The show rooms offer dancing girls and top musical entertainment, the gardens flash with lasers and the Chinese restaurant is one of the best in the country.

Daily 3pm–3am, floor shows nightly at 11pm

CLUBE DE GOLF DO ESTORIL

Avenida da República, Estoril
Tel 214 680 054, 214 660 367 or 214 680 176
www.portugalgolf.pt

Designed by Mackenzie Ross in 1945, this club underwent several changes owing to the construction of the Cascais highway in the 1960s. But it remains a great par-69 course, with the 16th hole considered by many to be Portugal's best.

Daily 7.30–7 18 holes Mon–Fri €54, Sat–Sun reserved for members; club rental €15; hand trolleys €4

Take Estoril/Sintra turn-off from the A5 highway. Turn right on the EN9 towards Sintra. The course is 200m (218 yards) on the left

SINTRA

CASA BRANCA I

Rua Consiglieri Pedroso 12, Sintra
Tel 219 230 528
www.portugueseembroidery.com

Opened in 1987, this shop sells high-quality linens and embroidery. Tablecloths, place mats, bedding, towels and robes are all exquisitely crafted using the best materials. There is also Casa Branca II at Praça da República 6–10.

Daily 10–7

PIRIQUITA

Rua das Padarias 1–7, Sintra
Tel 219 230 626

Piriquita started making its famously delicious *queijadas* (cheesecakes in a pastry shell) in the 1860s. It is also known for its almond *travesseiros*.

Thu–Tue 9am–11pm

CENTRO HÍPICO O PADDOCK

Rua do Alecrim, Janas
Tel 219 2834 308

The stables at Janas organize guided horse-riding trips in the Parque Natural de Sintra-Cascais, or along the coast.

Jun–end Sep 10–1, 4–7; Oct–end May 10–1, 3–6, 7.30–7 €25 per hour

About 10km (6 miles) from Sintra towards Praia da Almoçagem

Take a punt on a slot machine at the celebrated casino in Estoril

HORSE AND CARRIAGE

Sintra
Tel 219 231 157 (tourist office)

One of the most romantic ways to see Sintra is by horse-drawn carriage. Rent one by the *pelhourino* (pillory) just below the National Palace, or from the entrance to the Parque da Liberdade. It's worth checking prices at the tourist office in advance.

All year round

MUSEU DO BRINQUEDO

Rua Visconde de Monserrate, Sintra
Tel 219 242 171
www.museu-do-brinquedo.pt

In a converted fire station, this museum has more than 20,000 toys, including clockwork trains, tin soldiers, dolls and model airplanes. There is also a restoration workshop.

Tue–Sun 10–6 Adult €3, child (3–16) €1.50

FESTIVALS AND EVENTS

JUNE–JULY

FESTIVAL DE MÚSICA

Mid-Jun to mid-Jul, Sintra
Tel 219 231 157 (information from the tourist office at Praça da República) or 219 107 117 (Centro Cultural Olga Cadaval at Praça Francisco Sá Carneiro)

This music festival is held mainly in the Centro Cultural Olga Cadaval in Praça Francisco Sá Carneiro and is the highlight of Sintra's cultural calendar, attracting dance and classical music performances from around the world.

ESTORIL JAZZ FESTIVAL

July, Estoril
Tel 214 663 813 (tourist office)

This laid-back festival brings top international jazz names to perform in Estoril throughout July. Weekend performances are held in several venues, so for full details contact the tourist office, opposite the train station on Avenida Marginal.

JULY–AUGUST

FEIRA DO ARTESANATO

Summer, Estoril
Tel 214 663 813 (tourist office)

Held during the summer, this crafts fair sets up daily in the area beside the casino. It offers a selection of regional crafts, as well as paintings, hand-made jewellery, leather goods and other souvenirs.

Daily 6pm–midnight

THE ALENTEJO

WHAT TO DO

Traditional crafts are alive and well in the Alentejo and you'll find good buys in the form of pottery, textiles, foodstuffs and carpets. For the last, head for Arraiolos, but the biggest range of local buys can be found at Évora. Good purchases here include leather, pottery, cork and woollens, though don't forget the *doces conventuais*, the ultimate in sweetmeats that are also an Évoran speciality. The region's liveliest market is at Estremoz, where local ceramics and cheeses feature strongly. Or you could opt to drive a wine route—there are three from which to choose. For the energetic, there's swimming, golf, and canoeing on the Guadiana, or you could take a cycle trip and explore some prehistoric sites.

KEY TO SYMBOLS

- Shopping
- Entertainment
- Nightlife
- Sports
- Activities
- Health and Beauty
- For Children

ALTER DO CHÃO

COUDELARIA REAL

Alter do Chão
Tel 245 610 060

The Royal Stud at Alter was founded in 1748 by João V to breed and train horses for the House of Bragança. Pure Andalucian stock was used to breed the now world-famous performing Lusitanians, which can be seen here during training sessions.

Tue–Fri 9.30–4.30, Sat–Sun 11–3.30 Guided visits: Tue–Fri €3, minimum 20 people 4km (2.5 miles) northwest of Alter do Chão; follow signs to the Coudelaria

ARRAIOLOS

CALIFA

Rua Alexandre Herculano 34, Arraiolos
Tel 266 499 277

Founded in 1916, Califa is the oldest rug manufacturer in Arraiolos. Its showrooms, furnished with antiques, have fantastic displays of traditional handcrafted rugs, while in the studio you can see the craftsmen at work on the intricate and individual designs. Shipping service available.

Mon–Fri 10–1, 2–7, Sat 10–5

BEJA

CAFÉ LUIS DA ROCHA

Rua Capitão João Francisco de Sousa 63, Arraiolos
Tel 284 323 179

The Alentejo is renowned for its *doces conventuais* (sweet eggy desserts, traditionally made by nuns in local convents), and this art deco-style shop, along from the tourist office, is one of the best places to buy them. Also try their unique *porquinhos doces* (sweet pigs), made with marzipan, eggs and squash.

Apr–end Sep daily 8am–10pm; Oct–end Mar Mon–Sat 8am–10pm

CASA DE CHÁ MALTESINHAS

Rua dos Açoutados 35, Arraiolos
Tel 284 321 500

This tea house specializes in *doces conventuais*, but deliberately limits what it makes to typical Beja recipes handed down from the convents in the immediate vicinity. Try *toucinho do céu*, a fine pastry with a rich almond filling, or *queijinhos de hóstia,* made with a sweet egg custard.

Mon–Sat 9–7.30

IGREJA DA MISERICORDIA

Praça da Républica, Arraiolos
Tel 284 389 545

For the best selection of crafts in town, this converted church, which is now dedicated to

promoting the work of artisans of the southern Alentejo region, should be your first port of call. Don't miss the delicate linen embroideries, considered to be Beja's strong point.
Mon–Fri 9.30–12.30, 2–5.30

DORTE LARSSEN
Monte Gravia dos Pisões, Quintos
Tel 284 893 121 or 965 724 642
For tailored horse rides through the Alentejo plains or beside the River Guadiana, it's worth making for these stables in the village of Pisões, east of Beja. With about two days' notice, Dorte Larssen will arrange excursions personally designed to suit each client.
Daily 9–9 €12.50 per hour, €33 with picnic lunch Go south out of Beja on the IP2, then turn left onto the EN391 to Quintos/Pisões. Pisões is at the end of the road about 17km (10.5 miles) from Beja

OS SOZINHOS
Beja
Tel 968 516 177 or 969 022 122
Os Sozinhos organizes mountain-bicycle rides in the Guadiana region. The varied itineraries cover such options as the Alqueva Dam, frontier fortifications and watermills, and are always accompanied by helpful explanations from the guides. Book by phone, two days in advance. They have no office, but provide a pick-up service.
Daily 9–9 €10–€20 according to activity

CASTELO DE VIDE

CASA DA VILA
Largo Dr. José Frederico Laranja 4, Fonte da Vila, Castelo de Vide
Tel 245 919 169
Near the worn 16th-century marble town fountain, this ceramics shop sells pottery, most of which is hand-painted in the back workshop. If you are staying in the area for a while, speak to Claudina about decorating your choice of plain pieces, which can then be fired and collected a few days later.
Apr–end Sep daily 10–7; Oct–end Mar daily 10–1.30, 3.30–7

PARQUE NATURAL DA SERRA DE SÃO MAMEDE
Centro de Interpretação do Parque de São Mamede, Rua de Santo Amaro 27, Castelo de Vide
Tel 245 905 299
For a hike in the Serra de São Mamede, start at the park office, which has information on flora and fauna and semi-reliable maps of marked trails, often along medieval cobble-ways, tracks and paths.
Mon–Fri 9.30–12.30, 2–5.30
Walk along the back of the church in the middle of town. Rua de Santo Amaro is the last road on the right

Saturday is market day at the walled town of Estremoz

ELVAS

ANTAS DE ELVAS
Castelo de Elvas, Sítio do Castelo, Elvas
Tel 268 626 403
www.ippar.pt
Organized by the Portuguese Institute for Architectural Heritage (IPPAR), these half-day 4x4 trips visit some of the best megalithic menhirs and neolithic granite portal dolmen in the area; some are believed to date from around 3800BC. They leave from the castle.
Jun–15 Oct Wed, Sat, Sun and national holidays 10am and 5pm; Apr, May Wed, Sat, Sun and national holidays 10am and 3.30pm Adult €17.50, child €10

ESTREMOZ

JOÃO PORTUGAL RAMOS-VINHOS, S. A.
Monte do Serrado Pinheiro, Santa Maria, EN4, Estremoz
Tel 268 339 910
www.vinhosdoalentejo.pt
A stop along one of the three wine routes in the region, the João Portugal Ramos winery began production in 1997 using a selection of noble grape varieties, such as Aragonez, Trincadeira and Antão Vaz. Book a day ahead for a tour and tasting.
Mon–Sat 9–11.30, 2–4.30 Visit free; wine tasting €5.50 Head out of town on the EN4 towards Montemor. The winery is signed about 1.5km (1 mile) after the Galp fuel station

MERCADO TRADICIONAL
Rossio do Marquês de Pombal, Estremoz
Tel 268 333 541 (tourist office)
Held along the southern side of the Rossio, Estremoz's market is especially noted for its crafts, rustic antiques and unglazed earthenware pottery, including typical Estremoz terracotta figurines. It is also a good place to buy local goat's- and ewe's-milk cheese.
Sat 8–1

ÉVORA

ARTESANATO DIANA
Rua Cinco de Outubro 48, Évora
Tel 266 704 609
For a selection of good-quality regional crafts, try this shop to the east of Praça do Giraldo. As well as leather, cork and sheepskin items, it also sells the typical Alentejan *capotes*: heavy woollen capes with fur collars, ideal for cold winters.
Daily 9.30–7

MARKETS
Tel 266 702 671 (tourist office)
Évora's main market is held on the second Tuesday of each month at the Rossio de São Brás. Its endless stands sell everything from shoes and clothes to agricultural

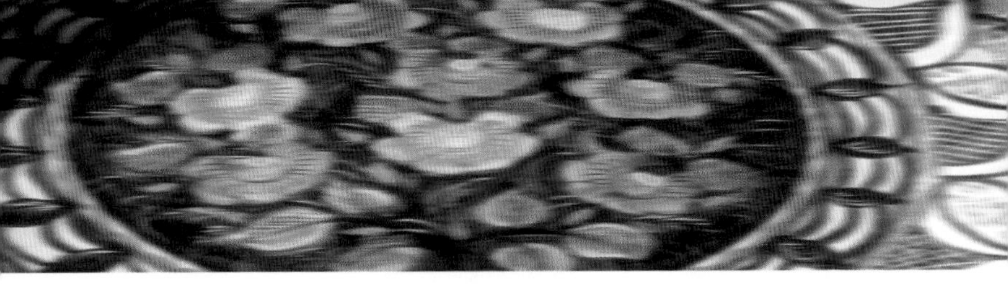

hardware and fresh produce. On the second Sunday of the month there is an antiques market at the Lgrgo do Chão das Covas near the aqueduct.

OFICINA DA TERRA
Rua do Raimundo 51A, Évora
www.oficinadaterra.com
If you are interested in ceramics, it's well worth visiting this gallery and workshop off the western side of the Praça do Giraldo. The hand-made ceramics, especially its terracotta character figures made by Tiago Cabeça, have won several national prizes.
Mon–Sat 10–7

PASTELARIA PÃO DE RALA
Rua do Cicioso 47, Évora
Tel 266 707 778
This tile-panelled cake shop is the best place in Évora to buy *doces conventuais*. As well as trying the *paõ de rala*, made with marzipan, almond and squash, don't miss the less sweet *cerica*, a dense cinnamon-flavoured sponge.
Daily 7.30am–8pm

TEÓFILO BILOU SANTANA
Rua da Républica 7–9, Évora
Under the arches in the main square, this hat store is the only shop in Évora to have preserved its traditional interior. Ceilings are decorated with stucco reliefs and the walls are lined with old wooden cabinets displaying a huge range of hats for all tastes.
Mon–Fri 9.30–1.30, 3–7, Sat 9.30–1

CONCERTOS DE MUSICA CLÁSSICA
Tel 266 702 671 (tourist office)
Promoted by the Duchess of Cadaval, these classical concerts are held outdoors in the Jardim do Paço or in the Loios church and are considered to be the highlight of Évora's cultural calendar. For tickets and information, contact the tourist office.
Evenings in July

CASA DO VINHO
Praça 1º de Maio, Évora
Tel 266 709 445
With its bare stone walls and tasteful lounges, this is a great place to try Alentejo wines. In addition to some 200 different wines, the bar also serves great *petiscos* (tapas) until 2am. Try the grilled cheese with oregano.
Mon–Sat 7pm–2am

OFICÍN@BAR
Rua da Moeda 27, Évora
Tel 266 707 312
Just off Praça Giraldo and playing a mix of music—jazz, blues and Lou Reed—this friendly bar attracts all ages; especially student and artist types who browse newspapers, check emails and enjoy the fabulous *shoarma* (spit-roasted lamb), which is served late into the evening.
Tue–Fri 8pm–2am, Sat 9pm–2am

These prize-winning figures from Oficina da Terra make unusual gifts

BIKE LAB
Centro Comercial da Vista Alegre, Lote 14, Rua Diogo do Couto, Évora
Tel 266 735 500
Bicycling is a great way to explore Évora's narrow cobbled streets. To rent a bicycle, head out to the northwest side of town and the Vista Alegre shopping mall, where Bike Lab rents out adult mountain bicycles and organizes guided tours.
Mon–Fri 9–7, Sat 9–1 €2 per hour, €20 per day. Helmets provided
Take the Arraiolos road out of town; the shopping mall is second left

PISCINAS MUNICIPAIS
Avenida Eng. Arantes e Oliveira, Évora
Tel 266 777 186
These municipal pools have something for everyone. There is a baby and toddler pool, a pool for people learning to swim, a diving pool and an Olympic-size pool for adults.
Jul–end Sep Tue–Sun 10–8
€2.25 Outside the town walls; follow signs to 'Piscinas Municipais'

ROTA DOS VINHOS DO ALENTEJO
Praça Joaquim António de Aguiar 20–21, Évora
Tel 266 746 498 or 266 746 609
www.vinhosdoalentejo.pt
Contact this establishment for information, driving instructions and lists of wineries on the area's three wine routes: the São Mamede route, the Historic route and the Guadiana route.
Mon–Fri 9–12.30, 2–5.30

TURAVENTUR
Quinta do Serrado, Senhor dos Aflitos, 7000-1734, Évora
Tel 266 743 134, 266 758 642 or 967 600 089
www.turaventur.com
Based just outside Évora (they will pick you up in town), this company organizes canoeing, mountain bicycling, and 4x4 trips to archaeological sites.
Office: Mon–Fri 9.30–6
€25–€75 according to activity

MARVÃO

AMMAIA CLUBE DE GOLF DO MARVÃO
Quinta do Prado, São Salvador de Aramenha, Marvão
Tel 245 993 755
www.portugalgolf.pt
For a practically empty golf course, come to Ammaia on a weekday. Nestling below the medieval fortified village of Marvão, this 18-hole, par-72

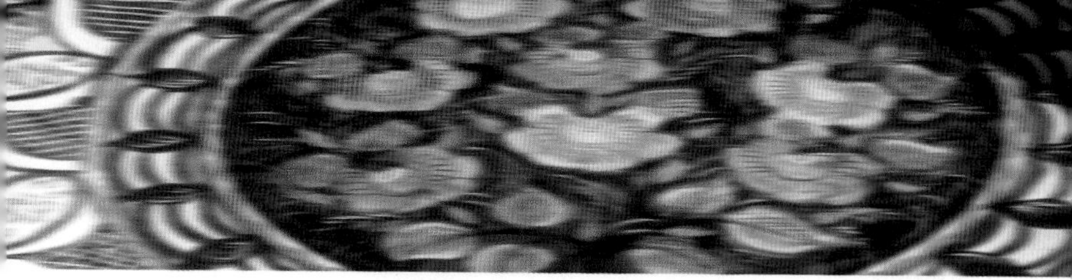

course has water hazards and some challenging steep sections, especially at holes 12 and 15.

 18 holes Mon–Fri €35, Sat–Sun and national holidays €45; club rental €15; buggy €30; trolley €4 From Marvão, go down to the bottom of the hill. In Portagem, turn right just before the main junction; the golf club is on the left. From Castelo de Vide, follow directions to Marvão, then turn left where signed

MONSARAZ

LOJA DA LIZETTE

Rua dos Celeiros, Monsaraz
Tel 266 557 159

This is a homey little store producing *mantas alentejanas* (heavy loom-woven blankets) in traditional and modern patterns. They make great gifts to take home.

Mon–Fri 9.30–1, 2.30–6, Sat–Sun 10–1, 2.30–8

OLARIA CARTAXO

Rua da Primavera 23, São Pedro do Corval, Reguengos de Monsaraz
Tel: 266 549 681

In the most important pottery area in the region, this is a good place to purchase patterned or plain plates, pots and floor tiles.

Daily 8–6 5km (3 miles) northeast of Reguengos de Monsaraz

PORTALEGRE

ADEGA DA CABAÇA

Quinta da Cabaça, Portalegre
Tel 245 207 217
www.vinhosdoalentejo.pt

Part of the northern São Mamede Wine Route, Quinta da Cabaça is owned by the Avillez family, who moved to the area in 1369. Today, the estate provides tours (book one day in advance), tastings and great regional food at a state-of-the-art winery.

Mon–Fri 9–12.30, 2–5.30. Restaurant: Tue–Sun 12–2pm, Fri–Sat 12–2, 7–10 Visit free; tastings €5–€7.50 Take the southeasterly road out of Portalegre towards Alegrete. Watch for *Rota dos Vinhos* signs for Adega da Cabaça

FESTIVALS AND EVENTS

MARCH

OVIBEJA

Last two weeks in March, Beja
Tel 284 311 913 (tourist office)

The biggest fair south of the Rio Tejo is held yearly at the Parque de Feiras e Exposições. Originally a livestock market, it has grown to include fishing contests, equestrian events, bullfights and interesting displays of regional crafts, dance and music.

APRIL–MAY

FEIRA INTERNACIONAL DE ARTESANATO E AGRO-PECUÁRIA DE ESTREMOZ (FIAPE)

Late April–early May, Estremoz
Tel 268 333 541 (tourist office)

This is Estremoz's biggest yearly event and is of great importance to the northern Alentejo region, as it promotes livestock and breeders from across the area. In addition to agricultural events, festivities include themed parties such as Fado Night and Spanish Night.

JUNE–JULY

FEIRA DE SÃO JOÃO

22 or 23 June–1 or 2 July, Évora
Tel 266 702 671 (tourist office)

The Fair of St. John, celebrated since 1569, is one of the Alentejo's biggest and best festivals. Traditionally agricultural, it now includes folk-dancing, crafts, fairground rides, food stands, music and, most importantly, bullfights, which take place from 24 to 29 June.

AUGUST

FESTIVAL INTERNACIONAL DE FOLCLORE DOS POVOS DO MUNDO

First two weekends in August, Elvas
Tel 268 622 236 (tourist office)

Usually held in the Praça da República, this international folklore festival hosts dance and musical groups from as far afield as Peru and Russia, plus national groups from up and down the country.

SEPTEMBER

FESTAS DAS FLORES DE CAMPO MAIOR

September Campo Maior (20km/12.5 miles north of Elvas on N373), Elvas
Tel 268 622 236 (tourist office)

This slightly random but spectacular festival is held in September if the inhabitants of Campo Maior decide to organize it. If you are lucky enough to catch it, it is well worth a detour to see the town's streets carpeted with hand-made and real flowers.

Amazing garlands of fresh flowers fill the streets during Campo Maior

FESTAS DO SENHOR DA PIEDADE E DE SÃO MATEUS

Last two weeks in September, Elvas
Tel 268 622 236 (tourist office)

Held towards the end of September in the Parque de Piedade, in honour of Our Lord of Mercy and St. Matthew, this is by far Elvas' biggest annual festival. In addition to elaborate religious processions, there are bullfights, folk-dancing, street performances, craft displays with examples of the crafts for sale, and food pavilions serving a huge range of local delicacies. Accommodation must be booked in advance.

THE ALGARVE

The Algarve is Portugal's holiday playground, so, as you'd expect, it is well served with shopping malls and offers plenty of activities and entertainments. For serious shopping you'd do best to head for Portimão or Faro, while if you're looking for regional crafts you could take in weekly markets up and down the coast, or head into the hills around Loulé. As a change from the beach you could go dolphin-watching, scuba-diving, surfing or fishing, or enjoy a cruise from the spectacularly beautiful coast around Albufeira. Golf is the obvious activity, with a clutch of Europe's best courses to hand. You can also bicycle, ride a horse and walk in unspoilt hill-country. Evenings could include listening to *fado*, some serious clubbing, or simply good eating in one the region's vast choice of restaurants.

KEY TO SYMBOLS

- Shopping
- Entertainment
- Nightlife
- Sports
- Activities
- Health and Beauty
- For Children

ALBUFEIRA

MARKET

Tel 289 585 279 (tourist office)

This twice-monthly market north of town near the new bus station sells mainly clothes and shoes, but, during summer, extra stands along the main shopping streets sell jewellery, ceramics, copper, leatherwear and souvenirs.

1st and 3rd Tue of month

RUA CÂNDIDO DOS REIS

Albufeira

This street off the Largo Engenheiro Duarte Pacheco is full of craft and souvenir shops. Among the best are Infante Dom Henrique (No. 40), which sells quality ceramics, and La Lojas (Nos 20–22), which has a great selection of lead crystal and fine porcelain.

Mon–Sat 10–8

SALGADOS GOLF CLUB

Herdade dos Salgados, Vale Rabelho

Tel 289 583 030

www.portugalgolf.pt

With 18 holes (par 72), this challenging lake-filled course is in a popular area of the Algarve between Albufeira and Armação da Pêra. In addition to the course there is a driving-range and a putting and chipping green.

Daily 8–4.30 18 holes €63.10; club rental €19.95; trolley rental €3.75; buggies €37.40 From the EN125, turn off at Vale da Parra exit. At the first traffic lights turn right

ZEBRA SAFARI

Apt. 836, Arcadas de São João, Areias de São João, Albufeira

Tel 289 583 300 or 965 040 225

www.zebrasafari.com

This outdoor pursuits company, with its convoy of distinctive zebra-patterned 4x4s, organizes guided day trips (9–5) to monuments, unspoilt hill-country and local craftsmen, such as basket-makers, beekeepers and cork

growers. It also provides a seemingly endless list of adventure activities.
Office: Mon–Sat 9–1, 3–7 1-day 4x4 tour €45 including lunch From Albufeira follow signs to Areias de São João. The office is on the main street next to the Caixa General de Depósitos bank

KRAZY WORLD
Lagoa de Viseu, Algôz
Tel 282 574 134
www.krazy-world.com
Started as a crazy-golf course, this park has expanded to include fairground rides and a mini-zoo. Its petting farm has llamas and pony rides; the lush Amazonia area houses Nile crocodiles, alligators and a 6m (20ft) Burmese python.
Jun–end Aug daily 10–7.30; Mar–end May and Sep daily 10–6; Oct–end Feb Wed–Sun 10–6 Adult €17, child €10, family €39.50 Head northwest from Albufeira towards Guia, then on to Algôz. Follow signs to Krazy World

THE BIG ONE
Alcantarilha
Tel 282 320 230
www.bigone-waterpark.com
One of several Algarve water parks, the Big One, just north of Albufeira, has attractions for everybody. There are wave pools and gentle rapids, twisting water slides or, for the totally intrepid, a 92m (300ft) kamikaze chute and a 23m (75ft) death drop.
May–end Oct daily 10–6 Adult €16, child €13 Just off the EN125 at Alcantarilha

ZOOMARINE
On the EN125 (km 65), Guia junction, Albufeira
Tel 289 560 300
www.zoomarine.com
At this oceanographic theme park the emphasis is on environmental conservation and education. A marine museum and cinema complement the large aquarium; daily attractions include the sea-lion and the dolphin show. There is also the chance to swim with bottlenose dolphins.
Easter–end Oct daily 10–6
Adult €17.90, child (5–10) €10.60; swimming with dolphins €125
Just off the EN125 between Guia and Alcantrilha

ALMANCIL

GRIFFIN BOOKSHOP
Rua 5 de Outubro 206-A, Almancil
Tel 289 393 904
This is probably the best place to find English-language books in the Algarve. In addition to a wide selection of fiction and non-fiction titles and plenty of children's books, it also sells second-hand books.
Mon–Fri 9.30–6, Sat 9.30–2

Say hello to a camel at the Krazy World petting zoo

CENTRO CULTURAL SÃO LOURENÇO
São Lourenço, Almancil
Tel 289 395 475
This cultural venue is near the 18th-century church of São Lorenzo, with its lovely blue-and-white tiled interior and has been converted from typical village houses. It hosts some great exhibitions and occasional concerts, and has metal animal sculptures in its garden.
Tue–Sat 10–7 Up to €30 according to exhibition or performance

ST. JAMES CLUB
Estação da Igreja, Almancil
Tel 289 393 300
In addition to its classy restaurant, St. James has a bar and disco. It attracts a slightly older crowd who enjoy its less frenetic pace and more intimate surroundings. Dress is smart.
Daily 10.30pm–4am Admission €5 (includes drinks) Take the N125 east out of Almancil towards Faro. The club is on the left

KARTING ALMANCIL
Sitio das Pereiras, Almancil
Tel 289 399 899
www.mundokarting.pt
This 760m (828-yard) track is a replica of a former Brazilian Formula 1 circuit and attracts more than 250,000 visitors a year. Set in a Western-style theme park, it has a saloon café, bar and restaurant. A children's circuit caters for younger visitors.
Jul to mid-Aug 10–midnight; mid-Aug to end Jun Tue–Fri 10–7, Sat–Sun 10–8 €14 Take Almancil turning off the EN125. Karting Almancil is on the right

FARO

O ATELIER
Rua Brites de Almeida 32, Faro
Tel 289 821 777
This Aladdin's cave of a shop, by the Largo do Pé da Cruz, has three rooms crammed with religious statuary, furniture, paintings and, perhaps more convenient for visitors, books, silverware, faïence ceramics, plates, postcards and some impressive antique watches.
Mon–Fri 10–1, 3–7

FORUM ALGARVE
On the EN125, Pontes de Marfil
Tel 289 889 300
This shopping mall on the outskirts of town has more than 120 shops, including well-known international chains. Although not particularly Portuguese, it makes a good wet-weather option, as its shopping, cinemas, restaurants, snack bars and parking are all housed under one roof.

Mon–Fri 10am–11pm, Sat–Sun 10am–midnight Minibus No. 1 runs Mon–Fri 8–8 every 15 min from several central pick-up points The mall is at km 103 of the N125 on the western side of town

TEATRO LETHES

Rua de Portugal 58, Faro
Tel 289 820 300

Once the site of a Jesuit church, this lovely Italianate theatre, with its frescoed ceilings and four-floor balconies, opened in 1845 and hosts theatrical performances, dance and classical music recitals. For information on current shows, contact the ticket office or the tourist office.

Ticket office: Mon–Fri 9–12.30, 2–5.30, Sat–Sun and show days 8–30 min after start of performance €10–€30 In auditorium

MEGASPORT

Rua Ataíde de Oliveira 39c, Faro
Tel 289 802 136
www.megasport.pt

For every type of bicycle rental, Megasport, a couple of blocks off Avenida 5 de Outubro, is the place to go. Their range of bicycles includes mountain, ladies', racing, downhill and bicycles of all sizes for children. They also have guides who will take you on escorted tours.

Mon–Fri 10–1, 3–7.30, Sat 10–1 1-day hire adult bicycle €9–€30 depending on type, child bicycle €9; guided tours €25 per hour; helmet €2; child seat €3

LAGOA

OLARIAS DE PORCHES

On the EN125, Porches

The village of Porches, to the east of Lagoa, is one of the few places in the region that sells genuine Algarve pottery, as opposed to imported Alentejo wares. It is best known for its good-quality, blue-and-green Mallorcan-style ceramics, which are usually decorated with naïve hand-painted motifs of sweeping leaves, fruits, birds and flowers. You can visit and choose what you want in any of the many shops that line the main road.

VALE DA PINTA GOLF

Carvoeiro Golf, Carvoeiro
Tel 282 340 900
www.pestana.com

Designed by Ronald Fream, this 18-hole, par-71 course is set amid a 1,500-year-old olive grove. Hilly and with plenty of bunkers, it is considered by some golfers to be one of the best courses in the country.

Daily 7.30–5.30 18 holes €90; club rental €22.50; hand trolley €5; buggy €40 From the EN125 follow signs to Carvoeiro at the Lagoa roundabout. The course is signed from there

Slide & Splash provides exactly that—sliding and splashing

SLIDE & SPLASH

On the EN125, Vale de Deus, Estombar
Tel 282 340 800

This is Portugal's largest water park, with around 6.5ha (16 acres) of children's pools, waves, rapids, twisting shoots and, for the more adventurous, the thrilling Kamikaze or the dark drop of the Black Hole. For the less crazy, there are great lawns for sunbathing.

Easter–end Oct daily 10–7 Adult €15.50, child €12.50 Go west from Lagoa on the EN125 towards Portimão. At a roundabout turn off to Estombar; after 0.5km (0.25 mile) Slide & Splash is signed to the left

LAGOS

CASA DO PAPAGAIO

Rua 25 de Abril 27, Lagos
Tel 282 789 666

Thanks to its live parrots standing guard at the door on the pedestrianized Rua 25 de Abril, this shop is easily recognized. Among the extensive collection of bric-à-brac, it is possible to find some genuine antiques, including old coins, religious statuary, African crafts and period furniture.

Mon–Fri 10–1, 3–7, Sat 10–1

MARKET

Rua das Portas de Portugal

Lagos's covered market has a good selection of fruit and vegetables, as well as fresh bread and some unusual cheeses. On the first Saturday of every month, there is an open-air gypsy market selling mainly shoes, clothes and textiles.

Mon–Sat 8–1

SIROCCO

Rua Cândido dos Reis 37, Lagos
Tel 282 762 306

This store offers something a little different, with a great choice of crafts reminiscent of North Africa. Moroccan stained-leather lamps, bright slippers and decorative mirrors are just a few of the items on sale.

Jun–end Sep daily 10–9; Oct–end May Mon–Sat 10–7

CENTRO CULTURAL DE LAGOS

Rua Lançarote de Freitas 7, Lagos
Tel 282 770 450

A cultural venue hosting art and photographic exhibitions in addition to regular music recitals and theatre performances. The snack bar also serves a great-value *prato do dia* (dish of the day) at lunchtime.

Jul–end Sep daily 1pm–midnight; Oct–end Jun daily 10–8 €2.50–€30 according to exhibition and performance In exhibition halls

WHAT TO DO

ADEGA DO PAPAGAIO
Rua da Adega 11, Espiche
Tel 282 789 423
If you want to listen to some good *fado*, visit this converted wine cellar to the west of Lagos on a Thursday or Saturday night. It is possible to come just for a drink, but the excellent cuts of meat grilled on hot rocks are also good.
Daily 7pm–midnight €25–€48 for 2 people Leave Lagos to the west on the N125. Turn off at Espiche and follow signs to the Adega

BOM DIA
Marina de Lagos, shop 10, Lagos
Tel 282 764 670 or 917 810 761
www.bomdia.info
This company organizes excursions along the Algarve coast in traditional Portuguese sailing ships. The multilingual crews sail the schooners down to Sagres for lunch, or offer shorter trips to explore the grottoes at Ponta da Piedade.
Jul–end Sep daily 9–8; Oct, Nov and Feb–end Jun daily 9.30–6 5-hour grotto and barbecue trip adult €37, child €18.50; full-day sail to Sagres adult €62, child €37 including lunch; 2-hour grotto trips adult €17, child €8.50 including wine Follow signs to the marina

DOLPHIN SEAFARIS
Marina de Lagos, Lagos
Tel 282 799 209 or 919 359 359
Based at the Lagos marina, this company organizes dolphin-watching excursions. Trips involve an exhilarating 90-minute RIB (rigid inflatable boat) ride; there is, they say, an 85 per cent chance of actually spotting some dolphins.
Apr–end Oct daily 9–6 €30
The office is well signposted within the Centro Comercial da Marinha at Lagos marina

MOTORENT
Rua Victor Coata e Silva, Ed. Vasco da Gama, Loja 8b, Lagos
Tel 282 769 716 or 282 416 998
One of the best ways to explore the narrow streets of Lagos' old town is by bicycle. Alternatively, head off to the hills behind the town on a motorcycle. Both engine- and leg-powered versions can be rented here.
24 hours Bicycle rental Apr–end Sep €13 per day, Oct–end Mar €10 per day (plus €50 deposit); helmet €2; child seat €2.50; motorcycle rental: €40–€60 depending on type of bicycle; quad bikes €50

TIFFANY'S
Vale Grifo, Almádena, Luz
Tel 282 697 395
www.valegrifo.com
Instead of kitting you out with diamonds, this Tiffany's organizes complete riding holidays and a variety of day rides.
Apr–end Sep daily 9–1, 3–7; Oct–end Mar daily 9–1, 3–5 1-hour country jaunt €25; Breakfast at Tiffany's (a 1.5-hour ride followed by breakfast) €38; 5-hour adventure ride €95
Head west out of Lagos on the EN125 towards Sagres. After passing through Espiche, watch for signs on the right to Tiffany's before Almadena

Get a different perspective on the Algarve from a traditional sailing ship

VIAGENS PORTITOURES
Alto do Quintão, Edifício Portimar, Portimão
Tel 282 470 063
If you'd like a day's guided bicycle ride in the Serra de Monchique, this travel agency will collect and transport you and your bicycle to the top and then escort you down to the village of Arão.
Mon–Fri 9–6, Sat–Sun and national holidays 4–6 €37–€40 depending on pick-up point Leaving Portimão on the new Avenida V6 towards Praia da Rocha and Lagos, the Portimar building is on the right

PARQUE ZOOLÓGICO DE LAGOS
Quinta Figueiras, Sítio do Medronhal, Barão de S. João, Lagos
Tel 282 680 100
www.zoolagos.com
This small zoo is home to about 120 animals, but the emphasis is on birds, which can be observed in a 60m (65-yard) walk-through aviary. There is a good farm for children, too.
Apr–end Sep 10–7; Oct–end Mar 10–5 Adult €8, child (3–13) €5, family of 4 €21 Take the EN120 northwest out of Lagos to Bensafrim. In Bensafrim turn left at the signs

LOULÉ

CENTRO DE ARTESANATO
Rua da Barbaça 11–13, Loulé
Tel 289 412 190
This street behind the castle is full of craftsmen, producing quality lace, leather goods, pottery, cane furniture, and brass- and copperware. The centre has a good collection of all of these, as well as fine displays of model wooden caravels.
Daily 8–1, 3–7

MARKETS
Tel 289 463 900 (tourist office)
Loulé's daily market (Mon–Fri 8–1) at the Praça da República sells tasty cheeses, olives, cured meats, produce and traditional crafts. The weekly market, held on a Saturday morning on the western side of the town, has clothes, shoes and inexpensive souvenirs.

AQUASHOW
On the EN125, Sitio Semino, Quarteira
Tel 289 389 396
www.aquashowpark.com
This water park also has a garden area with aviaries full of exotic birds.
Aquashow: May–end Oct daily 10–6. Aviary gardens: Nov–end Apr

daily 10–5 Aquashow: adult €18, child €14. Aviary gardens: adult €10.50, child €6.50 Take Quarteira turning off the EN125. Aquashow is signed 1.5km (1 mile) down this road

ATLANTIC PARK

On the EN125, Quatro Estradas
Tel 800 204 767 or 289 397 282

A water park with chutes, wave machines and twisting slides.

Mid-Mar to mid-Sep daily 10–6 Adult €12, child €10 Turn off the EN125 at Ferrieras/Quatro Estradas. At the traffic lights in Ferreiras follow signs to Albufeira. Atlantic Park is 1km (0.75 mile) from the junction on the right

MONCHIQUE

MONCHIQUE MARKET

Tel 282 911 189 (tourist office)

Monchique's monthly market is a good place to buy local crafts such as wooden items, cork and basketware. Particularly attractive are the naive hand-painted children's chairs and folding X-shaped scissor-stools, a design thought by some to be of Roman origin.

2nd Fri of the month

ALTERNATIV TOUR

Sitio das Relvinhas, Monchique
Tel 282 913 204 or 965 004 337

The wooded hills of Monchique are great for hiking and bicycling. If you prefer to take a guide, contact Alternativ, whose staff are experts on the wildlife, plantlife, geology and traditions of the region. They also provide information on independent routes and will arrange canoeing trips. Phone lines for booking are open daily all year round. There is no central office; staff arrange appropriate meeting places individually with you.

Guided walking tours €30 including picnic lunch; bicycle tours €37 including lunch; independent bicycle tours with maps provided €15; canoeing €30

TERMAS DE MONCHIQUE

Caldas de Monchique, Serra de Monchique
Tel 282 910 910
www.monchiquetermas.pt

Since Roman times, these hot springs have been used to help treat ailments. You can taste the waters free of charge; there is also a therapeutic spa clinic, which treats skin, digestive and rheumatic complaints. For something stronger, try a *medronho*, the local brandy, at one of the bars outside.

Mon 9–1, Tue 10.30–1, 3–7, Wed–Sun 9–1, 3–7 €23 minimum includes sauna, Turkish bath and hydromassage

OLHÃO

MARKET

Avenida 5 de Outubro, Olhão

The town is not geared to tourism, but its market gives a rare insight into day-to-day Algarve life. It is the biggest covered market in the region, with two enormous Moorish-style halls. One sells fresh fruit and vegetables and the other fish and meat.

Mon–Sat 8–1

Handpainted ceramics on sale at Monchique's market

PARQUE NATURAL DA RIA FORMOSA

Centro de Educação Ambiental de Marim, Quelfes
Tel 289 704 134

This unspoilt natural park is home to many wetland birds, including rare nesting gallinules. It consists of 80km (50 miles) of lagoons, marshes, beaches and dunes, and is a great area for hiking. For maps and information on waymarked paths, contact the park office on the above number.

Daily 9–5.30 Take EN125 east out of Olhão. Turn right at Cepsa fuel station. The office is 1km (0.75 mile) down the road towards the sea

PORTIMÂO

O AQUÁRIO

Rua Vasco de Gama 42–46, and Praça da República 42–46, Portimão
Tel 282 42 66 73

These central shops have a great selection of copper, brass and ceramics. They stock the highly regarded Atlantis full-lead crystal from Alcobaça, north of Lisbon (▷ 204), and the classically designed Vista Alegre porcelain.

Mon–Fri 9.30–1, 3–7, Sat 9.30–1

HOTEL ALGARVE CASINO

Praia da Rocha, Portimão
Tel 282 402 000

Nightlife is Praia da Rocha's forte, with a good supply of heaving bars and clubs. For something a little calmer (but no less expensive), it may be worth trying the casino. In addition to more than 300 slot machines and 10 gaming tables, it offers nightly floor shows and musical entertainment in sedate surroundings.

Daily 4pm–3am Floor show €10 (includes drinks); entry to gaming tables €4 The casino is on the seafront at the same end as the fort

DOLPHIN SEAFARIS

Marina de Portimão, Portimão
Tel 282 799 209 or 919 359 359

This company, which also operates from the marina in Lagos (▷ 225), organizes dolphin-watching excursions from the Portimão marina.

Mar–end Oct daily 9–6 €30 The office is next to Pizza Hut within the Centro Comercial da Marinha at Portimão marina

PRAINHA CLUB

Alvor, Prainha, Portimão
Tel 282 480 000
www.prainha.net

This Thalgo thalassotherapy clinic offers a range of sea-water treatments and health, beauty and relaxation therapies. Enjoy a relaxing seaweed poultice before being pummelled and then invigorated in a Scottish shower, or take it easy in the Turkish baths, Jacuzzis or hydromassage tubs.
Mon–Sat 9–9 €15–€85 according to treatment Leave Portimão in the direction of Alvor. Follow Prainha signs. The club is next to Hotel Prainha

QUINTA DO LAGO

GOLF QUINTA DO LAGO

Quinta do Lago, Almancil
Tel 289 390 700
www.portugalgolf.pt

Quinta do Lago has four immaculately maintained nine-hole golf courses dotted with umbrella pines looking out over the Ria Formosa Natural Park. Watch out for the lake at the sixth on 'C' course, which collects some 1,000 balls a week.
Daily 7–7 18 holes €150; club rental €40; trolley €7; buggy €55 From the EN125, take the Vale do Lobo turn at Almancil. Turn left at the sign for the course

SILVES

FÁBRICA DO INGLÊS

Rua Gregório Mascarenhas, Silves
Tel 282 44 04 40
www.fabrica-do-ingles.com

With a fine view of Silves castle, this converted cork factory now houses an informative cork museum and various restaurants. During the summer, it hosts outdoor concerts and performances in addition to the yearly *Festival da Cerveja* (Beer Festival) in late June.
Jul–end Sep daily 9am–midnight; Oct–end Jun Tue–Sun. Closed 1st 2 weeks Jan Jul, Aug €17–€27; Sep–end Jun free entry From Silves follow signs to São Bartolomeu de Messines. Fábrica do Inglês is signed

TAVIRA

AQUATAXIS

Tel 964 515 073 or 93 95 93 475

In order to get to the unspoilt beaches of the Parque Natural da Ria Formosa around Tavira you have to take a boat across the lagoons to the sand spits. Aquataxis has various pick-up points for rides to Tavira.
Jul, Aug daily 24 hours; Sep–end Jun daily 8–6 From Tavira fishing dock to Ilha de Tavira €15; from Quatro Águas quayside (1km/0.75 mile west of Tavira) to Ilha de Tavira €4; from Cabanas quayside (5km/3 miles east of Tavira) to Ilha de Tavira €15

RENT-A-BIKE

Rua do Forno 33, Tavira
Tel 281 321 973

For bicycling and hiking trips to the Ria Formosa Natural Park or around Tavira, Rent-a-Bike is the place. It offers four-hour guided bicycling trips and one- or two-day hikes with English-speaking guides.
Daily 9–9 Bicycle trip €25 per person; hikes €6–€10 Just off the bottom end of Rua Infante Dom Henrique.

Barringtons Golf and Health Spa offers both action or relaxation

VALE DO LOBO

BARRINGTONS GOLF AND HEALTH SPA

Vale do Lobo
Tel 289 351 940
www.barringtons-pt.com

For a daily membership fee, Barringtons, in sophisticated Vale do Lobo, offers an endless list of sports facilities, such as golf, squash, aerobics, swimming and a gymnasium, as well as a walk-in spa and beauty treatments that include massage and a sauna.
Daily 7.30am–10.30pm Daily adult membership €47; weekly adult membership €168 Take Almancil turning off the EN125. At the traffic lights in Almancil, turn left and take the right fork towards Vale do Lobo. At the end turn right then left into Vale do Lobo entrance. Go straight over the first two roundabouts, turning left at the third. Barringtons is on the left

VALE DO LOBO RIDING CENTRE

Avenida Ayrton Senna da Silva, Vale do Lobo
Tel 289 396 099

In addition to renting out horses by the hour for riding within the school, the centre offers escorted hacks through the surrounding countryside. At full moon you can go on a two-hour night ride around the lagoons and pine forests. Children are particularly well looked after, with half-hour escorted pony rides and half-day practical activity courses.
Apr–end Sep 7–12, 4–9; Oct–end Mar 8–12, 2–6 Adult €30 per hour, €50 for 2-hour group trek and full-moon ride; child €15 for half-hour ride, €25 for half-day activities, €55 for 2-hour beach ride Head out of town towards the N125. At the 2nd roundabout turn right then look for signs

VILA DO BISPO

SURF PLANET

EN268, nº268, Vila do Bispo
Tel 282 624 815
www.surfplanet-pt.com

This shop is close to the Costa Vicentina and has everything a surfing fanatic might need: surf-, body- and skimboards, fins, wetsuits and even surf-themed accessories and street wear. It also organizes surf lessons at nearby beaches.
Mon–Sat 9–8

VILAMOURA

CASINO DE VILAMOURA

Praça do Casino, Vilamoura
Tel 289 310 000
www.solverde.pt

Vilamoura's casino offers 350 slot machines and 14 gaming tables, including American and French roulette and blackjack. In addition to bars and a restaurant, there are floor shows and a disco.
Daily 4pm–3am Entrance to gaming tables €4 On the east side of the Vilamoura marina, between the Hotel Atlantis and Hotel Marina

JAZZ CLUB
Praça do Cinema, Edificio Pirâmides, Vilamoura
Tel 289 316 272 or 918 779 213
www.vilamoura-jazz-club.com
This welcoming bar near the Vilamoura cinema hosts live jazz four nights a week. The club's resident band plays on Monday and Thursday; guest performers appear on Friday and Saturday.
Mon–Sat 8pm–2am €5 entrance on live music nights

MILLENNIUM GOLF COURSE
Vilamoura
Tel 289 310 330
www.portugalgolf.pt
Millennium is made up of the nine holes of the old Laguna course plus nine new holes (par 72). The course was given a full overhaul in 1999, which involved laying new topsoil, planting more trees and improving drainage. There's a driving range, putting green, club house and restaurant.
Daily 7.30am–8pm 18 holes €90; club rental €27.50; trolley €5; buggy €45 From the EN125 take the Vilamoura turn. Take the first right and right again, and watch for signs to the club on the left

THE OLD COURSE
Vilamoura
Tel 289 310 333
www.portugalgolf.pt
Listed among Europe's top 100 courses, the Old Course, with its English school design, winds its way gently through umbrella-pine woods. The par-3, fourth hole, played over a small lake, and the back par-5 16th are considered to be the course's highlights.
Daily 8–7.30 18 holes €120; club rental €27.50; trolley €5; buggy €45 From the EN125 take the Vilamoura exit. Turn right and continue to the sign for the course on the left

FESTIVALS AND EVENTS

EASTER

CARNAVAL DE LOULÉ
Late February–early March, Loulé
Tel 289 463 900 (tourist office)
Loulé comes to life at *Carnaval* time, putting on the most impressive show in the Algarve. Costumed parades, samba dancers, live music, dancing, fireworks and themed tractor-drawn floats entertain the crowds.

FESTA DA MÃE SOBERANA
Easter and 2nd Sunday after Easter, Loulé
Tel 289 463 900 (tourist office)
This is the Algarve's biggest religious festival. The highly revered 16th-century image of Our Lady of Pity is carried in a procession along crowd-lined streets from her chapel to the parish church on Easter Sunday. The following week she is carried in a procession back to the chapel.

MAY–JUNE

FESTIVAL INTERNACIONAL DE MÚSICA
May–June, Região do Turismo do Algarve, Avenida 5 de Outubro 18, Faro
Tel 289 800 400
Running through May and June, this international music festival (partly sponsored by the Gulbenkian Foundation) attracts top classical performers, who play at a variety of venues. Contact the local tourist offices for details.
Tickets from regional tourist information office Mon–Fri 9–12.30, 2–5, or from concert venues €10, church concerts free

JUNE

FESTA DA CIDADE
24–25 June, Tavira
Tel 281 322 511 (tourist office)
Tavira's biggest yearly celebration is held in June, when the town's streets are lavishly decorated with paper flowers and myrtle leaves. Sardines are grilled and served free in the streets.

JULY

CONCENTRAÇÃO INTERNACIONAL DE MOTOS DO ALGARVE
Three days in July, Moto Clube de Faro, Sítio Vale da Amoreira 328A, Faro
Tel 289 823 845
www.motoclubfaro.pt
Taking place over three days in July, this rally attracts more than 30,000 bikers, who rev their mean machines up and down the Faro seafront. In addition to copious beer, the *motards*, as these enthusiasts are known, also come to the rally for rock concerts, to buy kit from bike-accessory stands, to get tattooed by tattoo artists and to attend live shows.

AUGUST

FESTIVAL DO MARISCO
Second week in August, Jardim Pescador Olhanense, Olhão
Tel 289 713 936 (tourist office)
This seafood festival attracts almost 100,000 people to its stands, which sell lobsters, prawns and all kind of shellfish. The eating is enhanced by live stage shows featuring a mixture of popular national and international bands.

This chapter describes 8 driving tours and 11 walks that explore the best of Portugal's beautiful countryside, its historic cities, its mountains, hills, forests and valleys and its spectacular Atlantic coastline. The location of each walk and drive is marked on the map on page 230, where you will also find the key to individual maps.

Out and About

WALK AND TOUR LOCATIONS

1. Drive
Through the Douro Valley (▷ 231–233)

2. Walk
Exploring Porto (▷ 234–235)

3. Drive
Through the Serra da Estrela (▷ 236–238)

4. Walk
A Circular Walk from Manteigas (▷ 239)

5. Drive
From Figueira da Foz to Mealhada (▷ 240–241)

6. Walk
In the National Forest of Buçaco (▷ 242–243)

7. Drive
A Coastal Drive from Alcobaça to Fátima (▷ 244–245)

8. Walk
Lisbon: The Chiado and Bairro Alto (▷ 246–247)

9. Walk
Through Lisbon's Alfama District (▷ 248–249)

10. Walk
Exploring the Parque da Pena (▷ 250–251)

11. Drive
The Lower Alentejo (▷ 252–253)

12. Drive
Into the High Algarve from Portimão (▷ 254–255)

13. Walk
In the Serra de Monchique Foothills (▷ 256)

14. Walk
Exploring the High Algarve (▷ 257)

15. Drive
Exploring the Barrocal Hills (▷ 258–259)

16. Walk
A Walk in the Barrocal Hills (▷ 260–261)

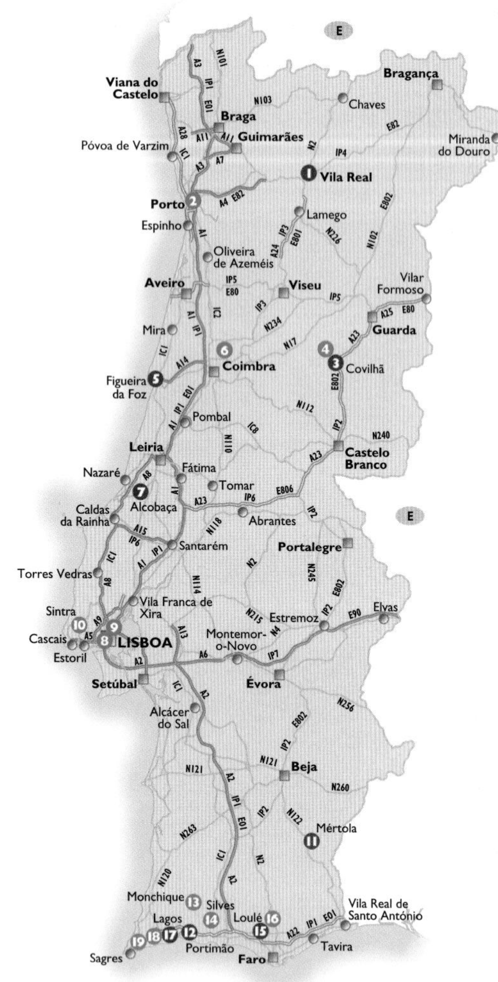

KEY TO THIS MAP

Drive
Walk
City
Town

17. Drive
A Trip Round the Western Algarve (▷ 262–263)

18. Walk
The Cliffs of Lagos and Praia da Luz (▷ 264–265)

19. Walk
A Coastal Walk in the Western Algarve (▷ 266–267)

KEY TO ROUTE MAPS IN THIS CHAPTER

Start point
Route
Alternative route
Route direction
Walk start point on drive
Featured sight along route
Place of interest in Sights section
Other place of interest
Viewpoint
621 Height in metres

1. DRIVE

THROUGH THE DOURO VALLEY

This spectacular drive takes you through the best parts of the port-producing valley of the river Douro, where steep hillsides are clothed from top to bottom with terraced vineyards. You will have the chance to visit a wine lodge, taste and buy port, and enjoy the beauty of the famous Solar de Mateus and its glorious gardens.

THE DRIVE

Distance: 130km (80 miles)
Allow: 4–5 hours
Start/end at: Vila Real

From Vila Real (▷ 83) take the IP4 towards Porto and Amarante. Follow this road for 24km (15 miles). At the sign for '*pousada*', leave the main road and cross the river to reach the Pousada de São Gonçalo.

❶ The Pousada de São Gonçalo is a modern hotel, built as a base for visitors exploring the Serra de Marão mountains.

After leaving the *pousada*, turn left onto the N15, a minor road, and drive down through the pine forests of the Ovelha valley for 12km (7 miles) to Candemil.

❷ Candemil is in the heart of the Serra de Marão, a granite and shale mountain range whose highest point is the Pico de Marão (1,415m/4,642ft). You should be able to pick this out from the road between São Gonçalo and Candemil. It's an extraordinary landscape, with the road descending through an enclosed gorge above the Ovelha, a river that is noted for its trout fishing.

Just after Candemil, turn left in a tiny hamlet onto a steeply climbing road signposted for Bustelo. This descends to join the N101, where you turn left. At this point you have effectively crossed the Serra de Marão, but the N101 now recrosses it, traversing a plateau with superb views of the mountains before dropping down through vineyards to the small town of Mesão Frio on the river Teixera.

❸ At Mesão Frio, cross the river, drive through town and you'll get your first view of the vine terraces and the sweep of the river Douro far below. You're now right in the heart of the port country, where the steep valley sides have been painstakingly terraced into one of Europe's most fertile grape-growing areas. Carefully tended, the terraces themselves are a work of art; in the words of a local saying, 'God created Earth, but man created the Douro.'

At the intersection above the river turn left onto the N108 along the north bank of the Douro. Follow this road for 12km (7 miles) to Peso da Régua. Before the intersection, watch out for the Solar de Rede *pousada*, a fine old 18th-century manor house surrounded by 27ha (66 acres) of vineyards. It is a nice place to stop for a meal or to spend the night. You'll also drive through the spa town of Caldas de Moledo, before reaching Peso da Régua.

❹ Peso da Régua, a thriving provincial town, was once dubbed the 'Capital of the Upper Douro', when it was the up-river focus of the port trade. All port still passes through here on its way downriver, but Régua's role as the trade's hub has been taken over by Pinhão to the east. There are still ornamental *barcos rabelos*, the traditional port cargo boats, moored on the river; you can visit the Quinta de São Domingos, where you can tour the lodge and sample port.

Cross the river Douro on the lower of the two bridges, keeping right to swing back under the bridge and emerge next to the river onto the N222. Follow this road for 25km (15 miles) to Pinhão.

❺ Pinhão is the main focus for quality port production, and several of the leading

The gardens of Solar de Mateus are probably Portugal's finest

houses have *quintas* (wine lodges) here. The section of the drive leading to the town is particularly attractive, running alongside the river with views of the terraced vineyards, olive groves and a steady procession of lodges, each with the name of the producer who owns it emblazoned on the hillside.

At Pinhão cross the Douro and return to the north bank. Leave Pinhão and take the N323 north, signposted for Sabrosa and Vila Real. At Sabrosa ❻, the birthplace of the explorer Ferdinand Magellan, turn left onto the N322 following the sign for Vila Real.

Above: A wine lodge near Pinhão. Left: The Dão valley is the second most productive wine area in Portugal. Most Dão wine is red

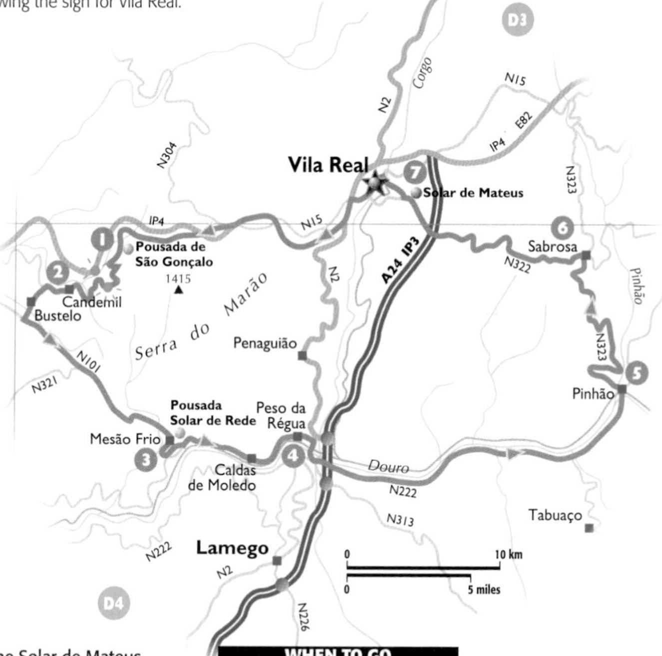

❼ The Solar de Mateus (▷ 82) is the highlight of this part of the tour. It is a magnificent country manor house whose outside is familiar from the labels on millions of bottles of Mateus Rosé wine.

Past here, turn right and follow the signs back to Vila Real.

WHERE TO EAT

Try the Pousada do São Gonçalo (open daily for lunch noon–2.30pm), just over halfway between Amarante and Vila Real, or the Pousada Solar da Rede (also open daily noon–2.30pm) in Peso da Régua. Both serve tasty regional food.

WHEN TO GO

The best times for this drive are late summer and autumn.

PLACES TO VISIT

Solar de Mateus (▷ 82)

Quinta de São Domingos
Aptdo. 130, 5050 Pasoragua
☎ 254 320 100 🕐 Mon–Fri 9–12.30, 2–5 ✋ Free

Quinta do Panascal
Valanca do Douro, 5120 Tabuaco
☎ 254 732 321 🕐 Mon–Fri 10–7.30
✋ Free
A short detour up the Távora valley will take you to this port vineyard; audio-tours and vineyard walks are available.

A roadside grape seller at Régua, with his offerings of fresh black, red and green grapes

2. WALK

EXPLORING PORTO

This walk through the heart of Porto gives you a taste of the highly individual character of Portugal's vibrant second city and its wonderful old quarter. There is also the bonus of stopping off in some tempting cafés and bars for a breather along the way.

THE WALK

Distance: 2.6km (1.6 miles)
Allow: 2 hours
Start/end at: Praça da Liberdade

Start at the southern end of Praça da Liberdade. Cross the road and head left to get to Porto's mainline station, Estação de São Bento.

❶ Estação de São Bento's booking hall is worth taking a look at for its fantastic *azulejos* (tiles). There are more than 20,000—all of them painted between 1905 and 1930 by artist Jorge Colaço and depicting historical landscapes and northern rural traditions.

With the station on your left, walk along Avenida Dom Afonso Henriques, crossing the road to turn down Rua Dom Hugo, along which you will find the Historia do Porto exhibition and the Casa-Museu Guerra Junqueiro. Continue until you reach Porto's cathedral, the Sé (▷ 86–87).

❷ The Casa-Museu Guerra Junqueiro is a stunning collection of Islamic art assembled by the poet Abílio de Guerra Junqueiro (1850–1923).

Walk behind the Archbishop's Palace and plunge down to follow the steps and alleys through the atmospheric and medieval Barredo Bairro to the Cais da Ribeira on the waterfront—as long as you keep heading downhill the exact route doesn't matter. This is the waterfront's main street, the home to a weekday market. Turn right and walk alongside the river to Praça da Ribeira (▷ 87). From here head right and uphill along Rua dos Mercadores, and take the first left down Rua Infante Dom Henrique.

Above: The wonderful azulejos *in Estaçaõ São Bento's booking hall. Below: Running down to the waterfront is the Ribeira, Porto's oldest district*

❸ No. 47–53 Rua Infante Dom Henrique is a striking medieval house donated by João I to the city merchants, eventually to become Porto's first stock exchange. Look out, too, for the 18th-century English 'factory', designed by the British consul John Whitehead as a meeting place for English traders and port shippers. In the same street you'll also find the Igreja de São Francisco (▷ 88) and the Bolsa (▷ 88).

Next to the church, turn down Rua Ferreira Borges. Then go diagonally right across Largo São Domingos onto Rua das Flores.

❹ The Igreja da Misericórdia is on your left, a 16th-century church with a 17th-century façade designed by Nasoni. Next door is the Santa Casa da Misericórdia, which houses the *Fons Vitae*, one of Porto's most celebrated paintings.

Past the church take the second left up Rua Trindade Coelho,

dos Clérigos and its tower (▷ 88). Return to Praça da Liberdade along Rua dos Clérigos.

WHERE TO EAT

The Adega Vila Meã in Rua dos Clérigos serves good no-frills regional food (▷ 276).

WHEN TO GO

Either in the morning or mid-afternoon when the streets are busy and full of life.

PLACES TO VISIT

Casa-Museu Guerra Junqueiro

Rua Dom Hugo 32 ☎ 222 001 155

🕐 Tue–Sat 10–12.30, 2–5.30, Sun 2–5.30

€1

TIP

- **Be prepared for hilly walking.**

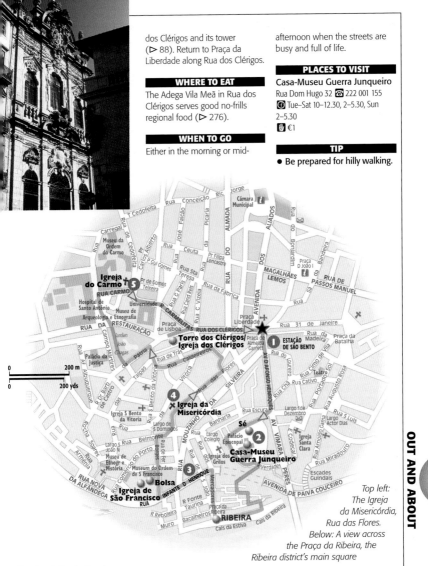

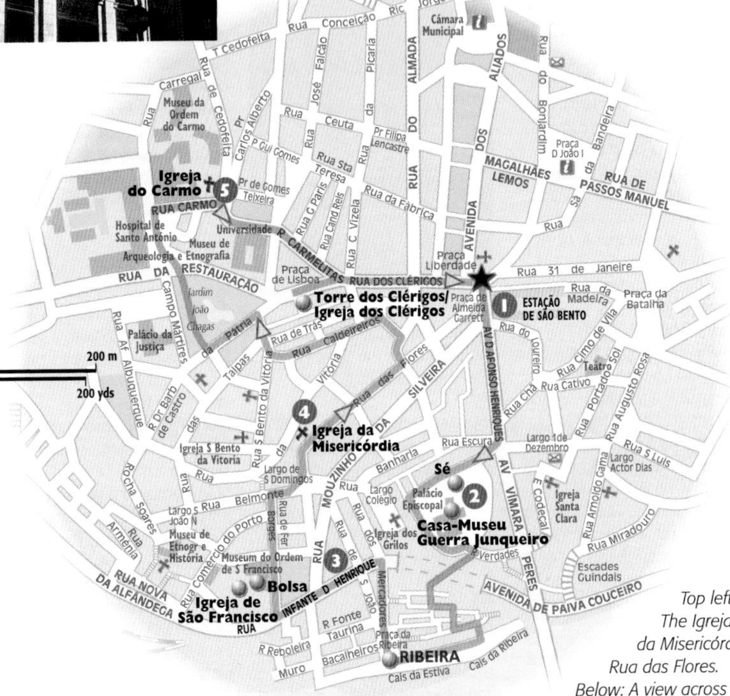

Top left: The Igreja da Misericórdia, Rua das Flores. Below: A view across the Praça da Ribeira, the Ribeira district's main square

then turn left onto Rua dos Caldereireiros and walk along to the Campo Mártires da Pátria. Walk through the garden then up to the Igreja do Carmo.

❺ The Carmo, built in the 18th century, is one of Porto's most exuberant churches, with a stunning façade dating from 1912, entirely covered with *azulejos* of the deepest blue. Next to the Carmo is the older Carmelitas church.

Leave the church and turn left past the Livraria Lello e Irmão, a famous bookshop with a superb interior (▷ 195), and head down Rua das Carmelitas to the Igreja

3. DRIVE

THROUGH THE SERRA DA ESTRELA

This is a high-altitude drive into the heart of the Serra da Estrela, Portugal's highest mainland mountain range. The route takes you up to Portugal's only ski area before following a dramatic glacial valley through the mountains and out into the fertile land below.

THE DRIVE

Distance: 38km (24 miles)
Allow: 1.5 hours without detours
Start at: Covilhã
End at: Belmonte

Covilhã, a textile town sprawled across the lower slopes of the *serra*, is popular all year with Portuguese visitors to the Parque Natural da Serra da Estrela (▷ 105). An old town, whose steep streets give glimpses of the plain below, it was the birthplace of the explorer Pêro de Covilhã, who reached India via the Cape of Good Hope in 1498.

Follow the brown signs marked '*Centro Historico*' and '*Serra da Estrela*' uphill through the town—keep your eyes open as the signs are few and far between. In the main square, Praça do Município, veer right to make a right turn (unsigned) along a busy shopping street and out of town. The street is steep and rapidly becomes steeper. Over the next 8km (5 miles) you'll gain a lot of altitude, so be prepared for a steep, twisting road, with plenty of hairpin bends and drops; although the road is relatively wide, it's not for the nervous.

The first 3km (2 miles) are lined with eucalyptus and acacia, but, once past the 1,200m (3,937ft) sign, which marks the start of the natural park, the trees thin out and you emerge onto a high, arid landscape, dotted with scrubby pines and littered with vast granite slabs and outcrops. Continue into Penhas de Saúde.

❶ Penhas da Saúde is a low-key mountain ski resort with a scattering of alpine-style chalets, hotels and cafés. This is where most of the accommodation is to be found for Portugal's only ski area. It is also a summer base for long-distance hiking in the *serra*.

The road climbs through the village and past a reservoir; ahead you'll see the peak of Torre, at

Above: Driving through the highest part of the Serra da Estrela as the sun sets

1,993m (6,537ft) the highest point in mainland Portugal. At the intersection, turn right onto the N338 but, in summer, it's worth taking a short detour to the left to take in Torre itself. The road pays avoidance in winter.

❷ Torre is named after the tower on its summit, added in the 19th century to bring the mountain's height up to a round figure. You can drive right to the top, passing a huge rock statue of Nossa Senhora de Boa Estrela, the focus of a huge pilgrimage each August.

If you have made the Torre detour, return to the intersection. The N338 descends from the heights into the Zêzere valley. Near the top is a series of stopping places where you can park and admire the wonderful views stretching down the valley.

❸ The Zêzere valley is a textbook example of a glacial geological feature. From the viewpoints along the road, you can see the spectacular valley encircled by dramatic mountains, with the road carved out of sheer walls of rock and scree. Tumbling streams run down the slopes.

Continue your descent. Once back below the treeline, you'll see stands of pine and beech, plus heather and broom.

❹ The lower reaches of the valley still have the remnants of the cultivated terraces that once provided a subsistence living for the locals. You'll also notice the last remaining traditional stone houses with their primitive thatched roofs.

The first settlement you'll come to is Caldas de Manteigas.

❺ Caldas de Manteigas, a lovely spa village with a gushing stream, merges into the small town of Manteigas. Set above the river Zêzere, Manteigas is home to the main office of the Parque Natural da Serra da Estrela, a good source of information if you're planning a stay. The town itself is a pleasant place to pause for a wander.

Take the N232 out of Manteigas towards Belmonte. From here, the road passes through a gentler valley, heavily forested with the river Zêzere at the bottom.

❻ The valley between Manteigas and Belmonte gives a great feeling of being deep in mountain territory, with the hills all round, the clear fast-flowing river, the little patches of cabbages, and tiny, isolated villages such as Sameiro.

As you lose altitude, the valley continues to open up, until you eventually cross the river and reach the fortress town of Belmonte (▷ 96).

Right: Looking down on the Zêzere valley, carved out of the mountain rock by glaciers many thousands of years ago

Above: A barn and other scattered buildings in the Zêzere valley, which is shaped just like a U

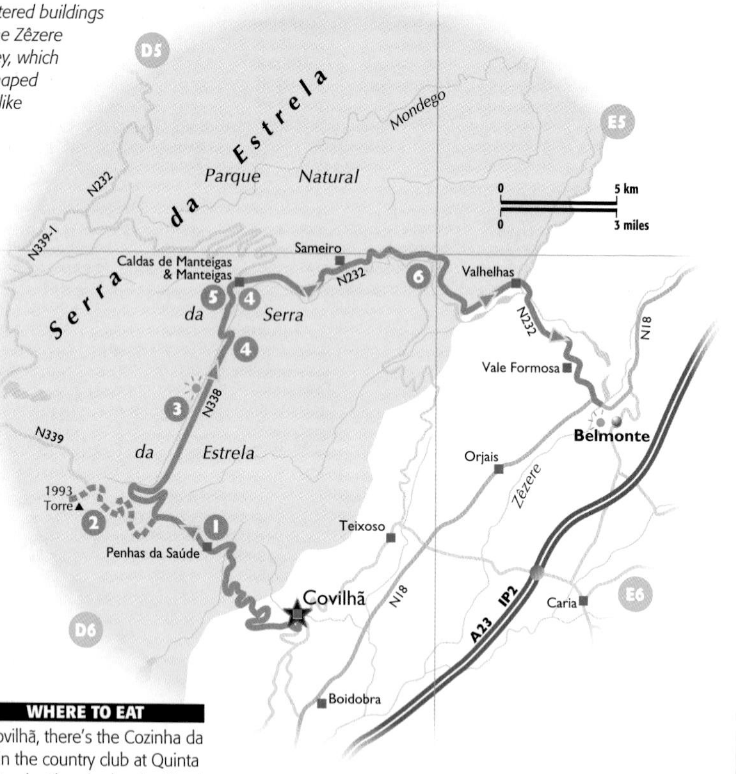

WHERE TO EAT

In Covilhã, there's the Cozinha da Avó in the country club at Quinta do Covelo. There's also the Hotel Serra da Estrela in Penhas de Saúde, the Pousada de São Lourenço at Caldas de Manteigas and, in Belmonte, the Pousada do Convento.

WHEN TO GO

The landscape is at its best in spring and autumn, while the cool mountain air is welcome in summer.

PLACES TO VISIT

Manteigas
Information Office, Parque Natural de Serra da Estrela
Rua 1º de Maio, 6260 Manteigas
☎ 275 980 060
Mon–Fri 9–12.30, 2–5.30

Castelo de Belmonte
6250 Belmonte ☎ 275 911 488
Tue–Sun 10–12.30, 2–5

TIP

- If you're intending to drive this tour in the winter or early spring, check the status of the roads. They may be closed due to snow blockage. Even if open, they may be treacherously slippery in icy or snowy conditions. Check at the tourist offices, or on the boards at the bottom of the access road.

A CIRCULAR WALK FROM MANTEIGAS

This straightforward walk from the village of Manteigas takes in a waterfall and swimming hole deep in the Parque Natural da Serra da Estrela.

The route is indicated by yellow markers like the one here

THE WALK

Distance: 10.7km (6.6 miles)
Allow: 3–4 hours without stops
Start/end at: Manteigas

Start in the middle of Manteigas, outside the park information office. Cross the road to the Galp service station and take the steep track on the right of the main road behind the tourist office. Follow this downhill, bearing right past the houses until you come to a bridge over the river Zêzere. Cross this and bear left past the factory at São Gabriel. Continue left, watching out for the yellow waymark arrows leading into the woods. Although not always easy to spot, these markers will take you all the way to the Poço do Inferno waterfall. The name is Portuguese for 'Hell's Gate.'

Poço do Inferno is a waterfall in an idyllic situation. It's a good place for a picnic and even a swim—but take care as the water is glacially cold. En route to the falls, you'll climb around 300m (1,000ft) as you walk through some fine woodland with pine, beech and birch. At the right times of year, particularly in spring, there are also some lovely wild flowers to spot.

At Poço de Inferno, you'll pick up the surfaced road that winds its way around the mountain above the river and into the valley of the Zêzere river.

As you come into more open country you'll see flocks of sheep; their milk is used to make the local cheese, *Queijo da serra*, which is famous all over Portugal. You might also catch sight of one of the celebrated Serra da Estrela dogs, a unique breed that was developed as guard dogs for the sheep of the area. The dogs can be long- or short-haired.

Follow the road down to join the N338. Turn right to descend to Caldas de Manteigas.

The cascading Poço do Inferno waterfall is the highlight of the walk

Caldas de Manteigas, a little spa town that spreads along the river valley, is now more or less part of Manteigas itself. It has two hot springs, both sulphurous, which are used to treat rheumatism and skin and lung diseases.

Follow the road downward into central Manteigas to regain your starting point.

WHERE TO EAT

Take a picnic, or, in Manteigas, try the Pousada de São Lourenço.

WHEN TO GO

Choose a clear, settled day any time between May and September. It's inadvisable to attempt the walk after snow, or in bad weather.

TIP

- Although this is a popular excursion, it is a mountain walk. This means being prepared, with stout footwear, suitable clothes (including waterproofs), and something to eat and drink.

5. DRIVE

FROM FIGUEIRA DA FOZ TO MEALHADA

A varied route that takes you from the typically Portuguese holiday resort of Figueira da Foz into the hills, with a great selection of places to visit along the way, including picturesque Montemor, historic Coimbra and the national forest of Buçaco.

THE DRIVE

Distance: 100km (62 miles)
Allow: 2–3 straight driving, 1–2 days if visiting everything
Start at: Figueira da Foz
End at: Mealhada
Overnight stop: Coimbra

The beach at Figueira da Foz, an ideal place for a pre-drive stroll

Take a stroll along the lovely beach at Buarcos ❶, on the northern outskirts of Figueira da Foz (▷ 102), before starting your drive at the central roundabout. Follow the brown signs for *outros direcções* (other directions) along the seafront until you see the lighthouse and the deep-water fishing port ahead. Follow the road round to the left, keeping the old castle on your right, and continue up-river.

On your right is the marina, the departure point for various boat trips. You'll notice the older part of Figueira to your left, set around the leafy greenery of the municipal gardens.

Follow the blue A1/A14 sign to Lisboa, Porto, Coimbra and Viseu past the port and under the cantilevered motorway bridge. At the roundabout turn left following the A14 Coimbra and Viseu signs, then fork right towards Coimbra and Viseu. Stay on this highway for 14km (8.6 miles) until you reach exit 4.

This stretch of the route runs through pine and eucalyptus woods above the Mondego estuary. The Mondego is one of Portugal's loveliest rivers, rising in the Serra da Estrela and running for much of its course through wooded country scattered with picturesque hamlets. The lower reaches are noted for waders and overwintering seabirds. Look out for herons and egrets feeding, and for storks' nests on chimneys and poles.

Take exit 4 to Montemor-o-Velho ❷ (▷ 104), which you'll see on a hill above the salt flats. Leaving Montemor, follow the signs to Soure round two roundabouts—the road crosses the river, and then the railway. Immediately after this, turn right, again following the signs to Soure. Drive up the hill and turn left at a T-junction signed 'Soure 14'. At the next roundabout follow the signs to Condeiso, crossing the railway again, then turn left onto the Granja ❸ road at the next roundabout.

You're now following the Mondego upstream along the south bank on a wonderfully rural road that crosses fertile alluvial agricultural land. The road undulates to give views left to the river and runs through a string of untouched farming villages. These give a real glimpse of traditional country life, where farms are little more than smallholdings growing a range of crops and supporting just a few animals. Farmers aim to be largely self-sufficient, growing food to feed their families and bartering or selling the surplus. From the

Figueira da Foz's lighthouse perches above the town walls

economic standpoint, it's inefficient, but it adds to the area's charm for visitors.

At the junction with the major road ❹, follow the signs on the wide, modern N341 towards Coimbra (▷ 98–101). If you're not visiting the city, skirt it on the ring road to pick up the IC2 and then the IP3.

Leave Coimbra on the IC2 and head north, turning off at exit 8 to join the IP3, a good road that runs over beautiful wooded hills. After 13km (8.6 miles) take the N235 left to Luso.

From here, you're climbing steadily up through gentle hill country on a shady road planted with eucalyptus on either side. The clearings are filled with olives, and you'll spot the terraces—once heavily cultivated and still used for grazing and food crops—that the locals created to make best use of the pockets of fertile soil. Tiny settlements, dripping with geraniums and ringed by orange groves, lie along the road—a landscape that's characteristically rural Portuguese.

The Palace Hotel do Buçaco was once a royal hunting lodge

Look out for the start of a high stone wall to your right; this rings the Mata Nacional (National Forest) of Buçaco ❺ (▷ 96).

Enter the forest through the main gate and drive up to the hotel, where you can park to stretch your legs or go for a walk in the woods (▷ 243). It is well worth allowing time for the latter, since the forest is one of Portugal's most important natural treasures.

After leaving Buçaco, drive downhill to the spa town of Luso ❻ (▷ 102), then take the N234 west to Mealhada ❼, a pretty drive that drops through the woods. Mealhada is famous for its *leitão*, which is considered to be the most delicious roast suckling pig in Portugal. The town is just five minutes from the A1, for the drive back to Figueira.

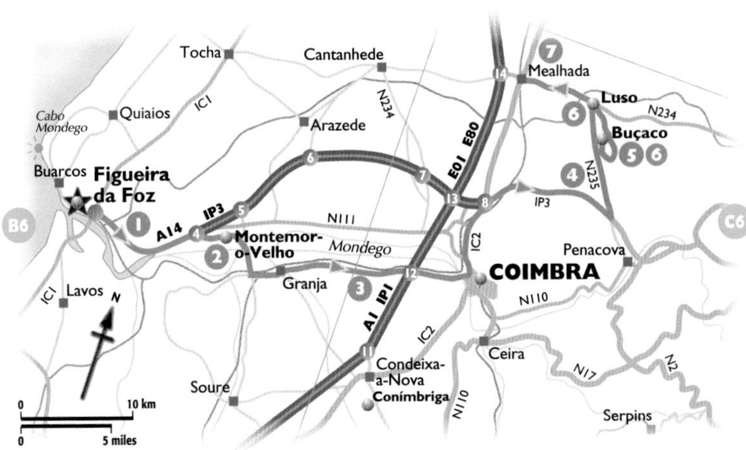

WHERE TO EAT

In Montemor-o-Velho, try Ramalhao in the Rua Tenente Valadim, which is renowned for its desserts. Buçaco has the Palace Hotel do Buçaco, where regional and international cuisine are served (▷ 301).

WHEN TO GO

Early summer or autumn are great times for this drive, as the weather should be settled, the countryside is at its best, and Coimbra itself will be relatively crowd-free. High summer is both busier and hotter.

TIP

- **It makes sense to spend a night in Coimbra, which deserves at least a couple of hours for a thorough exploration. You can leave the next morning for the second half of the drive, giving you plenty of time for a walk in the Buçaco forest.**

Street scene, Mealhada, where this drive ends

IN THE NATIONAL FOREST OF BUÇACO

On this shady walk in Portugal's best-known and best-loved woodland, you can see many varieties of shrubs and trees—it is estimated that there are around 700 varieties of trees here, some native and others exotic. The forest also harbours intriguing follies and water features.

THE WALK

Distance: 2.6km (1.6 miles)
Allow: 50 minutes with no stops
Start/end at: main parking area below Hotel Palace do Buçaco
Parking: Leave your car in the main parking area below the hotel

Look for the path down on the right, signed 'Fonte Fria'. Follow the steps leading down the hill, ignoring the turning to the left—you'll see a little hut off here. Keep to the path that circles the hut, continuing down until you reach the top of the Fonte Fria.

The Fonte Fria is one of the loveliest features of the forest, a water staircase with a series of steps on either side of a central cascade. The tumbling water forms a succession of pools and water terraces, all connected by the main stream. The combination of clear water and surrounding bosky green is wonderfully cooling in summer. Once you get to the bottom, there's a great view back up from the pool with its focal tree fern (if you don't want to do the full walk, you can access this directly from the road running up to the hotel).

Turn left near the pool, signposted 'Vale dos Fretos'.

From here the path leads through the Vale dos Fretos, an avenue planted with pines, sequoias and superb tree ferns, huge specimens as tall as 4–5m (13–16ft). The water running alongside the path feeds two lakes, while the area is planted with camellias and rhododendrons.

A tree fern in the Vale dos Fretos. Some ferns are giants

Keep on the left side of the second, larger lake and turn left up the steps, then right at the intersection. About 220m (240 yards) farther on, you'll come to a fork; take the wide dirt track on the left uphill.

Fork left again, climbing steadily, and then swing right onto a wide path. At the next intersection you'll see the first of a series of fascinating follies.

The little building decorated with pebbles is the Porta Pedron. Keeping this on your left, turn right along a wide path to reach the Porta de Siloa, a double-arched folly. Walk through this and turn left through the second arch, up the steps, and then on up a wide avenue, where you'll find another folly at the top.

Turn left along a wide level track near the last building. The track crosses a stream and continues uphill; at the next intersection bear right, then right again, continuing upwards. This path will take you back to your starting point in the parking area.

If you want to continue walking, there's a plethora of woodland paths through the forest. One option is to follow the route along the Via Sacra, lined with 17th-century chapels dedicated to Christ's journey to Calvary, as far as the Cruz Alta, a huge cross at the top of a hill, from where there are splendid views.

There are other viewpoints at the Portas de Coimbra, on the same side of the forest as the Cruz Alta, and at the Senhora da Vitória, just outside the walls on the other side of the enclosed area.

WHERE TO EAT

Palace Hotel do Buçaco (▷ 301). The hotel also sells maps of the forest.

WHEN TO GO

Good at any time in dry weather, and particularly pleasant on a hot afternoon.

TIP

• Throughout this walk the paths are a mixture of gravel, soft footing and steps, so wear flat, sensible shoes, particularly if it's been raining recently.

Left: The Fonte Fria. Below: The range of trees is tremendous

7. DRIVE

A COASTAL DRIVE FROM ALCOBAÇA TO FÁTIMA

Starting at Alcobaça, home to a superb monastic complex, this drive takes in the fishing village and resort of Nazaré, a stretch of little-known coast and aromatic pinewoods, and the magnificent abbey of Batalha, before reaching Fátima, the so-called 'altar of Portugal' and one of the world's most celebrated Catholic shrines.

THE DRIVE

Distance: 80km (50 miles)
Allow: 2 hours' straight driving, 2–6 hours with stops at Nazaré, beaches in the Pinhal, Leiria and Batalha
Start at: Alcobaça
End at: Fátima

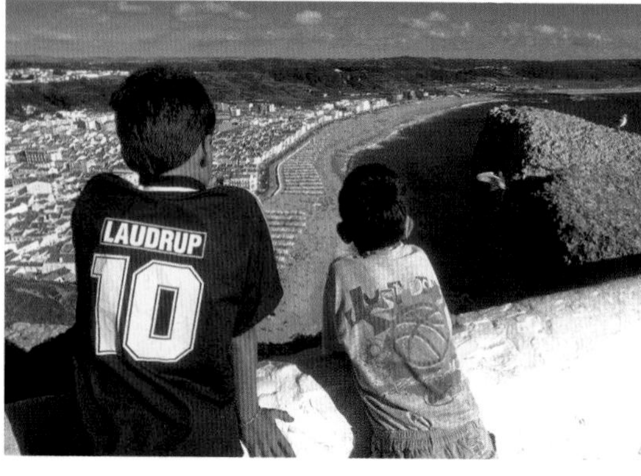

Above: Looking down on Nazaré, a popular resort with sandy beaches

In Alcobaça (▷ 110–111) follow the Nazaré signs out of town to the roundabout, where you'll pick up the signs to the A8, which will take you on to the N8-5. This crosses a wide fertile plain, planted with fruit trees, with rolling hills to the left.

After 5km (3 miles) you'll come to a roundabout; follow the brown signs for Nazaré and climb up through pines to the village of Tedeneira and on to Nazaré. Go downhill, following the signs marked '*Centro*' to the heart of the town. There, turn right along the waterfront.

❶ Nazaré (▷ 117) is a lively resort, a good place to stop and stretch your legs. The original fishing village has been all but swamped by holiday apartment buildings and the town bathing beach is likely to be packed, but there are fine stretches of sandy beach to the north and south. Note, though, that these beaches are dangerous for bathing.

Leave town following the signs uphill to Sítio and the N242 to Leiria. Look for a left turn above Sítio—ignoring the N242—towards Falor, Miradouro and Hospital; the orange sign marked 'Parque Aquatico' is useful here. A sign marked 'Praia da Légua', to the right, takes you onto the coastal road running north.

❷ The coastal road runs peacefully through the Pinhal de Leiria, a 700-year-old pine forest originally planted by Dom Dinis to protect the arable land from the encroaching dunes. Miles of aromatic trees are crisscrossed by sandy tracks, and side roads lead off to superb beaches and tiny holiday settlements. It's worth considering taking a detour to explore some of these—little Légua is particularly pleasant.

The main road drops right down to the sea at the lovely beach at Esteleira.

❸ Esteleira makes a good stop for a swim in the clear, clean sea, but bear in mind that these beaches are steeply shelving and currents and tides can be dangerous. There's another great beach farther north at Polvoeiro, a slightly more developed place with holiday apartments and villas.

Past here, and 30km (18 miles) from the start of the drive, turn right at the easy-to-miss sign to Marinha Grande along a road running inland through the woods. After 4km (2.5 miles), go straight over the crossroads across open, scrubby country towards Marinha. Bear right at the next intersection, then bear right again into Marinha Grande itself. At the roundabout in the middle of town, follow the signs to the A8 and Leiria, then, at the intersection with the A8/IC1, continue straight on to join the N242, a good shady road planted with pines and eucalyptus. Unless you intend to visit Leiria (▷ 117), take the slip road signed for Lisboa and Batalha (IC2 N1); you'll soon pick up the brown tourist signs for Batalha and Fátima. Batalha (▷ 112–115) is 8km (5 miles) farther on.

❹ Batalha, with its glorious Gothic/Manueline church, is visible from the busy road well before you reach it. Indeed, the church's outer fabric is beginning to suffer deterioration due to the proximity of the N1, with its polluting fumes from the constant heavy traffic.

Leave on the N356 for Fátima and turn left at the roundabout.

OUT AND ABOUT

❺ **The drive from Batalha to Fátima is a lovely section of the route, running across the northern tip of the Serra do Aire and passing through upland country scattered with villages and smallholdings.**

At the junction with the N357, follow the signs to '*Santuario*' to reach Fátima (▷ 116).

WHERE TO EAT

In Nazaré, there's the A Celeste in the Avenida da República, in Batalha the Pousada Mestre Afonso Domingues, and in Fátima the Tia Alice in the Rua do Adro (▷ 281).

Above: The main square, Marinha Grande. Below left: Vitrocristal from Marinha. Bottom: Leiria, with its castle, is well worth a stop

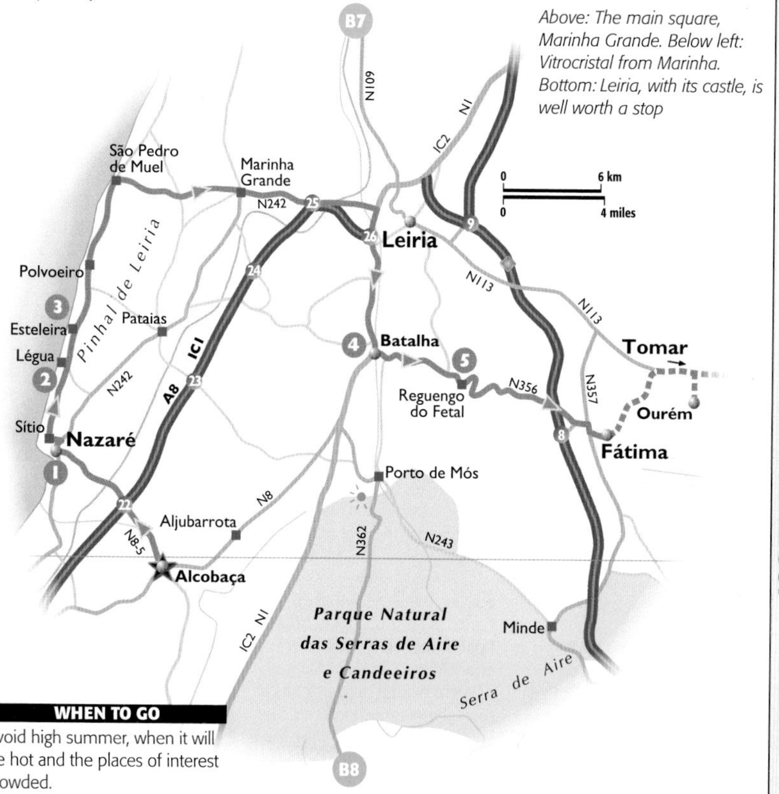

WHEN TO GO

Avoid high summer, when it will be hot and the places of interest crowded.

PLACES TO VISIT

Alcobaça (▷ 110–111)
Nazaré (▷ 117)
Leiria (▷ 117)
Batalha (▷ 112–115)
Fátima (▷ 116)

TIP

- You could continue to Tomar (▷ 118–121) via Ourém (▷ 122), an attractive drive through unspoilt hill-country sprinkled with tiny farms.

LISBON: THE CHIADO AND BAIRRO ALTO

On this varied walk in and around the Alfama quarter of the city, you'll take in some of Lisbon's ritziest stores as well as getting the chance to ride on the celebrated funiculars.

THE WALK

Distance: 2.4km (1.5 miles)

Allow: 1 hour without stops, 2–2.5 hours with visits

Start/end at: Praça dos Restauradores

Start in Praça dos Restauradores with the Palácio Foz on your left and walk round the corner to the Elevador da Gloria.

❶ The *elevador*, opened in 1885 as the second funicular railway to be built in the city, links the Bairro Alto with downtown Lisbon. Take your seat for a real Lisbon experience and turn left at the top of the steps when you get off.

Walk straight down Rua de São Pedro de Alcântara, keeping the side wall of the Igreja de São Roque to your left.

❷ The opulent Church of São Roque, with its sumptuous painted wooden ceiling, was built in the late 16th century by the Jesuits. The most ornate of the side chapels is the one dedicated to St. John the Baptist, which was built in Rome and shipped to Lisbon after a special papal blessing in 1749.

Turn left in front of the church and walk round the square to the far corner, where you'll see a flight of steps. Go down these, then take the second turning right along the Rua da Condessa, a quiet street with small workshops and a couple of bars. This leads onto the Largo do Carmo.

A statue of poet Fernando Pessoa outside his preferred café

❸ Largo do Carmo is an attractive square with benches and acacias, and is home to the Museu Arqueológico do Carmo.

Walk through the square and head down Calçado Sacramento until it meets Rua Garrett, where you turn right.

❹ Rua Garrett is one of Lisbon's ritziest shopping streets. Walk uphill, taking in the wonderfully traditional shop fronts along here and the elaborate façade of the Basílica dos Mártires across the way.

Just past the Mártires is Rua Serpa Pinto. You could detour right down it to visit the Museu do Chiado, or stay in Rua Garrett and pause for a drink or coffee at the Café A Brasileira at No. 120, famous for its literary associations (▷ 282).

With the café behind you, cross the road, walk through Largo do Chiado and head along Rua Duques de Bragança. A short way along you'll see Largo São Carlos below you on the left. Take the steps down to the square, which is dominated by the facade of the Teatro Nacional de São Carlos.

❺ The Teatro Nacional de São Carlos is Lisbon's opera house, built in the late 18th century and taking La Scala in Milan as its architectural model. It has a marvellous rococo interior, that you can experience during the winter opera season (▷ 211).

Past the theatre, continue straight ahead down Rua Capela, then turn left onto Rua Ivens, a fine street lined with harmonious early 19th-century buildings. This will take you back to the Rua Garrett. Turn right and you'll see the modern Chiado shopping area ahead.

❻ The Chiado shopping area was built during the massive reconstruction that followed a catastrophic fire in 1988. The design of the rebuilt district is by Alvaro Siza Vieira, a Porto-based architect who succeeded admirably in retaining a touch of tradition in this historic neighbourhood.

Turn left at the bottom of Rua Garrett and walk down Rua do Carmo, another classy shopping street. The viaduct of the Elevador de Santa Justa can be seen overhead.

The Elevador de Santa Justa towers over the Baixa district

❼ The Elevador de Santa Justa is a street elevator, designed in 1901 by a follower of Gustave Eiffel, the builder of Paris's Eiffel Tower, to link the Baixa with the Largo do Carmo above. The walkway from the elevator to the square has been closed for years, but you can take the elevator up for some great views—turn right down the steps to the entrance.

Right: Stylish art deco shopfronts in the Baixa. Below: Looking uphill from one of the city's famous traditional elevadores

At the bottom of Rua do Carmo, bear right onto the Rossio. You can simply walk up through the square to return to your starting point, bearing left past the station, or lengthen the walk by turning right and crossing Rua Aurea, Rua dos Sapateiros and Rua Augusta to reach Praça da Figueira. Turn left here and walk through the square, then take another left turn to bring you back onto the Rossio—and thence back to Praça dos Restauradores.

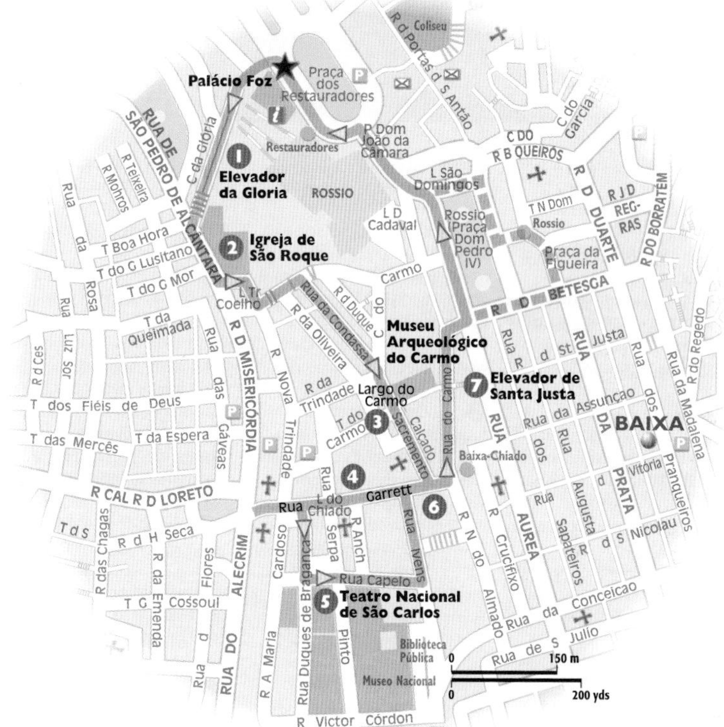

WHERE TO EAT

A Brasileira, on Rua Garrett, is great for snacks (▷ 282), while Cervejaria Trinidade on Rua Nova da Trinidade is good for prawns and ice-cold beer (▷ 283).

WHEN TO GO

During shopping hours is a good time for the walk as some of Lisbon's best shops provide temptation en route.

PLACES TO VISIT

Igreja de São Roque and Museu de Arte Sacra
Largo Trinidade Coelho, Lisboa
☎ 213 235 381 🕐 Church: daily 8.30–6. Museum: Tue–Sun 10–5
💰 Church: free. Museum: €1

Museu Arqueológico do Carmo (▷ 131)

Museu do Chiado (▷ 137)

THROUGH LISBON'S ALFAMA DISTRICT

On this varied walk in and around the Alfama, Lisbon's oldest quarter, you'll have the opportunity to visit several historic churches as well as enjoying some of the city's best views.

THE WALK

Distance: 3.7km (2.3 miles)
Allow: 1–1.5 hours without stops, 2–4 hours with visits
Start at: Praça do Comércio
End at: The Sé

Set off in Praça do Comércio with your back to the water, and turn left in the far right-hand corner to walk up Rua da Prata. Take the first right down Rua do Comércio and cross Rua dos Fanqueiros. Then take the first left and second right (following the brown signpost) uphill. You'll see the church of La Madalena on the right; follow the curve of the street up to the right onto Rua de Santo Antonio da Sé. Straight ahead you'll soon see the façade of the Sé (▷ 128). The cathedral's oldest parts date from 1150, when building on it started. Keeping the cathedral on your right, walk uphill following the tramlines along Rua da Augusta da Rosa.

❶ On Rua da Augusta da Rosa, the high wall on your right conceals the Law School, part of the University of Lisbon.

Continue uphill through Largo da São Martinho onto Rua da Limoeiro, then take the steps on the right next to the grassy bank to reach a *miradouro* (viewpoint) with splendid views.

❷ The Miradouro de Santa Luzia takes its name from the tiny church of Santa Luzia, whose exterior is decorated with 18th-century *azulejos* (tiles). Look out for the scene depicting Praça do Comércio. From the viewpoint, the domes and spires to the left are those of the Igreja de São Vicente de Fora (▷ 129). The steps opposite lead up to the Castelo de São Jorge (▷ 136).

Continue round the left-hand side of the church and walk up to Largo das Portas do Sol, home to the Museu-Escola de Artes Decorativas, housed in what was once a 17th-century palace (▷ 128–129), another *miradouro* with river views, and a statue of St. Vincent. Follow the road—and the tramlines—uphill, forking right and keeping to the cobblestones until you see a brown *miradouro* sign pointing to the right up Calçada da Graça. This street climbs fairly steeply to the Igreja da Graça, from where there's an outstanding view of the city below.

A tile detail from Santa Luzia shows pre-earthquake Lisbon

❸ The Graça church was founded in 1271 to house a sacred image of the Virgin, and enlarged in the 16th century. The great Lisbon earthquake of 1755 destroyed the original church; the present one is late 18th-century rococo. It's a real neighbourhood church, the scene of fervent Lenten processions. Have a peep inside before enjoying the views, which take in the castle, the river Tejo and its bridges, and the rooftops of the Baixa. The façade of Rossio station is easy to pick out, and you'll notice the easy-to-spot dome of the Estrela church on the skyline.

With the Graça church behind you, walk along the south side of Largo da Graça and take a right, down the steps and onto Rua da Voz do Operário—look for the tramlines again as a guide. Walk downhill along the street until you get to the Igreja São Vicente de Fora to the left.

❹ The Church of São Vicente de Fora is dedicated to Lisbon's patron saint. According to legend, this fourth-century AD figure was martyred in Spain and his body found its way to Portugal in a boat guided by two ravens, making landfall at Cabo de São Vicente in the far southwest. His remains were brought to Lisbon in 1173.

Continue downhill, following the tramlines round to the right. About 300m (330 yards) on, where the road swings right, cross over and walk down the Escadinhas das Escolas, a long flight of steps. At the bottom of the steps turn right onto Largo del Salvador, where you fork left and head downhill. These steep, narrow streets penetrate right into the heart of the historic Alfama district (▷ 128).

❺ The Alfama is Lisbon's oldest quarter, Moorish in appearance and consisting of a warren of alleyways called *becos* and *travessas*. It is full of vibrant life, much of it played out in the streets and squares.

Continue down to a tiny square with the Centro Paroquial de Alfama across the corner on the right; turn right next to this and head along a row of shops. You'll emerge onto Largo São Miguel.

❻ Largo São Miguel is another small square, with a church on the right and a solitary, lofty palm tree planted in its middle.

Walk across the square, keeping the church on the right, and carry straight ahead onto Rua do São Miguel. This becomes Rua do São João da Praça, named after the unpretentious 18th-century church along it. Bear left along the side of the church, gradually heading uphill. In a few minutes you'll emerge along the south side of the cathedral.

WHERE TO EAT

There is lots of choice, but try Lautasco in the Beco do Azinhal, with its lovely shaded patio, or Malmequer-Bemmequer in the Rua São Miguel.

WHEN TO GO

This is a good walk at almost any time in daylight hours, except perhaps in the middle of the day. Many people claim the *miradouro* at the Graça is the best place in Lisbon from where to enjoy the sunset.

PLACES TO VISIT

Ingreja de São Vicente de Fora
(▷ 129)

Igreja da Graça
Largo da Graça, 1170 Lisboa
☎ 218 873 943 🕐 Mon–Sat 9.30–12.30, 2.30–7, Sun 9.30–12.30, 5.30–8 Free

Left: Lisbon's great medieval cathedral. Below: Rooftops in the Alfama. Bottom: The view from Largo das Portas do Sol

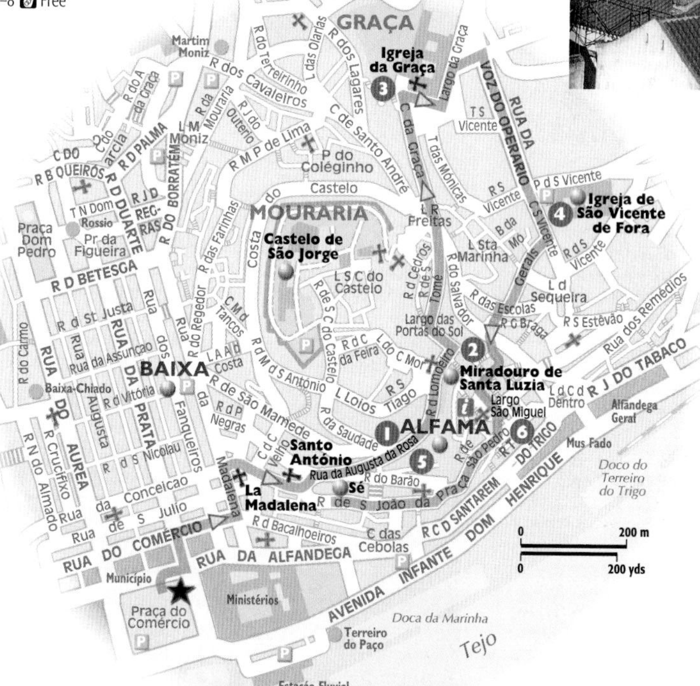

EXPLORING THE PARQUE DA PENA

This is a waymarked circular walk through the wooded grounds of the Parque da Pena. Perfect on a hot summer's day, the route winds downhill through cool, shady woods, giving tantalizing views and taking in an exotically planted valley and four bird-haunted lakes.

THE WALK

Distance: 3.3km (2 miles)
Allow: 1 hour or 1–2 hours if visiting the Palácio da Pena en route
Start at: Main entrance
End at: The bottom gate near the fourth lake

Left: The paths through the park are well signed. Right: Oriental lilies

Walk through the main entrance and follow the green signs uphill along the tarmac path. Shortly you'll see a sign for the Picadeiro at an intersection.

The Picadeiro was once a venue for small bullfights and still retains its original shape.

As the path reaches the road, walk straight across and up the steps if you're visiting the Palácio Nacional de Pena (▷ 150, 152).

From outside the Palácio Nacional da Pena, there are wide views over a jumble of pinewoods and granite outcrops to the sea, scenery that typifies 19th-century Romantic taste and is perfectly in keeping with the excesses of the palace itself. Built over the ruins of a 16th-century monastery, the palace was the brainchild of Ferdinand of Saxe-Coburg-Gotha, the German husband of Dona Maria II. Helped by fellow-German architect Baron Eschwege, Ferdinand built a mock medieval extravaganza that, to today's eyes, is a masterpiece of kitsch.

Leave the palace and walk back downhill through the approach tunnel to the main road. Cross the road and walk down two steps to turn left onto the way-marked path—there's a green arrowed sign marked '*caminho pedona*'. At the next sign ('Alto de Santo Antonio') bear right to walk along the tarmac path through some heavy vegetation of pines and laurels.

The path swings left to an intersection, where you follow the green arrows left along a gravel path. Where the path branches, fork right and follow the arrows straight ahead.

In the depths of the park you can see how the inspiration for the design of the landscape came from the notion of combining elements of northern forest with typical Mediterranean and Asiatic plantings. One of the park's original purposes was for use as an acclimatization garden for the constant stream of new discoveries being brought back from China and the Far East by 19th-century plant hunters.

At the next intersection you could detour right to the *miradouro* (viewpoint) or continue the walk by following the sign (in English) to the Giant.

The Giant is an outlandishly large statue of a man perched on a granite outcrop above the path at 490m (1,600ft) above sea level.

Continue downhill to the intersection and bear right following the signs to the Alta de Caterinha. En route, a small path goes up to the left to the Cruz Alto, the highest point in the

The park combines European and Asiatic plantings

Above: The giant tree ferns in the Queen's Fern Valley

Top: Outside the Fonte de Passarinhos. Above: The fountain

park; do not follow this, but instead stick to the sandy path that wends its way through thick cover to an intersection with a tarmac track. Follow the signs downhill to the Queen's Fern Valley until you come to a clearing with a small pool surrounded by tree ferns. Leave the track here and take the two steps through the gap in the wall on the right onto a cobbled path.

The Queen's Fern Valley is one of the loveliest parts of the park, an area thickly planted with tree ferns, some of them reaching as high as 6–7m (20–23ft). Shelter for these delicate species is provided by mature beech, chestnut and oak trees, and by thickets of camellias. As the path gently meanders downhill you're accompanied everywhere by the rush and gurgle of the tiny streams that tumble through the valley. It's a maze of little paths, so follow your nose downhill, watching your footing as the cobbles can sometimes be slippery.

At the bottom, the path rejoins the main track near a magnificent red cedar. Turn right here and walk the 50m (55 yards) to the Fonte de Passarinhos, a Moorish-style tiled pavilion with benches and a fountain inside. Keep the pavilion on your right and continue downhill, following the signs to *lagos* (lakes). When you reach the lakes, follow the path down with the water on your left.

There are four man-made lakes, edged with walls and boulders and fed by the water from the Queen's Fern Valley. They're home to various water-birds, including a pair of black swans. The largest is the bottom lake, where there's a monument to Dom Fernando II, the initiator of the plantings here in 1839. Don't miss the duck houses, complete with crenellations, Moorish flourishes and ramps to give the ducks easy access to the water.

Leave the park through the bottom gate; a tourist bus runs from the stop just up to the right.

WHERE TO EAT

There is nowhere to eat in the park itself. Either take a picnic, or try a restaurant in Sintra town before or after the walk.

WHEN TO GO

With its shady paths and easy downhill walking, this walk is particularly enjoyable on hot summer afternoons.

PLACES TO VISIT

Palácio Nacional da Pena
(▷ 150, 152)

A memorial to Dom Fernando II (Ferdinand of Saxe-Coburg-Gotha), husband of Dona Maria II, who initiated the plantings in the east of the park

THE LOWER ALENTEJO

This drive takes you through the lonely country of the Baixo Alentejo, where villages and towns are few and far between and the landscape has a special and unique beauty—a real taste of the undiscovered Portugal many visitors miss.

THE DRIVE

Distance: 222km (138 miles)
Allow: 4–5 hours
Start/end at: Mértola

Leave Mértola (▷ 162) by crossing the river Guadiana to join the N265 towards Serpa. You'll get a good view back towards the town as you cross the bridge. The road climbs through an area that's designated as the Parque Natural do Vale do Guadiana.

❶ The Parque Natural do Vale do Guadiana is good for birds. Watch out for storks, azure-winged magpies, and egrets in the wetter areas. Once you've gained altitude, the road runs through shady avenues of eucalyptus, introduced here from the southern hemisphere in the early 20th century.

After 17km (10.5 miles) you'll come to the Barragem da Tapada reservoir, and the old copper-mining town of Mina de São Domingos. You're less than 5km (3 miles) from the Spanish border here, although there's no crossing point.

❷ Mina de São Domingos has been the focus of mining from Roman times right up to the 1960s. The mines themselves are being turned into a visitor attraction that traces the impact of more than 2,000 years of industrialization on the landscape. The site is well worth visiting, especially if you're interested in industrial archaeology.

Continue north on the N265 for 37km (23 miles) until you get to the sign for Serpa. Before entering the town, it's worth making a quick detour. Follow the *pousada* signs up the hill to take in the views over the plain. Also visit the little whitewashed chapel of Nossa Senhora da Guadalupe.

❸ Serpa (▷ 163) comes at the end of a stretch of road that passes through classic Alentejan landscape. It's an undulating country made up of huge wheat fields, dotted with cork oaks and interspersed with sheep pastures and olive groves. It has a beauty all of its own, part of which comes from the fact that it is virtually uninhabited. Santa Iria, just across the river Limas, relieves the monotony; it's a farming village that makes its living from the surrounding olive and orange groves.

Moura's faded elegance is a reminder of its fashionable past

Leave Serpa on the N255, signposted to Espanha.

❹ Pias is the first village on this lovely road. It's worth a stop to see the frescoes in the Igreja de Santa Luzia and to sample the local red wine.

From here, stay on the N255 through olive groves and vineyards until you reach Moura (▷ 162).

❺ Moura is a thermal spa town with Moorish roots. Its name, meaning 'Moorish Maiden' relates to a legendary tale of a Moorish girl who threw herself to her death from the tower of the castle when Christian knights killed her fiancé and captured the town on her wedding day.

Leave Moura on the N255. Just after crossing the river Ardila, turn left onto the N233 towards Alqueva and Portel. The Alqueva dam will soon come into view.

❻ The Alqueva dam is the result of a huge and contentious EU-funded project to dam the river Guadiana, with what could be hugely detrimental effects on the ecosystem of the whole area. Despite worldwide opposition from environmentalists, the dam gates closed and the reservoir started to fill in 2002. Once full, it will be Europe's largest reservoir, and it looks as if the best that campaigners against the project can hope for is a maximum water level of 139m (456ft), which would safeguard many of the threatened trees and wildlife habitats.

The bell-tower of São João Baptista, Moura. Like the main church, it is a fine example of medieval architecture

Follow the N384 to Portel then turn left onto the IP2 towards Beja (▷ 155), a pleasant little town at the heart of the Alentejo's southern plains.

7 Beja's story goes back to Roman times. In fact, its name is a corruption of the Latin *pax* (peace), given to the town in celebration of a peace treaty agreed here between Julius Caesar and the Lusitanians in 48BC.

Leave Beja on the IP2 south. After 15km (9 miles) turn onto the N122 for the journey back to Mértola.

Serpa is a bustling market town with fine views from its mainly Moorish castle. It is famous for its cheese-making

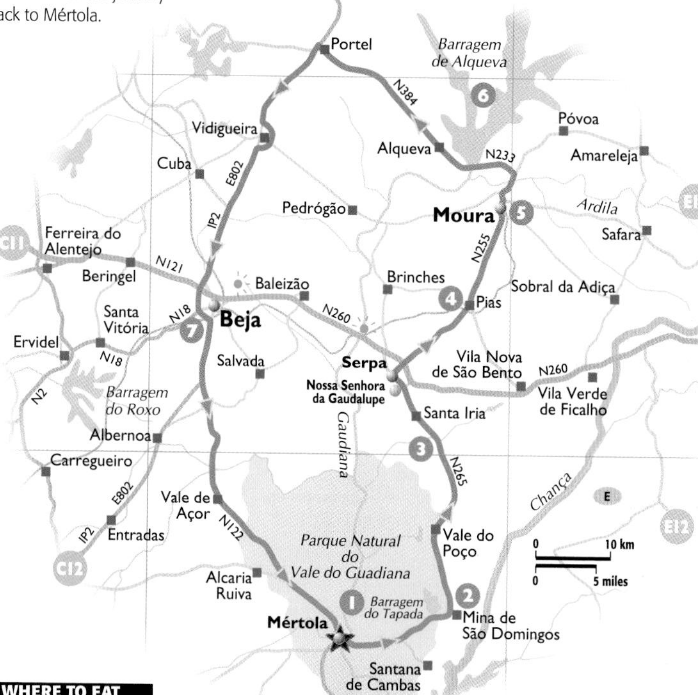

WHERE TO EAT

In Serpa, there's Molha o Bico in Rua Quente, in Pias the Restaurante O Lagar in the Estrada de Brinches, and in Moura there is O Triho on Rua 5 Outubro. In Beja, you could try A Esquina in Rua Infante D. Henrique (▷ 289), or, for something a little more sophisticated, the Pousada de São Francisco (▷ 311), which serves regional cuisine.

WHEN TO GO

Spring or autumn are the best times for this drive; avoid high summer, when the heat can be unbearable in this exposed countryside.

PLACES TO VISIT

Mértola (▷ 162)
Serpa (▷ 163)
Moura (▷ 162)
Beja (▷ 155)

Looking down on the pretty town of Mértola, which stands overlooking the confluence of the Guadiana and Oeiras rivers

12. DRIVE

INTO THE HIGH ALGARVE FROM PORTIMÃO

This drive runs inland from bustling Portimão to the historic town of Silves before taking you, via some attractive villages, to the Algarve's highest point for some tremendous views.

THE DRIVE

Distance: 80km (50 miles)
Allow: 2 hours without stops, 3–5 hours with stops
Start /end at: Portimão

Leave Portimão (▷ 173) on the N124 signposted for Monchique. (If you're accessing the road from the N125, take the slip road off the N125 in the northern outskirts of Portimão.) Head north for 6km (3.5 miles), then take a right turn at Porto de Lagos, continuing on the N124 to Silves. The road runs up the fertile Arade valley, an area of rolling citrus orchards. The local smallholders set up stands outside their houses where you can buy freshly picked fruit for about €1 per 2kg (4.4lb) bag.

❶ Silves (▷ 175), once a Moorish royal capital famed throughout the Islamic world, is worth a long stop. Park the car and explore the town on foot. Many old buildings were destroyed by the earthquake of 1755, but the great red sandstone fortress, symbol of Moorish dominance, remains.

On leaving Silves, retrace your route to the intersection with the N266 (same road, new number) and turn right up the valley of the Boina to head for Monchique.

The whitewashed bell-tower of the Igreja Matriz, Monchique

❷ The Boina valley is traced by a shady, wooded road, where acacia (mimosa) and eucalyptus predominate—a scented sea of soft yellow in early spring. Both these southern hemisphere species were discovered by the botanist Sir Joseph Banks, who accompanied Captain Cook on his epic Pacific voyage in 1770. Both trees adapted to life in Europe and there are large areas of the Algarve where they predominate over the native species. They are, however, a fire hazard, particularly the eucalyptus, which has high levels of natural oils.

Below: The spectacular suspension bridge over the river Arade, Portimão. Inset: Taking a welcome break in Monchique

After 11km (7 miles) look for the tiny slip road down to the spa village of Caldas de Monchique (▷ 175). Continue uphill to Monchique itself (▷ 175).

❸ Monchique holds a big market on the second Friday of the month, where you can buy the famous local ham, *presunto de Monchique* and—if you're brave enough—some *medronho*, the powerful local spirit distilled from the fruit of the arbutus, also called the strawberry tree. Look, too, for the traditional stools made to a design that originated with Roman furniture makers.

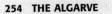

In the main square, turn steeply left uphill to leave town on the N266-3 towards the summit of Fóia—watch for the signs.

4 Fóia, at 902m (2,959ft), is the highest point in the Algarve, so on a clear day it's worth getting out a map at the summit to identify the landmarks that will be spread out at your feet. The whole of the southwestern tip of Portugal, with the sprawl of Portimão (▷ 173) and Lagos (▷ 172), should be visible to the south, with wild Cabo de São Vicente (▷ 174) at the farthest point. Fóia is a popular tour destination, so arrive early to miss the crowds, or, better still, late—it's a great place for sunsets.

Leave the summit and retrace your route to Portimão.

As an alternative you could turn left onto the N267 south of Monchique and continue to the tiny village of Casais, where you take the unclassified road that runs south via Montes de Cima. After about 3km (1 mile) you can either turn right to rejoin the N266 or continue south to hit the N125 to the west of Portimão.

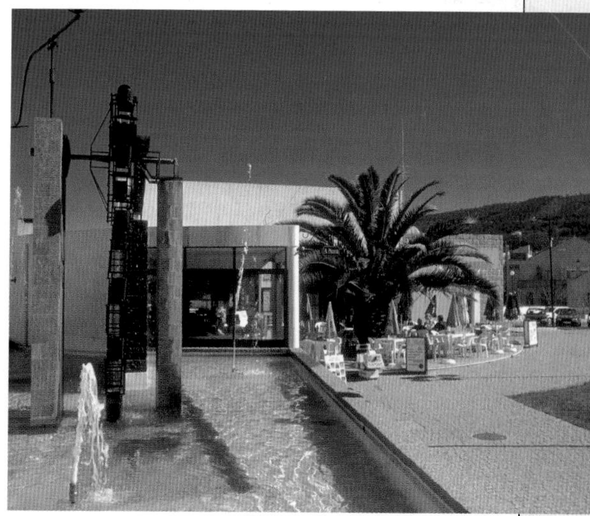

The main square in Monchique, with its intriguing modern fountain, immaculate lawns, palms and attractive paved walkways

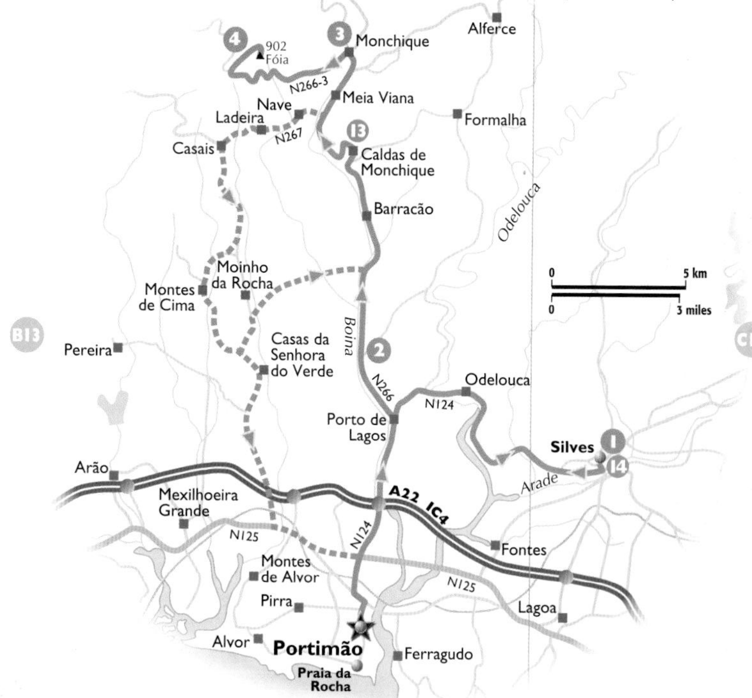

WHERE TO EAT

For light snacks in Silves, try the Café Inglês, Escadas do Castelo (▷ 293), and, in Caldas, the restaurant in the spa complex. Just beyond Monchique on the Fóia road, there's the Abrigo da Montanha (▷ 292), with superb views from its flower-filled terrace.

WHEN TO GO

This is a particularly appealing drive in late winter, when the almond blossom is out and the road between Silves and Caldas de Monchique is a sheet of mimosa. In summer, it's a great way to escape the crowds on the coast.

13. WALK

IN THE SERRA DE MONCHIQUE FOOTHILLS

On this lovely walk in the wooded foothills of the Algarve's Serra de Monchique you can escape from the crowds on the coast into a quieter, calmer world.

THE WALK

Distance: 7.5km (4.5 miles)
Allow: 2–3 hours
Start/end at: Caldas de Monchique

Set off from the red telephone box in Caldas de Monchique (▷ 175) and walk downhill through the village, past the spa buildings and on to the water bottling plant. The mineral water produced here is considered to be the best in Portugal. It's a sweet-tasting water that's high in minerals. Keeping the bottling plant on your left, turn right off the road onto a track that leads quite steeply downhill.

The path is lined with acacia trees, lovely in late winter when they're covered in fluffy yellow blossom. You'll be able to see or hear the river below you to the right as you walk.

Continue until you come to a bridge across the river. Walk over the bridge—take care if it has been raining as it may be slippery—and turn left along a narrow path that runs alongside the water.

In these hills, the greenery is incredibly lush during the late winter and spring. You'll see and smell almond as well as acacia blossom. Look out, too, for a small bush festooned with clusters of red fruit that vaguely resemble strawberries. This is *Arbutus unedo*, the strawberry tree, whose fruit is used to make the Algarve's best-known spirit, *medronho*. This ranges from a tastefully packaged 40°-proof version for tourist sale to a brain-numbing moonshine with a staggering 70°- to 90°-proof punch that's still brewed in the hills.

Caldas de Monchique, a tiny but friendly spa, viewed from above

Continue on the riverside path, passing a bridge on your left, and walk on until you see tiny fields above the river, planted with citrus trees, and a large house on the opposite bank. At the fork in the path, take the right branch uphill, away from the water. This path drops down to become a wide track, which runs fairly steeply uphill. Follow this as far as an intersection where another track comes in from the left. Turn right here and stay on this track for around 25 to 30 minutes.

There are many wildflowers to look out for along the way. Bright yellow Bermuda buttercups carpet the ground in late winter and spring, while the scents of lavender, thyme, rosemary and oregano fill the air during the hotter months.

A phone box marks the walk's start

When you reach a right-hand turn where you can see that the path climbs slightly before levelling off, take it—you'll shortly be able to enjoy a fine view down to Caldas de Monchique below. Follow the track steeply downhill, passing a small white house on the left at the bottom. The track bears right and you'll soon see the bridge over the stream that you took near the start of the walk. Cross it and retrace the route into Caldas.

WHERE TO EAT

There is nowhere to eat on this walk, so take a picnic with you. It's well worth carrying a bottle of water, especially in summer.

WHEN TO GO

This is a great walk to take at almost any time of year, but it is particularly enjoyable on a fine, crisp winter's day when the air is crystal clear—as a result, the views are even more spectacular.

EXPLORING THE HIGH ALGARVE

Good tracks and paths take you from the heart of the one-time Moorish capital of the Algarve, through smallholdings into the countryside, with lovely views along the way.

THE WALK

Distance: 7.5km (4.5 miles)
Allow: 2–2.5 hours
Start/end at: Silves

The view from the windmill ruins on this walk is spectacular

Start in Largo do Município in Silves (▷ 175). The town was once the Moorish capital of the Algarve until the Moors were driven out by the Christians in the 13th century. Head up Rua da Sé to the cathedral, a fine, originally Gothic building raised on the site of an old mosque. It was the Algarve's most important church until 1580, when the bishops moved their headquarters to Faro. Just past the cathedral, turn right and skirt the castle remains.

Keeping the castle to the left, head straight ahead downhill. After about 10 minutes, you'll come to an intersection. Here, turn left, then right onto a track running alongside an orange grove. This leads to a *levada*, the Portuguese name for a concreted water channel. Cross the footbridge and turn right, walking alongside the water channel.

Follow the path left towards some houses, where you turn left, then sharp right at the next intersection. To reach the ruined windmill you'll see from here, head for the aqueduct and go underneath it, before immediately turning left at the junction of several tracks and then right where the new track forks.

Continue along this fork up to the ruins. As you go, you'll walk through well-established groves of almond and fig trees and pass attractive traditional whitewashed cottages. In late winter, the ground here is yellow with Bermuda buttercups, while you should also look out for clumps of strongly scented wild narcissi. These are the ancestor of the cultivated garden variety.

Windmills are a common sight all over Portugal. The majority follow what was originally a Greek design dating from as far back as around 300BC, and are mainly used for pumping water. Here, few traces remain of the original superstructure, except for the solid stonework of the tower. It is a good place to pause and take in the superb views back towards Silves, down to Portimão (▷ 173) and into the hills of the Serra de Monchique (▷ 175).

There are plenty of wildflowers to look out for, including the pink, white and purple flowers of cistus and dense clusters of lavender. In spring, various orchids should be in bloom. In particular, try to spot the tiny green-winged orchid, which is quite a rarity.

With your back to the sea, follow the ridge north right to the end; the valley ahead on the right is the Bastos. At the end of the ridge, turn left downhill. At the bottom, turn right onto the lower track, then, shortly ahead, left at an intersection. Follow this path above a wooded valley, eventually dropping down to where several paths meet. Here, turn left onto the main track and follow this south downhill into more fertile countryside.

As you start to walk south, the landscape is one of olives, eucalyptus and aromatic shrubs. These soon give way to cultivated patches of vegetables and almond and citrus trees. The scene is a vivid contrast to the dusky brown scrub-covered hills you passed through earlier. The Portuguese call such scrubland *matos*, typically southern European vegetation that grows on poor soil. It varies in height, but is often composed of aromatic, low-growing shrubs like lavender, rosemary, cistus and the curry plant, interspersed with spring- and autumn-flowering bulbs, found in grassier, ungrazed areas.

Turn left when you reach the main track, which becomes a surfaced road as you approach the outskirts of Silves. Keep right at the first houses, then turn left and climb the steps you'll see in front of you. Turn left at the top of the steps, then go right. This takes you back to the water channel. Follow this until you reach the footbridge you crossed at the start of the walk, and then return to your starting point.

WHERE TO EAT

You can take a picnic with you to enjoy on the walk, or wait until you get back to Silves. There, the Café Inglês, in the Escadas do Castelo (▷ 293), serves light snacks and full meals.

WHEN TO GO

To enjoy the countryside at its best, take this walk in winter, spring or very early summer.

15. DRIVE

EXPLORING THE BARROCAL HILLS

This round trip north from Loulé takes in the fertile rolling hills of central Algarve, an unspoilt rural area known as the garden of the Algarve, rich in almond and orange groves.

THE DRIVE

Distance: 50km (30 miles)
Allow: 2–3 hours without stops
Start/end at: Loulé

❶ Loulé is a thriving market town. Lying inland and north-west of Faro, it was an important place long before the development of the coastal towns. Today, it is the administrative capital of the area. The old part is a grid of white-washed, cobbled alleyways focused on the 13th-century Gothic Igreja Matriz. The earlier bell-tower was once the minaret of a Moorish mosque, the only part of the Islamic building to survive. Round here are numerous craft shops, many devoted to copperware and hand-made lace. The castle ruins are home to an archaeological museum and you can climb the castle walls for fine views over the old town. Loulé has an excellent produce market, held in an eye-catching, domed Moorish-style building near the heart of town.

Follow the signs out of town for Querença/Ameixial onto the N396. After about 8km (5 miles) you'll see a fine old arched bridge and a sign marked '*fonte*' spring) Turn left (signed to Querença), then left again up into the heart of the village.

Lively Loulé is home to numerous craft shops and holds an excellent produce market

❷ Unspoiled Querença is a pleasant stop. You could have a peep into the church or enjoy a drink at a characterful bar. If the local sausage is available, it's really worth trying—it's so well known that the village feast day in January is devoted to its celebration.

Drive back down the hill and turn left to join the N524. About 3km (2 miles) along, you could park and take the short walk up to the Fonte da Benémola (▷ 260). Otherwise, continue left towards Salir (signposted).

❸ The road to Salir passes through typical Barrocal countryside. The land here is intensely fertile and farmed by smallholders, many of whom stick fervently to the historic ways of their peasant ancestors. Donkeys are still used for transportation, for instance, and you may even see older people proudly wearing traditional local costume. The main crops, apart from vegetables, are oranges, almonds, carobs and figs, and you'll also see plenty of cork oak stands. More than 50 per cent of the world's supply of cork oak comes from the inland Algarve and the Alentejo, the tree's spongy bark being harvested every nine years or so.

At the intersection with the N124 turn left to Salir, and follow the road steeply uphill to the middle of the village.

Looking down on the Barrocal countryside. The land is heavily cultivated, notably with olives and oranges

The white buildings of Salir, where the Moors once had a stronghold

❹ Salir is another traditional farming village, where you can stroll from the former church along flower-hung white alleys to the remains of the Moorish castle. There's not much to see, but the position is glorious, with fine views over the village and the valley beyond.

Leave Salir and take the unclassified road south for 16km (10 miles) back to Loulé.

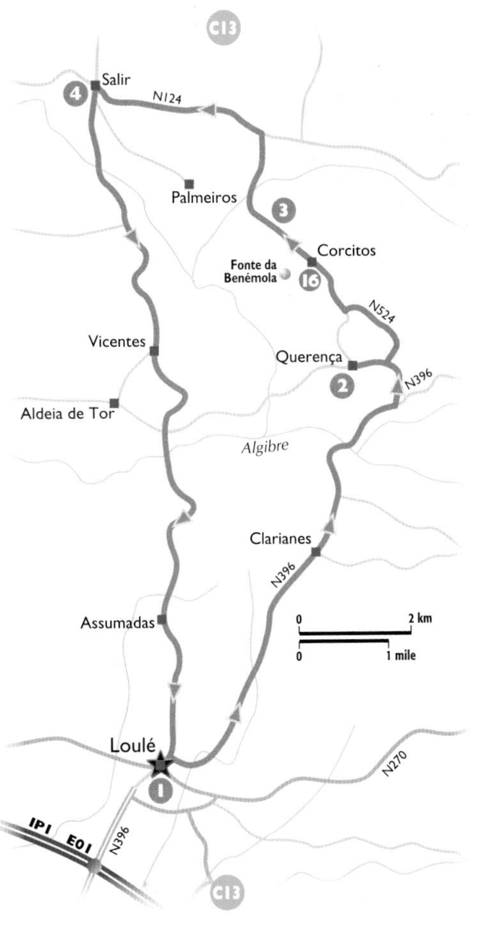

WHERE TO EAT

Just out of central Loulé, on the Clareanes/Querença road, is the Casa Paixanito (▷ 292). In Querença, try De Querença in the church square, and in Salir try the Mouro Bar Castelo by the castle.

WHEN TO GO

This pleasant drive is best in the spring when the almond trees are in blossom.

PLACES TO VISIT

Loulé

Largo Dom Pedro I, 8100 Loulé
289 463 900 or 800 296 296 (freephone information number)
Sep–end Jun Mon–Fri 9.30–1.30; Jul–end Aug Mon–Fri 9.30–7, Sat 9.30–3.30

Museu Arqueológico, Loulé Castle

Largo Dom Pedro 1
289 400 642
Thu 9–5, Sat 10–2

16. WALK

A WALK IN THE BARROCAL HILLS

This cool, leafy walk, with varied trees, shrubs and wildflowers along the way, takes you down a gentle valley to a little-known beauty spot.

THE WALK

Distance: 5km (3 miles)

Allow: 1 hour

Start/end at: 3km (2 miles) north of Querença on N524, at the sign 'Fonte de Benémola, *circulo pedestre*'

Parking: Off the road next to the ruined house on the left at the start of the track

Start walking at the sign marked '*circulo pedestre*' and follow the track—there's only one—for about 1km (half a mile). At the fork, head left and follow the signs to the *fonte* (spring) across a small bridge.

Along this first stretch you'll see two distinct types of vegetation: well-ordered fields of crops, fruit and olive trees, and vegetables planted among orange trees to the left of the track; and the *matos* (scrubland) to the right. The latter is rich in wildflowers; if you're walking in spring and early summer you should be able to spot several different varieties of orchid. Wild aromatic herbs also grow in abundance. Look out for rosemary, lavender, thyme and juniper, and enjoy their characteristic scents as they fill the balmy air.

Turn left beyond the bridge, then left again, keeping the river on your left. Here you're in a verdant haven, with the calming sound of running water and the pleasant scent of orange, lemon and carob trees to enjoy. You may also be able to hear, if not spot, a variety of warblers and other birds, while, after rain, there may be otter prints in the soft earth beside the water. The otters, which are shy and largely nocturnal, feed on the tiny fish in the river. Walk on for about five minutes to reach the Fonte de Benémola itself.

A donkey-drawn farm cart, still a widely used form of transportation in the Barrocal

Above: Oranges for harvest. Right: A view over the fertile countryside

The Fonte de Benémola spring is rich in minerals and there's a tradition of bathing in the water for health reasons—it's considered particularly good for arthritic conditions. There are picnic tables in an open clearing here. You can explore farther upstream, where you'll find caves as the river passes through a rocky ravine.

Cross the river on the stepping-stones and turn immediately left, following the water downstream and keeping it on your left.

A basketmaker's hut is a few minutes' walk farther along the river. The craftsman is usually there, selling a variety of traditional baskets.

Continue through a stand of cork oaks until you get back to the N124; turn left, cross the bridge and follow the road back to where you parked.

WHERE TO EAT

Take a picnic, or try De Querença back in the town in the Largo da Igreja before or after the walk.

TIPS

- If the river is high, the stepping-stones at the farthest point of the walk will be submerged and you'll have to retrace your steps.
- You'll see a variety of signs to the spring or red, white and yellow paint marks on walls and trees. Though locals drive down to the spring—the track is just wide enough to take a car—it's not recommended.

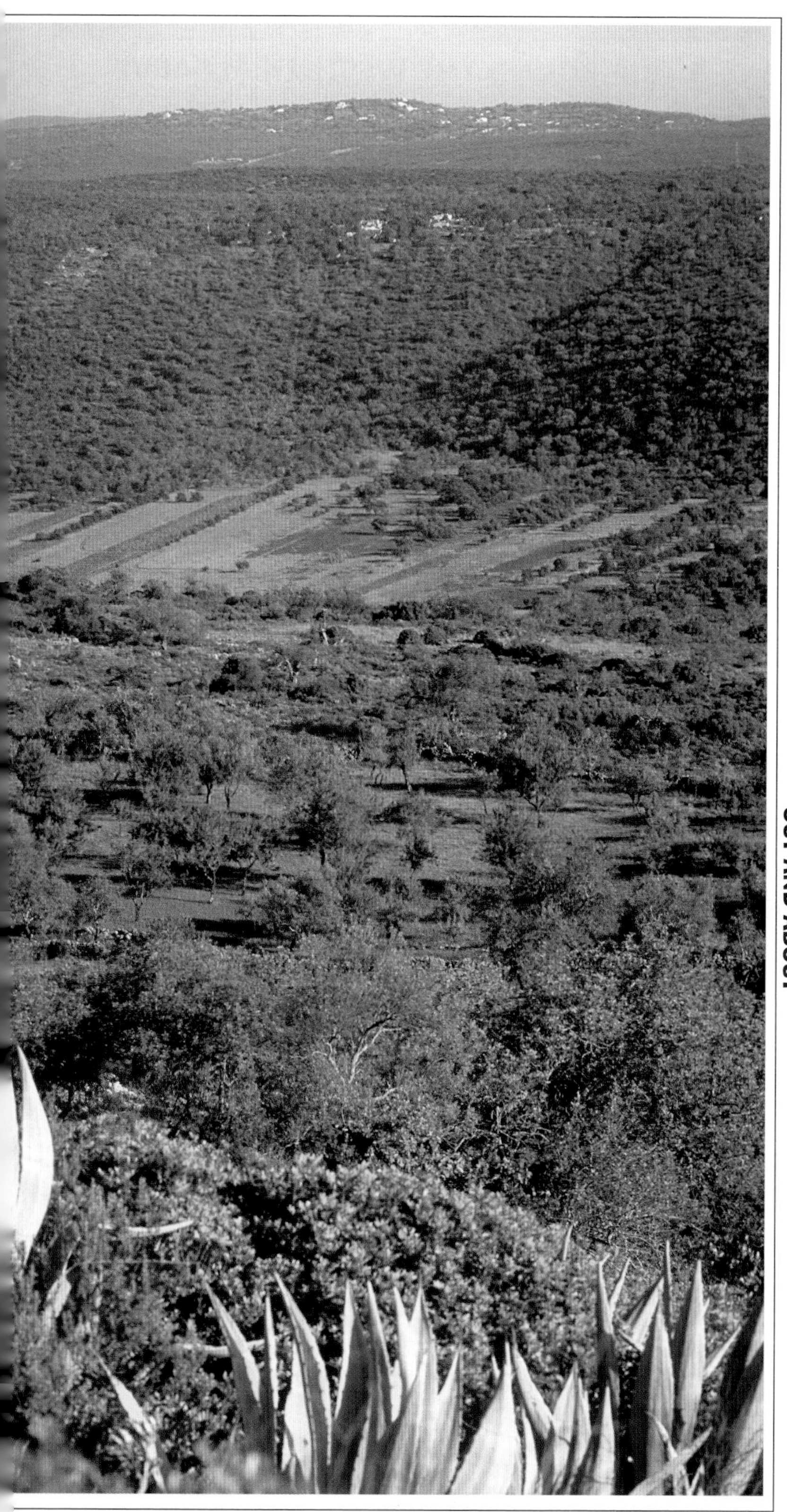

A TRIP ROUND THE WESTERN ALGARVE

In the undiscovered and undeveloped far western Algarve, you'll drive along deserted hill roads and experience the grandeur of the magnificent cliffs and wild scenery of the dramatic Atlantic coast.

THE DRIVE

Distance: 153km (95 miles)
Allow: 3 hours' straight driving, or 5–7 hours with stops and detours
Start/end at: Lagos

Leave Lagos (▷ 172) on the busy N125 and head west to Vila do Bispo.

❶ Vila do Bispo is a typical Algarve agricultural village, virtually untouched by modern tourism. While you are here, visit the ornate 17th-century parish church within the central core of whitewashed houses. Next, you could go surfing with Surf Planet (▷ 227), or head west across the hills for 5km (3 miles) to Praia do Castelejo, a huge sandy beach at the foot of dramatic, forbidding cliffs.

Leaving Vila do Bispo, turn left and follow the N268 south to Sagres (▷ 174).

❷ Sagres is believed to be the place where Prince Henry the Navigator established his headquarters when he became Governor of the Algarve in 1419. His settlement, known as Vila do Infante (Prince's Town), may have been on the site of Sagre's *fortaleza* (fortress).

From Sagres, go north along the coast for 6km (3.5 miles) to Cabo de São Vicente (▷ 174).

❸ Wild Cabo de São Vicente, is the site of Europe's second most powerful lighthouse. Though the lighthouse is not officially open to the public, the keeper will sometimes take visitors around it.

Return to Sagres, and retrace the route to the intersection with the N125 at Vila do Bispo. Turn left here and take the N268 north to Carrapateira.

❹ The road north from Vila do Bispo passes through a lusher landscape, with gently rolling hills, patches of eucalyptus and acacia, and neatly tended smallholdings. Little side roads off the N268 give access to superb beaches. For a real treat, take the turn-off to Praia do Amado, just south of Carrapateira. This broad sandy bay, backed by low hills and renowned for its excellent surf, has the bonus of being relatively quiet even in summer.

In Carrapateira turn left onto the loop road that runs round the headland and down to Praia da Bordeira.

❺ Praia da Bordeira is an unusual beach for the area. A broad stretch of sand, backed by dunes and a little river valley, it provides a pleasing contrast to the precipitous cliffs elsewhere on this coast.

Return to the main road (N268) and continue north to the intersection with the N120. Turn left towards Aljezur.

To explore more beaches, you could make a detour after approximately 1.8km (1 mile). Turn left onto an unclassified road signed '*arrifana*' (beach). Continue north through Vale da Telha to Praia de Monte Clérigo (great for families) and return up the river valley to the N120. Turn left and drive north to Aljezur.

❻ Aljezur, though little more than a large village, is the largest settlement on the

Above: A pavement mosaic, Lagos. Below: Rugged Cabo de São Vicente and its lighthouse

western Algarve coast. Park in the modern lower town, where you'll find most of the shops and restaurants, and walk up the steep cobbled streets of the old town to reach the ruins of the 10th-century Moorish castle, from where there are splendid views over the town and the surrounding countryside. There are also a couple of local museums.

At Aljezur turn right onto the N267 and continue for 10km (6 miles), before turning right down a minor road to Corsino and the Barragem da Bravura. This hilly road runs through lovely countryside between the western edge of the lower Serra de Monchique (▷ 175) and the Serra do Espinhaço de Cão. Follow the signs to the Barragem da Bravura on the N125-9.

❼ The huge Bravura reservoir is one of the finest in the Algarve, a smooth stretch of deep, green water backed by densely wooded hills. You can walk across the dam and along a track on the other side, or simply relax at the café.

Return to the N125-9 and head south back to the N125. Turn right to return to Lagos.

WHERE TO EAT

In Sagres, there's A Tasca in the Praia da Mareta (▷ 293). Praia da Bordeira has Sítio do Rio, which serves great charcoal grills (▷ 291), and Praia de Monte has Clérigo the Casa de Pasto O Zé and the Snack Bar a Rede. You can choose from several beachside bars in Praia do Amado, while in Aljezur itself there's the Restaurante Ruth in Rua 25 de Abril.

WHEN TO GO

Both Sagres and Cabo de São Vicente are popular tourist stops in summer, so aim to arrive early in the day to avoid the crowds.

TIP

- **The sea is much colder here than it is along the southern Algarve and currents and tides also can be treacherous. Take particular care if bathing.**

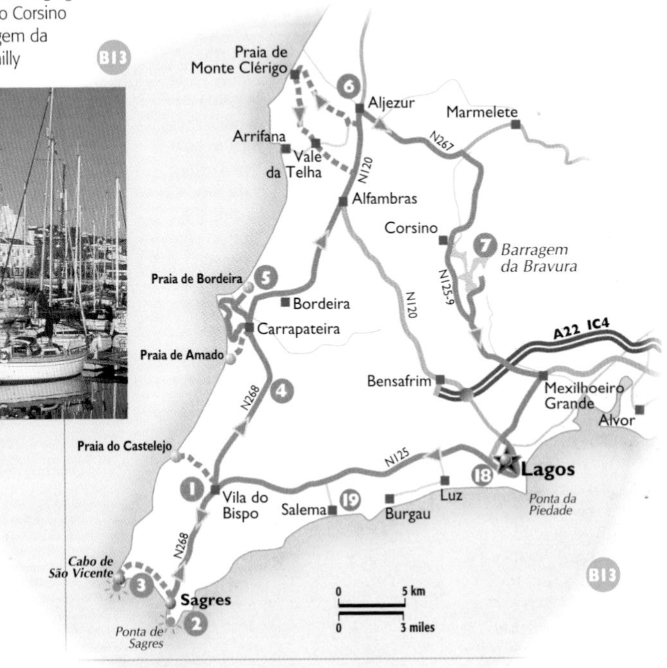

Above left: Lagos marina. Below: Looking up at hilltop Aljezur

18. WALK

THE CLIFFS OF LAGOS AND PRAIA DA LUZ

This invigorating clifftop walk encompasses a quintessential stretch of the western Algarve coastline. En route, you'll enjoy superb views of the coastal rock formations and the open Atlantic—and there's the bonus of escaping the worst of the crowds.

THE WALK

Distance: 6km (3.5 miles)
Allow: 2.5–3 hours
Start at: Lagos
End at: Praia da Luz

Start off on the riverside in Lagos (▷ 172), where the sweeping, palm-shaded Avenida dos Descobrimentos runs alongside the final reaches of the river Bensafrim.

Praça Dom Henrique, with its connotations of the great Age of Discoveries (look for the statues of Henry the Navigator and the explorer Gil Eanes nearby), is a good place from which to start. The waterfront is home to the market and marina, and you can look across the river to the Meia Praia, Lagos's long, sandy town beach.

Right: A statue of the boy-king Sebastian, Lagos. Below: The view down to Praia de Dona Ana, everyone's idea of beach perfection

Walk to the end of the promenade to the Forte da Ponta da Bandeira.

The 17th-century Forte da Ponta da Bandeira was built to guard the harbour entrance. Go inside the fort to enjoy the views; just below you is Praia da Batata, a sheltered, sandy cove.

Continue up the hill out of town until you reach the viewpoint, with its conspicuous stone monument.

The monument at the viewpoint commemorates São Gonçalo, a local fisherman's son who became a monk renowned for his sanctity. He is the patron saint of Lagos.

At the top of the hill look for a sign to the left marked 'Praia do Pinhão' and follow the path. It leads along the cliffs past tiny, sheltered Pinhão beach to Praia de Dona Ana.

Praia de Dona Ana is everything a beach in the Algarve should be: It has gently shelving sands and a good collection of the rock formations, sea stacks and caves so typical of this stretch of the coast. Inevitably, it attracts hordes of visitors and the clifftops have been developed with hotels, cafés and

apartment blocks. However, out of season, or late in the day, it's a real delight.

Cross the beach and the car parking area above it and make your way back up to the cliffs. There's a plethora of narrow tracks, but keep the sea on your left and you can't go wrong. The next cove is the Praia do Camilo, a classic beach that's often less crowded than some of the others along this stretch of coast. Continue to Ponte da Piedade.

Ponte da Piedade is a series of spectacular, red rock stacks rising from crystal-clear water and riddled with grottoes. In summer, local fishermen run trips to them from the foot of the cliffs. It's worth making a detour past the lighthouse for some wonderful coastal views.

Keep the sea on your left and continue along the cliffs, staying as close as possible to the sea to avoid the Porto de Mós resort development; at Praia de Porto de Mós the path drops right down to the sea. From here, follow the path steadily uphill for 40 minutes or so. You'll eventually reach an obelisk, at 109m (358ft) the highest point on the walk. Just past here, there's a gap in the bushes on the left. Go through the gap and scramble down the steep slope to a cobbled path that leads directly onto the beach at Praia da Luz.

Though development is increasing, Praia da Luz is an attractive, low-key resort with a pleasant promenade, a clutch of bars and restaurants, and a genuinely Portuguese heart.

To get back to Lagos, walk along the beach onto the promenade. Then head for the old fortress facing the parish church, from where there are regular buses (check the times in Lagos before you start out).

WHERE TO EAT

Praia da Luz has quite a few restaurants to choose from, but locals recommend the Restaurante Paraíso, which is open until midnight.

WHEN TO GO

This is a great walk for late afternoon when it's cooler. You may catch a fine sunset and you could have dinner in Praia da Luz before catching a bus or taking a taxi back to Lagos. It's also a superb winter walk.

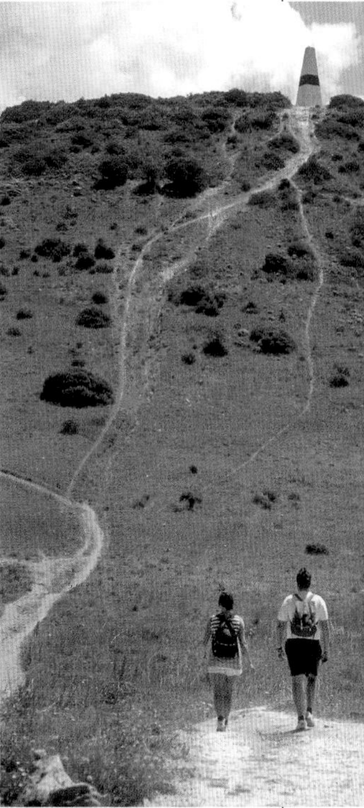

It's quite a stiff climb up to the obelisk outside Praia da Luz, but the view is well worth the effort

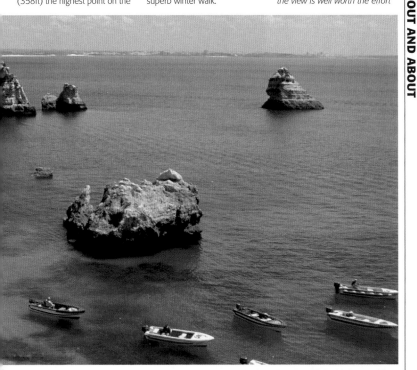

A COASTAL WALK IN THE WESTERN ALGARVE

This immensely varied walk takes in some great coastal scenery as well as wetlands rich in wildlife. If you fancy a swim, you can take a dip en route.

THE WALK

Distance: 8km (5 miles)
Allow: 2–3 hours
Start/end at: Boca do Rio beach
How to get there: Take the side road off N125, 14.5km (9 miles) west of Lagos; park at the beach

Walk inland to the river, cross the concrete bridge and then go back towards the sea.

Some large ruined sheds near the river mouth are reminders of the days when this was a celebrated tuna fishing coast—the sheds were used to store the cumbersome tuna nets. They were built on Roman foundations—the main Roman ruins are fenced off in the area around the sheds.

The large anchor and cannon nearby came from the French warship *L'Océan*, sent to the bottom of the sea by the British during the Battle of Lagos in 1759. The old wreck is now a popular dive site for trainee underwater archaeologists.

Just before the track reaches the sea, take the path leading uphill to the left. Turn right onto the wide track at the top. Follow this winding path until you come to the ruins of a 17th-century fortress, built on the orders of Dom Luís de Sousa, who was then the Governor of the Algarve. There are great coastal views from here.

Follow the line of the cliffs along any of the little paths that run left of the fort until you reach a large white house. Skirt this, and go down the track to the left of the garages. At the bottom, the route continues straight on and uphill.

Below: Look out for terrapins as you walk the marshy wetlands

The fortress ruins above Boca do Rio beach date from the 1600s

Cabanas Velha, an agreeably undeveloped beach, makes a good detour off the main route before the climb if you are ready for a rest, a drink, or even a quick swim.

Climb up to the cliff top, then head down until you meet another track coming in from the left. Turn left here and head uphill, climbing steadily and ignoring any turnings.

At the top you'll be rewarded with a superb view—on a clear day, you should be able to see right along the coast from Carvoeiro in the east to Sagres in the west.

Keep going along the cliff top for a short distance, then fork left through a stand of umbrella pines to an intersection with the old surfaced road that runs between Burgau and Salema. Turn left along the road, passing a restaurant on the right. Just past here, take the turning to the right (marked with hand-painted signs) and head downhill. The track bends right to an old

OUT AND ABOUT

farmhouse, but you should keep heading down through the almond and fig trees until you reach the wetland area at the bottom of the hill.

The marshy wetland next to the river was once used for rice growing. Today, however, the ever-increasing demand for water has increased its saltiness to the point where its agricultural use is impossible. The area is now a nature reserve, supporting an abundance of wildlife and a plethora of wildflowers, including superb wild euphorbia. Terrapins, otters and mongoose have been seen here, and there's excellent birdwatching to enjoy.

At the bottom of the hill, turn left. Cross the unsurfaced road and continue parallel with the river until you reach the bridge you crossed at the start of the walk.

WHERE TO EAT

Take a picnic with you or wait until you get back to Lagos, where you will find a wide range of eateries (▷ 292). The market in Lagos is a good place to pick up picnic supplies.

WHEN TO GO

In summer, avoid the middle of the day as there is no shade on the cliffs.

TIPS

- As the sun can be strong, take water with you, wear a hat and use sunscreen.
- *A Birdwatchers' Guide to Portugal and Madeira*, by H. Costa, C. C. Moore and G. Elias (Prion, 1997) is a useful book.

Above: There are fine views of beaches along the coast from the cliffs. Cabanas Velha is particularly attractive. Below: The wetlands

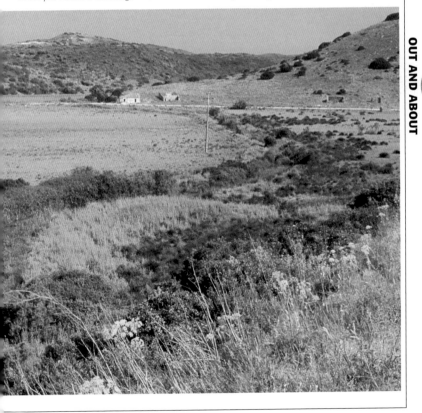

ORGANIZED TOURS

Many organized tours concentrate on villa/hotel sun-and-sea packages, but there is a great deal more to Portugal than simply its beaches, fine though these are. Whether you want to get to grips with Portugal's art and culture, eat and drink well, paint, play golf or tennis, or explore the heartland of the country, there will probably be a tour to suit you. Below are a few suggestions for specialized holidays, many of them led by experts in their fields.

Left: The old Alfama, Lisbon. Middle: Beyond Praia de Dona Ana. Right: The cliffs at Ponta da Piedade

You could start the search for something special by logging on to the two comprehensive official Portuguese websites:
www.portugalinsite.com
www.portugal.org

ART AND ARCHITECTURE

ACE Study Tours
Tel 01223 835055 (UK)
www.study-tours.org
A long-established charity that organizes guided art and architecture trips and makes donations to restoration projects throughout the world.

Martin Randall Travel Ltd
Tel 020 8742 3355 (UK)
www.martinrandall.com
A top-rated company specializing in themed art and cultural tours taken by leading academics; small groups and excellent accommodation.

GOLF

The two companies below are long-established specialists organizing custom-made golf packages and all-inclusive golfing holidays in the Algarve and around Lisbon.

The Algarve Golf Agency
Tel 08707 505450 (UK)
www.algarveagency.com/golf/home

Golf in the Sun
0845 600 3391 or 01327 350394 (UK)
www.golfinthesun.co.uk
www.premier.iberian.com

SAILING

Euro-Sail
Tel 01473 833001 (UK)
www.euro-sail.co.uk
A Faro-based British-run company that charters motorboats and yachts, and organizes independent and accompanied sailing holidays.

BICYCLING AND WALKING

Explore Worldwide
Tel 01252 760000 (UK)
www.exploreworldwide.com
Well-organized walking holidays for small groups in the Peneda-Gerês and the upper Douro valley.

Headwater's
Tel 01606 720099 (UK)
www.headwater-holidays.co.uk
Guided walking holidays in the Algarve, and walking tours in the Serra da Estrela and the Beiras.

Ramblers Holidays
Tel 01707 331133 (UK)
www.ramblersholidays.co.uk
Hiking holidays with an expert local guide based in two little-known rural areas: the Alentejo and the Parque Nacional da Peneda-Gerês.

US TOUR OPERATORS

Abercrombie and Kent
Tel 1-800/323-7308
www.abercrombiekent.com
Luxury tours with top-of-the-range accommodation and special features, such as private access and visits to museums, palaces and castles.

Abreu Tours
Tel 1-800/223-1580
www.abreu-tours.com
A company specializing in Portugal, which will customize holidays and organize *pousada* and *quinta* bookings.

Homeric Tours
Tel 1-800/223-1580
www.homerictours.com
Lisbon holidays and escorted tours to Portugal's main sights.

Magellan Tours
Tel 215/695-0330
www.magellantours.com
Portugal specialists offering escorted trips, fly-drive holidays, city breaks, golfing holidays and accommodation in *pousadas* and manor houses.

Maupintour
Tel 1-800/255-4266
www.maupintour,com
Escorted tours of Portugal, often including Spain as well.

Petrabax Tours
Tel 1-800/634-1188
Long-established Portugal specialists, who offer escorted tours, customized tours, and will organize fly-drive and accommodation bookings.

This chapter lists places to eat and stay by region and town.

Eating and Staying

EATING OUT IN PORTUGAL

The range of foods on offer reflects Portugal's history and culture, with the accent firmly on fresh, seasonal, local produce. The Moors, the Spanish and the British all left their mark on the country's food and drink, while the coast and great sea voyages of discovery produced a passion for fish and seafood, spices, and ingredients from across the globe. Cooking is intensely regional, with every area having its own special dishes.

Left to right: Seafood hot from the stove, saddle of lamb with artichokes and fresh grilled sardines

EATING

MEALS AND MEALTIMES

Pequeno-almoço (breakfast) is usually eaten between 8am and 9am by the Portuguese, often at a café or *pasteleria* (pastry shop), where some sort of cake or pastry is washed down by a cup of coffee. In remote areas you may still be served bread and soup for breakfast, or simply a hefty roll and a pat of butter.

Almoço (lunch) starts with bread, served with a selection of pâtés, olives, cheese and other titbits and perhaps soup. This is followed by a meat or fish dish, served with potatoes, vegetables and sometimes rice. Salad is rarely served, though you can ask for it as a side order. Puddings are generally sweet and simple

Jantar (dinner) normally starts around 7.30pm. Outside major cities and tourist resorts, it is not available much after 9.30pm; in rural areas it may well be served earlier.

Menus will sometimes advertise the *ementa turística*; this is not a tourist menu, but the set meal of the day. The price includes two courses plus beer or wine, and can be excellent value.

WHERE TO EAT AND WHAT TO EXPECT

The best and most typical food is often found in seemingly unpretentious eating establishments. These are the places to go to sample local dishes. Only the more expensive restaurants in larger cities and tourist areas take reservations. Book ahead in the peak season and at weekends.

- *Restaurantes* are straightforward restaurants, where you'll be served a two- or three-course meal. They're normally open from12am to 3pm for lunch and 7pm to 10pm for dinner. They may open longer in tourist areas or at peak season.
- A *casa de pasto* is an inexpensive, often family-run, local dining room, offering budget three-course meals, mainly at lunchtime only. They're excellent value for money.
- *Tascas* are small, inexpensive, family-run eateries. Expect huge portions of stews, grilled sardines, chicken, and bean soups.
- A *marisqueira* is a seafood restaurant, where both shellfish and fish are served. You can pick your own from the display, which will be cooked to order. Menu prices are in kilos, and will add up fast, so expect a fairly hefty bill.
- Lunch at a shared table in a *taberna* is a real Portuguese experience. Many serve a different regional dish daily. Service is fast and friendly.
- *Churrasqueiras* specialize in *frango no churrasco* (chargrilled chicken) with *batatas fritas* (fries), though they serve other grilled food too.
- *Cervejarias* primarily serve beer and snacks, and are open all day and late into the evening.
- *Pousadas,* the nationwide chain of deluxe hotels, all have restaurants serving regional food and wine, though standards vary.
- A *restaurante típico* serves regional food and wine and has, by law, to offer traditional entertainment and display local objects. Standards vary considerably, but it's worth looking at the menu.

LOCAL CUSTOMS

- Once you are seated, bread and nibbles will be placed on the table. These range from fish pâté and olives to cheese, *chouriço* (spicy sausage) and more elaborate dishes. You will be charged for what you eat (*couvert* on the bill).
- Smoking is the norm in all eating places.
- Most restaurants will have a TV playing.
- You may just get one knife and fork for the whole meal in smaller restaurants, so hang on to them between courses.
- It's quite acceptable to ask for a *meia dose*

(half-portion); Portuguese servings are large.

- If you share a table with people who are already eating, they may ask you *E servido?* (Have you been served?), meaning 'Would you like some of ours'? Just say *Não, muito obrigado* (No thank you)—it's just a way of saying 'Enjoy your meal'.

PAYING THE BILL

Ask for *la conta* (the bill) and check to see whether *serviço* (a service charge) has been included, as is more likely in more expensive restaurants. If not, it's customary to leave a 5–10 per cent tip.

SPECIAL REQUIREMENTS

Vegetarians may find eating out difficult, as even seemingly suitable soups, rice and bean dishes will be based on meat stock, or enlivened with small pieces of bacon or sausage. Even straightforward vegetable dishes may contain pork fat. If you eat fish there's no problem, but otherwise you may find there's little you can eat on the menu, except for cheese, an omelette or salad.

WHAT TO DRINK

- Coffee *(café)* in Portugal is excellent and inexpensive. It's served in cafés, *casas de chá* and

Left to right: Hot peppers, red and white wines, seafood, and an indulgent dessert

- Quite a few restaurants are cash only; check in advance to find out if they take credit cards *(Aceita cartões de crédito?)*.
- Many restaurants are closed all day Sunday, or on Sunday afternoon and evening.

CAFÉS

Cafés are open from early morning until late. Prices are generally higher if you sit down, so, if you just want a quick coffee, it's less expensive to drink it standing at the bar. Cafés also serve a wide variety of snacks, ranging from breakfast pastries to lunchtime specials, which can be anything from simple fare such as *prego no pão* (steak sandwich) to *pastéis de bacalhau* (salt-cod fishcakes).

TEA ROOMS

Casas de chá (tea rooms) serve a range of excellent teas, including herbal infusions, as well as coffee and a sometimes overwhelming range of sweet cakes and other indulgences. These are the places you need to go to when you are trying to track down *doces regional* or *doces conventuais*, the ultra-sweet sugar-and-egg-yolk confections that were originally made in the convents. Savoury snacks are also often served at lunchtime.

INTERNATIONAL CUISINE

Major Portuguese cities have French, Italian and other national restaurants, including a good selection serving South American—particularly Brazilian—food. Chinese restaurants also exist in larger towns and tourist resorts. As you would expect, the widest choice of international restaurants are to be found in Lisbon and Porto, and in places in the Algarve.

bars. The most popular varieties are *bica* or *café*, a short black espresso, and *café com leite* or *garoto*, coffee with hot milk.

- *Chá* (tea) is popular in Portugal and is normally served relatively weak without milk. If you like milk ask for a *chá com leite; chá com limão* is tea with a slice of lemon.
- Fruit juice can be *sumo de laranja fresca* (freshly squeezed orange juice), or one of the bottled varieties. Soft drink brands to look out for are Tri Naranjus and Sumol.
- *Cerveja* (beer) is widely drunk. The main brands are Sagres, popular in central and southern Portugal, and Super Bock, northern Portugal's favourite. Draft beer comes as *um imperial* (200ml/7fl oz), *um principe* (330ml/12fl oz) or *uma caneca* (500ml/18fl oz). The alcohol content is 5–6 per cent, depending on the brand.
- *Vinho da casa* (house wine) is usually good value, but it's worth paying more to sample some better wines. This is especially true as there is such a wide range to choose from, many of which are unavailable outside Portugal. The country is divided into eight wine regions; which region your wine comes from will be specified on the bottle. The DOC specification is a more specific guarantee of the provenance of the wine.
- Portugal's own spirit is *aguardente*, a variety of brandy. Types to look out for include *medronho*, made from the fruit of the strawberry tree, *aguardente de figo* (fig spirit) and *ginjinha* (cherry spirit).
- Port *(vinho do Porto)* makes a superb after-dinner drink; but don't miss the chance to try chilled *porto branco* (white port), not often available outside Portugal, as an aperitif. Madeira *(vinho da Madeira)* is also a delicious aperitif or after-dinner tipple.

MENU READER–PORTUGUESE FOOD AND DRINK

The best way to enjoy fine Portuguese cuisine is to venture off the tourist trail in favour of restaurants where the locals go. If you don't speak Portuguese this may seem a daunting prospect, but the knowledge of a few key words and names will help you track down regional dishes all over the country. Below is a menu reader to help you translate common words, get to grips with dishes and ingredients, and order the meals you are likely to see on a Portuguese menu.

Left to right: Ameijoas na cataplana, Queijo da serra *cheeses, and glasses of white and ruby port*

Courses and the Menu
Entradas e acepipes starters and hors d'oeuvres
Sopas soups
Peixes fish
Marisco e frutos do mar shell-fish and seafood
Aves e caça poultry and game
Carnes meat
Acompanhamento side dishes
Pratos completas complete dishes
Sobremesas e doces pudding, desserts
Fruta fruit
Lista de vinhos wine list
Por pessoa per person
2 pessoas dish for two people
Especialidades da casa special dish
Prato do dia dish of the day
Meia dose half-portion
Cozido boiled, stewed or poached
Assado roasted
Frito fried
Grelhado grilled
À casa in the house style
À moda da, a região in the regional style
Pão e manteiga bread and butter

Carnes Meat
Alheiras sausages
Bife steak
Borrego/cordeiro lamb
Cabrito kid
Carne de vaca beef
Carneiro mutton
Chouriços smoked sausages
Coelho rabbit
Cordoniz quail
Costeletas cutlets
Farinheiras pork-fat sausages
Fiambre cooked ham
Frango chicken
Javalí wild boar
Lebre hare
Morcelas blood sausage
Novilho veal
Pato duck
Peru turkey
Porco pork
Presunto air-dried cured ham
Toucinho bacon

Peixes Fish
Alabote halibut
Arenque/sável herring
Arinca haddock
Atum tuna
Bacalhau dried salted cod
Dourada bream/John Dory
Espardate swordfish
Linguado sole
Peixe-espada scabbard fish
Pescada whiting
Pescadinha whitebait
Pregado/rodovalho turbot
Raia ray
Robalo bass
Salmão salmon
Salmonete red mullet
Sardinha sardines
Solha flounder/plaice
Tamboril monkfish
Truta trout

Mariscos e Frutas do Mar
Seafood and Shellfish
Ameijoa clams
Anchova anchovies
Camarãos/gambas shrimps/prawns
Chocos cuttlefish
Enguia eel
Lagosta lobster
Lulas squid
Mexilhões mussels
Ostra oysters
Perceves barnacles
Polvo octopus
Sapateira crab
Vieira scallops

Hortaliças Vegetables
Abacate avocado pear
Abóbora pumpkin
Aipo celery
Alcachofra artichoke
Alface lettuce
Alho garlic
Arroz rice
Azeitona olives
Batata potato
Beringel aubergine/eggplant
Beterreba beetroot
Brúlos broccoli
Cebola onion
Cenoura carrot
Cogumelos mushroom
Corgete courgette/zucchini
Couve cabbage

Couve Galega Galician kale
Ervilhas peas
Espargo asparagus
Favas broad beans
Feijão beans
Feijão verde green beans
Grão de bico chickpeas
Lentilha lentils
Nabas turnip
Pepino cucumber
Pimento verde green pepper/capsicum
Figo fig
Framboesa raspberry
Laranja orange
Limão lemon
Maçã apple
Melão melon
Mirtilo blueberry
Morango strawberry
Pêra pear
Pêssego peach
Romã pomegranate
Salada de frutas fruit salad
Tâmaras dates
Feijoadas bean stew with lamb, seafood, pork or rabbit
Frango no Churrasco/Piri-piri charcoal-grilled chicken with chilli sauce
Polvo assado fried octopus
Sardinhas grilled sardines

Temperos Flavourings
Açúcar sugar
Alho garlic
Azeite olive oil
Caril curry

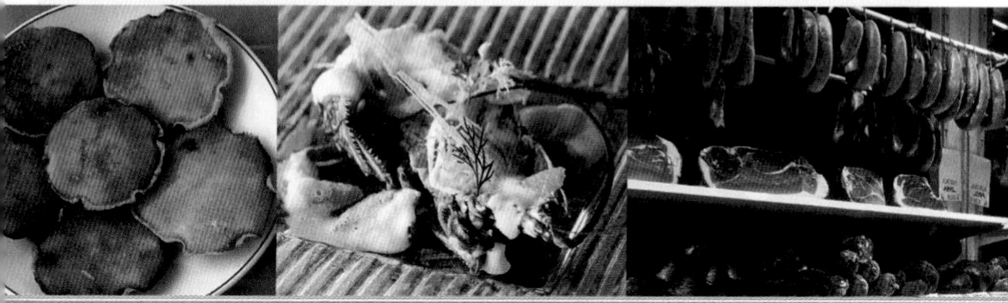

Left to right: Tasty cheese cakes from Serpa, lobster with citrus fruits, and hams and sausages

Pimento vermelho red pepper/capsicum
Piri-piri chilli
Porro leeks
Salada salad
Tomate tomato

Doces e Pastéis Sweets and Pastries
Arroz doce rice pudding
Bolos cakes
Doce jam
Doces de amêndoa marzipan sweets, often shaped as fruit
Doces conventuais sweet desserts, originally made by nuns
Doces de ovos egg-yolk sweets
Figos cheios dried figs with almonds
Fios de ovos sweetened egg-yolk threads
Gelado ice cream
Leite crème crème caramel
Mel honey
Ovos moles sweetened egg yolks
Pão-de-ló sponge cake
Pastéis de nata custard tarts
Queijadas sweet cheese tarts
Toucinho do céu sweet almond and cinnamon cake

Fruta Fruit
Ameixa plum
Ananás pineapple
Cereja cherry
Damasco/alperce apricot

Quiejo Cheese
Queijo de Azeitão cured sheep's-milk cheese from around Setúbal
Queijo de cabra fresh goat's-milk cheese
Queijo da ilha island cheese from the Azores
Quiejo do Monte sheep- and cow's-milk cheese from the Trás-os-Montes
Queijo de ovelha sheep's-milk cheese
Queijo da Serra/Estrela sheep's-milk cheese fermented with cardo thistles

Especialidades Special dishes
Açorda bread soup
Arroz complete rice dishes cooked with seafood, duck or goat
Bacalhau dried salt cod
Bolo Rei (King's Bread) spiced bread with dried and crystallized fruit eaten during Christmas season
Caldo verde Galician kale and potato soup
Canja de Galinha chicken broth with rice and lemon
Carne de porco à Alentejano pork cooked with clams
Cozida à Portuguesa stew with meat, offal, sausages, green vegetables, rice and potatoes
Empadas de galinha small chicken pies

Especiaries spices
Mostarda mustard
Pimenta pepper
Piri-piri chilli sauce
Sal salt
Vinagre vinegar

Bebidas Drinks
Água fresca water served chilled
Água mineral com/sem gás fizzy or still mineral water
Água natural water served at room temperature
Aguardente brandy-like spirit
Bica, café small, black coffee
Café coffee
Café descafeinado decaf-feinated coffee
Cerveja beer
Chá tea
Chá com leite tea with milk
Chá com limã tea with lemon
Garoto, café com leite long filter coffee with hot milk
Gelo ice
Sumo de laranja orange juice
Sumo de maçá apple juice
Vinho branco white wine
Vinho doce sweet wine
Vinho da Madeira fortified white wine from the island of Madeira
Vinho do Porto port
Vinho seco dry wine
Vinho tinto red wine
Vinho verde light white sparkling wine

THE MINHO AND TRÁS-OS-MONTES

This is the best part of Portugal to sample *caldo verde*, a potato and cabbage soup made with Galician kale that goes well with the region's *broa de Milho*, solid country corn bread. The latter appears at every meal, and is particularly good as an accompaniment to the region's pork dishes. Every scrap of the pig is used, so look out for *bicas* (spicy blood sausages), *cozido à Portuguesa* (boiled meats, sausage and vegetables) and *chouriço* (spicy sausage with mild chilli). *Presunto* (smoked ham) is particularly good in both the Minho and Trás-os-Montes; the country's finest is said to come from Chaves. Ham is even used in puddings—try *pudim do Abade de Priscos*, a spice-and-port-flavoured crème caramel that's spiked with bacon, in the Minho, or *toucinho do-céu* (bacon from heaven), an egg, pumpkin and cinnamon cake with a touch of ham that's traditional to Murça in the Trás-os-Montes.

PRICES AND SYMBOLS

The restaurants are listed alphabetically. The prices given are for a two-course lunch (L) and a three-course dinner (D) for two people, without drinks. The wine price is for the least expensive bottle.

For a key to the symbols, ▷ 2.

BARCELOS

PEDRA FURADA

Lugar da Rua Nova, Pedra Furada, Barcelos
Tel 252 951 144

South of Barcelos in the village of Pedra Furada, this rustic restaurant serves a vast range of regional Minho dishes. For the more daring, there are the famous river Minho lampreys when in season, or the undisputed national favourite, *cozido à Portuguesa*, a selection of boiled meats, sausages and vegetables served in their own broth. For the more faint-hearted, there is succulent roasted pork or kid.

Tue–Sun 12–3, 7–10, Mon 12–3 L €24, D €35, Wine €5 Take N306 south from Barcelos to Pedra Furada

BRAGA

ABADE DE PRISCOS

Praça Mouzinho de Albuquerque 7, Campo Novo, Braga
Tel 253 276 650

The restaurant serves not just regional food, but also dishes from farther afield, such as prawn or squid curry, Azorean beef, *galinha mourisca* (a chicken dish dating back to Moorish times seasoned with cinnamon), and rabbit with savoury herbs. To finish, try the region's most famous dessert: a sticky milk pudding made with eggs, lemon and cinnamon called *abade de Priscos* in honour of the gourmet cleric after whom the place is named. Credit cards are not accepted.

Tue–Sat 12–3, 7.30–10, Mon 7.30–10. Closed last 2 weeks Jun, 1st week Aug L €30, D €40, Wine €9

CAFÉ VIANNA

Praça da República, Braga
Tel 253 619 233

A good place for a light snack, this art nouveau café in the heart of town serves excellent coffee and irresistible savoury pastries and cakes. Try a *prego* (fine slices of beef inside a bread roll) or an *empada de galinha* (small chicken pie). Sweet treats include *charutos de chila* (pastry tubes filled with sweet pumpkin), or *rabanadas* (cinnamon French toast). If Vianna is full, try the Astória next door. Both are great places to people-watch.

Daily 9–7 Light snack and drink approx. €5 per person

CASA DAS ARTES

Rua Costa Gomes 353, Real, Braga
Tel 253 622 023

Mixing the pleasures of food with the exhibition of art and strange objects, this is a great option for late-night diners. Rustic, with dark-wood dressers and long, trestle-style tables, the Casa das Artes focuses on game dishes when in season. Year-long favourites include *rojões* (casseroled pieces of pork, often seasoned with garlic and bay leaves). Finish with *abade de Priscos*, the local egg-and-milk pudding. There is an attractive terrace for outside dining, weather permitting.

Mon–Sat 12–3.30, 7.30–12 L €30, D €40, Wine €7.50 Valet parking Take EN201 northwest out of Braga towards Ponte de Lima, following signs to Real. In Real the restaurant is signed

SAMEIRO

Lugar de Sameiro, Braga
Tel 253 675 114

Right by the Santuário de Sameiro and with fantastic views is this old-fashioned dining room, which has been serving meals for more than 90 years and is known for its excellent salt-cod dishes. Try the delicious *bacalhau à Sameiro* (cod steak fried with onions and potato) or *bacalhau com natas* (cod with cream). Roast beef and duck with rice are two great meat options, and the house wine, a white *vinho verde*, is excellent; it comes by the pitcher.

Tue–Sun 12–3, 7–10. Closed last week in Oct L €24, D €30, Wine €4 a glass Take EN309 southeast out of Braga following signs to Sameiro for about 10km (6 miles). Restaurant is next to the Santuario de Sameiro

BRAGANÇA

LÁ EM CASA

Rua Marquês do Pombal 7, Bragança
Tel 273 322 111

This congenial dining room in a townhouse in the heart of Bragança showcases Trás-os-Montes cooking. A selection of local cheeses, sausage meats, and garlic and olive oil soup make tasty starters. For mains, choose from *arroz de polvo* (rice with octopus), roasted

salt cod stuffed with air-cured ham, trout with ham, rabbit, partridge and wild boar. Apple or pumpkin tart make a good pudding.
Daily 12–4, 7–11
L €25, D €34, Wine €6.50

REAL FEITORIA
Quinta Braguinha, Lote A R/C, Bragança
Tel 273 323 050
The cuisine here has Transmontana roots, presented with an innovative twist that has won the restaurant many awards. Well-known regional delicacies appear on the menu: excellent cod dishes, beef stuffed with air-cured ham and, when in season, conger eel Bragança style. There are also some inventive suggestions, such as onion au gratin soup or mushroom stew. The tables are laid with linen and contemporary designer tableware, and the lavatories are luxurious.
Mon–Sat 12–3, 7–10.30 L €24, D €30, Wine €8 Rua Dr. Abílio Vas Dias, to the right of the tourist office, leads north to Quinta Braguinha

SOLAR BRAGANÇANO
Praça da Sé 34, Bragança
Tel 273 323 875

This 18th-century manor house in the middle of town has two spacious dining rooms and a fine garden terrace. Gentle classical music and elegant tableware give a home-from-home feel. The menu is a tribute to the regional cuisine with a strong emphasis on game. Try chestnut soup, braised wild boar with cabbage and fried apple, pheasant with chestnuts, or partridge with grapes. The fixed-price menu is good value.
Daily 12–3.30, 6.30–11. Closed Mon in winter L €24, D €40, Wine €8; three-course fixed-price meal €12.50 per person inc. a bottle of wine

CHAVES

ADEGA FAUSTINO
Travessa do Olival, Chaves
Tel 276 322 142
This no-frills restaurant is a fun place to come for an inexpensive but cracking meal. Rustic tables with paper tablecloths and somewhat uncomfortable wooden stools make it seem a little sparse and impersonal, but the menu, with little egg tarts, air-cured ham, home-made sausages, octopus and onion vinaigrette, stewed pork morsels, salt cod and so on, is great. The local red wine comes straight out of the barrels that line the walls.
Mon–Sat 10am–midnight L€16, D€20, Wine €4

GUIMARÃES

FLORÊNCIO
Madre de Deus, Guimarães
Tel 253 415 820
From ancient eatery to café to restaurant, Florêncio has transformed itself over the years, but the old wood-burning oven still rules the roost. The numerous starters could form a meal in themselves, but the roasts, thanks to the long hours spent in the famous oven, are superb. Try *bacalhau*, octopus, lamb, kid, or beef with *leite creme* (crème brûlée) to finish. The *vinho verdes* are well worth trying.
Daily 12–11 L€30, D€40, Wine €6 Head north out of Guimarães to São Torcato. The restaurant is about 2km (1.5 miles) out of Guimarães on the left, next to a small chapel

SÃO GIÃO
Avenida Comendador Joaquim, Almeida de Freitas, Moreira de Cónegos, Lugar das Vinhas, Guimarães
Tel 253 561 853
Considered by one national paper to be the best restaurant in the Minho, this dining room is modern with elegant lines and simple furnishings. Long, low windows give uninterrupted views over the next-door vineyard. The menu is vast, its roots firmly fixed in traditional Minho cuisine. There are spectacular meat, game and fish dishes, a tempting dessert trolley, fine cheeses and a first-rate wine list.
Tue–Sat 12–3.30, 7.30–10.30, Sun 12–3.30 L€40, D€50, Wine €10 Take the N105 south towards Santo Tirso. Moreira de Cónegos is on this road and the restaurant is next to the Moreirense Stadium

SOLAR DO ARCO
Rua Santa Maria 48–50, Guimarães
Tel 253 513 072
Solar do Arco is off the Praça de Santiago just before the stone arch in one of the most picturesque streets in town. It is popular with tourists, but also has a firm following among locals—so don't be put off by the multilingual menus. Opt for the roasted salt cod, which comes in gargantuan portions, or *picanha* (Brazilian-style grilled beef), served with black beans and spiced with *chouriço* sausage.
Mon–Sat 12–3, 7–11, Sun 12–3
L€20, D€40, Wine €6

MIRANDA DO DOURO

CAPA D'HONRAS
Travessa do Castelo 1, Miranda do Douro
Tel 273 432 699
This typical village house has a modern and bright interior. The regional food it serves is not the least expensive in town, but the quality is good. The menu leans heavily towards roasted and stewed meat dishes. The friendly owners take pride in their locally prized, home-made sausages and cured meats, produced from their own free-range pigs. There are some great salt-cod options too.
Daily 12–3, 7–10 L €25, D €30, Wine €4 Enter the old walled town and take the first right. Restaurant is on the right

PONTE DE LIMA

CARVALHEIRA
Arcozelo, Ponte de Lima
Tel 258 742 316
A rustic dining room with an open log-burning fire in winter, Carvalheira is somewhat more sophisticated than many and offers the best in Minho cooking. Varied starters, such as broad beans with *chouriço*, *pataniscas* (cod fritters) and octopus vinaigrette, can be followed by *bacalhau com broa* (salt cod with maize bread), roast pork loin, or duck with rice. Service is attentive and the wine list is of good quality.
Tue–Sun 12–3, 7.15–10
L €30, D €40, Wine €12 In Ponte de Lima cross the new bridge and follow signs to Arcos de Valdevez.

At the roundabout turn right. Restaurant is 700m (770 yards) past traffic lights on the right

VIANA DO CASTELO

CAMELO DA AMPÚLIA
Rua do Facho 14, Lj 3 (shop No. 3), Ampúlia, Viana do Castelo
Tel 253 987 600
An offshoot of the highly respected Restaurante Camelo, up the river in Santa Maria de Portuzelo (tel 258 839 090, closed Mon), Camelo da Ampúlia has the advantage of a fine sea view from its panoramic windows. Interiors in both mix traditional materials with modern, and the cuisine is regional and of exceptional quality. *Petiscos* (tapas), grilled or baked fish and roasted meats are all excellent, as is the *leite creme* (crème brûlée) to finish.
Tue–Sun 12–3, 7–10.30 L €30, D €40, Wine €7 From Viana take the IC1 towards São Ampúlia/Porto. Exit at São Ampúlia; the restaurant is next to the windmills

VILA REAL

PASOS PERDIDOS
Vilarinho de Samardã, Vila Real
Tel 259 347 322
This gently lit restaurant is decorated with warm yellows, deep blues and terracotta, its tables dressed with rough linen cloths. Despite a change of management, the current owners share the vision of the previous proprietors, which was to promote traditional dishes, such as *porco no borralho* (grilled pork served with black-eyed beans and cabbage or with rice and chestnuts) and cod with maize bread.
Wed–Mon 12–2.30, 7–10.30 L €18, D €30, Wine €4.75 Take N2 north out of town towards Chaves. After 10 km (6 miles) turn off to Vilarinho de Samardã. The restaurant is signed at the far end of the village

EATING

PORTO AND THE DOURO

Porto has a great choice of restaurants, serving everything from traditional cuisine to contemporary cooking with a twist. The city's most famous staple is tripe, which is why its natives are affectionately dubbed *triperios* (tripe eaters) by other Portuguese. It's prepared in a number of ways, with *tripas à moda do Porto*, a slow-cooked dish of tripe, sausage, pigs' trotters, beans and vegetables, heading the list. Definitely one for the stronger stomach.

PRICES AND SYMBOLS

The restaurants are listed alphabetically. The prices given are for a two-course lunch (L) and a three-course dinner (D) for two people, without drinks. The wine price is for the least expensive bottle.

For a key to the symbols, ▷ 2.

AMARANTE

TASQUINHA DA PONTE
Rua 31 de Janeiro, Amarante
Tel 255 433 715

Across the bridge from the church, the Tasquinha has a rustic interior with white ceramic wine mugs hanging on the walls and lots of wood. It caters not so much for visitors, but for locals in search of hearty, regional food, and serves substantial amounts of authentic dishes that may be unsophisticated but are full of flavour. The menu lists all the regular choices, as well as several unidentifiable pork-based dishes for the intrepid.
Daily 9am–midnight L €15, D €20, Wine €3.50

PORTO

For all restaurants in Foz do Douro, either take bus 1 or tram 1E from the middle of the city, or a taxi, which will cost approximately €10.

ADEGA VILA MEÃ
Rua dos Clérigos 62, Porto
Tel 222 082 967
This not-to-be-missed *adega* (wine cellar) near the famous Torre dos Clérigos, serves unadorned regional food in massive portions *a moda antiga* (as in the old days). Ask for a quarter-portion if you are on your own—that's how big they are! Each day of the week has its special dish: salt-cod fritters on Mondays, roast octopus on Tuesdays, *cozido à Portuguesa* (boiled meats and vegetables) on Thursdays, roast veal on Fridays and roast kid on Saturday. Credit cards are not accepted.
Mon–Sat 12–3, 7–11 L €20, D €30, Wine €6

BULL AND BEAR
Avenida da Boavista 3431, Boavista, Porto
Tel 226 107 669
Acclaimed in the national press, this has become one of Porto's most popular restaurants. Its modern wood and stone interior is elegant, and its menu—a fusion of Portuguese tradition and international innovation—changes with the seasons. There is foie gras terrine served with 10-year-old port, roe and beer blinis, hake in olives and maize bread, duck and truffle pie, and more than 400 wines to choose from. The service is excellent.
Mon–Fri 12.30–3, 8–12, Sat 8–12 L €46, D €60, Wine €10 Bus 3 from Avenida da Liberdade

CAFÉ MAJESTIC
Rua de Santa Catarina 112, Porto
Tel 222 003 887
www.alvo.com/majestic/index.htm
At its opening in 1921, this luxurious art nouveau coffee house attracted intellectuals and politicians. Complete with stucco cherubs, magnificent chandeliers, leather upholstery,

Indian marble floors and huge Antwerp mirrors, the Majestic was meticulously restored to its former glory in the 1990s. Now probably the most beautiful café in the country, it is an ideal place to stop for a coffee and a pastry, although the liveried waiters also serve light meals at lunchtime, including salads and a dish of the day.

Mon–Sat 9.30am–midnight
Light snack and drink €9 per person

CAFEÍNA
Rua Padrão 100, Foz do Douro, Porto
Tel 226 108 059
At weekends you should book in advance at this landmark restaurant with its signature dark green walls and large, modern art panels. As well as being known for its fine steaks served with a variety of sauces, there are also French and Italian influences, as seen in the foie gras with bacon and mushroom, truffle tagliolini and grilled bream with risotto. The desserts include a delicious pear and almond tart with vanilla ice cream.
Daily 12.30pm–1.30am L €40, D €60, Wine €12

CAFETARIA DA FUNDAÇÃO DE SERRALVES
Rua Dom João de Castro 210, Foz do Douro, Porto
Tel 226 156 500
There is no need to pay the museum entry charge to eat in this lovely café-cum-restaurant, which is a masterpiece of art deco architecture. The Sunday buffet is good value, with hot and cold options and a fine spread of desserts, including the famous *doces conventuais*.
May–end Sep Tue–Thu 10–7, Fri–Sat 10–10, Sun 10–8; Oct–end Apr Tue–Fri 10–7, Sat–Sun 10–8 L €24, D €50, Wine €14 Bus 3, 18, 19, 21, 35, 78 from middle of city

CASA AGRÍCOLA
Rua do Bom Sucesso 241–243, Porto
Tel 226 053 350
Inside an original 18th-century building (onto which the Bom Sucesso shopping mall has been added), the first-floor Casa Agrícola, with its ox-blood walls and wooden floors, is an elegant establishment. It has a choice of grilled fish, meats (including duck and succulent peppered steaks) and, most unusually for Portugal, a vegetarian menu. For dessert, try the port pudding with mango ice cream.
Mon–Sat 12–3, 8–12 L €36, D €47, Wine €12

O COMERCIAL
Rua Ferreira Borges, Palácio da Bolsa, Porto
Tel 223 322 019
One of the city's classic restaurants is inside the impressive stock exchange building down towards the Ribeira. Here, monumental granite pillars and fine old tiles grace the floors and walls. Chestnut and onion soup, *pataniscas de bacalhau* (cod and potato fritters) and stuffed grilled aubergine (eggplant) make great starters, to be followed by salt cod with broad beans and sweet potato, sautéed monkfish with mustard sauce and irresistible chocolate fondue with fresh fruits. The wine list is extensive.
Mon–Thu 12–2.30, 8–10.30, Fri 12–2.30, 8–11.30, Sat 8–11.30 L €30, D €40, Wine €5

COZINHA DO MANEL
Rua Heroísmo 215, Porto
Tel 225 363 388
Rustic, with tiles and beamed ceilings, this is a good place to experience genuine Porto cuisine. Start with tasty home-made sausages, such as *salpicão* and roasted *morçela* (blood sausage), then move on to one of the dishes of the day. Wednesdays and Saturdays are tripe days, served Porto style, Tuesday is duck with rice, Thursday *cozido* (boiled meats and vegetables), and Fridays salt cod with maize bread. For dessert, try *rabanadas* (cinnamon French toast).
Mon–Sat 12.30–3, 7.30–10
L €40, D €46, Wine €8

DOM TONHO
Cais da Ribeira 13–15, Ribeira, Porto
Tel 222 004 307

The atmospheric granite interior of this converted salt-cod warehouse is complemented by sharp white ceilings and large windows looking out onto the river Douro. Recipes are traditional, heavy and full of flavour; they include beef or wild boar roasted in a wood-burning oven, baked octopus and salt-cod fritters. In addition to the regular menu, there are always two daily specials, one meat, the other fish.
Daily 12.30–2.45, 7.30–11.15
L €48, D €64, Wine €12

ESCONDIDINHO
Rua Pasos Manuel 144, Porto
Tel 222 001 079
Escondidinho serves perfectly prepared French food in a great country house-style setting. Here you can try all manner of fish grilled, cooked in wine or in soup. Be sure to leave room for dessert, such as the *folhada de maçã* (apple tart).
Mon–Sat 12–2, 8–10.30

FILHA DA MÃE PRETA
Cais da Ribeira 40, Ribeira, Porto
Tel 222 086 066
Of the traditional Ribeira eateries, Filha de Mãe Preta is one of the best loved. Established more than 30 years ago and run by the same friendly family ever since, it serves good-quality home cooking to a loyal clientele. For those brave enough, there is the obligatory tripe; for others, there are fillets of bream and tender roast beef or pork loin. A lavish dessert made with dried and fresh fruits and ice cream is aptly named 'end of the world.'
Mon–Sat 12–3, 6.30–10 L €24, D €30, Wine €8

FOZ VELHA
Esplanada do Castelo, Foz do Douro, Porto
Tel 226 154 178

This is one of Porto's newest and hippest restaurants. Frequented by the young affluent crowd, the period dining room has rough wooden floors, enhanced by deep purple walls and fuchsia lamps. The cuisine is avant-garde. Cold melon, mint and almond soup; escalopes with foie gras and cherries; sautéed octopus on a bed of sweet potato; and fresh raspberries with cream and almond crunchies give an idea of what you can expect on the menu.
Thu–Mon 12.30–3, 7.30–11, Fri–Sat 12.30–3, 7.30–midnight, Wed 7.30–11
L €50, D €60, Wine €10

GARDEN'S
Beco das Carreiras 65, Parque da Cidade, Aldoar, Porto
Tel 226 151 609
For a peaceful retreat in the heart of the city, head for this restored *quinta* in the Parque da Cidade. Here you can sample fried camembert, steamed skate with lemon and capers, and hot crêpes with fresh cheese and raspberry coulis while sitting on cool granite verandas overlooking the park. Alternatively, stay inside, where the traditional dining room with its shuttered windows and stone frames is given a contemporary twist with vivid hues and matching chairs.
Mon–Sat 12.30–3, 9–12 L €50, D €60, Wine €11 Bus 52 from Avenida dos Aliados

HOMEN DO LEME
Avenida de Montevideu, Foz do Douro, Porto
Tel 226 181 847
Protected from the occasional rough seas by a large beach, the open terraces at Homen do Leme are also protected from the wind by glass panels. The simple modern interior is warmed by an open fire. Come here for a quick drink and snack, or for a full meal of pâté, prawn crêpes, freshly grilled fish, mango mousse and orange cake, and enjoy the stunning sunsets.
Daily midday–2am
L €25, D €50, W €10
On the Homen do Leme beach, below the statue *Fisherman at the Helm*, on the seaside promenade

MUSEU DOS PRESUNTOS
Rua Padre Luís Cabral 1070, Foz do Douro, Porto
Tel 226 106 965
On a narrow street in the old part of Foz, this rustic restaurant is named after the *presuntos* (air-cured hams) that hang from its walls. You can expect the usual regional dishes, such as beef with mushrooms and monkfish with rice, but you might prefer one of the long list of starters (home-made sausages, black-eyed bean vinaigrette, and, of course, air-cured ham). It is a good place for late meals as it serves into the early hours. Credit cards are not accepted.
Tue–Sun 8pm–4am D €30, Wine €4

ORIENTAL
Rua do Padrão 103, Foz do Douro, Porto
Tel 226 177 339
The food at the Oriental is mainly Japanese and Thai with Indian and Chinese influences. Tofu soup, sushi and sashimi, and caramelized tiger prawns with sweet and sour sauce are all worth trying, as is the warm chocolate cake with ice cream (not strictly Asian but divine nevertheless). The restaurant can also prepare food for you to take out.
Daily 12.30–3.30, 7.30–1.30
L €40, D €50, Wine €10

PEIXES E COMPANHIA
Rua do Ouro 133–135, Foz do Douro, Porto
Tel 226 185 655
For a great selection of fresh fish, try Peixes e Companhia. Fresh bream, bass, mullet and monkfish come grilled, baked or boiled, accompanied by sautéed vegetables and *batatas a murro* (literally, 'bashed potatoes'). Finish with fresh tropical fruit, almond tart or, if you dare, chocolate *brigadeiros*. The first-floor position has great views of the river and out to sea.
Mon–Sat 12–3.30, 7.30–11.30
L €30, D €40, Wine €10

PRAIA DA LUZ
Rua Coronel Raul Peres, Foz do Douro, Porto
Tel 226 173 234
This is undoubtedly one of the best restaurants along the seafront, attracting a young and beautiful crowd. For cooler days there is a chic, glassed-in dining room, but the best spot is outside on the deck, looking out over the rocks to the sea. At meal times a variety of pasta dishes and more traditional options, such as baked salt cod, are available, while light snacks are served all day.
Daily 9am–2am L €20, D €40, Wine €12.50

RESTAURANTE CAFETARIA DA FUNDAÇÁO DE SERRALVES
Rua Dom João de Castro 210, Foz do Douro, Porto
Tel 226 156 500
Furniture designed by Siza Vieira and amazing views of the park through massive plate-glass windows make this a privileged spot. The Sunday buffet is particularly good, with hot and cold options and a fine selection of puddings, including the famous *doces conventuais* (egg-based convent desserts).
Tue–Sat noon–7, 8–midnight
L €24, D €50, Wine €14

SURIBACHI
Rua do Bonfim 134–140, Porto
Tel 225 106 700
This flower-filled restaurant, near the central 24 de Agosto Stadium, is one of the few vegetarian eateries in this meat-mad city. Spread over two floors, it is always filled with the relaxing sound of running water, thanks to a small waterfall and fish-filled pond. It is also non-smoking throughout. Macrobiotic meals are served throughout the day and into the evening. Try the seaweed soup or one of the tofu dishes. For fish-eaters there is a great mixed seafood stew.
Mon–Sat 9am–10pm L €12, D €20, Wine €6

THE BEIRAS

Some of the region's finest foods come from the Serra da Estrela, home of Portugal's most famous cheese, *Queijo da Estrela*. Look out, too, for *requeijão*, a ricotta-style cheese that's eaten with local honey and cinnamon. Goat and lamb turn up as *chanfana* (stews) or roasted, and you should certainly not miss the chance to try *leitão assado* (roast suckling pig). Aveiro and the other western coastal towns are noted for *enguias* (eels).

PRICES AND SYMBOLS

The restaurants are listed alphabetically. The prices given are for a two-course lunch (L) and a three-course dinner (D) for two people, without drinks. The wine price is for the least expensive bottle.

For a key to the symbols, ▷ 2.

AVEIRO

SALPOENTE

Canal de São Roque 83, Aveiro
Tel 234 382 674

On the ground floor is a display of regional costumes and salt-gathering implements, while upstairs there are good views of the famous salt flats. The menu concentrates on fish and seafood cooked in copper *cataplanas* and (when in season) the local eels.

Mon–Sat 12–2.30, 7.30–10.30
L €25, D €30, Wine €8

A TASCA DO CONFRADE

Rua dos Marnotos 34, Aveiro
Tel 234 386 381

This restaurant, next to the Rossio fish market, has a true Beiras theme, with wine barrels on the counter, typical northern terracotta crockery on the tables and slightly comic regionally costumed mannequins. The wood-panelled bar and floors complement the arched brown-and-white tile panels depicting local daily activities. The menu consists of *petiscos* (tapas), local dishes and a daily set menu. Try baked octopus, monkfish with rice and prawns, or roast kid.

Tue–Sun 12.30–3, 7.30–11
L €30, D €36, Wine €8 Next to the fish market in the Rossio

COIMBRA

ARCADAS DA CAPELA

Hotel Quinta das Lágrimas, Rua António Augusto Gonçalces, Santa Clara, Coimbra
Tel 239 802 380

The restaurant in this famous palace-hotel combines refined surroundings with excellent service. Wooden floors, warm tones and fine tableware complement the quality international cuisine. Try ravioli stuffed with lobster, goat's cheese with saffron sauce or venison medallions with roast potatoes. For puddings, there's an excellent tangerine tart with mandarin and chocolate sauce.

Tue–Sat 7.30–10 D €90, Wine €15 Cross the Santa Clara bridge, turning left then right at the sign

CAFÉ SANTA CRUZ

Praça 8 de Maio, Coimbra
Tel 239 833 617

This is the most famous and imposing coffee house in town. Housed in a 15th- to 16th-century chapel next to the cathedral, it has a heavy, dark-wood panelled interior with old mirrors. A constant flow of students, professors and visitors passes through its Manueline doorway—there's no better place to stop for a coffee and snack.

Summer Mon–Sat 8am–1.30am; rest of year Mon–Sat 8am–11.30pm
Drink and snack €5 per person

A TABERNA

Rua dos Combatentes da Grande Guerra 86, Coimbra
Tel 239 716 265

All the food in this small restaurant comes out of the wood-burning oven or off the charcoal grill—both of which are in full view. The home-baked bread is a treat, as is the chargrilled octopus served with spring greens and *batatas a murro* ('bashed' potatoes). The roast kid and casseroled beef are also much praised. To finish, there is *leite creme* (crème brûlée) or crêpes.

Sun–Fri 12.30–3, 7.30–10.30
L €34, D €44, W €8 Between the university and the football stadium, southeast of the heart of the city

ZÉ CARIOCA RESTAURANTE

Avenida Sá de Bandeira 89, Coimbra
Tel 239 835 450
www.zecarioca.pt.vu

For a break from Portuguese cooking, try this Brazilian restaurant between the Praça da República and the Avenida shopping mall. They recommend fillets of grouper with a prawn sauce, *rodizio de picanha (*cuts of grilled meat) and *feijoada à Brasileira* (typical black-bean stew). Live music is played nightly.

Mon–Sat 12–3, 7–10.30 L €25, D €38, Wine €6

FIGUEIRA DA FOZ

CAÇAROLA

Rua Cândido dos Reis 65, Figueira da Foz
Tel 233 424 861

In the road running along the southern side of the impossible-to-miss casino building, this restaurant may not win any interior decorating prizes with its mix of nautical memorabilia and plastic plants, but the food is superb. It specializes in fish and seafood, all of which is simply prepared to preserve its natural flavour.

Daily 10am–3.30am L €20, D €30, Wine €5.50

GUARDA

O BULE

Rua Dom Miguel de Alarcão 25–27, Guarda
Tel 271 214 392

Up from the cathedral square, these tea rooms decorated in warm tones, with wood panelling and framed engravings, are just right for morning coffee or afternoon tea. It's hard to resist the counter full

of freshly made cakes and local delicacies, such as *pão lô de ovar* (light sponge made with eggs). Credit cards are not accepted.
Daily 8–8 Coffee and cake €2.50 per person

RESTAURANTE BELO HORIZONTE
Largo de São Vicente 2, Guarda
Tel 271 211 454
For true northern cooking, come to the Belo Horizonte, on the corner down from the cathedral square, and with an austere stone façade and white linen curtains in the door. Here, friendly staff will serve you any number of regional dishes, including roasted, grilled and stewed meats and fresh fish. The restaurant's pièce de résistance, though, is *bucho recheado*, a huge homemade sausage big enough for four.
Sun–Fri 12.30–2.30, 7.30–10
L €20, D €30, Wine €6

RESTAURANTE CAFÉ MONTENEVE
Praça Luis de Camões 24, Coimbra
Tel 271 212 799
In front of the cathedral, inside a prominent *casa senhorial* (manor house), this establishment serves snacks and full meals. Climb the exterior granite stairs into the modern café, with light wood chairs and old black-and-white pictures of Guarda, for sandwiches and pastries. For more formal service and a full meal, opt for the restaurant at the back. There, you can choose from various meat dishes, salt cod, or, when available, grilled squid.
Café: Tue–Sun 9am–11pm; Restaurant: Tue–Sun 12–3, 7–10
Café: snack with drink €5 per person. Restaurant: L €15, D €25, Wine €4

LAMEGO

O LAMPIÃO
Rua Direita 30, Lamego
Tel 254 612 550
In the heart of town behind the cathedral, the Lampião is small and in no way sophisticated. However, thanks to its generous portions of simple yet high-quality country food, it is popular with the locals. On Sundays the house special is oven-roasted kid with potatoes. During the week choose from *arroz de pato* (duck with rice), roast lamb or beef, salt-cod with cream sauce, or, when in season, fresh trout or river lampreys. Credit cards are not accepted.
Sun–Fri 12.30–2.30, 7.30–10
L €20, D €34, Wine €5

TURISERRA
Serra das Meadas, Lamego
Tel 254 609 100
Huge panoramic windows give this restaurant an outstanding view of the river Douro, Régua and the *serra*. Roast kid and *bacalhau à Turiserra* (salt cod) are always popular, but be sure to go with a good appetite or order half-portions as servings are large. Alternatively, stick with the starters, which are a meal in themselves—especially good are the croquettes and *bolinhos de bacalhau* (salt cod and potato fritters). It is best to avoid weekends, when the restaurant can be overwhelmed by wedding parties.
Daily 12–3, 7–10 L €40, D €46, Wine €15 From the municipal council buildings in Lamego, follow signs to Serra das Meadas. Turiserra is about 6km (4 miles) out of town on the left

SORTELHA

RESTAURANTE DOM SANCHO I
Largo do Corvo, Sortelha
Tel 271 388 267
The fortified hamlet of Sortelha, perched on its massive boulders, is a fantastic place, and a meal at Dom Sancho will serve to add to the experience. The restaurant is up a flight of stone steps in one of the tiny village houses, its bare granite walls softened by low beamed ceilings and rustic cabinets. The menu is divided into 'stewed' (lamb and kid), 'grilled' (cod, lamb or pork) or 'game' (hare, boar, venison). Regional desserts are displayed on the dresser. Credit cards are not accepted.
Wed–Sun 12.30–3, 7–9, Mon 12.30–3 L €25, D €45, Wine €6
Go through the main gateway and the restaurant is on the right

VISEU

CLUBE DE CAÇADORES
Muna, Lordosa, Viseu
Tel 232 450 401
As its name suggests, this restaurant is attached to a hunting/shooting club next to the practice range. Its three dining rooms each have their own open hearth, and walls are lined with fine bottles of red wine and—as suits the nature of the club—several trophies lovingly preserved by local taxidermists. The game theme continues, with rabbit salad, hare and rice, wild duck with pine nuts and partridge with onions appearing on the menu regularly.
Thu–Tue 10–3, 7–10 L €25 D €40, Wine €5 Take EN2 north out of Viseu towards Lamego. After 10km (6 miles) follow signs to '*autódromo*'. Restaurant is next to the *autódromo*

O CORTIÇO
Rua Hiário Augusto, Viseu
Tel 232 423 853
Owned by the same family for 35 years, this is the restaurant that many locals recommend for a memorable and not too expensive meal. The food is simple, hearty and, above all, delicious. Some dishes are given humorous names, such as *bacalhau podre* (stale salt cod) and *coelho bêbado* (drunken rabbit), but there is no need to worry. The rest are regular regional dishes, including roast kid, fried *chouriço* (smoked sausage), cheeses and air-cured ham. Cottage cheese served with pumpkin jam makes a superb dessert.
Daily 12–3, 7.30–10
L €30, D €35, Wine €4.75
In middle of town next to the Dom Duarte statue

MURALHA DA SÉ
Adro da Sé 24, Viseu
Tel 232 437 777
Down to the left of the Misericórdia church, Muralha da Sé serves great regional food. The interior is granite with terracotta floors and red drapes, which highlight the dark red window frames. In summer there is seating on the terrace. In the evening, the *menu desgustação*, the special tasting menu that showcases the best the restaurant has to offer, is the one to go for, provided you are hungry enough to do it justice. Dishes that appear on the menu regularly include fish fritters, pork chops and fried octopus.
Tue–Sat 12.30–2.30, 7.30–10.30, Sun 12.30–2.30 L €25, D *menu desgustação* €34.40 for two (includes *couvert*, starter, main course, dessert), Wine €5

ESTREMADURA AND THE RIBATEJO

Sandwiched between the coast and interior, Estremadura has a cuisine that reflects its position, with fish definitely having the upper hand. Here you'll find *sopas de mariscos* (seafood soups) and *caldeiradas de peixe* (fish stew) alongside oily fish, such as herring, sardine and mackerel. In the Ribatejo, the food is straightforward, so expect plenty of plainly cooked meat, grilled *bacalhau* (dried salt cod) and vegetables, such as turnip tops, cabbage and carrots.

PRICES AND SYMBOLS

The restaurants are listed alphabetically. The prices given are for a two-course lunch (L) and a three-course dinner (D) for two people, without drinks. The wine price is for the least expensive bottle.

For a key to the symbols, ▷ 2.

ALCOBAÇA

TRINDADE

Praça Dom Afonso Henriques 22, Alcobaça
Tel 262 582 397

Thanks to its hearty food and central location in a tree-shaded square near the monastery, this little eatery often gets packed with visitors. It serves a great *frango na púcara* (chicken stew), grilled fish such as sole and bream, roast chicken and rabbit. There are also light snacks, such as toasted sandwiches and pastries. The crush is relieved in the summer by extra tables set out in the shady square.

Daily 7am–1am L €17, D €37, Wine €8

FÁTIMA

TIA ALICE

Rua do Adro, Fátima
Tel 249 531 737

Tia Alice opened in 1988 inside a humble townhouse next to Fátima's parish church. The bare stone walls have been left as they were and gentle lighting added to give a relaxed feel. Thanks to its wood-oven-baked bread, excellent soups, roasts and *açordas* (bread stews) the reputation of its fine Serra de Aire cooking has spread the length and breadth of the country. There are only 12 tables, so be sure to book in advance.

Tue–Sat 12–3, 7.30–10, Sun 12–3. Closed Jul L €60, D €80, Wine €12 Leave the Fátima sanctuary on the EN356 towards Tomar. Restaurant is on right-hand side by the parish church

LEIRIA

TROMBA RIJA

Rua Professores Portela 22, Marrazes, Leiria
Tel 244 855 072

People come from all over the country to eat in this renowned restaurant. One of the two fixed-price menus offers a choice of 50 starters from the buffet: cheeses, homemade sausages, octopus, chickpeas *(grão de bico)*, salt-cod salads and more. If you are still hungry, you can order a main course from a tempting selection of regional dishes on the à la carte menu.

Tue–Sat 1–3.30, 8–10.30. Closed 1st 2 weeks in Jul Mixed buffet with dessert and house wine €50 for two; mixed buffet plus main course from à la carte menu and house wine €80 for two; à la carte wine €10 Take Figueira da Foz exit from the A1 highway. Follow signs to Marrazes

ÓBIDOS

A ILUSTRE CASA DE RAMIRO

Rua Porta do Vale, Óbidos
Tel 262 959 194

Inside the ancient town walls, this rustic split-level dining room is painted in pink terracotta throughout. It has a medieval atmosphere, with its solid pillars, deep arches and alcoves filled with giant ceramic pots. The food is regional, with special dishes such as garlic fried prawns, stuffed squid, grilled grouper kebabs and duck with rice. The extensive wine list includes wines from all over the country. Finish with *crêpes à Ilustre*.

Fri–Wed 12.30–3, 7–10.30
L €50, D €60, Wine €7

PENICHE

ESTELAS

Rua Arquitecto Paulino Montez 21, Peniche
Tel 262 782 431

One of the best dishes at Estelas is the delicious steamed lobster Peniche-style, which must be ordered in advance to ensure total freshness. Alternatively, try *sequinho de cherne*, a grouper fish dish invented by the local fishermen. Other dishes include *caldeiradas* (mixed fish and seafood stew), plain grilled fish and a variety of fresh seafood.

Daily 12–3, 7–12. Closed 2nd 2 weeks Aug L €40, D €53, Wine €9 Next to the municipal market and courthouse

TOMAR

CHICO ELIAS

Rua Principal 70, Algarvias, Tomar
Tel 249 311 067

People come to Tomar just to eat at this fine restaurant. Chickpea broth, pumpkin stuffed with rabbit, salt cod with *presunto* and corn bread are just some of the delights on offer. Book and order in advance to give them time to marinate food overnight. Credit cards are not accepted.

Wed–Mon 1–3, 8–11. Closed 2nd 2 weeks in Jul and 1st 2 weeks in Sep L €50, D €55, Wine €14 Take Torres Novas road out of Tomar. Restaurant is 1.5km (1 mile) on the left

LISBON

You'll eat well in Lisbon, which not only serves Portuguese dishes from all over the country, but also has a good selection of restaurants specializing in international cuisine. Look for the lunchtime *pratos do dia* (daily specials) available at many restaurants, and for *menus de prova* (tasting menus), which allow you to try servings of several Portuguese dishes at one meal.

PRICES AND SYMBOLS

The restaurants are listed alphabetically. The prices given are for a two-course lunch (L) and a three-course dinner (D) for two people, without drinks. The wine price is for the least expensive bottle.

For a key to the symbols, ▷ 2.

1º DE MAIO

Rua Atalaia 8, Bairro Alto
Tel 213 426 840

The menu of this informal regional eatery changes from day to day, but often includes *açorda* (bread-based stew), fried squid or fresh tuna. Finish off with caramel cream or forest-fruits tart. The service is friendly and there is a great selection of wines.

Mon–Fri 12–3, 7–10.30, Sat 12–3. Closed 1st 3 weeks in Aug L €25, D €40, Wine €12 Baixa-Chiado

O ACONTECIMENTO

Clube dos Jornalistas, Ruas das Trinas, 129-r/c (ground floor), Lapa
Tel 213 977 138

This restaurant, with its verdant flower-filled patio, provides some of the best outdoor dining in the city, although in cooler weather the interior rooms are an attractive alternative. Begin with *pão com azeite*, large slices of rustic bread with a generous splash of olive oil, then try cod with rosemary and honey or maybe duck with air-cured ham and fine herbs. The *delirium de chocolate* for dessert lives up to its name.

Mon–Thu 12.30–3, 8.30–11, Fri 12.30–3, 8.30–11.30, Sat 8.30pm–11.30pm L €36, D €44, Wine €10 Bus 27; tram 25 Santos

ALI-À-PAPA

Rua da Atalaia 95, Bairro Alto
Tel 213 474 143

With a warm candlelit interior, somewhat reminiscent of a tent, the Moroccan Ali-à-Papa offers a limited but quality menu late into the night. *Tagine moderbel*, made with lamb and fried aubergines (eggplant), is always in great demand, as is the exotic *cous-cous tifaya*, made with lamb and raisins and spiced with cinnamon. The vegetarian vegetable and chickpea couscous is also good. To finish, try the yoghurt mousse with condensed milk, lemon and strawberries. It's advisable to book during the summer.

Wed–Mon 7.30pm–1am D €30, Wine €10 Baixa-Chiado

ANTIGA CONFRARIA DE BELÉM

Rua de Belém 84–88, Belém
Tel 213 637 423

A visit to Belém would not be complete without stopping at this nationally famous establishment for a coffee and *pastel de nata* (custard tart). Not even the owners of this cake shop know the secret recipe for the crisp pastry of these egg-custard-filled tarts, which has been guarded by the master pastry-makers since 1837. Served warm out of the oven, the tarts should be liberally sprinkled with the icing sugar and cinnamon provided.

Daily 8am–11pm €1.25 for custard tart and coffee Bus 27, 28, 29, 43, 49, 51; tram 15

BBC—BELÉM BAR CAFÉ

Avenida Brasília, Pavilhão Poente
Tel 213 624 232

This chic restaurant, housed in a converted warehouse to the east of Belém, offers riverside seating indoors and out. In the evening it attracts a young, lively crowd, and as the night wears on it begins to function primarily as a bar, often with live bands. This in no way detracts from the quality of the immaculately presented Portuguese cuisine. Grilled Barrosã beef and Katif prawns wrapped in crispy pastry are two popular dishes.

Mon–Sat 12–3, 8–12 L €50, D €80, Wine €20 Bus 28 Belém

BICA DO SAPATO

Avenida Infante Dom Henrique, Armazém B, Cais Pedra, Santa Apolónia
Tel 218 810 320

Bica do Sapato is one of the trendiest of Lisbon's trendy restaurants. At a prime dockside location just across from the Santa Apolónia train station, and with a riverfront terrace and super-modern interior, it encompasses three different eating areas: the restaurant, offering the popular *sugestão da semana* (dish of the week); the café, serving traditional Portuguese dishes; and the sushi bar, where on Wednesday the fixed-price *dia dos sabores* (day of flavours) menu is good value.

Restaurant: Mon 8pm–11.30pm, Tue–Sat 12–2.30, 8–11.30. Café: Mon 7.30pm–1am, Tue–Sat 12.30–3.30, 7.30–1. Sushi bar: Mon–Sat 7.30pm–1am L €76, D €110, Wine €10 Terreiro do Paço Bus 9, 12, 28, 46, 81, 90

A BRASILEIRA

Rua Garrett 120, Chiado
Tel 213 469 541

This Chiado café is one of Lisbon's most venerable coffee houses, complete with original wooden and mirrored interior. Once the retreat of artists and writers, such as 20th-century poet Fernando Pessoa (whose statue stands outside), the café continues to serve excellent coffee and cakes. The terrace is a good place to watch the world go by.

Daily 8am–2am €9 for light snack and drink Baixa-Chiado

CASA DA COMIDA
Travessa das Amoreiras 1 (off Avenida Alexandre Herculano)
Tel 213 885 376
From outside, the 'House of Food' seems somewhat unimpressive, but pass the doorman and descend the wooden staircase and you enter a sophisticated eatery. In the two dining rooms, separated by an attractive patio, the food is traditional Portuguese with a French twist. Clam soup, anglerfish with leek and lemon, or duck with olives are all regulars. There is an excellent wine cellar and the place serves delicious desserts.
Mon–Fri 12–3, 8–11, Sat 8pm–11pm L €60, D €80, Wine €18 Rato Bus 12, 18, 42, 51

CASANOVA
Cais Pedra à Bica Sapato, Armazém B-Lj.7 (warehouse B, shop No. 7), Santa Apolónia
Tel 218 877 532
In a converted warehouse, across the road from the Santa Apolónia train station, this genuine Italian eatery is an inexpensive alternative to a characterless fast-food joint. There is an extensive range of pizzas on offer, all thin crust and cooked in a traditional pizza oven in front of you. You can also enjoy fine crostini, bruschettas and other traditional Italian dishes, such as Neapolitan sausage with beans, or mozarella with aubergine (eggplant).
Tue–Sun 12.30pm–1am. Closed Tue lunch L €24, D €28, Wine €10 Terreiro do Paço Bus 9, 12, 28, 46, 81, 90

O CASEIRO
Rua de Belém 35
Tel 213 638 803
This restaurant near the Jerónimos monastery is attractive yet unpretentious. Simply grilled fish and meat, or more elaborate dishes such as oven-roasted lamb or *açorda de marisco* (bread stew with prawns), come in generous portions. Try the almond pudding to finish.
Mon–Sat 12–3, 7–10.30. Closed Aug L €35, D €45, Wine €9 Tram 15 Belèm

CERVEJARIA TRINIDADE
Rua Nova da Trindade 20c, Bairro Alto
Tel 213 423 506, 213 423 356

In business since 1836, this restaurant and beer hall is one of the city's oldest. The food here is nothing particularly out of the ordinary—grilled beef fillets, omelettes and fresh, though somewhat overpriced, seafood. However, the place itself is a classic Lisbon landmark. Housed in what was once a convent, it has vaulted ceilings, magnificent tile panels and noisy crowds that make it worth a visit, even if it's just for a quick, ice-cold *imperial* (a small glass of beer). There is a non-smoking section.
Daily midday–1am L €24, D €41, Wine €10 Baixa-Chiado Tram 28, 58

CHÁ DA LAPA
Rua do Olival 8–10, Lapa
Tel 213 900 888
This is an ideal place for a quiet lunch or afternoon tea if you are visiting the Museu Nacional de Arte Antiga (▷ 137). It is half tea room, half *belle époque* restaurant, with red velvet sofas, wood panelling and printed wallpaper, where everything is freshly made. At lunchtime they offer a couple of *pratos do dia* (dishes of the day), and there is always a great selection of cakes and desserts. The apple pie and cheesecakes are particularly good.
Daily 9–7 Bus 27, 40, 49, 60; tram 25 Santos Turn right out of museum then left up right side of square. At top turn right. Chá da Lapa is on the right-hand side

A CHARCUTARIA
Rua do Alecrim 47A, Bairro Alto
Tel 213 423 845
The owner-chef of the Charcutaria started cooking originally for friends but was persuaded to open to the public. Natural tones with light wooden panelling, original brick arches and basketware chairs create a calming atmosphere. Choose from game dishes, such as miniature partridge pies and hare with beans, or stick to old stalwarts like *carpaccio de bacalhão* (salt cod). Finish with the highly prized *doces conventuais*—desserts with eggs and lots of sugar originally made in convents.

Mon–Fri 12.30–4, 7–12, Sat 7pm–midnight L €50, D €70, Wine €15 Bus 58, 100 Cais do Sodré

COMIDA DE SANTO
Calçada Engenheiro Miguel Pais 39, Rato
Tel 213 963 339
Off the Rua da Escola Politécnica, this lively Brazilian restaurant brings a touch of the jungle to the Lisbon scene. It specializes in deceptively powerful caipirinha cocktails made with limes and *cachaça* (sugar-cane liquor). Brazilian dishes, such as chicken *muquecas*, cooked in coconut milk, and delicious *feijoada* (pork and black bean stew) accompanied by toasted manioc and orange, are served in generous portions. Try fresh mango and papaya to finish. There are only 12 tables, so booking is essential.
Daily 12.30–3.30, 7.30–1 L €40, D €48, Wine €7 Rato Bus 58

A CONFRARIA AT YORK HOUSE
Rua das Janelas Verdes 32, Lapa
Tel 213 962 435
Tucked away in a former 17th-century Carmelite convent in the Lapa district, this hotel and restaurant, with its oasis-like courtyard shaded by a giant palm, has transformed its cuisine over the last few years and now attracts diners from around the city. A selection of

traditional, although increasingly creative, Portuguese dishes are elegantly served. Cod and game dishes, when in season, are highly commended, as is the extensive wine list. There is a non-smoking section.
Mon–Sat 12.30–4, 7.30–10.30
L €52, D €64, Wine €15 Bus 27, 40, 49, 60; tram 25 Santos

CONVENTUAL
Praca das Flores 44–45, Rato
Tel 213 909 246
On one of the prettiest squares in town, this pious-sounding restaurant offers some of the best dining in the city. Appropriately decorated with antique and modern sacred art, it continues the religious theme in the names of some of its dishes, such as Pope of Avignon snails, and its excellent *doces conventuais*, highly prized egg-and-sugar-based puddings traditionally made by convent nuns. The *arroz de pato* (duck with rice) is superb.
Tue–Fri 12.30–3.30, 7.30–11, Sat, Mon and national holidays 7.30–11. Closed Aug. L €40, D €50, Wine €10 Rato Bus 100

ENOTECA–CHAFARIZ DO VINHO
Rua Mãe d'Água/Praça da Alegria
Tel 213 422 079
www.chafarizdovinho.com
Off the Praça da Alegria, Chafariz do Vinho is an excellent place for a tapas-style meal of cured ham, spicy sausages, cheeses and a good bottle of wine. Alternatively, there's the *menu de prova*, which offers a choice of three excellent Portuguese dishes plus dessert.
Tue–Sun 6pm–2am. Closed 23 Dec–10 Jan D €23, Wine €15
Avenida

GAMBRINUS
Rua Portas de Santo Antão 23, Baixa
Tel 213 421 466

In a street packed with restaurants and eateries, Gambrinus is the most expensive and the best. With its comfortably sedate interior, sporting wood-beamed ceilings and huge fireplaces, it's a popular retreat for politicians, journalists and other Portuguese celebrities. Sit at the bar counter or in one of the two dining rooms and choose from a huge selection of seafood (prawns, lobster and crab are always available), fresh fish (seasonsal choices include sea bream, sea bass and sole), and meat and game. For dessert, try the crêpes suzette. There is a non-smoking section.

Daily noon–1.30am L €70, D €100, Wine €20 Restauradores

MARTINHO DA ARCADA CAFÉ
Praça do Comércio 3, Baixa
Tel 218 879 259
Like the Nicola Café on the Rossio and A Brasileira in the Chiado, this old coffee house, founded in 1782, was a gathering place for Lisbon's literati–it was here, for instance, that poet Fernando Pessoa would enjoy his daily glass of absinthe. The restaurant has smartened itself up in recent years and is now fairly expensive, but the bar, with its fine wood-panelled counter, is still a good spot for a coffee and light snack. Try the *cataplana* (clam stew) from the Algarve.
Mon–Sat 7am–11pm €14 for drink and snack Baixa-Chiado

MEZZALUNA
Rua Artilharia Um 16, São Sebastião
Tel 213 879 944
A couple of blocks to the west of the Parque Eduardo VII, up the hill, this Italian restaurant is one of the best in town, attracting a quiet crowd in search of genuine Italian cuisine. The chef, who is Italian, offers mozarella in breadcrumbs, tagliatelli with prawns and vodka sauce, and risotto, plus some more unusual dishes, such as salmon with orange sauce and chicken thighs stuffed with spinach.
Mon–Fri 12.30–3, 7–11, Sat and national holidays 7pm–11pm L €40, D €54, Wine €12 Rotunda Bus 11, 23, 48, 53

NICOLA CAFÉ
Praça Dom Pedro IV 24, Baixa
Tel 213 460 579

This city landmark dates from 1777 and, like Brasileira and Martinho da Arcada, gained its fame as one of the café haunts of the literary and liberal set. Its impressive art deco interior is filled with linear patterns and huge mirrors. The location makes it one of the most popular cafés in the city, although the service is not particularly attentive. Diners can enjoy light and somewhat unimaginative meat-with-fries meals on the busy pavement terrace.
Mon–Fri 8am–10pm, Sat 9am–10pm, Sun 10–9 €16 for light snack and drink Rossio

PAP' AÇORDA
Rua da Atalaia 57–59, Bairro Alto
Tel 213 464 811
In a converted bakery in the Bairro Alto, this fashionable restaurant has managed to maintain its iconic status. Choose from oysters, mussels or a variety of *açordas* (thick bread-and-egg stews to which such ingredients as prawns and lobster are added). The chocolate mousse is reputed to be the best in town.
Tue–Sat 12–2, 8–1. Closed 1st 2 weeks of Jul and Nov L €50, D €70, Wine €20 Baixa-Chiado
Bus 58, 100

LA PAPARRUCHA
Rua de Dom Pedro V 18–20, Bairro Alto
Tel 213 425 333

As would be expected of an Argentinian restaurant, beef features heavily on the menu. Served with potato, grill-roasted corn and black beans, the high-quality selection of beef cuts grilled *a la parilla* is reason enough to come here, but what sets La Paparrucha apart from any of the other Argentinian restaurants in the city is its magnificent terrace and view. With its late opening hours it attracts the younger partying set, especially over the weekend. There is a non-smoking section.
Daily noon–12.30am, Sat 7..30pm–1.30am L €40, D €50, Wine €8 Baixa-Chiado Bus 100

PAVILHÃO CHINÊS
Rua Dom Pedro V 89, Bairro Alto
Tel 213 424 729
One of Lisbon's eating eccentricities, this café-cum-cocktail bar a few blocks up from the Gloria elevator in the Bairro Alto is worth popping into just for a look. Every available inch of wall space is covered with an eclectic selection of bric-à-brac, collected by Luis Pinto Coelho, the place's owner, from around the world. The result is a mish-mash of fine oriental porcelain hanging alongside tin soldiers, iron helmets, fans, statues and dolls. It will certainly keep you entertained while you enjoy a cup of coffee or an aperitif.
Mon–Sat 6pm–2am, Sun 9pm–2am Baixa-Chiado or Restauradores, then Gloria Elevator

PORTUGÁLIA RIO
Cintura do Porto de Lisboa, Armazém 63
Tel 213 422 138
Part of a chain of *cervejarias* (beer houses) dotted around the city, Portugália Rio has one of the best positions of them all, right on the riverfront. These establishments have limited menus of steaks, served with chips and rice, prawns and, of course, beer. They are good places for a quick, reasonably priced meal late into the night, but are not a viable option for vegetarians.
Mon–Thu noon–1am, Fri–Sat noon–2am L €24, D €40, Wine €5.80 Cais do Sodré Cais do Sodré

SOLAR DOS PRESUNTOS
Rua das Portas de Santo Antão 150
Tel 213 424 253
This is among the best of the many restaurants that line this popular street. You will recognize it by the air-cured hams hanging on display in the window; inside, the walls are covered with football memorabilia and tributes to the restaurant from famous patrons. The kitchen specializes in traditional Minho dishes, including roast kid and, when in season, highly prized fresh lampreys. Excellent fresh fish and seafood is stewed in a *caldeirada* or simply grilled. Service is friendly and, at the same time, highly professional.

Mon–Sat 12–3.30, 7–11. Closed Aug L €40, D €50, Wine €10 Restauradores

A SEVERA
Rua das Gáveas 51–61
Tel 213 428 314
Named after the gypsy singer and Portugal's first great *fado* performer Maria Severa, who died in 1836 at the age of only 26, this restaurant serves traditional Portuguese cuisine accompanied by live folk dancing and *fado* shows. Don't be put off—it has a great atmosphere and the professionally staged shows contribute greatly to what will prove a fun evening. Interesting *fado* paraphernalia decorate the alcoves.
Fri–Wed 12.30–3, 8–2am L €50, D €72, Wine €14 (meal prices include an €18 charge for the *fado* and folk show) Baixa-Chiado

SUA EXCELÊNCIA
Rua do Conde 34 , Lapa
Tel 213 903 614
The atmosphere of Sua Excelência is relaxed and intimate, and the flamboyant owner-cum-chef is an attraction in himself. He often greets guests at their tables, and can recite the entire menu in five languages, enthusiastically describing each dish in detail. Many of these have a strong African influence, such as the Mozambique prawns and Angolan-style chicken; others are innovative modern Portuguese creations.
Mon–Tue, Thu–Fri 1–3, 8–10.30, Sat–Sun 8pm–10.30pm. Closed Sep L €60, D €80, Wine €15 Santos Bus 27, 40, 49, 60

TÁGIDE
Largo da Academia Nacional de Belas Artes 18
Tel 213 420 720
The renowned Tágide serves fine, classic Portuguese cuisine with a French influence, and if you happen to get a seat by the window you will be treated to a spectacular view of the city and river. The *bacalhau da casa* is the house special, or try the hare in red wine, or baby octopus Azores style. The wine cellar is one of the most refined in the city and you will have no trouble finding a suitable accompaniment to your meal.
Mon–Fri noon–2, 8–10.30 Baixa-Chiado

OS TIBETANOS
Rua Salitre 117, Rato
Tel 213 142 038

In the Buddhist Centre off the Avenida de Liberdade, Os Tibetanos is the best—and almost the only—fully vegetarian restaurant in the capital. Dining rooms are spread over several floors, with agreeable views over the city and a pleasant interior patio. The menu is extensive and inexpensive, and includes such dishes as fresh cheese lasagne, vegetable curry and *momos Tibetanos* (steamed Tibetan pasties). This is also currently the only eating establishment in town that is

completely non-smoking. However, credit cards are not accepted.
Mon–Fri 12–2, 7.30–9.30
L €22, D €36, Wine €12
Avenida or Rato

VALLE-FLÔR
Pestana Palace Hotel, Rua Jau, 54
Santo Amaro
Tel 213 615 600
For a special occasion, it is worth splashing out on a meal at Lisbon's most luxurious restaurant. In what is now the Pestana Palace Hotel (▷ 307), the nationally acclaimed Valle-Flôr has polished wooden floors, high gilded ceilings and period furniture. The French chef creates exquisitely elaborate tastes and textures from traditional ingredients, varying the menu on offer with each week and season. There is a non-smoking section.
Daily 12.30–3, 7–10.30 L €60, D €100, Wine €15 Bus 22; tram 18

XL
Calçada da Estrela 57, Estrêla
Tel 213 956 118
XL is around the corner from the National Assembly building, with a closing time that makes it a good late-night dining spot. The restaurant has a home-like feel, thanks to its ochre-painted walls, rustic furniture and the antique curios with which it is decorated. Soufflés are the kitchen's particular forte. Also worth trying are the Camembert in breadcrumbs with raspberry sauce and the traditional Portuguese dishes, which include good salt cod. Finish off the meal with a delicious crêpe or crème brûlée.
Mon–Wed 8pm–midnight, Thu–Sun 8pm–2am. Closed 3 weeks Aug
D €50, Wine €17 Bus 6, 13, 49; tram 25, 28

AROUND LISBON

The resorts of Estoril and Sintra boast some of the best restaurants in Portugal. Both places are only a short train ride from Lisbon, making it perfectly feasible to head out to them for lunch or dinner. Food from all over the world features on restaurant menus, but look out, too, for local specialities, notably *caldeirada rica*, a superbly rich traditional stew that can include up to as many as eight different varieties of fish.

PRICES AND SYMBOLS

The restaurants are listed alphabetically. The prices given are for a two-course lunch (L) and a three-course dinner (D) for two people, without drinks. The wine price is for the least expensive bottle.

For a key to the symbols, ▷ 2.

All listings in Cascais, Carcavelos and Estoril can be reached from Lisbon by train from the Cais de Sodré station. Listings in Guincho are best reached by taxi from Cascais (approximately €6), although bus numbers from Cascais are given. Listings in Sintra can be reached from Lisbon by train from the Rossio train station.

CASCAIS

BANGKOK
Rua Bela Vista 6, Cascais
Tel 214 847 600

This restaurant, in the middle of Cascais, is arguably the best place to eat Thai food in the country. The interior resembles nothing less than a sophisticated oriental palace; everything from the welcoming waiters to the exotic dancing girls—and, naturally enough, the food—are genuine Thai. To sample a full range of the Bangkok's varied cuisine, come at the weekend for the special buffet, which includes a variety of delicious soups and green and red Thai curries. The friendly staff are always on hand to talk guests through some of the more exotic dishes.
Daily 12.30pm–1am L €60, D €100, Wine €8 Cascais

BRAZILIAN
Marina de Cascais, Cascais
Tel 214 835 939
For a change of scene, try this interesting place in the marina. To get there, walk up past the fort of Nossa Senhora da Luz, keeping left until you reach the marina compound. There are many restaurants, *cervejarias* and bars to choose from here, but the Brazilian, on the first floor, has some of the best views of the fort and bay of Cascais from its large terrace. It serves snacks and more substantial meals. There is a non-smoking section.
Sun–Mon, Wed–Thu 10am–midnight, Fri–Sat 10am–2am L €30, D €45, Wine €11 Cascais

CARVOARIA
Rua João Luís de Moura 24, Cascais
Tel 214 830 406
Just beyond the Visconde da Luz garden, this is a great option if you're looking for plainly grilled, resonably priced fresh fish. You can choose from a selection of sea bass, bream, or whatever has been freshly caught that day, all cooked over hot coals as the restaurant's name implies—*carvoaria* means coal-house. For dedicated meat-eaters, there are several cuts of beef and pork available, which are also served grilled.
Mon–Sat 12–3, 7.30–10.30. Closed 1st 2 weeks Apr, 1st 2 weeks Oct
L €24, D €30, Wine €7.50
Cascais

CASA DA GUIA
Estrada do Guincho, Cascais
Out on the Guincho road, the group of eateries known collectively as Casa da Guia is a great place for lunch or afternoon tea. Choose from

pastries and quiches at Confeitaria do Monte, or sample a slice of cake at Chá da Guia and watch the sun set from this great spot perched on the cliffs above the ocean. At night, you could try Dom Grelhas or Prazeres da Carne for grilled fish and meat.
Daily 10–10 L €12, D €30, Wine €7 Bus 415, 405 from Cascais

FORTALEZA DO GUINCHO
Estrada do Guincho, Cascais
Tel 214 870 491
Perched above the ocean inside an imposing 16th-century fort, this exclusive restaurant looks straight onto the ocean and the cliffs. Its award-winning cuisine is in no way overshadowed by these grand surroundings. The prices are high, but reflect the quality of the experience and the impeccable service. Try gilt-head sea bream with stewed fennel and anise, or their roast partridge, and, for dessert, chocolate truffles with lemon sorbet. There's an extensive list of Portuguese and foreign wines.
Daily 12.30–3, 7.30–10.30 L €86, D €114, Wine €15 Bus 415, 405 from Cascais

MELTING POT
Rua da Alfarrobeira 4A, Cascais
Tel 214 820 627, 919 916 123
In downtown Cascais above the Largo de Camões, this candlelit restaurant serves a set menu of 10 courses, ranging from cold starters through main courses to dessert. Dishes vary daily according to what the owner and chef select in the market, and all are expertly prepared and deliciously cooked. A typical menu might include an inventive salad or two, breaded grilled cheese with wild berries, and stewed partridge. Credit cards are not accepted.
Tue–Sat 7.30pm–10pm D €35, Wine €11 Cascais

PEREIRA
Rua Visconde da Luz 43, Cascais
Tel 214 831 215
This simple eatery provides reasonably priced traditional cooking with few frills. As is common in such places, food arrives on metal serving platters in large portions, so ask for a half-serving or share. Roast kid and duck with rice are popular, as are the other meat dishes, which are served (as always in Portuguese eateries), with chips and rice. From the typical list of desserts, the *leite creme* (crème brûlée) is popular. Credit cards are not accepted.
Fri–Wed 12–3, 7–10.30 L €24, D €48, Wine €6 Cascais

PORTO DE SANTA MARIA
Estrada do Guincho, Guincho, Cascais
Tel 214 879 450
One of the most respected (and expensive) of the exclusive fish restaurants along this promenade, the award-winning Porto de Santa Maria is set above the ocean with views of the *serra*. After a glass of champagne, choose from the wide range of seafood and fresh fish on offer, which is simply grilled over hot coals, or lightly fried so as not to detract from the subtle natural tastes. When it comes to dessert, soufflés are the house forte.
Tue–Sun 12.15–3.30, 7–10.30 L €90, D €110, Wine €11 Bus 415, 405 from Cascais

XAROPE
Travessa dos Navegantes 13, Cascais
Tel 214 840 154
Run by an English/Canadian couple, this cheerful and bright establishment is particularly popular among Cascais' expatriate community. The award-winning English chef prepares modern European cuisine with an emphasis on seasonal ingredients. Try the herb-crust salmon with oven-roasted vegetables in a pistachio sauce. They make a good Bucks Fizz (champagne and fresh orange juice) and Bloody Mary.
Tue–Sat 12–3, 7..30–1 L €20, D €30, Wine €9 Cascais In old Cascais between the police station and Igreja dos Navegadores

COLARES

COLARES VELHO
Largo Dr. Carlos França 1–4, Colares
Tel 219 292 406
This excellent little restaurant is in the old village square, behind the bandstand. The dining room was once the village store and is still lined with the original wooden cabinets. The chef and owner, Carlos Moreira, combines traditional Portuguese ingredients with his own innovative culinary touches. Try pear and smoked salmon salad with Azorean cheese, steamed monkfish with coriander (cilantro) and, for dessert, the delicious frozen chocolate mousse served in a biscuit shell with wild berries.
Tue–Fri 7–11, Sat–Sun 12–3, 7–11 L €40, D €60, Wine €15 Bus 403 from Sintra or Cascais train station

MOINHO DOM QUIXOTE
Estrada do Cabo da Roca, Azóia, Colares
Tel 219 292 523
If you are driving from Cascais around to Colares and Sintra via Cabo de Roca, this is a superb place for lunch or afternoon tea, especially in good weather. As its name implies, the Moinho is a converted windmill. Both the mill and its beautiful terraced gardens have magnificent views over the Sintra hills and the cliffs of the Cascais coastline. The salads and hamburgers are equally excellent, and the bar attracts a lively crowd in the evening.
Daily noon–2am L €26, D €30, Wine €8 Bus 403 from Sintra or Cascais station Take the Cabo da Roca turn-off from the main Cascais–Colares coastal road and then 1st left, signed to Moinho

ESTORIL

AL FRESCO
Centro Comercial Galerias, Lj 45 (shop 45), Rua de Lisboa 5, Estoril
Tel 214 676 770
Although situated inside a somewhat unattractive shopping mall just up from the casino, this restaurant serves genuine Italian cuisine as opposed to the fast-food variety. You could start with delicately seasoned carpaccio, then move on to one of the many delicious pasta dishes. It was its superb risottos that put this restaurant on the map, and there are several varieties to choose from, including *funghi porcini* (dried mushrooms) and prawns with mint.
Tue–Sun 12.30–3.30, 7.30–11.30 L €40, D €60, Wine €8 Estoril

MANDARIN SOL
Praça José Teodoro dos Santos, Casino do Estoril, Estoril
Tel 214 667 270
The classy Mandarin Sol offers some of the best Chinese food in the country. Housed within the Estoril casino complex, it has great views down the length of the park to the sea. At night, the trees and fountain are lit up and lasers flash (there's a laser show nightly at 9.30pm). The dining rooms are large and airy, and the menu is predominantly Cantonese. Dim sum and Peking duck are popular choices. Finish off with banana, apple and pineapple *fasi* (fritters).
Wed–Mon 12–3, 7–11 L €50, D €60, Wine €10 Estoril

PRAIA DO TAMARIZ
Praia do Tamariz, Estoril
Tel 214 681 010

A good spot for lunch along the seaside promenade from Cascais to Estoril, the place where exiled European monarchs, politicial refugees and spies took up residence during the 1940s and 1950s. Set above the sandy Tamariz beach, the place provides quick snacks as well as more substantial meals for the visitors and locals who come to enjoy the beach and ocean views from its terraces.
Apr–end Sep daily 12–12; Oct–end Mar daily 12–6 L €16, D €24, Wine €7 Estoril

LA VILLA
Praia do Tamariz, Estoril
Tel 214 680 033
Perched above the main beach, this lovely 1930s villa is decorated in tones of cream and white. The main restaurant, on the first floor, specializes in nouvelle cuisine, while on the top floor there is an excellent sushi bar and art gallery. Regardless of where you decide to sit, you may order from either menu, where you will find such dishes as fresh Brittany oysters, roasted breast of chicken and, of course, sushi and sashimi.

Tue–Thu 1–3, 8–12, Fri–Sat 1–3, 8–1, Sun 1–5, 8–12 L €70, D €90, Wine €30 Estoril

SINTRA

BICA DE SÃO PEDRO
Rua 1º de Dezembro 16c, São Pedro de Sintra
Tel 219 232 514
Housed in the same ochre-painted building as the Barro e Seda shop just off the main road, this rustic-chic café prides itself on its cooking. Try vegetable quiche or mozzarella and tomato tart with various different salads, and, not so healthy but totally irresistible, their own chocolate cake and apple tart. It is the ideal lunch stop for shoppers browsing the chic stores here.

Mon–Sat 8–7 (lunch menu served 12–3) L €16, Wine €4.50 Bus 433 from Sintra-Vila (old town)

LAWRENCE'S HOTEL
Rua Consiglieri Pedroso 38–40, Vila Velha, Sintra
Tel 219 105 500
www.lawrenceshgotel.com
This fine 17th-century building was patronized in its time by the likes of Lord Byron, Eça de Queiroz and other prominent literary figures of the 19th century. You can choose between eating in one of the the classic dining rooms, made welcoming by their warm decoration schemes, or in good weather, opt for the terrace, with its great views of the *serra*. Try the salt cod à la Lawrence's, or the delicious fish soup served with a crust of puff pastry. (▷ 310 for accommodation details.)

Daily 12.30–2.30, 7.30–9.45
L €60, D €80, Wine €12

TACHO REAL
Rua da Ferraria 4, Vila Velha, Sintra
Tel 219 235 277

Decorated with old green-and-white tiles that complement the dark-wood furniture, this restaurant is situated in the historic heart of old Sintra, just 50m (55 yards) away from the Palácio Nacional. It offers patrons a variety of traditional Portuguese dishes, including salt cod, squid, *caçao* (skate) on a bed of clams, prawn curry and beef medallions Tacho Real style. For vegetarians there is a good selection of roasted vegetables. The pears stewed in red wine make a great finish. There is a non-smoking section.
Thu–Tue 12.30–3, 7.30–10.30
L €50, D €70, Wine €18

THE ALENTEJO

The dry, hot summers of the Alentejo are reflected in its cooking, in which olive oil is extensively used, wild herbs are featured heavily and the pork is some of the best you'll ever eat. The signature dish here is *carne de porco Alentejana*, marinated pork cooked in white wine with clams being added just before serving. Summer is also *gaspacho* time, while wild game features on the menu in season. Other delights include *bolo podre* (spiced honey cake) and the superb *empadas de galinha*, the rich little chicken pies that are special to Évora.

PRICES AND SYMBOLS

The restaurants are listed alphabetically. The prices given are for a two-course lunch (L) and a three-course dinner (D) for two people, without drinks. The wine price is for the least expensive bottle.

For a key to the symbols, ▷ 2.

BEJA

A ESQUINA

Rua Infante Dom Henrique 26, Beja
Tel 284 389 238

This restaurant just north of the tourist office is not much to look at, with its modern interior and stainless-steel counters, but the service is friendly and it has a loyal following among locals looking for quality food. Begin with soup or *petiscos* (tapas) of homemade sausages and cheeses from Serpa. Then try *migas com carne de porco* (roast pork with clams) or *cação de coentrada* (skate with coriander/cilantro).

Mon–Sat 12–3, 7–10 L €16, D €20, Wine €4.50

CASTELO DE VIDE

MARINO'S

Praça Dom Pedro V 6, Castelo de Vide
Tel 245 901 408

Tucked away in a corner of the main square, this restaurant is owned by a charming Italian couple who were attracted to the northern Alentejo by its peace and quiet. The owner, Marino, is formal and professional, while Roberta, his wife, whose cooking has strong Italian influences, usually remains tucked away unseen in the kitchen downstairs. Try *osso buco*, the great pastas, flambéed steak, or succulent roast lamb with fresh herbs, which they will cook to order. Roberta also makes a mean apple pie and a memorable tiramisu.

Mon 7pm–10pm, Tue–Sat 12.30–2.30, 7–10 L €34, D €44, Wine €7

ELVAS

A BOLOTA

Quinta das Janelas Verdes, Terrugem, Elvas
Tel 268 657 401

Terracotta floors, wooden latticework and dressers holding regional ceramic plates give this place a country feel. Tables are simple yet refined, with linen cloths and fine tableware, and staff are happy to offer advice. Either stick with the delicious starters, such as spinach with prawns, salt cod with asparagus, and mint and partridge soup, or move on to one of the superb main courses, such as wild boar with chestnut purée or duck stuffed with raspberries.

Tue–Sat 12–12, Sun 12–3 L €50, D €64, Wine €13 Terrugem is just off the N4 between Elvas and Estremoz. The *quinta* is well signposted

TABERNA DO ADRO

Largo João Dias de Deus, Vila Fernando, Elvas
Tel 268 661 194

For a snack, a light tapas-style lunch or a main meal, try this taberna. Its rustic interior, with green stained-wood panelling, is crammed with regional ceramics of every shape and size. Roasted red peppers, spicy sausages, cheese and cured meats are just a few of the *petiscos* (tapas) on offer. For something more substantial, order fish stew with coriander (cilantro) or casseroled lamb, but make sure to leave room for one of the convent desserts, which are generously drowned in *ginjinha*, the Portuguese cherry brandy. Credit cards are not accepted.

Thu–Tue 9–2.30, 4.30–10 L €22, D €26, Wine €5 From the western roundabout, by the Hotel Dom Luís, take the EN372 following signs to Vila Fernando (14km/8 miles from Elvas).

ESTREMOZ

SÃO ROSAS

Largo Dom Dinis 11, Estremoz
Tel 268 333 345

São Rosas is located within the medieval walls in a modest townhouse next to the *pousada*. It has a country feel thanks to its whitewashed walls, wood-beamed ceilings and the solid wooden chairs with which it is furnished. Bread comes wrapped in linen and pâté is served in individual little pots. In season, wild asparagus and mushrooms feature prominently on the menu. Also try partridge pie or the pork loin with plums, choosing one of the fine regional wines on offer to accompany them. It's worth booking ahead at weekends.

Tue–Sun 12.30–3.30, 7.30–10.30. Closed 1st 2 weeks in Jan and 1st 2 weeks in Jul L €50, D €70, Wine €15

ÉVORA

BOTEQUIM DA MOURARIA

Rua da Mouraria 16A, Évora
Tel 266 746 775

This family eatery is in the Moorish quarter; it has no outside sign other than its street number, so you need to look carefully for it. The interior is tiny, but it serves some of the best food in town. Try a selection of the cured meat and cheese appetizers, then one of the soups or *açordas* followed by roast lamb. Finish with a homemade dessert.

Mon–Fri 12–3, 7–10, Sat 12–3. Closed Aug L €32, D €36, Wine €12

O FIALHO
Travessa Mascarenhas 14–16, Évora
Tel 266 703 079

A landmark among Alentejo restaurants and one of the best places to experience the local cuisine, Fialho attracts customers from far and wide. Owned by the same family since 1945, its forte is the huge number of starters it offers, which you will see on display in the front dining room. There is octopus vinaigrette, stuffed mushrooms, prawns, beans, peppers and many more. The daily specials include all the usual Alentejan delicacies, while there are superb wines on offer as well as deliciously sweet and sticky desserts.
Tue–Sun 12–12. Closed 1–25 Sep, 23 Dec–2 Jan L €70, D €80, Wine €11 In a narrow lane near the Garcia de Resende theatre

O FORCADO
Rua dos Mercadores 26, Évora
Tel 266 702 566
The menu at O Forcado, in this row of humble eateries, is somewhat limited, but the food is fresh, wholesome and good value for money. Try the soup, *bacalhau* and almond tart, washed down with wine or sparkling water. Popular with the locals.
Mon–Sat noon–2, 8–10.30

O MOINHO
Rua Santo André 2A, Bairro Nossa Senhora do Carmo, Évora
Tel 266 771 060
Part of a working mill, this cottage-like restaurant near the Campo do Juventude to the south of the city hub was once a grocery store. Its small dining rooms with rough terracotta floor tiles, wood-beamed ceilings and blue gingham tablecloths, are decorated with interesting collections of copper cooking pots, pottery and other local craft items. All the usual Alentejo dishes are on the menu, including a great pork loin with *migas de batata*, a mix of tomato with potatoes typical of the area. The wine list is stunning.
Mon–Sat 12–3, 7–10 L €16, D €27, Wine €6 Head south out of town towards the Ibis hotel. After the hotel turn right. The restaurant is just past the Campo do Juventude

TASQUINHA DO OLIVEIRA
Rua Cândido dos Reis 45A, Évora
Tel 266 744 841

This place is noted for its innovative and original cooking, and has numerous newspaper accolades and local gastronomy awards decorating its walls. Cold starters include artichokes with ham or stuffed crab, or, on colder days, try prawn soufflé with spinach, or chickpea and mint stew. In season, there is usually partridge or rabbit, or, if not, the more traditional roast lamb. There is a wide selection of wines to complement the food and the owner is only too happy to suggest which goes best with what. Book ahead at weekends.

Mon–Sat 12.30–3, 7.30–10. Closed 1st two weeks Aug L €50, D €60, Wine €10

MARVÃO

POUSADA DE SANTA MARIA
Rua 24 de Janeiro 7, Marvão
Tel 245 993 201
www.pousadas.pt
Marvão is an obligatory stop on any tour of the fortified hill towns, and this *pousada* is a magnificent viewpoint. The regional food here is great, especially the cream of pea soup and the excellent local cheeses. The tables with printed fabrics are attractive, and the staff are friendly, but the lasting impression is that of the marvellous views that open up before you, looking out across the olive trees and cork oaks of the Alentejo. (▷ 312 for accommodation details.)
Mon–Fri 12.30–3, 7.30–10, Sat–Sun 1–3, 7.30–10 L €48, D €58, Wine €13.50 At the double-gated town entrance follow signs to the *pousada*–down to left if in car or up to right if walking

VILA VIÇOSA

POUSADA DOM JOÃO IV
Terreiro do Paço, Vila Viçosa
Tel 268 980 742
www.pousadas.pt

Inside the main *pousada* building, this welcoming dining room with its polished terracotta floors and latticed shutters has wood-panelled ceilings and high frescoed vaulting. It serves traditional yet inventive culinary creations that are all delivered with an appealing combination of professionalism and flair. Pheasant with port and chestnut purée, cabbage stuffed with lamb and potatoes, and roast lamb in a pastry crust with artichokes and pine nuts are among the place's signature dishes. In the summer there is the option of alfresco dining on the terrace. (▷ 312 for accommodation details.)
Daily 1–3, 7.30–10 L €50, D €70, Wine €12 Next to the Paço Ducale

THE ALGARVE

Eating in the Algarve is perhaps the most varied in Portugal, with international cuisine from all over the world served up in its sophisticated restaurants. If you're looking for the region's own cookery, it's best, on the whole, to head away from the major tourist venues and track down places frequented by the locals and others in the know. Here you'll find great dishes based around fresh local produce—pork, game and, above all, fish and seafood.

PRICES AND SYMBOLS

The restaurants are listed alphabetically. The prices given are for a two-course lunch (L) and a three-course dinner (D) for two people, without drinks. The wine price is for the least expensive bottle.

For a key to the symbols, ▷ 2.

ALBUFEIRA

PÁSSARO AZUL

Praia Olhos d'Agua, Albufeira
Tel 289 502 852

This wooden restaurant sits above Olhos d'Agua beach, east of Albufeira, with great views of the Atlantic. The menu leans heavily towards fresh fish; sea bass, sole, gilt-head bream and sardines are some of the most popular choices, as is the grilled squid kebab. There are also meat dishes—try the beef loin.

Daily 10am–midnight. Closed Dec–end Feb L €35, D €40, Wine €12 Head east out of Albufeira and follow signs to Olhos d'Agua

A RUÍNA

Praia dos Pescadores, Largo Cais Herculano, Albufeira
Tel 289 512 094

Set into the cliff face of the Praia dos Pescadores, where the old Albufeira castle once stood, this restaurant has a terrace at beach level, an indoor dining room on the middle floor and a rooftop patio. Inside, the fare is straightforward and unpretentious, but it's all top quality. Fresh fish is seasoned with sea salt and plainly grilled, while there is a good choice of other seafood on the menu.

Daily 12–2.30, 7–11 L €46, D €66, Wine €12

VILA JOYA

Praia da Galé, Albufeira
Tel 289 591 795
www.vilajoya.de

A luxurious atmosphere, flawless service and exquisite cooking by Austrian chef Dieter Koschina make this one of the country's top restaurants. The dining room extends onto the terrace, which looks over palm-filled gardens and down onto the sea. The modish cuisine is ultra-sophisticated, uses the freshest ingredients and is priced accordingly. Try prawn rosti with avocado or fish with pasta and basil. You can also stay in the hotel here (▷ 313). There is a non-smoking section.

Daily 1–2.30, 7.30–8.30 (arrival time). Closed 15 Nov–1 Mar L €100, D €190, Wine €30 10km (6 miles) west of Albufeira towards Armação de Pêra. Follow signs to Praia da Galé. Restaurant is on the left just before the beach

ALJEZUR

SÍTIO DO RIO

Praia Bordeira, Carrapateira, Aljezur
Tel 282 973 119

Patrício Ferreira is the grill-master here. Bream, bass, mullet, beef, pork or kid are all expertly cooked over the hot coals. Salads are dressed simply with fine olive oil and vinegar; all vegetables come from the garden and their chickens are all free range. Credit cards are not accepted.

Wed–Mon 12–12. Closed Nov–end Jan L €28, D €32, Wine €5 Take N125 to Vila do Bispo, then north on N268 to Carrapateira. Just after Carrapateira, turn left to beaches. Restaurant is last building on the right before the beach

ALMANCIL

AUX BONS ENFANTS

Sítio das Areias, Almancil
Tel 289 396 840

Whether you eat in the charming dining room or on the pleasant terrace, this candlelit restaurant serves some of the best French cuisine in the Algarve and has a wine list to match. Snails or fresh foie gras are good starters, followed by Chateaubriand steak in pepper sauce and *confit de canard*. There is a mouthwatering list of desserts and, most agreeably, port is available by the glass to complete your meal. There is a non-smoking section.

Tue–Sat 7–10 D €60, Wine €12 Take the Quinta do Lago road out of Almancil. About 1km (0.75 miles) outside Almancil turn left; Aux Bons Enfants is down on the right

HENRIQUE LEIS

Vale Formoso, Almancil
Tel 289 393 438

This exclusive restaurant, set inside a small yellow house in Almancil, serves fine international cuisine. In season, the chef recommends his special truffle menu, which includes seven different truffle-based dishes, including dessert. Also much recommended are the langoustines with endive and lemon, and the lobster with asparagus ravioli.

Mon–Sat 7pm–10.30pm. Closed 15 Nov–27 Dec D €60, Wine €18 From the middle of Almancil, head out of town on the Loulé road, pass under the EN125; Henrique Leis is on the corner of the 2nd left turn

TRADICIONAL

Estrada Fonte Santa, Escanchinas, Almancil
Tel 289 399 093

In summer, book ahead to get a table on this restaurant's lovely terrace, or in its light, airy dining room with its huge Algarvian carved fireplace. The signature dishes of the Swiss chef, Cédric Blanc, include apples with foie gras and Parma ham, followed by sea bass stuffed with leek, or roast breast of duck with honey. The crunchy apple crêpe is a fine way to round off a meal. The extensive wine list is superb.

Mon–Sat 7pm–10pm. Closed last 3 weeks of Jan D €76, Wine €15 Head south out of Almancil towards Vale do Lobo. The restaurant is next to the Avia service station

FARO

A TASKA

Rua Alportel 38, Faro
Tel 289 824 739

Not far from the Largo do Carmo, this no-frills Portuguese eatery is popular among locals. Dining rooms are split between two floors and there is an open fire in winter. The walls are decorated with the work of local artists and with verses by António Aleixo, a popular 20th-century Algarvian poet. The kitchen serves up regional food in healthy sized portions, including bean rice with razor fish, prawn curry, fried squid and much more. Credit cards are not accepted.

Mon–Sat 12.30–3, 7.30–11.30
L €20, D €40, Wine €3.50

LAGOS

RESTAURANTE FLORESTAL

Mata Nacional, Barão de São João
Tel 282 687 204

This restaurant can be a little hard to find, so it's sensible to call ahead and speak to the English-American owners to get directions at the same time as booking a table. It's well worth the effort, as the restaurant's country location and the spectacular views you will get from the patio are fantastic, as is the food: a range of tasty soups, salads, eggs Benedict, fish, homemade burgers, steak and grilled rack of lamb. There is a non-smoking section.

Tue–Sat 12–2.30, 7–10. Closed Nov–end Mar L €24, D €34, Wine €8.50 From Lagos take N120 to the northwest towards Aljezur until you reach the village of Bensarfim. Turn left towards Barão de São João, about 3km (2 miles) down the road. The restaurant is on the hill above Barão de São João

RESTAURANTE PARAÍSO

Praia da Luz, Lagos
Tel 282 788 246

One of hundreds of Algarve beach terraces, this relaxed, wooden *esplanada* sits directly on the sand of the attractive and popular Praia da Luz beach a stone's throw from the ocean. The informal deck is ideal for those coming straight off the sand in search of refreshment, while the inside is a little more formal. Both offer a selection of light snacks, sandwiches, soup or salads, or something more substantial, such as grilled fish or seafood.

Daily 10am–midnight L €12, D €30, Wine €7.20 On the Praia da Luz, west of Lagos

LOULÉ

CASA PAIXANITO

Estrada Querença, Loulé
Tel 289 412 775

Passed down from father to son for decades, this place has a friendly atmosphere, its beamed ceilings and yellow walls enlivened by bright framed prints. Choose from a large variety of tapas, such as octopus salad, pâtés, homemade sausages, cured meats and more; or from some notable main courses, such as the house's wild boar, venison, roast duck or lamb dishes. The partridge in red wine marinade is also highly praised. American Express is the only charge card accepted.

Daily 12–3, 7–10.30 L €60, D €80, Wine €9 Take the Clareanes/Querença road north. The restaurant is 2km (1.5 miles) on the right, just after the Centro de Saúde

MONCHIQUE

ABRIGO DA MONTANHA

Corte Pereiro, Estrada da Fóia, Monchique
Tel 282 912 131
www.abrigodamontanha.com

This restaurant is superbly located in the Monchique hills, with panoramic views over the *serra* towards the coast. Popular with visitors on excursions from the coast, it serves good-value regional food, such as *assadura*—pork grilled with an olive oil, parsley and lemon dressing. There is also a great monkfish stew cooked in a copper *cataplana*. You can also stay here (▷ 315).

Daily 12.30–3.30, 7–9.30 L €30, D €38, Wine €8 West on the Fóia road, about 3km (2 miles) on from Monchique

PORTIMÃO

ADEGA VILA LISA

Rua Francisco Bívar 52, Mexilhoeira Grande, Portimão
Tel 282 968 478

This is a temple to traditional Algarve cooking, established more than 25 years ago by Vila and Lisa, two friends who shared the same dream of sparking a local culinary revival. Take the chef's tapas suggestions, which may include rice with cockles, roasted octopus or beef with coriander (cilantro), accompanied by one of the excellent red wines. Finish off with fig and almond dessert and a local liqueur. Credit cards are not accepted.

Jul–end Sep daily 8pm–midnight; Oct–end Jun Fri–Sat 8pm–midnight
Fixed four-course menu including wine €55 per person Between Lagos and Portimão

DONA BARCA

Largo da Barca 9, Portimão
Tel 282 484 189

In the middle of town behind the sardine quay, this place is great value for money. Fish is brought directly from the quay to the terrace grill, so the *prato do dia* (dish of the day) is always super-fresh.

Daily 12–3, 6–10.30. Closed 2 weeks Jan L €18, D €24, Wine €8

FORTE E FEIO

Largo da Barca 1, Portimão
Tel 282 413 809

In what was once a dockside warehouse, subtle lighting and long dark wood tables create a sociable welcoming feel. The old underground saltwater tanks, originally used for storing fish, now house lobsters and crabs, ready to be served fresh. Their *arroz de mansco* (seafood with rice) is particularly good.

Daily 12–3, 6.30–10 L €20, D €30, Wine €6

QUINTA DO LAGO

CASA VELHA

Quinta do Lago
Tel 289 394 983

Thanks to chef Jean-François Renard, the cuisine here is French-influenced. To begin, try sautéed prawns with coconut sauce, then fresh cod and fennel, followed by cheesecake with cinnamon and raspberries. Casa Velha boasts a formidable selection of wines on display along one wall.

Mon–Sat 7.30pm–10.30pm. Closed Jan–end Feb D €120, Wine €25
Heading into Quinta do Lago on the road from Almancil, cross over the first 5 roundabouts, turn right at the 6th, then first left. The restaurant is at the end of this road

SAGRES

A TASCA

Praia da Mareta, Sagres
Tel 282 624 177

Overlooking the marina, this place has a slightly eccentric feel. Its walls are covered with a profusion of bottles, pebbles and ceramic plates set decoratively into the plaster, in stark contrast to the black-painted tables and chairs. However, the service is friendly and the food, though simple, is of a high quality. Try the grilled oysters, lobster, crab, tuna fish stew, squid kebabs or fresh grilled fish, with almond or orange tart to finish.

Thu–Tue 10–10 L €24, D €30, Wine €12 At the fishing port of Sagres

SÃO BRÁS DE ALPORTEL

ADEGA NUNES

Sítio dos Machados , São Brás de Alportel
Tel 289 842 506

For regional cooking, reasonable prices and interesting surroundings, try Adega Nunes, housed in an old *adega* (winery)—the barn-like room still contains wine barrels, brick vats and other tools of the trade. Start with the homemade bread and anchovy vinaigrette, followed perhaps by *açorda de galinha* (thick bread and chicken stew), succulent wood-oven-roasted lamb or fried rabbit. Credit cards are not accepted.

Mon–Sat 9–3, 6.30–11.30 L €20, D €24, Wine €8 From the main Via do Infante highway, take the São Braz de Alportel exit, just north of Estói. At the junction, follow signs to Barracha. The restaurant is 150m (160 yards) down this road on the right

SILVES

CAFÉ INGLÊS

Escadas do Castelo 11, Silves
Tel 282 442 585

Behind the cathedral, on the steps below the castle, this elegant 1920s house is now a popular English-run café and restaurant, which makes a good place to stop off on a day's sightseeing. Sit inside or outside on the terrace for a mid-morning reviver of fine coffee and a slice of cake from the homemade selection. For something bigger, choose from the salads, pastas, pizzas or traditional Portuguese dishes on offer.

Tue–Fri, Sun 9.30am–10pm, Sat 6pm–10pm, Mon 9.30–5.30 L €14, D €30, Wine €7

TAVIRA

AQUASUL

Rua Dr. A. Silva Carvalho 13, Tavira
Tel 281 325 166, 967 915 222

Aquasul has a fresh and cheerful, southern European feel to it. The cuisine is mainly Italian and Mediterranean, which provides a welcome break from tasty, but heavy, traditional Portuguese food and the ever-present grilled fish. Choose from a variety of fresh leafy salads, pasta dishes and pizza from the wood-fired oven. Credit cards are not accepted.

Wed–Mon 7pm–10.30pm D €30, Wine €7.50 From the Roman bridge head down the pedestrian street. Aquasul is just down the pedestrian street on the left

CASA DA IGREJA

Largo da Igreja, Cacela Velha, Tavira
Tel 281 952 126

Martim's, as it is known by the locals, can be recognized by its wooden tables, set on the cobbled village street beside the church. These are in great demand in the height of summer, when you can sit outside and enjoy what seems like an unending supply of *petiscos* (tapas).

15 Jun–30 Sep 4.30–10.30; 1 Oct–14 Jun Sat–Sun 4.30–10.30 D €20, Wine €3 Take EN125 east out of Tavira. Turn right at sign to Cacela Velha. The restaurant is next to church overlooking the Ria

O PÁTIO

Rua António Cabreira 30-1º, Tavira
Tel 281 323 008

Winner of several local gastronomy awards, O Pátio serves hearty regional food. House specials include fish or seafood *cataplana* (stew cooked in large copper pans), prawns fried in cognac and chicken with almonds. Finish with toasted almond cake and a tot of *aguardente*, a local fig and wild strawberry liqueur.

Mon–Sat 5–11.30 L €24, D €36, Wine €15 Near the Roman bridge in the old town

VALE DO LOBO

ERMITAGE

Estrada Almancil, Vale de Lobo
Tel 289 355 271

This highly acclaimed (and expensive) restaurant is owned and run by a couple from the Netherlands; Vincent cooks, while Willemina looks after the restaurant. Vincent recommends the set menu, which may include terrine of goose-liver pâté with blackberries, or fillets of John Dory with leek and truffle sauce.

Tue–Sun 7pm–10pm. Closed mid Nov to mid Jan D €80, Wine €20 3km (2 miles) out of Vale de Lobo on the Almancil road, in Escanchinas. Watch for the sign

SÃO GABRIEL

Estrada Quinta do Lago, Vale de Lobo
Tel 289 394 521

Less formal than some, São Gabriel is one of the top restaurants in the area. French, Italian and Swiss influences on its cooking have been joined in recent years by lighter Mediterranean dishes, such as lobster with fresh vegetables and lemon sauce, and sautéed sole with asparagus. Credit cards are not accepted. There is a non-smoking section.

Tue–Sun 7.30pm–10.30pm. Closed 20 Nov–14 Feb D €86, Wine €18.50, set menu approx. €100 for 2 excluding wine From Vale do Lobo take the road to Quinta do Lago. The restaurant is 2km (1.5 miles) down this road on the left

EATING

STAYING IN PORTUGAL

There is a wide range of accommodation all over Portugal. For budget travellers, there is plenty of choice in the shape of clean, simple pensions and a wealth of self-catering options. Accommodation overall is excellent value, and even top-notch options cost appreciably less than elsewhere in Europe. Expect to pay more in Lisbon and the Algarve in high season, but even then you may be pleasantly surprised by how far your money goes.

Left to right: Hotel Vila Vita Parc, Porches; Palace Hotel do Buçaco; Hotel Quinta do Lago

TYPES OF ACCOMMODATION

Pousadas, a chain of more than 40 nationwide luxury state-run hotels, are wonderful places to stay, and, in remote areas, provide levels of comfort you won't find elsewhere. Prices vary considerably depending on where they are, so there's no need to dismiss the idea even if you're travelling on a tight budget. They run seasonal promotions, while over-65s can get discounts of as much as 35 per cent.

Hotels in Portugal are graded from between 1 and 5 stars, with comfort, facilities and service reflected in the price and rating. It's quite acceptable to ask to see the room before you take it; the official price list (which includes IVA–the equivalent of VAT) must be displayed inside the door. Extra beds can normally be provided for a small charge, but children under four years can usually stay free in their parents' room. Simpler hotels, particularly in remote areas, are often quite basic and have little in the way of heating–worth bearing in mind if you're travelling in winter.

Pensões and **residenciais** are a good budget choice, their main distinction being that *residenciais* are unlikely to serve meals other than breakfast. They are classified from 1 to 3 stars. A 3-star *pensão* costs roughly the same as a 1-star hotel. Not all rooms will have private bathrooms, but the accommodation will be simple, clean and reasonably comfortable. **Hospedarias** are very similar in style, with even lower prices.

Privately owned country and manor houses provide superb accommodation at excellent prices, and are ideal if you are touring outside the cities. They are promoted and inspected by the government tourist office and vary from simple farmhouses *(casas rústicas)* to country manor houses *(quintas)* and even palaces *(casas antigas)*. Rooms and facilities obviously vary, but must meet certain standards and are categorized on a scale of A–C. You can find out more and make bookings through the various marketing companies. **Country guesthouses** are classified as *turismo rural*. They are government-inspected and awarded a green tree symbol if approved.

VILLAS AND SELF-CATERING

Self-catering options are available all over Portugal, particularly in coastal areas. They range from simple one-room, studio-type apartments in soulless blocks to luxurious houses with a pool, gardens and maid service. If you want plenty of choice, it's advisable to book months ahead, using one of the many specialist holiday or tour operators. You can often get all-in packages that include flights and car rental, which are a good bet if you want total independence, or are travelling with children and want to base yourself in one place.

You can arrange to rent a property yourself–a much less expensive option–either by obtaining a list of properties from the local tourist board or going on-line and checking out the websites devoted to private house rentals.

CAMPSITES

There are official campsites *(parques de campismo)* all over Portugal, many of them open year round. The pick of the bunch are operated by Orbitur and can be huge; these also have spaces for camper vans (RVs) and caravans, and some have permanent caravans and bungalows you can rent. They can be very crowded during the summer months, particularly in the Algarve, where you should also be aware that theft is becoming an increasing problem.

YOUTH HOSTELS

Portugal has around 30 youth hostels *(pousadas de juventude)*, all offering excellent value, though those in Lisbon, Porto and the Algarve are more expensive than elsewhere. They're clean, safe and friendly, with dormitory-style accommodation. Most have a curfew (11pm or midnight) and all require a valid Hostelling International card.

FINDING A ROOM

- Advance booking is vital in July and August or if your stay coincides with important local festivals or pilgrimages.
- If you haven't booked in advance, start by asking at the tourist office; they will have lists of accommodation and may be willing to book for you.
- You'll be asked to leave your passport when you check in; don't forget to collect it later.
- In larger towns and cities there's always plenty of downtown *pensão* accommodation, as well as pricier hotels, so don't assume you'll have to stay out of town if you're on a budget.
- If you're visiting rural areas out of season you may find that many hotels are closed; this also applies to many coastal resorts.
- Check-out time is normally noon, but some hotels will keep luggage until the end of the day.
- In smaller places, pay your bill the night before if you want to make an early start.
- Many hotels and self-catering apartments in the Algarve are block-booked by travel operators during the summer, so book well ahead.

PRICING

- Portuguese hotels are legally required to post the room rates on the back of the bedroom doors; prices should also include IVA (VAT).
- Rates vary according to season, sometimes by as much as 40 per cent.
- Agree a price before you make a reservation, and ask for written confirmation if you're booking ahead from home.
- Hotels will often quote their most expensive rates; ask if they have cheaper rooms.
- Hotels will put an extra bed in the room for a small charge—ideal for families with children.

ACCOMMODATION INFORMATION

HOTELS

The following are quick, efficient, on-line booking sites for hotel accommodation and all-in holidays across Portugal, offering good value for money and a wide range of options.
www.hotelopia.co.uk
www.magicbreaks.com
www.strawberry-world.net

POUSADAS

- Avenida Santa Joana Princesa 10, 1749-090 Lisboa ☎ 218 442 001, fax 218 442 085
- Keytel, 402 Edgeware Road, London W2 1ED, UK ☎ 020 7616 0300, fax 020 7616 0317
- Marketing Ahead, 433 Fifth Avenue, New York, NY 10016 ☎ 212/686-9213, fax 212/686-0271

or try **www**.pousadas.pt

COUNTRY HOUSE ACCOMMODATION

- Solares de Portugal, Praça da República, 4990 Ponte de Lima ☎ 258 741 672, fax 258 741 444; **www**.solares-de-portugal.com
- Privetur, Largo das Pereiras, 4990 Ponte de Lima ☎ 258 743 923, fax 258 741 493; **www**.manorhouses.com
- ANTER, Quinta do Campo, Valado dos Frades, 2450 Nazaré ☎ 262 577 135, fax 262 577 555

SELF-CATERING AND VILLA HOLIDAYS

- CV Travel, 43 Cadogan Street, London SW3 2PR, UK ☎ 020 7591 2800
- The Manor Stables, Great Somerford, Chippenham, Wiltshire SN15 5EH, UK ☎ 01249 712494; **www**.cvtravel.net; specialists in luxury villas in the Algarve
- The Villa Holiday Centre, 12 Headlands Business Park, Salisbury Road, Ringwood, Hampshire BH24 3PD, UK ☎ 01425 484434; **www**.villaholidaycentre.co.uk; a wide selection of villas around Carvoeiro in the Algarve
- Holidaylets.Net, NetSquared Ltd, Cranfield Innovation Centre, Cranfield, Bedfordshire MK43 0BT, UK ☎ 01234 757281; **www**.holidaylets.net; a good selection of privately ownedvillas and apartments all over Portugal
- Selfcatering Hols, Pinetrees, Old Road, Wrinehill, Crewe CW3 9BW, UK ☎ 0871 711 3039; **www**.selfcateringhols.com; villas and apartments in the Algarve and northern Portugal
- **www**.portugalvirtual.pt/_lodging; a comprehensive site with self-catering options all over Portugal

CAMPING

- The booklet *Roteiro Campista* (€10) is available from tourist offices, bookshops and newsstands, or from Roteiro Campista, Apartado 3168, 1301-902 Lisboa; **www**.roteiro-campista.pt
- Orbitur, Rua Diogo Couto 1–8, 1149-02 Lisboa; **www**.orbitur.pt; operates campsites all over Portugal

You can get an international camping carnet from:

UK

- Camping and Caravanning Club, Greenfields House, Westwood Way, Coventry CV4 8JH ☎ 024 7669 4995; **www**.campingandcaravanningclub.co.uk
- The AA; **www**.theAA.com

USA

- Family Campers and RVers, 4804 Transit Road, Building 2, Depew, NY 14043 ☎ 800/245-9755; **www**.frcv.org

YOUTH HOSTELS

- Movijovem, Avenida Duque de Avila 137, 1069-017 Lisboa ☎ 213 559 081

UK

- YHA, Trevelyan House, 8 St. Stephen's Hill, St. Albans, Hertfordshire AL1 2DY ☎ 0870 870 8808; **www**.yha.org.uk
- SYHA, 7 Gelbe Crescent, Stirling, Scotland FK8 2JA ☎ 0870 155 3255; **www**.syha.org.uk

USA

- HI-AYH, 733 15th Street NW, Suite 840, PO Box 37613, Washington, DC 20005 ☎ 202/783-6161; **www**.hiayh.org

THE MINHO AND TRÁS-OS-MONTES

Braga makes a good base for a night or so, but, as it's also a business destination, prices can be steep, so Guimarães, a lovely and historic city far better geared to tourists, may be a better alternative. To the northeast, Bragança is a good base for touring the remote country in Montesinho, while, to the south, Vila Real gives easy access to the Solar de Mateus and is well connected by road to the coast. Viana do Castelo is the big draw here, a beautiful old coastal town that makes a good base for exploring the Costa Verde. From Viana, the river Lima cuts inland to Ponte de Lima and Ponte de Barca, both lovely places to stay for a few days. This is prime *quinta* country, with a superb choice of country house accommodation.

PRICES AND SYMBOLS

Prices are for a double room for one night. All the hotels listed accept credit cards unless otherwise stated. Note that rates vary widely throughout the year.

For a key to the symbols, ▷ 2.

BARCELOS

QUINTA DO CONVENTO DA FRANQUEIRA

Carvalhal CC 301, Barcelos
Tel 253 831 606
www.quintadafranqueira.com

Owned by an English couple, this superb *quinta* was built in the 1560s by Franciscan monks, drawn here by the healing waters of the ancient Fonte da Vida spring. It has a 16th-century cloister and an adjoining chapel (open to guests). Rooms are furnished with antiques, paintings and fine old Portuguese rugs. The estate boasts extensive woodlands, a vineyard and a modern winery, along with a lovely outdoor pool filled with gushing spring water. Credit cards are not accepted. The hotel is closed from November to April.

€100 including breakfast
5
Outdoor
From ring road, go right for Póvoa de Varzim, under bridge, then left to Franqueira. Through village, take middle road of three uphill into woods. Turn right then left after the church

BRAGA

CASTELO DO BOM-JESUS

Turismo de Habitação, Bom Jesus do Monte, Braga
Tel 253 676 566
www.armilarworldusa.com

This 18th-century, neo-Gothic building has a solid gated entrance and provides outstanding views of Braga and, on clear days, the sea. The interior, with its air of faded grandeur, is stylishly decorated with drapes, antiques and reproduction period furniture. Some of the bedrooms are particularly elegant, especially the presidential suite with its gilded bed head and *trompe l'oeil* frescoes. The Castelo has extensive gardens filled with 100-year-old trees and a large swimming pool.

€100–€125 including breakfast
12
In suites Outdoor
In Braga follow signs to Bom Jesus. At top of hill turn right just before Sanctuary parking area

HOTEL DO ELEVADOR

Parque do Bom Jesus do Monte, Braga
Tel 253 603 400
www.hoteisbomjesus.web.pt

Enjoying the same splendid location as the Castelo (above), this fine hotel is named after the 19th-century water-powered elevator that was built to take pilgrims up to the Sanctuary. It is still in use today. Behind the period façade of the hotel is an elegant interior, including a superb glassed-in arched walkway serving as the acclaimed restaurant's dining room. Rooms have been renovated recently and provide all the modern comforts.

€90 including breakfast
22

In Braga follow signs to Bom Jesus

POUSADA DE SANTA MARIA DO BOURO

Amares, Braga
Tel 253 371 971
www.pousadas.pt

This monumental granite *pousada*, northeast of Braga, was a Cistercian monastery, built in the 12th century. An ingenious transformation in 1997 fused the plant-covered ruins with modern plate glass and wood, and converted monks' cells into contemporary bedrooms with fantastic views of the countryside. The huge granite water tank still feeds the system of channels that runs through the convent, including the monastery kitchens that now house a restaurant specializing in Minho cuisine. There are tennis courts on site.

€169–€178 including breakfast
30 rooms, 2 suites
Outdoor
From N101 north of Braga, turn right onto EN206 to Amares. Approximately 14km (9 miles) from Braga

BRAGANÇA

POUSADA DE SÃO BARTOLOMEU

Estrada do Turismo, Bragança
Tel 273 331 493
www.pousadas.pt

On the hill across from the castle, this *pousada* has superb views of the city and old town. The public areas have a mountain-lodge feel to them, with lots of wood and stone—especially local slate. The interiors throughout are a little dated, but the rooms are welcoming and all have balconies with good views.

€92–€144 including breakfast
28
Outdoor
Cross to the south bank of the river Fervença on the main road, Alexandre Herculano. Turn left following signs to the *pousada*

QUINTA DA AVOZINHA
Cabeça Boa, Samil, Bragança
Tel 273 331 101
www.quintadavozinha/planeta.clix.pt
If you'd rather stay outside the city, try the Quinta da Avozinha in Cabeça Boa, just a short drive away. Painted in a welcoming shade of yellow with light wood trim, the house was built in the 1930s and has been added to over the years. Thanks to its hillside position, it enjoys great views of the valley and river Sabor, and the hosts are happy to help organize walks and off-road bicycle trips. Credit cards are not accepted.
€75–€100 including breakfast
4 rooms, 1 suite
Outdoor
Cross to the south bank of the river Fervença on the main road, Alexandre Herculano. Turn left following signs to the *pousada*. Go past the *pousada* and continue to Cabeça Boa. The *quinta* is on the left just after the church

RESIDENCIAL TULIPA
Rua Dr. Francisco Felgueiras 8–10, Bragança
Tel 273 331 675
Tulipa is simple, but agreeable and offers extremely good value if you want to base yourself right in the heart of old Bragança. All the rooms are modern with bathroom and shower facilities, and some have balconies (though these are quite tiny). There is a regional restaurant on the ground floor that serves copious portions of traditional northern dishes. Breakfast is also served here.
€38 including breakfast
28

CHAVES

ALBERGARIA JAIME
Rua Joaquim José Delgado, Chaves
Tel 276 301 050
www.albergariajaime.com.pt
There has been an Albergaria Jaime since 1874, though in a different place and with different owners. The main building, now in front of the medieval city walls, dates from the 1940s and has been extended several times. Rooms are co-ordinated and contemporary. The hotel retains its home-like feel and does much to promote its family history.
€68–€98 including breakfast
61

HOTEL FORTE DE SÃO FRANCISCO
Alto da Pedisqueira, Chaves
Tel 276 333 700
www.forte-s-francisco-hoteis.pt
Head for the highest point in town to find the Forte de São Francisco, with its imposing stone walls and cannon; the hotel grounds occupy the whole of the fort's interior. The main hotel building is in the converted Franciscan monastery, where graceful modern structures have been built around ancient ruins. Rooms are well furnished in period style. Be sure to visit the chapel, its cloisters and the interesting centuries-old water cistern. There is tennis on site.
€95–€140
53 rooms, 5 suites
Outdoor

HOTEL VIDAGO PALACE
Parque de Vidago, Chaves
Tel 276 990 900
This colossal palace, 20km (12.5 miles) to the south of Chaves, was built in 1910 as a spa resort. It sits amid 40ha (100 acres) of rolling parkland, and the spa waters are believed to have medicinal properties. The palace is glamour itself; the sumptuous double staircase, shimmering chandeliers and polished marble were all carefully restored in the 1990s. Bedrooms are furnished in period style, and the restaurant serves a mix of regional and international food. Tennis court and nine-hole golf course.
€76–€140 including breakfast
83 rooms, 10 suites
Outdoor
In Vidago, just off the IP3 between Chaves and Vila Real

GUIMARÃES

CASA DE SEZIM TURISMO DE HABITAÇÃO
Lugar de Santo Amaro, Nespereira, Guimarães
Tel 253 523 000
www.sezim.pt
Casa de Sezim, an aristocratic 18th-century ochre home since 1376, is reached via a grand gateway, with an imposing coat of arms. Spacious salons are decorated with ancestral portraits, exquisite chandeliers and rare 19th-century wallpapers; some bedrooms have four-poster beds. Even the pool is surrounded by grass rather than concrete. The estate has produced wine since 1390 and provides tours for enthusiasts.
€110 including breakfast
8 rooms, 1 suite
Outdoor
Head south from Guimarães on the N105 signed to Santo Tirso. In Covas turn right to Santo Amaro. The house is 1.5km (1 mile) after Santo Amaro on the left

PAÇO DE SÃO CIPRIANO TURISMO DE HABITAÇÃO
Tabuadelo, Guimarães
Tel 253 565 337

This family home with an impressive tower and granite exterior dates from the 1400s with 18th-century additions, including a baroque chapel. For many years it was a resting place for pilgrims on their way to Santiago de Compostela in Spain. The old kitchen has a massive hearth and is now the sitting room, while in the tower is an amazing bedroom with an elaborate four-poster bed. In the gardens are azaleas and camellias.
€100–€110 including breakfast
7 Outdoor

Head south out of town on the N105 signed to Santo Tirso. Turn left to Tabuadelo. In the village turn right where signed

POUSADA DA NOSSA SENHORA DA OLIVEIRA
Rua de Santa Maria, Guimarães
Tel 253 514 157
www.pousadas.pt

In the middle of the historic old town (the so-called 'birthplace of Portuguese nationality)', this *pousada* was converted in 1973 from a row of 18th-century townhouses. Today, it is a welcoming place with low beamed ceilings, old floorboards, leather armchairs and, in the bedrooms, attractive soft furnishings and fine bed linen. In summer, the restaurant tables spill out on to the medieval square, and in winter a welcoming open fire blazes.
€92–€144 including breakfast
9 rooms, 6 suites

POUSADA DE SANTA MARINHA
Largo Domingos Leite Castro, Guimarães
Tel 253 511 249
www.pousadas.pt
The monks made a good choice for the site of this 10th- to 12th-century monastery: on a hill with fine views over Guimarães. The reconstruction of the surviving 17th-century buildings preserves monastic sobriety while providing modern comforts. Fine tiles, stone fountains and cloisters are just a few of the features. Some rooms in the old wing are the former monks' cells, so are small, but are well appointed. The restaurant serves a selection of high-quality Minho dishes.
€112–€214 including breakfast
49 rooms, 2 suites
Outdoor

MIRANDA DO DOURO

ESTALAGEM DE SANTA CATARINA
Largo da Pousada, Miranda do Douro
Tel 273 431 005
This *estalagem* (inn) looks out over the Miranda dam and river Douro to Spain. Bedrooms have wooden floors and wood panelling. The furnishings are somewhat dated, but from the windows and balconies there are some breathtaking views. The restaurant serves quality Transmontano cuisine.
€68–€122 including breakfast
12

PESO DA RÉGUA

POUSADA DO SOLAR DA REDE SANTA CRISTINA
Mesão Frio, Peso da Régua
Tel 254 890 130
www.pousadas.pt
A huge baroque gateway leads to this beautiful palace and its spectacular 18th-century chapel, with fine tiles and a gilded altarpiece. Inside the *quinta* proper, there is a French influence in the opulent lounge and in the elaborate beds in the suites. There are other rooms in buildings in the garden, reached along cobbled, flower-lined paths.
€112–€228 including breakfast
19 rooms, 10 suites
Outdoor
On the N101 between Peso da Régua and Amarante

PINHÃO

HOTEL VINTAGE HOUSE
Lugar da Ponte, Pinhão
Tel 254 730 230
www.hotelvintagehouse.com
This idyllic place on the banks of the river Douro was once a port warehouse. The bedrooms still have original 18th-century features and each has a private balcony overlooking the river. The fine arched dining room serves traditional yet innovative dishes, and you can enjoy a glass of port on the shaded terrace. There is tennis on site.
€116–€163 including breakfast
37 rooms, 6 suites (non-smoking rooms available)
Outdoor

PONTE DE LIMA

PAÇO DA GLÓRIA
Lugar da Portela, Jolda, Ponte de Lima
Tel 258 947 177
Most of the bedrooms in this majestic 18th-century palace are in the converted outbuildings and are warm and comfortable. It makes a great base from which to explore the area. Credit cards are not accepted.
€80–€110 including breakfast
9
Outdoor
Just off of the N202 between Arcos de Valdevez and Ponte de Lima. Coming from Arcos, turn right at the village of Jolda

VIANA DO CASTELO

ESTALAGEM CASA MELO ALVIM
Avenida Conde Carreira 28, Viana do Castelo
Tel 258 808 200
www.meloalvimhouse.com
The Melo Alvim was built in 1509 in the Manueline style, and is one of the oldest buildings of its type in Viana. Added to over the years, it has a lovely façade with arched Manueline windows, a neo-baroque fountain and peaceful cloisters. In keeping with the original architecture, the modern interior is sober yet elegant. Bedrooms, reached by a stone staircase, are individually decorated with differing periods of the house's history in mind.
€115–€140 including breakfast
16 rooms, 4 suites
P

VILA REAL

CASA AGRÍCOLA DA LEVADA
Lugar da Timpeira, Vila Real
Tel 259 322 190
www.casadalevada.com
A short distance out of Vila Real, this is a peaceful haven located at the end of a 400m (440-yard) driveway. There are three guest rooms in the main house, which dates from 1922 and has an attractive decorative façade; the apartments in the grounds were converted from various outbuildings. In summer, enjoy breakfast on the patio and savour the home-made bread, jams and honey.
€55–€65 including breakfast
4 rooms, 3 2-roomed apartments
Outdoor
Coming from Porto towards Vila Real on the IP4, turn off at Vila Real Norte. Turn left to *'centro'* then left at the roundabout signed 'Mateus/ Sabrosa'. At 2nd left look for 'Casa Agrícola/Turismo de Habitação' signs

PORTO AND THE DOURO

Porto has plenty of accommodation at every level, whether you're looking for ultra-modern luxury and comfort, or an inexpensive yet friendly place for just a night. It's best to stay right in the middle of the city, and there are plenty of options in the streets on either side of the Avenida dos Aliados. It's worth bearing in mind that Porto's streets are noisy, so it might be better to do without a view and ask for a quieter room at the back. If you're driving, check ahead to see if your hotel has its own parking; paying extra for this makes sense rather than spending hours hunting for a space in the street.

PRICES AND SYMBOLS

Prices are for a double room for one night. All the hotels listed accept credit cards unless stated otherwise . Note that rates vary widely throughout the year.

For a key to the symbols, ▷ 2.

AMARANTE

CASA DA CALÇADA

Largo do Paço 6, Amarante
Tel 255 410 830
www.casadacalcada.com

This imposing building, painted in highly individual yellow, is one of the loveliest places to stay in Portugal. Sitting on the banks of the river Tâmega, overlooking Amarante's church and baroque bridge, the hotel is furnished with a harmonious blend of period and contemporary pieces. Warm and sumptuous tones fill the public spaces and rooms, and the luxurious fabrics, graceful ornaments and flowers make the rooms seem like those of a private house. The fine garden has age-old camellias, a granite water tank with a fountain, and a tennis court. The elegant restaurant serves national and international cuisine.

€118.50–€171.50 including breakfast
30 rooms, 3 suites, 1 presidential suite
Outdoor
The hotel is a conspicuous yellow building in the middle of town

POUSADA DE SÃO GONÇALO

Curva do Lancete, Ansiães, Amarante
Tel 255 461 113
www.pousadas.pt

This *pousada* is (unusually) not in a historic building, but it has outstanding views of the river Tâmega and Serra do Marão, and is just 20km (12.5 miles) from Amarante. All the rooms enjoy valley views and have been refurbished in country style; the dark wooden furniture and plaid bedspreads make them welcoming and comfortable. The restaurant serves high-standard regional fare with the fabulous *serra* as a backdrop.

€92–€122
14 rooms, 1 suite
Leave Amarante on IP4, and go east towards Vila Real. Turn right at the sign to the *pousada*

PORTO

ALBERGARIA MIRADOURO

Rua da Alegria 598, Porto
Tel 225 370 717

This slim 13-storey hotel with its 1950s–1960s feel seems uninspiring, until you see the views. Spread out beneath it are the city and river Douro with the Gaia port warehouses on the opposite bank. Many of the rooms are large and well appointed; the corner rooms with dual aspect are the best. Day or night, enjoy a sunny breakfast or leisurely dinner in the highly acclaimed Restaurante Portucale.

€65 including breakfast
30
P

CASA DO MARECHAL

Avenida da Boavista 2674, Porto
Tel 226 104 702

Built in the 1940s, this charming house sits proudly among the imposing private homes on Porto's exclusive Avenida da Boavista. A superb example of art deco, it is set amid a well-maintained garden, and has five rooms. They are all painted in different shades, have hardwood floors, large comfortable beds and bathrooms with a Jacuzzi, and are furnished with period pieces. The restaurant serves innovative French-Portuguese dishes.

€160 including breakfast
5
Closed Aug
P

CASTELO DE SANTA CATARINA

Rua de Santa Catarina 1347, Porto
Tel 225 095 599

For an original place to stay, this flamboyant Gothic Revival villa really takes some beating. The building is surrounded by palms and covered in tiles depicting scenes from Portuguese history. Built in the 1920s a short distance from the heart of the town, the hotel's interior is a warren of stucco and chandeliers, gilt mirrors and fine faded salons. Art nouveau bathroom fittings,

reproduction beds and wardrobes, and bright carpets grace the bedrooms. The villa is ostentatious and some might say even gaudy, but mostly a stay here is an unforgettable experience.
€63–€75 including breakfast
26
P

HOTEL BOA VISTA
Esplanada do Castelo 58, Foz do Douro
Tel 225 320 020
www.hotelboavista.com
This classic hotel was purpose-built during Porto's heyday at the end of the 19th century, and its position, looking over the river mouth and the Atlantic, could not be better. The elegant architecture, typical of that era, has in no way been compromised by the renovations, which added a modern wing and rooftop swimming pool to the villa. The views from some of the rooms, the restaurant and the rooftop terrace are quite stunning.
€79.80–€89.80 including breakfast
67 rooms, 4 suites
Outdoor
P
From the middle of Porto, follow the riverside road all the way to Foz at the mouth of the river. The hotel is up behind the fort on the right

HOTEL DA BOLSA
Rua Ferreira Borges 101, Porto
Tel 222 026 768
www.hoteldabolsa.com

Down towards the Ribeira, right next to the fine stock exchange building and just 50m (55 yards) from the Port Wine Institute, the Hotel da Bolsa was built on the site of the old São Francisco monastery. Its archetypal 19th-century façade with decorative lintels and arched windows gives way to a modern and comfortable interior. The bedrooms, though unexceptional, have all the facilities you would expect of a 3-star hotel.
€68–€80 including breakfast
36

HOTEL INFANTE SAGRES
Praça Dona Felipa de Lencastre 62, Porto
Tel 223 398 500
www.hotelinfantesagres.pt
Built by a wealthy industrialist in the 1950s, this city landmark is just off the Avenida dos Aliados. Its sumptuous furnishings, draped fabrics and 17th-century Chinese porcelain recall a lost age of elegance. The delicate and sinuous wrought-iron staircase is worthy of special attention, as is the interior courtyard, which is used for alfresco meals as well as being a sun trap in the summer. Rooms are dressed in the same vein, with period-style furniture. The opulent dining room serves international and Portuguese cuisine and there's also an intimate cocktail bar.
€200–€350 including breakfast
72 rooms, 9 suites
P Limited

HOTEL MERCURE BATALHA
Praça da Batalha 116, Porto
Tel 222 043 300
www.mercure.com

A couple of minutes up from the Baixa, right in the middle of Porto's main commercial district and just opposite the national theatre, the Mercure offers quality surroundings and service. The rooms are large and modern, yet traditional in style, and the bathrooms have been newly tiled. The restaurant serves good-quality Portuguese dishes.
€93 excluding breakfast (€7.50)
140 rooms, 9 suites (non-smoking available)

RESIDENCIAL DOS ALIADOS
Rua Eliseo de Melo 27, Porto
Tel 222 004 853
www.residencialaliados.com
This *residencial* is great value for money. It is conveniently located in the heart of town, and the service is friendly. Rooms are simply but adequately furnished and all have their own bathroom. Some have small balconies and overlook the Ávenida; the ones at the back are slightly smaller, but much quieter.
€47.50–€70 including breakfast
43

RESIDENCIAL REX
Praça da República 117, Porto
Tel 222 074 590

On the north side of one of the most attractive garden squares in the city is the Rex, providing low-cost accommodation amid the faded grandeur of yesteryear. The art nouveau exterior is decorated with beautiful emerald-green tiles, while an impressive marble staircase leads up to the reception area. Inside, the public rooms are equally grand, with intricate stucco ceilings. The bedrooms, though fairly basic, are furnished with a well-judged mix of modern and antique pieces.
€45–€55 including breakfast
21
P

VILA DO CONDE

FORTE DE SÃO JOÃO
Avenida Brasil, Vila do Conde
Tel 252 240 600
www.hotelfortesjoao.com
This 18th-century fortress has been converted into a delightful, small hotel. The bedrooms have goose-feather pillows and covers, bath robes and atmospheric candles, and the paintings, by young Portuguese artists, are for sale.
€100–€150 including breakfast
7 suites

STAYING

THE BEIRAS

Coimbra and Aveiro have a good range of accommodation at all prices, while the smaller towns and villages have some wonderful character-packed places to stay. Book ahead in summer, and remember that Coimbra will be jammed with visitors at the end of May, when the end-of-year academic celebrations get underway. If you want to avoid staying in large towns, you could base yourself in the green hills around the national forest of Buçaco, or in Guarda, the highest town in Portugal and a great base for exploring the Serra da Estrela. For a beach break, try Figueira da Foz, a quintessentially Portuguese seaside resort.

PRICES AND SYMBOLS

Prices are for a double room for one night. All the hotels listed accept credit cards unless stated otherwise. Note that rates vary widely throughout the year.

For a key to the symbols, ▷ 2.

AVEIRO

HOTEL MERCURE

Rua Luís Gomes de Carvalho 23, Aveiro
Tel 234 404 400
www.mercure.com

This imposing 1930s townhouse was formerly known as the Hotel Paloma Blanca. Recently bought by the Accor Group, it has thankfully retained its charm and individuality. An attractive tiled stairwell with a stained-glass window leads to the large bedrooms, which have all been redecorated in gentle, welcoming tones. Some rooms overlook the goldfish pond and an attractive conservatory has a garden view.

€64–€68 excluding breakfast
49

P

HOTEL MOLICEIRO

Rua Barbosa de Magalhães 15–17, Aveiro
Tel 234 377 400
www.hotelmoliceiro.com

In the middle of the old town, in front of the main canal, this modern hotel has elegant lodgings along with a family atmosphere and personal service. Public areas have polished wood and marble with gentle lighting, while large, sunny bedrooms have wrought-iron beds, coordinated fabrics, and views over Aveiro's old quarter. The best rooms are on the top floor in a 'penthouse' style and have small balconies. Port and *ovos moles* (traditional cakes) are served on arrival, and there's complementary tea and biscuits.

€85–€97.50 including breakfast
20

P Limited

BELMONTE

POUSADA DO CONVENTO DE BELMONTE

Serra da Esperança, Belmonte
Tel 275 910 300
www.pousadas.pt

South of Belmonte, this *pousada*, one of Portugal's most attractive hotels, was built on the ruins of a 13th-century Franciscan monastery and the restoration is first class. The granite chapel and sacristy are now home to a snug, rustic-style bar and lounge, with antiques and choice printed fabrics. The individually designed bedrooms all have panoramic views of the Zêzere valley and the Serra de Estrela, and the restaurant specializes in traditional local recipes.

€140–€186 including breakfast
23 rooms, 1 suite
P Outdoor

BUÇACO

PALACE HOTEL DO BUÇACO

Mata do Buçaco, Luso
Tel 231 937 970
www.almeidahotels.com

This outstanding building, created as a hunting lodge for the Portuguese royal family, shows neo-Gothic, neo-Manueline architect Manini at his best. Set in 100ha (250 acres) of protected forest, it became a hotel in 1917 after the fall of the monarchy. Its profusion of carved stone, wood panelling, painted tiles and priceless furnishings is overwhelming. The restaurant, with a superb Manueline window and terrace, serves Portuguese-French cuisine and has an impressive wine list.

€95–€220 including breakfast
60 rooms, 4 suites
P

COIMBRA

HOTEL ASTÓRIA

Avenida Emídio Navarro 21, Coimbra
Tel 239 853 020
www.almeidahotels.com

The wedge-shaped Astoria, with its distinctive cupola, has provided fine service since 1926. Restored in 1990, it has kept its original art deco charm. The period elevator—the oldest in the city—takes guests from the marble-and-wood lobby to art deco bedrooms. The dining room has beautiful wooden floors and panelling.

€80–€99 including breakfast
60 rooms, 2 suites

HOTEL QUINTA DAS LÁGRIMAS

Santa Clara, Coimbra
Tel 239 802 380
www.quintadaslagrimas.pt

Across the river from the heart of the town, this wonderful 17th-century palace with its double-staired entrance is now a luxury hotel. The delicately hand-painted breakfast rooms and impressive library are particularly noteworthy; the latter opens out onto the gardens,

which are packed with rare plants. Sadly, an incongruous new bedroom wing and the surrounding high-rises detract a little from the romantic atmosphere. Tennis is available.
€133–€195 including breakfast
48 rooms, 5 suites (non-smoking available)
Outdoor and indoor
Cross the Santa Clara bridge, turn left, then turn right at the sign

PENSÃO LAR BELO
Largo da Portagem 33, Coimbra
Tel 239 829 092
For an inexpensive and central choice, try Lar Belo, on the west side of the old town by the Santa Clara bridge. Rooms have plain, somewhat dated furniture, but they are clean and all have private facilities. Front rooms have views of the river Mondego and are double-glazed to keep out street noise. Bedrooms are on the first to third floors, and there's no elevator. Credit cards are not accepted.
€35–€45 including breakfast
17

FIGUEIRA DE CASTELO RODRIGO

ESTALAGEM FALCÃO DE MENDONÇA
Rua Alvaro Castelões 20, Figueira de Castelo Rodrigo
Tel 271 319 200
www.falcaodemendonca.com
The bedrooms in this 19th-century manor house are well equipped with rustic wooden furniture, and there is a terrace bar and regional restaurant. It is a great place to break a journey from Guarda to Miranda do Duoro.
€70–€90 including breakfast
11 rooms
Outdoor

FIGUEIRA DA FOZ

CASA DA AZENHA VELHA
Turismo Rural, Caceira de Cima
Tel 233 425 041
With its outdoor pool, tennis, horses and bicycles, this is a great place for children, and is a good base for exploring the Beiras. The bedrooms are in beautiful outbuildings, with breakfast served in the main house. There is a comfortable lounge, plus a good restaurant. Credit cards are not accepted.
€75–€90 including breakfast
6 rooms, 1 suite
Outdoor
From Coimbra, take N111 to Figueira da Foz. Shortly before Figueira turn towards Caceira, then immediately left following signs 'Turismo Rural'. After 2km (1.25 miles) turn right for 500m (550 yards); the house is on the left.

GUARDA

QUINTA DA PONTE
Faia, Guarda
Tel 271 926 126
www.quintadaponte.com
In the main house (dating from the 18th century) are two bedrooms plus an attractive salon with a fine Italianate painted ceiling. It looks out over the formal gardens. Five apartments are housed in a modern building overlooking the pool. All have a lounge, log fire, small kitchen, double room and bathroom. Tennis is available on site. It is closed from October to Easter.
Rooms €85, apartments €92, including breakfast
2 rooms, 5 apartments
Outdoor
Leave IP5 at exit 26. Join EN16 for Porto da Carne. The house is signed 'Turismo de Habitação' to the right

RESIDENCIAL SANTOS
Rua Tenente Valdim 14, Guarda
Tel 271 205 400
This great-value *residencial* is close to the central arched gateway of the Torre dos Ferreiros. It's worth a visit just for its architecture, particularly the granite exterior. The modern multilevelled interior has been expertly constructed around medieval features. Rooms are simple, with matching fabrics; breakfast is served in a bright and cheerful room on the top floor.
€40 including breakfast
27 rooms, 1 suite

LAMEGO

CASA DOS VISCONDES DA VÁRZEA HOTEL RURAL
Várzea de Abrunhais, Lamego
Tel 254 690 020
www.hotelruralviscondesvarzea.com
The ruins of an 18th-century ancestral home have been lovingly restored and now stand proudly in formal gardens. Granite balustrades and a veranda lead to an interior filled with period furniture and antiques. The dining room has a wood-panelled ceiling and exquisite antique tiles, and bedrooms, all with two double beds, are large and well furnished. There is tennis on site.
May–end Oct, *Carnaval*, Easter and New Year €160; Nov–end Apr Mon–Thu €110, Fri–Sun €140; all including breakfast
30 rooms, 5 suites
Outdoor saltwater
Leave Lamego southeast on the N226. At Britiande turn left and follow the road to Várzea. The house is signed

MONSANTO

POUSADA DE MONSANTO
Monsanto
Tel 277 314 471
www.pousadas.pt
In what has been called the 'most Portuguese village in Portugal', this *pousada* has a modern exterior. Inside, stone rooms are softened with light wood and bright fabrics. For a view, ask for the corner room upstairs. The restaurant serves regional dishes.
€78–€105 including breakfast
10

VISEU

HOTEL AVENIDA
Avenida Alberto Sampaio 1, Viseu
Tel 232 423 432
www.turism.net/avenida
Off the Rossio, this friendly, family-run hotel has employed the courageous use of rich, bright tones, so often lacking in Portuguese interior design. The first-floor lounge is a welcoming mix of deep green walls, comfortable sofas and an open fire, while the stylish bedrooms are in warm tones of red, blue, green or caramel. This hotel is superb value for money.
€40–€50 including breakfast
29

HOTEL GRÃO VASCO
Rua Gaspar Barrieros, Viseu
Tel 232 423 511
This central, modern hotel has all the usual 4-star facilities. Its stone façade and surrounding gardens are easily spotted, just up from the Rossio. The lobby has marble and wood panelling, and the wide staircase leads to rooms with period-style furniture and coordinated fabrics. The restaurant, with smart furniture and terracotta floors, serves regional cuisine.
€75–€86 including breakfast
106 rooms, 3 suites
Outdoor

ESTREMADURA AND THE RIBATEJO

As Alcobaça, Batalha and Fátima are only a short distance apart, you could base yourself in Alcobaça or Fátima for a couple of nights, though the latter is packed during the pilgrimage season. Alternatively, you could head a little farther east to Tomar, home to the Convento de Cristo, where there's usually plenty of accommodation. Coastal villages all happily combine their original role as fishing ports with that of modern holiday resorts. The pick of these is Peniche. Just inland, Óbidos is central Portugal's biggest tourist magnet; to see it without the crowds, aim to stay at least one night, although advance booking is essential.

PRICES AND SYMBOLS

Prices are for a double room for one night. All the hotels listed accept credit cards unless stated otherwise. Note that rates vary widely throughout the year.

For a key to the symbols, ▷ 2.

ALCOBAÇA

HOTEL SANTA MARIA

Rua Francisco Zagalo 20–22, Alcobaça
Tel 262 597 395

This is the best of Alcobaça's modern hotels. In a quiet corner of the old town, just above the monastery, its rooms are relatively small but are adequately furnished and kept spotlessly clean. Several of them have small balconies looking over the flower-filled square. The hotel has underground parking and, although it has no restaurant of its own, there are several good eateries nearby.

€50–€60 including breakfast
73 rooms, 2 suites

FÁTIMA

HOTEL DOM GONÇALO

Rua Jacinta Marto 100, Fátima
Tel 249 539 330
www.estalagemdomgoncalo.com

The Sanctuary of Our Lady of Fátima is visited by thousands of pilgrims every year, yet accommodation in the area is uninspiring. The best is probably the Best Western Dom Gonçalo, set amid well-tended lawns some 400m (440 yards) from the basilica precinct. The rooms have all modern amenities and staff are welcoming and efficient. The restaurant is known in the area for its traditional cuisine and extensive selection of regional wines.

€75–€82 including breakfast
42

ÓBIDOS

CASA D'ÓBIDOS

Turismo de Habitação, Quinta de São José, Óbidos
Tel 262 950 924
www.casadobidos.com

Built by 19th-century railway engineers, and with great views up to the fortified town of Óbidos, this *casa* offers the choice of double rooms and cottages with kitchens. Rooms in the main house are classically furnished with attractive printed fabrics, while those in the annexe and cottages are more country in style. There isn't a restaurant on site, but there are several within 10 minutes' walk and the English-speaking owner will help with recommendations. Tennis is available on site.

€80 including breakfast
6 rooms, 3 garden cottages
Outdoor

HOTEL REAL D'ÓBIDOS

Rua Dom João de Ornelas, Óbidos
Tel 262 955 090
www.hotelrealdobidos.com

The oldest part of this hotel is believed to date from the 14th century, although its most outstanding feature is the imposing façade, added in the 1700s. Rooms are named after Portuguese kings and queens, and decorated in the style of the appropriate era. The sitting room is rustic, with a big granite fireplace and heavy old beams; outdoors there is a heated pool and a sun terrace overlooking the village.

€130–€185 including breakfast
15 rooms, 2 suites
Outdoor saltwater

POUSADA DO CASTELO

Castelo de Óbidos, Óbidos
Tel 262 959 105
www.pousadas.pt

The *pousada* at Óbidos, within the town's medieval castle, was the first to be converted from a historic building classified as a national monument. The main entrance and windows are noteworthy examples of Manueline carving. The best rooms are the duplex suites in the towers, which have medieval furniture and four-poster beds. Standard rooms are more modest but still comfortable. The limited number of rooms makes advance booking essential.

€149–€207 including breakfast
6 rooms, 3 duplex suites

PENICHE

QUINTA DO JUNCAL

Turismo de Habitação, EN144 Serra d'El Rey, Peniche
Tel 262 905 030
www.quintadojuncal.com

Just 2km (1.25 miles) from Peniche, this *quinta* makes a great base, especially for independent travellers who want to cater for themselves. Three cottages, converted from the old outbuildings, provide fully equipped accommodation for up to six people each. The main house, dating from the 1800s, has double suites,

STAYING

some of which are decorated in 18th-century style with classical furniture, while others are more rustic. All have use of the kitchen. There is tennis on site, plus a golf driving range.

€45–€60 including breakfast, €70–€119 for cottages sleeping up to 6, excluding breakfast

8 suites, 3 cottages

Outdoor

TOMAR

CASA DA AVÓ GENOVEVA

Rua 25 de Abril 16, Curvaceiras, Tomar
Tel 249 982 219

This 17th-century country house, with a gentle pink façade, palm trees and potted flowers, provides a quiet retreat. The cobbled courtyard leads to a series of public rooms—the music room, library and snooker room, small bar, dining room and lounge, where you can take a look at the family photos. Bedrooms, whether doubles in the main house or in the apartments in the converted granary, are decorated with wood-panelled ceilings, antiques and oil paintings. Tennis is available on site.

€70 including breakfast; apartment €80 for 2 people, €130 for 4 people

3 rooms, 2 apartments

Outdoor

Head south out of Tomar on N110. Turn right onto N358 to the village of Curvaceiras

ESTALAGEM DE SANTA IRIA

Parque do Mouchão, Tomar
Tel 249 313 326
www.estalagemiria.com

Although dwarfed by the luxurious Hotel dos Templários nearby, this inn, with its ancient water wheel, has much more character. It sits on a wooded island in the river Nabão, peacefully removed from the hustle and bustle of the nearby town of Tomar. The bedrooms are unpretentious, light and airy, and look out onto the park or across the river. Almost all have balconies that are large enough to sit out on and enjoy a drink or two. The restaurant serves a selection of typical regional dishes.

€53–€85 including breakfast

13 rooms, 1 suite

LISBON

Lisbon's busiest months are from Easter to the end of October, with a lull in August as many people head for the coast. There's accommodation to suit everyone, from luxury hotels to a huge range of *pensões*, many of them in the historic heart of the city. Choose the Baixa, Chiado or Alfama districts to be in the thick of things, though be aware that rooms overlooking the street can be very noisy. Otherwise, check out the hotels on and just off the Avenida de Liberdade, or head out to Lapa, where some of Lisbon's best hotels are to be found.

PRICES AND SYMBOLS

Prices are for a double room for one night. All the hotels listed accept credit cards unless stated otherwise. Note that rates vary widely throughout the year.

For a key to the symbols, ▷ 2.

ALBERGARIA SENHORA DO MONTE

Calçada do Monte 39, Graça
Tel 218 866 002
www.maisturismo.pt/sramonte.html

In a prime location up in the quiet Graça district, this hotel has uninterrupted views of the city. The rooftop breakfast bar looks across the River Tagus to the Christ statue and Ponte 25 de Abril. It's worth paying extra for a south-facing room with a terrace from where you can watch the sun set, or, even better, the sun rise. It's a short tram ride to the heart of the city.

€105–€175 including breakfast

28 (4 with terrace)

Martim Moniz

Tram 28, 12

HOTEL AMERICANO

Rua 1º de Dezembro, Rossio
Tel 213 474 976

Although the furnishings are a little mismatched and the furniture a little old, the bedrooms and bathrooms here are spotlessly clean and its position, just behind the Rossio, couldn't be better. All rooms are double-glazed and have air conditioning and central heating. A few of the rooms share bathroom facilities, so be sure to specify if you want your own bathroom. The hallways and public areas add a touch of elegance, with art deco wooden door frames and a graceful staircase.

€40–€50 including breakfast

50 (10 share facilities)

Rossio

HOTEL AVENIDA PALACE

Rua 1º de Dezembro 123, Rossio
Tel 213 218 100
www.hotel-avenida-palace.pt

Built in 1892, this is Lisbon's only palace and was the first luxury hotel in the city. It still provides palatial opulence in the heart of cultural and business Lisbon, having maintained its characteristic romanticism from the days of the *belle époque*. The bedrooms and public areas are lavishly decorated and packed with 18th-century French and Portuguese Empire-style furniture, and all rooms are equipped with modern facilities, including triple-glazing. Especially enchanting are the fairy-tale black and gilded staircase, magnificent salons and wood-panelled breakfast room with huge, delicate chandeliers and views up the Avenida da Liberdade towards the Parque Eduardo VII.

€165–€375 including breakfast

65 rooms, 17 suites

P

Rossio

HOTEL BORGES

Rua Garrett 108–110, Chiado
Tel 213 461 951

This hotel in the exclusive Chiado district, next to the art

STAYING

nouveau A Brasileira café (▷ 282), with its statue of Fernando Pessoa sitting outside, is good value for money. Don't be put off by the mirrored lobby with its dated furnishings, as most rooms have been refurbished and are now freshly carpeted and well coordinated. Light sleepers should avoid the front rooms, especially at the weekend, when the café stays open late.
€65–€75 including breakfast
96
Baixa-Chiado
Tram 28

HOTEL BRITANIA
Rua Rodrigues Sampaio 17
Tel 213 155 016
www.heritage.pt
For fantastic art deco architecture, this is the place to stay, just off the Avenida da Liberdade. It was built in 1944 by modernist architect Cassiano Branco and, though restored, retains all its charm. Rooms are large and decorated in gentle tones with burnished red and gold details; facilities include a safe and Internet connection. Notice the superb 1940s chandeliers in the polished marble entrance hall, and the symmetry of the breakfast and reading room—this is almost a museum.
€156–€230 excluding breakfast (€12.50)
30 (non-smoking and anti-allergic available)
Limited garage, €9 per day
Avenida

HOTEL DOM CARLOS PARK
Avenida Duque de Loulé 121
Tel 213 512 590
www.domcarloshoteis.com

At the top end of the Avenida da Liberdade, this 3-star hotel has more competitive rates than others in the area and is efficiently run. Rooms are well equipped with a safe and Internet connection; the front-facing twin rooms are more spacious but a little noisier than the back-facing doubles, although double-glazing cuts out much of the street noise. Breakfast and light meals are served throughout the day in the ground-floor restaurant.
€81–€209 including breakfast
76 rooms (non-smoking available)
€10 per day
Marquês de Pombal

HOTEL DUAS NAÇÕES
Rua da Vitoria 41, Baixa
Tel 213 460 710 or 213 460 714
www.duasnacoes.com

In the middle of the pedestrian Baixa shopping district, Duas Nações represents good value for money. Set in a smart 19th-century townhouse with a solid marble and stone entrance, it has simple rooms, some of which share bathroom facilities. All of them, however, have been refurbished and, while modest, are kept impeccably clean. A buffet breakfast is served in a large, bright dining room decorated with tile panels and furnished in dark wood.
€50–€60 including breakfast
69 (24 with shared facilities)
Baixa-Chiado

HOTEL JORGE V
Rua Mouzinho da Silveira 3
Tel 213 562 525
www.hoteljorgev.com
In a 1960s building just off the Avenida da Liberdade is this well-established hotel. The bedrooms are not big and the furniture is not particularly modern—the patterned carpets can clash a little with the riotous curtains and bedspreads—but all have modern marble bathrooms, a safe and some have small balconies. A buffet breakfast is served in the ground-floor dining room and there is 24-hour bar service. Most importantly, the hotel staff are friendly and helpful.
€65–€95 including breakfast
43 rooms, 6 suites (non-smoking available)
€10.50 per day
Avenida

HOTEL LISBOA PLAZA
Travessa do Salitre 7
Tel 213 218 218
www.heritage.pt
Off the Avenida da Liberdade, the Plaza was built in 1953 and elegantly updated in 1988 by Graça Viterbo, one of Portugal's most famous interior designers. The large, modern rooms are decorated in warm tones with sumptuous fabrics. All are equipped with Internet connection. The public areas feel like private sitting rooms, with book-filled cabinets, pictures and ornaments. The restaurant, which serves all meals, including breakfast, has buffet and à la carte menus. Guests can swim at the nearby Sheraton.
€156–€280 excluding breakfast (€12.50)
94 rooms, 12 suites (non-smoking and anti-allergic available)
Limited
Avenida

HOTEL LISBOA REGENCY CHIADO
Rua Nova do Almada 114, Chiado
Tel 213 256 100
www.regency-hotels-resorts.com

The Regency Chiado is in the exclusive Chiado shopping district, inside the reconstructed Armazens do Chiado buildings that were destroyed by fire in 1988. Its main attraction is the awe-inspiring view over Lisbon and its castle from public areas and the private terraces of superior rooms. Decorated according to feng shui principles, the bedrooms are a fusion of Portuguese and oriental design, using rich tones of red, deep greens and dark woods; they also have Internet connection. The breakfast buffet is lavish.

€154–€244 including breakfast

38 rooms, 2 suites

Baixa-Chiado

HOTEL LISBOA TEJO

Rua dos Condes de Monsanto 2

Tel 218 866 182

www.hotellisboaTejo.com

Well priced and well positioned off the Praça da Figueira, the Lisboa Tejo has public areas decked out in a modern mix of stone and glass. Upstairs is predominantly blue: blue corridors lead to blue-and-white rooms equipped with blue furniture. The rooms are comfortable and clean, and all have Internet connection.

€85–€135 including breakfast

58

Rossio

HOTEL MÉTROPOLE

Praca Dom Pedro IV 30, Rossio

Tel 213 469 164

www.almeidahotels.com

An imposing, yet elegant hotel, with a triangular pediment above its main entrance, the Métropole has a prestigious location on the western side of the Rossio. It opened in 1917, and a complete refurbishment in 1993 restored many of the original features. The best rooms are on the top floors facing the square, as they have great views of the castle. All the bedrooms are elegantly furnished in 1920s style and have double-glazing so you sleep easier.

€130–€168 including breakfast

36

Rossio

HOTEL NH LIBERDADE

Avenida da Liberdade 180 B

Tel 213 514 060

www.nh-hotels.com

This boutique hotel on Lisbon's main street is decorated in neutral, muted tones of grey, black and white. Rooms are large, chic and kitted out with many modern facilities, including games consoles. For the best views, choose a room on the seventh floor or higher. The outdoor pool on the roof terrace is open in summer. Breakfast, lunch and dinner are served as a buffet or à la carte in the dining room.

€100–€292 including breakfast

58 rooms, 25 suites (non-smoking available)

Outdoor

Avenida

All Avenida de Liberdade services

HOTEL OLISSIPO

Rua Costa do Castelo 112–126, Mouraria

Tel 218 820 190

www.olissipohotels.com

Named after the city's original Roman hillside settlement, this hotel is located high in the Bairro do Castelo against the medieval city walls. The bedrooms are all decorated with classic furnishings and some have large private terraces. This is a great place to be in June, when the *bairros* of Mouraria and Alfama celebrate the *festas populares* in honour of Lisbon's patron saints (▷ 214).

€135–€165 including breakfast

22 rooms, 2 suites (non-smoking available)

Tram 12, 28

HOTEL REAL PALÁCIO

Rua Tomás Ribeiro 115

Tel 213 199 500

In the Avenidas Novas area, the modern Palácio Real sets a luxurious tone with its black-and-pink marble entrance. This is continued in the warm ochre restaurant, complemented by terracotta tiled floors. All the bedrooms are tastefully decorated with light wood and earthy orange tones, and there is a health club with a Jacuzzi and a massage service.

€130–€200 including breakfast

145 rooms, 4 suites (non-smoking available)

Picoas

HOTEL VENEZA

Avenida da Liberdade 189

Tel 213 522 618

www.3khoteis.com

Housed in what was a palatial 19th-century townhouse, this hotel is really something out of the ordinary. As you go in, notice the façade with its Moorish-influenced arches, especially over the main entrance. The interior is lavishly decorated with wrought iron, polished wood and stained glass, while bright murals of Lisbon adorn the monumental staircase. Some of the 37 rooms overlook the Avenida da Liberdade and all are well coordinated and attractively furnished.

€90–€130 including breakfast

37

€10.50 per day

Avenida

Tram 45

AS JANELAS VERDES

Rua da Janelas Verdes 47, Lapa
Tel 213 968 143
www.heritage.pt

This 18th-century mansion, near the Museu Nacional de Arte Antiga, provides personal service in intimate surroundings. The sumptuous public rooms could easily be mistaken for those of a private house, and the home-away-from-home feeling is encouraged further by the self-service honour bars and the extra-friendly staff. The well-equipped rooms have Internet connection. In summer, breakfast is served on an ivy-clad patio, and on the top floor the library and terrace offer uninterrupted views over the River Tagus.

€182–more than €280 excluding breakfast (€12.50)
29 (non-smoking available)

Bus 27, 40, 49, 60; tram 25
Cais do Sodré

LAPA PALACE

Rua do Pau da Bandeira 4, Lapa
Tel 213 949 494
www.lapapalace.com

Converted from what was once the 19th-century residence of the Count of Valença, and set amid tranquil gardens overlooking the River Tagus, this is one of Lisbon's plushest and most expensive hotels. At the time of writing, it is also the only one with a heated outdoor pool. Inside, the original opulence has been lovingly restored, especially in the splendidly frescoed Columbano room and the Count of Valença suite, the most luxurious room of them all. Others are decorated in art deco, *belle époque* and oriental styles; their facilities, somewhat incongruously, include Internet connection.

€325–€550 including breakfast
109
Indoor and outdoor
Bus 13, 27; tram 25
Santos

PALÁCIO DE BELMONTE

Páteo Dom Fradique 14, Alfama
Tel 218 816 600
www.palaciobelmonte.com

If money is no object, take the opportunity to stay here, at the 500-year-old home of the earls of Belmonte. This national monument has undergone a US$24 million restoration using ancient building methods alongside state-of-the-art energy-saving systems. The bedrooms are peaceful, simple and dressed in rich silks, with great views of Lisbon or the gardens. Even the outdoor pool is lined with black marble. Take your breakfast on the terrace.

€300–€1200 including breakfast
10 suites
Outdoor

PENSÃO ALEGRIA

Praca de Alegria 12
Tel 213 220 670

Set in a pleasant square off the Avenida da Liberdade, this lemon-painted *pensão* provides fairly basic, though friendly, service. All the rooms have been redecorated and have private facilities. The wooden floors and furniture are simple, but fabrics are coordinated and everything is spotlessly clean. The dining room offers breakfast, but no other meals.

€38–€63 including breakfast
35
Avenida

PENSÃO LONDRES

Rua Pedro V 53, 1st–4th floors, Bairro Alto
Tel 213 462 203
www.pensaolondres.com.pt

In the famous area of Principe Real on the northern fringes of the Bairro Alto, this *pensão* is housed in what was once a town mansion. It is good value for money–and is also gay-friendly. The rooms are pleasantly furnished with slightly old-fashioned pieces; those on the fourth floor have good views over the Castelo de São Jorge and Ponte 25 de Abril. Breakfast is served in a sunny dining room at the back.

€60–€70 including breakfast
40
Rossio then Glória elevator
Bus 58

PENSÃO RESIDENCIAL ROYAL

Rua do Crucifixo 50, 3rd floor, Baixa
Tel 213 479 006

Pensão Royal offers one of the best budget deals in town. Its rooms are simple, yet freshly painted and decorated with attractive fabrics. They all have their own bathroom and many are decorated with beautiful antique tiles. Breakfast is not served, but there are plenty of cafés to explore right on the doorstep. If the Royal is full, try Pensão Galicia upstairs, which is run by the same family. It is older, has lino floors and not all rooms have private facilities, but it is clean and friendly (€25–€30, tel 213 428 430).

€30–€45 excluding breakfast
9
Baixa-Chiado

PESTANA PALACE HOTEL

Rua Jau 54, Santo Amaro
Tel 213 615 600
www.pestana.com

About 5km (3 miles) west of the city, this fabulous 19th-century palace has been restored to its former Romantic Revivalist glory. Most rooms are in modern wings that blend effortlessly into the extensive gardens, these sporting exotic specimens and a fine Chinese pavilion. The chandeliered public rooms are particularly opulent, as are the four suites in the main palace building. The hotel's Valle-Flôr restaurant serves outstanding internatinal cuisine (▷ 284).

€265–€280 including breakfast
173 rooms, 17 suites
Indoor and outdoor
Bus 22; tram 18

POUSADA DE JUVENTUDE DE LISBOA

Rua Andrade Corvo 46
Tel 213 532 696
www.pousadasjuventude.pt

Lisbon's 170-bed youth hostel has double rooms with private facilities as well as dormitory accommodation. The rooms are simple, youth-hostel style; if you are sharing a dormitory, remember to bring a padlock for your locker. The bar is open from 6pm to midnight.

€35–€42 for double with private facilities, €12.50–€15 in shared dormitory, including breakfast
170 beds, including 9 doubles
Picoas
Bus 46, 90

RESIDENCIAL AVENIDA PARQUE

Avenida Sidónio Pais 6
Tel 213 532 181
www.avenidaparque.com

On the east side of the Parque Eduardo VII, this unpretentious *residencial* provides efficient service and good value for

money. Rooms are comparable in standard to those in many 3- and 4-star hotels, with matching soft furnishings, modern light wood furniture and double-glazing. This *residencial* has an elegant wooden staircase that leads to the first floor from the black, white and brown marbled entrance hall. Breakfast is served in the ground-floor dining room.
€50–60 including breakfast
44
Parque, Marquês de Pombal

RESIDENCIAL CAMÕES
Travessa do Poço da Cidade, 38, 1º Esq (1st floor, left-hand door), Bairro Alto
Tel 213 467 510
In the heart of the Bairro Alto, this well-priced *residencial* has simple, somewhat dated furniture, but is friendly and clean. Some rooms have private shower facilities and others have sink and bidet combinations with shared lavatories. It is worth remembering that from Thursday to Saturday night the street-side rooms are likely to be noisy well into the early hours owing to late-night revellers. Breakfast is available between 1 March and 30 September for an extra charge. Credit cards are not accepted.
€25–€50 excluding breakfast
10 rooms with private facilities, 8 rooms with shared facilities
Baixa-Chiado Bus 58

RESIDÊNCIA ROMA
Travessa da Gloria 22a, 1º (1st floor)
Tel 213 477 621
Off the Avenida da Liberdade, Residência Roma is unbeatable value if you are visiting in a group and are prepared to self cater. Standard rooms are available, but, for the same price and a walk up an extra flight or two of stairs, there are apartments for up to five people that come complete with a fully equipped kitchenette. The deal is great value for money for stays of three days or more. The interiors of the apartments are simple and slightly old-fashioned, but nevertheless the place is spotless.
Rooms or apartments (up to 5 people) €48–€80 including breakfast
20 rooms, 20 apartments
Avenida

SOLAR DO CASTELO
Rua das Cozinhas 2
Tel 218 806 050
www.heritage.pt
This 18th-century palace shares its ancient walls with the Castelo de São Jorge, and its many medieval elements have been made into interesting architectural features. With only 14 intimate rooms and professionally discreet service, it feels like a private home. Bedrooms are decorated in warm tones with fine fabrics in a mix of modern and classical styles, and the Pombaline-style windows look out onto an attractive tiled patio where a good breakfast is served in warm weather.
€182–€280 excluding breakfast (€12.50)
14 rooms (non-smoking available)
Limited street parking
Bus 37

SOLAR DOS MOUROS
Rua do Milagre de Santo António 6
Tel 218 854 940
www.solardosmouros.pt

Below the Castelo de São Jorge, inside a bright yellow, steeply perpendicular building, this hotel is decorated in wild shades and outlandish modern paintings adorn the walls. The rooms are starkly modern with minimalist furniture, bright art and African sculptures. Some rooms have steep spiral staircases (which may be a problem for small children or people with disabilities) and loft-style ceilings. The breakfast room has great views over Lisbon and the river.
€126–€156 including breakfast
11
Bus 37

VIP EDEN APARTHOTEL
Praça dos Restauradores 24
Tel 213 216 600
www.viphotels.com
This pink art deco building was once one of the city's best-known cinemas. Redeveloped in 1996, it now provides quality self-catering accommodation in studios and apartments, which sleep two to four people each. All are modern and functional, with fitted bathrooms and fully equipped kitchens, including everything from dishwashers to ironing boards. The roof terrace and outdoor swimming pool look straight out onto the Castelo de São Jorge. Breakfast is available on the terrace at an extra charge.

Studios €79–€89, apartments €99–€129, excluding breakfast (€5)
75 studios sleeping up to 2 people, 59 apartments with 2 rooms sleeping up to 4 people
Public parking in front of hotel, €39 per day Outdoor
Restauradores

YORK HOUSE
Rua das Janelas Verdes 32, Lapa
Tel 213 962 435
www.yorkhouselisboa.com
It is essential to book in advance if you want to stay in this tranquil and elegant 17th-century former Carmelite convent tucked away in a discreet location in classy Lapa. Some of the bedrooms are decorated in traditional style, while others have been given the minimalist-chic treatment, combining neutral tones and vibrant hues. On sunny days, you can eat your breakfast under the huge palm in the flower-filled courtyard. A first-rate restaurant, which is frequented by many non-residents, serves a refined version of traditional Portuguese cuisine.
€140–€200 excluding breakfast (€14)
32
€6 per day
Bus 27, 40, 49, 60; tram 25
Santos

AROUND LISBON

Some of Portugal's best accommodation is found around Lisbon, so it's worth considering staying in one of the outlying towns and tackling the capital on a day-trip basis. Verdant Sintra, set in the hills, cooled by fresh breezes, and with frequent trains to central Lisbon, is a good choice. On the coast, smart Estoril has some very fine hotels, where prices can drop by as much as 40 per cent out of season. The same goes for Cascais. Cascais and Estorial can be reached by train from Cais de Sodré train station, Sintra from Lisbon by train from the Rossio train station.

PRICES AND SYMBOLS

Prices are for a double room for one night. All the hotels listed accept credit cards unless stated otherwise. Note that rates vary widely throughout the year.

For a key to the symbols, ▷ 2.

AZOIA

CONVENTO DE SÃO SATURNINO

Azoia
Tel 219 283 192
www.saosat.com

Clinging to the hillside overlooking the Atlantic, this 12th-century convent is an oasis of calm, just the place to relax after a busy day touring. The interiors are simple, but exquisite; in the bedrooms, the atmosphere created by the combination of old ceiling beams and beautiful fabrics is unbeatable. Breakfast is served in the converted kitchen and chapel, or on sunnier days in the garden under the lemon trees. Dinner can be ordered in advance and eaten while admiring the sunset. Beside the pool is a pavilion where an open fire is laid on cooler days.

€145–€160 including breakfast
6 rooms, 3 suites
Outdoor
Turn off the main Cascais–Colares road at the left turn signed 'Cabo de Roca'. Take the first left, go past Moinho de Don Quixote and look for the sign for the *convento* on the left-hand side

CASCAIS

CASA DA PÉRGOLA

Avenida Valbom 13, Cascais
Tel 214 840 040
www.ciberguia.pt/casa-da-pergola

This *casa* in central Cascais is easily recognized by the vivid blue, white and red decorative tiles adorning its façade (not to mention many local postcards). The interior is fairly formal, while the bedrooms have carved wooden beds, stucco ceilings and beautiful old light fittings. The hotel is closed from mid-December to the end of January.

€74.80–€122.20 including breakfast
8

ESTALAGEM DO FAROL DESIGN HOTEL

Avenida Rei Humberto II de Itália 7, Cascais
Tel 214 823 490
www.cascais.org

Close to the marina and the Boca do Inferno, this 19th-century building was once the home of the Count of Cabral. It has now been stylishly refurbished and a modern wing has been added. Seven of the rooms were designed by well-known Portuguese fashion designers, some using vibrant hues and others soft pastel shades. An outdoor saltwater pool and full spa facilities add to the pleasures of this fabulous homage to design. The ultra-modern black, white and shocking-red restaurant, the Rosa Maria, has sea views and a menu of dishes described as 'Mediterranean fusion'. A summer bed terrace and ocean terrace are both perfect for evening drinks. In fact, they boast that you can 'practically touch the sea' from here.

€125–€255 including breakfast
34
Outdoor saltwater

ESTALAGEM SENHORA DA GUIA

Estrada do Guincho, Cascais
Tel 214 869 239
www.senhoradaguia.com

Some 3km (2 miles) from Cascais, on the Guincho road, this fine 1970s building was once the country retreat of the Sagres brewery family. As a hotel it's impressive, offering the most sophisticated accommodation in the area, with immediate access to the sea and several golf courses. Set in pretty gardens with a panoramic saltwater pool and large restaurant terrace, the hotel is tastefully furnished with both period and contemporary pieces.

€125–€250 including breakfast
40 rooms, 3 suites (non-smoking available)
P Outdoor

ESTALAGEM VILLA ALBATROZ

Rua Fernandes Tomás 1, Cascais
Tel 214 863 410
www.albatrozhotels.com

Set right above Cascais bay, this delightful 18th-century villa was built by the dukes of Palmela, and at one time was

frequented by novelists and poets. It now offers some of the most stylish boutique accommodation in Cascais. Rooms in this 5-star hotel are fresh and airy, and are decorated in a Dona Maria style with exquisite fabrics and prints. The equally elegant restaurant serves both national and international cuisine.

€170–€285 including breakfast
11

HOTEL ALBATROZ AND ALBATROZ PALACE

Rua Frederico Arouce 100, Cascais
Tel 214 832 821
www.albatrozhotels.com

The oldest and architecturally most impressive part of this hotel, which is made up of three buildings set on the rocks above the beach, is the duke's palace, dating from 1873. Here, neo-Manueline meets neo-Gothic with a hint of Arab influence. The design of the spacious interior shows great attention to detail. The terrace bar is a great place to watch the sun set and the restaurant offers a fine international menu.

€205–€280 excluding breakfast (€15)
53 rooms, 10 suites
Outdoor

ESTORIL

HOTEL PALÁCIO DE ESTORIL

Rua do Parque, Estoril
Tel 214 680 400
www.hotelestorilpalacio.pt

This hotel was opened in 1930 as part of a plan to encourage tourism in the area, and during World War II it became a haven for many well-heeled refugees from across Europe, including several exiled monarchs. From those who had escaped to safety but had run out of cash, the understanding hotel management accepted payment in diamonds, rubies or gold. Thankfully, much of the hotel's old-world charm remains intact. Its splendid Pompeian public rooms and intimate salons lead gracefully to Regency-style bedrooms, many with superb views.

€250–€300 including breakfast
129 rooms, 32 suites
Outdoor

SINTRA

LAWRENCE'S HOTEL

Rua Consigliéri Pedroso 38–40, Sintra
Tel 219 105 500
www.lawrenceshotel.com

Opened in 1764, this inn is the oldest hotel on the Iberian peninusla, and soon became a haunt of such 19th-century literary figures as Lord Byron. Closed for many years, it was restored to its former state in 1999 and is often referred to as a 'restaurant with rooms'. The wood-panelled library has an open fire, and there are welcoming bedrooms, hand-painted walls and breathtaking views. The superb restaurant serves modern Portuguese cooking (▷ 288).

€185–€290 including breakfast
16

PALÁCIO DE SETEAIS

Rua Barbosa do Bocage 8–10, Sintra
Tel 219 233 200
www.tivolihotels.com

Set in classically landscaped gardens surrounding the pool, this 18th-century palace is a relaxing haven. The public rooms, furnished with period furniture and elaborate hand-painted murals, once hosted parties in honour of the royal family, who used to spend the summer at nearby Sintra. Sash-windowed bedrooms are all lavishly furnished with period-style furniture, and the grand marble staircase descends to the Panoramic restaurant, decorated with 18th-century-style murals. The covered terrace beyond overlooks the gardens. Staff are friendly and helpful, and there is a tennis court.

€240–€285 including breakfast
30
Outdoor

QUINTA DA CAPELA

Turismo de Habitação, Estrada Velha de Colares, Monserrate, Sintra
Tel 219 290 170

This one-time ducal home on the mossy country lane linking Sintra with Colares was practically destroyed in the 1755 earthquake. The façade you see today dates from the 18th-century rebuilding, when the chapel was lined with fine decorative tiles. Rooms are furnished with a mixture of antique and country-style pieces; breakfast is served in the attractive dining room looking out over the quiet gardens. Modern additions include a pool, gym and sauna, but the *quinta* still remains the epitomy of a Sintra country house. Closed November to February.

€140–€160 including breakfast
6 rooms, 3 self-catering cottage suites
Outdoor

THE ALENTEJO

There's plenty of accommodation in Évora, much of it in lovely old buildings in the heart of town, though the place gets crowded during its late June festival and it is expensive compared with elsewhere. Northeast, towards some of Portugal's finest border country, the towns of Estremoz and Vila Viçosa have good places to stay, as does Arraiolos to the north. Farther north again, there's a treat in the shape of hilltop Marvão and Castelo do Vide; make a point of spending the night in one of these picturesque towns. Or you could head for the coast and its resort villages. Fashionable Vila Nova de Milfontes makes a good base. Moura lies to the east towards the border, while farther north is Monsaraz, a fortified village with some of Portugal's finest views.

PRICES AND SYMBOLS

Prices are for a double room for one night. All the hotels listed accept credit cards unless stated otherwise. Note that rates vary widely throughout the year.

For a key to the symbols, ▷ 2.

ARRAIOLOS

POUSADA DE NOSSA SENHORA DA ASSUNÇÃO

Vale das Flores, Arraiolos
Tel 266 419 340
www.pousadas.pt

In the valley below Arraiolos, surrounded by silence and the rolling plains of the Alentejo, this former 16th-century Renaissance Manueline monastery has been gracefully transformed. Cloisters and the exquisitely tiled chapel remain, but they now sit alongside avant-garde extensions and contemporary interior design. Rooms are large and minimalist, with panoramic windows and balconies facing out over the plains. The restaurant serves regional Alentejo cuisine to a high standard. Tennis is available on site.

€112–€186 including breakfast
30 rooms, 2 luxury rooms
Outdoor
From Évora take the N114-4, then the N370, to Arraiolos. Follow signs to the *pousada*. From the A6 take exit 4 and the N4 to Arraiolos

BEJA

POUSADA DE SÃO FRANCISCO

Largo Nuno Álvares Pereira, Beja
Tel 284 313 580
www.pousadas.pt

In the heart of the old town, this former 13th-century Franciscan convent is now an impressive *pousada*. Its most outstanding feature is the splendid frescoed vaulting in the former chapter room, which now serves as a public lounge. Appropriately, the old refectory houses the restaurant, which acts highly acclaimed regional cuisine. The bedrooms, with their locally produced carpets, are stylishly furnished and many look out over the large outdoor swimming pool and palm-filled gardens. Tennis is available.

€112–€178 including breakfast
34 rooms, 1 suite
Outdoor

CASTELO DE VIDE

ALBERGARIA EL-REI DOM MIGUEL

Rua Bartolomeu Álvares da Santa 45, Castelo de Vide
Tel 245 919 191

One of the Alentejo's most attractive hilltop towns, Castelo de Vide makes a good base from which to explore the area. On the town's main street, this village house has been converted into a family-run inn. The owner's passion for antiques is demonstrated in the lounge and passages, while bedrooms are more contemporary with plentiful use of coordinated fabrics. The wooden flooring is stunning.

€50–€60 including breakfast
7

CRATO

POUSADA FLOR DA ROSA

Mosteiro da Santa Maria de Flor da Rosa, Crato
Tel 245 997 210
www.pousadas.pt

Built in the 14th century as the headquarters of the warrior knights of Malta, this restored castle monastery, with cloisters and superb brick vaulting, has managed to maintain the feel of an ancient ruin while providing modern and elegant lodgings. A surprisingly unobtrusive extension contains large minimalist rooms with panoramic windows looking out across the olive groves. Bedrooms in the old part are smaller, yet more atmospheric. The elegant restaurant serves local cuisine.

€112–€186 including breakfast
24
Outdoor
From Castelo de Vide take the N246 to Alpalhão, then N245 to Crato. Flor de Rosa and the *pousada* are signed right

ESTREMOZ

MONTE DA FORNALHA TURISMO RURAL

Arcos, A. Maria Ruiva, Estremoz
Tel 268 840 314
www.montedafornalha.com

Lime-washed walls and fine linen give the rooms of this converted blacksmith's house a Mediterranean feel. The public areas are large and airy in summer and warmed by large fires in winter. As with the rest of the house, the guest rooms are simple yet attractively decorated in warm, natural tones beneath wood-beamed ceilings.

€80–€120 including breakfast
2 rooms, 3 suites, 1 self-contained unit
Outdoor
Turn off the A6 at the Estremoz/Borba exit. Follow signs to Estremoz. After 500m (550 yards), look for the sign to the right

ÉVORA

POUSADA DOS LÓIOS

Largo Conde de Vila Flor, Évora
Tel 266 730 070
www.pousadas.pt

This fine *pousada* is one of Évora's most impressive buildings. Originally a 15th-century monastery, it encompasses several architectural styles; as is fitting, furnishings are sombre and classical. Rooms on the first floor, most of which have been expertly converted from the original monks' cells, are reached by way of an impressive marble staircase. Regional cuisine is served in the old refectory or in the glassed-in cloister. Note, too, the ornately painted walls and ceilings in the main lounge.

€149–€201 including breakfast
30 rooms, 2 suites
Outdoor
Follow signs to *centro histórico* and Templo de Diana. The *pousada* is in the same square as the temple

RESIDENCIAL RIVIERA

Rua 5 de Outubro 49, Évora
Tel 266 737 210

This guest house is on one of the prettiest streets in Évora, just down the cobbled hill from the cathedral. The rooms are bright, clean and airy (although not always well coordinated), and each has a big spotless bathroom. Service is professional and they serve a good breakfast. Originally a private house, it retains many of its design features, such as stone window frames, decorative ironwork and attractive tiling in the entrance hall.

€55–€75 including breakfast
22

SOLAR DE MONFALIM

Largo da Misericórdia 1, Évora
Tel 266 750 000
www.monfalimtur.pt

In a jacaranda-lined square in the heart of Évora, this 16th-century building has been receiving paying guests since 1892. Its arched first-floor arcade and coat of arms make it easy to recognize; a solid granite staircase leads from the cobbled street to reception. Bedrooms have crisp, geometric bedspreads that contrast with the old wrought-iron and brass bedsteads. Breakfast is served in the large airy dining room, or if you prefer, out on the terrace.

€60–€85 including breakfast
25
Limited, outside hotel

MARVÃO

POUSADA DE SANTA MARIA

Rua 24 de Janeiro 7, Marvão
Tel 245 993 201
www.pousadas.pt

This is one of the snuggest *pousadas* in the country, and has some of the most magnificent views. Built within a group of medieval village houses, it is warm and welcoming and the staff seem eager to please. The bedrooms have enchanting Alentejan hand-painted beds.

€92–€144 including breakfast
28 rooms, 3 suites
At double-gated entrance follow signs to the *pousada*. Take the left fork if driving, the right fork if on foot

MONSARAZ

ESTALAGEM DE MONSARAZ

Largo de São Bartolomeu 5, Monsaraz
Tel 266 557 112
www.estalagemdemonsaraz.com

This small, whitewashed and blue-trimmed village inn is near the main entry point to the medieval cobbled village of Monsaraz. The public lounge area has a rustic, lived-in look, with mock-leather sofas, heavy archways and a substantial fireplace, while the bedrooms are decorated in matching fabrics. All have well-kept private bathrooms. The pool and sun terrace have spectacular views. There is also a restaurant.

€84–€90 including breakfast
8 rooms, 4 suites
Outdoor

REDONDO

HOTEL CONVENTO DE SÃO PAULO

Aldeia da Serra, Redondo
Tel 266 989 160
www.hotelconventospaulo.com

Built in 1182, this peaceful one-time convent is a gem. Lime-washed vaulting, a frescoed chapel, fountains and cloisters are just a few of its fascinating features. Old cells have been converted into nicely furnished guest rooms and there is a first-class regional restaurant.

€125–€195 including breakfast
27 rooms, 3 suites
Outdoor
Go south out of Estremoz on the EN381. The *convento* is signposted from this road

VILA NOVA DE MILFONTES

CASTELO DE MILFONTES

Largo Brito Pais, Vila Nova de Milfontes
Tel 283 998 231

This lovely hotel makes a great stop on the Alentejo coast. The rooms have vaulted ceilings, parquet floors and outstanding views, while the restaurant serves top-quality Portuguese cuisine. Credit cards are not accepted.

€155–€166 for 2 people, including breakfast and lunch or dinner
7 doubles, 1 self-catering apartment, 1 room with kitchenette

VILA VIÇOSA

POUSADA DE DOM JOÃO IV

Terreiro do Paço, Vila Viçosa
Tel 268 980 742
www.pousadas.pt

This converted 16th-century convent, next to the imposing ducal palace in the middle of the town, has been a *pousada* since 1996. Public areas are furnished with 16th- and 17th-century pieces, while the large bedrooms have fine embroidered bedspreads and regional Arraiolos carpets. The restaurant serves traditional Portuguese cuisine.

€112–€178
34 rooms, 2 suites
Outdoor

STAYING

THE ALGARVE

This is undoubtedly the most popular part of Portugal as far as tourists are concerned, so when it comes to accommodation you might think that you would be spoilt for choice. Be careful, though. Certain areas, particularly on the central part of the coast, have fallen victim to modern mass tourism, so if you want to avoid the crowds and dislike being swamped by high-rise apartments and hotels, think carefully about where to stay. Inland Tavira, for instance, is one of the most beautiful towns in the Algarve and close to some great beaches. Alternatively, plan a visit in winter or spring, when the area is pleasantly warm, but relatively uncrowded.

PRICES AND SYMBOLS

Prices are for a double room for one night. All the hotels listed accept credit cards unless stated otherwise. Note that rates vary widely throughout the year.

For a key to the symbols, ▷ 2.

ALBUFEIRA

MONTE DAS CORTELHAS

Caminho do Monte, Guia
Tel 289 561 487
www.montecortelhas.com

This attractive farmhouse to the northwest of Albufeira is surrounded by protected agricultural land. Single-storey and whitewashed, with traditional light blue trim, it sits among shady gardens and cobbled courtyards filled with palms and trellises. Rooms are rustic and simple, with terracotta floors, rough wooden beams and patches of bright paint and fabrics. Just minutes away from popular beaches, this tranquil haven, with its views of the Serra de Monchique, remains unaffected by the bustle of the nearby town. Credit cards are not accepted.

€460–€475 including breakfast
4 rooms, 1 apartment
Outdoor
From Albufeira take the EN125 west towards Guia. At the traffic lights in Guia follow signs to Portimão. Monte das Cortelhas is signed about 150m (155 yards) after the lights

SHERATON ALGARVE HOTEL AT PINE CLIFFS RESORT

Praia da Falesia, Albufeira
Tel 289 500 100
www.pinecliffs.com

Standing on a cliff top overlooking the Atlantic Ocean, the Sheraton Algarve is surrounded by pine trees and is part of the impressive Pine Cliffs Resort. The hotel overlooks miles of unspoilt beaches and clear blue seas. The Moorish-influenced architecture results in airy interiors, open patios and gardens, with well-equipped, enticing bedrooms and excellent services–just as you would expect from a world-class hotel chain. A health club, children's village, mini golf and tennis are complemented by several 18-hole PGA gold courses nearby and hotel's own nine-hole golf course and academy. No fewer than six restaurants and bars cater to your every need, from snacks by the pool to cocktail bars and a gourmet meal accompanied by fine wines.

€130–€200
215
3 outdoor, 1 indoor
In Albufeira, follow the blue Sheraton signs

VILA JOYA

Praia da Galé, Albufeira
Tel 289 591 795
www.vilajoya.de

The most exclusive hotel in the Algarve, this Moorish-style villa is perched on a bluff above the shimmering ocean to the west of Albufeira. Its peaceful gardens, shaded by palms, bougainvillea and agaves, lead into sumptuous bedrooms. The decorative keynote here is formal elegance. Richly hued, tile-clad bathrooms, reminiscent of Arab bath houses, exquisite bedlinens and fine furnishings all contribute to the overall feeling of understated luxury. The terrace is home to one of Portugal's best restaurants (▷ 291), and the resort has its own tennis courts.

€400–€580 including breakfast and lunch or dinner
11 rooms, 6 suites
Outdoor
Praia da Galé is 10km (6 miles) west of Albufeira towards Armação de Pêra. Follow signs to Praia da Galé; the hotel is signed

ALMANCIL

QUINTA DOS AMIGOS

Escanxinas, Almancil
Tel 289 395 269
www.quintadosamigos.com

Within a 1ha (3-acre) estate, just 10 minutes from the beach and the resort facilities of Vale do Lago, this is a great place for a family holiday. Simple but comfortable apartments in converted farm buildings provide good self-catering accommodation in an attractive rural setting. In the pretty gardens there is a swimming pool, and the *quinta* has its own stables and riding centre. Credit cards are not accepted.

€41–€82 excluding breakfast
18 apartments sleeping 2–6 people
2 Outdoor pools
From Almancil follow signs south to Quarteira/Vale do Lobo. Keep right to Quarteira. The *quinta* is on the right

QUINTA DOS ROCHAS

Fonte Coberta, Almancil
Tel 289 393 165
www.geocities.com/quintadosrochas

This whitewashed, flower-covered *quinta* is a small and welcoming spot, with covered outdoor terraces where you can enjoy a drink and some peace and quiet. It is close to beautiful beaches and historical and scenic spots, as well as plenty of leisure activities, including tennis, fishing, watersports and the inevitable golf. The farm nearby supplies the oranges that in turn supply your breakfast marmalade.

€45–€70
6
Outdoor
On the road between Almancil and Quarteira, just after Escanxinas

CARRAPATEIRA

MONTE VELHO

Carrapateira, Aljezur, Costa Vicentina
Tel 282 973 207, 966 007 950

This simple, informal hotel stands in the Costa Vicentina Natural Park between the beaches of Amado and Carrapateira. Opened in 2001 by a keen surfer, it is powered by wind and solar energy and the decoration is simple and brighty. Bedrooms are painted in warm tones, with mosquito nets protecting the beds and hammocks on the porch. In warm weather, breakfast is served outside; otherwise it is taken in the vivid yellow dining room with fun fish paintings on the walls. Credit cards are not accepted.

€90–€100 including breakfast
2 rooms, 7 suites
From Carrapateira head south following the signs to Vilarinha; watch for a right turn signed 'Monte Velho'

ESTÓI

MONTE DO CASAL

Cerro do Lobo, Estói
Tel 289 991 503
www.montedocasal.pt

This place offers a winning combination of excellent accommodation and intimate surroundings. The restaurant provides French-influenced meals that are served on the patio in warm weather, so you can enjoy your meal surrounded by palms, bougainvillea and honeysuckle. Breakfast, which consists of fresh orange juice and freshly baked croissants still warm from the oven, is served on bedroom balconies and terraces. All rooms are modern and attractively decorated. There are great sun decks, swimming pools and fountains in the gardens.

€116–€194 including breakfast. Lunch and dinner by request
10 rooms, 8 suites
Outdoor
Take Estói turning off IP1 or N125. Head towards the market, which is on the right-hand side. On the left is a sign to Monte do Casal

LAGOS

CASA GRANDE

Burgau
Tel 282 697 416
www.nexus-pt.com/casagrande

At the top end of the village of Burgau, this restored, English-owned, two-storey house has great character. Rooms in the main building have high ceilings and small balconies, and are furnished with faded antiques. Those in the converted barn at the back are more modern. The restaurant, called the Adega after the old winery in which it is housed, serves traditional Portuguese fare and a good choice of vegetarian dishes. It is open from March to November. Credit cards are not accepted.

€40–€80 including breakfast
3 rooms, 2 suites, 1 cottage
Burgau is 13km (8 miles) west of Lagos on the road to Praia da Luz

HOTEL LUZ BAY

Rua do Jardim, Praia da Luz
Tel 282 789 640
www.lunahoteis.com

Opened in 2003, this white-and-lemon hotel and villa complex has well-furnished, airy, Mediterranean-style interiors. There are family rooms, with refrigerators, for four people, and villa-apartments with two to four bedrooms and self-catering facilities, in addition to a restaurant. There are two adult pools, a fun children's pool with slide, and tennis and squash. The hotel is just 200m (220 yards) away from the popular and child-friendly beach at Praia da Luz.

€40–€153 including breakfast
23 rooms, 4 suites, 44 apartments, studios and villas for 2–10 people
Indoor (winter) and outdoor
The Luz Bay club is signed as you enter Praia da Luz, west of Lagos

QUINTA DAS ACHADAS

Estrada da Barragem, Odiáxere, Lagos
Tel 282 798 425
www.algarveholiday.net

The rooms and apartments here are all named after flowers, inspired by the lush setting. They have wooden ceilings, are simply decorated with modern art on the walls, and are furnished with rural antiques; all have terraces looking out onto the landscaped gardens. Apartments have self-catering facilities with small kitchen and dining areas, and the restaurant serves international cuisine. Credit cards are not accepted.

Rooms €70–€90, apartments €90–€160, including breakfast
3 rooms, 3 self-catering apartments
Outdoor
Exit IP1 at junction 3, signed to Odiáxere and Mexilhoiera. Go straight across 1st roundabout, then at 2nd roundabout take 1st exit right to Odiáxere. In Odiáxere turn right at traffic lights. Follow road for 1.3km (1 mile); the *quinta* is signed on the right

LOULÉ

LOULÉ JARDIM

Praça Manuel de Arriaga, Loulé
Tel 289 413 094
www.loulejardimhotel.com

This attractive building on the corner of a square has been refurbished to provide excellent-value accommodation within the historic heart of Loulé. The white-and-yellow Loulé Jardim has simple, modern rooms. The ones on the fourth floor have balconies that overlook the town, as does the pool terrace and bar on the floor below.

€48–€69 including breakfast
52
P
From the tourist office go left along Rua 5 de Outubro, then left into Rua Vasco de Gama. The hotel is on the corner of the Praça Manuel de Arriaga

MONCHIQUE

ESTALAGEM ABRIGO DA MONTANHA

Corte Pereira, Estrada da Fóia, Monchique
Tel 282 912 131
www.abrigodamontanha.com

Set in exquisite camellia gardens, this inn overlooks the village, the rolling hills of the *serra* and the coast beyond. Its solid granite exterior is softened on the inside by lots of

STAYING

wood and by a sitting room with an open hearth, where welcoming fires are laid in winter. All the pleasantly furnished rooms have balconies from which to enjoy the panoramic views. To preserve the peaceful atmosphere, there are no TVs in the rooms. There is also a restaurant (▷ 292).

€61–€96 including breakfast
11 rooms, 3 suites
Outdoor
Take N266 towards Monchique. At roundabout on far side of town follow signs to Foia; the inn is 2km (1.25 miles) down on the right

ESTALAGEM DAS TERMAS DE CALDAS DE MONCHIQUE
Caldas de Monchique
Tel 282 910 910
www.monchiquetermas.com

The originally Roman spa at Monchique was at its most fashionable back in the 19th century, when the rich and famous flocked to it from all over the country. Today, it is enjoying a new lease of life as spas once again become popular. There are several hotels all run by the same chain, but this one is probably the pick of the bunch, with stylish rooms and a good restaurant that, in winter, has a roaring log fire.

€66–€92 including breakfast
12
Take the N266 towards Monchique. The spa is just before the village, and the hotel is signed

OLHÃO

PEDRAS VERDES GUESTHOUSE
Sitio da Boavista, Quelfes, Olhão
Tel 289 721 343
www.pedrasverdes.com

If you want to stay somewhere that is unquestionably cool, you should try Pedras Verdes. The minimalist rooms of this trendy guesthouse take the themes of Asia, Africa, Arabia, the baroque and Zen as their decorative inspirations. Simple but with flashes of rich tones, they all have up-to-the-minute bathrooms and walk-in shower areas with pebble or slatted-wood floors. The low, Moorish-style building is surrounded by olive trees, and has outdoor terracing and a gorgeous pool.

€85–€95 including breakfast
6
Take the Olhão/Quelfes exit from the IP1, then the N398 south. Follow signs for Quelfes. On entering the village, take a sharp right turn at the grocery store and continue for 1.5km (1 mile)

PORCHES

CASA BELA MOURA
Estrada de Porches, Alporchinhos, Porches
Tel 282 313 422
www.casabelamoura.com

Within minutes of beautiful beaches and good coastal walks, this modern villa, with both a main house and garden rooms, is a peaceful spot. To avoid noise, garden rooms have no TV; all are furnished with traditional hand-painted wooden furniture. Breakfast is a feast, with freshly squeezed orange juice, cereals, and a wide selection of cold meats and cheeses. In the afternoons, complementary tea and cakes are served in the lounge, where, in the cooler months, there is a welcoming open fire.

€70–€130 including breakfast
14
Outdoor
At Porches take Armação de Pêra turn off N125. Casa Bela Moura is on the right after about 3km (2 miles)

HOTEL VILA VITA PARC
Alporchinhos, Porches
Tel 282 310 200
www.vilavita.com

If what you're looking for is a luxury resort with every conceivable facility, then the Vila Vita Parc fits the bill. It is expensive, but what you get compensates. The immaculate cliff-top gardens have steps to the beach and are home to a seawater spa, tennis, squash, swimming pools and a nine-hole pitch-and-putt golf course. The elegant rooms are in the main four-storey building, or in Moorish-style bungalows and villas scattered throughout the grounds. The restaurants serve a variety of cuisines.

€176–€520 including breakfast
87 rooms, 83 suites, 12 apartments
Indoor and outdoor
At Porches take Alporchinhos/Armação de Pêra turn off N125. Follow signs to Vila Vita Parc

PORTIMÃO

CASA TRÉS PALMEIRAS
Praia do Vau, Apartado 84, Portimão
Tel 282 401 275
www. casatrespalmeiras.com

Sitting low on the cliff tops above an attractive rocky cove, this 1960s villa, with its arched colonnades and the three palms from which it gets its name, looks more North African than Portuguese. Views of both the ocean and the cliffs are superb. The rooms, with marble bathrooms and large, luxurious beds, have direct access to the sun terrace, which offers private sun-loungers and a saltwater pool close by. There is no restaurant, but Dolly, the owner, is always ready with a recommendation. Credit cards are not accepted and the hotel is closed from the end of November to the beginning of February.

€170– €200 including breakfast
5
Outdoor saltwater
From Portimão follow signs to Praia do Vau. After 100m (110 yards), turn right up a slope, then left down a dirt track. Casa Trés Palmeiras is 50m (55 yards) ahead through black gates

QUINTA DAS FLORES
Vale de Dega, Mexilhoeira Grande, Figueira
Tel 282 968 649

This delightful Algarvian villa is owned by a landscape gardener by the name of David and, as you would expect, is carefully planned, with swaying palms, a pretty pool, shady corners and bougainvillea trellises. Artist Gealle is responsible for the interior design, with its warm tones of yellow, bright printed fabrics and examples of her lively paintings, which are often African in theme. There are tennis courts on site, too. Credit cards are not accepted.

Rooms €85, cottage €120 per person (minimum 3 nights)

38 rooms, 1 self-catering studio, 1 self-catering cottage (sleeps 4)

Outdoor

Take the Figueira turning off the N125 between Portimão and Lagos. Pass the church and take the right turn just before Café Ceélia

QUINTA DO LAGO

QUINTA DO LAGO

Quinta do Lago
Tel 289 350 350
www.hotelquintadolago.com

This well-known hotel is set in around 800ha (2,000 acres) of rolling hills and pine woods, overlooking the Ria Formosa. The sun shines all year round here, and is especially perfect for golf lovers, who can play a round or two on some of Europe's best courses–four championship courses are within reach of the hotel. There's also a lake for windsurfing, riding stables and tennis. The spa offers health and beauty therapies in relaxing surroundings. There are two restaurants, one elegant and Italian, the other Portuguese and international.

€200–€500

121 rooms, 20 suites

Outdoor and indoor

From Almancil follow signs to Quinta do Lago. Turn left at 2nd traffic lights, take left fork and carry on for 2km (1.25 miles) to the roundabout, the entrance to Quinta do Lago

SAGRES

POUSADA DO INFANTE

Sagres
Tel 282 620 240
www.pousadas.pt

Strategically positioned on the rugged cliffs above the Atlantic, this *pousada*'s decoration is themed around early discoveries. Guest rooms have balconies or terraces overlooking the ocean. The building is attractive; long, low and whitewashed, with a red-tiled roof, arched colonnades and decorative chimneys. The restaurant serves regional Portuguese cuisine.

€97–€157 including breakfast

38 rooms, 1 suite

Outdoor

In Sagres, follow signs leading to the *pousada*

SILVES

QUINTA DO RIO

Sítio São Estevão, Apt 217, Silves
Tel 282 445 528

To the northeast of Silves, this rural guest house enjoys a peaceful setting in the rolling hills. It is surrounded by attractive orange groves. The original house has been enlarged to accommodate six guest bedrooms, each with a shower room. All the rooms are simple and clean, and four of them have their own terraces. Evening meals can be arranged in advance. The hotel is closed for two weeks in December.

€40–€80

6

TAVIRA

CONVENTO DE SANTO ANTÓNIO

Cerro do Lobo, Tavira
Tel 289 990 140

This is a little gem of a hotel, which has been owned by the same family for the past 200 years. It started off life in the 17th century as a Capuchin convent and, from its exterior, it still retains a religious feel, the atmosphere and peace of the former convent having been carefully preserved–most of the rooms are converted monks' cells. The large white portal of the chapel hides the garden and the original cloisters. Breakfast is served in the arched courtyard and guests are free to linger here or by the pool. Advance booking is essential and there is a minimum stay requirement of two to four nights, depending on the season.

€120–€180 including breakfast

6 rooms, 1 suite Outdoor

PENSÃO RESIDENCIAL CANTINHO DA RIA FORMOSA

Ribeiro de Junco, Cacela Velha, Tavira
Tel 966 172 717
www.cantinhoriaformosa.com

This is the Algarve as it used to be–simple guest houses and tiny, untouched fishing villages. Close to the idyllic Cacela Velha in the Parque Natural da Ria Formosa, this whitewashed and blue-trimmed house has simple but spotless rooms with fine views over the countryside. The beach is on the Ilha de Tavira sand spit, a short walk down the lane, followed by a ferry ride across the lagoon (runs Jun–Sep).

€45–€75 including breakfast

8

Turn off the N125 at Cacela Velha between Vila Real de Santo António and Tavira. Just before reaching the village, turn right to Fábrica. Stay on this road until you reach the *pensão*

QUINTA DA LUA

Bernardinho, Santo Estevão, Tavira
Tel 281 961 070
www.quintadalua.com.pt

The lasting impression of this peaceful haven is of the quality of the service provided by the friendly hosts, Miguel and Vimal. The rooms are a very harmonious mix of simple rustic furniture and boutique-style chic. Outside, shady gardens, bamboo-covered decks for alfresco breakfasts and saltwater pool complete the picture. No children. Credit cards are not accepted.

€60–€130 including breakfast

6 rooms, 2 suites (all non-smoking)

Outdoor

From Tavira take the N125 towards Olhão. Turn right to Santo Estevão, then 1st left and next right. Look out for the arched entrance

Planning

BEFORE YOU GO

CLIMATE

Despite its Atlantic position, Portugal's climate is predominantly Mediterranean, with the characteristic warm, dry summers and mild, wet winters. Its geographic position on Europe's western edge ensures that the average rainfall is far higher than that of Spain to the east, which means that the landscape is verdant year-round over most of the country. Much of the rain falls between November and March, with levels increasing as you move north; showers are possible throughout the year in the far north, particularly in the higher areas of the Douro and Trás-os-Montes. Winters in the latter can be bitter, with low temperatures and snow. In central and southern Portugal, especially on the coast, it's mild throughout the year, though it is often cloudy in winter. Summers are hot and sunny all over the country, the high temperatures pleasantly tempered by cooling breezes along the coast.

WHEN TO GO

Most seasoned visitors to Portugal agree that spring and autumn are the best times to go; the weather is at its best and you'll escape the huge influx of high-summer tourists. In late spring the whole country looks superb, with sheets of brilliant wildflowers. Autumn is warm but not too hot. It is a particularly good time to visit the Douro and the wine-producing areas as the grape harvest is in full swing and the red and gold shades of the season are at their best.

July and August are prime vacation time, with millions of foreign visitors flocking into the country and many Portuguese themselves on holiday. The Algarve, in particular, is at its busiest: Prices are at their peak, and bars, shops and beaches are packed to bursting point. This time of year is ideal for exploring northern Portugal, however, as the days are hot and sunny and there's less chance of rain than during the rest of the year.

Lisbon and the southern third of the country have mild winters, so this is an excellent time to explore the capital, the Alentejo and the Algarve. A few tourist facilities may be closed, but there's the huge advantage of dramatically reduced prices and few other visitors. The Algarve, in particular, feels like a different place without the crowds, and there's the bonus of hillsides pink and yellow with almond blossom and acacia.

WEATHER REPORTS

BBC World news and CNN have websites and broadcast regular global weather updates in English, and the Weather Channel and the Met Office in the UK also have global weather websites:
www.bbc.co.uk/weather
www.CNN.com
www.weather.com
www.metoffice.com

WHAT TO TAKE

- Clothing requirements will differ depending on the time of year and where you're going.

TIMES ZONES

CITY	TIME DIFFERENCE	TIME AT 12 NOON IN PORTUGAL
Auckland	+12	midnight
Berlin	+1	1pm
Brussels	+1	1pm
Chicago	-6	6am
Dublin	0	noon
Johannesburg	+2	2pm
London	0	noon
Madrid	+1	1pm
Montreal	-5	7am
New York	-5	7am
Paris	+1	1pm
San Francisco	-8	4am
Sydney	+10	10pm
Tokyo	+9	9pm

Portugal uses GMT in winter, moving the clocks forward one hour between the last Sunday in March and the last Sunday in October. The 24-hour clock is generally used in Portugal.

WEATHER STATIONS

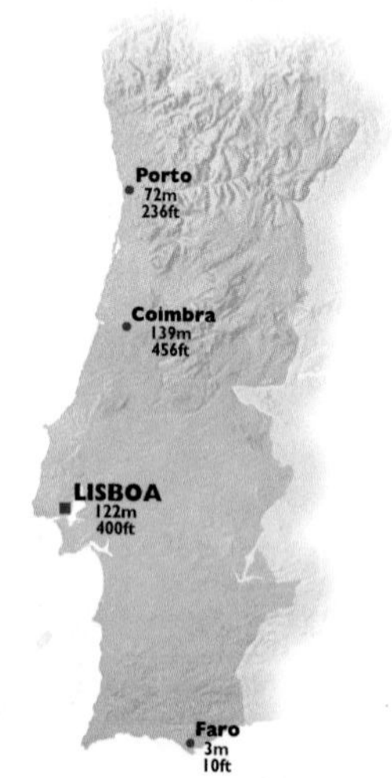

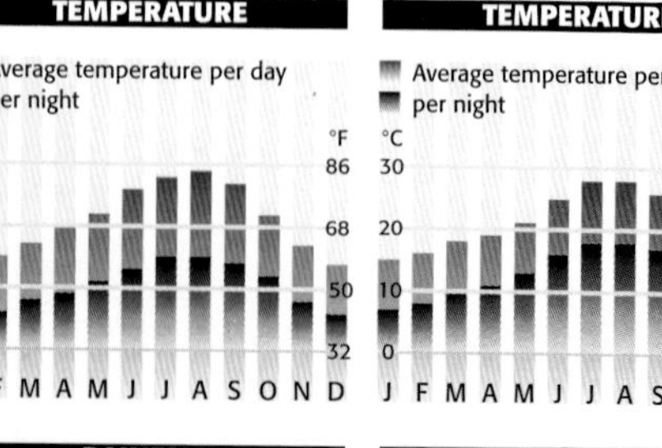

RAINFALL **RAINFALL**

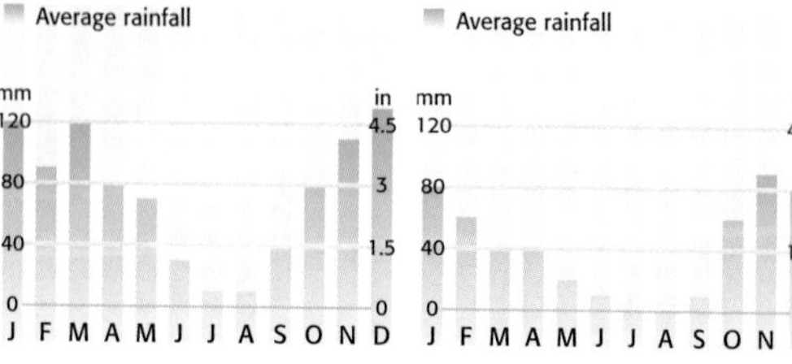

PLANNING

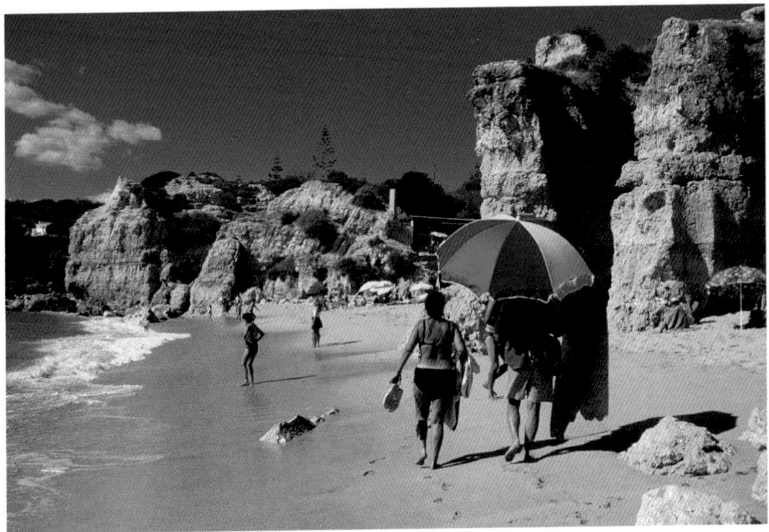

Praia do Castelo, Algarve, one of the region's best beaches

Take lightweight cotton and linen to wear during the summer, with some light wool garment or a cotton jacket for cooler evenings in the north. Waterproofs and an umbrella are essential for winter and make sense if you're in northern Portugal at any time of the year.

- If you intend to visit churches or other religious buildings, take some clothes that cover your shoulders and knees.
- Casual clothing is the norm during the day, but take more formal clothes for the evening, particularly for Lisbon, Porto and the classier Algarve resorts.
- Comfortable shoes are essential for sightseeing.
- Take emergency contact telephone numbers and addresses, the numbers of your travellers' cheques in case of loss or theft, the numbers of credit/debit cards, and registration numbers of mobile phones, cameras or expensive equipment (in case you need to report their loss or theft).
- Carry your travel insurance details; you will need to clear any medical emergency payments with your insurers, and you will need to notify them immediately in case of theft or loss.
- If you are taking any prescribed medication, bring enough for the duration of your trip. If you do need to replace medicine, you should have a note of the pharmaceutical name of your medication, as trade names may differ in Portugal.
- If you forget to take anything, you should be able to buy most things you are likely to need in Portugal, although the choice may be limited in some of the more remote areas.

REMEMBER TO PACK

- Waterproofs and a folding umbrella.
- A secure bag for daily use, large enough to hold camera, books, maps etc.
- Your driver's licence.
- Your address book.
- A torch (flashlight) and binoculars.
- A first-aid kit, including plasters (Band Aids), antiseptic and antihistamine creams, and painkillers.
- A Portuguese phrasebook—any efforts to speak Portuguese are much appreciated; English may not be spoken in the remoter rural areas. See also pages 335–338.

PASSPORTS AND VISAS

- All visitors to Portugal must carry a valid passport or identity card at all times.
- UK citizens need a passport to enter Portugal, but visitors from other EU countries need only an identity card. No visa is necessary if you're from the EU, and there is no time limit to your stay.

LISBOA

TEMPERATURE

Average temperature per day
per night
°C °F
30 86
20 68
10 50
0 32
J F M A M J J A S O N D

PORTO

TEMPERATURE

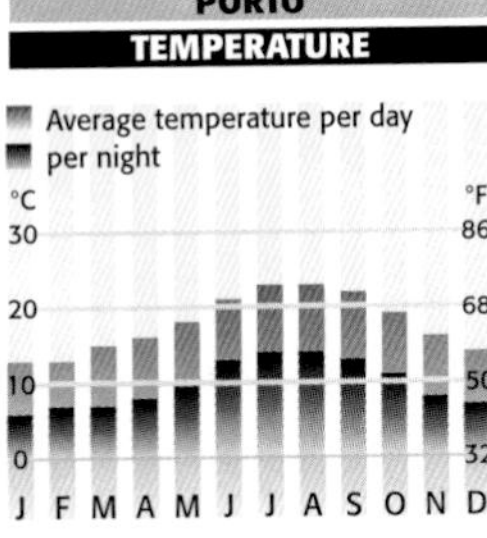

RAINFALL

RAINFALL

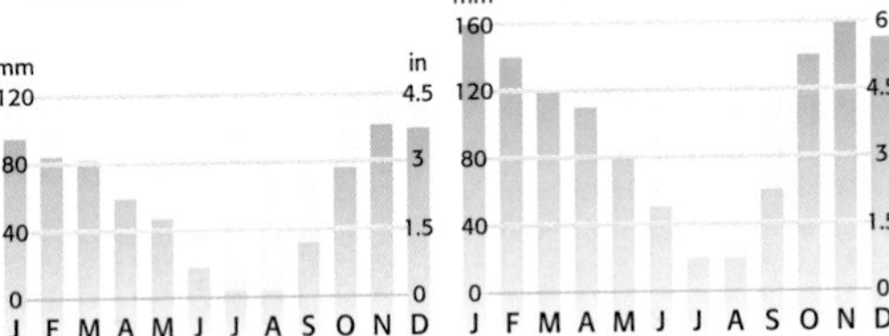

PLANNING

- US, Canadian, Australian and New Zealand visitors need a passport valid for a further six months from the date of entry into Portugal. Visitors from those countries can stay for up to 90 days without a visa.
- US, Canadian, Australian and New Zealand visitors can extend their stay by obtaining an extension from district police headquarters or a branch of Servico de Estrangeiros e Fronteiras (Foreigner's Registration Service), which has offices in the most popular tourist areas. Applications should be made at least a week before the entry permit runs out, and applicants should be prepared to offer proof that they can support themselves without working.
- Visa rules can change at short notice and you should check with the Portuguese embassy in your home country.

TRAVEL AND HEALTH INSURANCE

- Take out travel insurance as soon as you book your trip to ensure you will be covered for cancellations and delays.
- Make certain your policy includes repatriation, medical expenses, baggage and money loss, accident compensation and personal liability.
- Keep all receipts in case you need to make an insurance claim.
- Report losses or theft to the police and make sure you obtain a written report from them. No insurers will consider your claim without this.
- If you have private medical coverage, check your policy, as you may be covered while you are away.
- If you travel a lot, consider taking out an annual travel insurance policy.

DUTY-FREE GUIDELINES

Duty-free allowances for US citizens

You may take home up to $800 of duty-free goods, providing you have been out of the country for at least 48 hours and have not made an international trip within the previous 30 days. This limit applies to each member of the family regardless of age, and allowances may be pooled. For the most up-to-date information, see the US Department of Homeland Security's website: www.customs.treas.gov

- **1 litre of alcohol**
- **100 cigars (non-Cuban)**
- **200 cigarettes**
- **1 bottle perfume (if trademarked in the US)**

Duty-free guidelines for EU citizens

You cannot buy goods duty-free if you are journeying within the EU. You can take home unlimited amounts of duty-paid goods, as long as they are for your personal use. For UK visitors, anything more than the following is considered to be for commercial use:

- **3,200 cigarettes**
- **3kg of tobacco**
- **400 cigarillos**
- **200 cigars**
- **110 litres of beer**
- **10 litres of spirits**
- **90 litres of wine**
- **20 litres of fortified wine (such as port or sherry)**

Whatever your entitlement, you may not bring back goods for payment (including payment in kind) or for resale. For the most up-to-date information, see the H. M. Customs and Excise website: www.hmce.gov.uk

A selection of port, Portugal's premier drink, on display, Lisbon

PORTUGUESE EMBASSIES AND CONSULATES ABROAD

COUNTRY	ADDRESS AND TELEPHONE NUMBER	WEBSITE
Australia	23 Culgoa Circuit, O'Malley, ACT, tel 02 6290 1733	www.consulportugalsydney.org.au
Canada	645 Island Park Drive, Ottawa K1Y OB8, tel 613/729-0883	www.embportugal-ottawa.org
Ireland	Knocksinna House, Knocksinna, Fox Rock, Dublin 18, tel 01 289 3375	
New Zealand	PO Box 305, 33 Garfield Street, Parnell, Auckland, tel 09 309 1454	
	PO Box 1024, Suite 1, 1st Floor, 21 Marion Street, Wellington, tel 04 382 7655	
South Africa	1006 Main Tower, Standard Bank Centre, Hertzog Boulevard, 8001 Cape Town, tel 421 4560/1/2	
UK	11 Belgrave Square, London SW1X 8PP, tel 020 7235 5331	www.portembassy.co.uk
USA	2125 Kalorama Road NW, Washington DC 20008; tel 202-328 8610	www.portugalemb.org

PRACTICALITIES

ELECTRICITY

- Electricity in Portugal is 220/380 volts. Electric sockets follow European regulations and take plugs with two round pins. If your appliances are manufactured for 240 volts, you will need a plug adaptor, which is best bought before you leave home.
- North American visitors, whose voltage is different, will also need to bring a transformer; this should be bought before leaving home, as they are hard to find in Portugal.

LAUNDRY

Many middle- to top-range hotels have a laundry service, where your clothes are collected from your room and returned there, and the (often high) charge added to your bill. There aren't many self-service launderettes, but *lavandarias* are common. These provide a *roupa branca* (general laundry service), which includes overnight washing, ironing and mending (if necessary) at a relatively low cost, or *limpeza a seco* (dry cleaning). Some *lavandarias* do only dry cleaning.

PUBLIC LAVATORIES

You'll find the most hygienic facilities in museums, restaurants and shopping malls. Otherwise, public lavatories are few and far between and hygiene levels may leave a lot to be desired. It's acceptable to use the lavatories in bars, but they may be less than pristine, and toilet paper may not be provided. Look for signs saying *Banheiro*, *Lavabos*, *Retretes* or WC; once inside, it's *homens* or *cabalheiros* for men and *senhoras* or *mulheres* for women. Ask for a *casa do banho* or *um banheiro* if in doubt.

SMOKING

- Smoking is universal in Portugal, and is still permitted in most hotels and restaurants. Non-smoking areas are few and far between.
- Smoking is not permitted in museums, inside airport buildings, or on some forms of public transportation.
- You can buy cigarettes at tobacconists, or from vending machines in bars and cafés.

The Portuguese as a nation are child-tolerant

WC - Público

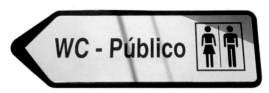

Most public facilities in Portugal's towns and cities are clearly signed

CONVERSION CHART

FROM	TO	MULTIPLY BY
Inches	Centimetres	2.54
Centimetres	Inches	0.3937
Feet	Metres	0.3048
Metres	Feet	3.2810
Yards	Metres	0.9144
Metres	Yards	1.0940
Miles	Kilometres	1.6090
Kilometres	Miles	0.6214
Acres	Hectares	0.4047
Hectares	Acres	2.4710
Gallons	Litres	4.5460
Litres	Gallons	0.2200
Ounces	Grams	28.35
Grams	Ounces	0.0353
Pounds	Grams	453.6
Grams	Pounds	0.0022
Pounds	Kilograms	0.4536
Kilograms	Pounds	2.205
Tons	Tonnes	1.0160
Tonnes	Tons	0.9842

CLOTHING SIZES

Clothing sizes in Portugal are in metric. Use the chart below to convert the size you use at home.

UK	Metric	USA	
36	46	36	SUITS
38	48	38	
40	50	40	
42	52	42	
44	54	44	
46	56	46	
48	58	48	
7	41	8	SHOES
7.5	42	8.5	
8.5	43	9.5	
9.5	44	10.5	
10.5	45	11.5	
11	46	12	
14.5	37	14.5	SHIRTS
15	38	15	
15.5	39/40	15.5	
16	41	16	
16.5	42	16.5	
17	43	17	
8	36	6	DRESSES
10	38	8	
12	40	10	
14	42	12	
16	44	14	
18	46	16	
20	46	18	
4.5	37.5	6	SHOES
5	38	6.5	
5.5	38.5	7	
6	39	7.5	
6.5	40	8	
7	41	8.5	

VISITING PORTUGAL WITH CHILDREN

You should have no serious problems if you are on a package holiday, as these are organized by foreign tour operators with their own nationals in mind. Independent holidaymakers in Portugal with children may find a few pointers useful.

- Like many other southern Europeans, the Portuguese adore children and are tolerant towards

Disability need not be a barrier; facilities and access are improving

them, fussing over them everywhere and welcoming them into bars and restaurants.

- Despite this, facilities such as changing rooms, high chairs and special children's menus are virtually non-existent.
- Portuguese children stay up late—if parents are eating out, the kids go too. This means that most hotels do not have a baby-sitting/listening service.
- In summer, adjust to the local routines, making sure your children have a quiet time out of the heat during the afternoon siesta hours.
- Most hotels, if notified in advance, will put up to three or four beds in a room so families can stay together; there is usually no charge for children under 6 sharing their parents' room, while discounts for kids aged between 6 and 12 can be as much as 50 per cent.
- Disposable nappies (diapers) and other baby requisites are available everywhere, but if you are bottle-feeding your baby you might want to bring your usual formula with you. *Leite do dia* (fresh milk) is sold in larger shops and supermarkets only. You can buy *fraldas* (nappies/diapers) in supermarkets and pharmacies.
- Children aged between 5 and 11 qualify for a 50 per cent discount on trains, but must pay full fare on buses and metros; under-5s go free.
- Museums and most sights are usually free for small children.
- Pushchairs (strollers) can be hard work on cobbled streets.
- In traffic-heavy areas, keep a close eye on your children; Portuguese drivers often ignore pedestrian crossings.
- Remember the strength of the sun in Portugal; use a high-factor sun cream and keep the children covered up until they acclimatize. Get them to stay in the shade during the middle of the day when the sun is at its hottest, and if they're swimming, persuade them to cover up—better a wet T-shirt than a sunburned and miserable child.
- Don't be surprised if total strangers pick up your baby or talk to your children. This is quite normal in Portugal.

VISITORS WITH DISABILITIES

- Portugal's facilities for visitors with disabilities are not extensive and you should not expect standards as high as those at home. However, the situation is slowly improving, and major hotels in the main cities and visitor areas usually provide good access, as do official buildings, including some museums.
- Portuguese national tourist offices abroad can supply lists of wheelchair-accessible hotels.
- Airports and major railway stations generally have good disabled facilities.
- The Portuguese will often go out of their way to help make your visit problem free.

Contact addresses

- Secretariado Nacional Para a Reabilitação e Integração das Pessas com Deficiêcia in Portugal is an organization that produces a comprehensive, accessible tourism guide, with good hotel and restaurant listings and much more (Avenida Conde Valbom 63, Lisboa, tel 217 929 500 or 217 959 545, www.snripd.mts.gov.pt).
- Holiday Care is an organization in the UK that publishes a range of information about accessibility for holidaymakers with disabilities (Holiday Care, 7th Floor, Sunley House, 4 Bedford Park, Croydon, Surrey CR0 2AP, tel 0845 124 9972, www.holidaycare.org.uk).
- In the US, SATH (the Society for Accessible Travel and Hospitality) has lots of tips for holidaymakers with visual impairment or poor mobility (347 5th Avenue, Suite 610, New York, NY 10016, tel 212/447-7284, www.sath.org).

PLACES OF WORSHIP

If you are a Roman Catholic you will have no problem celebrating your faith in religious Portugal. You will find Catholic churches in even the smallest towns and villages, and there are some famous pilgrimage sites to track down. Numerous religious festivals are celebrated all over the country throughout the year, and tourist offices can give details about local places of worship and service times.

With its large expatriate communities, the Algarve is also well served with places of worship for other religiions and religious denominations, and you'll be able to get details at tourist offices and in the foreign-language local press.

The following are places of worship in Lisbon:

Anglican

St. George's Church, Rua São Jorge, Jardim de Estrela, tel 213 906 248.

Baptist

Igreja Evangélica Baptist da Graça, Rua Capitão Humberto Ataíde 28, Santa Apolónia, tel 218 132 889.

Islamic

Mesquita Central de Lisboa, Avenida José Malhôa, Praça de Espanha, tel 213 874 142.

Jewish

Comunidade Israelita de Lisboa, Rua Alexandre Herculano 59, Rato, tel 213 858 604.

Ismaeli

Centro Cultural Ismaelita, Rua Abranches Ferrão, laranjeiras, tel 217 229 000.

MONEY

LOST/STOLEN CREDIT CARDS

American Express
800 205 598

Diners Club
21 315 98 56

MasterCard
800 8 11 272

Switch
+44 8457 203 099

Visa
0800 895 082

Like many other EU countries, Portugal has adopted the euro as its official currency. Outside larger cities and the main tourist areas, cash is still widely used, although the majority of hotels will accept credit and debit cards. You will need cash to pay for small transactions, and market traders don't accept credit cards. It's a good idea to make certain you are carrying some euros before you leave your arrival airport, although larger hotels will change money for you.

It makes sense to use a combination of cash, travellers' cheques and credit cards rather than relying on just one form of payment during your trip. Before departure, check with your bank that you can withdraw cash from cash machines (ATMs) in Portugal. You should also ask what charge is made for this service and make a note of an emergency telephone number to call if your card is lost or stolen.

Travellers' cheques are by far the safest way of carrying money, because you are insured against loss. Remember to keep a separate note of the cheque numbers and the telephone number you need to call if they are stolen.

You will need to show your passport when cashing travellers' cheques.

Banks in Portugal normally open at 8.30am, closing at 3pm

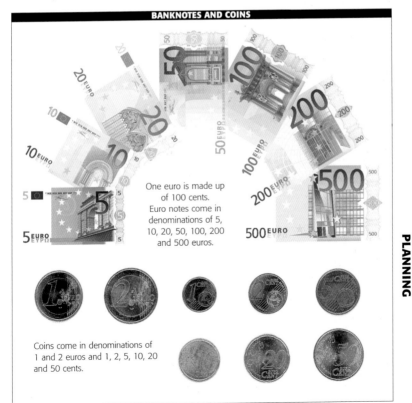

BANKNOTES AND COINS

One euro is made up of 100 cents. Euro notes come in denominations of 5, 10, 20, 50, 100, 200 and 500 euros.

Coins come in denominations of 1 and 2 euros and 1, 2, 5, 10, 20 and 50 cents.

The easiest way of getting cash is to use a multibanco *(ATM)*

ATMS

Cash machines, called *multibancos*, are by far the easiest way of withdrawing cash in Portugal. You'll find ATMs in even the most remote places and you can withdraw up to €200 a day. They are accessible 24 hours a day and most have onscreen instructions in English and other languages.

Check with your bank before you leave that you will be able to use your debit card for transactions in Portugal, and make certain that you have a 4-digit PIN number. You will normally be charged a cash-handling fee on credit card withdrawals as well as the usual currency conversion charge.

BANKS

There are *bancos* (banks) in all but the smallest towns in Portugal. They are normally open Monday to Friday 8.30–3, but in Lisbon and some of the Algarve resorts they may also be open in the evening for exchange. Commission rates for changing money stand at around €3–€5; some banks have automatic exchange machines for different currencies. Commission rates for changing travellers' cheques in a bank can be exceptionally high—it's better to head for a *caixa* (savings bank) or a *câmbio* (exchange bureau).

BUREAUX DE CHANGE

There are *câmbios* (exchange bureaux), where you can change cash and travellers' cheques, in all cities and resort areas; the commission for changing travellers' cheques will be lower than that charged by a bank.

CREDIT CARDS

American Express, MasterCard and Visa are the most widely used credit cards, but are still not accepted by smaller establishments or for small purchases. Look for the credit card logos in shop and restaurant windows, or check with the staff before making your purchase. You can use your credit card to withdraw cash, although your card issuer will charge it as a cash advance. Make sure you have a 4-digit PIN number if you intend to use this service. Banks will also advance cash against your credit card at the counters.

TAX REFUNDS

Sales tax or VAT (known in Portugal as IVA) is added to the price of services and goods in Portugal. This is non-refundable to residents of EU member states. Visitors from the US can claim back sales tax on goods purchased from shops that participate in the tax-free scheme; these will have a sticker displayed in their windows. Keep the receipts and fill in the claims form at the tax-free counter at the airport before your departure. You can find out more at www.portugalrefund.com.pt.

WIRING MONEY

You can have money wired to you from your home country in an emergency, but this can be expensive and will entail much lengthy telephoning. The main agents are Western Union (www.westernunion.com) and Moneygram (www.moneygram.com).

10 EVERYDAY ITEMS AND HOW MUCH THEY COST

Sandwich	€2.50
Bottle of water	50¢
Cup of tea or coffee	€1–€3
0.5 litre of beer	€1–€3
Glass of wine	60¢–€4.50
Daily newspaper	€1–€1.50
Roll of camera film	€4
20 cigarettes	€2.50
An ice cream cone	€1–€2
A litre of petrol (gas)	90¢

Shopping in Lagos. Small stores may not take credit cards

TIPPING

The Portuguese do not tip heavily, and service is often included in your hotel or restaurant bill, although it's usual to give a little extra if the service has been particularly good. The following is a general guide:

Bars and cafés:	round up to the nearest euro
Restaurants:	10%
Taxis:	only tip if service has been exceptionally good
Porters and chambermaids:	50¢–€1 per day
Cloakroom and lavatory attendants:	20¢–50¢

HEALTH

MEDICAL ASSISTANCE
Ambulance (emergencies)
112

Look for the green cross sign if you need to visit a pharmacy

BEFORE YOU GO

- If you are likely to need a repeat prescription during your trip, apply for this well before you travel. Also ask your doctor to give you a note of the pharmaceutical name of any medications you are taking in case your medicine goes missing. Trade names for various medicines may differ in Portugal.
- If you are planning a long visit, have a health check, an eye test and a dental check-up before you leave home.
- No inoculations are required for visiting Portugal, although it is a good idea to check the date of your last tetanus shot and have a booster if necessary.

INSURANCE

- As part of the European Union, Portugal has free reciprocal health agreements with other member states. To take advantage of this, UK citizens should take form E111 (EHIC–European Health Insurance Card–from 2006), which must be stamped by the post office before you travel. This new form is issued on an individual, instead of a family, basis. Though having such a form is not essential, it is a good idea to get one as it makes dealing with the red tape easier. One form is valid for an indefinite period and allows reduced-cost medical (including hospital) treatment while you are in Portugal. The reduced fee, however, must be paid, plus part of the cost of any prescribed medicines.
- In many parts of Portugal, public health care lags behind that of other European countries and you are strongly advised to take out insurance to cover the cost of private treatment. This is essential for US citizens, who must pay for all medical treatment in Portugal. Check to see if your existing health cover is valid when abroad.
- For up-to-date information, see the Department of Health's website on www.doh.gov.uk (in the UK) or the National Center for Infectious Diseases on www.cdc.gov/travel (in the US).
- If you need treatment, take a copy of your insurance documents to the doctor or hospital–they may be able to bill your insurance company direct.
- You may need to contact your insurance company for clearance before treatment, so make sure you have their 24-hour emergency number to hand.
- If you have to pay for treatment or medicines, keep all receipts for your insurance claim.

WHAT TO TAKE WITH YOU

- Mosquitoes can be bad in Portugal, so stock up with insect repellent and coils or electric zappers for use in bedrooms at night.
- A small first-aid box is a good idea, particularly if you have children with you. This should include painkillers (Paracetemol or Tylenol), antiseptic and antihistamine cream, sunburn lotion and plasters (Band Aids).
- A spare pair of glasses or contact lenses (if worn).
- Prescription medication.

FINDING A DOCTOR OR GETTING HOSPITAL TREATMENT

- Go to the local *centro de saúde* (health clinic) closest to where you are staying. You'll find one in every town, and some provide a 24-hour emergency service, called SAP/CATUS.
- Ask at the local *farmácia* (pharmacy).
- Ask your hotel to call a *médico* (doctor) for you.
- For an ambulance call 112.

PHARMACIES (FARMÁCIAS)

- Pharmacies are designated by a green cross on a white background.
- They are open 9–1 and 3–7 Monday to Friday and 9–1 on Saturdays.
- Every *farmácia* displays in its window or on its door the address of the nearest pharmacy with a 24-hour service, and a list of those open until 10pm.

PLANNING

SELECTED HOSPITALS WITH EMERGENCY DEPARTMENTS

CITY	ADDRESS	TELEPHONE
Lisbon	Hospital de Santa Maria, Avenida Prof. Egas Moniz	217 975 171
Porto	Hospital Santo António, Largo Prof. Abel Salazar	222 077 500
Coimbra	Hospital de Universidade de Coimbra, Praça Prof. Mota Pinto	239 400 400
Lagos	Hospital Distrital, Rua do Castelo dos Governadores	282 763 034
Portimão	Hospital Distrital de Portimão, Sítio do Poço Secos	282 450 300

• Portuguese pharmacists are highly trained and can give medical advice and dispense drugs, such as antibiotics, that would be available only on prescription in many countries.
• For many minor ailments it is worth consulting a pharmacist before looking for a doctor; many speak English.

WATER

• Portugal's tap water is generally safe to drink, but be careful in small or remote villages.
• You'll see roadside fountains all over Portugal, where people fill bottles with local spring water; if you follow suit, always fill from the running water just below the spring itself.
• Bottled water is cheap; it comes *com gás* or *sem gás* (sparkling or still).
• If you're out and about, always have a supply of bottled water with you—and make sure you drink it when temperatures soar. Sugary drinks, coffee and alcohol are diuretics and will add to, rather than slake, your thirst.
• If you're feeling thirsty, it's a sign you're already mildly dehydrated.

SUMMER HAZARDS

Portugal is extremely hot in summer, so you will need to protect yourself against the heat and the sun.
• Dress in loose clothing, keep the back of your neck covered and wear a sunhat.
• Apply high-factor (SPF 15 +) sun cream at frequent intervals.
• Drink about 2 litres (4 US pt) of water a day during hot weather.
• Keep out of the sun when it's at its strongest—between midday and 3.30pm.

ALTERNATIVE MEDICAL TREATMENTS

Portugal has no tradition of complementary medicine, apart from the widespread use of traditional herbal remedies in rural areas. Alternative medicine is only now starting to catch on, with a growing interest in homoeopathic and holistic treatments. The best way to track down practitioners is to look in the Yellow Pages under *Homeopatia*.

SUNBURN INDEX

	SKIN TYPE			
Index	**Fair, burns**	**Fair, tans**	**Brown skin**	**Black skin**
1/2	Low	Low	Low	Low
3/4	Medium	Low	Low	Low
5	High	Medium	Low	Low
6	Very high	Medium	Medium	Low
7	Very high	High	Medium	Medium
8	Very high	High	Medium	Medium
9	Very high	High	Medium	Medium
10	Very high	High	High	Medium

Low risk: the sun is not likely to harm you but you should still use sunscreen.
Medium risk: do not stay in direct sunlight for more than 1–2 hours.
High risk: you could burn in 30–60 minutes. Avoid direct sunlight, cover up and use sunscreen of SPF 15+.
Very high risk: you could burn in 20–30 minutes. Avoid direct sunlight, cover up and use sunscreen of SPF 15+.

HEALTHY FLYING

• People visiting Portugal from places like the US, Australia or New Zealand may be concerned about the effect of long-haul flights on their health. The most widely publicized concern is deep vein thrombosis, or DVT. Misleadingly called 'economy class syndrome', DVT is the forming of a blood clot in the body's deep veins, particularly in the legs. The clot can move around the bloodstream and could be fatal.
• Those most at risk include the elderly, pregnant women and those using the contraceptive pill, smokers and the overweight. If you are at increased risk of DVT see your doctor before departing. Flying increases the likelihood of DVT because passengers are often seated in a cramped position for long periods of time and may become dehydrated.

To minimize risk:
Drink water (not alcohol)
Don't stay immobile for hours at a time
Stretch and exercise your legs periodically
Do wear elastic flight socks, which support veins and reduce the chances of a clot forming

EXERCISES

1 ANKLE ROTATIONS

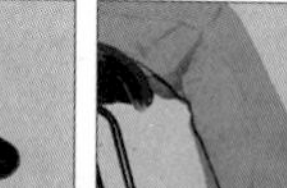
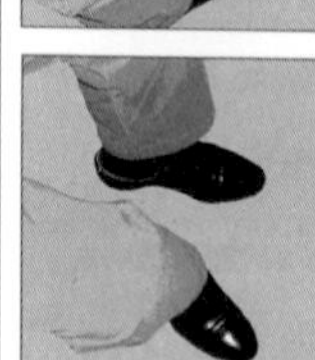

Lift feet off the floor. Draw a circle with the toes, moving one foot clockwise and the other counterclockwise

2 CALF STRETCHES

Start with heel on the floor and point foot upward as high as you can. Then lift heels high keeping balls of feet on the floor

3 KNEE LIFTS

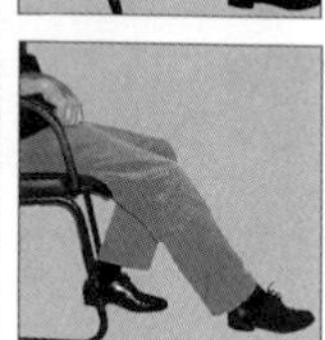

Lift leg with knee bent while contracting your thigh muscle. Then straighten leg pressing foot flat to the floor

Other health hazards for flyers are airborne diseases and bugs spread by the plane's air-conditioning system. These are largely unavoidable, but seek advice from a doctor before flying if you have a serious medical condition.

COMMUNICATION

USEFUL TELEPHONE NUMBERS
Emergency services 112
International operator-assisted service 179
Directory enquiries (directory assistance) 118
International directory enquiries 177
Speaking clock 151
Tourist enquiries (freephone) 800 296 296

TELEPHONING

- All calls are most easily made using card-operated *credifones*.
- Cards are available from post offices, newspaper shops, kiosks and tobacconists, and come in denominations of €3, €6 and €9.
- You'll find *credifones* on the street, in bars and cafés and in some tourist information offices.
- Main post offices also have telephone cabins where you can make your call and pay afterwards. The clerk will assign you a cabin.
- The cheap rate for national and international calls runs from 9pm to 9am Monday to Friday and all day on weekends and public holidays.
- Hotel charges for telephoning from your room are high.
- You can make a reverse-charge (collect) call *(chamada cobrar ao destinatório)* from any telephone. Dial 120 for a European connection and 172 for the rest of the world.
- If you have problems, dial 179 to speak to an operator.

MOBILE PHONES

- It can be expensive to use your mobile phone abroad as you will often be charged for receiving as well as making calls.
- If your mobile phone SIM card is removable, it makes sense to remove it and replace it with a local card on arrival. You will then be able to use the Portuguese mobile telephone system and pay at local rates.

AREA CODES FOR MAJOR CITIES	
Aveiro	234
Beja	284
Braga	253
Bragança	273
Coimbra	239
Évora	266
Faro	289
Guarda	271
Leiria	244
Lisbon	213
Portimão	282
Porto	222/223

To call from outside Portugal, dial 00 351 + the 9-digit number.

CALLING ABROAD

To call the UK from Portugal, dial 800 800 440 + the area code (omitting the first 0) + the number.
To call the USA from Portugal, dial 800 800 + your telephone company's US code (see right) + the area code + the number.

COUNTRY CODES FROM PORTUGAL

Portugal's international dial code is 800 800.
The international dial code for mobile phones is 268.

Australia	800 800 610
Belgium	800 800 320
Canada	
(via AT&T Canada)	800 800 124
(via Stentor)	800 800 122
France	800 800 330
Germany	800 800 490
Greece	800 800 300
Ireland	800 800 353
Netherlands	800 800 310
New Zealand	800 800 640
Spain	800 800 340
Sweden	800 800 46 00
UK	800 800 440
USA	
(via AT&T)	800 800 128
(via Ameritech)	800 800 119
(via Bellsouth)	800 800 117
(via MCI)	800 800 123
(via Southwestern Bell)	800 800 115
(via Teleglobe USA)	800 800 118
(via TRT)	800 800 188
(via USSprint)	800 800 187

You need a card (which is easy to buy) for Portugal's credifones

PLANNING

USING A COIN-OPERATED PHONE

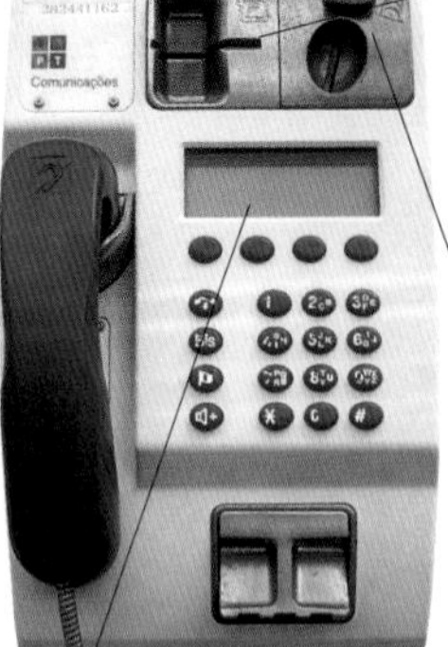

1 Lift the receiver and listen for the dial tone.

2 Insert phone card or coins. The coin drops as soon as you insert it.

3 Dial or press the number.

4 If you want to cancel the call before it is answered, or if the call does not connect, press the coin release lever or hang up and take the coins from the coin return.

5 Once your call is answered, the display will show how much money or units you have left. Unused coins will be returned after the call.

POSTAGE RATES	
Within Portugal	45¢
Within Europe	56¢
To America	72¢
To Africa	72¢
To Asia	72¢
To Australia	72¢

COURIERS	
DHL	800 345 345
Federal Express	800 833 040
UPS	199 199 345
EMS–International Express Courier	800 009 966

SENDING A LETTER

- *Selos* (stamps) can be bought at *correios* (post offices), kiosks, tobacconists, automatic dispensing machines and anywhere that has the sign of a red horse on a white circle against a green background and the words 'Correio de Portugal'.
- There are two levels of mail service: *correio azul* (blue mail) for urgent letters, which must be weighed and posted in a blue box; and regular mail, which is collected from red boxes. Letters within the EU will normally arrive in 6 to 8 days, and to the USA in 10 to 14 days.

POST OFFICES

- Post offices are normally open 8.30–6 Monday to Friday; larger offices may also be open on Saturdays, while the main post offices in Lisbon and Porto have much longer opening hours.
- You can have mail delivered *poste restante* (general delivery) to yourself at any post office in Portugal. You will need to go to the counter marked *Encomendas* and show your passport. Filing may be erratic, so get the clerk to check under all your initials or other possible letters when you collect mail. There is a small charge (about €1) for the service. *Encomendas* letters should be addressed as follows:

LAST NAME first name
Encomendas
Correio de Portugal
Praça dos Restauradores
1200 Lisboa

Blue post boxes are for overseas and urgent mail, red ones for regular post

INTERNET ACCESS AND CAFÉS

- Internet cafés can be found in larger Portuguese towns and resorts. Most charge around €2.50–€4 per hour.
- It may be cheaper to buy a debit card for use at internet stations in post offices; these give you up to 3 hours' access for around €5.50.
- You'll need a web-based email account if you want to send or receive email from abroad (hotmail, Yahoo etc.).
- The netcafeguide.com website lists internet cafés in Portugal and around the world (www.netcafeguide.com/countries/Portugal).
- Remember to log out when you've finished and close the browser to dump your session cookies (temporary files). These are shared computers and you don't want someone else reading your emails, or accessing your personal information.
- If you have Bluetooth technology you can access the internet using your mobile phone.

LAPTOPS

If you intend to use your own laptop computer in Portugal, remember to bring a power converter for re-charging and a plug socket adaptor. You will also need an adaptor for the telephone socket, and it's also a good idea to bring a surge protector.

PERSONAL SECURITY

Although Portugal is a safe country with low levels of crime, particularly against visitors, you should still take common-sense precautions:

- Take care around main railway stations, on public transportation in cities, and in areas full of visitors in larger towns, where pickpockets and bag-snatchers may be operating.
- Beware of thieves operating in pairs; one may try to distract you with a question or remark while the other robs you.
- Never carry more cash than you need and keep passports, credit cards and travel tickets separate from your money.
- Never carry a wallet, money, or credit cards in a back pocket.
- Place valuables in a hotel safe-deposit box.
- Wear your bag or camera slung diagonally across your chest, rather than hanging loose from one shoulder; knapsack-type bags are also good.
- Always lock your car, even if you intend leaving it for only a short time, and make certain luggage and other valuables are kept securely out of sight in the boot (trunk).
- Take especial care if your journey includes a night train, as thieves sometimes target sleeping passengers. Take it in turns with a companion to watch the luggage. Keep an eye on suitcases during daytime journeys as well.
- Never leave valuables on a bar, a restaurant table or hanging from the back of a chair.
- Leave valuable jewellery at home.
- Stick to brightly lit main thoroughfares at night.
- If you are robbed, whatever you do, don't resist.

EMERGENCY NUMBERS

From anywhere in Portugal
112
Dial this number and ask for the emergency service you need—Polícia (the police), Ambulância (ambulance), or Bombeiros (fire service)

Police stations, pharmacies and health clinics are clearly signed

LOST PROPERTY

- If you lose money or other items, inform the police and contact your insurance company as soon as possible.
- If your travellers' cheques are stolen, notify the issuing company, quoting the numbers of the first and last cheque and the numbers of those you have already cashed.
- If your debit or credit card is stolen, report it to the police and phone your bank/credit card emergency number to cancel the card as soon as possible. Emergency lines are open 24 hours a day and have English-speaking staff.
- If you want to make an insurance claim for theft, you will have to get a written report from the police. This can be a time-consuming business, so it's not usually worth reporting the loss of inexpensive items or small amounts of money.

LOSING A PASSPORT

- If you lose your passport or it is stolen, report it to the police and then contact your embassy or consulate for assistance (see panel below).
- Keep a separate note of your passport number and a photocopy of the page that carries your personal details.

POLICE

There are three different types of police force in Portugal. It's worth noting that Portuguese police sometimes retain traces of the authoritarian attitudes that were common during the Salazar dictatorship. If you are stopped, don't argue, and treat the police with courtesy. Politeness will ensure that you're quickly on your way.

- The PSP (Polícia de Segurança Pública) wear blue uniforms and police the cities. Among other duties, they are responsible for incidents involving visitors.
- The GNR (Guarda Nacional Republicana) wear blue-grey uniforms and knee-high boots; they operate in rural areas and patrol the roads and motorways for traffic offenders.
- The Serviço de Estrangeiros e Fronteiras is a specialist police force dealing with foreign and border affairs, such as work permits.

FIRE

- When checking into your room, read the fire instructions on the back of the door and check the location of the nearest fire escapes.
- Never use lifts (elevators) during a fire emergency.
- If you are trapped, block the bottom of the door with wet towels and remember that the air closest to the floor will be relatively smoke free.

EMBASSIES AND CONSULATES

Australian Embassy	Avenida da Liberdade 200, 2nd Floor, 1250-147 Lisbon, tel 213 101 500, fax 213 101 555 Consulate services at same address
Canadian Embassy	Avenida da Liberdade 200, 4th Floor, 1269-121 Lisbon, tel 213 164 600, fax 213 164 655 Consulate services at same address
Irish Embassy	Rua da Imprensa a Estrela 1-4, 1200-684 Lisbon, tel 213 929 440, fax 213 977 363 Consulate services at same address
UK Embassy	Rua de São Bernardo 33, 1249-082 Lisbon, tel 213 9240 00, fax 213 924 183/184/188 Consulate services at same address
USA Embassy	Avenida das Forças Armadas, 1600-081 Lisbon, tel 217 273 300 , fax 217 279 109 Consulate services at same address

MEDIA

NEWSPAPERS

If you read Portuguese, there's a wide choice of newspapers available. Even if your command of the language is less than perfect, local papers can be a good way to find out what's on in the way of entertainment. Portugal's main daily papers include:

- *Público*: A quality daily with comprehensive coverage; good on international news. It issues a Friday guide to the arts (www.publico.pt).
- *Diário de Notícias*: A long-established Lisbon-based paper, a big seller and noted for its classified ads (www.dn.pt).
- *Jornal de Notícias*: Sister paper to the *Diário*, published in Porto. It produces local sections for virtually every area of the country. (www.jnoticias.pt).
- *Diário Económico*: A national daily business paper that also covers international finance (www.de.iol.pt).
- *Expresso*: Weekly, multi-sectioned paper that summarizes the week's news. Its political analysis is considered good and it runs excellent cultural listings. (www.expresso.pt).
- *A Bola*, *Record* and *O Jogo*: A trio of sports dailies that concentrate on the Portuguese obsession with soccer—although some other sports news does creep in. Each is packed with photos and graphics and concentrates respectively on Benfica, Sporting (the two Lisbon soccer teams) and Porto (www.abola.pt, www.record.pt, www.ojogo.pt).

ENGLISH-LANGUAGE NEWSPAPERS

There are a few local English-language newspapers for Portugal's expatriate communities. The *Anglo-Portuguese News* is published in Estoril and re-hashes local and foreign events. It's good for listings and residents swear by the classified ads. In the Algarve you should be able to buy *The News*, another weekly with listings, classified ads and good news coverage. The *Algarve Resident* is a free monthly paper aimed at resident Britons. You'll find international newspapers on sale in Lisbon, Porto and some other major cities, and on the Algarve, though the quality papers usually arrive a day or more late. Tabloids, such as the UK's *Sun*, *Daily Mirror* and *Daily Mail*, are published in Spain, and are normally on sale the same day on the Algarve. The *International Herald Tribune* and *USA Today* are available in Lisbon, Porto and other major towns.

It's worth checking Portuguese newspapers to find out what's on

MAGAZINES

On Portuguese newsstands and kiosks, television dominates the magazine genre. The immensely popular *TV Mais* comes out weekly, presenting news of schedules and gossip; *Caras* is another popular weekly with plenty of gossip and pictures. Quality publications include *Visão*, a respected news weekly similar to *Time* or *Newsweek*, and *Grande Reportagem*, which, despite its glossy looks, is a serious monthly magazine with similar coverage. *Activa* and *Cosmopolitan* are aimed at women and cover fashion and beauty, while *Boa Mesa*, *Caras Decoração* and *Casa Claudia* concentrate on food, home and design. For a real taste of TV obsessiveness, take a look at *Telenovelas*, which is entirely devoted to the super-popular Portuguese soaps. Disney publishes no fewer than four titles aimed at younger readers.

TELEVISION

Portugal has two state-run television channels, RTP1 and RTP2, and two private channels, SIC and TV1. The public-service channels have strong news reporting and investigative journalism, and also show imported US and UK shows, which are subtitled in Portuguese rather than dubbed. This also applies to all films shown on television. SIC and TV1 are unashamedly lowbrow, the former devoting hours to Brazilian *telenovelas* (soap operas) and ludicrous game shows—riveting viewing even if you don't understand a word. Cable and satellite channels in bars and restaurants are mostly tuned to sport, but better hotels will generally have CNN and BBC World available.

RADIO

Portuguese radio concentrates on music, with the occasional bursts of news, soccer and traffic reports. Rádio Cidade (107.2FM) gives a good taste of what's popular in music, and you'll hear international hits alternating with distinctive Latin American and local sounds. The church-owned Rádio Renascença has a huge following for its talk shows; there's also a 24-hour news channel, TSF (89.5FM). The BBC World Service broadcasts on 648KHz medium wave and 15.00MHz short wave, and the Voice of America is on 553KHz to 1700KHz.

OPENING TIMES AND TICKETS

Most shops and businesses in Portugal close during the siesta period, usually from around 12.30pm to 2.30 or 3.

BANKS
Banks are open Monday to Friday 8.30am–3pm. Some branches in big towns may stay open until 6.

BARS
Bars open around 8.30am and close any time between 10pm and midnight. Opening hours may vary in rural areas or holiday resorts. In summer they may be open until 3–5am.

CAFÉS
These are usually open from about 7am onwards.

CHURCHES
Most churches open early in the morning for Mass, though some are kept locked and can be visited only by prior arrangement with the caretaker. Others have specific opening times and may charge a fee for entry to their cloisters, treasuries etc. Churches that are open regularly will close for a couple of hours in the middle of the day, opening again between approximately 3 and 6pm. Check the Sights section of this book for specific times, or contact the church concerned.

MUSEUMS AND GALLERIES
Museums and monuments are normally open from 10–12.30 and 2–6, though times vary according to the season and location. Check the Sights section of this book, or contact the museum, gallery, or local tourist office. Almost all Portuguese museums are closed on Mondays, and national palaces on Wednesdays.

OFFICES
Opening hours are usually 9–1 and 3–7.

POST OFFICES
Post offices are normally open 8.30am–6pm Monday to Friday; larger ones may also be open on Saturdays, and the main offices in Lisbon and Porto have much longer opening hours.

SHOPS
Shops are generally open between 9 and 1 and again from 3 to 7. Outside larger towns and cities they often close on Saturday afternoons and Sundays. Shopping malls stay open seven days a week, often until midnight, and large supermarkets are open every day from 9 to 10 (5pm on Sundays).

PHARMACIES
Pharmacies are open from 9 to1 and 3 to 7 Monday to Friday, 9 to 1 on Saturdays. Every *farmácia* displays a card in the window or on the door giving the address of the nearest pharmacy with a 24-hour service and a list of those open until 10pm.

RESTAURANTS
Restaurants that serve lunch open from 11am and usually close for a while during the afternoon. They reopen—along with those that serve dinner only—around 7pm, staying open until 10–11; in remote or rural areas they may close earlier. Restaurants catering for visitors in the Algarve are often open throughout the day. Most restaurants in Portugal are closed on one evening during the week—often Sunday.

The bright sign to the Museu de Arte Popular, Lisbon

NATIONAL HOLIDAYS

On public holidays almost everything is closed and transportation services are reduced

1 Jan	New Year's Day
Mar/Apr	Good Friday
25 Apr	Liberty Day (commemorating 1974 Revolution)
1 May	Labour Day
Late May/ early Jun	Corpus Christi
10 Jun	Camões Day
15 Aug	Feast of the Assumption
5 Oct	Republic Day
1 Nov	All Saints' Day
1 Dec	Independence Day (from Spain in 1640)
8 Dec	Immaculate Conception
25 Dec	Christmas Day

ENTRANCE FEES
Many sights, museums and galleries charge admission fees, but these are generally moderate or inexpensive (approximately €1.50–€3). Recreational facilities aimed at holidaymakers, such as waterparks in the Algarve, tend to be more expensive.

COMBINED TICKETS
Both Lisbon and Porto have combined tickets—the *Cartão Lisboa* (Lisbon Card) and the *Passe Porto* (Porto Pass)—giving free access to public transportation and reduced admission charges to museums, monuments and places of interest. If you intend to do a lot of sightseeing, both cards are excellent value and well worth purchasing.

DISCOUNTS
Discounts on travel and entrance to museums, galleries and other sights of interest are available both to students and senior citizens. Senior citizens are entitled to a range of reductions in Portugal, so it's always worth showing your senior citizen's card or passport when asking for tickets. Offers include 50 per cent off the cost of the *bilhete turístico* (tourist ticket) rail pass, and discounts of up to 35 per cent on seasonal promotions at *pousadas*. Museums have reduced entry charges for students on production of a student identity card (International Student ID Card).

TOURIST OFFICES

Cities, towns and villages all over Portugal have tourist offices—look for the word *turismo*—and even in the smallest places there will usually be at least one English-speaking staff member. They can supply local information of every kind as well as help with finding accommodation; some offices will actually make reservations, while others simply supply accommodation lists. In addition, they should have up-to-date information about opening hours of local museums and sights (which can fluctuate), town plans and various brochures about the local area.

Tourist offices in the big towns and major resorts have longer opening hours than those in remoter areas: They are generally open all day, while rural offices will normally close for a couple of hours in the middle of the day and may be closed at weekends.

The Portuguese National Tourist Board operates an excellent tourist freephone telephone number (*Linha Verde Turista*, tel 800 296 296), which operates Monday to Saturday 9–midnight, Sunday and holidays 9–8. English-speaking operators have information about everything from transportation and accommodation to museum opening times and the whereabouts of English-speaking doctors.

You will find that the information provided by different tourist offices varies immensely. Some places have an excellent range of good, free information, while others apparently have little on offer. If the latter is the case, persevere—a smile and a few words of Portuguese may produce a plethora of maps, brochures and leaflets from under the counter.

OVERSEAS TOURIST OFFICES

Australia
Suite 201, 234 George Street, Sydney NSW 2000
Tel 12 9241 2710

Canada
60 Bloor Street West, Suite 1005, Toronto, Ontario M4W 3B8
Tel 416/921-7376

Republic of Ireland
54 Dawson Street, Dublin 2
Tel 01 670 9133

New Zealand
The office in Sydney, Australia (see above) is responsible also for New Zealand

UK
22–25a Sackville Street, London W1S 3LY
Tel 020 7201 6666

USA
4th Floor, 590 Fifth Avenue, New York, NY 10036
Tel 212/354-4403

TOURIST OFFICES

Albufeira
Rua 5 de Outubro,
tel 289 585 279

Alcobaça
Praça 25 de Abril,
tel 262 582 377

Amarante
Câmara Municipal,
Praça da República,
tel 255 420 246

Arraiolos
Praça Lima Brito,
tel 266 499 105

Aveiro
Rua João Mendonça 8,
tel 234 420 760

Beja
Rua Capitão João Francisco de Sousa 25,
tel 284 311 837

Braga
Avenida da Liberdade 1,
tel 053 262 550

Bragança
Avenida Cidade de Zamora,
tel 273 381 273

Cascais
Avenida Combatentes da Grande Guerra,
tel 214 868 204

Castelo Branco
Alameda da Liberdade,
tel 272 330 339

Castelo de Vide
Posto de Turismo de Castelo de Vide,
tel 245 901 361

Coimbra
Largo da Portagem,
tel 239 488 120,
Largo Dom Dinis,
tel 239 855 930,
Praça de República,
tel 239 833 202

Elvas
Praça de República,
tel 268 622 236

Estoril
Arcadas do Parque,
tel 214 663 813

Estremoz
Praça de República 26,
tel 268 333 541

Évora
Praça do Giraldo 73,
tel 266 702 671

Faro
Rua da Misericórdia 8,
tel 289 803 604

Fátima
Avenida Dom José Correia da Silva,
tel 249 531 139

Guarda
Praça Luís de Camões,
tel 271 205 530

Guimarães
Alameda de São Damaso 83,
tel 253 412 450,
Praça de Santiago,
tel 253 518 394

Lagos
Largo Marquês de Pombal,
tel 282 764 111

Lamego
Avenida Visconde Guedes Teixera,
tel 254 612 005

Leiria
Jardim Luís de Camões,
tel 244 848 770

Lisboa
Praça do Comércio,
tel 210 312 810,
Palácio Foz, Praça dos Restauradores,
tel 213 463 314

Mafra
Avenida 25 de Abril,
tel 261 812 023

Marvão
Posto de Turismo,
tel 245 993 886

Miranda do Douro
Largo do Menino Jesus da Cartolinha,
tel 273 431 132

Monsaraz
Largo Dom Nuno Alvares,
tel 266 557 136

Nazaré
Avenida da República,
tel 262 518 790

Óbidos
Rua Direita 51,
tel 262 955 060

Peniche
Rua Alexandre Herculano,
tel 262 789 571

Ponte de Lima
Torre da Cadeia,
tel 258 942 335

Portalegre
Palácio Póvoas, Rossio,
tel 245 331 359

Portimão
Avenida Zeca Afonso,
tel 282 470 732

Porto
Rua Clube dos Fenianos 25,
tel 223 393 472,
Rua Infante Dom Henrique,
tel 222 009 770

Sagres
Rua Comandante Matoso,
tel 282 624 873

Santiago do Cacém
Praça do Mercado,
tel 269 826 696

Sesimbra
Avenida dos Náufragos,
tel 212 288 540

Setúbal
Casa do Corpo Santo,
Praça do Quebedo,
tel 265 534 402

Sintra
Praça da República 23,
tel 219 231 157

Tavira
Rua da Galeria 9,
tel 281 322 511

Tomar
Avenida Dr. Cândido Madureira,
tel 249 329 000,
Rua Serpa Pinto 1,
tel 249 329 823

Valença do Minho
Avenida de Espanha,
tel 251 823 329

Viana do Castelo
Rua do Hospita Velho (off Praça da Erva),
tel 258 822 620

Vila Nova de Gaia
Avenida Diogo Leite 242,
tel 223 759 042

Vila Viçosa
Praça da República,
tel 268 881 101

Viseu
Avenida Calouste Gulbenkian,
tel 232 420 950
Piazza Castelnuovo,
tel 091 583 847

BOOKS, MAPS AND FILMS

BOOKS

Reading enriches your knowledge of a country and its history, people and culture, and the following suggestions may help whet your appetite before you go to Portugal, or answer a few questions and amuse you once you're there.

- *Backwards Out of the Big World* —Paul Hyland. A journey through Portugal by an author who knows the country as few other foreigners do.
- *The Portuguese: the Land and its People*—Marion Kaplan. Excellent overview of every aspect of the country.
- *Journey to Portugal*—José Saramago. Story of a journey round Portugal in the 1990s by Portugal's Nobel prize-winning author.
- *Ricardo Reis*—José Saramago. Saramago's easiest-to-read novel focuses on the pre-Salazar years.
- *Portugal: A Companion History*—José Hermano Saraiva. Excellent, concise and up-to-date history written for non-specialist foreign readers.
- *The Lusiads*—Luis de Camões. Portugal's great 16th-century epic poem celebrating Vasco da Gama's voyage to India.
- *The Wines and Vineyards of Portugal*—Richard Mayson. All you need to know about what's best to drink.
- *The Taste of Portugal*—Edite Vieira. A lovely cookery and food history book that will have you reaching for your knives and pans.
- *Living in Portugal*—Anne de Stoop. A beautiful picture book to whet your appetite or bring back memories.
- *A Small Death in Lisbon*—Robert Wilson. A contemporary murder mystery, set in Lisbon and Cascais, by a British author resident in Portugal.

MAPS

An atlas can be found at the back of this book, and there are other maps integrated throughout the text. The Portuguese National Tourist Board and *turismos* in larger towns can give you a useful free map of the whole country, with main topographical features, railways, motorways (expressways) and main roads clearly marked. You'll be able to augment this from local *turismos*, which will have regional maps and plans, though these are often less than detailed.

It's worth looking at www.geocid-snig.cnig.pt for its satellite and aerial images, as well as maps of virtually all of Portugal.

If you plan to hike, ask at local visitor information offices, or contact the Instituto Geográfico do Exercito, Avenida Dr. Alfredo Bemsaúde, Olivais Norte (tel 218 520 063, www.igeoe.pt), but be warned that many of their maps, though excellently detailed, are very out of date. A new series is in preparation and some maps in it have already appeared; look for the Serie M888.

SPECIALIST MAP SHOPS

UK	USA
National Map Centre 22–24 Caxton Street London SW1 0QU Tel 020 7222 2466 www.mapsnmc.co.uk	The Complete Traveler 199 Madison Avenue New York, NY 10022 Tel 212/685-9007
Stanfords 12–14 Long Acre London WC2 9LP Tel 020 7836 1321 www.stanfords.co.uk	Map Link Inc. 30 La Patera Lane Unit 5 Santa Barbara, CA 93117 Tel 805/692-6777 www.maplink.com

An eye-catching display of theatre and concert posters, Lisbon

FILMS

Portuguese films rarely reach a wide international audience, and there are few films that have made it onto the big screen overseas. The genre tends to reflect political concerns dating from the 1974 revolution and—oddly in this light-drenched country—there's a distinct emphasis on gloomy interiors and shadowy landscapes.

Portugal's big-name director is Manoel de Oliveira, whose work spans 70 years of the 20th century. His debut feature film, *Aniki-BóBó* (1942), is a delicate story of poor children in Porto, which was panned by Portuguese critics but highly praised abroad. Unable to work for much of the Salazar era, he became the standard-bearer for Portuguese cinema with *Amor de Perdição (Love of Perdition)* in 1978. The 1990s saw the release of *O Convento (The Convent),* starring Catherine Deneuve and John Malkovich, and *Viagem ao Princípio do Mundo (Journey to the Beginning of the World)*, the Italian actor Marcello Mastroianni's last film.

On a lighter note, Portugal occasionally makes an appearance in mainstream commercial movies, notably a couple of the James Bond epics.

WEBSITES

TOURISM

www.portugalinsite.com
Main tourist board site.
www.portugal.org
Major tourist board site, aimed at US.
www.portugalvirtual.pt
Information about all Portuguese regions.
www.orderportugal.com
Brochure ordering online for North Americans.
www.obrigado.com
General independent site.

REGIONAL TOURISM

www.rt-atb.pt
www.bragancanet.pt
Both cover northeast Portugal; in Portuguese only.
www.rtam.pt
Alta Minho.
www.rtvm.pt
Verde Minho Northeast of Porto; in Portuguese only.
www.cm-guimaraes.pt
Guimarães.
www.portoturismo.pt
Porto.
www.cm-gaia.pt
Vila Nova de Gaia.
www.rotadaluz.aveiro.co.pt
Aveiro and around.
www.turismo-centro.pt
Coimbra and around.
www.rt-dao-lafoes.com
Viseu area; in Portuguese only.
www.serra-caramulo.com
Serra de Caramulo.
www.rt-serradaestrela.pt
Serra da Estrela.
www.cm-covilha.pt
Covilhã and Serra da Estrela.
www.mun-guarda.pt
Guarda.
www.visitlisboa.com
Lisbon.
www.costa-azul.rts.pt
Costa Azul, south of Lisbon.
www.rt-leiriafatima.pt
Leiria and around; includes Alcobaça, Fátima and Batalha.
www.rt-oeste.pt
North of Lisbon; in Portuguese only.
www.mafra.net
Mafra.
www.estorilcoast-tourism.com
Estoril and around; includes Mafra and Sintra.
www.rtsm.pt
Northern Alentejo.
www.cm-evora.pt
Évora; in Portuguese only.
www.rt-planiciedourada.pt
Southern Alentejo.
www.rtalgarve.pt
Algarve.

TRANSPORTATION

www.ana-aeroportos.pt
Airports.
www.tap.pt
TAP Air Portugal.
www.cp.pt
Portuguese trains.
www.rede-expressos.pt
Countrywide express bus services.
www.rodonorte.pt
Express bus services in northern and central Portugal.
www.carris.pt
Lisbon public transportation.
www.metrolisboa.pt
Lisbon metro system.
www.eva-bus.com
Bus travel to and in the Algarve.
www.ranstejo.pt
Ferries and cruises on the Tejo.
www.stcp.pt
Porto public transportation.

ACCOMMODATION

www.maisturismo.pt
Hotel booking site.
www.pousadas.pt
Pousada booking site.
www.roteiro-campista.pt
Campsite booking site.

SPECIAL INTEREST

www.icn.pt
National parks and nature reserves. Portuguese only.
www.ippar.pt
Portuguese National Trust.
www.ipmuseus.pt
Museum site with links to individual museums; in Portuguese only.
www.termasdeportugal.pt
Portuguese spas site.
www.vinhoverde.com
Vinho verde site.
www.ivp.pt
Port and Douro region site.
www.wannasurf.com
Surfing information.
www.portugalgolf.pt
Golf tourism.

GENERAL

www.fco.gov.uk
www.travel.state.gov

MAJOR SIGHTS QUICK WEBSITE FINDER

SIGHT	WEBSITE	PAGE
Braga	www.com-braga.pt	68
Porto	www.portoturismo.pt	86
Aveiro	www.rotadalero.aviero.co.pt	94
Coimbra	www.com-coimbra.pt	98
Alcobaça	www.ippar.pt	110
Batalha	www.ippar.pt	112
Fátima	www. santuarro-fatima.pt	116
Tomar	www.rttemplarios.pt	118
Lisbon	www.visitlisboa.com	123
Sintra	www.cm-sintra.pt	150

WORDS AND PHRASES

Even if you're far from fluent, it is always a good idea to try to speak a few words of Portuguese. The words and phrases on the following pages should help you with the basics, from ordering a meal to dealing with emergencies.

CONVERSATION

I don't speak Portuguese.
Não falo português.

Do you speak English?
Fala inglês?

I don't understand.
Não compreendo.

Please repeat that.
Por favor repita isso.

Please speak more slowly.
Por favor fale mais lentamente.

My name is ...
Chamo-me ...

Hello, pleased to meet you.
Olá, prazer em conhecê-lo(a).

I'm on holiday.
Estou de férias.

I live in ...
Vívo em ...

Good morning.
Bom dia.

Good afternoon.
Boa tarde.

Good evening/night.
Boa noite.

Goodbye.
Adeus.

See you later.
Até logo.

May I/Can I?
Posso?

How are you?
Como está?

I'm sorry.
Desculpe.

Excuse me.
Com licença.

SHOPPING

Could you help me, please?
Podia ajudar-me, por favor?

How much is this?
Quanto custa isto?

I'm looking for ...
Preciso de ...

This isn't what I want.
Não é isto que eu queria.

When does the store open/close?
Quando é que a loja abre/fecha?

I'm just looking, thank you.
Estou só a ver, obrigado(a).

Do you accept credit cards?
Aceitam cartões de crédito?

This is the right size.
Este é o tamanho certo.

Do you have anything less expensive/smaller/larger?
Tem algo mais barato/mais pequeno/maior?

I'll take this.
Levo este(a).

Do you have a bag for this?
Tem um saco para isto?

I'd like ... grams please.
Queria ... gramas, por favor.

I'd like a kilo of ...
Queria um quilo de ...

What does this contain?
O que é que isto contém?

I'd like ... slices of that.
Queria ... fatias disto.

bakery
padaria

bookshop
livraria

chemist
farmácia

market
mercado

NUMBERS

1	**um**
2	**dois**
3	**três**
4	**quatro**
5	**cinco**
6	**seis**
7	**sete**
8	**oito**
9	**nove**
10	**dez**
11	**onze**
12	**doze**
13	**treze**
14	**catorze**
15	**quinze**
16	**dezasseis**
17	**dezassete**
18	**dezoito**
19	**dezanove**
20	**vinte**
21	**vinte e um**
30	**trinta**
40	**quarenta**
50	**cinquenta**
60	**sessenta**
70	**setenta**
80	**oitenta**
90	**noventa**
100	**cem**
1000	**mil**

USEFUL WORDS

yes	**sim**
no	**não**
there	**ali**
here	**aqui**
where	**onde**
who	**quem**
when	**quando**
why	**porquê**
how	**como**
later	**mais tarde**
now	**agora**
open	**aberto**
closed	**fechado**
please	**por favor**
thank you	**obrigado(a)**

HOTELS

Do you have a room?
Tem um quarto?

I have made a reservation for … nights.
Fiz uma reserva para … noites.

How much each night?
Quanto é por noite?

double room
quarto de casal

twin room
quarto duplo

single room
quarto individual

with bath/shower/lavatory
com banho/duche/sanita

Is there a lift in the hotel?
O hotel tem elevador?

Is the room air-conditioned/heated?
O quarto tem ar condicionado/aquecimento?

Is breakfast/lunch/dinner included in the cost?
O pequeno-almoço/almoço/jantar está incluído no preço?

Is room service available?
Tem serviço de quarto?

When do you serve breakfast?
Quando servem o pequeno-almoço?

May I have breakfast in my room?
Posso tomar o pequeno-almoço no quarto?

Do you serve evening meals?
Servem jantares?

The room is too hot/cold.
O quarto está demasiado quente/frio.

May I see the room?
Posso ver o quarto?

May I have my room key?
Pode dar-me a chave do quarto?

Will you look after my luggage until I leave?
Pode olhar pela minha bagagem até eu partir?

Where can I park my car?
Onde posso estacionar o carro?

Do you have a babysitting service?
Tem serviço de babysitting?

Could I have another room?
Pode dar-me outro quarto?

Please can I pay my bill?
Posso paga a conta?

swimming pool
piscina

sea view
vista para o mar

RESTAURANTS

I'd like to reserve a table for … people at …
Gostaria de reservar uma mesa para … pessoas às ….

A table for …, please.
Uma mesa para …, por favor.

We have/haven't booked.
Temos reserva/não temos reserva.

Could we sit there?
Podemos sentar-nos ali?

Is this table taken?
Esta mesa está ocupada?

Could we see the menu/wine list?
Pode trazer-nos a ementa/lista dos vinhos?

Are there tables outside?
Há mesas lá fora?

Do you have nappy-changing facilities?
Tem fraldário?

Where are the toilets?
Onde ficam as casas de banho?

We'd like something to drink.
Gostávamos de tomar uma bebida.

Could I have bottled still/sparkling water?
Pode trazer-me uma garrafa de água sem gás/com gás, por favor?

Is there a dish of the day?
Tem prato do dia?

I can't eat wheat/sugar/salt/pork/beef/dairy.
Não posso comer trigo/açúcar/sal/carne de porco/carne de vaca/lacticínios.

What do you recommend?
O que recomenda?

I am a vegetarian.
Sou vegetariano(a).

How much is this dish?
Quanto custa este prato?

The bill, please.
A conta por favor.

Is service included?
A taxa de serviço está incluída?

FOOD AND DRINK

breakfast	**pequeno-almoço**	knife	**faca**	cheese	**queijo**
lunch	**almoço**	fork	**garfo**	soups	**sopas**
dinner	**jantar**	spoon	**colher**	sandwich	**sanduíche**
starters	**entradas**	salt	**sal**	cod	**baclhau**
main course	**prato principal**	pepper	**pimenta**	sardines	**sardinhas**
dessert	**sobremsa**	bread	**pão**	wine list	**lista de vinhos**
		sugar	**açúcar**		

GETTING AROUND

Where is the information desk?
Onde é o guichet das informações?

Where is the timetable?
Onde está o horário?

Does this train/bus go to ...?
Este comboio/autocarro vai para ...?

Do you have a metro/bus map?
Tem um mapa do metro/ dos autocarros?

train/bus/metro station
estação dos caminhos-de-ferro/terminal dos auto carros/estação de metro

Where can I buy a ticket?
Onde posso comprar bilhete?

Where can I reserve a seat?
Onde posso reservar um lugar?

Please can I have a single/ round-trip ticket to ...?
Pode dar-m um bilhete/ bilhete de ida e volta para ...?

Is this seat free?
Este lugar está ocupado?

Do I need to get off here?
Tenho que sair aqui?

Where can I find a taxi?
Onde posso encontrar um táxi?

How much is the journey?
Quanto é a corrida?

I'd like to rent a car.
Gostaria de alugar um carro.

no parking
estacionamento proibido

I'm lost.
Estou perdido(a).

Is this the way to ...?
É este o caminho para ...?

Go straight on.
Vá sempre em frente.

Turn left.
Vire à esquerda.

Turn right.
Vire à direita.

traffic lights
semáforos

intersection
Cruzamento

corner
esquina

one way
Sentido único

DAYS/MONTHS/TIMES

Monday	**segunda-feira**
Tuesday	**terça-feira**
Wednesday	**quarta-feira**
Thursday	**quinta-feira**
Friday	**sexta-feira**
Saturday	**sábado**
Sunday	**domingo**
January	**janeiro**
February	**fevereiro**
March	**março**
April	**abril**
May	**maio**
June	**junho**
July	**julho**
August	**agosto**
September	**setembro**
October	**outubro**
November	**novembro**
December	**dezembro**
spring	**primavera**
summer	**verão**
autumn	**outono**
winter	**inverno**
Easter	**Páscoa**
Christmas	**Natal**
morning	**manhã**
afternoon	**tarde**
evening	**noitinha**
night	**noite**
today	**hoje**
yesterday	**ontem**
tomorrow	**amanhã**
day	**dia**
month	**mês**
year	**ano**

MONEY

Is there a bank/currency exchange office nearby?
Há um banco/uma agência de câmbio aqui perto?

Can I cash this here?
Posso levanta isto aqui?

I'd like to change sterling/ dollars into euros.
Gostaria de cambiar libras/dólares para euros.

Can I use my credit card to withdraw cash?
Posso usar o meu cartão de crédito para levantar dinheiro?

What is the exchange rate today?
Qual é a taxa de câmbio hoje?

POST AND TELEPHONES

Where is the nearest post office/mail box?
Onde fica a estação de correios/a caixa de correio mais próxima?

How much is the postage to ...?
Qual é a franquia para ...?

I'd like to send this by air mail/ registered mail.
Quero mandar isto por avião/registado.

Can you direct me to a public phone?
Pode indicar-me onde fica uma cabina telefónica?

Where can I buy a phone card?
Onde posso comprar um cartão telefónica?

What is the number for directory enquiries?
Qual é o número das informações dos telefones?

Where can I find a telephone directory?
Precisava de consultar uma lista telefónico?

Please put me through to ...
Por favor ligue para ...

Can I dial direct to ...?
Posso ligar directamente para ...?

What is the charge per minute?
Quanto é por minuto?

I would like to speak to ...
Podia falar com ...

TOURIST INFORMATION

Where is the tourist information office, please?
Onde é o Turismo, por favor?

Do you have a city map?
Tem um mapa da cidade?

Where is the museum?
Onde fica o museu?

Can you give me some information about ...?
Pode dar-me algumas informações sobre ...?

What are the main places of interest here?
Quais são as atracções principais aqui?

Please could you point them out on the map?
Podia mostrar-me onde ficam no mapa?

What sights/hotels/restaurants can you recommend?
Que atracções/hotéis/restaurantes me recomenda?

I am interested in ...
Estou interessado(a) em ...

Do you have any suggested walks?
Pode sugerir alguns passeios?

Are there guided tours?
Há excursões organizadas?

Does the guide speak English?
Há um guia que fale inglês?

Are there organized excursions?
Há excursões organizadas?

Can we make reservations here?
Podemos fazer reservas aqui?

What time does it open/close?
A que horas abre/fecha?

What is the admission price?
Quanto custa a entrada?

Is there a discount for senior citizens/students?
Há desconto para reformados/estudantes?

Do you have a brochure in English?
Tem um folheto em inglês?

What's on at the cinema?
Qual é o filme que estão a passar no cinema?

Where can I find a good nightclub?
Onde posso encontrar um bom nightclub?

Do you have a schedule for the theatre/opera?
Tem algum programa para o teatro/a ópera?

Should we dress smartly?
Decemos vestir roupa de cerimónia?

What time does the show start?
A que horas começa o espectáculo?

How do I reserve a seat?
Como posso reservar um lugar?

Could you reserve tickets for me?
Pode reservar-me bilhetes?

How much is a ticket?
Quanto custa um bilhete?

ILLNESS AND EMERGENCIES

I don't feel well.
Não me sinto bem.

Could you call a doctor?
Pode chamar um médico, por favor?

Is there a doctor/pharmacist on duty?
Há médico/farmacêutico de serviço?

I feel sick.
Estou mal disposto(a).

I need to see a doctor/dentist.
Preciso de um médico/dentista.

Please direct me to the hospital.
Por favor indique-me onde é o hospital.

I have a headache.
Tenho dor de cabeça.

I am diabetic.
Sou diabético.

I'm asthmatic.
Sou asmático.

I've been stung by a wasp/bee/jellyfish.
Fui picado por uma vespa/abelha/alforreca.

I have a heart condition.
Tenho um problema de coração.

I'm on a special diet.
Estou a seguir uma dieta especial.

I am on medication.
Estou a tomar medicamentos.

I have left my medicine at home.
Deixei os meus medicamentos em casa

I need to make an emergency appointment.
Preciso de marcar uma consulta de emergência.

I have bad toothache.
Tenho uma grande doe de dentes.

I don't want an injection.
Não quero injecções.

Help!
Socorro!

I have lost my passport/wallet/purse/handbag.
Perdi o meu passaporte/a minha carteira/bolsa/mala de mão.

I have had an accident.
Tive um acidente.

My car has been stolen.
Roubaram-me o carro.

I have been robbed.
Fui assaltado.

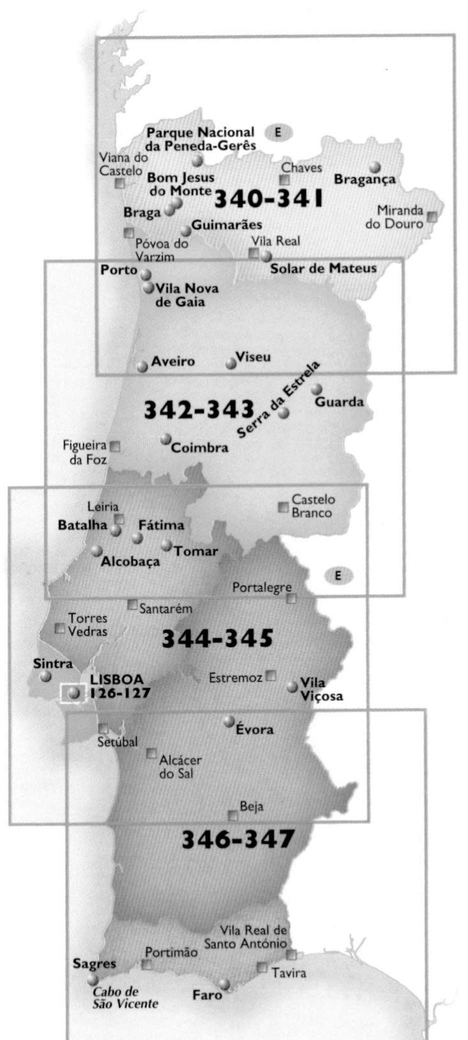

Toll motorway (Turnpike)

Motorway (Expressway)

Motorway junction with and without number

National road

Regional road

Railway

International boundary

Administrative region boundary

Built-up area

City / Town

National park

Featured place of interest

Airport

Height in metres

Mountain pass

Viewpoint

340-347	0 — 20 km 0 — 10 miles

Maps

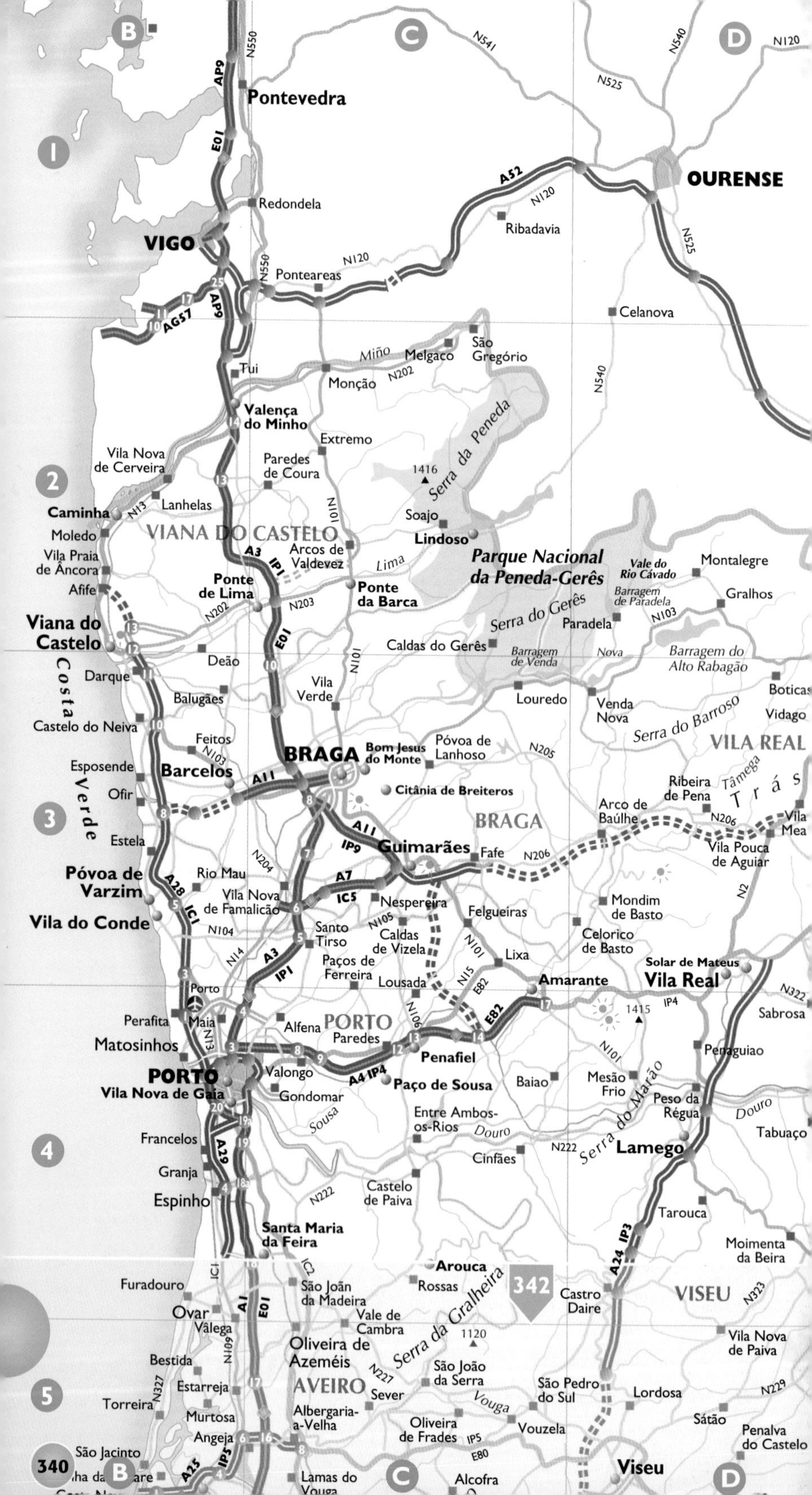

B
C
D
1
2
3
4
5
Pontevedra
OURENSE
Redondela
VIGO
Ribadavia
Ponteareas
Celanova
Tui
Melgaço
São Gregório
Monção
Miño
Valença do Minho
Extremo
Vila Nova de Cerveira
Paredes de Coura
Serra da Peneda
1416
Caminha
Lanhelas
Moledo
VIANA DO CASTELO
Soajo
Lindoso
Vila Praia de Âncora
Arcos de Valdevez
Lima
Parque Nacional da Peneda-Gerês
Vale do Rio Cávado
Montalegre
Afife
Ponte de Lima
Ponte da Barca
Barragem de Paradela
Gralhos
Viana do Castelo
Serra do Gerês
Paradela
Deão
Caldas do Gerês
Barragem de Venda
Nova
Barragem do Alto Rabagão
Darque
Costa Verde
Vila Verde
Louredo
Venda Nova
Boticas
Balugães
Vidago
Castelo do Neiva
Serra do Barroso
Feitos
BRAGA
Bom Jesus do Monte
Póvoa de Lanhoso
VILA REAL
Esposende
Barcelos
Ribeira de Pena
Tâmega
Citânia de Breiteros
Trás
Ofir
Arco de Baúlhe
Vila Mea
BRAGA
Estela
Guimarães
Fafe
Vila Pouca de Aguiar
Póvoa de Varzim
Rio Mau
Vila Nova de Famalicão
Nespereira
Mondim de Basto
Vila do Conde
Felgueiras
Santo Tirso
Caldas de Vizela
Celorico de Basto
Paços de Ferreira
Lixa
Solar de Mateus
Lousada
Amarante
Vila Real
Porto
1415
Sabrosa
Perafita
Maia
Alfena
PORTO
Paredes
Matosinhos
Penafiel
Peso da Régua
PORTO
Valongo
Baiao
Mesão Frio
Vila Nova de Gaia
Paço de Sousa
Gondomar
Serra do Marão
Peniguiao
Sousa
Entre Ambos-os-Rios
Douro
Tabuaço
Francelos
Lamego
Cinfães
Granja
Castelo de Paiva
Espinho
Tarouca
Santa Maria da Feira
Moimenta da Beira
Arouca
Furadouro
São Joãn da Madeira
Rossas
Serra da Gralheira
342
Castro Daire
VISEU
Ovar
Vale de Cambra
Vâlega
1120
Vila Nova de Paiva
Bestida
Oliveira de Azeméis
São João da Serra
Estarreja
AVEIRO
Sever
São Pedro do Sul
Lordosa
Torreira
Vouga
Murtosa
Albergaria-a-Velha
Vouzela
Sátão
Angeja
Oliveira de Frades
Penalva do Castelo
São Jacinto
340
Viseu
Lamas do Vouga
Alcofra
AP9
E01
A52
N120
N550
N541
N525
N540
AG57
N202
A3
IP1
N13
N101
N203
N205
A11
IP9
A7
IC5
N206
A28
IC1
N104
N14
N105
N2
N15
E82
N106
N322
IP4
A4
N222
A29
IC2
A1
N109
N327
N227
A24
IP3
N323
N229
A25
IP5
E80

Ponferrada
Monforte de Lemos
E
F
G
N120
C536
I
1778
E
Viana do Bolo
C533
A52
C622
N525
N525
Verín
2
Landedo
Parque Natural de Montesinho
Portelo
1243
N103-7
Vila Verde da Raia
Tronco
N103
Vinhais
N103
Bragança
N218
E82
Chaves
Rebordelo
Quintanilha
Rabaçal
Serra da Nogueira
Torre de Dona Chama
1321
Alcañices
N122
Vilarandelo
IP4
Santa Comba de Rossas
Montes
Oura
Valpaços
Podence
Vimioso
Izeda
Malhadas
N218
Carrazedo
Macedo de Cavaleiros
Miranda do Douro
3
Alfarela de Jales
Mirandela
Algoso
IP4
E82
IP2
BRAGANÇA
Duas Igrejas
N212
1199
Serra de Bornes
Peredo
N221
N216
Murça
Tua
Trindade
Douro
Santiago
Vila Flor
N102
E802
Mogadouro
Brunheda
Alfândenga
Fermoselle
Alijó
Castelo Branco
Barragem de Aldeiadavila
Junqueira
Parque Natural do Douro Internacional
Tua
Carrazeda de Ansiães
Ervedosa
Carviçais
N220
N222
São João da Pesqueira
Torre de Moncorvo
Freixo de Espada-à-Cinta
C525
Vilarouco
IP2
Vila Nova de Foz Côa
E
4
N102
E802
Barca de Alva
Penedono
Almendra
Parque Arqueológico do Vale do Côa
Vitigudino
Meda
C517
Antas
Longroiva
Lumbrales
Barragem de Vilar
N332
343
N226
Marialva
Sernancelhe
Figueira de Castelo Rodrigo
San Felices de los Gallegos
Côa
Aguiar da Beira
Trancoso
GUARDA
Pinhel
5
Freixedas
Almeida
Celorico da Beira
Fornos de
E
Vilar
F
E80

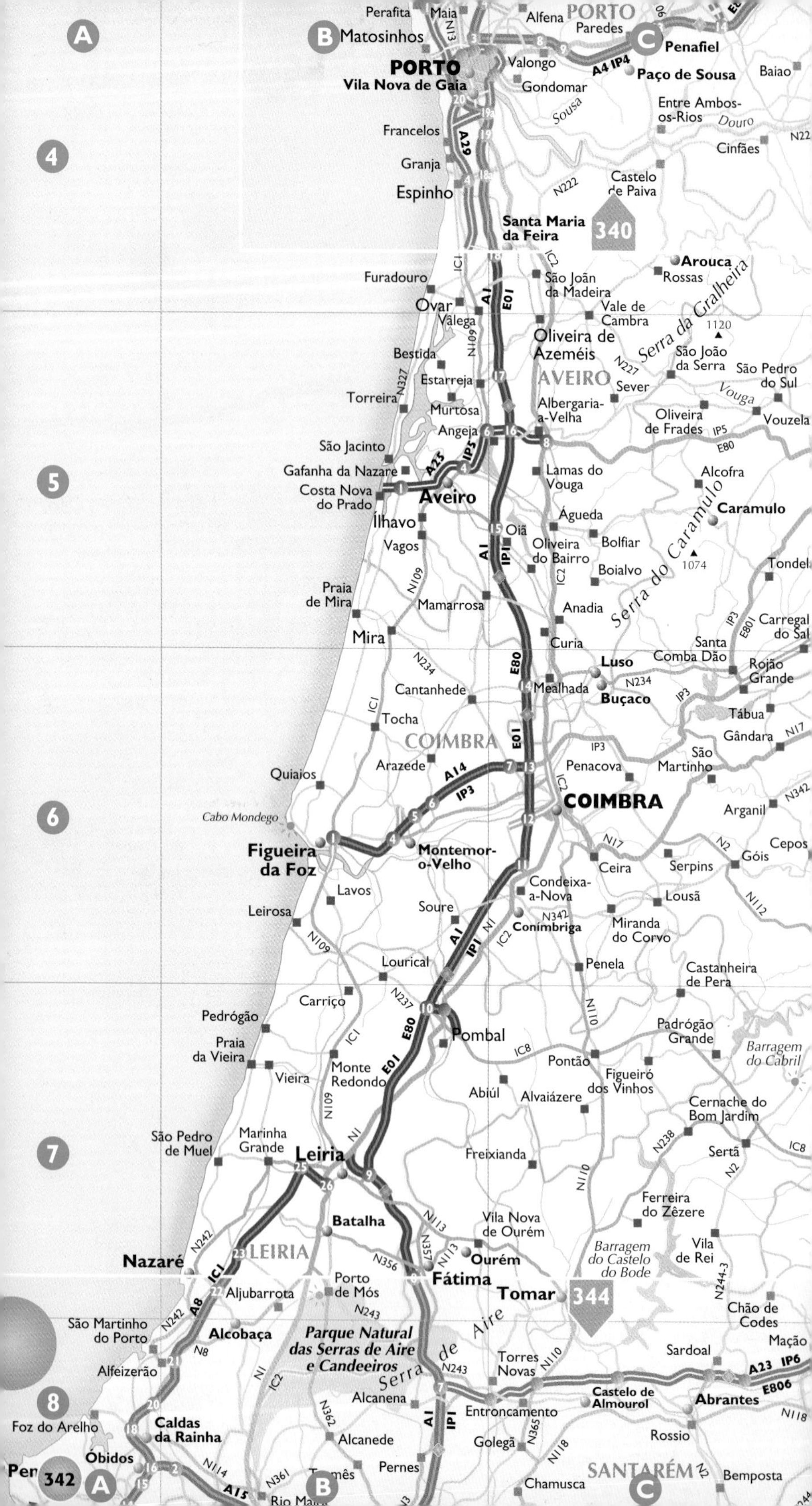

A
B
C
4
5
6
7
8
PORTO
Perafita
Maia
Alfena
Paredes
Matosinhos
Penafiel
Valongo
A4 IP4
Paço de Sousa
Baiao
Vila Nova de Gaia
Gondomar
Sousa
Entre Ambos-os-Rios
Douro
Francelos
A29
Cinfães
N22
Granja
Castelo de Paiva
N222
Espinho
Santa Maria da Feira
340
Arouca
Rossas
Furadouro
São Joãn da Madeira
Serra da Gralheira
A1
E01
Ovar
Vale de Cambra
Válega
1120
Oliveira de Azeméis
Bestida
N109
São João da Serra
São Pedro do Sul
N227
AVEIRO
Estarreja
Sever
Torreira
N327
Vouga
Albergaria-a-Velha
Murtosa
Oliveira de Frades
Vouzela
Angeja
IP5
E80
São Jacinto
A25
Lamas do Vouga
Alcofra
Gafanha da Nazare
Costa Nova do Prado
Aveiro
Caramulo
Serra do Caramulo
Águeda
Ílhavo
Oiã
Bolfiar
Vagos
IP1
Oliveira do Bairro
IC2
Boialvo
1074
Tondela
Praia de Mira
N109
Mamarrosa
Anadia
Carregal do Sal
Mira
Curia
Santa Comba Dão
Luso
N234
Rojão Grande
Cantanhede
Mealhada
Buçaco
IP3
IC1
Tocha
Tábua
COIMBRA
Gândara
N17
Arazede
São Martinho
A14
Penacova
Quiaios
IP3
N342
COIMBRA
Cabo Mondego
Arganil
Figueira da Foz
Montemor-o-Velho
N17
N2
Cepos
Góis
Ceira
Serpins
Lavos
Condeixa-a-Nova
Lousã
Soure
N112
Leirosa
N342
Conímbriga
Miranda do Corvo
N1
IC2
N109
Lourical
Penela
Castanheira de Pera
Carriço
N237
N110
Pedrógão
Padrógão Grande
Pombal
Praia da Vieira
IC8
Barragem do Cabril
Pontão
Vieira
Monte Redondo
Figueiró dos Vinhos
Abiúl
Alvaiázere
Cernache do Bom Jardim
N109
São Pedro de Muel
Marinha Grande
N238
IC8
Leiria
Freixianda
Sertã
N2
Ferreira do Zêzere
Batalha
N113
Vila Nova de Ourém
N357
Barragem do Castelo do Bode
Vila de Rei
N242
LEIRIA
N356
Ourém
Nazaré
IC1
Fátima
Porto de Mós
Tomar
344
N244-3
Aljubarrota
N243
Chão de Codes
São Martinho do Porto
A8
Alcobaça
Parque Natural das Serras de Aire e Candeeiros
Serra de Aire
Sardoal
Mação
Alfeizerão
N8
Torres Novas
N243
A23 IP6
E806
Alcanena
Castelo de Almourol
Abrantes
Foz do Arelho
Caldas da Rainha
Entroncamento
N118
N362
Alcanede
Golegã
N365
Rossio
Óbidos
N114
A15
N361
Pernes
SANTARÉM
Bemposta
Chamusca
342
Rio Maior

Douro Internacional
Tua
de Ansiães
Carviçais
N220
Torre de Moncorvo
Freixo de Espada-à-Cinta
Ervedosa
N222
São João da Pesqueira
Vilarouco
Peso da Régua
Douro
Tabuaço
Lamego
Serra do Marão
N101
Mesão Frio
Vila Nova de Foz Côa
IP2
N102
E802
Barca de Alva
Almendra
Parque Arqueológico do Vale do Côa
341
Lumbrales
C517
Tarouca
Penedono
Meda
Moimenta da Beira
Antas
Longroiva
Barragem de Vilar
N332
Castro Daire
A24
IP3
VISEU
N323
N226
Sernancelhe
Marialva
Figueira de Castelo Rodrigo
San Felices de los Gallegos
Côa
Vila Nova de Paiva
Aguiar da Beira
Trancoso
GUARDA
Pinhel
Lordosa
N229
Sátão
Penalva do Castelo
Freixedas
Almeida
Viseu
Celorico da Beira
Fornos de Algodres
IP5
E80
E802
Mangualde
A25
E80
Vilar Formoso
Ciudad Rodrigo
N620
Pinzio
N234
Nelas
Mondego
N17
Rio Torto
Gouveia
Guarda
Cerdeira
N231
Canas de Senhorim
Parque Natural da Serra da Estrela
N233
Vila Fernando
Aldeia da Ponte
Alfaites
Oliveira do Hospital
Seia
Manteigas
Serra da Estrela
Pega
Belmonte
Sabugal
Vide
1993
Torre
N18
IP2
Caria
N18-3
Santo Estevão
Aldeia do Bispo
C526
Vendas de Galizes
N230
Covilhã
A23
1492
Tortosendo
Valverde del Fresno
Capinha
1418
Penamacor
EX205
Silvares
Fundão
CASTELO BRANCO
E
Alpedrinha
N233
Serra da Guardunha
Pampilhosa da Serra
Orca
Medelim
Moraleja
EX109
Monsanto
Orvalho
São Vicente da Beira
São Miguel de Acha
Zêzere
Lardosa
Termas de Monfortinho
Foz Giraldo
Alcafores
N238
Barragem de Idanha
N112
Oleiros
E802
Idanha-a-Nova
Zebreira
Sarzedas
N240
N233
Segura
Ladoeiro
N233
Castelo Branco
Proença-a-Nova
A23 IP2
Sobreira Formosa
Monforte da Beira
Rosmaninhal
Alcántara
N241-1
Perdigão
Vila Velha de Ródão
EX207
Fratel
345
Montalvão
N18
IP2
Belver
Tejo
Nisa
Barragem da Póvoa
N521
Gavião
Parque Natural de Serra de São Mamede
Castelo de Vide
Tolosa
Valencia de Alcántara
N521
Alpalhão
Marvão
Vale do Arco
Monte
N245
IP2
E802
N246
624
D
E
F
4
5
6
7
8

A
B
C
7
8
9
10
11
Praia da Vieira
Vieira
E01
IC8
Pontão
Abiúl
Alvaiázere
N109
São Pedro de Muel
Marinha Grande
Leiria
N1
Freixianda
N110
Ferreira do Zêzere
Batalha
N113
Vila Nova de Ourém
N242
LEIRIA
N357
Ourém
342
Nazaré
IC1
N356
Fátima
Porto de Mós
Tomar
A8
Aljubarrota
N243
São Martinho do Porto
Alcobaça
Parque Natural das Serras de Aire e Candeeiros
Serra de Aire
N8
Torres Novas
Farilh'es
Alfeizerão
IC2
N243
Ilha Berlenga
Alcanena
Entroncamento
Castelo de Almourol
N362
A1
IP1
Foz do Arelho
Caldas da Rainha
N365
Alcanede
Golegã
Cabo Carvoeiro
Óbidos
N118
Peniche
N114
N361
Tremês
Pernes
Chamusca
A15
Rio Maior
N3
SANTARÉM
IP6
N247
Bombarral
Ulme
Cadaval
N366
N114
Santarém
Lourinhã
Quebradas
Costa de Prata
Cercal
Alcoentre
Almeirim
Porto Novo
N8-2
N115
Tejo
Marianos
Praia de Santa Cruz
Torres Vedras
Aveiras de Cima
N3
Cartaxo
N9
E01
E80
Muge
São Pedro da Cadeira
Sobral de Monte Agraço
Alenquer
Azambuja
Raposa
N114
Salvaterra de Magos
Marinhais
Lamarosa
N247
LISBOA
A10
Ericeira
Arruda dos Vinhos
Vila Franca de Xira
Benavente
N251
Mafra
Coruche
Couço
Sorraia
Malveira
Alverca do Ribatejo
Montelaver
N10
Porto Alto
Santana do Mato
Lousa
N119
Praia Grande
Loures
N118
Sintra
A9
Lisboa
N10
Cabo da Roca
Colares
Odivelas
Sacavém
Infantado
N247
A13
Cacém
Palácio Nacional de Queluz
A21
Alcochete
Canha
Lavre
Charneca
A5
Amadora
LISBOA
Atalaia
Taipadas
Cascais
Estoril
Belém
Almada
Montijo
N4
N114
Trafaria
Barreiro
Moita
A12
Vendas Novas
Seixal
Poceirão
Pegões
N4
N10
A6
IP7
Arrentela
N252
E90
Costa da Caparica
E90
Coina
A2 IP7
IP7
Cabrela
N10
Palmela
Quinta da Bacalhoa
Marateca
São Romão
Vila Nogueira de Azeitão
Setúbal
IC1
Serra da Arrábida
Tróia
Praias-Sado
São Cristóvão
Nossa Senhora do Cabo
N379
Portinho da Arrábida
Rio Sado
N261
Barragem Pego do Altar
Cabo Espichel
Sesimbra
A2
E01
Comporta
Montalvo
N253
IP1
Alcácer do Sal
Costa Azul
SETÚBAL
Casa Branca
Torrão
N5
346
N261-1
São Romão
Barragem de Vale de Gaio
N261
326
IC33
Grândola
Alentejo
Melides
Serra de Grândola
IC1
Santa Margarida do Sado
São Francisco da Serra
Lagoa de Santo André
10
Azinheira dos Barros
IP8
Santo André
N121

Barragem do Cabril
Oleiros
D
N112
E802
Idanha-a-Nova
Barragem de Idanha
E
Zebreira
Cernache do Bom Jardim
Sarzedas
N233
N240
Segura
Ladoeiro
N238
Sertã
IC8
N233
A23 IP2
Castelo Branco
N2
Sobreira Formosa
Monforte da Beira
7
Proença-a-Nova
Rosmaninhal
N241-1
Perdigão
Alcántara
Vila de Rei
Vila Velha de Ródão
343
N244-3
Fratel
Montalvão
Chão de Codes
N18
Maçao
Sardoal
IP2
Nisa
Barragem da Póvoa
N521
A23 IP6
Belver
Tejo
E806
Parque Natural de Serra de São Mamede
Abrantes
Gavião
N118
Castelo de Vide
Valencia de Alcántara
Rossio
Tolosa
Alpalhão
Marvão
N2
Bemposta
IP2 E802
N246
E
8
N244
Vale do Arco
Monte da Pedra
N245
Serra de São Mamede
1025
Crato
Portalegre
EX110
Domingão
Ponte de Sôr
Albuquerque
Seda
N119
N369
Alter do Chão
Pernacha de Cima
Galveias
N370
PORTALEGRE
N2
IC13
Cabeço de Vide
Barragem do Maranhão
N245
Arronches
Benavila
Barragem de Montargil
Barragem do Caia
Fronteira
Montargil
Avis
Monforte
N246
Campo Maior
N243
IP2 E802
EX100
Santa Eulália
Cabação
Sousel
Santo Aleixo
9
Mora
Casa Branca
Veiros
9
10
11
12
13
Pavia
N251
A6
N4
Elvas
N2
Estremoz
E90
BADAJOZ
N370
Vimieiro
8
N432
Ciborro
7
Borba
EX107
Évoramonte
Vila Viçosa
São Geraldo
N4
Arraiolos
Santa Justa
Alandroal
Azaruja
ÉVORA
Olivenza
Barragem do Divor
4
A6
6
E802
N254
Redondo
Montemor-o-Novo
5
São Miguel de Machede
Cromeleque do Almendres
N114-4
N18
N254
N381
Guadiana
Pias
Santiago do Escoural
Évora
IP2
E802
Montoito
10
Casa Branca
N380
São Manços
N256
Monsaraz
Xarrama
N257
Reguengos de Monsaraz
EX107
Villanueva del Fresno
Alcáçovas
Barragem do Alqueva
Mourao
Viana do Alentejo
N2
Degebe
EX112
Barragem do Alvito
Portel
Granja
Alvito
347
Póvoa
Barragem de Odivelas
Vidigueira
N2
Alqueva
Amareleja
Cuba
IP2
E802
Odivelas
Ardila
Barrancos
11
Moura
Safara
Pedrógão
Ferreira do Alentejo
N255
N258
N121
N121
Beringel
Brinches
Baleizão
D
Pias
E
Sobral
Santa
N118

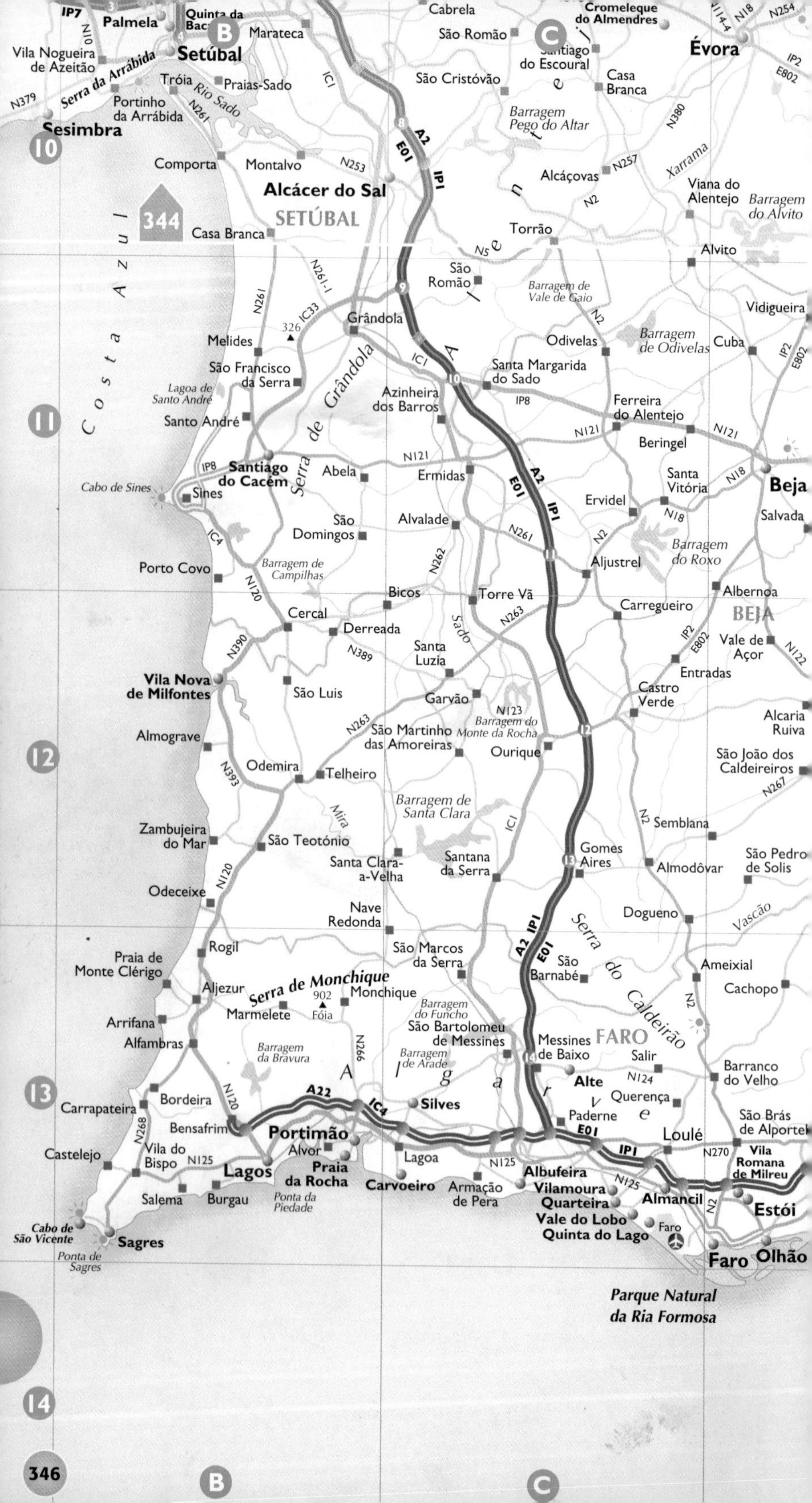

Palmela
Setúbal
Évora
Sesimbra
Serra da Arrábida
Alcácer do Sal
SETÚBAL
Costa Azul
Grândola
Serra de Grândola
Santiago do Cacém
Sines
Beja
BEJA
Alentejo
Vila Nova de Milfontes
Odemira
Ourique
Castro Verde
Aljustrel
Serra de Monchique
Monchique
Serra do Caldeirão
FARO
Algarve
Silves
Portimão
Lagos
Sagres
Cabo de São Vicente
Albufeira
Vilamoura
Quarteira
Vale do Lobo
Quinta do Lago
Loulé
Faro
Olhão
Estói
Parque Natural da Ria Formosa

de Machede
D
E
F
Pias
Montoito
Guadiana
Barcarrota
N435
N432
Monsaraz
N256
Zafra
10
São Manços
Reguengos de Monsaraz
Mourao
EX107
Villanueva del Fresno
Barragem do Alqueva
Degebe
345
EX112
Jerez de los Caballeros
EX101
Portel
Granja
Póvoa
Alqueva
Amareleja
N435
Fregenal de la Sierra
Barrancos
EX201
Ardila
Pedrógão
Moura
Safara
11
N255
N258
Baleizão
Brinches
Pias
Sobral da Adiça
N260
N433
Rosal de la Frontera
Vila Nova de São Bento
N260
Serpa
Vila Verde de Ficalho
959
E
N433
Guadiana
Santa Iria
N265
Chança
A493
N435
Vale do Poço
Paymogo
Nerva
Mina de São Domingos
Mértola
12
Santana de Cambas
Puebla de Guzmán
Valverde del Camino
Espírito Santo
N435
Alcoutim
San Bartolome de la Torre
A493
A499
Pereiro
N124
Martim Longo
A495
Gibraleón
A472
A49
E01
N122
Guadiana
Odeleite
N431
A49
E01
Huelva
Portos dos Fusos
13
Castro Marim
Ayamonte
A22
IP1
E01
Monte Gordo
Vila Real de Santo António
Cacela Velha
A494
N125
Tavira
Moncarapacho
A483
103
Asperillo
Fuzeta
14
D
E
F

T

U

V

Z

Page numbers in bold indicate the main reference.

A

B

D

E

M

ACKNOWLEDGMENTS

Abbreviations for the credits are as follows:
AA = AA World Travel Library, t (top), b (bottom), c (centre), l (left), r (right), bg (background)

UNDERSTANDING PORTUGAL

4cl AA/A Mockford & N Bonetti; **4c** AA/M Chaplow; **4cr** AA/P Wilson; **5cl** AA/J Edmanson, **5c** AA/A Mockford & N Bonetti; **5cr** AA/A Mockford & N Bonetti; **6cl** AA/T Harris; **6c** AA/A Mockford & N Bonetti; **6cr** AA/A Mockford & N Bonetti; **8tr** AA/A Mockford & N Bonetti; **8cl** AA/A Mockford & N Bonetti; **8cr** AA/T Harris; **8br** AA/A Mockford & N Bonetti; **9tl** AA/J Tims; **9tr** AA/A Kouprianoff; **9cl** AA/T Harris; **9cr** AA/T Harris; **9bl** AA/L Allen; **10tc** AA/M Birkitt; **10tr** AA/A Mockford & N Bonetti; **10cl** AA/M Chaplow; **10cr** AA/C Jones; **10br** AA/T Harris.

LIVING PORTUGAL

11 AA/A Mockford & N Bonetti; **12/13bg** AA/M Chaplow; **12tl** AA/T Harris; **12tr** AA/A Mockford & N Bonetti; **12c** AA/M Birkitt; **12bl** AA/C Jones; **12r** AA/A Kouprianoff; **12tl** AA/A Kouprianoff; **13r** Rex Features Ltd; **13c** Bruce Coleman Ltd; **13cl** Getty Images/Paulo Cunha/AFP; **14/15** AA/A Kouprianoff; **14t** AA/A Kouprianoff; **14tl** AA/J Tims; **14c** J Edmanson; **14b** AA/M Chaplow; **14r** AA/A Mockford & N Bonetti; **15tl** AA/A Kouprianoff; **15tc** Rex Features Ltd; **15cl** Jan Butchofsky-Houser/Corbis; **15tr** AA/M Chaplow; **15cr** AA/A Mockford & N Bonetti; **16/17** AA/A Mockford & N Bonetti; **16t** AA/A Kouprianoff; **16cl** AA/J Edmanson; **16cr** AA/J Edmanson; **16b** AA/M Chaplow; **17tl** AA/M Chaplow; **17cl** AA/A Mockford & N Bonetti; **17tr** Bruce Coleman Ltd; **17ctr** Pinto/ASP Europe; **17cb** Pinto/ASP Europe; **18/19bg** AA/A Mockford & N Bonetti; **18tl** José Manuel/ICEP; **18ct** AA/A Mockford & N Bonetti; **18tr** AA/A Mockford & N Bonetti; **18crl** ModaLisboa; **18crc** ModaLisboa; **18cr** ModaLisboa; **18br** ModaLisboa; **19tl** Rex Features Ltd; **19tr** Getty Images Sport/Laurence Griffiths; **19c** AA/C Jones; **20/21bg** AA/A Kouprianoff; **20tl** Rex Features Ltd; **20tr** AA/A Mockford & N Bonetti; **20cl** Getty Images Sport/Alex Livesey; **20r** AA/A Mockford & N Bonetti; **21tl** AA/A Kouprianoff; **21cl** AA/A Kouprianoff; **21c** AA/C Jones; **21r** Metro do Porto, SA; **22/23bg** AA/T Harris; **22tl** Joao Paulo/ICEP; **22cl** AA/A Mockford & N Bonetti; **22tr** AA/T Harris; **22cr** World Pictures Ltd; **22br** AA/J Edmanson; **23tl** AA/P Wilson; **23tr** Getty Images/ The Image Bank/Joe Patronite; **23c** AA/M Chaplow; **24bg** AA/A Kouprianoff; **24tl** Getty Images Sport/Alex Livesey; **24cl** Getty Images Sport/Alex Livesey; **24c** Getty Images; **24ctr** AA/A Kouprianoff; **24cbr** AA/C Jones; **24b** AA/A Mockford & N Bonetti.

THE STORY OF PORTUGAL

25 AA/A Kouprianoff; **26/27bg** AA/A Kouprianoff; **26cl** AA; **26bl** AA/A Kouprianoff; **26c** AA/A Kouprianoff; **26br** AA/C Jones; **27bl** AA/A Kouprianoff; **27ctr** AA/A Mockford & N Bonetti; **27cbr** AA/C Jones; **27br** AA/A Kouprianoff; **28/29bg** AA/A Kouprianoff; **28cl** AA; **28bl** AA/A Mockford & N Bonetti; **28cr** AA/I Burgum; **28/29b** AA/A Mockford & N Bonetti; **29ctl** Getty Images/Hulton; **28cbl** AA/A Kouprianoff; **29cb** AA/A Kouprianoff; **29cr** AA/A Kouprianoff; **29br** Mary Evans Picture Library; **30/31bg** AA/T Harris; **30c** AA; **30bl** AA/C Jones; **30/31b** AA/P Wilson; **31cl** Getty Images/Hulton; **31c** AA; **31cr** Roy 14 IV f.244v Duke of Lancaster dines with the King of Portugal, from Vol. III 'From the Coronation of Richard II to 1387', by Jean de Batard Wavrin, English School, (15th century) / British Library, London, UK/www.bridgeman.co.uk; **31bl** AA; **31bc** AA/J Edmanson; **31br** AA/A Kouprianoff; **32/33bg** AA/A Kouprianoff; **32cl** AA; **32c** AA/A Kouprianoff; **32bl** Mary Evans Picture Library; **32/33b** AA; **33cl** AA; **33c** AA; **33bl** AA; **33cr** AA/A Kouprianoff; **33br** AA/I Burgum; **34/35bg** AA/A Mockford & N Bonetti; **34cl** AA/A Mockford & N Bonetti; **34cr** AA; **34bl** AA; **34br** Mary Evans Picture Library; **35ctl** AA; **35c** AA; **35cr** AA/A Mockford & N Bonetti; **35cbl** AA; **35bl** AA/A Kouprianoff; **35br** AA/A Kouprianoff; **36/37bg** AA/T Harris; **36cl** Mary Evans Picture Library; **36cr** Getty Images/Hulton; **36bl** AA/A Kouprianoff; **36/37b** AA/A Kouprianoff; **37cl** Getty Images/Hulton; **37cr** Getty Images/Hulton; **37bl** AA/T Harris; **37br** AA/F Dunlop; **38/39bg** AA; **38cl** Getty Images/Hulton; **38bl** AA/J A Tims; **38br** Getty Images/Hulton; **39bl** Rex Features Ltd; **39cl** Getty Images/Hulton; **39cr** Getty Images/Hulton; **39cbr** Getty Images/Hulton; **39cbl** AA/A Mockford & N Bonetti; **40bg** AA/A Mockford & N Bonetti; **40cr** AA/A Mockford & N Bonetti; **40cl** AA/A Kouprianoff; **40bl** AA/A Mockford & N Bonetti; **40bc** AA/M Birkitt; **40br** AA/C Jones.

ON THE MOVE

41 AA/A Mockford & N Bonetti; **42t** Digitalvision; **43t** Digitalvision; **43l** Aeroporta de Lisboa; **44t** Digitalvision; **44c** Faro Airport/Ana-Aeroporta; **44b** TAP Air Portugal; **45t** Digitalvision; **45c** AA/C Jones; **46t** Digitalvision; **46b** Rail Europe Ltd; **47t** AA/A Mockford & N Bonetti; **47c** AA/A Kouprianoff; **47b** Communicarta Ltd/Robin Woods; **48t** AA/A Mockford & N Bonetti; **48c** AA/A Mockford & N Bonetti; **48b** AA/A Kouprianoff; **49t** AA/A Mockford & N Bonetti; **50t** AA/A Mockford & N Bonetti; **50c** AA/A Mockford & N Bonetti; **50b** Metro do Porto, S.A; **51t** AA/A Mockford & N Bonetti; **51cl** Metro do Porto, S.A; **51b** AA/A Mockford & N Bonetti; **52t** Digitalvision; **52c** AA/A Mockford & N Bonetti; **52b** Carole Philp; **53t** Digitalvision; **53c** AA/C Jones; **54t** Digitalvision; **55t** Digitalvision; **55cl** Communicarta Ltd/Robin Woods; **56t** Digitalvision; **56cl** AA/A Mockford & N Bonetti; **56ccl** AA/A Mockford & N Bonetti; **56ccr** AA/A Mockford & N Bonetti; **56cr** AA/A Mockford & N Bonetti; **56btl** AA/A Mockford & N Bonetti; **56btc** AA/A Mockford & N Bonetti; **56btr** Carole Philp; **56bl** AA/A Mockford & N Bonetti; **56br** AA/A Mockford & N Bonetti; **57t** Digitalvision; **57c** AA/A Mockford & N Bonetti; **58t** Digitalvision; **58c** AA/M Jourdan; **58b** AA/A Mockford & N Bonetti; **59t** Digitalvision; **59c** AA/A Kouprianoff; **60t** Digitalvision; **61t** Digitalvision; **61c** Communicarta Ltd/Robin Woods; **61b** AA/A Mockford & N Bonetti; **62t** Scotturb; **62ct** AA/A Mockford & N Bonetti; **62cb** Communicarta Ltd/Robin Woods; **62b** Scotturb; **63t** Scotturb; **63cr** Communicarta Ltd/Robin Woods; **63b** TAP Air Portugal; **64t** Scotturb; **64cl** Wheeling Around the Algarve; **64br** Wheeling Around the Algarve; **64b** Wheeling Around the Algarve.

THE SIGHTS

65 AA/A Kouprianoff; **67tl** AA/A Mockford & N Bonetti; **67tr** AA/A Kouprianoff; **67b** AA/A Mockford & N Bonetti; **68t** AA/A Mockford & N Bonetti; **68cl** AA/A Mockford & N Bonetti; **68cc** AA/A Kouprianoff; **68cr** AA/A Kouprianoff; **69** AA/P Wilson; **70tl** AA/A Mockford & N Bonetti; **70tr** AA/A Mockford & N Bonetti; **70b** AA/A Mockford & N Bonetti; **71** AA/A Mockford & N Bonetti; **71b** AA/A

Kouprianoff; **72t** AA/A Mockford & N Bonetti; **72c** AA/A Mockford & N Bonetti; **73tl** AA/A Kouprianoff; **73tr** AA/A Mockford & N Bonetti; **73b** Pictures Colour Library; **74t** AA/A Mockford & N Bonetti; **74cl** AA; **74cc** AA/A Mockford & N Bonetti; **74b** AA/A Kouprianoff; **75t** AA/A Kouprianoff; **75cr** AA; **76tl** AA/A Kouprianoff; **76tr** AA; **77tl** AA/A Kouprianoff; **77tr** World Pictures Ltd; **78** AA/T Harris; **79t** AA/T Harris; **79c** AA/A Mockford & N Bonetti; **79b** AA/A Mockford & N Bonetti; **80c** AA/A Mockford & N Bonetti; **80b** AA/A Kouprianoff; **80/81** AA/A Mockford & N Bonetti; **81cl** AA/T Harris; **81cr** AA/A Mockford & N Bonetti; **81b** AA/T Harris; **82t** AA/T Harris; **82c** AA/T Harris; **83tl** World Pictures Ltd; **83tr** AA/P Wilson; **85tl** AA/A Mockford & N Bonetti; **85tc** AA/A Kouprianoff; **85tr** AA/A Mockford & N Bonetti; **85b** AA/A Mockford & N Bonetti; **86/7** A Kouprianoff; **87** AA/A Mockford & N Bonetti; **88l** AA/A Mockford & N Bonetti; **88c** AA/A Mockford & N Bonetti; **88r** AA/A Mockford & N Bonetti; **89** AA/A Mockford & N Bonetti; **90t** AA/T Harris; **90cl** AA/T Harris; **90cr** AA/A Mockford & N Bonetti; **91t** AA/A Mockford & N Bonetti; **91cr** AA/T Harris; **91b** AA/T Harris; **92tl** AA/A Mockford & N Bonetti; **92tr** AA/A Mockford & N Bonetti; **92b** AA/A Mockford & N Bonetti; **94t** AA/A Kouprianoff; **94cl** AA/P Wilson; **94/95** AA/A Mockford & N Bonetti; **95cr** AA/A Mockford & N Bonetti; **95br** AA/A Mockford & N Bonetti; **96tl** Bob Krist/Corbis; **96tr** AA/A Kouprianoff; **96b** AA/A Mockford & N Bonetti; **97tl** AA/P Wilson; **97tc** AA/A Mockford & N Bonetti; **97tr** AA/A Kouprianoff; **98t** AA/A Kouprianoff; **98cl** AA; **98/9** AA/A Kouprianoff; **99** AA; **100tl** AA/A Kouprianoff; **100tr** AA/A Kouprianoff; **100b** AA/A Kouprianoff; **102tl** AA/A Kouprianoff; **102tc** AA; **102tr** AA; **102b** AA/A Kouprianoff; **103t** AA/A Kouprianoff; **103cr** AA/A Kouprianoff; **103b** AA/A Kouprianoff; **104tl** AA/A Mockford & N Bonetti; **104tr** Visionarium; **105t** AA/T Harris; **105c** AA/T Harris; **106tl** AA/A Mockford & N Bonetti; **106tc** AA/A Mockford & N Bonetti; **106tr** AA/A Mockford & N Bonetti; **106cl** AA/A Mockford & N Bonetti; **107t** AA; **107cr** AA/A Kouprianoff; **109tl** Hans Georg Roth/Corbis; **109tc** AA/A Kouprianoff; **109tr** Kevin Schafer/Corbis; **109b** Dennis Marsico/Corbis; **110t** AA; **110l** AA/A Kouprianoff; **111l** AA/A Kouprianoff; **111r** AA/A Kouprianoff; **111b** AA/A Kouprianoff; **112t** AA/A Kouprianoff; **112/113** AA/A Kouprianoff; **113l** AA/A Kouprianoff; **113r** AA/A Kouprianoff; **114l** AA/A Kouprianoff; **114/5** AA/A Kouprianoff; **116t** AA/A Kouprianoff; **116cl** AA/A Mockford & N Bonetti; **117tl** AA; **117tc** AA/A Kouprianoff; **117tr** AA/A Kouprianoff; **117br** AA/A Kouprianoff; **118tc** AA/T Harris; **118cl** AA; **118cc** AA/T Harris; **118cr** AA/A Kouprianoff; **119** AA/A Kouprianoff; **120cl** AA/T Harris; **120/121** AA/T Harris; **121tl** AA/A Kouprianoff; **122tl** AA/A Mockford & N Bonetti; **122tc** AA/A Mockford & N Bonetti; **122tr** AA/A Kouprianoff; **122bc** AA/A Mockford & N Bonetti; **124ctl** AA/A Mockford & N Bonetti; **124cbl** AA/A Mockford & N Bonetti; **124b** AA/A Kouprianoff; **125tr** AA/A Mockford & N Bonetti; **125ct** AA/A Mockford & N Bonetti; **125c** AA/A Mockford & N Bonetti; **128tc** AA/A Mockford & N Bonetti; **128cl** AA/T Harris; **128cc** AA/A Mockford & N Bonetti; **128cr** AA/A Kouprianoff; **129tl** AA/A Mockford & N Bonetti; **129tr** AA/A Kouprianoff; **130** AA/A Kourpianoff; **130cl** AA/A Kouprianoff; **130cc** Museu de Marinha, Lisbon; **130cr** AA/A Kouprianoff; **130c** Museu de Marinha, Lisbon; **131t** AA/T Harris; **131cl** AA/T Harris; **132t** AA/A Mockford & N Bonetti; **130cl** AA/A Kouprianoff; **132bl** AA/A Kouprianoff; **133t** AA/A Mockford & N Bonetti; **133cr** AA/A Kouprianoff; **133br** AA/A Kouprianoff; **134tc** AA/A Kouprianoff; **134c** AA/A Kouprianoff; **135bl** AA/A Kouprianoff; **135** AA/A Kouprianoff; **135bc** AA/A Kouprianoff; **137tl** AA/A Kouprianoff; **137tr** AA/A Kouprianoff; **138tc** Fundação Calouste Gulbenkian; **138/139** AA/A Kouprianoff; **139t** Fundação Calouste Gulbenkian; **139br** AA/A Kouprianoff; **140tl** Fundação Calouste Gulbenkian; **140c** Fundação Calouste Gulbenkian; **140/141t** Fundação Calouste Gulbenkian; **140b** Fundação Calouste Gulbenkian; **141tr** AA/A Kouprianoff; **141c** Fundação Calouste Gulbenkian; **142/143** AA/A Mockford & N Bonetti; **142c** AA/T Harris; **143c** AA/T Harris; **144t** AA/T Harris; **144br** AA/A Mockford & N Bonetti; **145tr** AA/A Mockford & N Bonetti; **145cl** AA/T Harris; **145clc** AA/A Mockford & N Bonetti; **145crc** AA/A Mockford & N Bonetti; **146tl** AA/A Kouprianoff; **146tr** AA/A Kouprianoff; **148tl** AA/A Kouprianoff; **148tc** AA/A Mockford & N Bonetti; **148tr** AA/A Mockford & N Bonetti; **149tl** AA/A Mockford & N Bonetti; **149tc** AA/A Kouprianoff; **149tr** AA/A Mockford & N Bonetti;**149bc** AA/A Kouprianoff; **150tc** AA/A Kouprianoff; **150cl** AA/A Kouprianoff; **150cc** AA/A Kouprianoff; **150/151** AA/A Kouprianoff; **151** AA/A Kouprianoff; **152** AA/A Mockford & N Bonetti; **153tc** AA/A Mockford & N Bonetti; **153bc** AA/A Mockford & N Bonetti; **155tl** AA/J Edmanson; **155tc** AA/A Mockford & N Bonetti; **155tr** AA/A Kouprianoff; **156tl** AA/A Mockford & N Bonetti; **156tc** AA/A Mockford & N Bonetti; **156tr** AA/J Edmanson; **157tl** AA; **157tr** AA/A Kouprianoff; **157bc** AA/A Mockford & N Bonetti; **158tc** AA/A Mockford & N Bonetti; **158cl** AA/A Mockford & N Bonetti; **158cc** AA/A Mockford & N Bonetti; **158/159** AA/A Kouprianoff; **159** AA/A Mockford & N Bonetti; **160cl** AA/J Edmanson; **160br** AA/A Kouprianoff; **161cr** AA/P Wilson; **162tl** AA/P Wilson; **162tc** AA/A Kouprianoff; **162tr** AA/A Mockford & N Bonetti; **163tl** AA/A Kouprianoff; **163tc** AA/A Mockford & N Bonetti; **163tr** AA/P Wilson; **163cl** AA; **164tl** AA/A Mockford & N Bonetti; **164tr** AA/P Wilson; **165t** AA/A Mockford & N Bonetti; **165cr** AA/A Mockford & N Bonetti; **165br** AA/A Kouprianoff; **167tl** AA/C Jones; **167tr** AA/C Jones; **168tc** AA/C Jones; **168cl** AA/C Jones; **168cc** AA/C Jones; **168cr** AA/C Jones; **169br** AA/C Jones; **170cl** AA/C Jones; **170cc** AA/C Jones; **170br** AA/A Kouprianoff; **171tl** Carole Philp; **171tr** AA/M Chaplow; **171b** AA/C Jones; **172tl** AA/A Mockford & N Bonetti; **172tc** AA/C Jones; **172tr** AA/A Mockford & N Bonetti; **172bc** AA/A Mockford & N Bonetti; **173tl** AA/C Jones; **173tr** AA/M Birkitt; **174t** AA/A Kouprianoff; **174cl** AA/C Jones; **175lt** AA/M Chaplow; **175tc** AA/M Chaplow; **175tr** AA/M Chaplow; **175bl** AA/A Kouprianoff; **176tl** AA/C Jones; **176tc** AA/M Birkitt; **176tr** AA/C Jones; **176c** AA/M Birkitt.

WHAT TO DO

177 AA/C Jones; **178t** AA/A Mockford & N Bonetti; **179t** AA/A Mockford & N Bonetti; **179c** www.oficinadaterra.com; **180t** Digitalvision; **180cl** AA/A Mockford & N Bonetti; **180cr** Coliseu Lisboa; **181t** Digitalvision; **181cl** AA/T Harris; **181cr** AA/A Mockford & N Bonetti; **182t** Brand X Pics; **182cl** AA/C Jones; **182cr** Brand X Pics; **183t** Corbis; **183cl** AA/C Jones; **193cr** AA/C Jones; **184t** Corbis; **184cl** Villa Termal of Caldas de Monchique Spa Resort; **184cr** Photodisc; **185t** Corbis; **185cl** Photodisc; **185cr** ICEP Portugal; **186t** João Paulo/ICEP Portugal; **186cl** Aquashow Park; **186cr** Aquashow Park; **186br** Aquashow Park; **187t** João Paulo/ICEP Portugal; **187cl** AA/P Wilson; **187cr** António Sacchetti/ICEP Portugal; **188t** João Paulo/ICEP Portugal; **188c** AA/A Mockford & N Bonetti; **189t** João Paulo/ICEP Portugal; **189c** AA/P Wilson; **190t** João Paulo/ICEP Portugal; **190c** AA/A Kouprianoff; **191t** João Paulo/ICEP Portugal; **191c** AA/M Chaplow; **192t** João Paulo/ICEP Portugal; **192c** Cavaleiros do Mar; **193t** João

Paulo/ICEP Portugal; **193br** João Paulo/ICEP Portugal; **194t** AA/A Mockford & N Bonetti; **194c** AA/A Mockford & N Bonetti; **195t** AA/A Mockford & N Bonetti; **195c** Taylors Fladgate & Yeatman Vinhos S.A; **196t** AA/A Mockford & N Bonetti; **196c** AA/T Harris; **197t** AA/A Mockford & N Bonetti; **197c** João Paulo/ICEP Portugal; **198t** AA/A Kouprianoff; **198c** AA/A Kouprianoff; **199t** AA/A Kouprianoff; **199c** Região Turismo Centro/ICEP Portugal; **200t** AA/A Kouprianoff; **200c** AA/A Kouprianoff; **201t** AA/A Kouprianoff; **201c** Photodisc; **202t** AA/A Kouprianoff; **202c** Corbis; **203t** AA/A Kouprianoff; **204t** Vitrocristal; **204c** AA/A Kouprianoff; **205t** Vitrocristal; **205c** Vitrocristal; **206t** Vitrocristal; **206c** João Barbosa/ICEP Portugal; **207t** Vitrocristal; **207cl** José Manuel/ICEP Portugal; **207b** Photodisc; **208t** AA/A Mockford & N Bonetti; **208c** AA/A Mockford & N Bonetti; **209t** AA/A Mockford & N Bonetti; **209c** ModaLisboa; **210t** AA/A Mockford & N Bonetti; **210c** AA/A Kouprianoff; **211t** AA/A Mockford & N Bonetti; **211c** Coliseu Lisboa; **212t** AA/A Mockford & N Bonetti; **212c** Photodisc; **213t** AA/A Mockford & N Bonetti; **213c** AA/L Allen; **214t** AA/A Mockford & N Bonetti; **215t** João Barbosa/ICEP Portugal; **215** Joào Barbosa/ICEP Portugal; **216t** João Barbosa/ICEP Portugal; **216c** AA/A Mockford & N Bonetti; **217t** João Barbosa/ICEP Portugal; **217c** Casino Estoril; **218t** AA/A Kouprianoff; **218c** AA/A Mockford & N Bonetti; **219t** AA/A Kouprianoff; **219c** AA/A Kouprianoff; **220t** AA/A Kouprianoff; **220c** www.oficinadaterra.com; **221t** AA/A Kouprianoff; **221cr** João Paulo/ICEP Portugal; **222t** AA/C Jones; **222c** Algarve Airsports Centre, Lagos; **223t** AA/C Jones; **223c** Krazy World; **224t** AA/C Jones; **224c** Bom Dia Sailing Cruises; **225t** AA/C Jones; **225c** AA/C Jones; **226t** AA/C Jones; **226c** Barringtons Golf & Health Spa; **227t** AA/C Jones; **227c** AA/M Chaplow; **228t** AA/C Jones.

OUT AND ABOUT

229 AA/M Chaplow; **231b** AA/T Harris; **232** AA/T Harris; **233tr** AA/T Harris; **233br** AA/A Kouprianoff; **234cl** AA/A Kouprianoff; **234br** AA/A Mockford & N Bonetti; **235tl** AA/A Mockford & N Bonetti; **235br** AA/A Mockford & N Bonetti; **236c** AA/A Mockford & N Bonetti; **237** AA/T Harris; **238t** AA/A Mockford & N Bonetti; **239tl** AA/A Mockford & N Bonetti; **239br** AA/A Mockford & N Bonetti; **240tr** AA; **240b** AA/A Kouprianoff; **241tc** AA/A Kouprianoff; **241b** AA/A Mockford & N Bonetti; **242** AA/A Mockford & N Bonetti; **243c** AA/A Mockford & N Bonetti; **243bl** AA/A Mockford & N Bonetti; **243br** AA/A Mockford & N Bonetti; **244tr** AA; **244br** Vitrocristal; **245tr** AA/A Mockford & N Bonetti; **245br** AA/P Wilson; **246cr** AA/A Kouprianoff; **246bl** AA/A Mockford & N Bonetti; **247tr** AA/A Kouprianoff; **247br** AA/A Mockford & N Bonetti; **248c** AA/A Mockford & N Bonetti; **249tc** AA/T Harris; **249tr** AA/A Mockford & N Bonetti; **249b** AA/A Mockford & N Bonetti; **250tl** AA/L Allen; **250tc** AA/L Allen; **250b** AA/L Allen; **251tl** AA/L Allen; **251tr** AA/L Allen; **251trb** AA/L Allen; **251b** AA/L Allen; **252c** AA/J Edmanson; **252bc** AA/J Edmanson; **253tr** AA/J Edmanson; **253br** AA/A Kouprianoff; **254c** AA; **254cr** AA/A Kouprianoff; **254b** AA/C Jones; **255tr** AA/A Kouprianoff; **256tr** AA/J Edmanson; **256bl** AA/J Edmanson; 257tr AA/A Mockford & N Bonetti; **258c** AA/M Chaplow; **258b** AA/M Chaplow; **259t** AA/M Chaplow; **260tr** AA/M Chaplow; **260br** AA/M Chaplow; **261** AA/M Chaplow; **262c** AA/C Jones; **262b** AA/C Jones; **263cl** AA/C Jones; **263br** AA/J Edmanson; **264/5** AA/M Chaplow; **264c** AA/C Jones; **265tr** AA/M Chaplow; **266c** AA/A Mockford & N Bonetti; **266bl** AA/C Sawyer; **266/7** AA/A Mockford & N Bonetti; **267cr** AA/A Mockford & N Bonetti; **268cl** AA/A Mockford & N Bonetti; **269c** AA/M Chaplow; **268cr** AA/C Jones.

EATING AND STAYING

269 AA/C Sawyer; **270cl** AA/M Chaplow; **270ccl** IVO SOL/Vila Joya; **270ccr** AA/C Jones; **270cr** AA/M Chaplow; **271cl** AA/C Jones; **271ccl** AA/M Chaplow; **271ccr** AA/A Kouprianoff; **271cr** IVO SOL/Vila Joya; **272cl** AA/M Chaplow; **272c** AA/A Kouprianoff; **272cr** AA/ T Harris; **273cl** AA/J Edmanson; **272c** IVO SOL/Vila Joya; **273cr** AA/A Mockford & N Bonetti; **274** AA/A Mockford & N Bonetti; **275** AA/A Mockford & N Bonetti; **276** AA/A Mockford & N Bonetti; **277t** AA/A Mockford & N Bonetti; **277b** AA/A Mockford & N Bonetti; **278** AA/A Mockford & N Bonetti; **279** AA/A Mockford & N Bonetti; **281tl** AA/A Mockford & N Bonetti; **281tr** AA/A Mockford & N Bonetti; **282** AA/A Mockford & N Bonetti; **283tl** AA/A Mockford & N Bonetti; **283tr** AA/A Mockford & N Bonetti; **284tl** AA/A Mockford & N Bonetti; **284tr** AA/A Mockford & N Bonetti; **285tl** AA/A Mockford & N Bonetti; **285c** AA/A Mockford & N Bonetti; **285b** AA/A Mockford & N Bonetti; **286** AA/A Mockford & N Bonetti; **288tc** AA/A Mockford & N Bonetti; **288tr** AA/A Mockford & N Bonetti; **288cl** AA/A Mockford & N Bonetti; **288c** AA/A Mockford & N Bonetti; **288cr** AA/A Mockford & N Bonetti; **289** AA/A Mockford & N Bonetti; **290tl** AA/A Mockford & N Bonetti; **290tr** AA/A Mockford & N Bonetti; **290c** AA/A Mockford & N Bonetti; **290b** AA/A Mockford & N Bonetti; **292** Sao Gabriel; **293** AA/A Mockford & N Bonetti; **294cl** Vila Vita Parc; **294c** AA/A Mockford & N Bonetti; **294cr** AA/C Jones; **296cl** AA/A Mockford & N Bonetti; **296b** AA/A Mockford & N Bonetti; **297t** AA/A Mockford & N Bonetti; **297br** AA/A Mockford & N Bonetti; **298t** AA/A Mockford & N Bonetti; **299t** AA/A Mockford & N Bonetti; **299cl** AA/A Mockford & N Bonetti; **299b** AA/A Mockford & N Bonetti; **300t** AA/A Mockford & N Bonetti; **300bc** AA/A Mockford & N Bonetti; **300cr** AA/A Mockford & N Bonetti; **301cr** AA/A Mockford & N Bonetti; **301bl** AA/A Mockford & N Bonetti; **303bl** AA/A Mockford & N Bonetti; **303br** Quinta do Juncal; **304** AA/A Mockford & N Bonetti; **305c** AA/A Mockford & N Bonetti; **305b** AA/A Mockford & N Bonetti; **306tl** AA/A Mockford & N Bonetti; **306tc** AA/A Mockford & N Bonetti; **306tr** AA/A Mockford & N Bonetti; **306b** AA/A Mockford & N Bonetti; **307** AA/A Mockford & N Bonetti; **308c** Solar dos Mouros; **308r** AA/A Mockford & N Bonetti; **309t** AA/A Mockford & N Bonetti; **309b** AA/A Mockford & N Bonetti; **310tl** Estalagem Vila Albatroz; **310cl** Estalagem Vila Albatroz; **310c** AA/A Mockford & N Bonetti; **310cr** AA/A Mockford & N Bonetti; **310b** AA/A Mockford & N Bonetti; **311** AA/A Mockford & N Bonetti; **312t** AA/A Mockford & N Bonetti; **312b** AA/A Mockford & N Bonetti; **313bc** Vila Joya; **313br** Vila Joya; **314** Hotel Luz Bay; **315t** Estalagem das Termas de Caldas de Monchique; **315b** Vila Vita Park; **316b** Quinta da Lua.

PLANNING

317 AA/C Sawyer; **319** AA/C Jones; **320** AA/A Kouprianoff; **321t** AA/A Mockford & N Bonetti; **321b** AA/A Kouprianoff; **322** Wheeling Around the Algarve; **323** AA/J Wyand; **324t** AA/A Mockford & N Bonetti; **324b** AA/C Jones; **325** AA/A Mockford & N Bonetti; **327** AA/T Harris; **328t** AA/A Mockford & N Bonetti; **328bl** AA/A Mockford & N Bonetti; **328br** AA/A Mockford & N Bonetti; **329** AA/A Mockford & N Bonetti; **330** AA/A Kouprianoff; **331** AA/A Kouprianoff; **333** AA/A Mockford & N Bonetti; **334** Photodisc.

Project editor
Jeremy Harwood, Nicola Lancaster

AA Travel Guides design team
David Austin, Glyn Barlow, Kate Harling, Bob Johnson,
Nick Otway, Carole Philp, Keith Russell

Additional design work
Katherine Mead, Jo Tapper

Picture research
Liz Allen

Internal repro work
Susan Crowhurst, Michael Moody, Ian Little

Production
Lyn Kirby, Helen Sweeney

Mapping
Maps produced by the Cartography Department of AA Publishing

Main contributors
Jo Chapman, Charlotte Elmer, Emma Rowley-Ruas, Sally Roy

Copy editors
Audrey Horne, Jo Perry

Published by AA Publishing, a trading name of Automobile Association Developments Limited, whose registered office is Southwood East, Apollo Rise, Farnborough, Hampshire, GU14 0JW. Registered number 1878835.

A CIP catalogue record for this book is available from the British Library.

ISBN-10: 0-7495-4513-5
ISBN-13: 978-0-7495-4513-0

Colour separation by Keenes
Printed and bound by Leo, China

Find out more about AA Publishing and the wide range of travel publications and services the AA provides by visiting our website at www.theAA.com/bookshop

A01618
Maps in this title produced from:
mapping © Mairs Geographischer Verlag / Falk Verlag, D-73751 Ostfildern, Germany
and with reference to mapping © GEOnext - ISTITUTO GEOGRAFICO DE AGOSTINI, Novara

Relief map images supplied by Mountain High Maps® Copyright © 1993 Digital Wisdom, Inc
Weather chart statistics supplied by Weatherbase © Copyright 2004 Canty and Associates, LLC
Communicarta assistance with distance/time charts gratefully acknowledged

We believe the contents of this book are correct at the time of printing. However, some details, particularly prices, opening times and telephone numbers do change. We do not accept responsibility for any consequences arising from the use of this book. This does not affect your statutory rights. We would be grateful if readers would advise us of any inaccuracies they may encounter, or any suggestions they might like to make to improve the book. There is a form provided at the back of the book for this purpose, or you can email us at Keyguides@theaa.com

COVER PICTURE CREDITS
Front cover: AA/A Kouprianoff
Back cover, top to bottom: AA/A Mockford & N Bonetti, AA/C Jones, AA/A Mockford & N Bonetti, AA/T Harris

Dear Key Guide Reader

Thank you for buying this Key Guide. Your comments and opinions are very important to us, so please help us to improve our travel guides by taking a few minutes to complete this questionnaire.

You do not need a stamp (unless posted outside the UK). If you do not want to cut this page from your guide, then photocopy it or write your answers on a plain sheet of paper.

Send to: Key Guide Editor, AA World Travel Guides
FREEPOST SCE 4598, Basingstoke RG21 4GY

Find out more about AA Publishing and the wide range of travel publications the AA provides by visiting our website at **www.theAA.com/bookshop**

ABOUT THIS GUIDE

Which Key Guide did you buy? ______________________

Where did you buy it? ______________________

When? _ _ month/ _ _ year

Why did you choose this AA Key Guide?

❑ Price ❑ AA Publication
❑ Used this series before; title ______________________
❑ Cover ❑ Other (please state) ______________________

Please let us know how helpful the following features of the guide were to you by circling the appropriate category: very helpful (**VH**), helpful (**H**) or little help (**LH**)

Size	**VH**	**H**	**LH**
Layout	**VH**	**H**	**LH**
Photos	**VH**	**H**	**LH**
Excursions	**VH**	**H**	**LH**
Entertainment	**VH**	**H**	**LH**
Hotels	**VH**	**H**	**LH**
Maps	**VH**	**H**	**LH**
Practical info	**VH**	**H**	**LH**
Restaurants	**VH**	**H**	**LH**
Shopping	**VH**	**H**	**LH**
Walks	**VH**	**H**	**LH**
Sights	**VH**	**H**	**LH**
Transport info	**VH**	**H**	**LH**

What was your favourite sight, attraction or feature listed in the guide?

Page ______________ Please give your reason ______________

____

Which features in the guide could be changed or improved? Or are there any other comments you would like to make?

____

____